Japanese/Korean Linguistics

Volume 9

Japanese/Korean Linguistics

Volume 9

Edited by
Mineharu Nakayama &
Charles J. Quinn, Jr.

Published for the
Stanford Linguistics Association by
CSLI Publications
Center for the Study of Language and Information
Stanford, California

Printed in the United States
04 03 02 01 00 5 4 3 2 1

Library of Congress Cataloging-in-Publication Data

Conference on Japanese/Korean Linguistics (1st : 1989 : University of Southern California)
Japanese/Korean Linguistics/edited by Hajime Hoji
p. cm.
Includes bibliographical references and index.
ISBN 1-57586-263-8
ISBN 1-57586-264-6 (pbk.)
1. Japanese language—Congresses. 2. Korean language—Congresses.
3. Japanese language—Grammar, Comparative–Korean–Congresses.
4. Korean language—Grammar, Comparative–Japanese–Congresses.
5. Linguistics–Congresses. I. Hoji, Hajime. II. Stanford Linguistics Association.
III. Center for the Study of Language and Information (U.S.) IV. Title.
PL503.C6 1989
495.6–dc20 90-2550
CIP

∞ The acid-free paper used in this book meets the minimum requirements of the American National Standard for Information Sciences—Permanence of Paper for Printed Library Materials, ANSI Z39.48-1984.

CSLI Publications reports new developments in the study of language, information, and computation. In addition to conference proceedings, our publications include lecture notes, monographs, working papers, revised dissertations, and Studies in Logic, Language and Information. Our aim is to make new results, ideas, and approaches available as quickly as possible. Please visit our website at
http://www.csli-publications.stanford.edu
for comments on this and other titles, as well as for changes and corrections by the author and publisher.

Contents

Preface

It is our distinct pleasure to present with this volume the papers delivered at the Ninth Japanese/Korean Linguistics Conference, which met from July 31 through August 2, 1999 at The Ohio State University in Columbus, Ohio. All papers delivered at the conference are included, with the exception of Noriko Yoshimura's. The ninth "J/K" followed J/K 8 (held in conjunction with the LSA Linguistics Summer Institute at Cornell in 1997), and a 1998 hiatus when no conference met. The J/K Linguistics Conference is set to return to the West Coast and convene for the tenth time at UCLA, in October 2000. This makes the 1999 J/K 9 the last of the millennium.

The following scholars judged the 125 abstracts submitted for J/K 9: Hee-Don Ahn, Mary Beckman, Nick Cipollone, Chang Chung, Stuart Davis, Stanley Dubinsky, Takao Gunji, Sungshim Hong, Masayo Iida, Shoichi Iwasaki, Keith Johnson, Kimberly Jones, Brian Joseph, Sun Ah Jun, Youngjoo Kim, Masatoshi Koizumi, Hyo-Sang Lee, Robert Levine, Bart Mathias, Yoshiko Matsumoto, Kazumi Matsuoka, Hiromi Morikawa, Mari Noda, Peter Sells, Natsuko Tsujimura, Jennifer Venditti, John Whitman, Hiroko Yamashita, Kiyoko Yoneyama, Lindsay Yotsukura, and Etsuyo Yuasa. They helped us to ensure that the quality of the conference papers remains high. For this they have our sincere gratitude, as do all of those who submitted abstracts. There were more quality abstracts than places in the timetable, and we did not invite a guest lecturer, instead opting for a program of refereed papers only. Eleven of the papers presented research on Korean, sixteen on Japanese, and two papers investigated matters related to both languages. As is usual at J/K conferences, variety was the rule, both in terms of subfields and theoretical frameworks.

J/K 9 was scheduled so as to come on the heels of the 1999 LSA Summer Linguistics Institute, and a number of colleagues in fact joined us on their way back from the LSA Institute. The J/K 9 sessions also occupied the middle spot (and hottest days) in a week-long program entitled Full Week Focus on East Asian Languages, which opened with Performative Perspectives for East Asian Language Pedagogy: a Workshop, and closed with the first International East Asian Psycholinguistics Workshop. A few hearty souls stayed the week, despite the record-setting heat; the American Association of

Teachers of Korean also held their annual national meeting at Ohio State, immediately following the other three meetings.

We're not sure we would want to try anything like a Full Week of meetings again, but thanks to our colleagues and graduate students at Ohio State, the week went smoothly and quickly. Here we thank those who helped with J/K 9: Jeff Angles, Eve Catus, Marjorie Chan, Noriko Chino, Peter Culicover, Brad Dielman, Sanae Eda, Stephen Filler, Yu Hirata, Stephen Horn, Soyoung Kang, Satoko Katagiri, Mark Knauf, Debbie Knicely, Scott Langton, Peace Lee, David Liu, Jennifer Nakayama, Chan Park, Koichi Sawasaki, Misako Terashima, Jim Unger, Shravan Vasishth, WenLan Yang, Leo Yip, and Etsuyo Yuasa. We would also like to thank Craig Thiersch for creating a web announcement in GLOW.

J/K 9 enjoyed the support of several units at Ohio State, namely the Department of East Asian Languages and Literatures, the Department of Linguistics, the College of Humanities, the Office of International Studies, the East Asian Studies Center, and the Institute for Japanese Studies. We are also deeply indebted to The Japan Foundation and The Korea Research Foundation for their generous support.

At J/K 9 we mourned the passing of a teacher who inspired many of us, regardless of whether we had the good fortune to study in his classes. James D. McCawley, late Andrew McLeish Distinguished Professor of Linguistics at the University of Chicago, remains with us in his many writings and in his former students, but as many of us can attest, those are just part of the Real McCawley. The Tenth J/K, first of the new millennium, will be dedicated to his memory. See you at UCLA!

Mineharu Nakayama
Charles J. Quinn, Jr.
The Ohio State University

Part I

Historical Linguistics

Toward Common Japanese-Koguryoic: A Reexamination of Old Koguryo Onomastic Materials

CHRISTOPHER BECKWITH
Indiana University

1. Introduction

According to mythological and historical accounts, a branch of the 夫餘 Puyo (Korean: Puyŏ) people of Manchuria named 高句麗 Koguryo (Korean: Koguryŏ) appeared in the area of southern Manchuria and northwestern Korea in the first century B.C. They rapidly grew in power and threatened the Chinese commanderies in northern Korea and the Liaotung (Liaodong) Peninsula. After several centuries of alternating expansion and retreat, in the fourth century Koguryo subdued the Chinese commandery of 樂浪 Lolang based in P'yongyang and successfully dominated northern Korea and the neighboring areas of southern Manchuria and the Liaotung Peninsula (Gardiner 1969). The Koguryo state maintained itself until its destruction by the allied forces of the Chinese T'ang dynasty and the southeastern Korean state of Silla in the year 668. Within a few years, Silla forced China out and established sole *de facto* rule over most of the Korean peninsula. The language of Silla, known today as 'Korean', ultimately from the *name* 'Koguryo', spread northward across the entire peninsula and eventually supplanted all other languages spoken there.

There is little data on the Puyo language, but it does seem to be closely related to Old Koguryo, as the sources claim (Kiyose 1998). In fact, the Chinese sources claim that the Puyo language, the Koguryo language, the language of the Paekche ruling class, and the language of the 夫租 Putsu or

沃沮 Okcho[1]--were all mutually intelligible. The same sources distinguish these languages from the 韓 Han languages, including the language of Silla and the subservient class of Paekche. We unfortunately know very little about the language of 任那 Mimana or 加羅 Kara (Korean: Kaya), located between Paekche and Silla on the south coast.[2] Our main source, the 三國史記 *Samguk Sagi*, or *History of the Three Kingdoms*, written in Chinese by 金富軾 Kim Pu-sik in 1145 on the basis of earlier sources, most of which are now lost, refers to the names of the different regions of Korea according to *political* geography. It almost never explicitly says, for example, that a given name is in the Koguryo language, but only that it was a Koguryo name--this could mean the Koguryo state or people as well as the language, and indeed, a large number of 'Koguryo' names are purely Chinese. It is because of this unclarity that it has been possible to make other arguments about the identity of the language usually called Koguryo or Old Koguryo today.[3]

2. Sources and Previous Studies

Except for a few words found elsewhere in Chinese, Korean, and Japanese sources, the Old Koguryo language is known only from a small number of glosses[4] to place names in the geographical section of the *Samguk Sagi*. Both the Old Koguryo names and their glosses are written exclusively in Chinese characters. However, many of the names are purely Chinese, or they have no glosses, or there are other problems, so that only a limited corpus of usable material remains.

Recognition of the importance of the Old Koguryo materials is due to early twentieth century scholars (Miller 1979:349). Most recent scholarship has consisted of the publication of lists of Old Koguryo words with putative correspondences in Japanese, Korean, and other languages of Northeastern Eurasia (Lee 1964; Lewin 1973; Whitman 1990; Kiyose 1986, 1991).[5]

---

1 The traditional name, 沃沮 Okcho, appears to be a graphically corrupt form of the early name recorded on bricks found at Lolang (Gardiner 1969b: 164). The Putsu, who lived on the northeast coast of Korea, were dominated by the Koguryo.

2 Toh Soo-hee, author of a monumental three-volume study of this material, considers the language of Kara to have been a Han-type (i.e., Korean-type) language (Toh 1989:465-484).

3 Toh argues throughout his work (1987-1994) that the language called Koguryo is really a 'Paekche' language. Accordingly, he has unfortunately lumped the presumably mixed (Han-type and Puyo-type) Paekche material together with the Koguryo material in his study and calls it all 'Paekche'. Kim (1981) argues, along similar lines, that the language called 'Koguryo' was really the indigenous language of most of the Korean peninsula.

4 I use the term 'gloss' loosely here to include both gloss-like translations of place names and instances where place names have been converted or translated into Chinese.

5 Much of the recent attention to Old Koguryo is due to a series of papers published in the early 1960s by Lee Ki-moon and Muryama Shichirô (Lewin 1973:23-24).

However, many Old Koguryo words have been incorrectly identified etymologically, or remain unidentified.[6]

The fundamental problem is the phonological interpretation of the data. Scholars have largely based their interpretations on *modern Korean* readings of the Chinese characters used to transcribe Old Koguryo.[7] However, this is methodologically incorrect, since there was little contact between Old Koguryo and the language of Silla until after the fall of the Koguryo kingdom. The Koguryo place names were mostly converted into Chinese a century later,[8] in the year 757 (Toh 1987: 387), the probable date when the literary source for the *Samguk Sagi*'s geographical material on Koguryo was composed. The transcriptions basically reflect mid-T'ang Chinese values, though the underlying dialect does not have the prenasalised initials of the northwestern dialect of Late Middle Chinese such as was spoken in Ch'ang-an and is represented in Japanese by the *kan on* or 'T'ang pronunciation' layer of Middle Chinese loanwords.[9]

When Silla changed the Koguryo place names, some of them were translated. Old Koguryo 烏斯含達 *☆ɔsiɣam ☆taδ* ~ *☆usiχam ☆tar*,[10] for example, was translated literally into Chinese as 兔山 'Rabbit Mountain'.[11]

---

6 The monumental publication by Toh (1987-1994), the only large-scale study of the material in its own right, suffers from its assumption first of all that all the languages of Korea were related, if distantly, to each other and to Japanese, and secondly that what everyone else calls (Old) Koguryo was really Paekche, even though Toh himself is aware of the fact that the Paekche material includes names in at least two languages, one a Puyo (Koguryo, Japanese) type language and the other a Han (Korean) type language.

7 Toh (1987-1994) is an exception to this practice. One problem related to it has already been raised by Miller (1979), namely the questionable 'traditional' reading of the transcription character 尸 MChi *☆śi*, as both a palatal sibilant and a liquid.

8 Nearly all of the conversions are recorded as having taken place in the mid-eighth century reign (742-765) of King 景德 Kyŏngdŏk (cf. Miller 1979: 348-349, 364).

9 All unnoted reconstructions are mine, generally based on the 'Early Middle Chinese' (EMC) and 'Late Middle Chinese' (LMC) forms in Pulleyblank (1991), but influenced by, among other things, the Old Northwestern Mandarin dialect (which in Pulleyblank and other works is considered to be the northwestern dialect of Late Middle Chinese) written in Old Tibetan script (Takata 1988); it is the earliest phonetically secure transcription of any variety of Chinese. Pulleyblank's transcription system has been altered when necessary to conform to the system used here. The Old Koguryo reconstructions are given in both a 切韻 *Ch'ieh-yün* ('EMC') form and a T'ang ('LMC') form, both based largely on Pulleyblank's Middle Chinese dictionary (1991), but it is notable that the readings appropriate for Old Koguryo are almost always much closer to the T'ang reconstruction. New Mandarin forms are given in the Pinyin spellings of Pulleyblank's dictionary.

10 Non-Chinese forms attested in Chinese transcription are marked with a star; reconstructions are marked with an asterisk regardless of the basis for the reconstruction.

11 In fact, there are also complications involving the administrative unit names. In Chapter 35, the Old Koguryo place is a 縣 'County', while the new Chinese name is a 郡 'Commandery', but in Chapter 37, which tends to be more reliable for the Old Koguryo forms of the place names, the name is only 烏斯含達, without 縣 'County' and without any gloss.

However, this strict calque is an ideal example; most are far from this simple. The philological problems involved in the interpretation and analysis of the Old Koguryo corpus are formidable; some may never be solved.

3. Phonology

With the help of Chinese reconstructions and the clearly identifiable cognates with Japanese, it is possible to reconstruct the elements of Old Koguryo phonology.

3.1. Syllable structure

Many words (or stems) are monosyllabic in Old Koguryo, as in Old Japanese; but unlike Old Japanese, Old Koguryo has both open- and closed-syllable nominal stems. Old Koguryo monosyllabic words with final consonants correspond either to Japanese words with no final--as in example (1), OKog 斤 ☆*kin* 'tree, wood', corresponding to OJpn 紀 ☆*ki* 'tree, wood'--or to Japanese words with an additional vowel after the consonant in question, giving a disyllabic form. This is because Old Koguryo permits both open and closed syllables, but Old Japanese permits only open syllables. Although in (1) the final could theoretically be the result of epenthesis from an original **ki* with the addition of a so-called 'weak' final *-n*, as in Mongolian, while in (2) the final consonant could be the result of deletion, OKog 但 ☆*tan* 'valley' descending from a Common Japanese-Koguryoic **tani*, the data indicate that most such words were probably closed monosyllables in Common Japanese-Koguryoic, as in (3), where the Japanese toponym *Toba* reflects a Pre-Old Japanese **təwr* (rather than a disyllabic **tori*), corresponding to the Old Koguryo cognate ☆*tawr*. In general, many of the disyllabic Japanese forms seem to be the result of epenthesis.

(1) OKog 斤 ☆*kin* (many examples; also written [illegible] ☆*γεy* ~ ☆*χi*) 'tree, wood (木)': OJpn 紀 ☆*ki*, also 許 ☆*kü-* 'id.' > NJpn 木 *ki, ko-* (Mar. 449: < *ko-Ci[12]) < CJK **kin*.

(2) OKog 但 ☆*dan* ~ ☆*tan* (many examples variously written) 'valley (谷)': OJpn 多尒 ☆*tani* 'id.' > NJpn 谷 *tani* < CJK **tan*.

(3) OKog 刀臘 ☆tawrap 'Pheasant Mountain (雉嶽)' < ☆*tawr* 'pheasant' + ☆*ap* (~ ☆*yap* (see example (8)): OJpn 登利 ☆*təŋri* (*[tə wri]) 'chicken (雞); bird (鳥)' > NJpn *tóri* 'id.', < CJK **tawr*.[13]

In most cases where there is a final consonant in Old Koguryo but not in Japanese it is likely that the Old Koguryo form preserves the earlier state

12 Martin's suprasegmental feature markings are omitted in citations of his work.

13 Cf. 鳥羽 *Toba* 'P.N.' (lit., 'Bird-feather') < OJpn ☆*təwba* < Pre-OJpn **təwr* 'bird' + **pa* 'feather'. Ccf. MChi 鳥 ☆*tew* ~ ☆*tiaw* 'bird' (NMan *niǎo* is irregular); Common Japanese-Koguryoic (CJK) **tawr* is apparently a loan from the Old Chinese word, which seems to have had a final liquid.

of affairs. It is known that Old Japanese verbs usually have consonant stems, unlike the nouns, which exclusively have vowel stems. However, of the five clearly attested Old Koguryo verbs, only one, in (22), has a stop final; three have vowel or nasal stems, as shown in examples (4) through (6), and one, in (7), has a nasal-final root. Moreover, even in Japanese many verbal stems clearly are composed of previously simpler roots with the later addition of derivational extensions, one of the most common of which, based on many examples in Martin's analysis, is **-ra-* (Martin 1987). This means that any Old Japanese verb with stem-final *-r* might originally have lacked that final, or indeed any final. This unfortunately makes reconstruction of Proto-Japanese even more difficult than it already is. Moreover, the correspondence of words in Old Koguryo and Japanese for which the Chinese transcription syllables record a final velar nasal for both languages forces us to reconsider the previously accepted interpretation of such transcriptions, which indicate a nasalized coda or nucleus, perhaps even an articulated nasal consonant final. Since both transcriptions occur in Old Japanese, it would seem that there are grounds for considering the possibility of variation (presumably dialect-based) having existed among zero, glides, nasalized vowels, and articulated nasal finals.

(4) OKog 伊 *☆i* 'enter (入)': OJpn 伊理 (J. 106) *☆ir-i* > NJpn 入 *ir-* 'id.' < (Mar. 698: "ir-u < *ira-") < CJK **i.*

(5) OKog 金 *☆kim* 'rest, cease, stop': OJpn **kim-* (unattested) > NJpn *kim-* in *kimaru* 'to be fixed, settled, sure' (Cf. Mar. 710).

(6) OKog 冬 *☆tawŋ* ~ *☆təwŋ* 'take': OJpn 登良 *☆təwŋ-ra-* > NJpn 取 *tor-* 'id. (Mar. 771: "< *t(w)oru < *t(w)ora-")[14] < CJK **təwŋ.*

(7) OKog 冬比 *☆tawŋpi* ~ *☆təwŋpi* 'to open': OJpn 登富禮 (J. 502) *☆təŋpuwr-i* (Mar. 770: < toforu < *topo-ra-) > NJpn 通 *toor-u* 'to pass through' < CJK **təwŋp(or)i* < PJK *☆tewŋ.* Cf. 通 MChi *☆t*^{h}*əwŋ* 'to pass through, penetrate, open'.

3.2. Syllable Initials

Syllables beginning with *☆a* ~ *☆ya* in Old Koguryo correspond to Old Japanese forms beginning with *☆ya,* while those beginning with **ü-* correspond to Old Japanese syllables with initial **ü-*. For example, OKog 押 *☆ap* ~ *☆yap* ~ Pre-OKog 蓋馬 *☆γapma* 'high mountain' corresponds to OJpn *☆yama* 'mountain', as in (8), while OKog 於 *☆ü* 'across, crosswise, horizontal' corresponds to OJpn 与許 *☆ükü,* which has the same meaning, in (9). While the conventional reconstruction of OJpn *☆ü* is **ö* or **yö,*

[14] John Bentley has recently argued persuasively that there were two Old Japanese verbs, 登-/等-/騰- *☆to*(*r*)- 'to take' and 斗-/刀- *☆two*(*r*)- 'to hold', which merged to become NJpn *tor-* (Bentley 1999).

based presumably on the fact that it usually corresponds to later Japanese [o] or [yo], since these and similar Old Koguryo and Old Japanese cognates are consistently transcribed with exactly the same vowel, ☆*ü*, one is forced to conclude that the vowel was, indeed, [ü] in both languages. There is in any case no reason why Old Japanese ☆*ü* could not become New Japanese *yo*, perhaps via **yö*.

(8) OKog 押 ☆*ap* ~ ☆*yap* 'high mountain (嶽)' and 蓋馬 Pre-OKog ☆*ɣapma* 'the high mountains of Koguryo': Pre-OJpn 邪馬 ☆*yama* > OJpn 夜麻 (J. 767) ☆*yama* 'mountain' > NJpn 山 *yama* 'id.' (Mar. 571: "< *dama") < CJK **ɣapma* (< PJK **ɣap*?)

(9) OKog ☆*ü* 於 'across, crosswise, horizontal (横)': OJpn 与許 (J. 793) ☆*ükü* 'id. (横)' (Mar. 576: "yoko < *doko 'side'") > NJpn 横 *yoko* 'id.'

For this reason, and because in some cases, as shown in (8), the Pre-Old Koguryo word had a velar initial, it is incorrect to reconstruct Proto-Japanese initial **d-* for all Old Japanese words that have initial ☆*y-*. Although Martin (1987: 571) reconstructs initial **d-* for *yama*, for example, he does not cite dialect words with initial *d-* to support this, and in his general discussion of initial **d-* he remarks that the Proto-Japanese initial "was surely palatalized and possibly affricated" (Martin 1987:20).

There are several possible solutions to this problem. For example, it could be that both *y-* and *d-* developed from a single initial that is no longer preserved as such in either Japanese or Ryukyuan, as Martin suggests (Martin 1987:20). However, as he also indicates several times, at least some instances of initial *y-* in Japanese definitely do not go back to initial **d-*, but to different initials in different words. In fact, the Old Koguryo evidence indicates that Japanese initial *y-* derives from at least three different Proto-Japanese-Koguryoic sources: the *y-* in *yama* from a voiced velar in example (8); the *y-* in *yoko* from vowel breaking in example (9);[15] and the *y-* in *yumi* 'bow' and *yugi* 'quiver' from an affricate in example (10).

(10) Puyo ~ Pre-OKog 鄒牟 ☆*tśuwmuw* ~ ☆*tśəwməw* ~ OKog 朱蒙 ☆*tśuməwŋ* ~ ☆*tśüməwŋ*) '(one who) shoots (arrows) well': OJpn 由美 (J. 788) ☆*yuwmi* ~ ☆*yiwmi* > NJpn *yumi* 'bow'; cf. NJpn *yugi* 'quiver', < Pre-OJpn **yu*(*m*?) + **ki* (Mar. 579: "? < *dum[i] k[aC]i") < CJK **dźum*?[16]

Although Old Japanese does not have voiced stop or affricate initials, it

---

15 However, it is possible that CJK **ü-* derives in this and some other cases from syllables that earlier had voiced velar initials. Further study is needed.

16 The gloss 善 'excellent' corresponds to the OKog word 買 ☆*mai* in two toponyms, so it should correspond to the second syllable here, 牟 ☆*muw* ~ ☆*məw*, which presumably has the same meaning. The relationship of the vowels in the two forms appears to parallel the contrast between words for 'water, river', OKog ☆*mai*, ☆*mi* ~ Jurchen ☆*mü* (Kiyose 1986:19).

does have voiced glides and nasals. The change of the initial in (8) CJK *γ- > OJpn *y- and in (10) CJK *tś- or *dź- > OJpn ☆y-, among other examples, appears to be evidence of a thoroughgoing sound-change that must have affected the entire language. More research, including study of the Old Chinese loanwords into Japanese-Koguryoic, is needed.

3.3. Phonological Changes from CJK to OKog and OJpn

There are several regular phonological differences between Old Koguryo and Old Japanese. One of the most interesting is a conditioned change that shows up in Japanese. There are a number of examples in which the first syllable in the Old Koguryo is ☆*kɔ* ~ ☆*ku*, while the Old Japanese has either ☆*kɔ* ~ ☆*ku* or ☆*ka*. When the second syllable in the Old Koguryo has the vowel ☆*i*, the corresponding syllable in the Old Japanese has ☆*ku* as in examples (11) to (13), but when the second syllable in the Old Koguryo has the vowel ☆*a*, as in (14) and (15), the first syllable in the Old Japanese is ☆*ka*. This vowel change occurs elsewhere and explains the apparent anomaly in the Japanese word for 'rabbit', *usagi*, from Old Japanese 宇佐岐 ☆*utsaki*, in (16). This is clearly from an earlier **utsika* (or **usika*), cognate with Old Koguryo 烏斯含 ☆*ɔsiγam* ~ ☆*usiχam* 'rabbit', where the high vowel in the second syllable influenced the initial vowel as in (11) through (13); the second and third syllable vowels subsequently metathesized[17] before the Old Japanese period. The same regressive assimilation seems to be reflected in several other cases.

(11) OKog 古次 ☆*kɔtsi* ~ ☆*kutsi* 'mouth' (also written 忽次 ☆*χwəδtsi* ~ ☆*χurtsi*): OJpn 久知 ☆*kuwtśi*[18] 'id.' > NJpn 口 *kutśi*.

(12) OKog 古所 ☆*kɔśi* ~ ☆*kuśi* 'roe-deer' (also written 古斯 ☆*kɔsi* ~ ☆*kusi*): OJpn **kusi* 'id.' (unattested) + ☆*ka* 'deer' > NJpn *kuzika*.

(13) OKog 古衣 ☆*kɔʔi* ~ ☆*kuʔi* (< **kɔγi* ~ **kuγi*) 'swan': OJpn 久久比 ☆*kuwkuwpi* 'id.' > NJpn *kugui* 'id.'[19]

(14) OKog 古麻 ☆*kɔma* ~ ☆*kuma* 'dragon': OJpn 加米 , 柯梅 (J. 225) ☆*kamey* < **kama-i* (Mar. 435: "< *kamaCi")[20] > NJpn 龜 *kame* 'tortoise', < CJK **kɔma*.

(15) OKog 古良 ☆*kɔ-lyaŋ* ~ ☆*ku-lyaŋ* 'unicorn (a mythical kind of deer) -virtue': OJpn 賀 (J. 170) ☆*γa* ~ ☆*χa* (*[ka]) 'deer' > NJpn 鹿 *ka* 'id.', < CJK **kɔ*.

---

17 The metathesis was first suggested by Miller (1971:117).

18 Note that the *man'yôgana* make it clear OJpn had the affricate [tśi] in the second syllable of this word, not the stop [t], as it is usually reconstructed.

19 Cf. the Chinese word 鵠 NMan *hú* 'swan' < MChi *γawk ~ *χəwk.

20 Cf. NJpn *kama-* in *kamakiri* 'mantis' and *kama-itachi* 'an invisible animal supposed to inflict wounds on people . . . without any apparent cause' (Hepburn 1983: 176).

(16) OKog 烏斯含 *☆ɔsiγam* ~ *☆usiχam* 'rabbit': OJpn 宇佐岐 (J. 114) *☆utsaki* (< Pre-OJpn **usika*) > NJpn *usagi* 'id.'[21] < CJK **ɔsika*.

4. Morphology

Earlier researchers have not recognized the presence of morphosyntactic markers in the Old Koguryo material, and have thus misidentified many items. There is one clearly identifiable function morpheme,[22] a genitive-attributive marker, which is identifiable partly due to the fact that some names omit it, leaving only the bare root, as in (17a).

(17) a. 烏生波衣 *☆ɔ śeŋ paʔi* ~ *☆u śeŋ paʔi* 'Pig Rail Rock (豬闌峴)'.

b. 烏斯迴 *☆ɔ-si γwai* ~ *☆u-si χwai* 'Pig's Foot' (豬足)'.

Failure to recognize this morpheme has resulted in incorrect segmentation and incorrect etymological identifications. For example, the word 仇斯 *☆guwsi* ~ *☆kiwsi* in the name 仇斯波衣 is identified as 'child' by Lee (1964:15). However, the syllable 斯 *☆si* in this instance is the genitive-attributive marker. Thus the root morpheme 'child' in example (18) is represented by the first syllable only, 仇 *☆guw* ~ *☆kiw* (i.e., *[ku]), which corresponds regularly to Old Japanese 古 *☆kɔ* ~ *☆ku* 'child'. Altogether the name thus means 'Child's Peak'. Lee also takes the entire sequence 古斯也 *☆kɔsiya* ~ *☆kusiya*, in (19), as 'roe-deer' (Lee 1964:15), despite the clear gloss, 'Roe-deer Nape'. Another transcription of the word for 'roe-deer' shows that the second syllable is in this instance part of the stem, though it is perhaps not part of the root.

(18) OKog *☆guw* ~ *☆kiw* (= *[ku]) 'child': OJpn 古 (J. 284) *☆kɔ* ~ *☆ku* (Mar. 452: "ko < kwo") > NJpn *ko* 'id.'

(19) OKog 古斯也 *☆kɔsiya* ~ *☆kusiya* 'roe-deer nape' (cf. 古所 *☆kɔśi* ~ *☆kuśi* 'roe-deer'): OJpn **kusi* 'id.' (unattested) + *☆ka* 'deer' > NJpn *kuzika* 'roe-deer'.

4.1 Genitive-Attributive marker

This morpheme has three allomorphs. All unambiguous examples found in the *Samguk Sagi* are listed here.

---

21 Although the OJpn *man'yôgana* transcribing the phone *[ts] seem uncontrovertible, the OKog and NJpn evidence indicates CJK **s*. Cf. Old Tibetan *yos-* 'rabbit, hare'.

22 There is one possible example of another grammatical morpheme, namely OKog 乃 *☆nəi* ~ *☆nai* in 骨乃斤 *☆kwəδnəi kin* ~ *☆kurnai kin* glossed as 黄驍 'yellow bravery (or 'steed')'. Since the syllable *☆kwəδ* ~ *☆kur* appears to correlate with NJpn *ki* < OJpn **ki* (J. 237; Mar. 449: "*kiy < *kɯ/${}_{o}$-Ci") 'yellow', while *☆kin* appears to correlate with NJpn *kimo* < OJpn 岐毛 (J. 46) *☆kimaw* 'liver, bravery', we are left with the syllable 乃 *☆nəi* ~ *☆nai*. If it is not part of either the word for 'yellow' or the word for 'bravery', it could be a function morpheme, perhaps an adjective marker, related etymologically to NJpn *no* 'genitive-attributive marker' < OJpn 乃 (J. 562-563) *☆nəi* ~ *☆nai* 'id.'

4.1.1. The Allomorph 斯 ⋆*si*.

Suffixed to open syllables with a rounded vowel, or closed syllables with a velar final:

烏斯押 'Pig's Den'

麻斯良 'Returning Virtue'

冬斯忽郡 'Mountain-Pass Fort Commandery'

仇斯波衣 'Child's Peak'

於斯內 'Hatchet Land'

伏斯買 'Deep River'

烏斯迴 'Pig's Foot'

於斯買 'Crosswise River'

冬斯肹 'Chestnut Tree'

去斯斬 'Willow Root'

4.1.2. The Allomorph 尸 ⋆*śi*.

Suffixed to open syllables with an unrounded or palatal vowel, or closed syllables with an alveopalatal final:

買尸達 'Garlic Mountain'

加尸達忽 'Plough Mountain Fort'

斤尸波兮 'Streaked/Veined Peak'

波尸忽 'Second-Growth-Paddy-Rice Fort'

骨尸押 'Rotten Peak'

皆尸押忽 'Royal-Camp Peak Fort'

4.1.2. The Allomorph 乙 ⋆*iδ* ~ ⋆*ir*.

Suffixed to 去聲 (Chinese 'departing tone', perhaps checked) syllables, and the closed syllable 達 ⋆*taδ* ~ ⋆*tar* 'high'.[23]

首乙呑 'Granary/Storehouse Valley'

助乙浦 'Road Overlook'

內乙買 'Sand River'

達乙斬 'High Root' (*'Mountain Root')

達乙省縣 'High Beacon County' (*'Mountain Beacon County')

---

23 The Chinese gloss in both examples is 高 'high, tall', but the story accompanying 達乙省縣 suggests that 'mountain' (OKog 達 ⋆*taδ* ~ ⋆*tar*) was the original sense.

5. Syntax

We unfortunately do not have a single sentence written in Old Koguryo. Nevertheless, several place names do reveal the language's basic syntax.

5.1. Noun Phrases

Numerous examples of adjective-noun collocations make it clear that NP internal syntax in Old Koguryo conforms to the pattern found in Japanese and other languages in the same region--that is, qualifiers precede the qualified. Consider (20) and (21), which show, respectively, an adjective with the genitive-attributive suffix qualifying a noun and a noun plus the genitive-attributive suffix qualifying another noun.

(20) OKog 伏 ☆*buwk* ~ ☆*puwk* 'deep', in 伏斯買 ☆*puwk-si mai* (deep-GEN/ATT water) 'Deep River': OJpn 布可 ☆*puka* 'deep' > NJpn *fuka-* 'id.'

(21) OKog 烏 ☆*ɔ* ~ ☆*u* (perhaps = **ui*; cf. OKog 烏 ☆*ɔ* ~ ☆*u* 'ford' ~ 唯 ☆*ui* 'ford') 'pig', in 烏斯迴 ☆*u-si χway* (pig-GEN/ATT foot) 'Pig's Foot': OJpn 為 ☆*wi* > NJpn 猪 *i* 'pig'.

5.2. Verb Phrases

Only one clear example of a collocation involving both a direct object and a verb exists in the data. This example, (22), unambiguously shows Object-Verb syntax in Old Koguryo.[24]

(22) OKog 伯 ☆*pak* ~ ☆*payk* 'to meet (someone)', in 皆伯縣 ☆*kay pak χian* (king meet county) 'Meet the King County (遇王縣)': OJpn 波加利 (J. 573) ☆*pakari* 'to confer together (相談)'.

6. Etymology

Careful examination of the entire Old Koguryo corpus allows the establishment of numerous clear cognates with Japanese, far more than can be presented here. At the same time, many previously proposed etymological identifications with words in Japanese, Korean, or other languages are in error. Earlier studies have generally argued for a common divergent relationship for all the languages in the area except Chinese. Yet considering the diverse linguistic map of Korea and southern Manchuria in the relevant times and places, it may be taken as a certainty that loanwords constitute an important part of the lexicon *whether or not* any or all of the languages are related. An important factor for determining the earlier history of Proto-Japanese-Koguryoic is the presence of close correspondences with Old Chinese, such as OKog ☆*tawr* 'pheasant' ~ OJpn ☆*təwri* 'chicken, bird' < Pre-

---

24 Cf. OKog 伊 ☆*i* 'enter (入)' in 買伊縣 ☆*mai i χian* water enter county '(Where) the Water Enters County (水入縣)': OJpn 伊理 (J. 106) ☆*ir*(*-i*) > NJpn 入 *i*(*r*)- 'id. OKog, OJpn, and Chinese all have Subject-Verb syntax.

OJpn **təwr* < CJK **tawr*: MChi **tew* 'bird' < OChi **tawr* in (3). Here only Japanese-Koguryoic reconstruction is attempted, but it must be borne in mind that some of these words are found also in other East Asian languages. They could be loans from those languages, inherited forms from a common proto-language, or even loans from Japanese-Koguryoic into the other languages. For the present, unless a divergent relationship with some other language can be established, all of them should be treated as loanwords between Japanese-Koguryoic and the other languages.

6.1. The Korean element in Old Koguryo

Although the majority of identifiable words in the Old Koguryo corpus are clearly related to Japanese, some are obviously related closely to Korean rather than to Japanese, as in (23), although the details are not always clear. The corpus also gives variant forms in some instances for semantically identical names or parts of names where one form is clearly related to Korean while the other is clearly related to Japanese, as in (24) to (26). This fact, combined with the high proportion of Japanese etymologies in general compared to the much smaller number of Korean ones, and the phonological closeness of Old Koguryo and Japanese as contrasted with Korean, would seem to indicate that the Korean-related words in Old Koguryo are either loans from a Korean-type language into Old Koguryo or loans from Old Koguryo or Puyo into Korean. Since there are some instances where the same word with the same meaning is found in Korean, Japanese, and Old Koguryo, as in (27), it has been thought that this constitutes proof of a genetic relationship. However, it must be noted that most, if not all, such words are well-known areal culture words, as in (27) and (28), and are found in many unrelated languages of eastern Eurasia. Finally, some interesting words, as in (29), remain etymologically unidentified.

(23) OKog 波 ☆*pa* ~ 波旦 ☆*patan* 'sea': NKor *pada* 'sea' < MKor *patah* 'id.' ≠ NJpn 海 *umi* 'sea' < OJpn 宇美 (J. 131) ☆*umi* 'id.' OJpn 和多 (J. 819) ☆*γwata* (*[wata]?) 'sea' is not directly cognate with the OKog word (OKog **p-* ~ OJpn **p-*); it would seem thus to be a loan into Japanese from, presumably, a Korean dialect.

(24) OKog 波兮 ☆*paγei* ~ 波衣 ~ 巴衣 ☆*paʔi* 'high mountain': MKor *pahoi* 'rock' ≠ OKog 押☆*ap* ~ ☆*yap* (~ Pre-OKog 蓋馬 ☆*γapma*) 'high mountain' (平淮押縣 = 別史波衣[縣]): NJpn 山 *yama* 'mountain' < OJpn ☆*yama* < Pre-OJpn ☆*yama*.

(25) OKog 夫斯 ☆*pusi* ~ 扶蘇 ☆*puso* 'pine': MKor *pus* 'id.' ≠ OKog 仇 ☆*guw* ~ ☆*kiw* 'pine' (松峴縣 = 夫斯波衣縣 = 仇史峴[縣]): NJpn *ko-*, *ki* 'tree, wood' < OJpn 許 (J. 236) ☆*kü* ~ 紀 (J. 285) ☆*ki* 'tree, wood'. Cf. OKog 斤 ☆*kin* 'tree, wood', 去 ☆*kï* ~ ☆*kü* 'willow tree'. Ccf. OJpn 麻紀 (J. 668) ☆*maki* > NJpn *maki* 'Chinese black pine'.

(26) OKog 息 ☆*sik* 'earth, dirt': MKor *hark* 'id.' < **siroga* (Lee 1964:16) ≠ OKog 內/奴/腦/乃 ☆*nɔ* 'land, earth, country': NJpn *no* 'field, plains, wild land' < OJpn 怒 ☆*nɔ* ~ ☆*nu* 'plains, wild land'. Cf. Southern Tungusic *na* 'earth', MKor *narah* 'land' (Kiyose 1986:19), OJpn ☆*naraŋ* 'Nara (P.N.)'.

(27) OKog 功 ☆*kəwŋm* (*[kəwm]) 'bear': NJpn *kuma* 'id.' < OJpn 久麻 ☆*kuma*[25]: NKor *kom* 'id.' < MKor *kuma* 'id.' Cf. Evenki *kuma* 'seal', Lamut *kuma* 'id.' (Kiyose 1986:19).

(28) OKog 內米 ☆*nɔmei* 'rough water (pool below a waterfall)'[26]: OJpn 那美 ☆*nami* 'wave'. Cf. Tungusic *nâmu* 'sea' (Kiyose 1986:20).

(29) OKog 非 ☆*pwi* ~ ☆*pʰyi* (*[pi]) 'soybean (大豆, lit., "big bean")'.

7. Conclusion

The relationship between Old Koguryo and Japanese demonstrated here has serious implications for Japanese ethnolinguistic history. Not only are some vocabulary items (such as the numerals) peculiar to Japanese--and apparently unrelated to Korean or other languages--also found in Old Koguryo, there is also a systematic phonological relationship between Old Koguryo and Japanese.

It has been thought that Proto-Japanese generally had closed syllable verb stems but only open syllable nouns. However, some open syllable verb stems do occur in Japanese, and some nominal compounds reflect underlying closed syllable roots, as in the Japanese word *tori* 'chicken, bird' from Pre-OJpn **təwr*, in (3) above.

In Old Koguryo we find four possible syllable structures for *both* nouns and verbs: V, VC, CV, and CVC. This distribution is essentially that found in Chinese from Late Old Chinese to the present, and supports recent arguments that *typologically* Proto-Japanese (or better now, Proto-Japanese-Koguryoic) must have been akin to Chinese and the languages of Southeast Asia (Sakakura 1993:30-31; Janhunen 1997; Kiyose 1997:42-43) rather than Korean and other languages of Northeast Asia, to which it now seems to belong according to typology. As there is also a deep layer of very ancient Chinese words in Japanese-Koguryoic (Beckwith 1998), there can be no doubt that Common Japanese-Koguryoic once had an intimate relationship with Chinese.

The language of the Wa, or early people of Japan, recorded in the *San kuo chih*, or 'Records of the Three Kingdoms' (220-265 A.D.) of China, by

---

25 The ☆*-m* is from the initial of 木 ☆*məwk*. This example has been taken as **kumok* by other scholars, but they ignore the character 閃 in the gloss (功木達 = 熊閃山). The present treatment accounts better for the data and the OKog preference for monosyllables.

26 In the light of OKog 內/奴/腦/乃 ☆*nɔ* 'earth' : OJpn 怒 ☆*nɔ* ~ ☆*nu* wild land' in (26), it would seem possible that CJK **nɔmei* meant, literally, 'wild water'.

the contemporaneous historian Ch'en Shou (233-297 A.D.), seems already to be Japanese--indeed, it appears to be very close to Old Japanese. Since it is virtually certain that the Japanese and Koguryo languages are 'genetically' related to each other, perhaps exclusively, it would now seem necessary to reexamine all existing theories about Japanese ethnolinguistic origins.

Abbreviations

CJK: Common Japanese-Koguryoic, EMC: Early Middle Chinese, J.: *Jidai betsu kokugo daijiten* (Omodaka 1967), LMC: Late Middle Chinese, NJpn: New Japanese, NMan: New Mandarin, OJpn: Old Japanese, OKog: Old Koguryo, Mar.: Martin 1987, MChi: Middle Chinese, OChi: Old Chinese, PJK: Proto-Japanese-Koguryoic, P.N.: Place Name.

References

Beckwith, Christopher I. 1998. Old Chinese Initial **m-* and Early Loanwords in Japanese and Tibeto-Burman. Paper presented at the 31st International Conference on Sino-Tibetan Languages and Linguistics, Lund.

Bentley, John R. 1999. The Verb *toru* in Old Japanese. *Journal of East Asian Linguistics* 8. 131-146.

Gardiner, K.J.H. 1969. *The Early History of Korea.* Canberra: Australian National University Press.

Gardiner, K.J.H. 1969b. The *Hou-Han-Shu* as a Source for the Early Expansion of Koguryŏ. *Monumenta Serica* 28. 148-187.

Hepburn, James Curtis. 1983. *A Japanese and English Dictionary with an English and Japanese Index.* Tokyo: Tuttle.

Janhunen, Juha. 1997. Problems of Primary Root Structure in Pre-Proto-Japanic. *International Journal of Central Asian Studies* 2. 14-30.

Kim, Bang-han. 1981. The Relationship between the Korean and Japanese Languages. *Hangeul* 173-4. 657-667.

Kim, Pu-sik. 1971. *Samguk Sagi.* Dong-kwun Im, et al., eds. *Korean Folklore Texts in Chinese Characters: History and Folklore of the Three Kingdoms of Korea (Sam-guk sa-gi).* Taipei: The Orient Cultural Service.

Kiyose, Gisaburo N. 1986. Tunguz and Other Elements in the Languages of the Three Kingdoms. *Korean Linguistics* 4. 17-26.

Kiyose, Gisaburo N. 1997. Yamatökoku no gengo o ronji gen-Nippongo no kochi ni oyobu. *Gogen tankyû* 5. 1-43. Tokyo: Meiji Shoin.

Kiyose, Gisaburo N. 1998. Puyŏ-Koguryŏ Languages: The Fourth Altaic Stock. Paper presented at the 41st PIAC Meeting, Helsinki.

Lee, Kee-moon. 1964. Materials of the Koguryo Language. *Bulletin of the Korean Research Center: Journal of Social Sciences and Humanities* 20. 11-20.

Lewin, Bruno. 1973. Japanese and the Language of Koguryo. *Papers of the C.I.C. Far Eastern Language Institute* 4. 19-33.

Martin, Samuel E. 1987. *The Japanese Language Through Time*. New Haven: Yale University Press.

Miller, Roy Andrew. 1979. Old Japanese and the Koguryo Fragments: a resurvey, in George Bedell et al., eds., *Exploration in Linguistics: Papers in Honor of Kazuko Inoue*, 348-368. Tokyo: Kenkyusha.

Omodaka, Hisataka, et al. 1967. *Jidai betsu kokugo daijiten, jôdaihen.* Tokyo: Sanseido.

Pulleyblank, Edwin G. 1991. *Lexicon of Reconstructed Pronunciation in Early Middle Chinese, Late Middle Chinese, and Early Mandarin.* Vancouver: UBC Press.

Sakakura, Atsuyoshi. 1993. *Nihongo hyôgen no nagare.* Iwanami Seminâ Bukkusu 45. Tokyo: Iwanami Shoin.

Toh, Soo-hee. 1987. *Paekcheŏ yŏn'gu*, I. Seoul: Paekche Munhwa Kaebal Yŏn'gu wŏn.

Toh, Soo-hee. 1989. *Paekcheŏ yŏn'gu*, II. Seoul: Paekche Munhwa Kaebal Yŏn'gu wŏn.

Toh, Soo-hee. 1994. *Paekcheŏ yŏn'gu*, III. Seoul: Paekche Munhwa Kaebal Yŏn'gu wŏn.

Whitman, John. 1990. A Rule of Medial *-*r*-loss in Pre-Old Japanese, in Philip Baldi, ed., *Linguistic Change and Reconstruction Methodology*, 511-545. Berlin: Mouton de Gruyter.

Rendaku and Proto-Japanese Accent Classes

J. MARSHALL UNGER
The Ohio State University

1. Introduction

Rendaku (or sequential voicing) in Japanese refers to the voicing of the initial obstruent of a morpheme when it comes second in a compound. It never occurs in non-mimetic native compounds when there is a medial voiced obstruent in the second morpheme (Lyman 1894), but no one has found a rule that predicts when it does occur. Contrasting pairs like *hanazi* 'nosebleed' (< *hana* + *ti*) vs. *hanasaki* 'tip of the nose' and *hiragana* 'cursive syllabic script' (< *hira* + *kana*) vs. *katakana* 'angular syllabic script', compounds like *Nakata* ~ *Nakada* (family name), and the fact that some neologisms do exhibit *rendaku* while others do not all make it doubtful that a purely phonological explanation for the distribution of *rendaku* in the modern language will ever be found. The same is true for earlier stages of the language (Unger [1977] 1993).

Consequently, if we tabulate all the noun-compounds attested in Old Japanese documents by some phonological feature of their constituents, we expect to find *rendaku* distributed randomly over all combinations. Using a list of 908 noun compounds culled from Omodaka 1967 by Timothy J. Vance, my research assistant Yu Hirata created a "flat" database for testing this prediction. For each compound, he checked Vance's data, entered the meaning of the constituent nouns (to facilitate separation of homophones), and looked up their reconstructed accent classes (Martin 1987). I used Excel 97 to analyze this database.

2. Findings

In 826 (90.97%) of the 908 OJ compounds, the second noun lacked a medial *b*, *d*, *g*, or *z*, which would have blocked *rendaku* (Lyman's Law). Of those 826 compounds, the first and second nouns in 683 (82.69%) contained one or two syllables each. In fact, no second-position noun contained more than two syllables whereas 143 compounds had first-position nouns of three or more syllables. Because such long nouns fall into a large number of low-frequency accent classes and because the accent of first- with second-position nouns must be compared, I restricted my attention to the 683 compounds with mono- and dissyllabic constituents.

Table 1 shows how these are distributed with respect to the accent classes of their constituents. The 220 compounds that exhibit *rendaku* are tabulated in array R; all 683 observed compounds are tabulated in array O. In both arrays, the rows (columns) correspond to the accent classes of the nouns in first (second) position. In the accent class designator *n.k*, the number to the left of the point counts the syllables in the noun; the number to the right is the class number. An *x* instead of a number means that, for these nouns, Martin could not narrow down the reconstruction to one specific class. Thus 1.*x* and 2.*x* are not actual classes, like 1.1, 2.1, etc.

Instead of discarding the *n.x* data, we can distribute them over the real classes. There are two ways to do this (Table 2). One is to use the accent class percentages found in Martin's 1987 noun inventory (excluding borrowings); the other is to use percentages based on the set of all constituents actually found in OJ compounds. The advantage of using Martin's inventory is that we get a larger sample, including many nouns that do not begin with voiceless obstruents, as all the second-position nouns in the OJ data must. To obtain array R′ (O′) in Table 3, we multiply the numbers in the 1.*x* and 2.*x* rows (columns) of R (O) by the percentage of nouns in each class 1.1–1.3 (2.1–2.5) and add the products to the corresponding cells in that column (row). The advantage of using only the constituents found in OJ compounds is that we can obtain separate percentages for each class in first and second position; these figures lead to R″ (O″) in Table 4. In this case, the sample size for each class is smaller, but it turns out that the results of both procedures are in good agreement.

To compute the expectation arrays E′ (Table 5) and E″ (Tables 6), we multiply the entries in arrays O′ and O″, respectively, by 220/683 (32.21%), the ratio of *rendaku* compounds to all compounds. These arrays therefore reflect the hypothesis H_0 that *rendaku* is distributed randomly regardless of constituent accent. To check H_0, we perform χ^2 tests on the row and column sums of arrays E′, R′ and E″, R″, respectively. As shown in Tables 5 and 6, H_0 is confirmed for the row sums in both cases, but not for the column sums.[1] The probability that the columns sums differed from the expected values by chance alone is less than 5 percent for R′ and E′, and only slightly more than 5 percent for R″ and E″. In both cases, the number of *rendaku* compounds with a monosyllabic noun in second position was significantly lower than expected.

3. Accounting for the discrepancy

3.1 Merging mono- and dissyllabic nouns

This is a puzzling result because it suggests some sort of phonological conditioning of *rendaku*, yet the presence of a monosyllabic noun in second position merely makes it less likely. Moreover, since the number of syllables in the second constituent seems to affect the occurrence of *rendaku* significantly, it is strange that the number of syllables in the first constituent does not. Finally, why should we get fewer cases of *rendaku* than expected? If there were a preference for inserting *no* in *X.Y* compounds when *Y* was monosyllabic, then we would expect to find *more* cases (since reductions of *X.no.Y* would look like *rendaku* compounds).[2]

All these problems can be solved if we rearrange the data in accord with two ideas developed in Martin 1987. One is that class 1.3 is the result of a merger of two classes, 1.3a and 1.3b, that were distinct in proto-Japanese.

> Though the modern dialects require the reconstruction of only three accent types for monosyllabic nouns, both evidence from [Ruiju] Myōgi-shō and structural considerations indicate that earlier kinds of Japanese must have had four types. (Martin 1987, 180)

The other is that all pJ monosyllabic nouns were bimoraic, as they are in many Western Japanese dialects even now. When uttered in isolation, their vowels were prolonged so that they could carry any of the pitch contours HH, HL, LH, or LL, just like dissyllabic nouns. Furthermore, in terms of pitch contours, the 1.*k* and 2.*k* classes corresponded to one another in the following way (Martin 1987, 251):

---

[1] Although there are eight rows and columns, there are 6 degrees of freedom , not 7, because no expected value can be less than 5; hence, the 1.1 and 1.2 row sums and 2.4 and 2.5 column sums must be combined.

[2] Since we find *rendaku* randomly distributed when *Y* was dissyllabic, it can't be that there was a preference for inserting *no* in those cases.

Accent	Class	Noun		Class	Noun
HH	1.1	ki 'spirit' k̄īī	=	2.1	hana 'nose' p̄ān̄ā
LL	1.3a	ki 'tree' k̲i̲i̲	=	2.3	hana 'flower' p̲a̲n̲a̲
HL	1.2	ha 'leaf' p̄āa̲	=	2.2	hasi 'bridge' p̄ās̲i̲
LH	1.3b	ha 'tooth' p̲a̲ā	=	2.4	hasi 'chopstick' p̲a̲s̄ī

Using these correspondences, we can reorganize the data into arrays R″′ and O″′, calculate E″′, and carry out χ^2 tests on row and column sums as before (Table 7). This time H_0 is confirmed.

3.2 No alternative solution

Is there any other way we could achieve the same result? Since Martin's correspondences do the job, there is no point trying others if we accept his 1.3a ≠ 1.3b distinction. The critical test is to check whether combining two of the three original classes 1.2–1.3 also restores random distribution to *rendaku*. Table 8 summarizes the χ^2 results for each of the three possible cases. The only one that satisfies H_0 at the 5 percent level is the combination of 1.1 and 1.2 versus 1.3, but with $p < .07$, it just barely does so. Furthermore, combining 1.1 and 1.2 raises more questions than it answers. What could have caused these classes to split? If there were a split, why didn't it skew the distribution of *rendaku* when monosyllabic nouns came first as well as when they came second?

Classes 1.2 and 2.5 contain nouns that have distinctive falling pitch on the last syllable when uttered in isolation in Kyōto-type dialects. This alone distinguishes them from nouns in classes 1.1 and 2.4 (Martin 1987, 346 n. 1 to Chapter 4, §4). Japanese linguists have long struggled to interpret the 2.4 ≠ 2.5 distinction as the result of a phonemic split. Sakurai (1974) thinks it was conditioned by contrasting vowel distributions, but fares no better than the earlier scholars whose studies he reviews in detail. The Russian linguist Polivanov speculated that final falling pitch is a trace of a "truncated" nasal phoneme. Martin (1987, 361 n. 1 to Chapter 4, §14) thinks he got the idea by comparing Korean *achom* 'morning' with Japanese *asa* id., which is 2.5 and could be taken back to an earlier **asa.m*.[3] However, Martin found that the

---

[3] Actually, as Murayama shows, Polivanov got the final-nasal idea from an article by E. A. Meyer (1906), a phonetician interested in the origins of tones in Northern Germanic.

handful of Ryūkyū words with final nasals unreflected in main-island cognates are scattered randomly across reconstructed accent classes, and Hirata and I have hunted in vain for additional Korean matches with final nasals for Japanese 2.5 nouns. Polivanov's explanation for class 2.5 is therefore dubious. (In any case, he suggests no link between classes 1.2 and 2.5, and apart from falling pitch in Kyōto-type dialects, there seems to be none.) The present study adds to the doubt by showing that 2.5 nouns are unexceptional with respect to the distribution of *rendaku*. On that basis at least, the fact that class 2.5 is relatively small and distinctive only in one dialect group suggests that its origins should be sought in relatively recent developments within that group.

4. Significance of the results

If we don't adopt Martin's reconstruction of OJ monosyllabic noun accent, we cannot explain the non-random distribution of *rendaku* in those OJ noun compounds in which the second constituent is monosyllabic. Since we have strong independent reasons for thinking that *rendaku* has always been lexical, this strongly supports Martin's reconstruction, even though it was based solely on unrelated "evidence from Myōgi-shō and structural considerations." This surprising congruence of results has far-reaching implications for the reconstruction of early stages of the Japanese language.

In Unger ([1977] 1993), I showed that the internal reconstruction of OJ verb paradigms requires rules for reducing vowel sequences that depend on whether a vowel belongs to a mono- or polysyllabic morpheme. I also showed that the so-called *-ramu* forms of OJ verbs are evidence of a pre-OJ stage during which the *rentaikei* of *yodan* and *rahen* verbs ended in **-uru*, which shortened to *-u* in Old Japanese.[4] Whitman (1985, 1990) proposed that this change was a special case of a more general rule of *r*-deletion conditioned by the length of the preceding pre-OJ vowel. He reconstructed long vowels to block *r*-deletion, noting that they often matched rising pitch in Middle Korean cognates. But if vowels could be distinctively long or short before pre-OJ **r*, there is no reason that vowel length could not be distinctive in other environments, and, in Unger 1998, I explained how the rules of vowel sequence reduction could be recast in terms of vowel length provided that every monosyllabic morpheme was bimoraic. I also showed that, without that assumption, one is forced to give up other sound changes postulated by Whitman on the basis of Korean-Japanese matches. These changes—pre-OJ

---

[4] OJ *nahen*, *sahen*, *kahen*, and *nidan* verbs all have *rentaikei* in *-uru*. Likewise, they have *izenkei* in *-ure*, to which *yodan* and *rahen* answers with *-e*. The *-rasi* forms also preserve the **-ur-* sequence.

**ti* > OJ *si*, **ni* > *i*, and **ri* > *i*—help explain how the collapse of the so-called *kō-otsu* (or A-B) distinctions among pre-OJ *i*-ending syllables began, but lead to contradictions in the internal reconstruction of OJ verb paradigms unless pre-OJ vowel length is taken into account.

Thus, the assumption that vowels were automatically lengthened in pre-OJ monosyllabic morphemes forms a vital link between Korean-Japanese comparisons and the internal reconstruction of pre-OJ verb paradigms. The fact that it is supported by observations about the unrelated matter *rendaku* distribution is quite unexpected and therefore considerably strengthens our confidence that the proto-Korean-Japanese reconstruction reflects a real prehistoric language.

References

Lyman, Benjamin Smith. 1894. *Change from surd to sonant in Japanese compounds*. Philadelphia: Oriental Club of Philadelphia.

Martin, Samuel E. 1987. *The Japanese language through time*. New Haven: Yale University Press.

Meyer, Ernst Alfred. 1906. "Nihongo ni okeru ongakuteki go-akusento." *Nihongo kenkyū*, Murayama Shichirō (trans.), 1–10. Tōkyō: Kōbundō, 1976. Original in *Le monde oriental* (Uppsala: A.B. Lubdequistska Bokhandeln, 1906–41), 77–86.

Omodaka Hisataka et al., comps. 1967. *Jidaibetsu kokugo daijiten, jōdai hen*. Tōkyō: Sanseidō.

Sakurai Shigeharu. 1974. *Kodai kokugo akusento-shi ronkō*. Tōkyō: Ōfūsha.

Unger, J. Marshall. 1977. *Studies in Early Japanese morphophonemics*. Second edition, 1993. Bloomington: Indiana Linguistics Club.

——. 1998. "Reconciling comparative and internal reconstruction: the case of Old Japanese /ti, ri, ni/." Linguistics Society of America annual meeting (New York).

Whitman, John Bradford. 1985. "The phonological basis for the comparison of Japanese and Korean." Cambridge, MA: Harvard University dissertation.

——. 1990. "A rule for medial *-r- loss in pre-Old Japanese." *Linguistic change and reconstruction methodology*, ed. Philip Baldi, 511–45. Berlin: Mouton de Gruyter.

R	1.1	1.2	1.3	1.*x*	2.1	2.2	2.3	2.4	2.5	2.*x*	Total
1.1	1	0	2	0	4	2	2	2	0	0	13
1.2	0	0	0	0	0	2	1	0	0	0	3
1.3	0	1	1	0	9	3	3	2	2	0	21
1.*x*	0	0	1	0	3	3	4	1	0	0	12
2.1	0	2	3	0	6	9	10	2	0	0	32
2.2	0	2	3	0	4	7	10	0	0	0	26
2.3	0	1	4	0	6	11	10	9	1	1	43
2.4	0	0	2	0	2	4	4	3	0	1	16
2.5	0	2	0	0	6	2	2	3	0	0	15
2.*x*	2	2	4	0	9	6	12	4	0	0	39
Total	3	10	20	0	49	49	58	26	3	2	220

O	1.1	1.2	1.3	1.*x*	2.1	2.2	2.3	2.4	2.5	2.*x*	Total
1.1	3	1	6	0	9	5	12	5	1	2	44
1.2	1	0	0	1	1	3	3	0	0	0	9
1.3	2	3	5	1	15	8	7	5	2	1	49
1.*x*	2	0	3	0	6	5	8	2	0	0	26
2.1	2	5	10	1	21	25	34	7	0	1	106
2.2	5	4	8	2	12	18	26	6	1	1	83
2.3	7	5	9	4	27	33	35	17	2	3	142
2.4	4	0	4	2	3	7	8	3	0	1	32
2.5	3	4	3	4	16	11	18	3	1	1	64
2.*x*	7	5	22	3	26	24	29	10	0	2	128
Total	36	27	70	18	136	139	180	58	7	12	683

Table 1

pJ nouns reconstructed by Martin (1987)				OJ noun compound constituents				
Class	Distinct nouns (total)		Class	Distinct nouns in 1st position		Distinct nouns in 2nd position		
1.1	32	30.77%	1.1	18	31.03%	5	17.24%	
1.2	12	11.54%	1.2	8	13.79%	6	20.69%	
1.3	60	57.69%	1.3	32	55.17%	18	62.07%	
Total	104			58		29		
1.*x*	30		1.*x*	23		6		
Grand total	134			81		35		
2.1	239	31.20%	2.1	65	29.28%	43	31.85%	
2.2	111	14.49%	2.2	38	17.12%	23	17.04%	
2.3	264	34.46%	2.3	76	34.23%	48	35.56%	
2.4	90	11.75%	2.4	20	9.01%	17	12.59%	
2.5	62	8.09%	2.5	23	10.36%	4	2.96%	
Total	766			222		135		
2.*x*	40		2.*x*	99		8		
Grand total	806			321		143		

Table 2

R'	1.1	1.2	1.3	1.*x*	2.1	2.2	2.3	2.4	2.5	2.*x*	Total
1.1	1.00	0.00	2.31		4.92	2.92	3.23	2.31	0.00		16.69
1.2	0.00	0.00	0.12		0.35	2.35	1.46	0.12	0.00		4.38
1.3	0.00	1.00	1.58		10.73	4.73	5.31	2.58	2.00		27.92
1.*x*											
2.1	0.62	2.62	4.25		8.81	10.87	13.74	3.25	0.00		44.17
2.2	0.29	2.29	3.58		5.30	7.87	11.74	0.58	0.00		31.65
2.3	0.69	1.69	5.38		9.41	13.21	14.48	10.50	1.08		56.44
2.4	0.23	0.23	2.47		3.37	4.85	5.75	3.59	0.08		20.58
2.5	0.16	2.16	0.32		6.73	2.49	2.97	3.32	0.00		18.16
2.*x*											
Total	3.00	10.00	20.00		49.62	49.29	58.69	26.23	3.16		220.00

O'	1.1	1.2	1.3	1.*x*	2.1	2.2	2.3	2.4	2.5	2.*x*	Total
1.1	3.62	1.00	6.92		11.47	6.83	15.15	5.85	1.16		52.00
1.2	1.54	0.12	0.92		1.69	3.58	3.92	0.23	0.00		12.00
1.3	3.46	3.12	7.31		18.77	11.03	11.96	6.27	2.08		64.00
1.*x*											
2.1	4.78	6.78	17.98		29.62	32.72	43.61	10.31	0.13		145.94
2.2	6.76	5.01	12.59		16.17	21.66	30.65	7.60	1.10		101.55
2.3	10.96	7.30	19.49		37.11	41.81	46.27	20.88	2.30		186.11
2.4	5.55	0.86	7.94		6.44	10.00	11.83	4.32	0.10		47.04
2.5	4.87	4.89	7.23		18.47	13.11	20.75	3.95	1.09		74.36
2.*x*											
Total	41.54	29.08	80.38		139.74	140.74	184.14	59.41	7.97		683.00

Table 3

R"	1.1	1.2	1.3	1.*x*	2.1	2.2	2.3	2.4	2.5	2.*x*	Total
1.1	1.00	0.00	2.31		4.93	2.93	3.24	2.31	0.00		16.72
1.2	0.00	0.00	0.14		0.41	2.41	1.55	0.14	0.00		4.66
1.3	0.00	1.00	1.55		10.66	4.66	5.21	2.55	2.00		27.62
1.*x*											
2.1	0.59	2.59	4.17		8.64	10.76	13.51	3.17	0.00		43.42
2.2	0.34	2.34	3.68		5.54	8.03	12.05	0.68	0.00		32.68
2.3	0.68	1.68	5.37		9.40	13.22	14.46	10.50	1.03		56.35
2.4	0.18	0.18	2.36		3.13	4.71	5.44	3.49	0.03		19.51
2.5	0.21	2.21	0.41		6.93	2.62	3.24	3.41	0.00		19.04
2.*x*											
Total	3.00	10.00	20.00		49.64	49.34	58.71	26.25	3.06		220.00

O"	1.1	1.2	1.3	1.*x*	2.1	2.2	2.3	2.4	2.5	2.*x*	Total
1.1	3.62	1.00	6.93		11.50	6.89	15.19	5.87	1.06		52.07
1.2	1.45	0.21	1.03		1.83	3.69	4.10	0.28	0.00		12.59
1.3	3.28	3.21	7.28		18.63	10.93	11.77	6.23	2.03		63.34
1.*x*											
2.1	4.37	6.85	17.61		29.12	32.30	43.05	10.13	0.05		143.48
2.2	6.63	5.38	13.33		16.88	22.34	31.44	7.88	1.04		104.91
2.3	10.26	7.75	19.65		37.07	41.84	46.24	20.89	2.11		185.82
2.4	5.02	0.92	7.39		5.72	9.36	11.03	4.05	0.03		43.53
2.5	4.47	5.41	7.95		19.08	13.69	21.43	4.19	1.04		77.26
2.*x*											
Total	39.10	30.72	81.17		139.82	141.04	184.27	59.51	7.36		683.00

Table 4

E'	1.1	1.2	1.3	1.*x*	2.1	2.2	2.3	2.4	2.5	2.*x*	Total
1.1	1.16	0.32	2.23		3.69	2.20	4.88	1.88	0.37		16.75
1.2	0.50	0.04	0.30		0.55	1.15	1.26	0.07	0.00		3.87
1.3	1.11	1.00	2.35		6.05	3.55	3.85	2.02	0.67		20.61
1.*x*											
2.1	1.54	2.19	5.79		9.54	10.54	14.05	3.32	0.04		47.01
2.2	2.18	1.61	4.06		5.21	6.98	9.87	2.45	0.36		32.71
2.3	3.53	2.35	6.28		11.95	13.47	14.90	6.73	0.74		59.95
2.4	1.79	0.28	2.56		2.07	3.22	3.81	1.39	0.03		15.15
2.5	1.57	1.58	2.33		5.95	4.22	6.68	1.27	0.35		23.95
2.*x*											
Total	13.38	9.37	25.89		45.01	45.33	59.31	19.14	2.57		220.00

	All rows
ChiSq =	6.36
d.f. =	6
p =	0.384

	All columns	1.*k* columns	2.*k* columns
ChiSq =	12.99	9.436	3.55
d.f. =	6	2	3
p =	**0.043**	**0.009**	0.314

Table 5

E"	1.1	1.2	1.3	1.*x*	2.1	2.2	2.3	2.4	2.5	2.*x*	Total
1.1	1.17	0.32	2.23		3.70	2.22	4.89	1.89	0.34		16.77
1.2	0.47	0.07	0.33		0.59	1.19	1.32	0.09	0.00		4.05
1.3	1.06	1.03	2.34		6.00	3.52	3.79	2.01	0.65		20.40
1.*x*											
2.1	1.41	2.21	5.67		9.38	10.40	13.87	3.26	0.02		46.22
2.2	2.14	1.73	4.29		5.44	7.19	10.13	2.54	0.33		33.79
2.3	3.31	2.50	6.33		11.94	13.48	14.89	6.73	0.68		59.85
2.4	1.62	0.30	2.38		1.84	3.02	3.55	1.30	0.01		14.02
2.5	1.44	1.74	2.56		6.15	4.41	6.90	1.35	0.33		24.89
2.*x*											
Total	12.60	9.90	26.15		45.04	45.43	59.35	19.17	2.37		220.00

	All rows
ChiSq =	6.50
d.f. =	6
p =	0.369

	All columns	1.*k* columns	2.*k* columns
ChiSq =	12.37	8.76	3.62
d.f. =	6	2	3
p =	0.054	**0.013**	0.306

Table 6

R'''	2.1+	2.2+	2.3+	2.4+	2.5+	2.x+	Total
2.1+	15.36	16.43	23.54	5.56	0.00		61.20
2.2+	5.98	12.56	15.97	1.71	0.00		36.35
2.3+	17.24	18.01	24.74	13.88	3.07		77.29
2.4+	7.05	7.51	8.96	3.74	0.07		27.46
2.5+	7.00	4.78	3.50	3.36	0.00		18.71
2.x+							
Total	52.62	59.28	76.70	28.25	3.14		220.00

O'''	2.1+	2.2+	2.3+	2.4+	2.5+	2.x+	Total
2.1+	49.50	47.38	75.02	24.67	1.40		198.28
2.2+	26.26	30.47	45.86	9.85	1.34		113.91
2.3+	62.46	56.34	75.83	31.84	4.70		231.52
2.4+	19.53	17.87	21.83	5.56	0.33		65.24
2.5+	23.59	18.18	27.02	4.81	1.38		75.05
2.x+							
Total	181.34	170.24	245.55	76.72	9.14		683.00

E'''	2.1+	2.2+	2.3+	2.4+	2.5+	2.x+	Total
2.1+	15.95	15.26	24.17	7.95	0.45		63.77
2.2+	8.46	9.82	14.77	3.17	0.43		36.65
2.3+	20.12	18.15	24.43	10.26	1.51		74.46
2.4+	6.29	5.76	7.03	1.79	0.11		20.97
2.5+	7.60	5.86	8.70	1.55	0.45		24.15
2.x+							
Total	58.41	54.84	79.09	24.71	2.94		220.00

	All rows
ChiSq =	3.44
d.f. =	4
p =	0.487

	All columns
ChiSq =	1.51
d.f. =	3
p =	0.680

Table 7

	Classes 1.1 & 1.2	Class 1.3	Classes 1.1 & 1.3	Class 1.2	Classes 1.2 & 1.3	Class 1.1
E'	22.75	25.89	39.27	9.37	35.26	13.38
R'	13.00	20.00	23.00	10.00	30.00	3.00
E''	22.49	26.15	38.74	9.90	36.04	12.60
R''	13.00	20.00	23.00	10.00	30.00	3.00
$p' =$	0.063		**0.034**		**0.012**	
$p'' =$	0.066		**0.041**		**0.016**	

Table 8

Forgotten Voices: Early Recordings of the Kawakami Troupe

J. PAUL WARNICK
Brigham Young University

1. Introduction

Just over 100 years ago, in May 1899, a group of 19 performers led by Kawakami Otojiroo sailed from Yokohama for the United States and Europe.[1] This group, known as the Kawakami Troupe, performed in several U.S. cities, including San Francisco, Chicago, Boston and New York. They arrived in London in May, 1900, a year after their departure from Japan. After performing for British audiences, including at Buckingham Palace, the group went on to perform in France and Belgium before returning to Japan by the end of the year. They were in Paris at the time of the Paris Exposition during the summer of 1900. This troupe was the first known group of Japanese actors to tour abroad (Salz 1993). Their various audiences included Gide, Debussy, Rodin, Degas, Yeats, and Picasso, who, at the age of 19, sketched Kawakami's actress wife Sadayakko.

Also at the Paris Exposition were two recording engineers sent from the U.S. to open the European market for a new development in recording technology, the disc-playing gramophone. While in Europe, they made a number of wax recordings, including some of the performance numbers of the Kawakami Troupe. These recordings were marketed in Europe

[1] The historical information regarding the tour is taken from Miller (1998). See Chiba (1992) and Salz (1993) for additional information.

beginning in February of the following year. Evidently, none of the recordings made it to Japan, however, and it seems that no one in Japan knew of their existence until recently.

A few years ago, J. Scott Miller of Brigham Young University happened across the 1901 catalogue on microfilm in the British Library National Sound Archive. Further investigation revealed that copies of the recordings were mostly intact. The existence of the recordings was brought to the attention of scholars in Japan, and in late 1997, the recordings were released on compact disc together with a booklet containing a description of the collection and a transcription of the recordings (Miller et al. 1997). Evidently, these recordings are the earliest extant recordings of Japanese voices. This discovery, as can be imagined, has piqued a great deal of interest in Japan and has received wide press coverage there in various print and broadcast media (e.g. Asahi Shinbun 1997, Katayama 1998, Ongaku Buyoo Shinbun 1998).

The recordings, essentially lost to the world for almost a century, are a veritable treasure for academic inquiry, of interest to actors, musicians, historians, and other scholars, including those interested in language and linguistics. Given the inclusion of the introductions to the recordings, made by the performers themselves, we have over two dozen samples of spoken Japanese from a century ago. Although the introductions are limited to language use in a particular kind of setting, the recordings do provide a fascinating glimpse into the language of the time.

There are many interesting issues related to the language used in these recordings, which are worthy of further study, however the purpose of this paper is to provide an introduction to a just a few of the lexical and syntactic features observed in the introductory segments.

2. Overview of the Recordings

There are 28 recordings in the collection, covering a variety of performances. Of these, 27 have accompanying comments, including 25 with introductions to the given performance and two which have comments following the performance.

There are 22 recordings which mention the performer(s) by name. There are 16 cases which are clearly self-introductions, and of these, three did not include the name. Several performers were involved in multiple recordings. In total, there were nine individuals mentioned a total of 31 times. All 25 recordings which included introductory comments mentioned affiliation with Kawakami's troupe, and in 19 of these, the speaker also made reference to the troupe's Western tour.

There were five cases where the performer mentioned previous stops on the group's tour. Fujikawa noted that on June 27 (1900) the troupe performed before the Prince of Wales at Buckingham Palace. He then goes on to perform the number, entitled *Bingo Saburoo* (備後三郎), which Kawakami had performed at that time, in an imitation of Kawakami's own voice (Track 3). In another recording, he announces that he will perform something he had done in New York (Track 18). Takanami, another member of the troupe, announces that he will perform a narrative that he did in San Francisco (Track 7). Wada explains that he will do a scene from the *Merchant of Venice* which he had performed at the Bijou Theater in New York (Track 19). Yamamoto speaks of visiting a drama school in New York and he announces that he will perform what they observed the students practicing, namely different ways to laugh (Track 14).

There were four introductions which referred to the circumstances of the recordings. The examples below note the performer and the track number of the recording on the compact disc.

(1) パリ府に於いて (Tsusaka, Track 8)
'In Paris, ...'

(2) 当フランスパリスに於きまして (Wada, Track 19)
'Here in Paris, France....'

(3) このパリスに於きまして「何か日本の唄のようなものを聞かせてくれ」ということでございますが. . . (Nogaki, Track 21)
'I was asked here in Paris to present some kind of Japanese song....'

(4) ランスのパリーの蓄音機会社の求めによりまして、皆今日（こんにち）うち連れて、蓄音機へ入れます中で. . .
(Fujikawa, Track 13)
'Due to a request by a gramophone company in Paris, France, we are all recording something today....'

The introduction by Fujikawa, shown in (4), is the most complete statement about the setting for the recordings. Interestingly, these introductions use three different terms to refer to Paris (*Pari-hu*, *Parisu*, and *Parii*). Presumably, the modern *Pari* had not been standardized by this point.

3. Linguistic Features of the Introductions

3.1 Personal Pronominal Reference

There were seven unique individuals represented in the 16 cases where performers were clearly introducing their own performance, with 13 of these mentioning the name explicitly. Of these, 11 also used a personal pronoun, which in each case was *watakusi*. There were two cases where this pronoun was used and the name was not mentioned (Tracks 9 and 27), which are both attributed to Nogaki. There was one introduction, attributed to Komai, which used neither pronoun nor name (Track 16)

Table 1 Occurrences of Names and Pronouns in Self-Introductions

Performer	Name & Pron	Name Only	Pron Only	Total
Fujikawa	2	1		3
Takanami	3			3
Tsusaka	1			1
Wada	1			1
Yamamoto	1			1
Nogaki	2		2	4
Komai	1	1	_	2
Total	**11**	**2**	**2**	**15**

There were three other cases where the performer used the personal pronoun in situations other than self-introduction. Fujikawa used *watakusi* in two different settings in introducing the given performance (Tracks 13 and 18), and Nogaki used it once in claiming that he was not skilled in singing (Track 21).

The personal pronoun *watakusi* is considered today to be the most formal pronoun for first person reference. Grammars of the time of Kawakami's tour list several first person pronouns, covering a range of social situations, including *watakusi*, *watasi*, *wasi*, *ware*, *boku*, *sessya*, *syoosei*, *ore*, and *temae*, and despite the number of variations, these grammars note the relative infrequency of these forms in Japanese (Aston 1873, 1877, 1904, Chamberlain 1898, Noss 1907, Akada and Satomi 1908). According to these early grammars for native English speakers, *watakusi* was the most common first person pronoun in spoken Japanese, particularly in polite conversation, and appears as the standard in examples in each text (Aston 1873, 1877, 1904, Chamberlain 1898, Kuroda 1901, Noss 1907). This preference for *watakusi* seems to be borne out in these recordings as well.

3.2 Verb Forms Used in Self-Introductions

Most of the introductions included a form of the copula (*desu*, *de arimasu*, and *de gozaimasu*). All forms are shown in Table 2 in polite style (discussed below). Akada and Satomi (1908) explain that *desu* is the "shortened" form of *de arimasu*, and *de gozaimasu* is the polite form of *de arimasu* (see also Chamberlain 1898, Kuroda 1901). Chamberlain (1898) explains that *de gozaimasu* is "fused" into *desu* in familiar conversation. He states that *de arimasu* is "rather polite" and *de gozaimasu* "truly polite". Noss (1907) points out that *desu* is a contraction of *de arimasu* (rather than *de gozaimasu*) and indicates that *de gozaimasu* is the most polite of the copula forms. Note that the form considered most polite (*de gozaimasu*) was used in a majority of the cases.

Table 2 Forms Used in Self-Introductions

Verb Forms	**Occurrences**	
Form of *desu*	1	
Form of *de arimasu*	1	
Form of *de gozaimasu*	15	
Form of *iimasu*	1	
Form of *moosimasu*	1	
Manner of Introductions		
surname + given name *de gozaimasu*	6	(5 individuals)
surname *de gozaimasu*	3	(2 individuals)
surname *de gozaimasuru*	1	
surname + given name *desu*	1	
surname + given name *to iu mono desu*	1	
surname + given name *to moosu mono de gozaimasu*	1	
Kawakami ikkoo no mono de gozarimasuru	2	(1 individual)
Individual Variation		
Fujikawa		
Huzikawa Iwanosuke de gozaimasu		(Track 3)
Kawakami no yahari ikkooin de gozaimasite, Huzikawa de gozaimasu		(Track 13)
Huzikawa de gozaimasuru		(Track 18)
Takanami		
Takanami Sadaziroo de gozaimasu		(Tracks 4, 22)
Takanami Sadaziroo desu		(Track 7)
Nogaki		
Nogaki Seiiti de gozaimasu		(Track 20)
Nogaki Seiiti to iu mono desu		(Track 21)
Kawakami ikkoo no mono de gozaimasuru		(Tracks 9, 27)

Moosimasu (*moosu*) is a deferential, humble form of *iimasu* (*iu*), each meaning 'named' or 'called'. There was one instance of each of these forms in the introductions. There were four occurrences of the somewhat self-deprecating *mono*, which means 'person'. One performer used the phrase *to iu mono*, literally 'person called...' and another used the more deferential *to moosu mono.* Anecdotal evidence suggests that in Japanese as used today, the use of *de gozaimasu* in self-introductions is not as common as the phrase *to moosimasu.* The literal meaning of the latter is something like '(I am) called (or named) X' rather than '(I am) X'. Based on these recordings, it would seem that the use of *de gozaimasu* was much more common in these contexts a century ago.

As seen in the lower part of Table 2, three individuals introduced themselves in different ways at different times in the recordings.

3.3 Style in Japanese

There are several aspects of style in Japanese which reflect social relationships. Respect, formality, and politeness can be shown through different conjugations and through the selection of variant forms. Discussion here will focus on two elements of style. First, politeness can be shown to the addressee through the use of the so-called *desu/-masu* style, which is often referred to as polite style. This is distinguished from plain style, which is more familiar and casual. It is the sentence-final form which determines the style of the utterance. As a result, the presence of a polite style form at the end of a sentence will render the entire utterance polite and respectful, suggesting social distance, even if there are plain style verb forms within the sentence. The presence of polite style forms within a sentence makes the sentence more formal.

Second, respect can be shown through the selection of honorific or humble forms of a verb, referred to here as 'deferential' terms. Honorific forms show respect to the subject of the sentence, and humble forms are used to show respect to the person filling the role of the direct or indirect object of the sentence. More will be said about these forms below.

In early grammars, *-masu* is described as an auxiliary verb (Aston 1877, Noss 1907, Akada and Satomi 1908) which attaches to the verbal stem. Aston (1873) states that it is used in polite conversation. Kuroda (1901) indicates this auxiliary is "required by the most elementary courtesy". Noss (1907) says that "ordinarily, politeness requires" the use of *-masu.* Chamberlain (1898) suggests that *-masu* is used to "make verbs polite" and that its use results in an "honorific conjugation, which sounds more courteous than the ordinary conjugation and which is therefore in particularly frequent use". He goes on to say that use of the plain form "is apt to strike the ear as curt, especially at the end of a sentence". He later makes a distinction between polite style and deferential terms by saying that *-masu* is "scarcely honorific in the proper sense of the word, that is to say that [polite style *-masu* forms] are more often simply marks of a courteous style than of any special respect paid to the person addressed". Akada and Satomi (1908) note that the use of *-masu* is a feature of the spoken language, rather than the written language.

Each of the comments in the recordings consistently used polite style in sentence-final forms, suggesting a certain level of formality due to a degree of social distance between the speaker and hearer(s).

3.3.1 Style Used in Linking Contexts

Generally speaking, in today's Japanese, the plain style is used to link a verb with other predicates in using the conjunctive *-te* form (the gerund form). Since an utterance is considered polite when the sentence-final form is in polite style, this style seemingly is used internally only in social contexts deemed to be quite formal. Table 3 shows the distribution of plain and polite style forms used in linking contexts in the recordings.

Table 3 Style in Linking Contexts

Form	Meaning	Style		Occurrences
utiturete	'accompany'	plain		1
kite	'come'	plain		1
motte	'have' 'hold'	plain		1
oite	'(bc) in'	plain		1
			Total	**4**
okimasite	'(be) in'	polite		4
yorimasite	'owing to'	polite		1
			Total	**5**

As seen in the table, the distribution is fairly even with four cases of plain forms and five cases of polite forms. Note that *oite* and *okimasite* are forms of the same verb; with this particular word, polite style was more prevalent (used four out of five times).

Early grammars generally do not explicitly discuss sentence-internal style. Several grammars discuss *-masu* generally, as noted above, with no specific mention of non-sentence-final forms. One exception is Noss (1907), who points out that in dependent clauses, plain style "may be used even in polite conversation if the principal verb is polite". He indicates, as noted above, that *-masu* forms are required by courtesy, "at least in those parts of a sentence on which stress is laid". He later suggests that for "variety's sake verbs in inconspicuous positions should ordinarily be plain", although he does not define such positions. Despite the general lack of discussion about the social distinction between internal linking forms in plain style as opposed to polite style, most grammars include examples of each style in linking contexts (Aston 1873, Chamberlain 1898, Kuroda 1901, Noss 1907, Akada and Satomi 1908).

3.3.2 Style Used in Adnominal Contexts

Use of the polite style is also relatively rare in adnominal uses of verbs in modern Japanese. Table 4 shows the number of these cases in the recordings.

Again there is a fairly even distribution between the two styles. The seven cases of polite forms used adnominally suggest a rather formal perception of the setting. Grammars of the period use both plain and polite forms in adnominal contexts in the examples they provide, without commenting on differences between the two (e.g. Chamberlain 1898, Kuroda 1901, Noss 1907, Akada and Satomi 1908).

Table 4 Style in Adnominal Contexts

Form	Meaning	Style	Occurrences
to iu koto	'thing called X'	plain	1
to iu mono	'thing called X'	plain	2
to moosu mono	'person called X'	plain	1
to moosu no	'one called X'	plain	1
gosyookai itasu mono	'thing (I)'ll introduce'	plain	1
		Total	**6**
itasimasita [title]	[title] which I performed'	polite	1
enzimasita [title]	[title] which [I] performed'	polite	1
hakusimasita [title]	'[title] met with (applause)'	polite	1
yatte orimasita koto	'thing which I did'	polite	1
iremasu naka de	'amidst recording'	polite	1
katazikenoo simasita [group]	'[group] favored with'	polite	1
mimasita toki	'time when X saw'	polite	1
		Total	**7**

3.3.3 Deferential Forms

Table 5 shows the verb forms used in sentence-final contexts and indicates whether each one is a deferential variant. Variations in tense and aspect are not reflected in the table.

Of the 55 sentence-final forms, all were in polite-style, showing respect to the addressee. In addition, the majority, 39 of the 55 (71%), were deferential forms, showing increased respect and politeness.

Table 5 Use of Deferential Verb Forms

Form		Deferential?	Occurrences
Copula forms			
desu		no	1
de arimasu		no	1
de gozaimasu		yes	20
Verbs meaning 'to present/perform/introduce'			
enzimasu		no	5
okurimasu		no	1
ome ni kakemasu		yes	1
okiki ni iremasu		yes	1
okiki ni tassimasu		yes	4
gosyookai itasimasu		yes	1
gosyookai moosimasu		yes	1
syookai itasimasu		yes	3
syookai simasu		no	7
Other forms			
yarimasu	'do'	no	1
itasimasu	'do'	yes	2
orimasu	'be'	yes	2
moosiagemasu	'say'	yes	2
gozaimasu	'exist'	yes	1
katazikenoo simasu	'be favored with'	yes	1
		Total	**55**

3.4 Notable Changes Over the Past Century

3.4.1 Adnominal Forms Ending a Sentence

There were several cases in the recordings where the adnominal form (the *rentai* inflection) of a predicate was used at the end of a sentence. Table 6 summarizes these occurrences.

Table 6 Adnominal Forms Used in Sentence-Final Position

Form	Meaning	Occurrences
de gozaimasuru	'be'	5
de gozarimasuru	'be'	2
moosiagemasuru	'say'	2
okiki ni tassimasuru	'present (for you)'	1
syookai simasuru	'introduce'	1
itasimasuru	'do'	1
	Total	**12**

In modern Japanese, there is no distinction between the conclusive form (the *syuusi* inflection) and the adnominal form. A century ago, as noted in these data, thc distinct adnominal form was still in use and used in sentence-final contexts. In these data, such adnominal uses account for 12 of the 55 sentence-final forms (22%). The distribution of these uses is shown in Table 7.

Table 7 Distribution of Adnominal Forms Used in Sentence-Final Position

Speaker	Track	# of Sentence-final Predicates	# of Sentence-final Predicates with *masuru*
Fujikawa	3	6	3
Fujikawa	13	2	1
Fujikawa	18	2	1
Nogaki	9	2	1
Nogaki	21	4	1
Nogaki	27	2	2
Yamamoto	14	2	1
?	1	1	1
?	24	2	1
Total		**23**	**12**

Note that those who used the *-masuru* form tended to use it about half of the time on average (12 times out of 23). Fujikawa accounts for five of the cases. He used adnominal forms in each of the three introductory segments he recorded, in five of ten total sentence-final predicates. Nogaki accounts for four of the instances of *-masuru* forms, using these forms in three of his four introductions, in four of eight cases. There were two predicates in his fourth introduction. Yamamoto used *-masuru* one time out of two in the one introduction clearly attributable to him. In two cases, the identity of the speaker is unclear.

Some early grammars make no mention of the adnominal *-masuru* form (e.g. Kuroda 1901, Akada and Satomi 1908). Others include examples using this form in sentence-final position, with varying degrees of explanation. Aston (1873) suggests that *-masu* and *-masuru* are used "indiscriminately". He states that the "latter form is affected by polite speakers". He later adds that *-masuru* is "more elegant, but less commonly used" than *-masu*. Chamberlain (1898) simply lists both forms for the "polite certain present" conjugation, with no explanation. Noss (1907) claims that *-masu* may become *-masuru* simply as a matter of euphony.

Research in recent years has examined more closely the uses of the adnominal inflection in Japanese. Quinn (1994) summarizes the various uses of this inflection and notes that all nonadnominal uses of the *rentai* inflection serve to nominalize a clause and index a certain level of commitment to the factuality of the information given. In main clauses, the nominalization serves as a referential predicate, presenting that predicate as established information and providing explanation linking the predicate with the discourse context. It has been argued that the modern *no da* construction is the functional counterpart of this use of the *rentai* inflection (see Horie 1993, Quinn 1987, 1993, Iwasaki 1993, Yamaguchi 1987).[2]

In examining the occurrences of the *-masuru* form in these data, five appeared in statements of identity, usually in stating affiliation with the Kawakami troupe. Five appeared in statements announcing the number to be performed. Of the other two cases, one was used in talking about the group appearing at Buckingham Palace, and one was used when the performer declared he was not generally adept at singing.

Future research will examine the use of *-masu* and *-masuru* forms in their specific contexts in these recordings in light of this research related to nominalized clauses and referentiality.

---

[2]Also see Prince (1978) and Kamio (1994) for discussion of the idea of established information and commitment to the factuality of information.

3.4.2 *De gozarimasu* Forms

As seen in Table 6, these data include uses of the *de gozarimasu* form in addition to the *de gozaimasu* form. In modern standard Japanese, only the latter is still in use. An examination of early grammars concerning the relative use of these forms shows that the examples in Aston (1873, 1877, 1904) favor *gozarimasu*. Chamberlain (1898) seems to favor *gozaimasu* in his examples. He states that the *r* is dropped in the Tokyo dialect when *-masu* is attached, pointing out that *gozarimasu* is the Kyoto pronunciation, still favored (at that time) by the Imperial Court. Kuroda (1901) uses both forms, with no explanation, although examples using *gozarimasu* seem to be more prevalent. Noss (1907) indicates that *gozarimasu* is usually "contracted" with the addition of *-masu*. The examples in his text seem to show a preference for *gozaimasu*. Akada and Satomi (1908) favor *gozaimasu*. Although both forms seem to have been used during this period, when viewed chronologically, these grammars seem to reflect a change to wider use of *gozaimasu* and less use of *gozarimasu* forms.

In the recordings, there was a definite preference for forms of *de gozaimasu*. Of 20 occurrences of the deferential form of the copula, only two were forms of *de gozarimasu*, and both appeared in introductions by Nogaki, who used the *de gozaimasu* form as well.

3.4.3 Adjective Forms

The use of adjective forms in the recordings was quite rare. There was only one case of an adjective used predicatively. This form, shown in Table 5, is the phrase *katazikenoo simasita* ('favored with'), which was used in stating that the group was favored with an audience with the Prince of Wales. This phrase seems to have become grammaticalized and appears as a unit in modern dictionaries (e.g. Kenkyusha 1974). The phrase is based on the adjective *katazikenasi*. The form in which it appears in these data is the result of a phenomenon of euphonic change (known as *onbin*) in the *ren'yoo* (adverbial) inflection.

Grammars of a century ago do include examples of adjectives as used today together with the copula to represent polite style (e.g. *omoi desu* 'is heavy'). Akada and Satomi (1908), however, point out that "it sounds better" to use *gozaimasu* rather than *desu*. In such cases, *onbin* forms are used (e.g. *omoo gozaimasu*). Most of the examples in these grammars use the *gozaimasu* forms (Aston 1873, Chamberlain 1898, Kuroda 1901, Noss 1907). In modern Japanese, the use of these *onbin* forms with *gozaimasu* is reserved for very polite or very formal situations, with the exception of certain formulaic utterances such as *arigatoo gozaimasu* ('thank you') and *ohayoo gozaimasu* ('good morning').

Chamberlain (1898) points out that the *ren'yoo* form is used when a verb other than *gozaimasu* follows. Such is the case in the example of *katazikenoo simasita.* The only grammar which specifically mentions *suru* (citation form of *simasita*) in combination with adjectival forms is Noss (1907). The meaning of this combination would be something like 'make it X' (X being the state described by the adjective) or 'do it in X manner'. The particular case in these data (*katazikenoo simasita*) has been derived in this way, although as noted, it seems to have become grammaticalized.

4. Conclusion

This paper has attempted to provide a preliminary analysis of some of the features of the Japanese language as it was used in these recordings of a century ago. These data present many possibilities for additional linguistic research. This paper has looked primarily at the forms. Future research will examine more closely the contexts in which these forms are used.

Salz (1993) suggests that given the many contributions of Kawakami and Sadayakko, their importance has yet to be fully realized. With the subsequent publication of early recordings of their troupe, his statement has proved prophetic in a way even he may not have realized. Future research, from a variety of fields and perspectives, will continue to underscore Kawakami's contributions and provide valuable insights into Japan and the Japanese language at the beginning of the twentieth century.

References

Akada K., and J. Satomi. 1908. *How to Speak Japanese Correctly*, 3rd Edition. Tokyo: R.Z. Okazakiya and Co., Ltd.

Asahi Shinbun. 1997. Nihonjin Saiko no Rekoodo Fukkoku. December 16. Pg. 1. Evening Edition.

Aston, W.G. 1873. *A Short Grammar of the Japanese Spoken Language*, 3rd Edition. London: Trubner and Co.

______. 1877. *A Grammar of the Japanese Written Language*, 2nd Edition. London: Trubner and Co.

_____. 1904. *A Grammar of the Japanese Written Language*, 3rd Edition. London: Luzac and Co.

Chamberlain, Basil Hall. 1898. *A Handbook of Colloquial Japanese*, 3rd Edition, Tokyo: Shuyeisha.

Chiba, Yoko. 1992. Sada Yacco and Kawakami: Performers of *Japonisme*. *Modern Drama* 35:1.35-53.

Horie, Kaoru. 1993. From Zero to Overt Nominalizer NO: A Syntactic Change in Japanese, in S. Choi, ed., *Japanese/Korean Linguistics 3*, 305-321. Stanford: CSLI.

Iwasaki, Shoichi. 1993. Functional Transfer in the History of Japanese Language, in P. M. Clancy, ed., *Japanese/Korean Linguistics 2*, 20-32. Stanford: CSLI.

Kamio, Akio. 1994. The Theory of Territory of Information: The Case of Japanese. *Journal of Pragmatics* 21.67-100.

Katayama, M. 1998. Nihonjin ni yoru Hatsu no Shoogyoo Rekoodo o Kiku Meiji Geinoo Mihon'ichi. *CD Jaanaru* . January. Pg. 50.

Kenkyusha. 1974. *New Japanese-English Dictionary*, 4th Edition. Tokyo, Japan.

Kuroda, Takuma. 1901. *The Spoken Language of Japan.* Tokyo: Kinkoodoo and Co.

Miller, J. Scott, Miyakoya Utaroku, et al. 1997. *Yomigaeru Oppekepee: 1900-nen Pari Banpaku no Kawakami Ichiza.* Toshiba EMI TOCG-5432.

Miller, J. Scott. 1998. Dispossessed Melodies: Recordings of the Kawakami Theater Troupe. *Monumentica Nipponica* 53:2.225-235.

Noss, Christopher. 1907. *A Textbook of Colloquial Japanese.* Tokyo: Methodist Publishing House.

Ongaku Buyoo Shinbun. 1998. Interumezzo. February 21. Pg. 1.

Prince, Ellen F. 1978. A Comparison of Wh-clefts and It-clefts in Discourse. *Language* 54.883-906.

Quinn, Charles J. 1987. *A Functional Grammar of Predication in Classical Japanese.* Doctoral dissertation, University of Michigan.

____. 1993. Clause as Text: The Staging of Information in Classical Japanese and Kakari-musubi. Ms., The Ohio State University.

____. 1994. Kodai Nihongo 'Kakarimusubi' Kinooron. *Nihon Bunka Kenkyuujo Kenkyuu Hookoku* 30.144-192.

Salz, Jonah. 1993. Intercultural Pioneers: Otojiro Kawakami and Sada Yakko. *The Journal of Intercultural Studies* 20.25-74.

Yamaguchi, Yoshinori. 1987. Kaku Katsuyookei no Kinoo, in A. Yamaguchi, ed., *Kokubunpoo Kooza* 2, 1-36. Tokyo: Meiji Shoin.

Part II

Phonetics, Phonology and Acquisition

Laryngeal Effects of Stop Consonants on Neighboring Vowels in /CV/ Sequences in Korean

HYUNKEE AHN
University of Texas

1. Aims and Motivations of the Study

This paper investigates the phonation modes of the vowels following the three phonemically different stop consonants in Korean, the tense stops, the lenis stops, and the aspirated stops. This study focuses on the acoustic differences of the vowels following the consonants in question, specifically in /_a/ sequences. The major acoustic measure employed in this study is the measurement of H1*-H2*, a normalized amplitude difference between the first and second harmonics that will be discussed in greater detail below. This analysis will allow us insight into the laryngeal settings made in the articulation of the three stop series without the use of fiberoptic measures of glottal width. The different articulatory gestures characterizing the three stop series in Korean have been described in previous studies (Kagaya, 1974) as follows: constricted glottis for tense stops, spread glottis for aspirated stops, and/or moderate glottis for lenis stops. This study also investigates the interrelationship among H1*-H2*, VOT, and F_0 measures. Particularly, the extent to which the different laryngeal settings are directly mapped to the durational difference in the Voice Onset Time (=VOT, henceforth) is still unknown. The mapping between laryngeal settings and VOT is important because VOT is the only well-known salient feature whereby the three stop series are acoustically distinguished. Specifically,

VOT is significantly longer in aspirated stops; VOT is shortest in tense stops; and VOT of the lenis stops is generally considered as in-between. Finally, based on acoustic findings, this paper suggests more plausible phonological representations for the three different stop classes in Korean.

2. The Obs(H1-H2) Measure

One way of determining a phonation type is by numeric measurements of the observed amplitude difference in decibels between the first and second harmonics (=Obs(H1-H2), henceforth). As clearly specified in Johnson (1997:127-130), the value of H1-H2 plays an important role as an index of the relative breathiness or creakiness of phonation. The general assumption is that the value of Obs(H1-H2) is much larger during breathy voice than during creaky voice. The difference in Obs(H1-H2) is mainly due to the difference in the shape of the glottal waveform. Specifically, the amplitude of the first harmonic in the breathy phonation is more dominant over the others because of these three phonations, the glottal waveform of breathy phonation is most like a sine wave. The creaky phonation does not show a difference in amplitude between the first few harmonics. Thus the creaky waveform is least like a sine wave. This is mainly due to the closing phase of the glottal waveform falling off abruptly.

On the assumption that the spectral characteristics of the glottal waveform are directly reflected in those of the following vowel, the value of Obs(H1-H2) can be used to determine the phonation type of that vowel. In this respect, the vowel in question should be a low vowel like [a], where the first formant (=F1), which is highest among the vowels, does not appear to boost up either the first or second harmonics very much.

3. The H1*-H2* Measure

However, the method of Obs(H1-H2) is not entirely reliable if it is measured at the voicing onset of a vowel in a /CV/ context. This is because the first and second harmonics undergo a 'boost effect' mainly by the amplitude of the first formant during the first formant transition in the initial part of a vowel that follows a consonant. Suppose, for example, that a first formant rises up from 200 Hz at the voicing onset to a stable state of 800Hz, this formant transition would affect the amplitude levels of the first few harmonics. This F1 amplitude perturbation effect is also clearly exemplified in Fant (1960:54-55), where the F1 downward shift in frequency with the rest of the formants being fixed results in an amplitude loss in the overall spectral envelope of the vowel. Thus, the Obs(H1-H2) measure is not dependable, since the main concern of this study is to observe the difference in phonation type at the voicing onset of the vowel following a stop. At this point the laryngeal influence of the preceding stop is supposedly most salient.

To correct this 'boost-up' effect at the voicing onset, Stevens and Hanson (1995) suggested a new method of H1*-H2*, a normalized amplitude difference between the first and second harmonics. The value of H1*-H2* is obtained by subtracting the expected value of H1-H2 (=Exp(H1-H2), henceforth) from the value of Obs(H1-H2), as shown in the formula (1) below.

(1) H1* - H2* = Obs(H1-H2) – Exp(H1-H2)

According to the acoustic theory of speech production (Fant, 1960), we can predict an expected value of Exp(H1-H2) if we know F_0 and the first few formant frequencies (Fant, 1960:49-60; 1972) (cf. for the detailed explanation, see Ahn (1999)). This prediction is based on the assumption that the glottal wave is characteristic of modal phonation. Hence, the spectral tilt of the glottal source is fixed at –12 dB/*octave*. Since H1*-H2* compares observed and expected differences, it provides an indication of how the source spectrum deviates from the reference. In this respect, the value of H1*-H2* naturally represents a normalized amplitude difference between the first and second harmonics. For example, a zero value of H1*-H2* indicates that the sound wave observed at that particular time point has a glottal spectrum of modal phonation; specifically, the spectral tilt of the waveform falls off at a rate of –12 dB/*octave*.

The H1*-H2* value is free from the variations of the F-patterns. Conversely, a value of Exp (H1-H2) varies depending on the F-pattern, so that the value naturally reflects the F1 amplitude perturbation effect. Because H1*-H2* is a value obtained by subtracting Exp(H1-H2) from Obs(H1-H2), this measure reflects the characteristics of pure glottal phonation, which is computed relative to modal phonation.

4. Experimental Method

A total of 6 male subjects participated in the recording. At the time of the recordings, all subjects with the exception of one visiting scholar were graduate students attending the University of Texas at Austin. None reported any medical problems influencing their language ability. The average age of the subjects was 36.5. They all speak standard Korean (Seoul dialect).

Speech samples were of CV structure with C being a stop consonant varying in place and manner and V being a fixed vowel [a]. Some of these items turned out to be real words, others nonsense words. For the data, the words in (2) were used, embedded in the carrier sentence in (3):

(2) a. tense series: /p'a/, /t'a/, /k'a/
b. lenis series: /pa/, /ta/, /ka/
c. aspirated series: /pʰa/, /tʰa/, /kʰa/

(3) Carrier sentence for the samples

sentence: /i+kəs+i ___ita/ [igəʃi ___ida]
gloss: this + thing + nominative marker ______ be (declarative ending)
meaning: This is ________.

The subjects were required to repeat each of the items in (2) in succession until 5 clear tokens of each sample had been obtained. Eventually, a total of 45 tokens was obtained from each subject (i.e., 3 manner categories * 3 places * 5 repetitions = 45 tokens). Subjects were recorded in a soundproofed room in the phonetics laboratory of the University of Texas at Austin. They were asked to speak the samples at normal speed and as naturally as possible in front of the microphone (Electro-Voice® 671A, Dynamic Cardioid, Electro-Voice, Inc.). The microphone was connected to a Power Mac computer (7100/80) via a stereo mixing console (Realisitc®, Model No. 32-1200B). The recording for each subject took approximately 30 to 45 minutes.

Since it was important to keep the amplitude level of each token constant, a method of on-line digitization was adopted. The digitization was made at a sampling rate of 22, 050 Hz with the aid of 'Sound Scope 1.43f (Macintosh software program from GW Instruments, Inc.)'. Those signals clipped either at the top or bottom were discarded. The amplitude level of each token was easily maintained within the range of +/- 10 volts. In addition, when the subject found the pronunciation of the token unnatural, that token was also discarded. Some subjects produced the speech sample more than five times in a row until five clear signals were obtained. The digitized tokens were analyzed using Sound Scope to obtain the following raw data in (4).

(4) a. VOT
b. Amplitude levels of harmonic 1 and 2
c. Fundamental Frequency
d. Frequency values of formant 1 through formant 4

The VOT value was obtained by measuring the durational length from the instant of the release of an articulator to the beginning of the first complete glottal pulse of the following vowel. To obtain the values of the various measures in (4 b, c, d), a digital signal program of 'Fast Fourier Transform

Routine' (=FFT, henceforth) included in Sound Scope was used with the following parameters in (5):

(5) a. FFT points: 1024
b. Bandwidth of Filter: 59Hz(25ms window)
c. 6 dB pre-emphasis: Off

The phonation mode (via H1*-H2*) and F_0 pattern at voicing onset position were most highly affected by the laryngeal settings of the preceding stop. To trace the extent to which they were maintained into a vowel, the values in (4 b,c,d) were obtained along a target vowel at the following five different time points as in (6) below:

(6) a. 13ms away from the voicing onset of the vowel (+13ms time point, henceforth)
b. 1/8 of the vowel (1/8 time point, henceforth)
c. 1/4 of the vowel (1/4 time point, henceforth)
d. 3/8 of the vowel (3/8 time point, henceforth)
e. 1/2 of the vowel (1/2 time point, henceforth)

The reason for measuring at +13ms point and not right on the first glottal pulse of a vowel (i.e., zero time point of a vowel), was that since the relevant FFT points that were collected centered around the marker on the source waveform in this particular software program, and since the window frame is fixed at 25ms, the +13ms point (i.e., around half of 25 ms window) could be the minimum distance used to identify a phonation mode of a pure vowel at its earliest position measurable. If the source marker was on the voicing onset position, it would include a mixture of the sound of aspiration and the vowel. Determining the remaining time points (i.e., 1/8, 1/4, 3/8, and 1/2 time points) was somewhat arbitrary and relational, and was mainly decided in reference to the whole length of a vowel.

The raw data were processed using 'Excel' (Microsoft Office 98 for Mac) in order to calculate the values of Exp(H1-H2), and H1*-H2*.

5. Statistical Treatment

For the statistical analyses, the present study used two different methods; Repeated Measures MANOVA and Regression Analysis. The former was conducted to test the significance of means of H1*-H2*, F_0, and VOT on three manner classes of stops across all subjects. The latter was performed to measure relationship between VOT and H1*-H2*values. This method was also adopted to determine the strength of the association among the two dependent variables as expressed in terms of R^2 values (the square of a correlation coefficient multiplied by 100). The repeated measures design is well known as one of the most powerful and efficient research designs. This design is employed in situations in which subjects are measured on more than one occasion – i.e., each subject participates in more than one experimental condition. This design is powerful because error variance is reduced substantially and efficient because fewer subjects are needed than in nonrepeated measures experimental design. In sum, the repeated measures MANOVA design employed in this study has the following parameters in (7).

(7) a. within-subject variables: 3
manner (3 levels) * place (3 levels) * time (5 levels)
b. between-subject variable: none
c. number of randomly selected subjects: 6
d. dependent variables:
3 (at +13ms time point): VOT, H1*-H2*, F_0
2 (at all other time points): H1*-H2*, F_0

6. Working Hypotheses

According to the fiberscopic studies (Kim C-W, 1965; Kagaya, 1974), the three Korean stop categories can be distinguished in terms of the glottal width during the stop closure; it is smallest for the tense stops, intermediate for the lenis stops, and largest for the aspirated stops. Since these distinct physiological characteristics are reflected most saliently in the H1*-H2* values at the +13ms time point, we can suggest the following working hypotheses for this measure as shown in (8):

(8) a. The H1*-H2* value should be larger in the aspirated class than in the lenis class at the +13ms time point.
b. The H1*-H2* value should be larger in the aspirated class than in the tense class at the +13ms time point.
c. The H1*-H2* value should be larger in the lenis class than in the tense class at the +13ms time point.

Following Ladefoged and Maddieson (1996)'s hypothesis that the wider the glottis at release, the longer the VOT, and on the assumption that glottal width is reflected in the H1*-H2* value, we suggest a working hypothesis in (9) below with regard to the interrelationship between H1*-H2* and VOT measure:

(9) The larger the H1*-H2* value, the longer the VOT duration.

7. Results

7.1 Results for the H1*-H2* Measure

A line graph in Figure 1 represents mean values of the Obs(H1-H2), Exp(H1-H2), and H1*-H2* measures for the three stop categories obtained at the +13ms time point. The numerical values for the means are presented in Table 1.

Figure1. Line graph with average data points for Obs(H1-H2), Exp(H1-H2), and H1*-H2* for the three stop categories. The observations were averaged over all 6 Korean subjects.

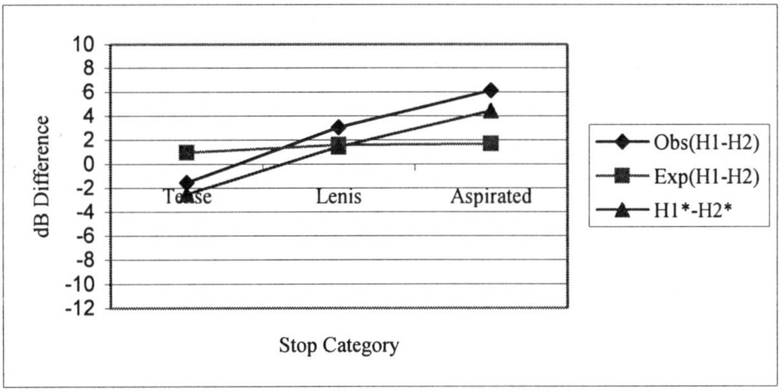

Table 1. Mean values of the Obs(H1-H2), Exp(H1-H2), and H1*-H2* measures at the +13ms time point

Manner Classes	Obs(H1-H2)	Exp(H1-H2)	H1*-H2*
Tense	-1.55	0.95	-2.50
Lenis	3.06	1.61	1.45
Aspirated	6.13	1.69	4.44

The F1 amplitude perturbation effects are reflected in the Exp(H1-H2) values. The post-lenis and post-aspirated vowels show somewhat higher values in this measure than the post-tense vowels. This is mainly because of the long duration of aspiration during which formant transition occurs simultaneously, as is usual for stops with long VOT's. Due to their short VOT, on the other hand, the post-tense vowels show Exp(H1-H2) values smaller than those of the other two classes. As for this class, the F1 transition is salient in the initial portion of the vowel, causing an amplitude perturbation effect on the first and second harmonics (especially, on the second harmonic). This is why at the +13ms time point the value of

Exp(H1-H2) of the post-tense class is smaller than those for the other two classes.

Temporal patterns of average H1*-H2* values are presented in figure 2.

Figure 2. The line graphs based on the average H1*-H2* values at the five time points.

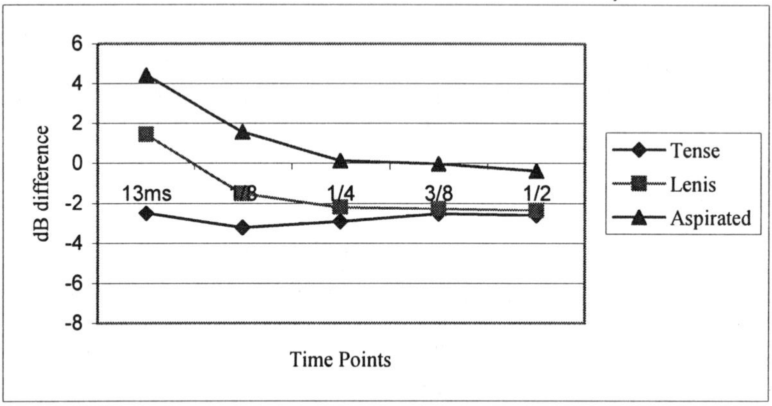

Figure 2 shows that the average H1*-H2* values tend to decrease as a function of time for the post-lenis and post-aspirated vowels, while the corresponding post-tense values stay relatively flat.

The graphic trends introduced in figures 1 and 2 should be evaluated statistically. Table 2 shows the results of the statistical analyses of the repeated measures ANOVA.

Table 2. Source table: analysis of variance with repeated measures for the H1*-H2* measure at the five time points

Time point	Sum of Squares	Degree of Freedom	Mean of Squares	F-statistic	p-value
+13	2175.51	2	1087.76	15.84	<.01*
1/8	1066.23	2	533.18	7.50	<.05*
1/4	459.65	2	229.82	2.57	.125
3/8	342.52	2	171.26	2.57	.126
1/2	269.47	2	134.73	2.85	.105

First of all, for an alpha level of .05, the results in table 6.2 show a strong main effect for the factor 'Manner' ($p < 0.01$*) at the +13ms and 1/8 time points, indicating a statistically significant difference in mean numbers between at least two manner classes. Statistically, the differences in this measure disappear among the three classes at and after the 1/4 time point.

As a next step, a pairwise Bonferroni test on estimated marginal means was performed as a post-hoc test to determine which means truly differ at the first two time points. The results of the pairwise comparisons are presented in table 3:

Table 3. The pair-wise comparisons (the Bonferroni test with adjusted alpha level = 0.05) of the estimated mean values of the three Korean manner classes at the +13ms and 1/8 time points.

Time points	Classes Compared	p-value ($\alpha = .05$)
+13ms	Tense vs. Lenis	<.05*
	Tense vs. Aspirated	<.01*
	Lenis vs. Aspirated	.365
1/8	Tense vs. Lenis	.462
	Tense vs. Aspirated	<.05*
	Lenis vs. Aspirated	.356

At the +13ms time point, the estimated mean value of the post-aspirated data is significantly higher than the mean values of the other two classes, while the difference in estimated means between post-lenis and post-aspirated classes is found to be non-significant. Consequently, the working hypothesis in (8a) is rejected. In a statistical sense, the lenis and aspirated classes are just variations of sampling distributions.

7.2 Results for the F_0 Measure

The course of F_0 during the vowel is diagrammed in figure 3.

Figure 3. Average F_0 values of the three manner classes plotted as a function of the five consecutive time points

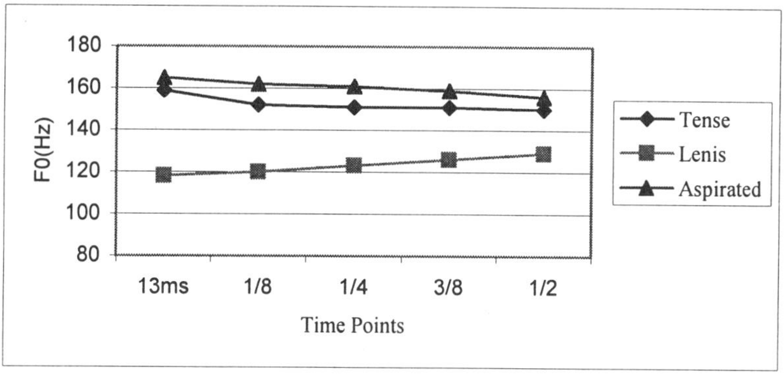

In terms of average values, F_0 is high for the post-aspirated, intermediate for the post-tense, and low for the post-lenis conditions. These conditions are consistently separated along the time scale. The univariate analysis with repeated measures is given in table 4 showing the Manner factor effect. The associated Bonferroni tests are provided in table 5.

Table 4. Analysis of variance with repeated measures for the F_0 measure at the five time points. Degrees of freedom are 2 at all time points.

Time points	+13ms	1/8	1/4	3/8	1/2
F-value	49.02	56.36	51.82	43.15	44.61
p-value	<.001*	<.001*	<.001*	<.001*	<.001*

Table 5. The pair-wise comparisons (the Bonferroni test with an alpha level .05) of the estimated F_0 mean values obtained at the five time points

	p-value ($\alpha = .05$)				
	+13ms	1/8	1/4	3/8	1/2
Tense vs. Lenis	<.01*	<.01*	<.01*	<.01*	<.001*
Tense vs. Aspirated	.633	.277	.191	.255	.304
Lenis vs. Aspirated	<.001*	<.001*	<.01*	<.01*	<.01*

According to the statistical results, for an alpha level of 0.05 there is no significant difference in mean values between post-aspirated and post-tense classes along all the 5 time points. On the other hand, the lenis F_0 values are significantly lower than those of the other two classes at all time points.

In the H1*-H2* patterns, differences between post-tense and the other two classes seem to statistically merge at and after the 1/4 time point. However, the F_0 patterns can be said to behave differently in that the significant low F_0's of the post-lenis vowels are maintained at all five time points. Therefore, it is possible that the laryngeal mechanism underlying glottal width is different from the one controlling F_0. A plausible explanation for the F_0 patterns of the Korean stops is as follows. For the lenis class, it seems that the laryngeal muscle activities resulting in a low F_0 are maintained throughout the vowels. For example, the post-suppression degree of vocalis muscle (=VOC, henceforth) reactivation is slight and slow for the lenis class, which produces a low F_0. In contrast, the quick and heightened post-suppression VOC activities appear to make F_0 high in the vowels following tense/aspirated stops (Hirose et al., 1981). The cricothyroid muscle (as well as the VOC muscle) has been assumed to facilitate a high F_0 for post-tense segments (Hirose et al. 1983). Regarding the aspirated class, it is highly possible that the aerodynamic mechanism helps increase F_0 on the adjacent vowels (Ladefoged, 1973).

7.3 Results for the VOT Measure

The descriptive statistics in table 6 below shows that there are considerable differences in VOT among the three classes.

Table 6. Descriptive statistics for the VOT measure

Manner Class	Mean Value (ms)	Standard Deviation (ms)
Unaspirated	13.46	7.81
Voiced	59.40	21.23
Aspirated	128.52	27.99

The result for the univariate test is: F-statistics 95.57 and p-value <.001*, showing that the main effect for Manner is highly significant for an alpha level of 0.05. The Bonferroni test in table 7 shows that the mean VOT values are significantly different from one another and descend in this order: aspirated, lenis, and tense stop categories.

Table 7. The pair-wise comparisons (the Bonferroni test with an alpha level .05) of the estimated VOT means among the three manner classes

Manner Class (i)	Manner Class (j)	Mean difference (i-j)	Standard Error	Signifi-cance
Tense	Lenis	-45.937	5.720	<.01*
Tense	Aspirated	-115.059	8.990	<.001*
Lenis	Aspirated	-69.122	9.852	<.01*

Summarizing the statistical results, we see that VOT duration can serve as an acoustic dimension between the three manner classes.

7.4 Correlation between H1*-H2* and VOT Measures

Figure 4 helps make the relationship between the two measures somewhat clearer:

Figure 4. A combination chart where the average H1*-H2* and VOT values are plotted on the primary and secondary y-axes, and the three manner classes are plotted on the x-axis.

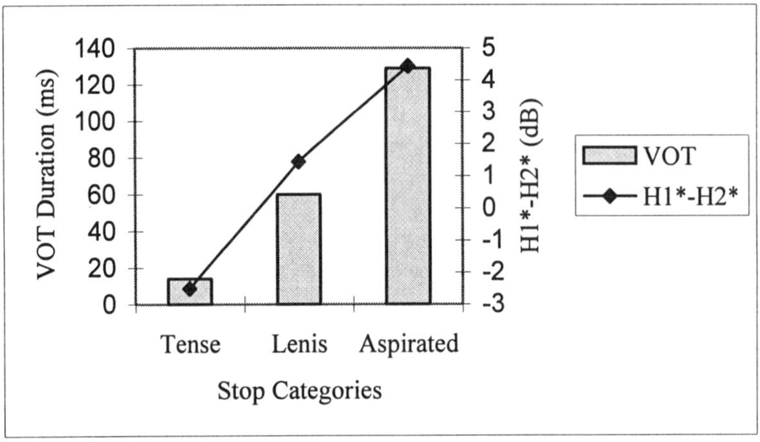

In figure 4, the correlation between VOT and H1*-H2* appears to be positive, showing that our hypothesis in (9) is roughly supported. However, it remains to be seen how strong this positive relationship is. To pursue this further, R^2 values were calculated in terms of regression analyses on the variously combined data for each subject. Table 8 shows the final outcomes.

Table 8. The R^2 values of the variously combined groups. These values are obtained from the data in a H1*-H2* vs. VOT scattergram.

	R^2 Scores (%)			
	Tense & Lenis & Aspirated	Tense & Aspirated	Lenis & Aspirated	Tense & Lenis
Subject 1	68	73	39	70
Subject 2	65	76	57	03
Subject 3	65	75	54	09
Subject 4	53	79	10	43
Subject 5	41	75	12	79
Subject 6	51	74	13	65
Mean	57.17	75.33	30.83	44.83
Standard Deviation	10.55	2.07	21.89	32.39
Max/Min Values	68/41	79/73	57/10	79/03

Table 8 shows two interesting patterns. First, the correlation between the H1*-H2* and VOT measures is overall strong for all subjects for the data of the three manner classes (see R^2=57.17 %). Second, surprisingly enough, as indicated in column B when the tense and aspirated classes are considered together, the percentage of variance that the two variables have in common is 75.33%. It is even more surprising that, as indicated by a standard deviation of 2.07, this score is consistently high across all subjects. This finding strongly implies that the Korean tense and aspirated stops are determined primarily in terms of the degree of glottal width at release. The corresponding VOT duration can be predicted in terms of a speaker-specific formula—i.e., each subject has his own pattern of laryngeal activities implying a proportionality between glottal width and VOT duration. This hypothesis is also supported by the observations of post-suppression VOC reactivations, where strength is almost the same for both classes (i.e., almost the same F_0's on neighboring vowels), and the time response is quick for both stops.

8. Conclusions

The fact that the tense stops are characterized by the smallest glottal opening at release (creaky phonation) was confirmed by the results of the H1*-H2* measure in this study, where the average value is significantly lower at the +13ms time point than that of the post-lenis class or the post-aspirated class. Also, the fact that post-aspirated vowels show the largest glottis at release (breathy phonation) is strongly implied by the H1*-H2* measure under study. Related to the correlation between H1*-H2* and VOT, the consistently high R^2 scores across subjects on the joint data of tense and aspirated classes show that these two classes can be systematically distinguished only in terms of one dimension; that is, the degree of glottal width at release. The VOT duration is a by-product that is naturally determined in proportion to the degree of glottal width, even though its determining strategy is subject-dependent. Also recall that these two classes show high F_0 measures which are not significantly different along the five time points. As for the lenis stop category, the main aim of its laryngeal activity lies in keeping F_0 low on the neighboring vowel. Without an intentional maneuver of controlling laryngeal actions set for this purpose, it is not easy to explain why the significantly low F_0 is maintained along the vowel at all five time points since the differences in H1*-H2* values among the three classes disappear from the 1/4 time point onward. Then, the further question as to why this class needs a breathy voice is clearly evidenced by the H1*-H2* measure, which is statistically as large as that of the aspirated stops. In actuality, the lenis class shows some phonetic characteristics closely approaching those expected for voicing. First, its closure duration is consistently short. Second, its production, compared to the tense or aspirated stop, involves lower air pressure in the cavity behind the point of articulation, a slower rate of pressure build-up, and a moderate rate of airflow after release. Because of these characteristics, the lenis stop tends to passively become voiced when it is flanked by sonorants (ex. /i+pal/ → [ibal] 'this + foot'). Returning to the question raised above, I suggest--as one plausible answer--that by making the glottis larger at release the lenis stops are able to maintain voicelessness during the stop closure. This functional reasoning seems to make sense, since this is one possible way to prevent the slackened vocal folds from vibrating.

The phonetic findings discussed so far naturally lead us to establish the phonological surface representations for the three stop categories of Korean as described below:

tense stops:	[constricted glottis]+[stiff vocal folds]
aspirated stops:	[spread glottis]+[stiff vocal folds]
lenis stops: word-initial	[spread glottis]+[slack vocal folds]
when voiced	[voice]+[slack vocal folds]

References

Ahn, Hyunkee. 1999. *Post-Release Phonatory Processes in English and Korean: Acoustic Correlates and Implications for Korean Phonology*. Doctoral dissertation, The University of Texas at Austin.

Fant, Gunnar. 1960. *Acoustic Theory of Speech Production*. Mouton: The Hague.

__________ 1972. Vocal Tract Wall Effects, Losses, and Resonance Bandwidths. *STL-QPSR* 2-3. 28-52.

Hirose, Hajime, Hea-Suk Park, Hirohide Yoshika, Masayuki Sawashima, and Hiroyuki Umeda. 1981. An Electromyographic Study of Laryngeal Adjustments for the Korean Stops. *Ann. Bull. RILP*. (Annual Bulletin, Research Institute of Logopedics and Phoniatrics) 15.31-43. Univ. of Tokyo.

Hirose, Hajime, Hea-Suk Park, and Masayuki Sawashima. 1983. Activity of the Thyroarytenoid Muscle in the Production of Korean Stops and Fricatives. *Ann. Bull. RILP* 17. 73-81.

Johnson, Keith. 1997. *Acoustic and Auditory Phonetics*. Cambridge: Blackwell.

Kagaya, Ryohei. 1974. A Fiberscopic and Acoustic Study of the Korean Stops. Affricates and Fricatives. *Journal of Phonetics* 2.161-180.

Kim, Chin-Wu. 1965. On the Autonomy of the Tensity Feature in Stop Classification. *Word* 21. 339-359.

Ladefoged, Peter. 1973. The Features of the Larynx. *Journal of Phonetics* 1.73-83.

Ladefoged, Peter and Ian Maddieson. 1996. *The Sounds of the World's Languages*. Cambridge: Blackwell.

Stevens, Kenneth N. and Helen M. Hanson. 1995. Classification of Glottal Vibration from Acoustic Measurements, in O. Fujimura & M. Hirano, eds., *Vocal Fold Physiology: Voice Quality Control*, 147-170. San Diego: Singular.

Acquiring Mora-timing: The Case of the Japanese Coda Nasal*

KATSURA AOYAMA
University of Hawaii

1. Introduction

This study investigates the acquisition of Japanese prosody, which is often considered to be mora-timed (Ladefoged 1993:251). Japanese has rhythmic characteristics, such as quantity contrasts in vowels and consonants, which are different from languages like English.

Studies utilizing a language game called *shiritori* suggest that the rhythm of young Japanese-speaking children may be based on a different timing unit compared to that of Japanese-speaking adults (Kubozono 1993, Ota 1993). It was found that 4- and 5-year-olds without solid knowledge of *kana* (Japanese mora-based orthography) sometimes used the syllable as the basic unit, unlike adults who use the mora as the unit for playing this game[1] (Ota 1993). Based on the observation of a 4-year-old's *shiritori,* Kubozono

* This paper is an expanded version of a poster presented at the thirtieth Child Language Research Forum held at Stanford University in April 1999. I am grateful to all the subjects for their participation, and to Diane Groves, Jaime Kuroiwa, Yumiko Sato, and Takaaki Suzuki for their assistance. I also thank Patricia Donegan, William O'Grady, and Ann Peters for their suggestions and discussions. Financial support for this research was provided by the College of Languages, Linguistics and Literature at the University of Hawai'i at Manoa.

[1] Although I know of at least one adult who sometimes uses the syllable in playing this game.

proposes the following developmental stages in the acquisition of Japanese prosody (Kubozono 1993:135, translation mine):

(1) Stage 1: Acquire consonants and vowels as segments
Stage 2: Acquire long vowels and coda consonants as segments
Stage 3: Acquire the sequence of CV as one (rhythmic) unit, the *mora*
Stage 4: Acquire the adult-like moraic status of coda consonants and long vowels

I observed three children, a 2-year-old (2;9), a 3-year-old (3;5), and a 6-year-old (6;4), and found that it was difficult for children around age three to distinguish contrasts between single and geminate nasals in Japanese (Aoyama 1999). Two pictures identified with the names *nene* and *nenne* were used to elicit a minimal pair, two words which differ only in the quantity of the nasal. The 3-year-old boy demonstrated considerable difficulty in distinguishing the minimal pair names both in perception and production. He claimed that the two names sounded the same, and his production of both *nene* and *nenne* indeed sounded like *nenne* to the adults. Similarly, the 2-year-old's utterances sounded like *nenne* to adult ears regardless of her intention. She seemed to avoid saying *nene* in her production.

My prediction was that the CVC.CV word (*nenne*) would be more difficult than CV.CV word (*nene*) for young children because of the coda consonant in the first syllable. The target word with geminates, however, seemed to be easier than the one with a singleton. The children had difficulty saying the CV.CV word (*nene*). It has been found that Japanese children's first words often include words like *nenne* 'do sleeping', or *pappa* 'do carrying a person on the back' (Yamashita 1995:55), which have CVCCV structure.

It seems that geminate consonants themselves are quite easy for young children to produce, but the difficulty seems to be due to the *contrastive moraic status* between single and geminate consonants. There is a possibility that children acquire the segments and syllables first and acquire the rhythmic characteristics of the segments later, as suggested in Kubozono 1993. If young children have acquired CVCCV structure, but not the adult-like rhythmic status of the coda consonant, this supports Kubozono's proposal of developmental stages in the acquisition of Japanese prosody.

The purpose of the experiment was to examine the acquisition of prosodic characteristics in Japanese by looking at the acquisition of the nasal quantity contrast. Children's production and perception of single and geminate nasals ([n] and [nn]) were investigated at different ages. A total of 96 subjects from 6 groups (3-, 4-, 5-, 6-, 7-year-olds and adults) participated. The subjects were all speakers of Japanese with limited influence from other languages. Three tasks, imitation, production and perception were employed to examine both production and perception of the nasal quantity contrast.

2. Research Questions and Hypotheses

This experiment is motivated by the following questions:

(a) Can children perceive and produce minimal pair words that contrast only in the quantity of the nasal consonant ([n] vs [nn])?

(b) If there is any difference between adults and children, by what age do children's perception and production become adult-like?

In order to investigate these questions, a 2-syllable, 2-mora word (CVCV; hana) and a 2-syllable, 3-mora word (CVCCV; hanna) were elicited from adults and children at different ages. Perception of these two words was also examined. My prediction was that there would be differences between adults and children of different ages both in their perception and production. In perception, younger children may have more difficulty in distinguishing the minimally contrasting words. In production, the durational ratio of a 2-syllable, 2-mora word (CVCV) to that of a 2-syllable, 3-mora word (CVCCV) may be more adult-like among the older group of children, while younger children may produce both 2-syllable 2-mora word and 2-syllable 3-mora words in a similar way.

More specifically, some children may be able to produce and imitate words with different rhythmic structures, but the distinction between the two may not be very clear for younger children. In other words, the mora may not have the same phonemic/rhythmic status in children's speech as in adults' speech.

It is also hypothesized that Japanese orthography could be an influence in reinforcing the moraic status of the coda nasal. Children who have learned Japanese orthography (*kana*) may have more adult-like durational ratio between 2-syllable 2-mora and 2-syllable 3-mora words in their production. Children start learning the Japanese orthography system in elementary school or shortly before that. Thus, there may be a difference between pre-schoolers and children in elementary school.

If the differences were found among children at different ages, it would provide a piece of evidence that Japanese-speaking children start with a different rhythmic structure from Japanese-speaking adults and that children gradually acquire the rhythmic characteristics of Japanese. The characteristics of a mora-timed language may develop later, and the phonemic importance of the moraic status of the coda nasal may not be clear for young children although they seem to be able to produce the quantity contrast.

3. Method

3.1 Subjects

Data collection was conducted in Osaka, Japan in summer 1998.[2] The data were collected from five groups of children: 3-, 4-, 5-, 6- and 7-year-olds.[3] They are all Japanese acquiring children. Data were also collected from adult native speakers of Japanese using the same procedure.

Age group	3	4	5	6	7	Adults
Participated	16	17	26	13	10	14
Completed imitation task	16	17	26	13	10	14
Analyzed	(7)	(7)	(7)	(7)	(7)	(7)
Completed production task	6	11	22	13	10	14
Analyzed	—	(7)	(7)	(7)	(7)	(7)
Completed perception task	15	17	26	13	10	14
Analyzed	(15)	(16)	(26)	(13)	(10)	(12)

TABLE 1. Number of subjects who participated.

A total of 96 subjects participated; the number of subjects in each group varied depending on age and kind of tasks. The number of subjects included in each group was determined by accessibility to the subjects and recording conditions. In addition, some subjects, especially the younger

[2] Osaka dialect was used throughout the experiment by both the experimenter and the subjects.

[3] An attempt was made to collect data from 2-year-olds. At least eight children participated, although a few imitated the target names a few times none of them completed the tasks.

ones, did not complete all the tasks. Table 1 summarizes the overview of subjects' information. Details will be described when the results are reported.

3.2 Procedure

The target words are two names that are minimally contrasting with the quantity of the medial nasal: *ha.na* (2-syllable, 2-mora) and *han.na* (2-syllable, 3-mora). *Hana* (or *hanako*) can be a real name for girls in Japanese, and *Hanna* is a relatively familiar foreign name for girls. Pictures of two girls were prepared accordingly; one girl with dark brown straight hair was identified as *hana*, and the other with yellow curly hair as *hanna*. Only one pair of names was used because having more than two names would be burdensome for younger children considering the time allocated for each subject.

Each experiment session started with two non-target questions that were intended to be practice for the following target tasks. The subjects were shown two pictures, apples and oranges, and asked to identify them. Then the first target task, an imitation task, was administered. The two names were introduced to the subjects, and they were asked to repeat the names after the investigator. Three imitative utterances each of *hana* and *hanna* were elicited from each subject. Next, pictures of *hana* and *hanna* were shown to the subjects, and they were asked to answer questions like 'What is her name?'. This task was to elicit non-imitative productions. Three non-imitative utterances each of *hana* and *hanna* were elicited from each subject. The last task was a perception task. Subjects were asked to point to the appropriate picture when asked 'Which one is *hana*/*hanna*?'. Different types of questions were asked randomly to prevent subjects from answering based on the order and patterns of the questions. Four questions were asked for each subject in the perception task.

Data from the production and perception tasks are less valid if children are not yet certain about the two target names. The production task was given prior to the perception task, because the picture-pointing task (perception task) would be easier than actually saying the names (production task) even when subjects are uncertain. Whenever it was evident that the two names were confused, the imitation task was repeated. If a subject seemed confused even after repeating the imitation task many times, the data were excluded from analysis.

Two puppets, a pig and a monkey, were used in order to capture the children's attention and elicit more utterances. Each session was audio-recorded.

4. Analysis

For the imitation and production tasks, durational measurements in milliseconds were carried out by using Signalyze.[4] Since it was difficult to determine the onset of /h/, the duration between the onset of the first vowel and the end of the second vowel ([ana] and [anna]) were measured instead of [hana] and [hanna]. The durations of the nasal portion of each word were also measured. The two names were uttered with a common ending for names '*-chan*' almost all the time. Data from only seven of the 7-year-olds were measurable; therefore, data from seven subjects from each age group were measured.[5] Since very few 3-year-olds (6 out of 16, 37.5%) completed the production task, only the data from the imitation task were analyzed for the 3-year-olds. A total of 231 tokens of *(h)ana* and 231 tokens of *(h)anna* were measured (imitation and production tasks combined) from 42 subjects (7 subjects each from 6 groups). The perception task was analyzed in terms of the number of correct responses.

5. Results

5.1 Production (Imitation and Production Task)

The data from both the imitation task and the production task will be reported as production data as opposed to perception data. Measurements were conducted on data from seven subjects from each age group. Only imitative utterances were measured for the 3-year-olds because many of them were not able to complete the production task. Thus, when a statistical analysis is reported on the production data, it is entirely based on the data from the imitation task. Data from the 3- and 4-year-olds were considered together as one group and that from 5- and 6-year-olds were grouped together as well for the statistical analysis. This is because the 3-year-olds' production data were available only from the imitation task and I regard seven subjects from each group too small a sample to conduct a separate statistical analysis.

[4] Signalyze is a product of the InfoSignal company. It is a speech analysis program for Macintosh which enables spectral analyses.

[5] The selection of the data was based on the quality of the recording.

The absolute durations of the target words across the subject groups are summarized in Tables 2 and 3. Adults' productions had shorter absolute durations in general, which is probably due to their faster rate of speech. In the imitation task, the 3- and 4-year-olds had longer absolute durations compared to adults and older children for the single nasal ([n]), and for the word containing the singleton [(h)ana] (see Table 2).

Imitation task						
Group	**Number of subjects**	**Mean age**	Whole word		Nasal portion	
			(h)ana	(h)anna	[n]	[nn]
3	7	3;6	355	414	101	137
4	7	4;4	390	447	100	144
5	7	5;6	301	391	82	146
6	7	6;5	322	415	83	146
7	7	7;5	301	410	82	136
Adults	7	36;6	267	353	65	134

TABLE 2. The mean duration of each whole word and the nasal portion of the target words (ms.).

Production task						
Group	**Number of subjects**	**Mean age**	Whole word		Nasal portion	
			(h)ana	(h)anna	[n]	[nn]
3	7	3;6	--	--	--	--
4	7	4;4	344	450	93	154
5	7	5;6	286	370	91	130
6	7	6;5	258	366	75	136
7	7	7;5	285	390	79	126
Adults	7	36;6	255	364	65	135

TABLE 3. The mean duration of each whole word and the nasal portion of the target words (ms.).

In order to examine whether the durations of (h)ana and (h)anna were significantly different, mean absolute durations of (h)ana and (h)anna from each of the 3- and 4-year-old's data (n = 14) were grouped together and paired t-test was conducted. The durations of (h)anna were significantly longer than the durations of (h)ana in the 3- and 4-year-olds' productions (t

= 4.581, p < 0.001). The duration of the geminate nasal is also significantly longer than the single nasal even among 3- and 4-year olds (t = 5.449, p < 0.000). This means that 3- and 4-year-old children are making distinctions of the quantity contrast in their productions, although the distinctions are not quite as clear as the adults' and older children's are.

Next, because there are variations in speech rate and it affects absolute durations, the data were analyzed in terms of durational ratios. Table 4 shows the durational ratios between (h)ana and (h)anna and between the single nasal and the geminate nasal. The 3- and 4-year-olds' ratios between (h)ana and (h)anna in the imitation task were small, 1:1.17 and 1:1.15 respectively. The 5-year-olds' ratio was similar to the older groups in imitation (1:1.30), although it was smaller compared to older groups in production (1:1.29). The ratios between (h)ana and (h)anna were similar among the 6- and 7-year-olds and adults, both in the imitation task (1:1.29 to 1:1.36) and the production task (1:1.37 to 1:1.43). When the data from the 3- and 4- year-olds, 5- and 6- year-olds, and 7-years-olds and adults were grouped together and statistically analyzed; the ratios between (h)ana and (h)anna are significantly different among the groups (F = 9.042, p < 0.001). The difference was significant between age 3-4 and 5-6 (F = 17.151, p < 0.001), but not between 5-6 and 7 and adults (F = 1.338, p > 0.05).

	Imitation task		**Production task**	
Age	(h)ana : (h)anna	[n] : [nn]	(h)ana : (h)anna	[n] : [nn]
3	1 : 1.17	1 : 1.35	--	--
4	1: 1.15	1: 1.44	1 : 1.31	1 : 1.66
5	1 : 1.30	1 : 1.77	1 : 1.29	1 : 1.43
6	1 : 1.29	1 : 1.76	1 : 1.41	1 : 1.82
7	1 : 1.36	1 : 1.65	1 : 1.37	1 : 1.60
Adults	1 : 1.32	1 : 2.06	1 : 1.43	1 : 2.08

TABLE 4. The ratios between (h)ana and (h)anna, [n] and [nn].

The ratios of the single nasal to the geminates ([n] to [nn]) were also examined (Table 4). The data from the imitation task produced the ratios that are similar between 3- and 4-year-olds (1:1.35 and 1:1.44 respectively), and among 5-, 6- and 7-year-olds. The adults' ratio was the largest: 1:2.06 in the imitation task and 1:2.08 in the production task. Again, when the ratios were statistically examined, the difference was significant among groups ($F = 5.303$, $p < 0.01$). The difference between 3-, 4-years and 5-, 6-years are significant ($F = 7.889$, $p < 0.01$), but the difference between 5-, 6-years and 7-years and adults was not ($F = 1.252$, $p > 0.05$).

Age	Imitation task		Production task	
	[n] in (h)ana	[nn] in (h)anna	[n] in (h)ana	[nn] in (h)anna
3	28.6%	33.0%	--	--
4	25.6%	32.2%	27.0%	34.3%
5	27.5%	37.4%	32.0%	35.3%
6	26.0%	35.3%	29.0%	37.3%
7	27.4%	33.2%	27.7%	32.5%
Adults	24.4%	38.1%	25.4%	37.1%

TABLE 5. The nasal portion in the whole word.

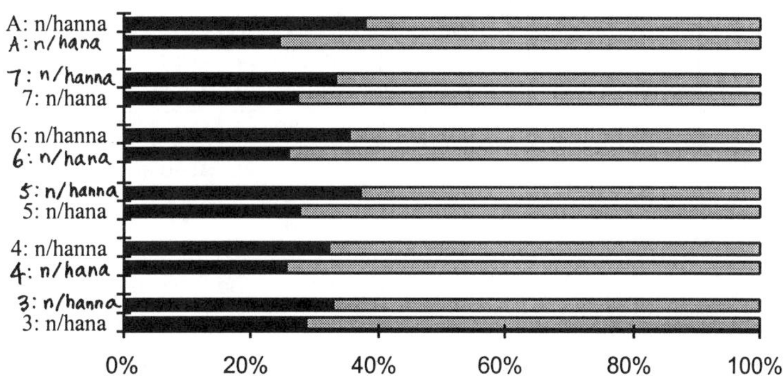

FIGURE 1. The percentages of nasal proportion in the whole word.

The proportion of the whole word taken up by the nasal was also examined in each target word. Adults made the clearest distinction between (h)ana and (h)anna; the nasal portion consisted of about 25% of (h)ana, and about 38% of (h)anna (Table 5, Figure 1). In general, the proportion of the nasal was larger in (h)ana and smaller in (h)anna when adult productions were compared to that of children. This means that children's productions of words that contain single and geminate nasals were similar to each other.

It is interesting that this difference was found between adults and all groups of children.

5.2 Perception

The results of the perception task are reported by the percentages of the responses to the designated pictures. The analysis was conducted on the data from subjects who completed the task (all except one 3-year-old). A 4-year-old's data were excluded since she looked uncertain even after repeating the imitation task for several times. The number of the subjects varied in each group from 10 (7-year-olds) to 26 (5-year-olds). One thing to note here is that the number of subjects was very different in the analysis of the perception task from the analysis of the production task. Thus, we cannot compare the results of these tasks directly.

Perception task					
Group	**Number of subjects**	**Mean age**	**Target: Hana**	**Target: Hanna**	**Overall**
3	15	3;6	66.7%	53.3%	60.0%
4	16	4;5	65.5%	71.4%	68.8%
5	26	5;4	84.3%	81.1%	82.7%
6	13	6;5	91.7%	95.8%	93.8%
7	10	7;5	100%	100%	100%
Adults	12	35;5	100%	100%	100%

TABLE 6. The percentages of correct response in the perception task.[6]

All of the 7-year-olds and adults correctly matched the picture with the names. The percentage of correct responses was the lowest among the 3-year-olds, and they gradually improve in accuracy according to their age group (Table 6, Figure 2). In fact, the 3-year-olds' responses were at chance-level ($t = 1.099$, $p = 0.29$). The 4-year-olds' responses proved better than chance ($t = 2.304$, $p < 0.05$), and therefore, all groups except the 3-year-olds performed better than chance. Neither target name seemed to be particularly more difficult than the other. The 3-year-olds did better on *hana*: the 4-year-olds did better on *hanna*.

[6] The data were reexamined and the percentages may differ from ones on the abstract.

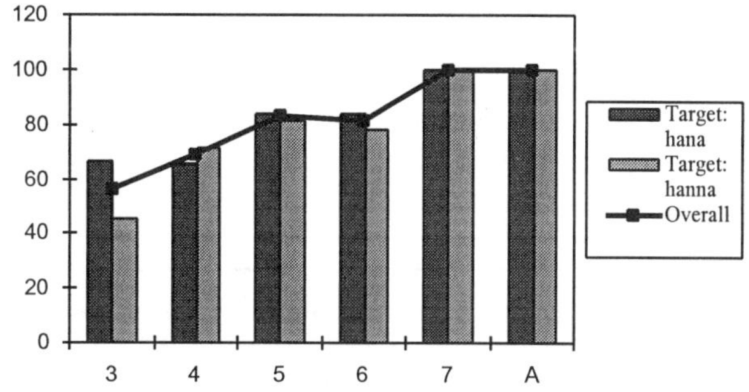

FIGURE 2. The percentages of correct response in the perception task.

6. Summary and Discussion

6.1 Summary of the Findings

The differences among the age groups were found both in production and perception of words contrasting by the moraic status of the coda nasal. The durational ratios in the 3- and 4-year-olds' productions were smaller compared to those of older groups, and the percentage of correct responses in the perception task was at chance level among the 3-year-olds.

It seems that 6- and 7-year-olds are closest to adults both in production and perception, and 5-year-olds are in between the younger groups and the older groups. Their productions were not so different from the adults' productions in comparison to the difference between the 3- and 4-year-olds and adults; however, the similarity between the 5-year-olds and adults' productions was not as consistent when compared to the similarity between the 6- and 7-year-olds and adults.

There are also differences between adults and every group of children; the adults made the clearest distinction between [n] and [nn]. Although statistically geminate nasals are significantly longer than the single nasal even among the youngest group, children's productions of single and geminate nasals were more similar to each other.

6.2 Stages of Prosodic Word Development

Overall results from this experiment are consistent with the developmental sequence for Japanese rhythm proposed by Kubozono (1993): the moraic status of the coda nasal is acquired at a late stage in the acquisition of phonology. Differences between children's and adults' productions of the nasal quantity contrast suggest that the phonemic/rhythmic status of the coda nasal in young children's language may differ from that in adult Japanese. It also suggests that children may indeed start out with a different type of timing than adults.

Observed ratios:	
English (stress-timed)	1 : 0.99 ~ 1 : 1.19
Korean (syllable-timed)	1 : 1.06 ~ 1 : 1.12
Japanese (mora-timed)	1 : 1.34 ~ 1 : 1.39

TABLE 7. Durational ratios of words containing a single nasal to words containing a geminate nasal in English, Korean and Japanese (Sato 1998:80).

According to Sato, durational ratios of similar pairs containing single/geminate nasal in Korean and English (classified as syllable-timed and stress-timed languages respectively) are smaller compared to those in Japanese. For instance, the whole word ratios ranged 1:1.06 to 1:1.12 in Korean, and 1:1.13 to 1:1.19 in English (Sato 1998:80). It is worth pointing out that the 3- and 4-year-olds' whole-word ratios in the imitation task in my study (1:1.17 and 1:1:15, respectively) were similar to the whole word ratios Sato found in Korean and English, which are not mora-timed languages. The similarity between these young children's ratios and those for Korean and English suggests that the rhythm of the young children's speech may not yet have characteristics of a mora-timed language. But their ratios are not as close to 1:1 as are in some of the ratios in the English and Korean data from Sato's study; thus it is possible that young Japanese children are developing the characteristics of mora-timing.

6.3 Influence of Orthography

It is important to note that the 6- and 7-year-olds' productions were similar to adults', and the 5-year-olds' productions were similar only for the imitation task but not for the production task. Children start learning *kana* systematically in elementary school, although they may have access to *kana* before they get into elementary school. In this experiment, all of the 7-year-olds were in elementary school, and all the 5-year-olds were in kindergarten. Some 6-year-old subjects were in the last year of kindergarten, while others were in the first year of elementary school. The results from the *shiritori* studies (Kubozono 1993, Ota 1993) also indicated the influence of mora-based orthography; 4- and 5-year-olds without a solid knowledge of *kana* treated the syllable as units in playing *shiritori*. The intermediate results among 5-year-olds' productions suggest that they were in transition from one stage to another, and that moraic status of the coda nasal was reinforced by learning the mora-based orthography.

6.4 Further Research Directions

It is reported that children's rhythmic structure may differ from that of adults in the target language (Allen and Hawkins 1978, Kubozono 1993, Ota 1993, Aoyama 1999). Examples in (2) also show difficulty in distinguishing the quantity contrasts found in a 2-year-old's data from naturalistic recordings.

(2) Japanese	M (2;1)	
Mother:	sore nani?	'What is it?'
Child:	kon.	'Corn (with a short vowel)'
Mother:	koon?	'Corn?'
Child:	kon.	'Corn.'
Mother:	koon?	'Corn?'
Child:	kon.	'Corn.'

Children around 3 years and younger may have difficulty in distinguishing a 3-mora word (*nenne, hanna*) from a 2-mora word (*nene, hana*). It is also possible that children are indeed making the distinctions but it is not as clear as adults' distinction; therefore, adults hear children's production as ambiguous.

Since only 3-year-olds and older were included in this study, we do not yet know how younger children perceive and produce the single and geminate contrasts. In order to capture the overall picture of the acquisition of prosody in Japanese, it is necessary to look at younger children's data using both longitudinal and experimental methods.

References

Allen, George D. and Sarah Hawkins. 1978. The Development of Phonological Rhythm, in A. Bell and J. B. Hopper, eds., *Syllables and Segments*. Amsterdam: North-Holland.

Aoyama, Katsura. 1999. Nene or Nenne?: The Acquisition of the Mora Nasal. Poster presented at International Association for the Study of Child Language, VIIIth International Congress. Donostia-San Sebastian Basque Country/Spain.

Kubozono, Haruo. 1993. Kodomo no shiritori to mora no kakutoku. *Nihongo no mora to onsetsu koozoo ni kansuru soogooteki kenkyuu* 2:130-7.

Ladefoged, Peter. 1993. *A Course in Phonetics.* Fort Worth, TX: Harcourt Brace.

Ota, Satoshi. 1993. Takaga 'shiritori' saredo 'shiritori' – yoochienji no shiritori asobi ga oshiete kureru koto. *Nihongo no mora to onsetsu koozoo ni kansuru soogooteki kenkyuu* 2:138-53.

Sato, Yumiko. 1998. *The Phonetic Reality of the Mora in Japanese: A Cross-linguistic Study of Timing in Japanese, English, and Korean.* Doctoral dissertation, University of Hawai'i at Manoa.

Yamashita, Yoshie. 1995. *The Emergence of Syntactic Categories: Evidence from the Acquisition of Japanese.* Doctoral dissertation, University of Hawai'i at Manoa.

The Role of the Prosodic Word in an Ordering Paradox of Korean

MI-HUI CHO & SHINSOOK LEE
Pukyong National University & Hoseo University

1. Introduction

Korean has Coda Neutralization in which obstruents in coda position surface as neither aspirated nor tensed but as unreleased lax stops (e.g., *k'oc* [k'ot˺] 'flower'). Korean also does not allow a consonant cluster within a syllable. Thus, underlying CVCC forms emerge as CVC when the cluster is in word-final position or when it is followed by a consonant-initial syllable (e.g., *saks* [sak˺] 'share'). In addition, sequences of /h/ plus voiceless obstruents such as /p, t, c, k/ or vice versa emerge as aspirated [p^h, t^h, c^h, k^h].

However, the interaction among Coda Neutralization, Cluster Simplification, and Aspiration Merger has posed a serious problem to the non-derivational approach of Optimality Theory (henceforth OT, McCarthy and Prince 1993a, b; Prince and Smolensky 1993). For example, in *olh+ko* [ol.k^ho] 'right-Connective' the second consonant /h/ in the cluster merges with the following consonant by progressive Aspiration Merger. This suggests that Coda Neutralization and Cluster Simplification occur after Aspiration Merger; otherwise, we would have a wrong output *[ol.go]. But unlike progressive Aspiration Merger, regressive Aspiration Merger shows that Coda Neutralization and Cluster Simplification apply before Aspiration Merger. For example, in *nas+hako* [na.t^ha.go] 'with a sickle', the fricative /s/ is neutralized into [t] before Aspiration Merger. Likewise, in *saks+hako* [sa.k^ha.go] 'with a share', not the second consonant but the first consonant in the cluster is merged with /h/, indicating that /s/ should be deleted before Aspiration Merger. Moreover, examples like [na.t^ha.go] and [sa.k^ha.go] may surface as [nat˺.t^{h}a.go] and [sak˺.k^{h}a.go], respectively, in extra, careful speech.

The interaction among Coda Neutralization, Cluster Simplification, and Aspiration Merger has been analyzed within a derivational model which assumes extrinsic rule ordering. For instance, Iverson and Kim-Renaud (1994) analyze Aspiration Merger by spreading the specified features (or nodes) to the unspecified features (or nodes). After this process, they claim that Coda Neutralization and degemination apply in turn. Likewise, focusing on the ordering problem, Shim (1995) claims that Korean needs derivational steps; Progressive Aspiration Merger precedes Coda Neutralization and Cluster Simplification, which in turn precede regressive Aspiration Merger. Thus, he contends that the nonderivational theory of OT is not compatible with the phonological phenomena of Korean.

In this paper, however, we argue that a constraint-based model provides a better account of the phenomena than a rule-based one does. Specifically, we propose that both progressive and regressive Aspiration Merger can be uniformly analyzed by a constraint ranking in which prosodic-word bounded constraints dominate markedness and faithfulness constraints. Namely, the undominated constraints accounting for Coda Neutralization and Cluster Simplification apply within a prosodic word, while the constraints accounting for Aspiration Merger apply both within and across a prosodic word. Furthermore, we demonstrate that facts concerning Coda Neutralization, Cluster Simplification, and Aspiration Merger cannot be accounted for by adopting a base-identity constraint (Kenstowicz 1995) or an output-output constraint (Benua 1997). Additionally, we show that alternative forms in extra, careful speech such as [nat˺.t^{h}a.go] and [sak˺.k^{h}a.go] are accounted for by the alternating ranking between faithfulness constraints.

The organization of this paper is as follows. Section 2 presents data concerning Coda Neutralization, Cluster Simplification, and Aspiration Merger. Section 3 examines previous analyses and problems. Section 4 provides a prosodically bounded constraint approach of the Korean facts. Section 5 concludes the paper.

2. Data Involving Coda Neutralization, Cluster Simplification, and Aspiration Merger

In Korean coda obstruents are realized as unreleased lax stops by Coda Neutralization, given below. ("˺" indicates the unreleasing of a segment in the coda.)

(1) Coda Neutralization

nas [nat˺] 'sickle'	nac [nat˺] 'day'	k'oc^h [k'ot˺] 'flower'
puək^h [pu.ək˺] 'kitchen'	pak' [pak˺] 'exterior'	saks [sak˺] 'share'

Thus, fricatives, affricates, and stops in coda position, regardless of being aspirated, tensed, or plain, surface as unreleased lax stops.

Korean also has Cluster Simplification which forces underlying CVCC forms to be realized as CVC when the cluster occurs word finally or when a consonant-initial syllable follows, as illustrated in (2).

(2) Cluster Simplification[1]

	UR	Suffix	PR	Gloss
a.	UR	Suffix	PR	Gloss
	saks		[sak˺]	'share'
	saks+	to	[sak˺.t'o]	'price-also'
	saks+	i	[sak˺.ʃi]	'price-Nominative'
b.	UR	Suffix	PR	Gloss
	anc		[an]	'to sit'
	anc+	ko	[an.k'o]	'to sit-Connective'
	anc+	a	[an.ja]	'to sit-Stative'

In (2) the underlying coda clusters /-ks/ and /-nc/ are simplified as [k] and [n], respectively.[2]

In Korean, sequences of heteromorphemic /h/ plus /p, t, k/ are merged into a single aspirated stop, as shown in (3). The reverse sequences of /p, t, k/ plus /h/ are also merged into a single aspirated stop, as in (4).

(3) Progressive Aspiration Merger

	Casual Speech	Careful Speech	
coh+ko	[co.kʰo]	[cot˺.kʰo], [cok˺.kʰo]	'like-Connective'
nah+ta	[na.tʰa]	[nat˺.tʰa]	'give birth-Declarative'
k'ɨnh+ca	[k' ɨn.cʰa]		'cut-Persuasive'
hɨnh+ko	[hɨn.kʰo]		'common-Connective'
silh+ta	[ʃil.tʰa]		'dislike-Declarative'
olh+ko	[ol.kʰo]		'right-Connective'

(4) Regressive Aspiration Merger

	Casual Speech	Careful Speech	
ip+hak	[i.pʰak]	[ip˺.pʰak]	'admission'
sok+hi	[so.kʰi]	[sok˺.kʰi]	'fast-Adverbial'
saks+hako	[sa.kʰa.go]	[sak˺.kʰa.go]	'with a share'
k'oc+hako	[k'o.tʰa.go]	[k'ot˺.tʰa.go]	'with a flower'
k'oc+hi+ta	[k'o.cʰi.da]	[k'o t˺.cʰi.da]	'insert-Passive-Declarative'

Here, progressive Aspiration Merger must precede Coda Neutralization and

---

[1] In Korean /s/ becomes [ʃ] before the high front vowel /i/. Also, obstruents become voiced while /l/ becomes [r] in intervocalic position. However, we will not deal with these phenomena since they are not relevant to our discussion.

[2] However, there is a dialectal difference in the realization of coda consonants. Namely, when the underlying coda cluster consists of a sonorant consonant and a stop such as /palp/ 'to step on', it is the stop that surfaces in Seoul dialect [pap˺], whereas it is the sonorant consonant that survives in Kyongsang dialect [pal]. For details, see Cho and Lee (1999).

Cluster Simplification (cf. *coh+ko* [co.k^{h}o], [cot˺.k^{h}o], *[cot˺.ko]; *olh+ko* [ol.k^{h}o] *[ol.go]). On the other hand, regressive Aspiration Merger must follow Cluster Simplification and Coda Neutralization (cf. *saks+hako* [sa.k^{h}a.go], *[sak˺.s^{h}a.go]; *k'oc+hako* [k'o.t^{h}a.go], *[k'o.c^{h}a.go]). Note that Coda Neutralization occurs in [k'o.t^{h}a.go], but not in [k'o.c^{h}i.da]. In addition, coda consonants resulting from Coda Neutralization and Cluster Simplification may survive in extra careful speech ([sak˺.k^{h}a.go]).

Coda Neutralization and Cluster Simplification interact with Aspiration Merger, as shown in (5).

(5) a. Coda Neutralization and Aspiration Merger

nas+hako	[na.t^{h}a.go], *[na.s^{h}a.go]	'with a sickle'
mos+hako	[mo.t^{h}a.go], *[mo.s^{h}a.go]	'with a nail'

b. Cluster Simplification and Aspiration Merger

kaps+hako	[ka.p^{h}a.go], *[kap˺.s^{h}a.go]	'with a price'
saks+hako	[sa.k^{h}a.go], *[sak˺.s^{h}a.go]	'with a share'

In (5a) /h/ is not merged with [s] but with the [t] that results from Coda Neutralization. In (5b) /h/ is merged with the surviving stop resulting from Cluster Simplification. This fact suggests that regressive Aspiration Merger must follow Coda Neutralization and Cluster Simplification (cf. *nas+hako* [na.t^{h}a.go]; *saks+hako* [sa.k^{h}a.go]). However, as mentioned above progressive Aspiration Merger must precede Cluster Simplification (cf. *olh+ko* [ol.k^{h}o] *[ol.go]). In the next section we will examine previous analyses concerning these phenomena as well as their shortcomings.

3. Shortcomings of Previous Analyses

Based on the ordering problem, the interaction among Aspiration Merger, Coda Neutralization, and Cluster Simplification has been analyzed within a derivational model which assumes extrinsic rule ordering. For instance, Iverson and Kim-Renaud (1994) analyze Aspiration Merger, either progressive or regressive, by spreading the specified features (or nodes) from coda to the unspecified onset. Thus, in the case of /coh+ko/ 'like-Connective', it first becomes /coh+k^{h}o/ by the spreading procedure, and then [cot˺.k^{h}o] by Coda Neutralization in extra, careful speech and [cok˺.k^{h}o] by optional place assimilation. It further becomes [co.k^{h}o] by simplification (i.e., degemination) in casual speech. Likewise, /ip+hak/ 'admission' becomes /ip+p^{h}ak/ by spreading and then it becomes [ip˺.p^{h}ak] by Coda Neutralization. Then it is simplified as [i.p^{h}ak] in casual speech. Their analysis, however, has serious problems. First, their analysis posits extrinsic rule ordering among Aspiration Merger, Coda Neutralization, assimilation and degemination. It also produces an intermediate stage, such as /coh+k^{h}o/ and /ip+p^{h}ak/, which is never surface-true.

Similarly, Shim (1995) contends that OT, which assumes a parallelistic mode of constraint interaction, cannot account for the ordering problems among Coda Neutralization, Cluster Simplification, and Aspiration Merger. This is because progressive Aspiration Merger precedes Coda Neutralization and Cluster Simplification, which in turn precede regressive Aspiration Merger. Thus, he claims that the rule-based model which assumes derivational steps provides a better account of Korean phonology than OT does.[3] However, Shim's analysis also has some drawbacks. Most importantly, his account cannot provide a unified analysis of Aspiration Merger since he treats progressive and regressive Aspiration Merger separately, although it can be viewed as a single phonological phenomenon. In addition, his analysis posits extrinsic rule ordering among Coda Neutralization, Cluster Simplification, and Aspiration Merger which imposes a burden on the Korean grammar. Thus, in the following section, we will provide an alternative to the derivational approach.

4. A Prosodically Bounded Constraint Approach

4. 1 Prosodic Structure in Korean

It has been well-known that mismatches exist between phonological rule domains and morphological constituent structure, as evidenced in Nespor and Vogel (1986), and Booij and Lieber (1993). For example, in Hungarian, although both prefixes and suffixes are bound morphemes, all suffixes belong to the linearly preceding adjacent stem with respect to the domain of vowel harmony, whereas a prefix and a stem form separate rule domains of vowel harmony.

Korean also exhibits similar prefix-suffix asymmetries with respect to several phenomena such as syllabification, Coda Neutralization, and Cluster Simplification. In particular, Kang (1992), among others, argues that in Korean a prefix in a prefix plus stem combination as well as each member of a compound forms a separate prosodic word (ω) in addition to lexical categories (i.e., N, V, A, Adv). She also claims that prosodically dependent elements such as derivational and inflectional suffixes are adjoined to a preceding prosodic word. Thus, in /təs/ 'outer' + /os/ 'cloth' the prefix and stem form a separate prosodic word ($(təs)_{\omega}$ $(os)_{\omega}$) whereas in /saks/ 'share' + /i/ 'nominative suffix' the noun and suffix form a single prosodic word ($(saksi)_{\omega}$). This also can account for the reason why Coda Neutralization occurs in *k'oc+hako* [k'o.t^{h}a.go], while it does not occur in *k'oc+hi+ta* [k'o.c^{h}i.da] in data (4) of Section 2. Namely, the former forms two prosodic words ($(k'oc)_{\omega}$ $(hako)_{\omega}$) and thus, the first constituent is subject to Coda Neutralization. In contrast, the latter forms a single prosodic word ($(k'ochita)_{\omega}$) and thus, the environment for Coda Neutralization may not be met.

[3] Shim (1995) also deals with the interaction between Cluster Simplification and Tensification, which seems to require derivational steps. Like other linguists, however, we assume that this phenomenon might be accounted for by adopting sympathy-related concepts (Davis 1997; McCarthy 1998; Walker 1998).

In order to derive prosodic structure in Korean, Kang adopts Selkirk's End-Based Theory (Selkirk and Shen, 1990) and the Prosodic Structure Well-Formedness Constraint (Nespor and Vogel, 1986). Unlike Selkirk, however, she claims that the X°[setting of the End-Based Theory, which derives a prosodic word, applies at the lexical level but not at the postlexical level, while the XP[setting, which generates a phonological phrase, applies at the postlexical level.[4] She also proposes a separate prosodic formation rule of prefixes since prefixes form their own prosodic words in Korean.

In this paper, we adopt Kang's prosodic theory of Korean and contend that Coda Neutralization, Cluster Simplification, and Aspiration Merger are prosodically bounded phenomena. We further assume that prosodic structures such as the prosodic word and the phonological phrase are bulit up simultaneously and constraint violations are checked whenever relevant prosodic structures are generated by Gen (cf. Kenstowicz, personal communication).

4. 2 Constraints

Correspondence Theory (McCarthy and Prince 1995) is a recent development of Optimality Theory. Like OT, Correspondence Theory is a model of constraints and constraint interaction which claims that an optimal form is selected through the evaluation of an array of candidate outputs in a parallel mode. In the context of Correspondence Theory, faithfulness constraints in OT are redefined as constraints on correspondence. Namely, the Parse and Fill constraints in OT are replaced by Max and Dep, respectively.

(6) a. The Max Constraint Family
Every element of the input has a correspondent in the output.
(No phonological deletion)
b. The Dep Constraint Family
Every element of the output has a correspondent in the input.
(No phonological insertion)

Now, let us consider constraints relevant to the Korean data. As seen in Section 2 (cf. (2)), Korean syllable structure does not allow onset or coda clusters. Thus, an underlyingly tautomorphemic sequence of CVCC is simplified when it occurs word-finally or when a consonant-initial syllable follows. This fact can be captured by the following undominated *Complex constraint, which is prosodic- word bounded. ("ω" indicates a prosodic word.)

(7) *Complex$_{\omega}$: No onset or coda clusters are allowed within a prosodic word.

---

[4] X^0 denotes a lexical category type while XP is a phrase type in the X-bar hierarchy. Readers may refer to Kang (1992) for details.

Syllable-final consonants in Korean are also subject to a coda condition by which obstruents in coda position emerge as neither aspirated nor tensed but as unreleased lax stops, as mentioned in Section 2. As a consequence, /p, p', p^h / are realized as the unreleased lax [p˺], /t, t', t^h, c, c', c^h, s, s', h/ as [t˺], and /k, k', k^h/ as [k˺]. We assume that the coda neutralization effect is captured by the following undominated constraint of Coda Condition, which is also prosodic-word bounded in Korean.

(8) Coda Condition$_\omega$: Only nonreleased lax stops are possible in the coda in a prosodic word.

As seen by the data given above, the segment /h/ tends not to be realized. Thus, there should be a markedness constraint *h which forbids the occurrence of /h/.

(9) *h: no /h/

The motivation for this constraint comes from the phonetic fact that the glottal fricative /h/ does not require a specific vocal tract configuration. Accordingly, the shape of the vocal tract during the production of /h/ is often determined by the adjacent segments.

The nonrealization of /h/ by the markedness constraint *h is penalized by the faithfulness constraint Max-IO(spread glottis) which prohibits the deletion of the feature [spread glottis], as shown in (10).

(10) Max-IO(spread glottis): The feature [spread glottis] in the input has a correspondent in the output.

Since /h/ tends not to be realized, the markedness constraint *h dominates the faithfulness constraint Max-IO(spread glottis).

Because the constraint *h is ranked higher than the constraint Max-IO(spread glottis), /h/ may be deleted or be coalesced with an adjacent obstruent becoming an aspirated stop, depending on the environment. When /h/ deletes, the constraint Max-IO(s.g.) is violated in order not to violate the constraint *h. However, there is a way not to violate both constraints *h and Max-IO(s.g.) when there is a neighboring obstruent. Namely, the constraint *h may not be violated by merging /h/ with a neighboring obstruent. At the same time, Max-IO(s.g.) is not violated since /h/ survives in the form of aspiration, even though this leads to a violation of the constraint *MC (Multiple Correspondence) in (11).

(11) *MC (Lamontagne and Rice 1995): Elements of input and output must stand in a one-to-one correspondence relationship with each other.

The constraint *MC is violated when elements in the input and output do not stand in an one-to-one correspondence relation.

The constraint of Agree given in (12) captures the fact that, in consonant sequences, the place feature of one consonant tends to assimilate to the place feature of a neighboring consonant due to ease of articulation. This constraint accounts for the place assimilation between the coda and the subsequent onset consonants.

(12) Agree: The coda and onset consonants should be agree in the place of articulation.

Note that the constraint of Agree which triggers place assimilation leads to a violation of the *MC constraint in that the place of the coda and the following onset in the input are linked in the output.

Another relevant faithfulness constraint is provided in (13).

(13) Max-IO(segment): A segment in the input has a correspondent in the output.

The constraint Max-IO(segment) penalizes the deletion of segments from the input.

Based on the discussion above, we tentatively propose the following ranking:*Complex$_\omega$, Coda Cond$_\omega$>>*h>>Max-IO(s.g.), Agree>>*MC>> Max-IO(segment).[5] In the following subsection we show that this ranking along with the use of prosodically bounded constraints provides a unified account of Aspiration Merger without derivational steps.

4.3 Analysis

Let us consider the following tableau in (14) which shows a form with an interaction among Coda Neutralization, Cluster Simplification, and regressive Aspiration Merger.[6] (*CC$_\omega$ = *Complex$_\omega$)

---

[5] We will show evidence for the ranking between *MC and Max-IO(segment) shortly. Also, the fact that Max-IO(s.g.) outranks *MC is discussed below.

[6] In principle, we may think of another candidate [sak˺.s^{h}a.go] which can be generated from (sak˺s)$_\omega$. However, [k˺] in (sak˺s)$_\omega$ is impossible since it violates both *CC and Coda Condition. Thus, [sak˺.s^{h}a.go] is excluded from consideration.

(14) Coda Neutralization, Cluster Simplification, and Regressive Aspiration Merger ("ϕ" indicates a phonological phrase.)

saks+hako 'with a share'	*CC$_\omega$	Coda Cond$_\omega$	*h	Max-IO (s.g.)	*MC	Max-IO (segment)
a. (saks)$_\omega$(hago)$_\omega$ (saks.ha.go)$_\phi$	*!	*	* *			
b. (sak)$_\omega$(hago)$_\omega$ (sak.ha.go)$_\phi$		*!	* *			* *
c. ☞(sak˺)$_\omega$(hago)$_\omega$ (sa.k^{h}a.go)$_\phi$			*		 *	* **
d. (sak˺)$_\omega$(hago)$_\omega$ (sak˺.k^{h}a.go)$_\phi$			*		 **!	* *
e. (sak˺)$_\omega$(hago)$_\omega$ (sak˺.ha.go)$_\phi$			* *!			* *
f. (sas)$_\omega$(hago)$_\omega$ (sas.ha.go)$_\phi$		*!	* *			* *
g. (sas)$_\omega$(hago)$_\omega$ (sa.s^{h}a.go)$_\phi$		*!	*		 *	* **

In this tableau /saks/ and /hako/ each form a prosodic word since they are independent words. Here we assume that prosodic words and phonological phrases are built up simultaneously. As a result, the constraint violations are checked whenever the prosodic constituents are built up. In the tableau the upper asterisks indicate violations that only occur in the prosodic word domain whereas the lower asterisks show violations incurred only in the phonological phrase domain. Therefore, the lower asterisks cannot count the violations of the *CC and Coda Condition because they are not phonological-phrase bounded. Candidate (a) incurs fatal violations of *CC and Coda Condition. Candidates (b), (f), and (g) lose out because they all fatally violate the undominated constraint of Coda Condition which is prosodic-word bounded. Candidate (e) with /h/ realized in the onset results in the violation of the markedness constraint *h, which is fatal. Candidate (d) is not optimal since it violates *MC twice. One violation of *MC is involved in the coalescence of /k/ with /h/. The other violation occurs because the input /k/ is realized as the onset of the second syllable and at the same time as the coda of the first syllable in the output. In contrast, candidate (c) emerges as the winner, because it violates *MC only once. Here note that *MC outranks Max-IO(segment), as suggested above, since candidate (c) incurs more violations of Max-IO(segment) than candidate (d) does, yet it is the winner.

An alternating form, which occurs in extra, careful speech, can be accounted for by the reverse ranking, between *MC and Max-IO(segment), as given in (15).

(15) An alternating form in extra, careful speech

saks+hako 'with a share'	$*CC_\omega$	Coda $Cond_\omega$	*h	Max-IO(s.g.)	Max-IO (segment)	*MC
a. $(saks)_\omega(hago)_\omega$ $(saks.ha.go)_\phi$	*!	*	* *			
b. $(sak)_\omega(hago)_\omega$ $(sak.ha.go)_\phi$		*!	* *		* *	
c. $(sak^{\urcorner})_\omega(hago)_\omega$ $(sa.k^hа.go)_\phi$			*		* **!	*
d.☞ $(sak^{\urcorner})_\omega(hago)_\omega$ $(sak^{\urcorner}.k^ha.go)_\omega$			*		* *	**
e. $(sak^{\urcorner})_\omega(hago)_\omega$ $(sak^{\urcorner}.ha.go)_\phi$			* *!		* *	
f. $(sas)_\omega(hago)_\omega$ $(sas.ha.go)_\phi$		*!	* *		* *	
g. $(sas)_\omega(hago)_\omega$ $(sa.s^ha.go)_\phi$		*!	*		* **	*

In (15) candidate (d) wins out as the optimal form since it violates Max-IO(segment) twice, whereas candidate (c) violates the same constraint three times. Thus, unlike (14), violations of the *MC constraint are rendered irrelevant to the selection of the optimal form. All other candidates also incur fatal violations of high-ranked constraints, and are not optimal forms.

Now, let us consider the following tableau in (16), which shows a form with a different prosodic structure.

(16) Coda Neutralization and Progressive Aspiration Merger

coh+ko 'like-Connective'	$*CC_\omega$	Coda $Cond_\omega$	*h	Max-IO(s.g.)	Agree	*MC	Max-IO (Segment)
a. $(coh.ko)_\omega$ $(coh.ko)_\phi$		*!	* *		* *		
b.☞ $(co.k^ho)_\omega$ $(co.k^ho)_\phi$						* *	* *
c. $(cot^{\urcorner}.k^ho)_\omega$ $(cot^{\urcorner}.k^ho)_\phi$					*! *	* *	
d. $(cok^{\urcorner}.k^ho)_\omega$ $(cok^{\urcorner}.k^ho)_\phi$						**! **	
e. $(co.go)_\omega$ $(co.go)_\phi$			*! *				* *
f. $(cot^{\urcorner}.ko)_\omega$ $(cot^{\urcorner}.ko)_\phi$			*! *		* *		

In (16) /coh+ko/ forms a single prosodic word since /ko/ cannot form a prosodic word on its own. Candidate (a) is ruled out because it violates the undominated prosodic-word bounded constraint Coda Condition. Even though candidates (e) and (f) satisfy high-ranked constraints of *CC and Coda Condition as well as *h, they are ruled out due to the violation of Max-IO(s.g.). Candidate (c) with different places of articulation between the coda consonant and the subsequent onset consonant is ruled out because it incurs a violation of the Agree constraint. Likewise, candidate (d) is not optimal, either, because of the multiple violations of the *MC constraint. As a consequence, candidate (b) wins out. Comparing candidate (e) with the optimal output the constraint Max-IO(s.g.) crucially outranks the constraint *MC.

In (17), however, candidate (d) is optimal since in careful speech Max IO(segment) is ranked higher than *MC.

(17) An alternating form in extra, careful speech[7]

coh+ko'like-Connective	$*CC_\omega$	Coda $Cond_\omega$	*h	Max-IO (s.g.)	Agree	Max-IO (Segment)	*MC
a.$(coh.ko)_\omega$ $(coh.ko)_\phi$		*!	* *		* *		
b.$(co.k^ho)_\omega$ $(co.k^ho)_\phi$						*! *	* *
c.$(cot^\urcorner.k^ho)_\omega$ $(cot^\urcorner.k^ho)_\phi$					*! *		* *
d.☞$(cok^\urcorner.k^ho)_\omega$ $(cok^\urcorner.k^ho)_\phi$							** **
e.$(co.go)_\omega$ $(co.go)_\phi$				*! *		* *	
f.$(cot^\urcorner.ko)_\omega$ $(cot^\urcorner.ko)_\phi$				*! *	* *		

Contrary to the tableau in (16), in (17) candidate (d) is the winning form because Max-IO(segment) outranks *MC in extra, careful speech. Thus, candidate (b), which incurs multiple violations of Max-IO(segment), loses out in the competition.[8]

---

[7] Candidate (c) also can be an optimal form in extra, careful speech. This can be accounted for by ranking the constraint Agree below the constraints Max-IO(segment) and *MC. Also, notice that in principle Agree can be ranked anywhere above *MC as in (16). However, we rank Agree immediately above *MC because it can move below Max-IO(segment) and *MC.

[8] When the Ejaculatory suffix /so/ is attached to /coh-/, [co.s'o] surfaces. This involves an opacity problem in that /h/, regardless of whether it undergoes Coda Neutralization, triggers tensification and then it disappears. The opacity problem can be accounted for by sympathy-related concepts, as mentioned above. However, we do not deal with this problem because it is beyond the scope of our paper. Also, [con.ne] is realized when the ending suffix /-ne/ is attached. The reason why [co.ne] is impossible is because nasal assimilation is obligatory when the trigger is in onset position. Thus, /h/ is not deleted but assimilated in this environment.

In sum, we propose the following constraint hierarchy for Coda Neutralization, Cluster Simplification, and Aspiration Merger in casual speech.

(18) The Constraint Hierarchy
$*CC_{\omega}$, Coda $Cond_{\omega}$>>*h>>Max-IO(s.g.), Agree>>*MC>>Max-IO(segment)

With the ranking above the rule interaction involving Coda Neutralization, Cluster Simplification, and Aspiration Merger can be accounted for without extrinsic rule ordering. We do not need to posit different rules for progressive and regressive Aspiration Merger. Further, the alternating form in extra, careful speech receives an explanatory account with the reverse ranking between *MC and Max-IO(segment). This is not uncommon given that in slow articulated speech speakers tend not to omit segments. Thus, degemination applied after Coda Neutralization and optional place assimilation in Iverson and Kim-Renaud (1994) is not necessary here.

Before we conclude this paper, let us consider the adequacy of Base-Identity constraints or output-output constraints for the Korean data given in this paper. Namely, facts concerning Coda Neutralization, Cluster Simplification, and Aspiration Merger cannot be accounted for by adopting Base-Identity constraints (Kenstowicz 1995) or output-output constraints (Benua 1997). This is because, for instance, the independent word /saks/ in /saks+hako/ is realized as [sak˺] by Cluster Simplification and Coda Neutralization, and thus there is no way of matching [sak˺] with [sa.k^ha.go] where the aspirated [k^h] surfaces instead of the related, unreleased output [k˺]. This suggests that neither Base-Identity nor output-output constraints are adequate for handling the Korean data.

5. Conclusion

A prosodically bounded constraint-based analysis has been shown to handle successfully phonological phenomena involving Coda Neutralization, Cluster Simplification, and Aspiration Merger in Korean. Specifically, we have shown that both progressive and regressive Aspiration Merger can be uniformly analyzed by a constraint ranking in which prosodic-word bounded constraints dominate markedness and faithfulness constraints, without extrinsic rule ordering as in a rule-based model. Thus, the ordering problem which seems to require derivational steps is easily resolved by making constraints sensitive to the independently motivated prosodic structures. We have also demonstrated that the alternating forms in extra, careful speech can be accounted for in a principled way by the alternating ranking between the faithfulness constraints *MC and Max-IO(segment). Furthermore, we have suggested that neither Base-Identity nor output-output constraints are adequate in dealing with the Korean facts.

References

Benua, Laura. 1997. *Transderivational identity: Phonological relations between words*. Doctoral Dissertation, University of Massachusetts, Amherst.

Booij, G. and R. Lieber. 1993. On the simultaneity of morphological and prosodic structure. *Studies in Lexical Phonology*. 23-44. New York: Academic Press.

Cho, Mi-Hui and Shinsook Lee. 1999. A Prosodically bounded constraint analysis of ordering problems. Presented at the Chicago Linguistic Society 35.

Davis, Stuart. 1997. The flowering of optimality theory: Ponapean nasal substitution and the problem of intermediate forms. Indiana University. MS.

Iverson, K.G. and Y-K Kim-Renaud. 1994. Phonological incorporation of the Korean approximant. Paper presented at the ninth International Conference on Korean Linguistics, London.

Iverson, K.G. and Shinsook, Lee. 1995. Variation as optimality in Korean cluster reduction. *ESCOL* 11. 174-185.

Kang, Ongmi. 1992. Word-internal prosodic words in Korean. *NELS* 22. 243-257.

Kenstowicz, Michael. 1995. Base-identity and uniform exponence: Alternative to cyclicity. *Current Trends in Phonology: Models and Methods*. 366-396. Paris: CNRS.

Lamontagne, Greg and Keren Rice. 1995. A correspondence account of coalescence. *UMOP* 18. 211-223.

McCarthy, John. 1998. Sympathy and phonological opacity. University of Massachusetts, Amherst. MS.

McCarthy John and Alan Prince. 1993a. Prosodic morphology I: Constraint interaction and satisfaction. University of Massachusetts, Amherst and Rutgers University. MS.

McCarthy John and Alan Prince. 1993b. Generalized alignment. *Yearbook of Morphology*. 79-153. Dordrecht, Boston, London: Kluwer Academic Publisher.

McCarthy John and Alan Prince. 1995. Faithfulness and reduplicative identity. *UMOP* 18. 249-384.

Nespor, M. and I. Vogel. 1986. *Prosodic Phonology*. Dordrecht: D. Reidel.

Prince, Alan and Paul Smolensky. 1993. Optimality theory: Constraint interaction in generative grammar. Technical Report #2 of the Rutgers Center for Cognitive Science, Rutgers University.

Selkirk, Elizabeth and T. Shen. 1990. Prosodic domains in Shanghai Chinese. *The Phonology-Syntax Connection*. Chicago: Chicago University Press.

Shim, Min-Su. 1995. Syllabification and consonant cluster simplification in Korean. *FLSM* 6. 51-61.

Walker, Rachel. 1998. *Nasalization, Neutral Segments, and Opacity Effects*. Doctoral dissertation, University of California, Santa Cruz.

Deriving Optionality in Korean Glide Formation

YOUNG-MEE YU CHO
Rutgers University

1. Data

We will begin with an overview of the Modern Standard Korean vowel system shown in (1). Korean has ten vowels on the surface. While it is widely acknowledged that the front rounded vowels /ü/ and /ö/ were pure monophthongs in all contexts in the earlier stages of Korean, the diphthongization process has been well under way for the past hundred years. As a result, the distribution of these monophthongs is quite limited. These marginal vowels alternate with diphthongs [wi] and [we] respectively in some contexts. We will assume in the paper that these vowels are underlying and the diphthongal counterparts are phonologically derived.

(1) Korean Vowels

	front		back	
		rd		rd
high	i	ü	ɨ	u
	e	ö	ə	o
low	ɛ		a	

In Korean verbal morphology there is a well-known process called Glide Formation (GF), which arises when the verb stem is concatenated with any suffix that begins with either -ə or -*a*. The choice between -ə or -*a* is determined by the so-called Vowel Harmony shown in (2), according to which the bright vowels /o/ and /a/ take the /-a/ suffix, whereas all the other vowels take /-ə/ as a default. The once productive Vowel Harmony is no longer productive except in the mimetic vocabulary in Korean (Cho and Inkelas 1993), and, though we use the commonly accepted term *Vowel Harmony*, we do not assume that there is synchronically valid vowel assimilation between vowels.

(2) Vowel Harmony in verbal morphology

Bright Vowels: /o/, /a/ + *a*		Dark Vowels: the others + ə	
c'o-a	'to peck'	chi-ə	'to hit'
cap-a	'to grab'	mut-ə	'to bury'
		pe-ə	'to cut'

As exemplified by the data in (3), Glide Formation changes the stem vowels, /i, u, o/ to a corresponding glide ([y] or [w]) before such suffixes such as continuative /-ə/ or /-a/, past tense /-əss/, /-ass/, causation suffix /-əsə/, /-asə/, concessive /-əto/, /-ato/, imperative /-əla/, /-ala/ and others.

(3) Glide Formation (GF):[1] i-ə → yə, u-ə → wə, o-a → wa
(W. Kim 1972, P. Lee 1979, E. Han 1990, Y. Lee 1997, H. Kim 1999, H. Kang 1998)

a. Obligatory (two consecutive onsetless syllables)

o-a → wa (*oa)	'to come'
pɛ.u-ə → pɛ.wə (*pɛuə)	'to learn'
s'a.u-ə → s'a.wə (*s'auə)	'to fight'
me.u-ə → me.wə (*meuə)	'to fill up'
mo.i-ə → mo.yə (*moiə)	'to gather'
chɛ.u-ə → chɛ.wə (*chɛuə)	'to fill'

b. Optional (one onsetless syllable)

po-a → poa, pwa	'to see'
pi-ə → piə, pyə	'to be empty'
phi-ə → phiə, phyə	'to bloom'
tu-ə → tuə, twə	'to put'

[1]Although the Korean orthographic convention does not illustrate Glide Formation for the high front rounded vowel, all high vowels can in fact undergo GF, as evidenced by the optional pronunciation of /cü-ə/ 'to grab' and /sü-ə/ 'to rest', in contrast to the front mid vowel (e.g. /cö-ə/ 'to tighten' and /sö-ə/ 'to celebrate (a holiday)').

titi-ə → titiə, tityə	'to step on'
t'i-ə → t'iə, t'yə	'to notice'
si-ə → siə, syə	'to be sour'
s'o-a → s'oa, s'wa	'to shoot'
c'o-a → c'oa, c'wa	'to peck'
kak'u-ə → kak'uə, kak'wə	'to adorn'
ki-ə → kiə, kyə	'to crawl'
k'u-ə → k'uə, k'wə	'to borrow'

What is of particular interest is the fact that there are two kinds of Glide Formation: one is obligatory while the other is optional. This distinction appears to be determined by the syllable structure of the stem-final syllable which undergoes Glide Formation. When the syllable in question does not contain an onset consonant (e.g. /o-a/), Glide Formation is obligatory, whereas the presence of an onset triggers optional resolution of the hiatus as in *po-a → poa, pwa* 'to see'.

Furthermore, Glide Formation interacts with Compensatory Lengthening (CL) for speakers who still have vowel length distinction. Vowel length plays only a marginal role in Modern Standard Korean. Although several processes have been identified as being sensitive to vowel length, the phonemic distinction of length is quite disputable. While older speakers of the Standard dialect and speakers of other dialects seem to have length as part of their system in the initial syllable of a word, most speakers, including myself find it difficult to distinguish long vowels from short vowels in all contexts. Not having the intuition (at least on the conscious level of perception), I base my analysis of compensatory lengthening on the data available from the written sources.

The data in (4) show the interplay between Glide Formation and Compensatory Lengthening. In (4a), the vowel is lengthened when GF applies. Contrary to what happens in most cases, (4b) lists one example showing the lack of Compensatory Lengthening, /o-a/ → wa. Surprisingly, it is the only counterexample to CL.

(4) Glide Formation and Compensatory Lengthening (CL)

a. <u>CL in initial syllable</u>

po-a → pwa: 'to see'	pi-ə → pyə: 'to be empty'
phi-ə → phyə: 'to bloom'	tu-ə → twə: 'to put'
titi-ə → tityə: 'to step on'	t'i-ə → t'yə: 'to notice'
si-ə → syə: 'to be sour'	s'o-a → s'wa: 'to shoot'
c'o-a → c'wa: 'to peck'	k'u-ə → k'wə: 'to borrow'

b. lack of CL
o-a → wa (*wa:) 'to come'

(5) shows that some potential cases of Compensatory Lengthening are neutralized in noninitial position. This is due to an independently operating general constraint that does not permit a vowel length contrast in non-initial syllables as shown.

(5) Neutralization of Vowel Length in non-initial syllables
a. lack of vowel length in verbal morphology
kak'u-ə → kak'wə 'to adorn' titi-ə → tityə 'to step on'
b. lack of vowel length in noun morphology
/nu:n+sa:ram/ → [nu:n saram] 'snowman'

Now we lay out three questions that need to be addressed in this paper. First, we should be able to point out the differences between optional vs. obligatory Glide Formation. Second, we need to accout for the lack of Compensatory Lengthening in /o-a/ → [wa]. Finally, we will characterize the nature of Glide Formation in Optimality Theory.

2. Past Analyses

Early analyses treated the difference between optionality and obligatoriness in terms of a rule feature [+optional] (P. Lee 1979:27). A typical example is shown in (6).

(6) Rule features (optional/obligatory, exception feature)

[u, i] → [w, y] / ____]Verbal suffix + ə (optional)

In more recent analyses, the lack of Compensatory Lengthening has been attributed to differences of syllabification in onsetless syllables (Han 1990).

Han treats (3a) and (3b) as a separate process based on the fact that the forms in (a) undergo compensatory lengthening after they undergo glide formation, but those in (b) do not. Even for those speakers who distinguish vowel length, the length distinction is valid only in initial syllables. So the only relevant form is *wa*.

Han's analysis is based on two different cycles of syllabification, as illustrated in (7). The words undergoing Glide Formation are syllabified in the later stage. Since moras are not present underlyingly but projected from vowels as part of syllabification, *po-a* undergoes early syllabification and gets demorified when Glide Formation applies. As a result, there is compensatory lengthening. On the other hand, verb stems which end with a syllable without an onset do not unergo early syllabification. The sequence of two vowels then obligatorily form a single syllable, thus accounting for the absence of CL.

(7) Han's (1990): Analysis of syllabification and resyllabification
a. po-a → po$a (syllabification)
→ pwa: (resyllabification and CL)
b. o-a (there is no stage o$a)
→ wa (syllabification and no CL)

An approach that shifts the burden of explanation to the representations rather than to rules is Kim (1999).[2] He proposes an opaque UR for the *o-a* case; /wʌ/ is assumed to be the underlying form for the verb stem /o-/. /ʌ/, as the bright counterpart of the least marked vowel /ɨ/, deletes when preceding a vowel in the Glide Formation context, while it surfaces as [o] in preconsonantal position. This approach explains the obligatory nature of GF and the lack of Compensatory Lengthening, but it posits the synchronically unmotivated /ʌ/ vowel, which disappeared from the language in the 18th century.

(8) H. Kim (1999): Opaque UR
o-ta (/wʌ-ta/) 'to come' /wʌ + a/ → [wa]

3. Deriving Optionality in Optimality Theory

In this paper, I propose that the apparent distinction between optionality and obligatoriness need not be stipulated but follows naturally from the basic principles of Optimality Theory.

(9) Optimality Theory (McCarthy and Prince 1993, Prince and Smolensky 1993, McCarthy and Prince 1995)
A grammar consists of three parts: (1) a generation function GEN whose input is an underlying form and whose output is a set of candidate forms derived from the input by unrestricted phonological operations, (2) a set of universal constraints on the output of GEN and (3) strict dominance ranking for resolving constraint conflicts.

---

[2]Kim (1999) contains a detailed analysis of variations of GF and CL. In particular, he cites one verb nobody seems to have accounted for /i-ə/ → [iə] ~ [yə:] 'to carry on one's head.' It is clear that a comprehensive analysis of GF and all the related processes is in order. For this particular verb, it might be possible to assume an UR that contains an onset consonant /yɨ-/, which surfaces as [i-] in the same way as the examples in (17b) and (19).

Capitalizing on the intuition that GF is a strategy which enhances syllable-wellformedness by creating an onset and avoiding vowel hiatus, we rely on those cross-linguistically well-motivated constraints in (10).

(10) Constraints at work

Onset: syllables must have onsets
***Complex:** complex onsets are not allowed
Max-μ: Every mora of the input has a counterpart in the output (mora-preservation)
License(length): long vowels only in initial position
***V̄** (No long vowels in the language)
DEP-IO: every segment of the output has a counterpart in the input (no epenthesis)
MAX-IO: every segment of the input has a counterpart in the output (no deletion)

For speakers who do not have the vowel distinction, the relevant constraint ranking is shown in (11). The two constraints, Onset and *Complex are not ranked with respect to each other, and their interaction yields the effects of optionality by allowing two optimal candidates in *po.a* and *pwa*, but in not in the /o-a/ → *wa* case. GF results when **Max-μ** is violated: i.e., an underlying mora does not have a counterpart in the output but the segment dominated by the mora is incorporated as a non-moraic segment into the adjacent syllable. Crucially for Korean, the two constraints **Onset** and ***Complex** are not ranked with respect to each other, thus yielding two equally harmonious outputs (*poa, pwa*) when there already is an onset consonant (*po-*). However, when there is no underlying onset (*o-*), GF does not create candidates with complex onsets, resulting in the single output (*wa*). Optionality is the result of the interaction between two unranked constraints (Onset, *Complex) while obligatoriness is due to inert *Complex in the onsetless syllable. Since there is no epenthesis in verbal morphology, we assume that DEP is higher ranked than the constraints discusssed here.

(11) Constraint Ranking

(*V, DEP-IO, MAX-IO>> Onset, *Complex >> Max-μ)

	Onset	*Complex	Max-μ
→ po.a	* !		
→ pwa		* !	*
o.a	* * !		
→ wa			*

Furthermore, GF in Middle Korean provides additional support for the present analysis. (12a) shows that GF was obligatory when there was no onset, the same pattern as in Modern Korean. As exemplified in (12b), GF was much more restricted in that only the /h/ onset allowed optional GF. I believe this has everything to do with /h/ weakening in intervocalic position. When /h/ deletes, the word patterns as an onsetless syllable. On the other hand, when /h/ is present, GF is blocked.

(12) GF in Middle Korean (Han 1988)

a. GF is obligatory when there is no onset.

o-a-n	→	wan	'to come'
ilu-ə-nɨl	→	ilwənɨl	'to rise'
kyeu-ə	→	kyeywa	'to exceed'
kyəlu-ə	→	kyelwə	'to compete'

b. GF is optional only when the onset is /h/.

moyho-a~	moyhwa	'to gather'
s'aho-a ~	s'ahwa	'to fight'
pʌyho-a ~	pʌyhwa	'to learn'
nʌnho-a ~	nʌnhwa	'to share'

(/h/ is weakened or deleted in intervocalic position.)

c. no GF but insertion of a glide when the onset is a C other than /h/

kətu-ə ~	kətuwə	*kətwə	'to take care'
tatho-a ~	tathowa	*tathwa	'to quarrel'

All other types of onset consonants blocked GF systematically, as in (12c). Instead of GF, Glide Insertion was an option. In contrast to Modern Korean, GF was more restricted in that only the /h/ onset allowed GF (e.g. *moyho-a* ~ *moyhwa* 'gather'); other types of onsets blocked GF systematically. These data find a natural explanation in the context of the historical /h/-weakening in the intervocalic position, and argue for the validity of a family of ***Complex** constraints as well as the dominance of ***Complex** over **Onset** in the earlier stage of Korean.

(13) illustrates the Middle Korean ranking. If we compare this with (11), we notice two differences: 1) the dominace of *Complex over Onset, which blocked GF when the result was a complex onset cluster such as *kətwə.* Another striking feature is that DEP-IO (which blocks epenthesis) is lower ranked in Middle Korean, producing outputs containing inserted [w] in *kətuwə.*

(13) Middle Korean Ranking:

***Complex >> Onset, DEP-IO, *VhV**

	*Complex	Onset	DEP-IO
/o-a/			
oa		* *!	
→ wa			
/kətu-ə/			
→ kətuə		*	
kətwə	*!		
→kətuwə			*

As in Modern Korean, optionality is the result of two unranked constraints (Onset, DEP-IO) while obligatoriness is due to inert *Complex in the onsetless syllable.

4. GF and Compensatory Lengthening

Now let us consider the data involving Compensatory Lengthening. Vowel length plays only a marginal role in Modern Standard Korean. While older speakers of the Standard dialect and speakers of other dialects seem to have length as part of their phonological system (at least in the initial syllable of a word), most speakers (including myself) find it difficult to distinguish long vowels from short vowels. J.-W. Park (1994) concludes that his subjects, when asked to identify vowel length in a list of words, failed to determine it with any systemacity. Not having the distinction, we base our analysis of CL on the data from the written sources. One major problem concerning the data involves frequent inconsistencies among speakers. Even dictionaries disagree in their specification of vowel length.

(14) presents data involving the interaction between GF and CL.

(14) Data

a. CL in initial syllable

po-a → pwa:	'to see'	cu-ə → cwə:	'to give'
i-ə → yə:	'to carry on the head'		
si-ə → syə:	'to be sour'	s'o-a → s'wa:	'to shoot'
t'i-ə → t'yə:	'to notice'	k'u-ə → k'wə:	'to borrow'

b. lack of CL

Initial Syllable

o-a → wa (*wa:)	'to come'

Non-initial Syllable

kak'u- ə → kak'wə	'to adorn'
titi-ə → tityə	'to step on'
kitali-ə → kitalyə	'to wait'

It is easy to see the competition between *pwa* and *pwa:*, as resolved by **Max-μ**; Underlying moras are realized as two moras with CL. For speakers who preserve vowel length, licensing length is higher ranked than the dominated constraint against a long vowel. **License(L)** allows long vowels in the initial syllable while long vowels in other syllables of a word are suppressed due to ***VV**.

(15) Constraint Ranking for CL:

License(L)>>*VV, DEP-IO, MAX-IO >>Onset,*Complex >>Max-μ

(16) shows that the outputs exhibiting CL are optimal candidates whether there is an initial onset consonant or not.

(16)

	Onset	*Complex	Max-μ
/po-a/			
pwa		*	*!
→ pwa:		*	
/i-ə/			
yə			*!
→ yə:			

In this context, the puzzle in /o-a/ → [wa] is harder to resolve unless for some reason the verb stem /o-/ ('to come') is not marked for an underlying mora, in which case [wa:] would be a DEP-μ violation. Whatever the proper solution might be, there is no doubt that this is an exception to the general CL phenomena.

There is another set of data that awaits explanation. Korean has a general constraint which prohibits /y/ from following a palatal onset (Cho 1988, Martin 1992). When such a sequence arises, /y/ deletes, thus motivating a ranking such as ***cy** >> **Max-(y)**. There are two distinct types of palatal merger, as shown in (17). (17a) are cases in which GF is optional. When GF applies, there are Palatal merger and CL, as expected.

On the other hand, for (17b) GF is obligatory and forms showing CL are ungrammatical.

(17) Palatal merger

a. Palatal merger and CL (Optional GF)

ci-ə → ciə, cə: 'to carry'

chi-ə → chiə, chə: 'to run over'

b. Palatal merger and lack of CL (Obligatory GF)

ci-ə → cə (*ciə, *cə:) 'to lose'

c'i-ə → c'ə (*c'iə, *c'ə:) 'to steam'

chi-ə → chə (*chiə, *chə:) 'to hit'

The solution lies in assuming different underlying representations for (17b). Following the suggestion made by Y-S. Kim 1984, we posit the as underlying /cɨ-, cɨ-, chɨ-/ for *ci-, c'i, chi-* in (17b). The high back unrounded vowel /ɨ/ occupies special status in Korean phonology. As the most unmarked vowel, it consistently deletes either before or after another vowel in verbal morphology (e.g. khɨ-ə → khə 'to be big', ka-ɨmyən → kamyən 'if..go'). It assimilates to the preceding labial or palatal consonant (e.g. təw+ɨn → təun 'to be hot', /chəchɨ/ → chəchi (from English *church*).) The underlying /cɨ/ ('to lose') loses its vowel when a suffix vowel follows. There is no CL for the loss of /ɨ/ in any case; not only syllables containing a palatal onset, but rather those containing any consonant onset do not permit lengthening, as shown in (18).

(18) /ɨ/ loss and lack of CL

khɨ-ə → khə (*khə:) to be big'

s'ɨ-ə → s'ə (*s'ə:) 'to use'

Moreover, a palatal consonant is not the only onset that shows this behavior. The verb, *phu-* does not conjugate like other *u*-final verbs, as illustrated in (19). Unlike a regular verb like /cu-ə/ → cuə ~ cwə: 'to give', this verb allows only one output (*pə*) when the suffix in question is attached. The stem-final /u/ never surfaces but deletes. There is neither GF nor CL. Again based on pervasive labialization of /ɨ/ in a labial context as well as its deletion in the vowel context , we can motivate /pɨ-/ as the underlying form of the verb stem. Under this assumption, this case exactly parallels (17b).

(19) phu-ta 'to ladle'
pu-ə → pə (*puə, *pwə, *pwə:, *pə:)
/pɨ-ta/ → puta (Labialization)
/pɨ-ə/ → pə

In addition to Palatal Merger, there are other processes of verbal morphology that closely interact with Glide Formation and Compensatory Lengthening. These are Vowel Contraction whose net effect is eliminating vowel hiatus and Deletion of a Medial Glide (/h/, /w/) which creates vowel sequences (C.-W. Kim 1980, H. Kang 1996, H. Kim 1999). The optimal resolution of these phenomena is closely related to the analysis of GF, but a comprehensive study of these phenomena is beyond the scope of this paper.

5. Conclusion

In this paper, we propose that the apparent distinction between optionality and obligatoriness need not be stipulated. The interaction between independently motivated constraints yields the effects of optionality by allowing two optimal candidates in one case but not in the other. This approach to variation or optionality has been validated for other processes within the Optimality-theoretic framework. The structure-dependence of synchronic variation and diachronic change is investigated by means of partially ordered constraint sets. Once we accept the fact that grammars impose structural constraints on variation and change, we need a theory which formally connects invariant and variable phenomena, synchrony and diachrony (McCarthy 1991, 1993, Kiparsky 1995, Anttila and Cho 1998, Cho 1998). These studies show that OT, combined with partial constraint ranking, permits one to model invariant and variable phenomena in the same framework.

In sum, the distinction between obligatory and optional application of rules in the derivational framework has no place whatsoever in Optimality Theory. The apparent distinction is an epiphenomenon derivable from the independently motivated constraint relation. In the optional case, GF creates a candidate with complex onsets, thus satisfying **Onset** but violating ***Complex**. When the two unranked constraints favor different competing candidates, variability is a natural outcome.

References

Anttila, Arto and Young-mee Yu Cho. 1998. Variation and Change in Optimality Theory. *Lingua* 104. 31-56.

Cho, Young-mee Yu. 1988. Syllable Structure Constraint in Korean. *The Proceedings of the International Conference on Korean Linguistics*. University of Toronto. 107-119.

Cho, Young-mee Yu. 1998. Language Change as Reranking of Constraints, in R. Hogg and L. van Bergen, eds., *Historical Linguistics* 1995. Amsterdam: John Bejamins.

Cho, Young-mee Y. and Sharon Inkelas. 1993. A Brief History of Korean Vowels. Paper presented at the Sound Change Workshop, Stanford University.

Han, Eunjoo. 1990. Glide Formation in Korean, in H. Hoji, ed., *Japanese/Korean Linguistics 1*. 173-186.

Han, Young-kyun. 1988. Piumcelhwa kyuchikuy thongsicek pyunhwawa ku uymi [The historical Change in Desyllabification Rules and Its Implication in Korean Phonology] *Ulsan Umwun-nwonchip* 4. 1-26.

Kang, Hyunsook. 1998. Glide Formation and Compensatory Lengthening within Sympathy Theory. *Studies in Phonetics and Phonology and Morphology* 4. 69-87.

Kang, Hyeon-Seok. 1996. The Deletion of w in Seoul Korean and Its Implications. *OSU Working Papers in Linguistics*. 56-76.

Kim, Chin-W. 1980. Abstractness and Distinctness in Korean Phonology. Reprinted in *Sojourns in Language II*. Tower Press. 1988. 587-596.

Kim, Hyung-Soo. 1999. Glide Formation and Compensatory Lengthening in Korean Revisited. Studies in *Grammar*. Vol 17. 15-31. Taeku, Korea: The Society of Modern Grammar.

Kim, Young-Seok. 1984. *Aspects of Korean Morphology*. Doctoral dissertation. University of Texas, Austin.

Kim, Wan-Jin. 1972. Hyungtayroncek hyunanuy eununronck kukpok-ul uyhaye. [Phonological solutions for morphological issues] *Dong-a Munhwa* 11. 273-299.

Kiparsky, Paul. 1993. Variable Rules. Rutgers Optimality Workshop Talk.

Kiparksy, Paul. 1995. The Phonological Basis of Sound Change, in J. A. Goldsmith, ed., *The Handbook of Phonological Theory*. 640-70. Oxford:Blackwell.

Lee, Yongsung. 1997. Glide Formation and Compensatory Lengthening in Korean Verbal Conjugation. *Studies in Phonetics, Phonology and Morphology*. 3 223-246. The Phonology-Morphology Circle of Korea.

Lee, Pyeng-Keun. 1979. *Umwunhyunsange Issosouy cheyak*. [Contraints on Phonological Phenomena] Seoul: Tower Press.

Martin, Samuel. 1992. *The Reference Grammar of Korean*. Tyoko, Japan: Tuttle.

McCarthy, John. 1991. Synchronic Rule Inversion. Berkeley Linguistics Society 17. 192-207.

McCarthy, John. 1993. A Case of Surface Constraint Violation. *Canadian Journal of Linguistics* 38. 169-195.

McCarthy, John and Alan Prince. 1993. Prosodic Morphology. Ms. RuCCS-TR-3.

McCarthy, John and Alan Prince. 1995. Faithfulness and Reduplicative Identity. *Papers in Optimality Theory*. University of Massachusetts Occasional Papers 18. 249-384.

Park, Jeong-Woon. 1994. Variation of Vowel Length in Korean. in Y. Kim-Renaud, ed., *Theoretical Issues in Korean Linguistics*. Stanford: CSLI. 175-187.

Prince, Alan and Paul Smolensky. 1993. Optimality Theory. Ms. RuCCS-TR-2.

More Acoustic Traces of "Deleted" Vowels in Japanese [1]

ALICE FABER & TIMOTHY J. VANCE

Haskins Laboratory & Connecticut College

1. Introduction

1.1 Devoiced vowels in Japanese

A number of well-known languages exhibit vowel devoicing, including Korean, but the phenomenon has been studied most intensively in Japanese (Jun, Beckman, Niimi, & Tiede, 1998:1). The standard allophonic account for Japanese says that a short high vowel, /i/ or /ɯ/, is devoiced when it is flanked by voiceless consonants or, word-finally, when it is preceded by a voiceless consonant (Nihon Onsei Gakkai, 1976: 748; Alfonso, 1971: xxviii), but this is just a crude first approximation. For one thing, non-high vowels occasionally exhibit devoicing as well, although not nearly as often as high vowels (Han, 1962: 84–85; Vance, 1987: 48–49). Several additional factors may also affect the probability of devoicing in high vowels. For example, it has long been claimed that devoicing is inhibited in an accented syllable (Han, 1962: 81–82; Kuriyagawa & Sawashima, 1989; Imai, 1997: 48), although some studies have challenged this conventional wisdom (Haraguchi, 1984; Tsuchida, 1997; Kitahara, 1998), and it may be that there

[1] The research summarized in this report was supported by grant HD-01994 from the National Institutes of Health to Haskins Laboratories and by an endowed chair research allowance from Connecticut College. We would like to thank Louis Goldstein, Cathi Best, and Kathy Harris for their helpful discussion concerning this project; none of these colleagues bear any responsibility for flaws in our presentation or reasoning. We would also like to thank Mike D'Angelo and Philip Rubin for a helpful modification of the HADES software package.

has been a diachronic weakening of the inhibiting power of accent in recent decades (Nihon Onsei Gakkai, 1976: 748; Kondo, 1997: 83–84). It has also been claimed that certain neighboring consonants favor devoicing more than others (Martin, 1952: 14; Han, 1962: 88–90), although the evidence for such differences is not very clear (Imai, 1997: 53). A third common claim is that devoicing in consecutive syllables is avoided (Martin, 1952: 14; Han, 1962: 91), but it can and does occur (Haraguchi, 1984; Imai, 1997: 50). When each of two or more consecutive syllables contains a short high vowel in the devoicing environment, the probability of devoicing in a particular syllable seems to depend on both accent and morphological structure (Vance, 1992; Kondo, 1997: 100–147).

There is no controversy about the relevance of tempo and style to the probability of devoicing in Japanese. Devoicing is less frequent in slower and more careful speech (Sakuma, 1929: 232-233; Kuriyagawa & Sawashima, 1989; Jun, Beckman, & Lee, 1998: 43). For example, professional teachers of hearing-impaired children devoice less in speech directed to such children than in speech directed to normal-hearing listeners (Imaizumi, Hayashi, & Deguchi, 1995).

There is also considerable variability in the phonetic realizations of devoiced vowels. Spectrograms sometimes show energy at the appropriate formant frequencies even in the absence of any voicing Han (1962: 83), and Jun, Beckman & Lee (1998: 50) sort tokens into three categories: voiced, partially devoiced, and completely devoiced. They define partial devoicing as "shorter than 30ms and show[ing] weak energy, at low frequencies only." Generally speaking, if the consonant preceding a devoiced vowel is a stop, an acoustic interval corresponding to the devoiced vowel is easily identifiable on waveforms and spectrograms, but if the preceding consonant is a fricative, such an interval is typically absent.

1.2 Evidence for the phonological presence of devoiced vowels

As far as phonological status is concerned, the consensus is that devoiced vowels, whether phonetically present or not, are allophones of the same phonemes as their voiced counterparts. This analysis certainly matches the intuitions of native speakers, and several lines of argument converge in supporting it. First, kana spelling makes no distinction between syllables with voiced and devoiced vowels; *tsuki* 'moon', which can be pronounced [ts·kʲi], begins with the same letter as *tsugi* 'next', normally pronounced [tsɯgʲi]. Of course, orthography raises a chicken-and-egg problem: it may be that kana spelling simply reinforces intuitions that speakers would have anyway, but it may also be that spelling determines those intuitions to some extent (Vance, 1987: 54). Incidentally, in 1900 Ueda Kazutoshi proposed a novel romanization for Japanese that simply left out devoiced vowels, but it was swiftly rejected (Takebe, 1977: 305).

A second argument in favor of ascribing phonological status to devoiced vowels involves phonotactics. Bloch (1950) consistently treats devoiced vowels in certain environments as phonologically absent (Vance, 1987: 52–54), and as a result, his phonemic transcriptions are full of word-final obstruents and obstruent clusters. Not only are these transcriptions phonotactically unwieldy, they are highly counterintuitive (Han, 1962: 82).

A third argument for phonemic status for devoiced vowels rests on anticipatory coarticulation. Studies using English speakers have shown that articulatory activity for a segment may begin several phonological segments earlier (Bell-Berti & Harris, 1982; Keating, 1988; Boyce, Krakow, & Bell-Berti., 1991) and that this articulatory pattern is reflected in spectral characteristics of these preceding segments (Yeni-Komshian & Soli, 1981; Nittrouer, Studdert-Kennedy, & McGowan, 1989; Goodell & Studdert-Kennedy, 1993). For example, Japanese /ç/ has lower frequency spectral peaks and edges when followed by /ɯ/ than when followed by /i/, even when the vowel is devoiced and seems to have disappeared into the frication noise (Beckman & Shoji, 1984; Endo, 1998). Similarly, release bursts for /k/ have lower frequency spectral prominences when followed by /ɯ/ than when followed by /i/, again regardless of vowel voicing (Endo, 1998; Faber & Vance, submitted).

Presumably as a consequence both of phonotactics and of anticipatory coarticulation, native speakers of Japanese perceive devoiced vowels as vowels and can discriminate between devoiced /i/ and devoiced /ɯ/, although not quite as accurately as between voiced /i/ and voiced /ɯ/ (Beckman & Shoji, 1984; Endo, 1998). Phonetic transcriptions such as Alfonso's (1971: xxviii), in which, for example, /Qk/, /kik/ and /kuk/ are all transcribed identically as [k̩k], are simply inaccurate. The perceptible effects of anticipatory coarticulation, together with the variability of devoicing (which means that a high vowel in the devoicing environment can be pronounced as a voiced vowel), leave no real doubt about the phonological existence of devoiced vowels.

1.3 A gestural overlap account of Japanese devoiced vowels, and its implications

Jun & Beckman (1993) conclude, on the basis of both acoustic and physiological evidence, that the observed distribution of devoiced and apparently deleted short high vowels in Japanese results from the degree of overlap between the supralaryngeal gestures responsible for the quality of the vowels in question and the laryngeal abduction required for the flanking voiceless consonants. Given sufficient overlap, there will be no acoustic interval in which vocal fold vibration is evident, and it may not even be possible to identify an interval—even a voiceless interval—containing noise-excited formants. Nonetheless, the presence of these supralaryngeal gestures can be inferred from their acoustic effects on immediately preceding consonants: [ç] has lower-frequency spectral peaks when followed by /ɯ/ than when followed by /i/, just what would be expected on the basis of the differing supralaryngeal configurations required for the two vowels (Beckman & Shoji, 1984).

This is not the only potential spectral effect of these obscured supralaryngeal gestures on adjacent consonants. Studies of anticipatory coarticulation in English and in other languages reveal that articulatory movements for a given target may begin early enough to influence several preceding segments (e.g., Boyce, Krakow, & Bell-Berti, 1991). Thus, the configuration of the various articulators during any one phonological segment may be influenced by the gestural requirements of multiple segments in a word; further, the number of segments so affected is a function both of the gestural needs of those segments and of the speech rate (reflected in the number of segments occurring in a given temporal interval).

It would not be surprising, then, if initial /s/ in the English words *stay* and *stow* were to differ acoustically due to anticipation of the vowels /e/ and /o/, despite the intervening /t/. But, because of the intervening /t/, the /s/s in *stay* and *stow* might be less different from each other than the /s/s in *say* and *sew*. If these English words are compared with the superficially similar Japanese words *sute* and *suto*, the initial /s/ in the Japanese items might well be influenced to some extent by the word-final /e/ and /o/. However, this influence might be lessened by the presence of *two* intervening segments: /t/, as in the English items, and an additional /ɯ/. As a result of this difference in phonological structure, /s/ should be more similar in Japanese *sute* and *suto* than in English *stay* and *stow* (or in Japanese *se* and *so*); that is, /s/ should be less influenced by the final vowel in the longer Japanese items than in the longer English items.

The goal of the present paper is to investigate this hypothesis. We do this by comparing acoustic characteristics of fricatives in English and Japanese and by looking at the magnitude of the differential effects of vowels differing in frontness on the fricatives. The gestural overlap account of vowel devoicing in Japanese predicts that the fricatives in Japanese *sute* and *suto* should be less different than those in English *stay* and *stow*, because the former contain four phonological segments while the latter contain three. If acoustic differences between /s/ in *sute* and /s/ in *suto* are observed, that by itself would not count as evidence against our hypothesis; our hypothesis is that such differences would be consistently smaller in magnitude than differences between /s/ in *se* and /s/ in *so*.

2. Methods

2.1 Participants

Four speakers of Japanese and three of English were recruited through acquaintance networks. The Japanese speakers are all from the greater Tokyo area, while the English speakers are from various parts of the US; none speaks with a marked regional accent. All speakers were naive to the purpose of the recording, and the Japanese speakers thought that our purpose was to test their choice of accent patterns. Demographic details about the seven speakers are provided in Table 1.

Table1: Participants in the study

	Speaker	Gender	Age	From
English	E1	Female	16	Connecticut
	E2	Male	42	Missouri
	E3	Female	45	Rhode Island
Japanese	J1	Female	50	Tokyo
	J2	Male	42	Tokyo
	J3	Female	23	Tokyo
	J4	Female	39	Tokyo

2.2 Corpus

Japanese test items consisted of pairs of words differing in the vowel in the final syllable. In addition to monosyllables *se/so* and *shi/shu*, there were four pairs typically produced with devoiced vowels in the first syllable: *sute/suto, suki/suku, tsute/tsuto, shitee/shitoo*. The corpus also contained two pairs of words typically produced with fully voiced vowels in the first syllable: *tsugi/tsugu* and *sude/tsudo*. Three additional items, *fuku, to,* and *mitee*, were included to facilitate some additional comparisons. Five additional items (*bi, ne, kugi, kizu, puro*) served as foils. Subjects produced ten tokens of each item in a carrier sentence "*Sore kara* _____ *da yo*", in two separate randomizations. The contrasting pairs were intended to have unaccented first syllables, because of reports in the literature that accented vowels are less likely to be devoiced than unaccented vowels are. However, two speakers consistently produced *tsudo* with an accented initial syllable; one speaker was so unsure of what accent pattern to use that she consistently tried out both versions between repetitions of the full list. This speaker also produced several tokens of *sute* with initial accent (and a devoiced vowel).

English test items likewise consisted of pairs of words differing in vowel quality. In addition to the CVs *see/sue, say/sew,* and *she/shoe*, there were three pairs with initial clusters: *steep/stoop, stay/stow,* and *scale/skoal*. Two items, *tee* and *two*, were included to enable some further comparisons. An additional ten items (*bee, kick, day, cake, peak, doe, mane, light, boat, good*) served as foils. Subjects produced ten tokens of each item in the carrier "*It's a* ______, *Helene*", in two separate randomizations.

2.3 Data handling

All items were recorded on a Sony portable DAT recorder, and converted to Haskins PCM format (Whalen, Wiley, Rubin, & Cooper, 1990) at a 20kHz sampling rate for acoustic analysis. While some acoustic information about fricatives, especially /s/, might appear at frequencies higher than 10kHz, the maximum observable with a 20 kHz sampling rate, this was the maximum usable sampling rate for the HADES (Rubin, 1995) waveform editing and analysis software available to us.

Fricative spectra are acoustically complex, and typically involve one or more high-amplitude bands of aperiodic noise. In addition, there may be a narrower-band resonance that is contiguous with one of the formants of an adjacent vowel. As a result, it is extremely difficult to provide an adequate characterization of individual fricatives in terms of just one or two parameters. Choice of measurement parameter has in the past been based on a combination of measurement ease (e.g., location of spectral peaks or boundaries of the fricative noise), computational ease, and theoretical considerations. Our strategy in the present investigation is somewhat different (see also Evers, Reetz, & Lahiri, 1998). While we include some measures of the computationally-simple sort (location of peaks in the fricative noise, spectral center of gravity (=centroid: Nittrouer, Studdert-Kennedy, & McGowan, 1989; Nittrouer, 1995)), these measures were not always informative, for reasons we will explain. Therefore, we derived some additional measures from systematically comparing fricative spectra from tokens that we expected might be different.

As evident from Figure 1, which compares the spectra of 10 tokens each of speaker J2's *se* and *so* at the midpoint of each fricative, fricatives may differ in the frequency and amplitude of spectral peaks. These tokens do differ significantly in centroid, as marked by the two vertical lines, but, because the peaks are closer together for *se* than for *so*, the spectra are more different globally than they appear to be based simply on the centroid. Further, even on these averaged cross-sections, it would be difficult to mark the lower boundary of the fricative noise with any degree of reliability; especially for *se*. However, the increase in amplitude is much steeper for *so* than for *se*. As a result of this difference in slope, combined with the shift downward in frequency of the first spectral prominence, these spectra can be divided into three regions: a low frequency range containing very little energy, a mid frequency range in which there is apparently more energy present in *so* spectra than in *se* spectra, and a high frequency range in which

Figure 1: Averaged and smoothed spectral cross-sections for /s/ in 10 tokens of se *(dashed line) and 10 tokens of* so *(solid line), at fricative midpoint, produced by speaker J2.*

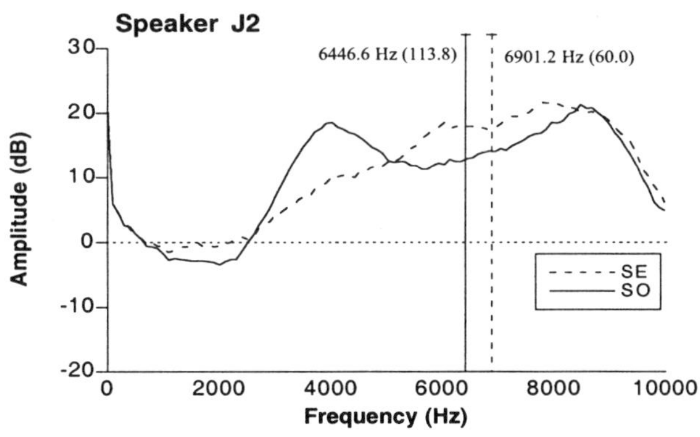

the reverse is true.

Because HADES can calculate centroids in batch mode, our first attack on analyzing the fricatives in the present corpus was to compare the centroids for the CV tokens in each speaker's corpus. If these were not different, we then proceeded to compare spectral cross-sections for these same tokens to see if there were spectral differences that would not be reflected in the centroids. If we could not identify a significant difference between spectra of CV tokens differing only in vowel (perhaps due to our limited sampling rate), we did not analyze that speaker's segmentally more complex tokens. However, if we found differences in the CV tokens, we then measured the more complex tokens, using the same measure, to determine whether vowel-conditioned differences, if any, were comparable in magnitude to those observed for the CV tokens.

Figure 2. Speaker J3: Sample waveform and pseudo-spectogram of a token of tsudo, *with phonetic transcription for orientation. Vertical lines represent the position of events in the token, from left to right: end of voicing for /a/, onset of frication for [s] in /ts/, end of frication (coinciding with onset of voicing for /ɯ/), beginning of closure for /d/, release of closure for /d/, onset of voicing for /o/, end of voicing for /o/, and release of closure for /d/ in the carrier phrase. The horizontal line in the closure interval for /ts/ represents 50 msec. The frequency range for the pseudospectrogram is from 0–10,000 Hz.*

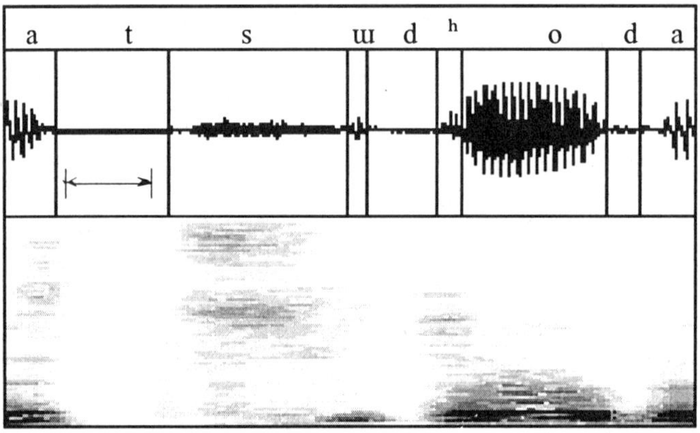

Analysis proceeded as follows: Individual tokens were excised from larger files after it was verified that they had been read as intended, and that the target items were not preceded or followed by a pause. The first stage in analysis was to delineate segmental boundaries, based on screen displays of waveforms and pseudo-spectograms.

Figure 2 illustrates the maximal set of landmarks, represented by vertical lines in the waveform portion of the display; a phonetic transcription is provided for ease in identifying individual segments. Based on the locations of these boundaries, durations of individual segments were calculated. In addition, centroids were automatically calculated from DFT spectral cross-sections[2] at five locations within each fricative: 15 msec after the onset of frication noise; 15 msec before the end of the frication noise; and, at three additional locations dividing the fricative into quarters. The edge measurements were offset 15 msec to avoid distortions based on formant excitation. If the CV tokens did not differ significantly in centroid frequency, complete spectral cross-sections at the same five frames were saved as text files, averaged, and plotted. On the basis of these plots, one of which appears in Figure 1, one or two spectral regions in which the two types appeared to contrast were identified. Using macros defined in Excel98 on the Macintosh, integrals[3] (representing the area underneath the spectral cross-section for these regions) were calculated for these frames.

In addition, formant frequencies were measured for two of the English speakers and one of the Japanese speakers. Because of the fronting of /u/ and, to a lesser extent, /o/ for many English speakers (Labov, 1991), it was important to verify that these two vowels did in fact differ from their front counterparts, especially at their onsets. If these vowels do not differ acoustically at their onsets, it would be unlikely that they would differentially affect the acoustics of preceding fricatives. For the Japanese speakers, the primary reason for looking at formant frequencies was to determine whether the formant frequencies for /ɯ/ in *tsugi/tsugu* and in *sude/tsudo* would be affected by the quality of the vowel in the second syllable.

3. Results

Some typical data are illustrated in Figure 3. In Figure 3A, each curve represents the mean centroids of the fricatives in ten tokens of one word produced by speaker E3, measured at the five locations indicated on the x-axis. The solid curves for *see* and *sue* are well separated, indicating that /s/ in *sue* indeed does have a lower frequency spectrum than that of /s/ in *see*. In addition, the dashed curves for *steep* and *stoop* are comparably separated. Figure 3B represents the integrals of the upper frequency range of the fricative spectra for the same words, produced by speaker E2. While these tokens are more variable, as evidenced by the size of the error bars associated with each point, the solid curves for *see* and *sue* are, nonetheless, distinct throughout the entire fricative. However, the dashed curves for *steep* and *stoop* are only distinct late in the fricative.

---

[2] DFT spectral cross-sections were calculated on windows of 1024 samples (50 msec), with an offset of 64 samples (3 msec). This relatively large temporal window was chosen to provide a high frequency resolution, as some of the hypothesized spectral differences between fricative types could have been of a relatively small magnitude. Centroids were calculated on the frequency range 1500–9999 Hz; the lower range was chosen to minimize the impact on the centroids of any voicing during the fricative as well as of any low frequency artifacts.

[3] Decibels represent relative rather than absolute amplitude, and the DFT routines in HADES sometimes return negative values, which confound the rather brute-force calculation of integrals used. To avoid these confounds, the DFT spectra were rescaled by adding 50 to each value, based on the minima observed in individual spectral slices.

Figure 3: A–Comparable difference in see/sue *and* steep/stoop *(Speaker E3); B–Vocalic influence on /s/ in steep/stoop is comparable in magnitude to that in* see/sue*, but starts later in the fricative (Speaker E2); C–Influence of final vowel on [s] starts later in* tsute/tsuto *than in* se/so *and is of smaller magnitude (Speaker J4); D–There is no influence of the final vowel on /s/ in* sute/suto*, while there is for* se/so *(Speaker J4).*

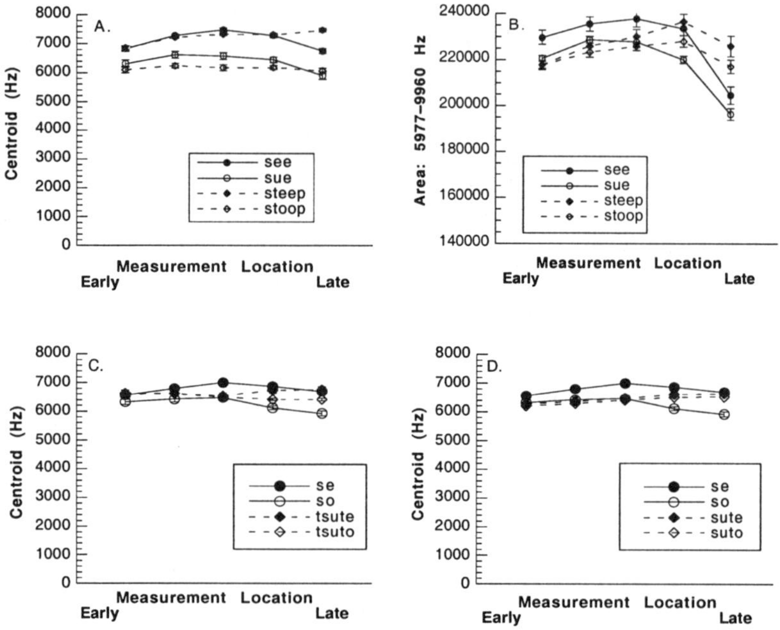

Figures 3C and 3D are comparable plots for tokens produced by speaker J4. The solid curves for the mean centroids of *se* and *so* show that the fricative spectra are influenced by the following vowel, at least in their second half. In contrast, the dashed curves for *tsute* and *tsuto* in Figure 3C show much less separation, and those for *sute* and *suto* in Figure 3D show none at all.

All such comparisons are summarized in Table 2. The number of plus signs provides a rough index of the magnitude of the differential effects of front and back vowels on fricative spectra, taking into account both the magnitude and the duration of differences like those illustrated in Figure 3. For the three English speakers, there was at least some acoustic difference between the fricatives in all word pairs for all speakers. Three of the six relevant comparisons showed approximately the same amount of difference in the longer pairs, and the other three comparisons showed somewhat less difference in the longer pairs than in the shorter pairs, but the fricatives in the longer pairs still differed based on vowel context.

Table 2: Results of study. A: English speakers; B: Japanese speakers. The number of +'s provides a rough indication of the extent to which the fricative in each pair reflects the influence of the last vowel in the word; '——' indicates no apparent difference.

A.	E1 area	E2 area	E3 centroid
say/so	+++	+	+++
stay/stow	++	+	+++
see/sue	+++	++	+++
steep/stoop	++	+	+++

B.	J1 area	J2 area	J3 centroid	J4 centroid
se/so	——	++	+++	++
sute/suto		+	——	——
tsute/tsuto		+	+	+
suki/suku		+	+	+
sude/tsudo		(+)	+	——
tsugi/tsugu		+	+	——
shi/shu	+++	+++	+++	+++
shitee/shitoo	——	(+)	——	——

For the Japanese speakers, in contrast, there was substantial acoustic difference between the fricatives in seven out of the eight CV pairs; Speaker J1's *se/so* showed no difference[4], either in the fricative centroids or in the calculated integrals in areas of the spectrum that appeared superficially different. For the remaining three Japanese speakers, none of the longer word pairs had fricatives that differed to the same extent as the fricatives in *se/so*, and, in four of the fifteen instances, there was no difference at all between the fricatives in the longer words. Likewise, for three of the speakers, there was no difference in the fricatives in *shitee* and *shitoo*, despite substantial difference between their fricatives in *shi* and *shu*; for J2, the fricatives in *shitee* and *shitoo* differed only slightly, and it is not clear that this particular difference would turn out to be statistically significant.

In the instances of longer Japanese words with initial fricatives not influenced by the vowel late in the word, the fricative shows a clear influence of the immediately following vowel, whether voiced or devoiced. That is, /ç/ in *shitee* and *shitoo* is, for all four speakers, more comparable to /ç/ in *shi* than to /ç/ in *shu*. As is evident from figures 3C and 3D, this is also the case for /s/ and /ts/. However, it is not the case that the supralaryngeal configuration for the later vowels has *no* influence earlier in the word. In fact, formant measurements taken during (voiced) /ɯ/ in J1's tokens of *sude/ tsudo* and *tsugi/tsugu* show that, even at the very beginning of the vowel, F2 is approximately 80 Hz higher in *sude* and *tsugi* than in *tsudo* and *tsugu*. At

[4] There are several possible accounts for this lack of difference. The first is that J1's fricatives did, in fact, differ in *se* and *so*, but that this difference was concentrated in areas of the spectrum above 10,000 Hz. The second is that because of dental abnormalities, her fricative spectra contained artifacts of sufficient magnitude to dilute any coarticulatory effects of the following vowel. Indeed, the spectral cross-sections for many of her tokens containing /s/ or /ts/ had an unusual relatively high amplitude peak at approximately 4,000 Hz.

the end of the vowel, immediately before the /g/ in *tsugi/tsugu* the difference is almost 500 Hz, while for the few tokens of *tsudo* with a long enough vowel for multiple measurements, F2 immediately before the /d/ is 175 Hz lower than immediately before the /d/ in *sude*. Thus, it is not that the final front and back vowels in these items do not exert a coarticulatory influence on preceding segments; rather, this influence does not extend into the initial consonant of the word, at least not measurably.

4. Discussion and Conclusion

The results of the present investigation are consistent with the gestural overlap view of Japanese devoiced vowels presented by Beckman and colleagues. Because the supralaryngeal gestures for short high vowels are *so* short—the ultra-short /ɯ/ in the token illustrated in Figure 2 is not atypical in our data, some of which are summarized in Table 3—it is relatively easy for these gestures to overlap totally with the flanking laryngeal abduction gestures required for adjacent voiceless obstruents. A schematic view of this overlap is presented in Figure 4 below.

Table 3: Mean duration (in msec) of first vowel in mitee, sude, tsudo, *for four Japanese speakers (standard deviation in parentheses).*

	J1	J2	J3	J4
mitee	83.3 (9.0)	73.2 (2.3)	51.3 (7.9)	71.2 (4.7)
sude	34.7 (9.1)	50.3 (17.8)	41.0 (12.3)	21.9 (5.9)
tsudo	26.7 (8.9)	53.2 (6.6)	34.2 (17.0)	34.9 (3.0)

The result of this overlap is not necessarily to extend the duration of the preceding consonant, but rather to shape its acoustic character (cf., Han, 1994); while the greater length of /ç/ in *shitee* relative to /m/ in *mitee* (see Table 4 on the following page) might give the impression that the duration of devoiced [i̥] is somehow incorporated into /ç/, some additional com-

Figure 4: Schematic of supra-laryngeal and laryngeal gestures for /sɯt/ in sute. *Arrows to the right indicate the direction of greater constriction of the vocal tract at the relevant location. Because of the overlap of the two larygeal abduction gestures for /s/ and /t/, the glottis does not ever reach the degree of constriction necessary for voicing during /ɯ/.*

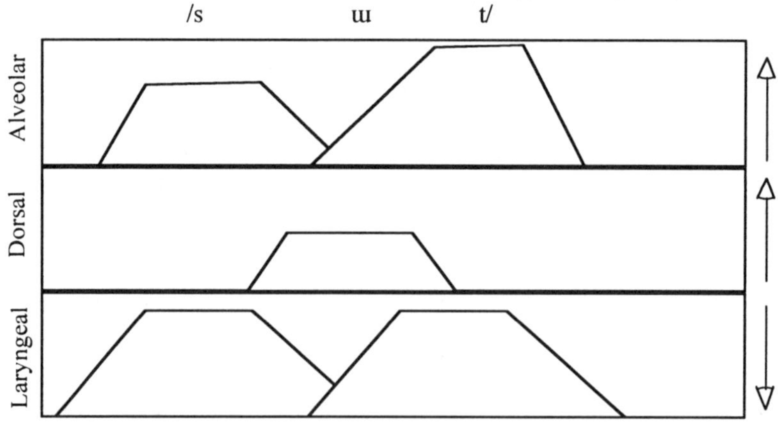

parisons, also presented in Table 4, make clear that this is not the case.

Table 4: Duration (in msec) of initial consonants in selected Japanese tokens (standard deviation in parentheses).

Speaker	*sute*	*so*	*sude*	*shitee*	*shi*	*mitee*
J1	138.39 (12.01)	106.28 (6.86)	139.78 (9.02)	125.78 (9.77)	128.55 (15.44)	77.90 (6.70)
J2	133.11 (15.95)	133.19 (9.58)	136.23 (13.94)	156.84 (18.60)	176.96 (30.02)	76.21 (16.62)
J3	83.30 (9.18)	88.59 (12.52)	113.94 (8.20)	98.93 (5.61)	123.18 (6.09)	76.30 (6.59)
J4	83.80 (5.20)	86.90 (9.63)	91.26 (16.34)	95.43 (10.93)	106.56 (10.25)	50.56 (4.75)

For speaker J1 only, [s] in *sute* is longer than [s] in *so*, while, for the other three speakers, there is absolutely no difference. Furthermore, [s] is virtually the same duration in *sute* and *sude* for J1 and J2, and substantially longer in *sude* than in *so* or *sute* for the other two speakers. Likewise, for all three of the four speakers, [ɕ] is shorter in *shitee* than in *shi*; for J1, there is no difference.

In any case, to the extent that Japanese morae are, in fact, of similar duration, it is not clear that onset consonants, which bear no metrical weight, ought to contribute to such isochrony or that surface acoustic duration is the appropriate measure thereof. Lehiste (1976) suggests that isochrony of phonological units, to the extent that it occurs, is a perceptual phenomenon. That is, units that are not physically comparable in duration are perceived by language users to be more comparable than they actually are. The duration of any given phonological segment, in Japanese as in other languages, depends on many factors, including at the very least phonological length, accent, phonological context, and intrinsic attributes of the segment. Listeners "parse out" these various factors, taking into account the contributions of each of these factors (Fowler, 1984). Thus, the perception of isochrony—of whatever level of phonological unit—should not be dependent solely on the surface durations of the phonological segments comprising that unit.

Our conclusions from the present study are simple: regardless of their surface duration, Japanese devoiced vowels maintain their supralaryngeal integrity, both in influencing the articulatory and acoustic characteristics of adjacent phonological units and in mediating longer-distance effects of one segment on another. The qualitative nature of this influence would be difficult to incorporate in a discrete, feature-changing account; rather, our findings complement those in other, superficially quite different, studies of anticipatory coarticulation (e.g., Fowler, 1980; Boyce, Krakow, & Bell-Berti, 1991) in supporting alternative models, such as that of Browman & Goldstein (1986, 1990; Surprenant & Goldstein, 1998), which explicitly specify the temporal extent of articulatory primitives. The superficial impression of vowel deletion results from the fact that the supralaryngeal gestures producing the vowels, whose presence is clearly deducible from their myriad acoustic consequences, may be fully masked by the supralaryngeal gestures associated with adjacent segments.

References

Alfonso, Anthony. 1971. *Japanese language patterns.* Tokyo: Sophia University.

Beckman, Mary & Atsuko Shoji. 1984. Spectral and perceptual evidence for CV coarticulation in devoiced /si/ and /syu/ in Japanese. *Phonetica* 41.61–67.

Bell-Berti, Fredericka & Katherine S. Harris. 1982. Temporal patterns of coarticulation. *JASA* 71.449–454.

Bloch, Bernard. 1950. Studies in colloquial Japanese IV: Phonemics. *Language* 26: 86–125

Boyce, Suzanne E., Rena A. Krakow, & Fredericka Bell-Berti. 1991. Phonological underspecification and speech motor organization. *Phonology* 8.219–236.

Browman, Catherine P. & Louis Goldstein. 1986. Towards an articulatory phonology. *Phonology Yearbook* 3.219–252.

Browman, Catherine P. & Louis Goldstein. 1990. Tiers in articulatory phonology, with some implications for casual speech. In *Papers in Laboratory Phonology I: Between the Grammar and Physics of Speech*, ed. by John Kingston & Mary Beckman. Cambridge: Cambridge University Press.

Endo, Yasuko Amy. 1998. Phonetic perception of Japanese devoiced vowels by English speakers. Wellesley College honors thesis.

Evers, Vincent, Henning Reetz, & Aditi Lahiri. 1998. Crosslinguistic acoustic categorization of sibilants independent of phonological status. *Journal of Phonetics* 26.345–370.

Faber, Alice & Timothy J. Vance. Submitted. Perception of Japanese devoiced vowels by native speakers of English. Manuscript submitted for publication.

Fowler, Carol A. 1980. Coarticulation and theories of extrinsic timing. *Journal of Phonetics* 8.113–133.

Fowler, Carol A. 1984. Segmentation of coarticulated speech in perception. *Perception & Psychophysics* 36.359–368.

Goodell, Elizabeth W. & Michael Studdert-Kennedy. 1993. Acoustic evidence for the development of gestural coordination in the speech of 2-year-olds. *Journal of Speech and Hearing Research* 36.707–727.

Han, Mieko S. 1962. Unvoicing of vowels in Japanese. *Onsei no Kenkyû* 10.81–100.

Han, Mieko S. 1994. Acoustic manifestations of mora timing in Japanese. *Journal of the Acoustical Society of America* 96.73–82.

Haraguchi, Shôsuke. 1984. Some tonal and segmental effects of vowel height in Japanese. In *Language Sound Structure*, ed. by Mark Aronoff & Richard T. Oehrle. Cambridge: MIT Press.

Imai, Terumi. 1997. *Vowel Devoicing in Japanese.* Michigan State University master's thesis.

Imaizumi, Satoshi, Akiko Hayashi, & Toshisada Deguchi. 1995. Listener adaptive characteristics of vowel devoicing in Japanese dialogue. *Journal of the Acoustical Society of America* 98.768–778.

Jun, Sun-Ah & Mary E. Beckman. 1993. A gestural-overlap analysis of vowel devoicing in Japanese and Korean. Paper presented at the 67th Annual Meeting of the Linguistic Society of America, Los Angeles, CA.

Jun, Sun-Ah, Mary E. Beckman, Seiji Niimi, & Mark Tiede. 1998. Electromyographic evidence for a gestural-overlap analysis of vowel devoicing in Korean. *UCLA Working Papers in Phonetics* 96.1–42.

Jun, Sun-Ah, Mary E. Beckman, & Hyuck-Joon Lee. 1998. Fiberscopic evidence for the influence on vowel devoicing of the glottal configurations of Korean obstruents. *UCLA Working Papers in Phonetics* 96.43–68.

Keating, Patricia A. 1988. Underspecification in phonetics. *Phonology* 5.275–292.

Kitahara, Mafuyu. 1998. The interaction of pitch accent and vowel devoicing in Tokyo Japanese. In: *Japanese/Korean Linguistics 8*, ed. by David J. Silva. Stanford: CSLI.

Kondo, Mariko. 1997. *Mechanisms of vowel devoicing in Japanese.* University of Edinburgh

Ph.D. Dissertation.

Kuriyagawa, Fukuko & Masayuki Sawashima. 1989. Word accent, devoicing and duration of vowels in Japanese. *Annual Bulletin: Research Institute of Logopedics and Phoniatrics* 23.85–108.

Labov, William. 1991. The three dialects of English. In *New Ways of Analyzing Sound Change*, ed. by Penelope Eckert. New York: Academic Press, pp. 1–44.

Lehiste, Ilse. 1976. Isochrony revisited. *Journal of Phonetics* 5.253–263.

Martin, Samuel E. 1952. *Morphophonemics of Standard Colloquial Japanese*. Supplement to *Language* (Language Dissertation No. 47).

Nihon Onsei Gakkai, ed. 1976. Onseigaku daijiten. Tokyo: Sanshûsha.

Nittrouer, Susan. 1995. Children learn separate aspects of speech production at different rates: Evidence from spectral moments. *Journal of the Acoustical Society of America* 97.520–530.

Nittrouer, Susan, Michael Studdert-Kennedy, & Richard S. McGowan. 1989. The emergence of phonetic segments: Evidence from the spectral structure of fricative-vowel syllables spoken by children and adults. *JSHR* 32.120–132.

Rubin, Philip E. 1995. HADES: A case study of the development of a signal analysis system. In *Applied Speech Technology*, ed. by A. Syrdal, R. Bennett, & B. Greenspan. Boca Raton, FL: CRL Press.

Sakuma, Kanae. 1929. *Nihon Onseigaku*. Tokyo: Kazama Shobô.

Surprenant, Aimée M. & Louis Goldstein. 1998. The perception of speech gestures. *Journal of the Acoustical Society of America* 104.518–529.

Takebe, Yoshiaki. 1977. Kokugo kokuji mondai no yurai. In *Iwanami Kôza Nihongo 3: Kokugo Kokuji Mondai*, ed. by Susumu Ôno & Takeshi Shibata. Tokyo: Iwanami.

Tsuchida, Ayako. 1997. Japanese vowel devoicing: Cases of consecutive devoicable syllables. Paper presented at the 8th Japanese/Korean Linguistics Conference, Ithaca, NY.

Vance, Timothy J. 1987. *An introduction to Japanese phonology*. Albany: SUNY Press.

Vance, Timothy J. 1992. Lexical phonology and Japanese vowel devoicing. In *The Joy of Grammar*, ed. by Diane Brentari, Gary N. Larson, & Lynn A. McLeod. Amsterdam: John Benjamins.

Whalen, D. H., Edward R. Wiley, Philip E. Rubin, & Franklin S. Cooper. 1990. The Haskins Pulse Code Modulation (PCM) system. *Behavioral Research Methods, Instruments, and Computers* 22.55–559.

Yeni-Komshian, Grace H. & Sigfrid D. Soli. 1981. Recognition of vowels from information in fricatives: Perceptual evidence of fricative-vowel coarticulation. *Journal of the Acoustical Society of America* 70.966–975.

Nasalization Before a Liquid in Yonbyon Dialect of Korean

HYUNSOOK KANG & SEO-HWA HAHN
Hanyang University

1. Introduction

In this paper, we examine phonological processes in a Korean dialect spoken in Yonbyon, China. Yonbyon is a district in China where, for political reasons, many Korean speakers have lived for a long time. Yonbyon speakers, however, did not have much contact with South Korean speakers until recently. Rather, they have had close contact with North Korean speakers. In this paper, we examine the phonological processes that take place when an /l/-initial morpheme is added to an obstruent-final morpheme in the Yonbyon dialect. We will then compare these phonological changes with those of the South Korean dialect.

This paper consists of the following. In section 2, we will discuss the phonological processes that occur when an /l/-initial morpheme is added to an obstruent-final morpheme in the South Korean and Yonbyon dialects. We will show how different surface forms can be derived in these two dialects. In section 3, we will discuss the implication of the aforementioned phonological processes in respect to the feature geometry. Contrary to McCarthy (1984), who argued that [sonorant] is a part of the root node, we will argue that [sonorant] feature should be represented on the separate tier. In section 4, we will discuss how different surface forms in the South Korean and Yonbyon dialects can be obtained within the Optimality Theory. Section 5 concludes the paper.

2. /Obstruent+lateral/ Sequence in Korean Dialects

In this section, we will examine some phonological changes that occur when an /l/-initial morpheme is added to an obstruent-final morpheme. This construction occurs only in a Sino-Korean word formation since no native Korean morpheme begins with an /l/. Let us first consider the South Korean dialect. Consider (1).

(1)	U.R.	P.R.	Gloss
	a. ko+lak	[korak]	'pain and pleasure'
	b. kyək+lyə	[kyəŋnyə]	'encouragement'
	c. lo+doŋ	[nodoŋ]	'work'
	d. an+lak	[allak]	'comfortableness'
	e. tal	[tal]	'moon'

As we see in (1a), /l/ becomes a flap [r] intervocalically, an [n] after a consonant and word initially as in (1b) and (1c), respectively, and remains as [l] if syllabified as a coda or as a member of a geminate. /l/-allophony rules are given in (2) (cf. Kang & Lee 1995).

(2) /l/-allophony rules
  a. /l/ → [r] / intervocalically
  b. /l/ → [n] / C ___
            ## ___
  c. /l/ → [l] / Otherwise

Interestingly, as we see in (1b), when a morpheme initial /l/ becomes /n/, the preceding obstruent also undergoes a change and become a nasal. Korean phonologists have assumed that /l/ in the morpheme initial position first becomes /n/ after a consonant as in (3a) (by rule (2b)) and then nasalization takes place, making the preceding obstruent a nasal as in (3b).

(3) INPUT	kyək+lyə	tæ+hak+lo	kuk+mul
a. /l/ → [n] / C ____	kyək+nyə	tæ+hak+no	-----
b. nasalization	kyəŋ+nyə	tæ+haŋ+no	kuŋ+mul

However, the same morpheme concatenation shows different surface forms in a Korean dialect spoken in China, namely the Yonbyon dialect. We tested two university students from the Yonbyon district who study at Handong University in Pohang, Korea. One speaker was male and the other was female. They are native Yonbyon dialect speakers and this was their first semester studying in Korea. We recorded their pronunciation of twenty words both in isolation and in natural speech context. Some of these words are given in (4).

(4) a. kyək+lyə 'encouragement'
b. kuk+ lyək 'a country's power'
c. tæhak+lo 'tæhak street'
d. yəkkok+lo 'yəkkok street'
e. tal+ lyək 'calendar'
f. tal 'moon'

After the recording, they were asked whether they thought their pronunciation of the words in (4) was the same as Korean students in South Korea. They answered that their pronunciation differed from their fellow South Korean students.

For the /obstruent+lateral/ sequence in (4), the female speaker consistently showed a nasal and a flap as in (5) but the male speaker showed several different surface forms shown in (6). In (6), all the surface forms of the male speaker are shown. However, the most frequent surface form for /obstruent+lateral/ is /nasal+flap/ for male speakers as well.

(5) Female Speaker
a. kyək+lyə [kyəŋryə] 'encouragement'
b. kuk+ lyək [kuŋryək] 'a country's power'
c. tæhak+lo [tæhaŋro] 'tæhak street'
d. yəkkok+lo [yəkkoŋro] 'yəkkok street'

(6) Male Speaker
/Obstruent + Lateral/ → [Nr] (frequent)
[NN] (somewhat frequent in fast speech)
[Or] [Nl] (rare)
a. kyək+lyə [kyəŋryə] 'encouragement'
b. kuk+ lyək [kuŋryək] 'a country's power'

In (7), we show one spectrogram of /O+l/ sequence.

(7) /yəkkok+lo/ → [yəkkoŋro]

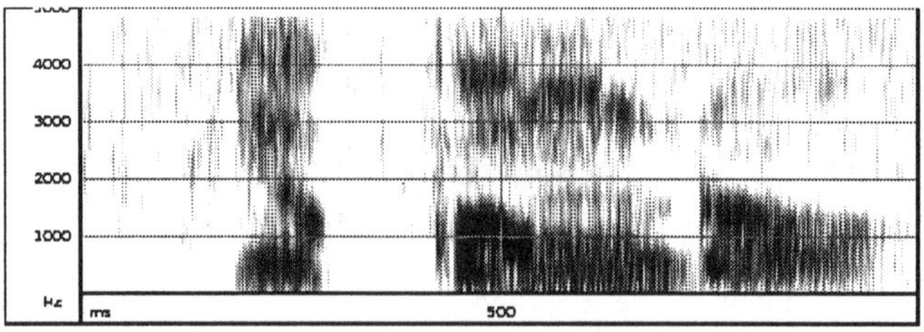

[yə kk o ŋ r o]

As we see in (7), the last /k/ in /yəkkok/ became a nasal. The spectrogram given in (7) has a lot of white noise due to the recording. However, this still shows that the obstruent is changed into a homorganic nasal while the following onset is changed into a flap [r].

Note that the phonological processes we considered in (3), namely nasalization of a liquid and the spreading of the [nasal] feature of nasal to a preceding obstruent, cannot apply for the surface forms given in (5): a lateral is not changed into a nasal after an obstruent. Consequently, there is no nasal to spread a [nasal] feature to a preceding obstruent.

Rather, we have to assume that the nasalization of the preceding obstruent is triggered by the most appropriate feature of the following lateral, namely a [sonorant] feature. We suggest the phonological processes in (8) and allophony rules in (9) for the Yonbyon dialect.

(8) INPUT kyək+lyə tæ+hak+lo
a. [sonorant] spreading kyəŋ+lyə tæ+haŋ+lo
b. /l/-allophony rules kyəŋ+ryə tæ+haŋ+ro

(9) /l/-allophony rules
a. /l/ → [r] / in the onset position if singly attached
b. /l/ → [l] / Otherwise

One might wonder whether morphemes which show a nasal coda such as /haŋ/ in (8) might have undergone a total change and is pronounced as /haŋ/ all the time. This is not the case as is shown in (10). The same morpheme appears with a final obstruent if the following phoneme is not a sonorant in the Yonbyon dialect.

(10) /l/-allophony rules
a. hak+ca → [hakca] 'scholar'
b. hak+kyo → [hakkyo] 'school'

Therefore, a segment which appears as a nasal or as an obstruent depending on the context should be represented as an underlying obstruent and its nasality should come from some feature of the following consonant. We, therefore, suggest that the sonorant feature of the second segment in an /Obstruent+Lateral/ sequence triggers nasalization of the preceding obstruent in the Yonbyon dialect.

3. Feature Geometry

In this section, we will consider how the sonorant feature of the following lateral can affect the preceding obstruent, changing it into a nasal within the framework of Feature Geometry.

Since the introduction of Feature Geometry into phonology, phonological processes that treat some features as a group has been understood as stemming from the structure of the feature geometry. That is, features that behave as a group in phonological processes are represented as dependents on a group node. For example, place features and laryngeal features are represented as dependents under Place and Laryngeal nodes and some phonological processes may affect the group node in their applications, rather than the dependent features.

Manner features, however, have been under some discussion. McCarthy (1988) argues that some manner feature like [nasal] should have its own tier whereas other manner features like [sonorant] and [consonantal should be located inside the root node as in (11); he could not find any evidence that supports an independent tier for these features. Therefore, he placed these features inside the root.

(11) McCarthy (1988)

```
            C
            |
      [son, cons]          root node
   /           |    \    \
Laryngeal Place [nas][cont]
     /  |  \
  Lab Cor Dor
```

Note that the assimilation has been defined as the spreading of the feature of the trigger to the target. For example, place assimilation can be represented as in (12).

(12) [kən+kuk] ----> [kəŋkuk]

```
          n        k   → [ŋk]
        Root    Root
     /   =|=   \    /
[nasal]Place Place
          |       |
        Cor     Dor
```

Therefore, if a [sonorant] feature is located inside the root node in a feature geometry, any phonological process where the sonorant feature spreads to the target would result in total assimilation. Therefore, [sonorant] feature spreading we argued in (8) would result in total assimilation, and produce the incorrect form as in (13); [kl] sequence will appear as an incorrect [ll] sequence.

```
(13) /kyək+lyə/ → *[kyəllyə]
        k      l   → *[ll]
        X      X
       =|=   \ |
     [-son] [+son]      Root node
        |      |
     Place   Place
        |      |
      Dor     Cor
```

In order to rectify the situation, we should separate a sonorant feature from the root node. It should be located as a dependent feature on the root node as in (14). When a sonorant feature spreads to a preceding obstruent, it is realized as a nasal, maintaining its original place. This would result in a correct surface form as shown in (14).

```
(14) /kyək+lyə/ → [kyəŋlyə]
             k       l   → [ŋl]
             X       X
          / =|=    \ |    \
     place [-son] [+son] place
       |                   |
      Dor                 Cor
```

[kyəŋlyə] would then undergo another rule and become [kyəŋryə].

Therefore, we propose that the [sonorant] feature should be separated from the root node and exist as a dependent feature on the root node.

4. Optimality Theory

In this section, we will consider how nasalization before a liquid in the Yonbyon dialect can be explained within the OT framework. It is known among Korean linguists that at least in South Korean dialect, some version of Syllable Contact Law in (15) is strictly enforced.

(15) Syllable Contact (SyllCon): When two syllables are in contact, the coda of the first syllable should be more sonourous than, or equally sonorous to the onset of the second syllable. (cf. Murray and Vennemann 1983)

When a consonant sequence which does not obey the Syllable Contact Law appears due to the morpheme concatenation, some phonological processes take place to remedy the situation. Consider (16).

(16) a. nasal spreading
obstruent + nasal → nasal +nasal
/kuk+mul/ → [kuŋmul] 'soup'
b. /l/-nasalization and nasal spreading
obstruent + liquid → nasal + nasal
/hyəp + lyək/ → [hyəmnyək] 'cooperation'
c. lateralization of /n/
nasal + lateral → lateral+lateral
/cən+lyək/ → [cəllyək] 'electricity'
d. nasalization of /l/
nasal + lateral → nasal + nasal
/ilbon#lyək/→ [ilbonnyəŋ] 'Japan's territory'

As we see in (16), if the coda is less sonorous than the onset, some phonological rules apply, making the coda and the onset sequence more desirable to the Syllable Contact Law. Based on this observation, Davis and Shin (1999) argues that with the constraint ranking in (17), surface forms for consonant sequences in the South Korean dialect can be explained. Consider /kyək+li/ in (17).

(17)

/kyək+li/	Syll Con	IdentOnset [son]	Ident [place]	Max [lat]	Max [nas]	Ident [son]
a. kyək.li	*!					
b. kyək.ni	*!			*		
c. kyəl.li			*!			*
d. kyəŋ.li	*!					*
e. kyəŋ.ni				*		*
f. kyək.ti		*!		*		*

As we see, (17a) and (17b) violate SyllCon and so are eliminated. Candidate (17d) which shows the nasalization of the /k/ and the maintenance of /l/ is also eliminated because it still violates SyllCon. Candidate (17c) violates Ident(place) whereas (17e) violates Max(lateral). Therefore, (17c) is eliminated. (17f) violates Ident-Onset[sonorant] which is ranked higher than Max(lateral). Therefore, Davis and Shin (1999) argues that the winner is (17e).

However, this constraint ranking does not fully account for the alternations of a liquid consonant in Korean. An underlying lateral sound in /lak/ does not always appear as /l/ or /n/. It appears as a flap /r/ intervocalically. With the constraint ranking in Davis and Shin (1999), the proper surface form for /l/ in intervocalic position does not occur. Consider (18).

(18)

/ko+lak/	Syll Con	IdentOnset [son]	Ident [place]	Max [lat]	Max [nas]	Ident [son]
a. ko.lak						
b. ko.rak				*		

As we see in (18), the expected winner is (18a) but (18b) is the correct surface form we get in the South Korean dialect. Therefore, we need a more elaborate constraint ranking for the South Korean dialect. Consider (1) again. We represent (1) as (19) for ease of reference.

(19)	U.R.	P.R.	Gloss
	a. ko+lak	[korak]	'pain and pleasure'
	b. kyək+lyə	[kyəŋnyə]	'encouragement'
	c. lo+doŋ	[nodoŋ]	'work'
	d. an+lak	[allak]	'comfortableness'
	e. tal	[tal]	'moon'

As we see, a lateral consonant appears on the surface only if it is aligned with the syllable final position. A flap appears intervocalically. We argue that there are constraints like (20) which align a lateral to a syllable coda position and a flap to a syllable onset position word medially. (21) shows a sample constraint tableau.

(20) a. Align-R([+lateral], syllable): A [+lateral] feature should be aligned with the syllable final segment. (Non-crisp alignment)

b. VflapV: a flap can appear only intervocalically. (undominated)

(21)

/ko+lak/	Align-R	Dep(nasal)	Dep(flap)
a. ko.lak	*!		
b. ko.rak			*
c. ko.nak		*!	

As we see in (21), /kolak/ in (21a) violates Align-R since a lateral feature is not aligned with the syllable coda position. /korak/ in (21b) violates Dep(flap) and /konak/ in (21c) violates Dep(nasal). Since Dep(nasal) is ranked higher than Dep(flap), /korak/ in (21b) is the optimal form. With the new ranking constraint we suggested in (21), the right surface forms for /l/ appear.

Let us now consider whether an input /kyək+li/ in the South Korean dialect will result in the right surface form if we adopt the new constraint ranking suggested in (21). Consider the constraint tableau (22).

(22)

/kyək+li/	Syll Con	Align-R	VflapV	Ident Place	Max [son]	Dep [nas]
a. kyək.li	*!	*				
b. kyək.ni	*!					
c. kyəl.li				*!		
d. kyəŋ.li	*!	*				
e. kyəŋ.ni						*
f. kyəŋ.ri			*!			

As we see in (22), (22a, b, d) are eliminated due to the violation of SyllCon. (22c) is eliminated because it violates Identity(place). (22f) violates VflapV. Therefore, (22e) is chosen as optimal since it violates the least fatal constraint. By adopting a new constraint ranking, we can explain the distribution of a lateral, a flap and a nasal in the South Korean dialect.

Let us now consider why the Yonbyon dialect shows different surface forms for these words. Note that as we have shown in (9), the /l/-allophony rules are different from those of the South Korean dialect. We present (9) as (23) for ease of reference.

(23) /l/-allophony rules
  a. /l/ → [r] / in the onset position if singly attached
  b. /l/ → [l] / Otherwise

Note that a lateral appears if it is syllabified as a coda, and a flap appears if it is syllabified as an onset. We suggest the following constraint.

(24) a. Align-R ([+lateral], syllable): A [+lat] feature should be aligned with the syllable final segment. (Non-crisp alignment)
  b. Align-L(flap, syllable): flap can appear only as syllable onset. (crisp alignment)(undominated)

A sample tableau for /ko+lak/ is given in (25).

(25)

/ko+lak/	Align-L	Align-R	Dep(nasal)	Dep(flap)
a. ko.lak		*!		
b. ko.rak				*
c. ko.nak			*!	

(25a) violates Align-R since a lateral appears as a singly attached onset. (25c) violates Dep(nasal). However, /korak/ in (25b) violates Dep(flap), the least fatal constraint and thus becomes the optimal candidate. Now, let us consider how /kyək+li/ is pronounced in Yonbyon.

(26)

/kyək+li/	Syll Con	Align-R	Align-L	Ident Place	Max [son]	Dep [nas]
a. kyək.li	*!	*				
b. kyək.ni	*!					
c. kyəl.li				*!		
d. kyəŋ.li	*!	*				
e. kyəŋ.ni						**!
f. kyəŋ.ri						*

As we see in (26), (26a, b, d) are eliminated due to the violation of SyllCon. (26c) is eliminated because it violates Identity(place). (26e) violates Dep(nasal) twice whereas (26f) violates Dep(nasal) only once. Note that (26e) shows the importance of the interpretation of the markedness constraints. We suggest that for (26e), each nasal segment receives a mark for the violation of Dep(nasal). If Dep(nasal) counted [nasal] autosegments instead of nasal segments as in (27), such a cluster would get only one mark for Dep(nasal). Given the assumption of the richness of the base in OT, a cluster with doubly linked [nasal] is a possible candidate and therefore, we have to decide which interpretation we will take in each case. For the Yonbyon dialect, Dep(nas) counts the nasal segments.

(27) kyəŋni
      \/
   [nas]

Also note that (26f) does not violate SyllCon because a flap [r] is less sonorous than a nasal. We suggest that a flap in Korean dialects should be classified as an obstruent rather than a sonorant. If so, /kyəŋri/ does not violate SyllCon. Lee (1999) shows that a flap [r] in Korean is hard to be classified as a sonorant. We believe that a flap [r] is less sonorous than a nasal if it is ever classified as a sonorant.

In addition, /kyəŋri/ does not violate Max[son] since a [son] feature of /l/ survives on the preceding segment, though it violates Ident[son]. Therefore, /kyəŋri/ in (26f) is more optimal than / kyəŋni/ in (26e).

In this section, we argued that different surface realizations for /obstruent+lateral/ sequence for the South Korean and Yonbyon dialects are a result of different constraint ranking in the Optimality Theory.

5. Conclusion

In this paper, we have examined some surface forms of /obstruent+lateral/ sequence in Korean dialects, especially the South Korean and Yonbyon dialects. We have argued that in order to explain the nasalization of an obstruent before a liquid in the Yonbyon dialect, we need to separate a [sonorant] feature from the root node. This sheds new light on the feature geometry. We have also shown that Optimality Theory can explain why different surface forms appear in different dialects. In doing so, we have shown that when we count the violations of a markedness constraint in the Yonbyon dialect, we should count how many segments violate the constraint, not how many autosegment violate the markedness constraint.

References

Benua, Laura. 1997. *Transderivational Identity: Phonological Relations between Words*. Doctoral dissertation, University of Massachusetts, Amherst.

Davis, Stuart and Seung-Hoon Shin. 1999. The Syllable Contact Constraint in Korean: An Optimality-Theoretic Analysis. MS. Indiana University.

Kang, Hyunsook and Borim Lee. 1995. Generalized Alignment and Prosodic Subcategorization in Korean, in H. Sohn and J. Haig, eds., *Japanese/Korean Linguistics* 6. 303-318. Stanford: CSLI.

Kang, Hyunsook and Seok-keun Kang. 1999. A Conjoined Constraint in Korean. MS. Hanyang University and Wonkwang University.

Kenstowicz, Michael. 1995. Base-identity and Uniform Exponence: Alternative to Cyclicity, in J. Durand and B. Laks, eds., *Current Trends in Phonology: Models and Methods*. 366-396. Paris: CNRS.

Lee, Sook-hyang. 1999. A Flap in Korean. Ms. Wonkwang University.

McCarthy, John. 1998. Sympathy and Phonological Opacity. MS. University of Massachusetts, Amherst.

McCarthy John and Alan Prince. 1993a. Prosodic Morphology I: Constraint Interaction and Satisfaction. MS. University of Massachusetts Amherst and Rutgers University.

McCarthy John and Alan Prince. 1993b. Generalized Alignment, in Geert Booij and Jaap van Marle, eds., *Yearbook of Morphology*. 79-153. Dordrecht: Kluwer Academic Publisher.

McCarthy John and Alan Prince. 1995. Faithfulness and Reduplicative Identity, in J. Beckman, S. Urbanczyk and L. Walsh, eds., *University of Massachusetts Occasional Papers in Linguistics* 18. 249-384. Amherst, MA: GLSA.

Murray, Robert and Theo Vennemann. 1983. Sound Change and Syllable Structure in Germanic Phonology. *Language* 59:3. 514-528.

Prince, Alan and Paul Smolensky. 1993. Optimality Theory: Constraint Interaction in Generative Grammar. Technical Report 2, the Rutgers Center for Cognitive Science, Rutgers University.

Vowel Devoicing and Syllable Structure in Japanese

MARIKO KONDO
University of Glasgow & University of Edinburgh

1. Introduction

Many dialects of Japanese have a phonological rule of high vowel devoicing. When high vowels /i, u/ occur between voiceless sounds, they are devoiceable, e.g. the underlined high vowels /i, u/ in *ashita* /as<u>i</u>ta/ 'tomorrow', and *kisha* /k<u>i</u>sja/ 'train'.

There has been a dispute as to whether Japanese vowel devoicing is a phonological or a phonetic process and whether it is 'devoicing' or 'deletion'. First of all, the process is not considered as vowel deletion because the durations of devoiced vowels were retained in the morae (Kondo, 1995). The quality of devoiced vowels were also manifested articulatorily in their preceding consonants, which made it possible to differentiate the morae without voiced vowels (Beckman & Shoji, 1984). Vowel devoicing is primarily a phonetic process because high vowels /i, u/ are intrinsically short in duration and the glottis is wide open during the production of voiceless consonants. Various studies found that devoicing occurred more often when voiceless fricatives preceded high vowels than voiceless plosives preceded (Takeda & Kuwabara, 1987; Yoshida & Sagisaka, 1990; Kondo, 1997). Jun and Beckman (1993) explained that preceding fricatives trigger devoicing more than preceding plosives because there was a greater degree of glottal gestural overlap between consonants and a following high vowel.

However, phonetic analyses cannot explain why there is not devoicing of all devoiceable vowels when devoiceable vowels occur in consecutive morae, e.g. *kashitsuchishi* /kasitutisi/ 'accidental death', *yushutsukichi* /jusjutsukiti/[1] 'exporting centre' and *fukushikikokyuu* /hukusikikokjuu/ 'abdominal breathing' where underlined vowels are devoiceable (the consecutive devoicing environment). Another problem is that devoicing rates at slow speaking rates were as high as at fast speaking rates as long as there were no devoiceable vowels in adjacent morae (the single devoicing environment)(Kondo, 1997).

It has been suggested that both phonetic and phonological factors can block vowel devoicing, including type of preceding consonant, presence of accent on the vowel and following word boundary (Sakurai, 1985; Vance, 1987; Maekawa 1989). Kondo (1997) showed that Japanese vowel devoicing was compulsory in the single devoicing environment, even when these proposed blocking factors were present. However, in the consecutive devoicing environment, some devoiceable vowels remain voiced. Phonetically ideal environments do not always trigger devoicing. Moreover, devoicing occurred in two consecutive morae in some samples, but not in three consecutive morae or more. The results indicated that vowel devoicing processes cannot solely be explained as a phonetic process.

One possible factor is the syllable. Vowel devoicing involves the change of syllable structure. When a vowel becomes voiceless, it loses its sonority. The preceding consonant in the devoiced syllable cannot constitute a syllable on its own. This process will cause a change of syllable structure.

Tranel (1987) proposed that in French schwa ([œ]) could be deleted, only if the remaining consonants were syllabified into an unoccupied coda of the preceding syllable, and the new consonant sequences satisfied French phonotactics. If the consonant preceding the schwa could not be syllabified with the preceding syllable, the consonant needed the assistance of the schwa to be syllabified as an independent syllable.

The syllable may also play a part in Japanese vowel devoicing. In this study, I will analyse the vowel devoicing process in relation to the mora and syllable, and examine how the process is constrained by Japanese syllable structure. I will also consider how the process causes changes to the Japanese syllable structure.

2. Japanese Mora and Syllable

Before examining vowel devoicing, I will briefly look at the mora and syllable in Japanese. The mora has been established in Japanese phonology principally as an important unit of speech rhythm which operates at the word level (Port, Dalby & O'Dell, 1987). The significance of the mora in Japanese phonology has also been manifested in other phonetic and

[1] The /sj-/ sequence is phonetically realised as [ç]: i.e. the /u/ occurs in the devoicing environment between voiceless consonants [ç] and [ts].

phonological processes such as speech perception (Cutler & Otake, 1997) and speech errors (Kubozono, 1989). The syllable is also important in Japanese as it is an accent baring unit (Shibatani, 1991). It also constrains various phonological processes, such as formation of loan words (Itô, 1990; Shinohara, 1997).

Although Japanese syllables can occur in a variety of structures (1a) ~ (1g), the predominant form is a light open syllable (Kubozono, 1995). The only possible consonants at the syllable final position are moraic nasal or the first element of geminate consonants (1c) and (1d). So called 'superheavy syllables' (1e)~(1f) can also occur, but their occurrence is limited to certain types of words such as the te-form, loan words and onomatopoeias. One of the typical characteristics of Japanese syllables is that consonant clusters do not occur within a syllable except for the rare occurrence of /-NC/ sequences in a syllable final position (1g). If we consider a glide /j/ as a consonant, another possible consonant cluster /Cj-/ sequence is found in a syllable initial position.

(1) a. (C)(j)V: /i/ 'stomach' /ki/ 'tree' /tja/ 'tea'
b. (C)(j)VV: /ai/ 'love' /koi/ 'carp' /gjoo/ 'line'
c. (C)(j)VN: /uN/ 'luck' /kaN/ 'can' /sjuNtoo/ 'general strike'
d. (C)(j)VC: /utta/ 'sold' /hotta/ 'dug' /sjotta/ 'burdened'
e. (C)(j)VVN: /saiN/ 'signature' /siiN/ 'scene' /tjeeN/ 'chain'
f. (C)(j)VVC: /kootte/ 'frozen' /kaette/ 'instead' /gjuutto/ 'tightly'
g. (C)(j)V(V)NC: /hoNtte/ 'Books are...' /rondoNkko/ 'Londoner'
/tjeeNtte/ 'Chain stores are...'

However, vowel devoicing creates other types of consonant sequences. When a high vowel is devoiced, it is acoustically manifested either as the continuation of a preceding fricative or as a preceding stop released into a fricative, which phonetically creates sequences of voiceless consonants.

This study examines how the processes of vowel devoicing change Japanese syllable structure, and considers its flexibility and the significance of the syllable in Japanese phonology. Whether wider varieties of syllable structures other than (1a)~(g) above are possible in Japanese will be discussed.

3. Vowel Devoicing Processes

3.1 Single Devoicing Environments

An earlier study demonstrated that at least in the single devoicing environment high vowel devoicing is a compulsory process in Japanese (Kondo, 1997). This process may be explained as resyllabification of the preceding consonant to an adjacent syllable.

For example, modifying the model by Hayes (1989)[2], the phonological structure of the word *akikan* /a.ki.kaN/ [akikaɯ̃] 'empty can' with devoiced [i̥] is represented as (2a) When the high vowel /i/ becomes voiceless, the devoiced mora /kˤ/ cannot be attatched to the syllable node because the syllable has lost its core element. Therefore, the second syllable cannot sustain its status as a syllable. As the remaining preceding consonant /k/ cannot constitute a syllable on its own, it has to be syllabified with an adjacent syllable as (2b). However, it becomes moraic since the mora keeps the duration of the devoiced vowel and the quality of the devioced vowel /i/ is reflected in the palatalisation of the preceding consonant as /kˤ/. The process creates a bimoraic heavy syllable /VC/ (which is permitted in Japanese), and reduces the number of syllables, but maintains the moraic structure of the word.

("σ" denotes a syllable, "μ" denotes a mora.)
(2a) *akikan* /akikaN/ [aki̥kaɯ̃][3] (2b)

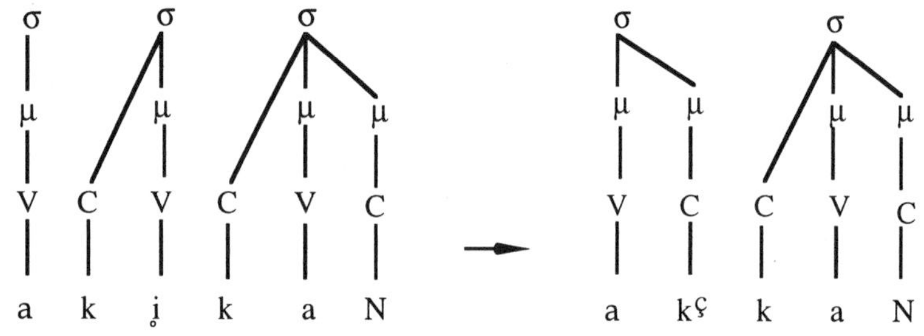

When devoicing occurs at the beginning of a word, such as *shita* /si.ta'/ [ç̥ita], 'below' and *hikari* /hikari/ [çi̥kari] 'light', the consonant in the devoiced syllable is syllabified with the following syllable as the syllable onset because this is the only possible place it can move to. As shown in (3), when the vowel /i/ becomes voicelss in the word *shita* /si.ta'/ (3a), the

[2] The mora tier usually represents an alternative rather than an addition to the CV tier, and onset consonants are attatched directly to the syllable node as they are nonmoraic (Hayes, 1989; Kenstowicz, 1994). However, I use a separate CV tier in order to present clearly the formation of moraic consonant and resulting syllable structures.

[3] For convenience, I used pseudo-phonemic transcriptions to describe devoiced vowels and resulting moraic consonants for convenience. The examples are the devoiced vowels /i̥, ɯ̥/, the allophones of consonants /ɕ/ instead of /s/ and /sju/ (in /si/ and /sju/), /ç/ and /ɸ/ instead of /h/ (in /hi/ and /hu/), /tɕ/ instead of /t/ (in /ti/) and /ts/ instead of /t/ (in /tu/). /kˤ/ was also used to indicate palatalisation of /k/ and its release into a palatal fricative [ç] in /ki/, and /kˣ/ for /k/ in /ku/ to indicate backness of the /k/ and its release into a velar fricative [x].

preceding consonant /s/ becomes moraic (3b) and is syllabified with the following syllable /ta/ (3c).

(3a) shita /sita/ [çita] (3b) [çi̥ta] (3c) [çta]

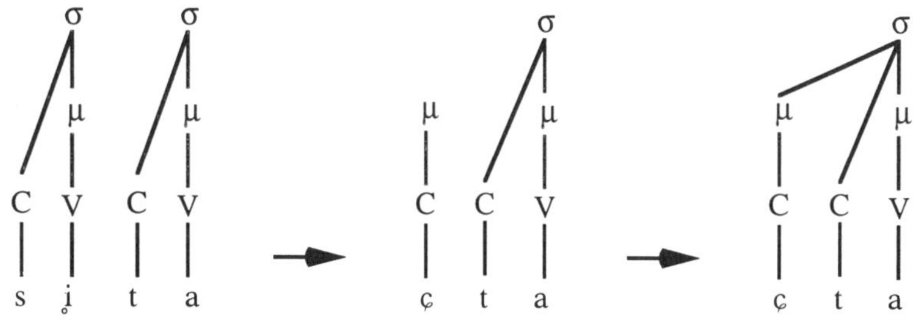

Application of this process must be restricted to certain positions as the resulting syllable structure is awkward. This process also reduces the number of syllables, but maintains the number of morae. A problem with this process is that consonant clusters do not occur in syllable initial positions in Japanese except for /Cj-/ sequence. Only if we consider the glide as another consonant, this sequence is possible in Japanese (see section 3.5).

When there is only one devoiced vowel in a word, the preceding consonant in the same mora can be syllabified to its preceding syllable or, in the case of word initial, to the following syllable. Therefore, vowel devoicing in the single devoicing environment is always possible.

One of the problems of above analysis is whether a devoiced mora really lose its syllabicity. Itô (1990) examined the process of loanword truncation in Japanese, and found that truncated words require a minimum of two syllables as shown in (4).

(4)					
a	/demoNsutoreesjoN/	'demonstration'	--->	/de.mo/	(2 syllables)
b.	/rokeesjoN/	'location'	--->	/ro.ke/	(2 syllables)
c.	/sutoraiki/	'strike'	--->	/su.to/	(2 syllables)
d.	/siNpoziumu/	'symposium'	--->	*/siN/	(1 syllable)
e.	/rooteisjoN/	'lotation'	--->	*/roo/	(1 syllable)

An example (4c) /su.to/ has two syllables. The vowel /u/ is in the devoicing environment, and normally devoiced. If a devoiced mora is non-syllabic, it contradicts Itô's claim. This is probably because the truncation process occurs before the devoicing process is applied to the word. When the word /sutoraiki/ is truncated, it becomes /su.to/ [sɯto] as it must have at least two syllables. It is perfectly all right to pronounce the word with a voiced [ɯ]. However, the devoicing rule is applied in some dialects to create a monosyllable form [sɯ̥to].

3.2 Consecutive Devoicing Environments

In the consecutive devoicing environment, not all devoiceable vowels become voiceless. It is not yet established exactly which vowel becomes voiceless and which vowel remains voiced. Some studies have suggested that fricatives trigger devoicing more than plosives (Sakurai, 1985; Maekawa, 1989), or that the accent blocks devoicing (Sakurai, 1985). However, these observations cannot explain voicing-devoicing patterns in unaccented words nor when all devoiceable vowels are preceded by the same type of consonants. In these environments, all devoiceable vowels should be equally likely to become voiceless. It is articulatorily easier and more sensible for all devoiceable vowels to become voiceless, but this does not always occur in normal speech.

For example, Kondo (1997) listed two kinds of pronunciations for the word *dookutsu* /dookutu/ (no accent) 'cave' where both underlined /u/s are devoiceable: [do:kɯ̥tsɯ] with the first /u/ devoiced occurred in 16 out of 18 samples and [do:kɯtsɯ] with both /u/s voiced in 2 out of 18 samples. The first pronunciation is possible because /k/ in /ku/ can be syllabified to the preceding syllable as shown in (5a). However, two consecutive devoicing [do:kɯ̥tsɯ̥] is not possible in normal speech. As shown in (5b), /k/ in /ku/ can be syllabified to the preceding syllable, but /t/ in /tu/ cannot because it would create sequences of */CVVCC/. This is not considered to be an acceptable superheavy syllable as the second last consonant is not a moraic nasal. The pronunciation of [do:kɯtsɯ] with both voiced vowels is more favourable than the clusters of three consonants.

(5a) [do:kɯ̥tsɯ]

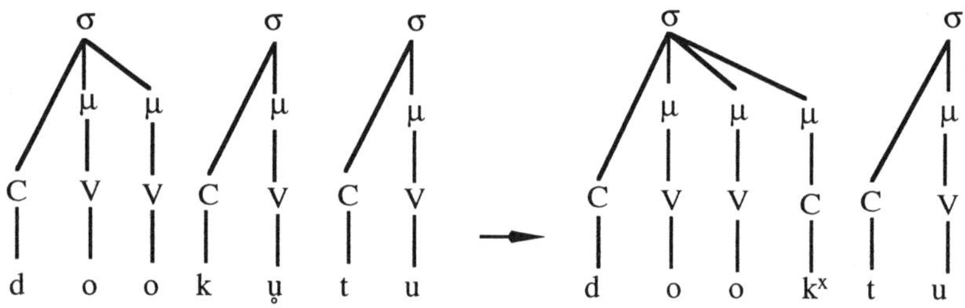

(5b) *[do:kɯ̥tsɯ̥]

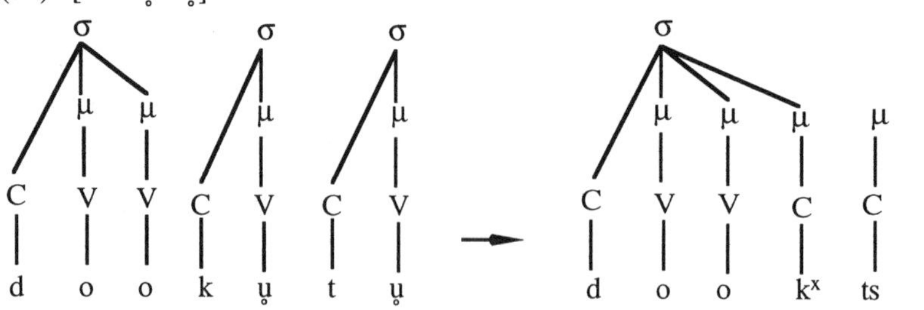

In the word *kutsushita(koujou)* /ku̲tu̲si̲ta (ko'odjoo)/ 'sock (factory)', where underlined vowels are devoiceable, unaccented and preceding consonants were the plosive [k], the affricate [ts] and the fricative [ç]. All 18 samples were [kɯ̥tsɯç̥ita (ko':dʑo:)] with the first and third vowels being devoiced and the second vowel being voiced. This process is also explained by the syllable structure as shown in (6a) and (6b). When the first vowel /u/ in /ku/ becomes voiceless, the preceding /kˣ/ becomes moraic and is syllabified to the beginning of the following syllable. The third vowel /i/ also becomes voiceless, and the /s/, becomes moraic /ç/ and is syllabified to the end of the preceding syllable. The process creates a new superheavy syllable /CCVC/. However, devoicing in three consecutive morae is not acceptable as shown in (6b). The first two consonants /kˣ/ and /ts/ cannot be syllabified to the following syllable, because it would create three consonant clusters. It is more acceptable to pronounce this word with all vowels voiced [kɯtsɯçita (ko':dʑo:)] rather than devoicing all three vowels .

(6a) [kɯ̥tsɯç̥ita' (ko':dʑo:)]

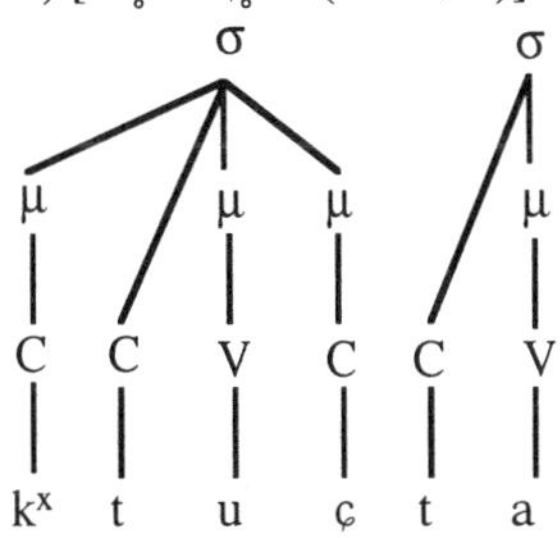

(6b) *[kɯ̥tsɯ̥ç̥ita (ko':dʑo:)]

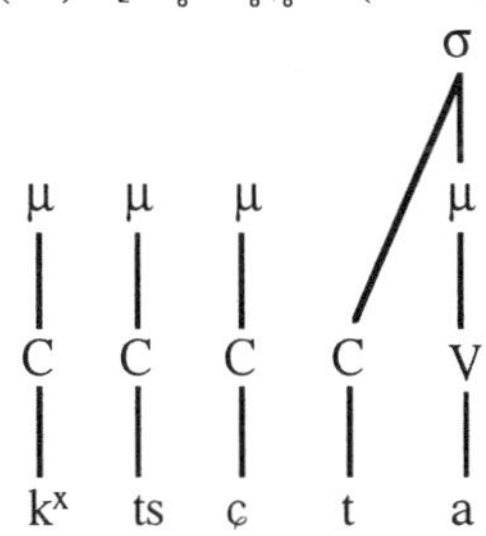

3.3 Devoicing in an Accented Syllable

All examples analysed above are unaccented words. Traditionally devoicing of an accented vowel was avoided either by shifting the accent to another syllable or the devoicing was blocked by the presence of an accent (McCawley, 1977; Sakurai, 1985; Vance, 1987). However, vowel devoicing in accented syllables can occur in normal speech (Hattori, 1989; Kondo, 1997). In Japanese a syllable carries the lexical accent and not a mora. When the vowel in an accented syllable is devoiced, and its preceding consonant cannot sustain its syllabic status, it can no longer carry an accent. The preceding consonant becomes moraic, but the mora is not an accent baring unit. For instance, the underlined /i/ in the word *shokikan* /sjo.ki̲'.kaN/ 'cabinet secretary' is devoiceable. When it is devoiced and loses its syllabicity, it cannot simply be syllabified to the preceding syllable /sjo/ as (7a). This is because it was the syllable /ki/ that carried the accent in the word and the accent baring syllable has now been lost.

The solution may be to syllabify the preceding /k/ to the following syllable /kaN/. Acoustically, there is no way to tell the presence of an accent on a voiceless vowel. Sugito and Hirose (1988) found that one acoustic cue of an accent is in the vowel of the following syllable. When there is an accent on a devoiced vowel, the perceptual cue for detection is not the fall of the fundamental frequency (F0) between the devoiced vowel and the vowel in the following syllable, but is the unusually high starting F0 of the following vowel which then falls very sharply. This finding supports syllabification of the preceding consonant to the following syllable as shown in (7b). This analysis seems more plausible since the accented syllable and acoustic manifestation of an accent match. In (7b), the superheavy syllable /kˤkaN/ (/CCVC/) carries the accent.

(7a) */sjoki'kaN/ [çoki̥'kaɯ̃]

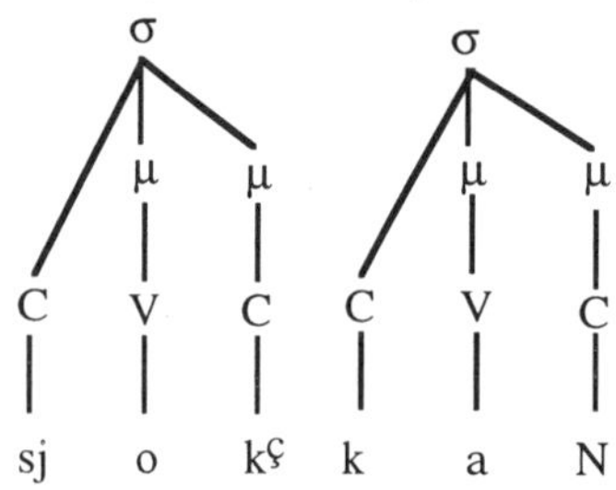

(7b)

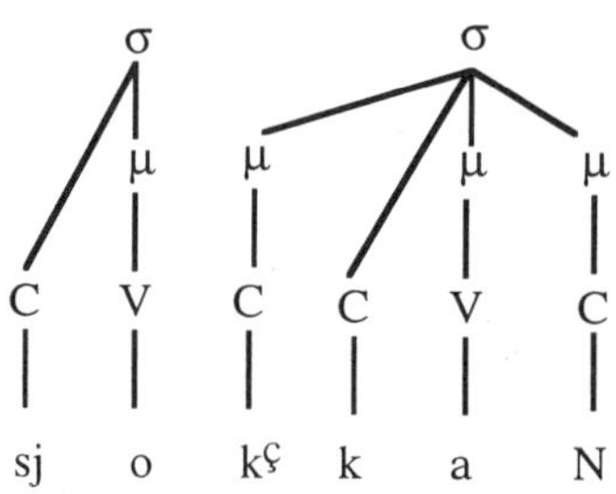

In the consecutive devoicing environment, syllabification of all consonants preceding voiceless vowels to their adjacent syllables would not be possible. In these cases, other factors such as the type of preceding consonants, position in the utterance and presence of accent will play a role determining devoicing pattern. In *shoohiti* /sjoohi̲'ti̲/ 'consumer belt' underlined high vowels are devoiceable, but *[ço:ç̥i̥'tç̥i̥] with consecutive devoicing is not favoured. First of all, it is not possible to syllabify both moraic /ç/ and /tç/ to the preceding syllable as shown in (8b). In addition, the syllabification of the moraic /ç/ is not allowed because the syllable /hi/ is accented. Either /hi/ or /ti/ needs to be syllabic to maintain the accent. The fricative [ç] is more likely to be devoiced than the affricate [tç], and the utterance final [i] in [tçi] is longer and less likely to be devoiced. Therefore, [ço:çi̥'tçi] with only one devoiced vowel as in (8a) is favoured.

(8a) [ço:çi̥'tçi]

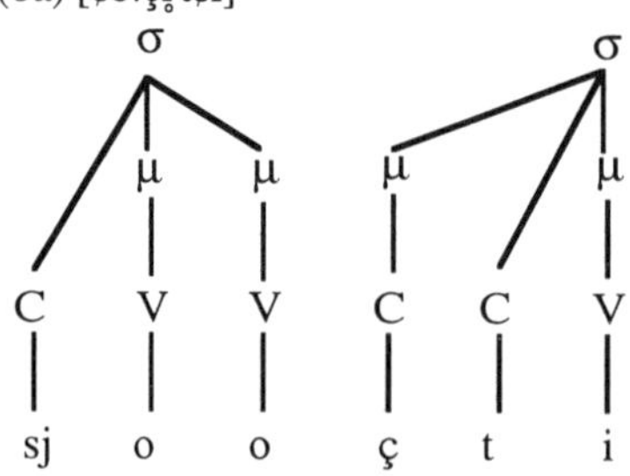

(8b) *[ço:ç̥i̥'tç̥i̥]

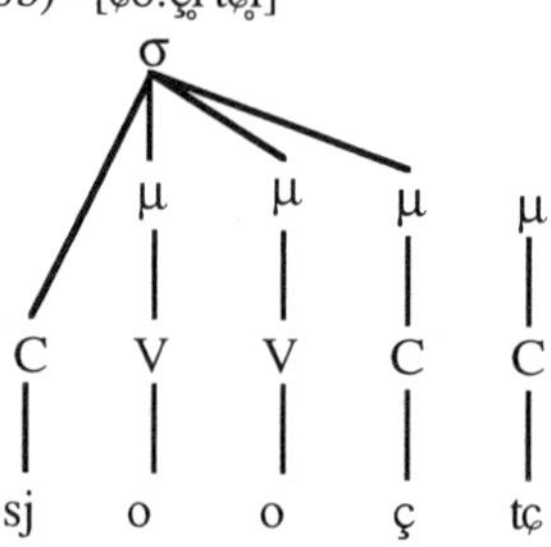

In the consecutive devoicing environment, phonetic factors such as the type of preceding consonants and utterance final lengthening, play a significant role. Every condition being equal, preceding fricatives trigger devoicing because of greater degree of glottal gestural overlap, and utterance final devoicing is less likely because of utterance final lengthening. Phonological factors other than syllable structure such as the presence of lexical accent also become effective. It is possible to devoice a vowel in an accented syllable, but the resulting syllable structure is not usually favoured. Therefore, accented vowels are likely to retain voicing in order to retain syllabicity.

3.4 Pre-geminate Consonants Environments

The syllable based analysis of the vowel devoicing process above is supported by the results of another experiment. Vowel devoicing in the pre-geminate environment, i.e. /V/ in /C̥VC̥C̥V/, was examined in words such as *kissaten* /kissateN/ 'coffee shop', *suppai* /suppa'i/ 'sour' and *goshikku* /gosi'kku/ 'gothic'.

Four native speakers of standard Japanese pronounced 44 words each with a vowel in the pre-geminate devoicing environment. In 22 test words, devoiceable vowels were accented as *chisso* /ti'sso/ 'nitrogen' and *goshippu* /gosi'ppu/ 'gossip', and in the other 22, devoiceable vowels were unaccented as *shippai* /sippai/ (no accent) 'failure' and *kukkiri* /kukki'ri/ 'clearly'. Initially sentences randomly containing the test words were presented, then the test words were presented in citation form in a random order. The subjects were asked to read the sentences and word list twice each. The results are presented in Table 1.

Table 1. Average devoicing rates of high vowels in the pre-geminate environment by four subjects. The numbers in brackets are the number of samples out of the total number of 176.

		clearly voiced	partially voiced	clearly voiceless
word in citation	accented	98.86% (174)	0.57% (1)	0.57% (1)
	unaccented	90.34% (159)	0.57% (1)	9.09% (16)
word in sentence	accented	85.80% (151)	0.57% (1)	13.64% (24)
	unaccented	65.34% (115)	6.58% (5)	31.82% (54)

One of the subjects showed a very high devoicing rate of 40.61% compared with the rates of the other three subjects which were 4.90%, 6.98% and 8.96%. A four factor analysis of variance found that there were significant effects of subjects [$F(3, 40)=22.713$, $p<0.0001$], presence of accent [$F(1, 40)=18.371$, $p<0.0001$], and context (citation or in sentence) [$F(1, 40)=27.134$, $p<0.001$]. The type of preceding consonants was found to be not significant [$F(2, 40)=1.938$, n.s.]. No significant interactions were found. The results showed that devoicing before geminate consonants is not generally favoured, despite The NHK Pronunciation and Accent Dictionary (1985) listing all pre-geminate devoiceable vowels as voiceless.

The pre-geminate devoicing process is also constrained by the syllable structure. The underlined vowel /u/ in *suppai* /suppa'i/ is in a typical devoicing environment surrounded by voiceless consonants, but the following consonants are geminates /pp/. If devoicing occurs as *[su̥p:a'i] as (9a), the preceding consonant /s/ can only to be syllabified to the following syllable. However, the first element of the geminates /pp/ would lose a link to the preceding syllable and would also have to be syllabified only to the following syllable. As a syllable cannot take three consonantal sequences in its onset position. The first two morae would be left unsyllabified as (9b). Therefore, the /u/ is not devoiced.

(9a) *suppai* /suppa'i/ [sɯp:a'i]

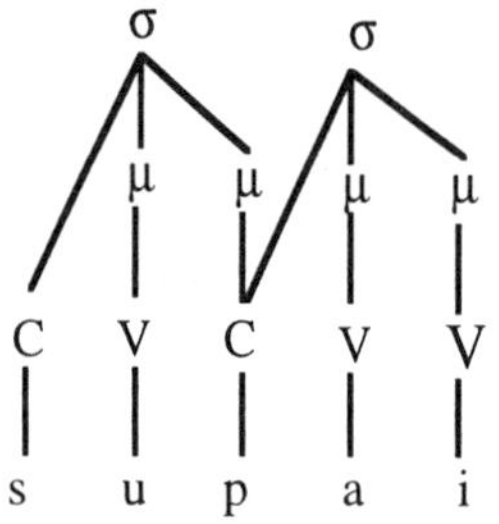

(9b) *[su̥p:a'i]

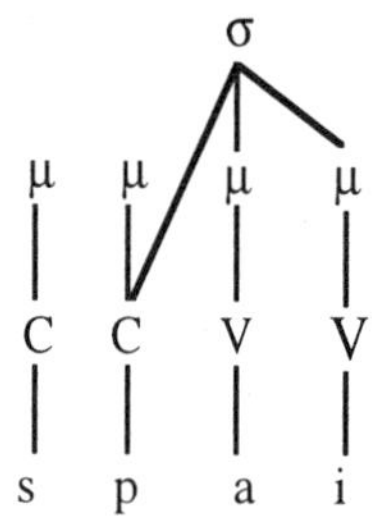

In the case of *goshikku* /gosi'kku/ 'gothic' as shown in (10a), devoicing of the /i/ is not favoured. First of all, the preceding /ç/ cannot be syllabified to the preceding syllable because the syllable /si/ carries the accent. Secondly, if the /ç/ were to be syllabified to the following syllable, both the /ç/ and the first element /k/ of the geminates would have to be syllabified to the following syllable, which would also cause a superheavy syllable with three consonant clusters. Therefore, devoicing the pre-geminate /i/ is not favoured as it would leave both /ç/ and /k/ left unsyllabified as (10b).

(10a) /gosi'kku/ [goçi'k:ɯ]

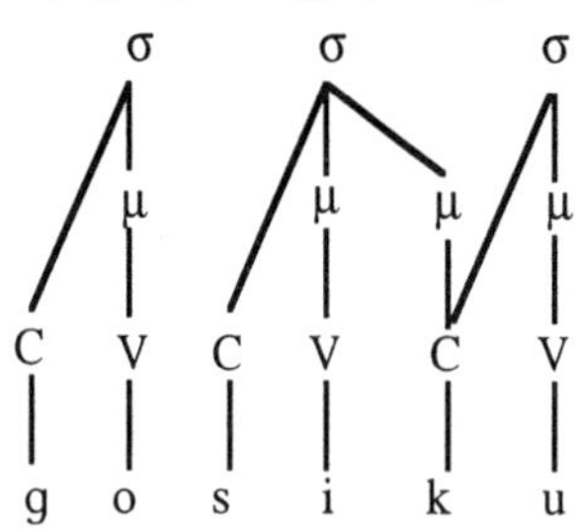

(10b) *[goçi̥'k:ɯ]

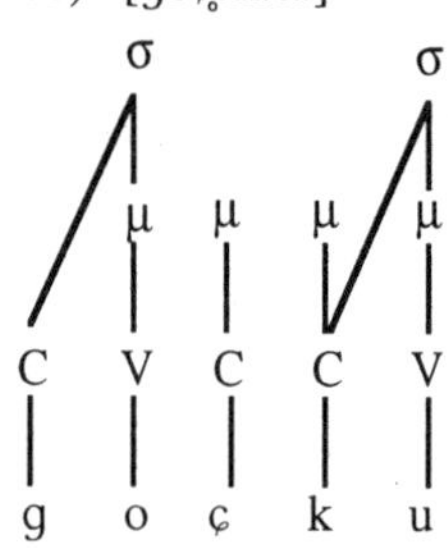

3.5 Bimoraic Syllable Onset

The analyses above only works if the Japanese syllable permits initial /CC/ sequences. The only consonant clusters permitted in the syllable initial position in Japanese are /Cj/ sequences. The phonological status of the /j/ in /CjV/ sequences is dubious because despite being voiced, when it occurs following /s/ in /sju/, it triggers devoicing. This may imply that the /j/ in /Cj/ sequence is just a reflection of palatalisation of preceding consonant, therefore the /j/ does not have a phonological status in Japanese.

It is difficult to check whether the /j/ in /Ç̥ju/ sequences blocks devoicing of following high vowels because there are very few Japanese words with /Ç̥juÇ̥/ sequence. The four subjects who participated in the experiment in section 3.4 above pronounced words with /Ç̥juÇ̥/ sequences. Most words of this kind are loan words: *kyupura* /kju̲'pura/ 'cupra', *chuchu* /tju̲'tju/ 'tutu (French)', *eguzekyutibu* /eguze'kju̲tibu/ 'executive', *okyupeeshon* /okju̲pe'esjoN/ 'occupation', *Machupichu* /matju̲pitju/ '*Machu Picchu* (Spanish)', Kyu̲kunosu /kju'kunosu/ 'Kyknos (Greek)' and Kyukuropusu /kju̲kuro'pusu/ 'Kyklops (Greek)'. There are a few more words such as *hjutte* /hju̲tte/ 'Hütte (German)' and *kyutto* /kju̲tto/ 'tightly (onomatopoeia)', where the high vowels are in the pre-geminate position. Therefore, devoicing was less likely to occur regardless of the presence of /j/ (see section 3.4). In their utterances, there were only 10 devoiced /u/ out of 56 /Ç̥juÇ̥/ environments in words in sentences, and there was no voiceless /u/ in samples of words in citation. It is difficult to generalise from these results as there as a limited number of samples and also all the words are loan words and are by no means common. However, the results indicated that a possible presence of the /j/ and that it blocks devoicing except in /sju/ sequences[4].

However, there is still a remaining problem because the /j/ in /CjV/ sequences is not moraic. The devoicing processes above caused two mora sequences in a syllable initial position. For example, the syllable structure of *shokikan* /sjo.ki'.kaN/ (3 syllables) [çoki̥kaɯ̃] in (7b) was reanalysed as two syllable /ço.kˤkaN/ with a /CCVC/ sequence. The sequence of /CCVC/ is allowed as long as the /CCV/ consists of one mora. However, the /kˤ/ in the /kˤkaN/ is moraic, which creates a new type of superheavy syllable /C-CV-C/ (3 morae) (hereafter "-" indicates a mora boundary).

Even if we do not accept the super-heavy syllable /kˤkaN/ and analyse the sequence as /sjo.kˤ.kaN/, one case which must have this syllable structure is word-initial devoicing as (3a) *shita* /sita/ [çita] 'below'. When the vowel /i/ in the initial mora is devoiced, there is no place other than the beginning of the following syllable for the preceding /s/ to move to, which

---

[4] Whether [ç] in [ça, çi, çu, (çe), ço] should be analysed phonologically as a sequence of /sj/ or an independent phoneme /ç/ (or /ʃ/) is a long standing argument. See Vance (1987) for detail.

causes a heavy syllable /ç-ta/ (/C-CV/). This violates the universal rule that a syllable onset consonant cannot constitute a mora on its own.

One possible reason why an onset consonant alone could constitute a mora in the case of word-initial vowel devoicing is that this consonant may not fully constitute a mora. The mora is a rhythmic unit in Japanese (see section 2). Durational adjustment of segments also operates at the mora level in Japanese, so that the durations of morae do not differ drastically (Campbell and Sagisaka, 1991; Sato, 1994; Han, 1994). Therefore, the presence or absence of an extra mora is crucial in terms of word duration. Durational comparison between the same morae with voiced and voiceless vowels showed that the durations of devoiced morae were significantly longer than their corresponding consonant's portion of /CV/ morae. However, morae with voiceless vowels were significantly shorter in duration than the same morae with voiced vowels. The average ratio of devoiced morae against their /CV/ counterparts was 83.93% (Kondo, 1995).

The same study found that the presence of devoiced vowels in words of one to three devoiced vowels did not significantly affect the duration of whole words. However, the rate of increase was not linear. When a word had more devoiced vowels, the whole word duration did not increase as much as it would have done if all the vowels had been voiced. Several devoiced vowels in a word did reduce word duration. Words with several devoiced vowels were unable to compensate for their short durations even at the word level. Devoiced morae have shorter durations.

This implies that a devoiced mora does not fully qualify as a mora, which is a unit of timing. This is why it may be allowed to be syllabified to the onset of a following syllable to form a syllable initial consonant cluster as the /j/ can form a part of a syllable onset cluster.

4. Devoicing, Syllable Structure and Speech Rhythm

Kubozono (1995) proposed that heavy syllables composed of two morae (/CVC/ or /CVV/) is the universally favoured syllable structure, and there has been a tendency for Japanese syllables to move towards bimoraic heavy syllables. The whole process of vowel devoicing creates new types of heavy syllables which do not normally occur in Japanese. The proposed new heavy syllables may not have been accepted unconditionally in Japanese and violate phonotactics. However, it is possible to pronounce these sequences. This may imply that Japanese syllable structure has become more flexible and is now in the process of changing. It should be noted that devoicing in consecutive three morae was not favoured in normal speech, because it would create a superheavy syllables of 3 or 4 morae which is a universally marked syllable structure. Clusters with more than two consonants are not permitted in Japanese and would also be difficult to pronounce or be perceived.

Moreover, superheavy syllables are not favourable because it would cause and uncomfortable speech rhythm. Ayusawa, Kitazawa & Toki (1999) studied Japanese speech rhythm using TEMAX (Tempo Evaluation and Measurement Algorithm by ks)[5] and found a tendency of bimoraic foot (Poser, 1990) in Japanese natural speech. Their results showed that in natural speech a high propotion of the units of rhythm consisted of 2 morae. Bimoraic heavy syllables such as /CVV/ and /CVC/ formed a rhythmic unit and also quite a large proportion of monomoraic light syllables joined with an adjacent mora and formed a bimoraic rhythmic unit. However, rhythmic units consisting of three morae or more were rare. Vowel devoicing of three morae or more would produce superheavy syllables of more than two morae. These are not favoured either in terms of rhythm or syllable structure.

5. Conclusion

I have examined the vowel devoicing process and how this is controlled by syllable structure. The results also suggested that the devoicing process may play a role in a change towards heavy syllable structures and establishing the speech rhythm of a bimoraic foot. Accented vowels tend to remain voiced in the consecutive devoicing environment, so that they can keep their syllabicity. However, it should be noted that there are also effects of phonetic factors. Every condition being equal, fricatives trigger devoicing more than plosives in the consecutive environment. Utterance final vowels are usually voiced even though they are easy to syllabify to the coda position of preceding syllable. This is probably because the vowels are lengthened in an utterance final position. Actual voicing/devoicing patterns in the consecutive devoicing environment may be determined by the combination of various phonetic and phonological factors such as the syllabification rule, the type of preceding consonants, accentedness and position in an utterance.

References

Ayusawa, Takako, Shigeyoshi Kitazawa and Satoshi Toki. 1990. A Study of Japanese Rhythm by Means of TEMAX. *Journal of the Phonetic Society of Japan* 2:1. 34-40.

Beckman, Mary E. and Atsuko Shoji. 1984. Spectral and Perceptual Evidence for CV Coarticulation in Devoiced /si/ and /syu/ in Japanese. *Phonetica* 4. 61-71.

Campbell, Nick and Yoshinori Sagisaka. 1991. Moraic and Syllable-level Effects on Speech Timing. *Journal of Electronic Information Communication Engineering* SP 90-107. 35-40.

Cutler, Anne and Takeshi Otake. 1997. Contrastive Studies of Spoken-language Perception. *Journal of the Phonetic Society of Japan* 1:3. 4-13.

Han, Mieko S. 1994. Acoustic Manifestations of Mora Timing in Japanese. *Journal of the Acoustic Society of America* 96:1. 73-82.

Hattori, Noriko. 1989. *Mechanisms of Word Accent Change: Innovations in Standard Japanese*. Doctral dissertation. University College London.

---

[5] See Ayusawa, Kitazawa & Toki (1999) for the explanation of TEMAX.

Haye, Bruce. 1989. Compensatory Lengthening in Moraic Phonology. *Linguistic Inquiry* 20. 253-306.

Itô, Junko. 1990. Prosodic Minimality in Japaneses, in K. Deaton, M. Noske and M. Ziolkowski, eds., *CLS 26-II: Papers from the Parasession on the Syllable in Phonetics and Phonology.* 213-239.

Jun, Sun-Ah and Mary E. Beckman. 1993. A Gestural-overlap Analysis of Vowel Devoicing in Japanese and Korean. Paper presented at the 1993 Annual Meeting of the Linguistic Society of America.

Kenstowicz, Michael. 1994. *Phonology in Generative Grammar.* MA: Blackwell.

Kondo, Mariko. 1995. Temporal Adjustment of Devoiced Morae in Japanese, *Proceedings of the 13th International Congress of Phonetic Sciences* 3. 238-241.

Kondo, Mariko. 1997. *Mechanisms of Vowel Devoicing in Japanese.* Doctral dissertation. University of Edinburgh.

Kubozono, Haruo. 1989. The Mora and Syllable Structure in Japanese: Evidence from Speech Errors. *Language and Speech* 32: 3. 249-278.

Kubozono, Haruo. 1995. *Gokeisei to On'in Koozoo.* Tokyo: Kuroshio Shuppan.

McCawley, James. 1977. Accent in Japanese, in M.L. Hyman, ed. *Studies in Stress and Accent, Southern California Occasional Papers in Linguistics No. 4.* University of Southern California. 261-302

Maekawa, Kikuo. 1989. Boin no musei-ka. in M. Sugito, ed. *Nihon-go no Onsei-On'in (1).* Tokyo: Meiji Shoin. 135-153.

Port, Robert F., Jonathan Dalby and Michael O'Dell. 1987. Evidence for Mora Timing in Japanese. *Journal of the Acoustic Society of America* 81: 5. 1574-1585.

Poser, William. 1990. Evidence for Foot Structure in Japanese. *Language* 66. 78-105.

Sakurai, Shigeharu. 1985. Kyootsuu-go no hatsuon de chuui subeki kotogara. Appendix to NHK, ed., *Japanese Pronunciation and Accent Dictionary.* Tokyo: Nihon Hoosoo Shuppan Kyookai. 128-143.

Sato, Yumiko. 1993. The Durations of Syllable-final Nasals and the Mora Hypothesis in Japanese. *Phonetica* 50. 44-67.

Shibatani, Masayoshi. 1990. *The Languages of Japan*, Cambridge: Cambridge University Press.

Shinohara, Shigeko. 1996 The Roles of the Syllable and the Mora in Japanese Adaptations of French Words. *Cahiers de Linguistique Asie Orientale* 25: 1. 87-112. Paris: CRLAO EHESS.

Sugito, Miyoko and Hajime Hirose. 1988. Production and Perception of Accented Devoiced Vowels in Japanese. *Annual Bulletin of Research Institute of Logopedics and Phniatrics* 22. 21-39. Tokyo: University of Tokyo.

Takeda, Kazuya and Hisao Kuwabara. 1987. Analysis and Prediction of Devocalizing Phenomena (in Japanese). *Proceedings of Acoustic Society of Japan.* 105-106.

Tranel, Bernard. 1987. French Schwa and Nonlinear Phonology. *Linguistics* 25. 845-866.

Vance, Timothy J. 1987. *An Introduction to Japanese Phonology.* Albany. NY: State University of New York Press.

Yoshida, Natsuya and Yoshinori Sagisaka. 1990. Factor Analysis of Vowel Devoicing in Japanese (in Japanese), *ATR Technical Report TR-I-0159.* Kyoto: ATR Interpreting Telephony Research Laboratories.

The Role of Syllable Weight and Position on Prominence in Korean*

BYUNG-JIN LIM
Indiana University

1. Introduction

This paper reports the results of an investigation into the production and perception of Korean word-level prosody. The production study examined the effects of syllable weight and syllable position on vowel duration, syllable duration, and fundamental frequency (F0) of Seoul Korean. We also examine what attributes of a syllable cause it to be perceived as prominent. The perception study examined how Korean word prominence is perceived by native speakers of English, Japanese, and Korean.

For the purpose of this paper, we assume that CVC syllables are heavy syllables and CV syllables are light syllables without any further explanation, since this is not the topic of the current paper[1]. In addition, since the vowel length distinction seems to be lost in Seoul Korean, the syllable structure with a long vowel, or CVV syllable structure, is not considered in this study, either.

---

* I would like to thank Kenneth de Jong, Stuart Davis, Yongsung Lee, Kwang-Chul Park, Chin Wan Chung, and Minkyung Lee for their valuable comments and encouragement.

[1] For the phonological status of coda consonant, J.H. Jun (1994) proposes that the Korean coda consonant is moraic; thus CVV and CVC syllables are heavy syllables. On the other hand, Tak (1997) analyzes that CV and CVC syllable as light in Korean.

1.1 Phonology of Prominence

H. B. Lee (1973, 1985, 1989) and H. Y. Lee (1990) suggest Korean is a stress language. They propose that Korean has a duration-based stress system where syllable duration plays a key role, while the role of pitch pattern is only marginal in the decision of stress position. Along this line, Kim (1998) claims that Korean has a rightward right-headed iambic foot structure and it has moraic coda consonants. Then, stress falls on the first syllable, if it is heavy. Or it falls on the second syllable if the first syllable is light. Some examples are given in (1).

(1)			
	kyó:.do.so 'prison'	sí:.caŋ 'market'	cám.ca.ri 'a dragonfly'
	$\underline{H}$ L L	$\underline{H}$ H	$\underline{H}$ L L
	nák.sən 'rejection'	i.yá.ki 'story'	kə.úl 'a mirror'
	$\underline{H}$ H	L $\underline{L}$ L	L $\underline{H}$

(H: heavy syllables; L: light syllables; data from Kim 1998)

For accent placement, Yu (1989) proposes Accent Placement Rules in Modern Korean: Accent falls on leftmost heavy syllable, otherwise rightmost light syllable. Some examples are shown below.

(2)			
	ba.rám 'wind'	sá:.ram ' people'	nún.bo.ra 'snow strom'
	L $\underline{H}$	$\underline{H}$ H	$\underline{H}$ L L
	a.ú. 'a younger sibling'	i.má 'forehead'	pi.hǽŋ.ki 'an airplane'
	L $\underline{L}$	L $\underline{L}$	L $\underline{H}$ L

Finally, in a recent study, Ko (1999) proposes a lexical stress system with the characteristics of a pitch accent based on vocative chant in Seoul and Chonnam Korean.

In sum, the above studies suggest that the internal structure of syllable is primary and stress and accent are a redundant feature concomitant to it.

1.2 The Phonetics of Prominence

In a phonetic study on Korean stress, Jun (1995a) reports that the second syllable is prosodically stronger, which is interpreted as stressed. She also mentions that stress exists in the language since a certain syllable within a prosodic unit the *Accentual Phrase* (AP) shows higher F0 and greater amplitude. Since prosodically strong syllable of a word changes depending on its position within the AP, stress is the property of the AP, not of the word.

Interestingly, de Jong (1994) suggests that Korean nouns do not have initial stress, and such an initial prominence marks the location of a prosodic phrase by initial high tone.

Finally, based on auditory and acoustic experiments, Seong (1991) concludes that the word in Standard Korean may have a fixed accent on one of the first two syllables in almost all words.

As mentioned, previous studies claim that Korean prominence is weight sensitive and duration-based. In addition, syllable position seems to play a role in attracting prominence on the words. Therefore, it this study, a production experiment was carried out to fulfill two functions: 1) it examines positional and weight effects on duration and fundamental frequency and 2) it determines acoustic correlates to be used in a following perception experiment.

2. Experiment 1: Production

To examine syllable position and weight effects in prominence, a production experiment by native speakers of Seoul Korean was conducted.

2.1 Subjects

Two male native speakers of Seoul Korean participated in the experiment. They were both graduate students at Indiana University. They were both in their late twenties and neither had any known speech or hearing disorders.

2.2 Stimulus Materials and Procedures

In a production experiment, stimuli included three syllable words composed of combinations of heavy and light syllables. Given three-syllable words, it is logically possible to have eight different combinations in terms of syllable weight, as in Table 1.

Table 1: Stimulus material

	Syllable weight	Word	Gloss
1	LLL	Ma.na.gwa	The capital of Nicaragua
2	LHL	Ja.jang.ga	A lullaby
3	LHH	Ma.gam.nal	A deadline
4	LLH	Na.ma.dam	Ms. Nah
5	HHH	Mal.jang.nan	A joke
6	HLL	Man.da.ra	The title of a movie
7	HLH	Kang.ma.dam	Ms. Kang
8	HHL	Man.dam.ga	A comedian

(H: heavy syllables; L: light syllables; '.' : syllable boundaries)

All test words had the vowel [a] only for minimizing inherent durational differences. Subjects were asked to read the test words five times at a comfortable speech rate. Test words were placed in two prosodic conditions, in isolation as a single IP, and in a sentential context as the first AP in a larger IP as in (3).

(3) a. [☞**(ja.jang.ga)**$_{AP}$]$_{IP}$ "A lullaby."
b. [☞**(ja.jang.ga)**$_{AP}$ (pul.reo.ju.se.yo)$_{AP}$]$_{IP}$ "Please, sing a lullaby."

The list of test words was presented in Korean orthography. Fillers were included to avoid list effects. Before recording, subjects practiced reading randomly ordered test words to familiarize themselves with the materials. All recordings were made in the recording room in the Indiana University Linguistics Department. Recordings were analyzed using the software *Sound Scope* on a Mac II in the Indiana University Phonetics Laboratory.

2.3 An Analysis

Measurements were taken of vowel, consonant, and syllable durations. In addition, the fundamental frequency of each vowel was measured. All data values reported here represent average values across the two subjects and test words. For the analysis of syllable weight effects, we combined light and heavy syllables each according to syllable position, and then compared them with each other.

3. Results

3.1 Durations

We turn to vowel durations first. As seen in Figure 1, the mean vowel duration of light syllables was significantly longer than that of heavy syllables. For the vowel duration of light syllables, an ANOVA revealed a significant difference among syllable positions [$F(2, 237)=10.221$, $p<0.01$]. The results of post hoc tests indicated that final syllables are significantly longer than other syllables ($p<0.01$).

There was also an effect of position in word [$F(2, 237)=45.045$, $p<0.01$]. Like light syllables, heavy syllables showed the longest final vowel duration. Of interest is that there was no significant difference in duration between initial vowels and medial vowels for the heavy syllables by each speaker ($p>0.5$)

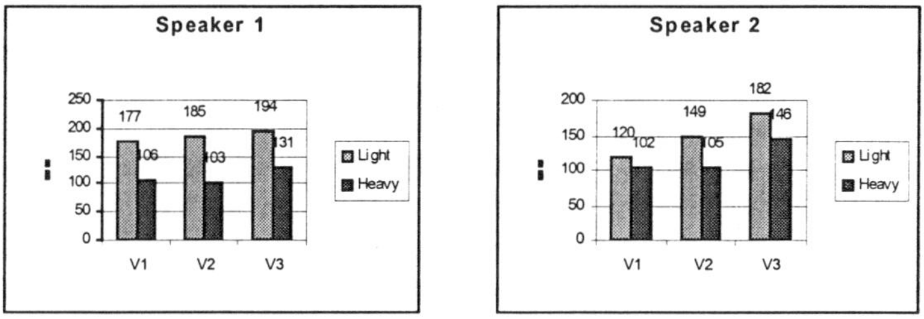

Figure 1: Mean vowel duration for each speaker

Since the longest vowel duration was found in final syllables, one might expect that syllable durations for each syllable might show the same pattern as the vowel duration, that is, with the longest final syllables. Interestingly, however, this was not the case. Data showing average syllable durations for each speaker are shown in Figure 2.

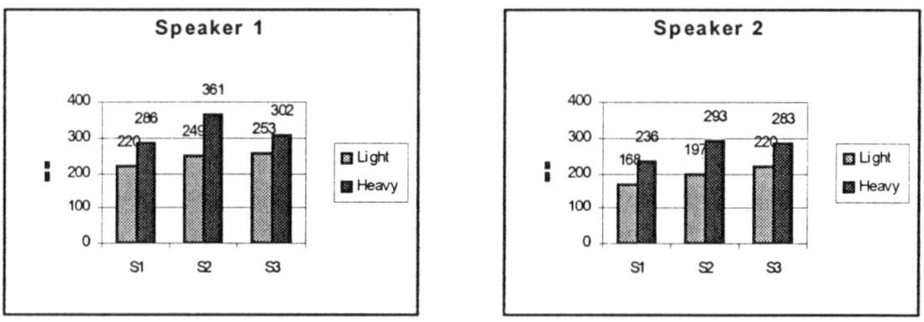

Figure 2: Mean syllable duration for each speaker

Unlike vowel durations, mean syllable durations indicated that heavy syllables are statistically longer than light syllables (t (478)=-13.071, p<0.001). This is not surprising since heavy syllables have more elements such as codas than light syllables. For the syllable duration of light syllables, an ANOVA revealed a significant difference among syllable positions [F (2, 237)=15.342, p<0.001]. There was a significant durational difference between the initial and final syllables (p<0.01), but no significant difference was observed between the medial and final syllables (p>0.1). However, heavy syllable durations did not show the same durational pattern as light syllables did. Of interest is that medial syllables were the longest, followed by final syllables [F (2, 237)=22.647, p<0.01]. That is, medial syllables were longer than final syllables, which, in turn, were significantly longer than initial syllables.

Contrary to expectation, heavy syllables showed the longest medial syllables with the longest final vowel duration. Thus, we turned to onset and coda durations for heavy syllables to see durational patterns for internal structure of syllables.

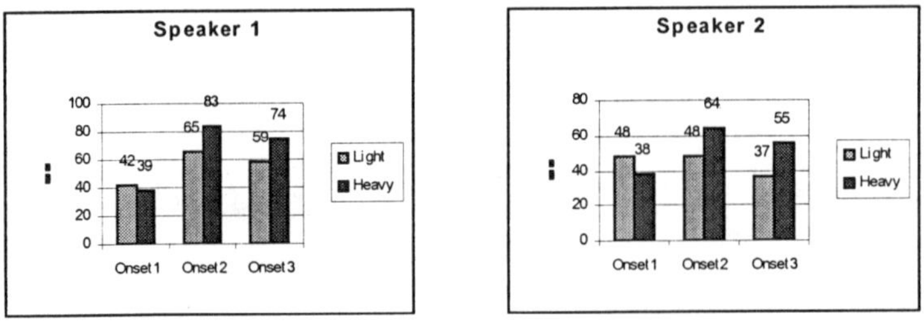

Figure 3: Mean onset durations for each speaker

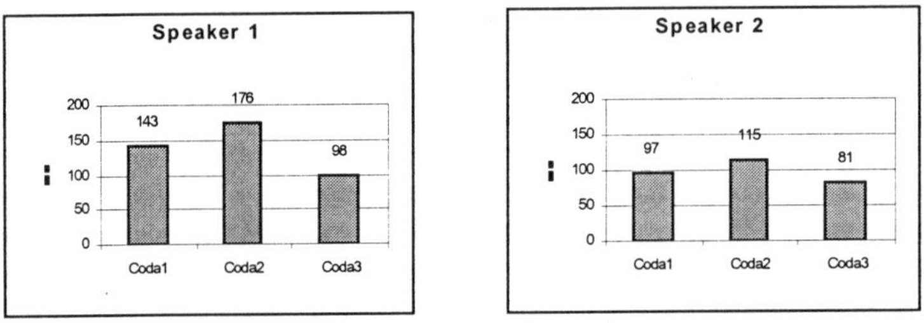

Figure 4: Mean coda durations for each speaker

Figure 3 shows average onset durations by each speaker. For onset durations, a significant difference was also found between medial and other syllables [F (2, 237)=35.948, p<0.01] except for the light syllables of speaker 2. For coda durations, medial codas are significantly longer than initial and final codas across speakers as in Figure 4 [F (2, 237)=25.304, p<0.01].

3.2 Fundamental Frequency

Before turning to the results of the fundamental frequency, it would be better to briefly mention the tonal patterns in Korean depending on prosodic units. According to Jun (1993, 1998), the AP has a phrase final rising pattern, a LH as in Figure 5 (b), and the IP may have one of several boundary tones such as L, H, LH, HL, LHL and HLH . However, when the final syllable of the AP is the IP final as in (4a), the final rise of the AP is preempted by the IP boundary tone as shown in Figure 5 (a).

(4) a. [(ma.mu.ri)$_{AP}$]$_{IP}$ "Finishing touches"
b. [(ma.mu.ri)$_{AP}$ (co.a.yo)$_{AP}$]$_{IP}$ "Finishing touches are satisfied"

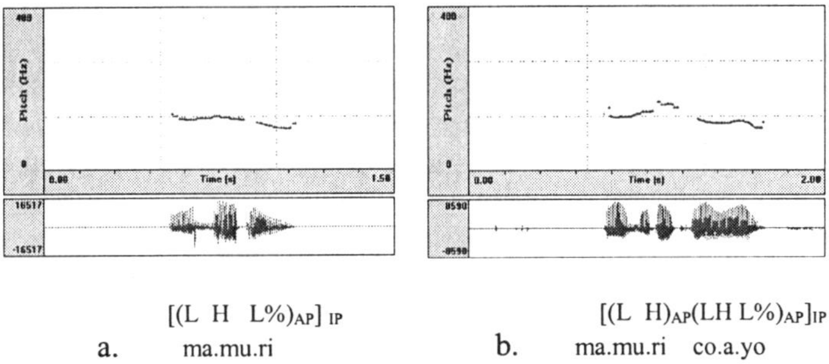

Figure 5: Fundamental frequency contours depending on prosodic units

Therefore, it might be expected that when the AP falls within the IP, initial or/and medial syllables show higher F0 as in Figure 5 (a), while within the AP, medial or/and final syllables indicates higher F0 as in Figure 5 (b).

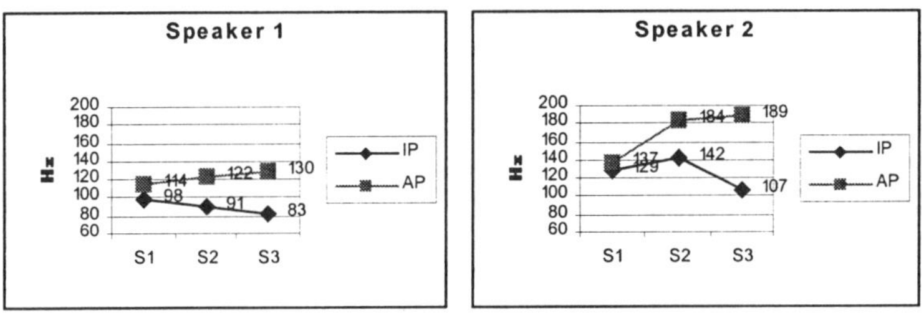

Figure 6: Fundamental frequency for each speaker

We turn then to the results of the fundamental frequency patterns. The fundamental contours by prosodic units are shown in figure 6. Since F0 patterns differ depending on their prosodic units, we distinguished F0 values of the AP from those of the IP, then compared by syllable positions and by syllable weight.

First, we turn to the F0 values for the IP prosodic condition. Interestingly, speaker 1 shows higher F0 values on the first syllables whereas speaker 2 shows highest values on the second syllables. Especially, for speaker 2, a significant difference in F0 between the first and the second syllables was observed ($p<0.01$).

As mentioned above, the AP final tonal pattern showed a rise, a LH, and the results confirmed this tonal pattern with the highest F0 value for final syllables across speakers. That is, final syllables show higher F0 values than initial syllables ($p<0.01$). Compared with medial syllables, however, there was no significant difference between the two ($p>0.1$).

3.3 Discussion

For durational patterns, the final vowels were significantly longer than the first two syllables. This durational difference turned out to be a final lengthening effect by the post hoc analysis. Interestingly, for heavy syllables, medial syllable durations were noticeably longer than other syllables as far as syllable durations were concerned. This could indicate that the second syllable position would be prominent or stressed. In addition, the durational patterns for the constituents of a syllable also showed that medial positions were different from other syllable positions. That is, coda durations and onset durations together seem to combine to increase syllable durations for medial syllables compared to other syllables. Therefore, it might be possible to say that a second syllable position seem to stand out for prominence or stress just based on the durational patterns for heavy syllables.

However, this is not the case for vowel durations. Final vowel lengthening might be an indicative for a boundary, which means that durational patterns of final vowels are sensitive to a coming boundary. Seemingly, there is a conflict in durational patterns between vowels and syllables: Vowel durations seem to reflect an edge effect, a pre-boundary lengthening effect, while syllable duration might reflect the prominence pattern of words, a head effect.

Fundamental frequency patterns also seem to support these conclusions. Regardless of prosodic units, the medial syllable position shows higher F0 than other syllables. That is, the peak of F0 is shown near onset of the second syllables.

Results of this study, however, seem to be problematic considering previous studies. According to Jun (1990, 1995b), the AP initial segments were lengthened, which implied that the IP initial segment duration would show greater lengthening since the IP is higher than the AP in a prosodic hierarchy. Compared to these studies, our results seem to be contradictory. Jun's argument was based on the durations of lenis stops in the AP while we measured initial sonorant segment durations in the IP. This difference might be a possible reason for different results.

4. Experiment 2: Perception

To examine which acoustic correlates are used as perceptional cues for Korean word prominence, a perception test was conducted. It seems reasonable to expect that a listener's linguistic background, to some extent, affects his judgment of prominence. The extent to which judgment is affected depends on the classification of the language in question as a stress, tone, or quantity language. It may be expected that listeners who speak a stress language, such as English, are more sensitive to some acoustic cues in stress judgment. In addition, the native speakers of pitch-accented languages like Japanese may use different acoustic cues in prominence perception.

In this perception test, native speakers of three different languages, English, Japanese, and Korean, participated as listeners. They were asked to indicate prominent syllables of utterances.

4.1 Subjects

Five native speakers of English and Japanese each, and six Korean native speakers participated as listeners in this perception test. They were selected from the Indiana University population. They were all naïve to the purpose of the test. They also reported no history of speech and hearing related impairments.

4.2 Stimuli and Procedures

As mentioned above, two subjects participated in the production experiment. Of the two, the speech data of speaker 2[2] were presented to the listeners using a Sony mini disk cassette player. Each word was repeated five times. Then, the listeners were asked to mark prominent syllables on answer sheets. If the listeners were not certain, the words were repeated once more. Then, the number of responses for each syllable were counted and were compared by syllable positions and by listeners.

4.3 Results

Figure 7 shows the responses for prominence in the IP by listeners. The results indicate that medial syllables were perceived as prominent or stressed across listeners. With a relatively high percentage, initial syllables were also responded as prominent following second syllables as shown below. Final syllables, however, did not seem to be favored for prominence for the IP. A small number of uncertainties for prominence were also observed. Especially, it is unlikely that Korean listeners are confident in responding to word prominence compared to other listeners.

[2] Compared to speaker 1, speaker 2 shows small range of variation in data values. Therefore, we used speaker 2's speech data for the perception test.

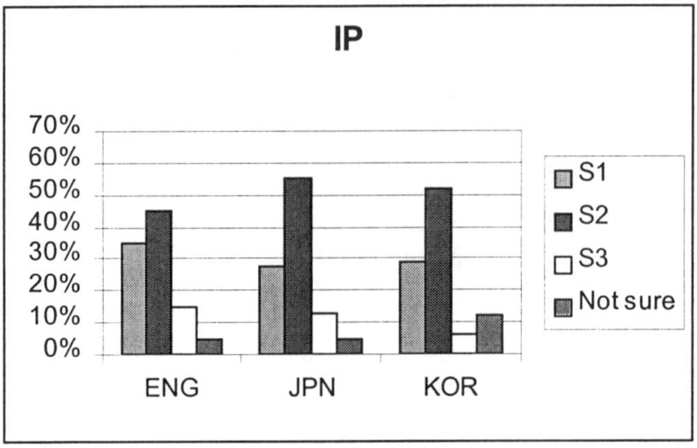

Figure 7: Percentage of prominence response by each listener in IP

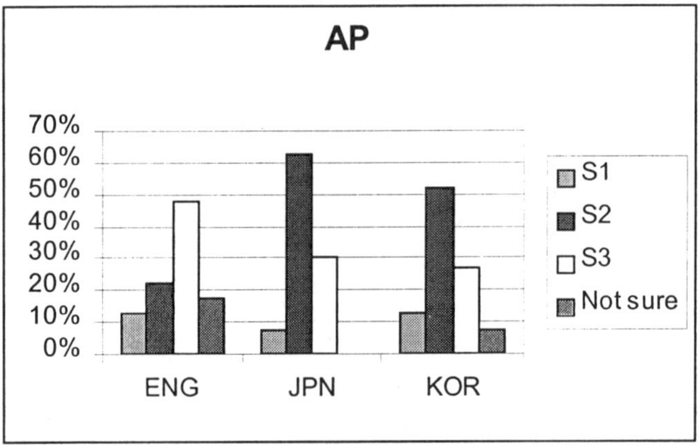

Figure 8: Percentage of prominence response by each listener in AP

For the results of AP, as seen in Figure 8, it was found that a greater number of responses indicated prominence on medial syllable positions regardless of listeners.

A closer examination, however, reveals differences among listener groups. In particular, English listeners chose final syllables as prominent, whereas Japanese and Korean listeners showed similar patterns by favoring medial syllables for the AP. Interestingly, no Japanese listeners showed any uncertainty for prominence.

4.4 Discussion

It is not surprising to find that different language speakers used different acoustic cues in perceiving prominence or stress. It is, however, interesting to see that they responded to the same speech data differently. As reported in the production experiment, the duration of final vowels showed longest values regardless of syllable weight. For the AP, English speakers preferred the final syllables to other syllables positions as prominent, which implies that they are sensitive to vowel duration as well as pitch change in prominence perception. It might be difficult to say that which acoustic factor has a primary function in prominence perception for English speakers based on the results of this study, though. However, it may not be difficult to say that they are very sensitive to these acoustic factors and using them as perceptional cues for word prominence. Compared to other language users, their perception results highly corresponded to the results of production experiment. Being speakers of an accent language, Japanese listeners showed that they are more sensitive to pitch movement between syllables as expected. Their perception data imply that they may use a relative change in pitch movement as a cue for prominence. In other words, they perceived as prominent or accented, if there is any significant increase or decrease in pitch movement available between syllables. Interestingly, Korean listeners showed a similar pattern to Japanese listeners, which indicates that they might be more sensitive to a relative pitch movement rather than to durational change. Related with recent studies where Korean seems to lose vowel length distinction, it suggests that durational factor do not play a role in prominence perception.

5. Conclusion

In this study, a production test was carried out to fulfill two functions; 1) to examine positional and weight effects on duration and fundamental frequency and 2) to determine which acoustic correlates could be used as perceptional cues in Korea word perception. Results indicate that syllable weight and syllable position play a key role in affecting durational patterns and intonational contours. The perception study examined the extent to which Korean word prominence is perceptible by native speakers of English, Japanese, and Korean. Results show that second syllables of three syllable words seem to be perceived as prominent in Korean. First syllable positions can also be a strong candidate for word prominence perception. However, it is also clear from the present results that the prominence perceived by Korean listeners is not the same as that found in English.

References

de Jong, Ken. 1994. Initial Tones and Prominence in Seoul Korean, in S. H. Lee and S. A. Jun, eds., *OSU Working papers in Linguistics* 43. 1-14.

Jun, Jongho. 1994. Metrical Weight Consistency in Korean Partial Reduplication. *Phonology* 11. 69-88.

Jun, Sun-Ah. 1990. The Domains of Laryngeal Feature Lenition Effects in Chonnam Korean. Paper presented at the 119th ASA meeting.

Jun, Sun-Ah. 1993. *The Phonetics and Phonology of Korean Prosody.* Doctoral dissertation, The Ohio State University.

Jun, Sun-Ah. 1995a. A Phonetic Study of Stress in Korean. Paper presented at the 130th meeting of the Acoustic Society of America, St. Louis. Mo.

Jun, Sun-Ah. 1995b. Asymmetrical Prosodic Effects on the Laryngeal Gesture in Korean. In B. Connell and A. Arvaniti, eds., *Phonology and phonetic evidence: Papers in Laboratory Phonology IV.* 235-253, Cambridge University Press, England.

Jun, Sun-Ah. 1998. The Accentual Phrase in the Korean Prosodic Hierarchy. *Phonology* 15. 189-226.

Kim, Jong-Kyoo. 1998. Anti-Trapping Effects in an Iambic System: Vowel Shortening in Korean, in D.J. Silva, eds., *Japanese/Korean Linguistics* 8. 289-302, Stanford: CSLI.

Ko, Eon-Suk. 1999. The Interaction of Tone and Stress in Seoul and Chonnam Korean. Paper given at the 18th WCCFL, the University of Arizona

Lee, Hyun-Bok. 1973. The Accent of Modern Korean (written in Korean), *Seoul-tae-hak-kyo-mul-ri-tae-hak-po* 19. 113-128.

Lee, Hyun-Bok. 1985. *Standard Pronunciation of Korean* (written in Korean). Seoul: Phonetic Society of Korea.

Lee, Hyun-Bok. 1989. *Korean Grammar.* London: Oxford University Press.

Lee, Ho-Young. 1990. *The Structure of Korean Prosody.* Doctoral dissertation, University of College London.

Seong, Chul-Jae. 1991. *Experimental Phonetic Study of Word Accent in Standard Korean* (written in Korean). MA thesis, Seoul National University.

Tak, Jin-young. 1997. *Issues in Korean Consonantal Phonology.* Doctoral dissertation, Indiana University.

Yu, Jaewon. 1989. A Study of the Accent-Placement Rules in Modern Korean (written in Korean). *Sungkoknonchong* 19. 293-322.

The Lexical Nature of *Rendaku* in Japanese*

KAZUTOSHI OHNO
University of Arizona

1. Issue

Japanese exhibits an interesting sound alternation in compounds which is called *rendaku*, also known as 'sequential voicing' after Martin (1952: 48). Rendaku is defined as "the replacement of a morpheme initial voiceless obstruent with a voiced obstruent" (Vance 1987: 133). That is, the phoneme /t/ alternates with /d/, /k/ with /g/, /s/ with /z/, and /h/ with /b/[1], when those sounds are the first sound of the second item in a compound, as illustrated in (1) below.[2] These examples in (1) are from Otsu (1980: 208–209).

---

* This paper is a partial development of my term paper "Rendaku -its complex status-" written in 1997. I gratefully thank Tsuyoshi Ono who was the instructor of the course and kept encouraging me to develop the paper to conference form through various means and enormous help. I also thank to George Bedell and Stephen Nolan for help with my talk, and to Peter Norquest and Keiichiro Suzuki for various valuable comments on the early versions of this paper.

[1] Historically, **/p/ > */F/ > /h/, where /F/ stands for a voiceless bilabial fricative. At first, the rendaku pattern was simply a voicing process of /p/ → /b/. This pattern still holds even though /p/ has been completely replaced by /h/ in modern Japanese. See Ueda (1898), Shinmura (1928, 1929), Hashimoto (1928, 1944), among others, for the detailed discussion of /p/ > /F/ > /h/.

[2] In this paper, *kunrei-shiki* romanization, i.e. phonemic representation, is used to describe Japanese sounds. Following tradition, the moraic nasal is represented by /n/. Readers who want

(1) a. *ko* 'small' + *taiko* 'drum' → *kodaiko* 'small drum'
b. *da* 'cheap' + *kasi* 'candies' → *dagasi* 'cheap candies'
c. *take* 'bamboo' + *sao* 'pole' → *takezao* 'bamboo pole'
d. *tabi* 'travel' + *hito* 'person' → *tabibito* 'traveler'

The appearance of rendaku, however, is not consistent. Some items such as *tuti* 'soil', *katati* 'shape', *sio* 'tide', *himo* 'string', etc. never undergo rendaku[3] as in (2) below.

(2) a. *aka* 'red' + *tuti* 'soil' → *akatuti* 'red clay'
b. *kao* 'face' + *katati* 'shape' → *kaokatati* 'face features'
c. *oo* 'big' + *sio* 'tide' → *oosio* 'spring tide'
d. *kawa* 'leather' + *himo* 'string' → *kawahimo* 'leather strap'

There are a large number of examples that sometimes undergo rendaku, and sometimes do not. Examples of this are given in (3) below.

(3)

		rendaku	**non-rendaku**
a.	*tama* 'ball'	*sirodama* 'white ball'	*siratama* 'white ball'[4]
		biidama 'marbles'	*mizutama* 'polka dots'
b.	*kusa* 'grass'	*igusa* 'rush'	*mizukusa* 'water plant'
		motigusa 'mugwort'	*hosikusa* 'hay'
c.	*soko* 'bottom'	*agezoko* 'false bottom'	*okusoko* 'depth'
		hunazoko 'bottom of a ship'	*sinsoko* 'bottom of heart'
d.	*hune* 'boat'	*turibune* 'fishing boat'	*ukihune* 'floating boat'
		kobune 'small boat'	*kurohune* 'black boat'

Some compounds can be read in either rendaku or non-rendaku forms (from Vance 1987: 148).

(4) a. *waru* 'bad' + *kuti* 'mouth' → *warukuti, waruguti* 'bad-mouthing'
b. *yoko* 'side' + *tura* 'face' → *yokotura, yokodura* 'side of the face'

Many scholars have been unable to make a solid generalization, due to many examples as in (3), and have merely made some notes on tendencies of rendaku appearance or blocking (Martin 1952, Hamada 1960, McCawley 1968, Tamura 1972, Okumura 1980, Vance 1987, among others). For

to know the actual sounds of examples are recommended to consult with an introductory text of the Japanese phonology, such as McCawley (1968), Vance (1987), Tsujimura (1994), etc.

[3] Vance's (1980b) experiments show that native Japanese speakers (from Tokyo) may pronounce those words in rendaku forms in novel compounds. However, Vance gives as the first element in compounds an old Japanese word. It is believed that old Japanese exhibits more rendaku patterns systematically (Hamada 1960, Endo 1989, and others. See also fn.18). Native speakers may have an intuition that old Japanese shows more rendaku patterns. This will be one area to explore in future research. See fn.17 for a comment on the view of Lyman's Law taken in this paper.

[4] This refers to a particular Japanese food (dumpling) made from rice-flour.

example, McCawley (1968: 87, fn.18) says: "I am unable to state the environment in which the 'voicing rule' applies. The relevant data are completely bewildering."

However, in some of the recent theoretical work which we will review in section 2, rendaku is assumed as a basic phonological rule in Japanese (Otsu 1980, Itô and Mester 1986, etc.). This fact is well represented by the following statement made by Itô and Mester (1986: 53): "Apart from sporadic and lexical exceptions, Rendaku is a productive phonological rule of Japanese."

In this paper, I question the validity of the recent view that rendaku is a productive phonological rule. Both the assumptions and the domain of the rule wiil be questioned, and a set of data will be included that has been rarely discussed: words that have exceptional rendaku or non-rendaku forms. Upon examining how native speakers make rendaku forms or non-rendaku forms when they face novel compounds, we will see that they do not follow the expectations of rule-based analyses. The results suggest that native speakers select rendaku/non-rendaku forms by analogy from existing compounds. This fact questions the recent view that rendaku is a productive phonological rule, but further supports the traditional view that rendaku is lexically determined.

The organization of this paper is as follows. First, a review of recent rendaku analyses is given (Section 2). Second, crucial flaws of recent rule-based analyses will be presented (Section 3). Third, the results of rendaku experiments are given and a proposal of the lexical nature of rendaku is provided (Section 4). Finally, it is concluded that rendaku is not a productive rule.

2. Rendaku as Rule-based

2.1 Rendaku and Lexical Strata in Japanese

The backbone of rule-based analyses is the stratification of lexical items. Let us briefly review the lexical strata of the Japanese vocabulary.

The Japanese lexicon has often been divided into three strata according to etymological history; these are native, Sino-, and foreign.[5]

[5] Usually a group of mimetics (onomatopoeia) is included as the fourth stratum. I do not include it in the strata in this paper for the following reasons. It is not a class according to an etymological background (it is a sub-stratum of the native stratum etymologically). In addition, mimetics do not form compounds, and therefore, do not undergo rendaku.

In Itô and Mester's (1995, 1999) most recent analyses, those four strata are based on violations of (morpho-)phonological constraints rather than etymology. I do not discuss the issue in this paper. See Rice (1997) for the counter-argument to Itô and Mester (1995).

(5) **Lexical strata in Japanese**

a. Native Japanese (NJ)

b. Sino-Japanese (SJ): historically of Chinese origin[6]

c. Foreign: borrowed from foreign languages other than Chinese

Hence, non-NJ, in this paper, refers to both (5b) and (5c) together.

There is a correlation between rendaku appearance and lexical information. It is reported that rendaku is observed more often in native vocabulary, while it occurs much less frequently in non-native vocabulary (Martin 1952, Okumura 1980, Vance 1996, etc.). Vance (1996: 25, and appendices) reports that 90 of 100 NJ items (90%) that are selected from a dictionary on a random basis can undergo rendaku, while just 13 of 100 SJ items (13%) that are chosen on the same basis can undergo rendaku.[7] It is obvious from the statistics that rendaku is more common in NJ than in SJ. There are only two reasonable rendaku examples from the foreign stratum; *kappa* '(rain)coat' and *karuta* 'card'.[8]

(6) a. *ama* 'rain' + *kappa* '(rain)coat' → *amagappa* 'raincoat'

b. *iroha* '(Japanese ABC)' + *karuta* 'card'→ *irohagaruta* 'Japanese traditional cards'

These two are some of the oldest foreign vocabulary that was borrowed from Portuguese (*capa* and *carta*, respectively) no later than the late sixteenth century (Umegaki 1980).

2.2 Analysis

Rule-based analyses take the following three steps. First, they restrict rendaku as a rule to NJ items. Second, they allow for some non-NJ items to undergo rendaku in an identical fashion with NJ items. Third and last, they provide supplemental conditions and sporadic lexical exceptions to cover the items that 'leak' out of the first two steps.

---

[6] Precisely, SJ refers to the lexical items which are pronounced in *on*. *On* refers to the original Chinese-based way of pronouncing kanji. That is, the lexical stratum of SJ includes items created in Japan and items that are originally NJ (switched pronunciation of kanji from the native way to *on*). In fact, the majority of the SJ words were created within a few decades after the Meiji Reformation in 1868 (Sato 1982). *On* has more than one layers such as *go'on* (older, and exhibits rather systematic rendaku), *kan'on* (less old, and exhibits few rendaku forms), etc. Thus the treatment of SJ is actually difficult both in etymology and rendaku, not knowing the background of each item. Due to limited space, I do not discuss the issue of SJ in this paper. See Okumura (1952), Numoto (1986), among others, for the detailed discussion of *on*, and rendaku of SJ.

[7] These numbers are out of potential rendaku candidates; that is, the items that start with a voiced sound and Lyman's Law (see 2.3 for discussion) candidates are not included in the original group of the selected items.

[8] Examples like the following are no longer used: *kuwae* 'having in the mouth' + *kiseru* 'pipe' (Cambodian: *khsier*) → *kuwaegiseru* 'pipe' and *aka* 'red' + *ketto* 'blanket' (English) → *akagetto* 'red blanket', 'countryman (who tended to come to Tokyo wearing a red blanket over the shoulder)'.

The assumption in the first step comes from the fact that the majority of NJ items can undergo rendaku (but non-NJ items mostly do not). Note that there are no similar kinds of restrictions on the first item of a compound. ((7c) is Otsu's (1980: 209) example (13).)

(7) a. *ura* 'back' (NJ) + *to* 'door' (NJ) → *urado* 'back door'
b. *koosi* 'lattice' (SJ) + *to* 'door' (NJ) → *koosido* 'latticed door'
c. *garasu* 'glass' (Foreign) + *to* 'door' (NJ) → *garasudo* 'glass door'

Supposing NJ items have the feature specification of [+wago] (Otsu 1980) or [+Yamato] (Itô and Mester 1986) (both of them mean [+(Japanese) Native]), then the rendaku rule is considered sensitive to this feature specification.

The second point is to justify non-NJ items that undergo rendaku. Otsu (1980: 209) assumes that non-NJ items undergo rendaku to the extent that they become 'Japanized'. Since rendaku is a rule for NJ items, the treatment seems to be the only way to save a group of non-NJ items that undergo rendaku. Itô and Mester (1986) do not actually mention non-NJ rendaku items, but the only way to justify their analysis would be to assign [+Yamato] to those non-NJ items.[9]

The final step is crucial because the two treatments above do not cover the whole rendaku (and non-rendaku) paradigm. For example, the lone rendaku trigger, being NJ, or having the feature specification of [+Native], is too strong because of the existence of non-rendaku NJ items. By giving supplemental conditions or rules and allowing some sporadic and lexicalized exceptions, the whole paradigm of rendaku becomes complete. We will see two of the supplemental factors in the next subsection.

2.3 Supplemental Conditions

There have been some rendaku-blocking conditions proposed so far in the literature (Okumura 1980, Tamura 1972, Vance 1987, Ohno 1997, etc.). The two conditions below strictly bleed rendaku.

One of the rendaku-blocking factors is Lyman's Law. This phonological stipulation states that a lexical item never undergoes rendaku if it contains a voiced obstruent,[10] as seen in examples (all items are NJ) in (8a) below.[11]

---

[9] Itô and Mester (1995) treat this issue as 'nativization' of non-NJ items, which seems to be parallel to Otsu's (1980) assumption of Japanization. As noted in fn.5, I do not discuss Itô and Mester's (1995, 1999) most recent analyses.

[10] This is the strong version of Lyman's Law. The weak version states that the second item of a compound never undergoes rendaku if the second mora contains a voiced obstruent. The weak version expunges the lone counterexample for the strong version, *hasigo* 'ladder' (e.g. *nawa* 'rope' + *hasigo* 'ladder' → *nawabasigo* 'rope ladder').

[11] But see Vance (1980b) for the possible incomplete application of Lyman's Law among native speakers. See also fn.3 and fn.17.

(8) a. *oo* 'big' + *kaze* 'wind' → *ookaze* 'big wind'
aka 'red' + *sabi* 'rust' → *akasabi* 'red rust'

b. *oo* 'big' + *sora* 'sky' → *oo**zo**ra* 'big sky'
aka 'red' + *tama* 'ball' → *aka**da**ma* 'red ball'

The morphemes *oo* 'big' and *aka* 'red' are not morphemes which block rendaku, as the examples in (8b) show. It is the voiced obstruents in the second item that block rendaku as in (8a).

Another example of rendaku bleeding is that of semantic factors of the pair of morphemes in the compound. If the pair is a coordinate (dvandva) compound, i.e., with meanings which are parallel or opposite, it never appears in a rendaku form, as given in (9a) below. The first items are not rendaku blocking factors as examples in (9b) show, and the second items are potential rendaku candidates, as examples in (9c) show. (Examples are all NJ.)

(9) a. *siro* 'white' + *kuro* 'black' → *siro**ku**ro* 'black and white'
asi 'foot' + *kosi* 'waist' → *asi**ko**si* 'legs and waist (lower body)'

b. *siro* 'white' + *sake* 'sake' → *siro**za**ke* 'white sake'
asi 'foot' + *kakari* 'holder' → *asi**ga**kari* 'foothold'

c. *iro* 'color' + *kuro* 'black' → *iro**gu**ro* 'dark skin'
yowa 'weak' + *kosi* 'waist' → *yowa**go**si* 'timid'

See Otsu (1980), which gives a few more instances of supplemental conditions.

Examples that are not covered by the supplemental conditions, such as the non-rendaku forms in (3), will be treated as lexical exceptions, e.g., those compounds such as *hosi**ku**sa* 'hay' are lexicalized in non-rendaku forms.

3. Crucial Flaws of Rule-based Analyses

We have seen how rule-based analyses of rendaku work: (i) regard rendaku as a basic rule of native vocabulary; (ii) treat some non-native items as part of the native vocabulary (so that they undergo rendaku); and (iii) set supplemental conditions and include lexicalized compounds to cover the exceptions to (i) and (ii).

It has been discussed that a rule or a small set of rules cannot cover the whole rendaku paradigm (contra (iii), see McCawley 1968, Okumura 1980, Vance 1987, Ohno 1997, among others). The fact itself can be a flaw in rule-based analyses, but in this paper, I would like to pose questions primarily to the assumption in (ii), which contains an undefined notion of Japanization. The questions about (ii) will trigger a question about the assumption in (i).

3.1 On Japanization

The step in (ii) that justifies a set of non-NJ items in undergoing rendaku is described as a Japanization (or nativization) process as illustrated in 2.2. However, the motivation for and definition of Japanization are actually unclear other than in reference to rendaku.

One possible interpretation of the term 'Japanized' is 'frequently used by' and/or 'familiar to' native speakers of Japanese. However, very familiar and frequently used non-NJ items in (10) below never undergo rendaku.

(10) a. *kyaku* 'guest' (SJ) → *tomarikyaku* 'guest who stays overnight'
b. *seeseki* 'result' (SJ) → *kooseeseki* 'good result'
c. *keeki* 'cake' (from English) → *musikeeki* 'steamed cake'
d. *toire* 'toilet' (from English) → *koosyuutoire* 'public restroom'

On the other hand, some 'unfamiliar' SJ items such as *kooyaku* 'plaster' (*hutamatagooyaku* '(a person who is) sticking to both sides'), and many 'less familiar' SJ items such as *hookoo* 'service' or *tooroo* 'lantern' undergo rendaku (*dettibookoo* 'apprenticeship', *isidooroo* 'stone lantern').

Another possible interpretation of the term 'Japanized' is 'old', i.e., having a long history as part of the Japanese lexicon. Remember that the lone two rendaku examples of foreign items, *kappa* '(rain)coat' and *karuta* 'card', given in (6), are the oldest among the foreign vocabulary. However, not all 'old' non-NJ items undergo rendaku. The foreign items *pan* 'bread', *kasutera* 'sponge cake', and *tenpura* 'tempura' that are loans from Portuguese (*pão*, *Castella*, and *tempera*, respectively) are as old as the two exceptional rendaku foreign items (Umegaki 1980). However, these three items never undergo rendaku. Quite large numbers of SJ items have an older history than *karuta* and *kappa*, but the majority of them do not undergo rendaku. For example, the SJ word *hakase* 'specialist' is a well-used word and is seen in the earliest Japanese literature in the eighth century[12] (Ide 1982: 55), but the word does not undergo rendaku.

In fact, as Vance (1996: 24) says, "there seems no non-circular way of determining whether an element is Japanized". In other words, it is not Japanization that determines rendaku, but it is rendaku that determines Japanization. This conclusion raises another issue: a set of NJ items that never undergo rendaku, as in (2), must be regarded as 'de-Japanized'. I cannot find any evidence confirming this 'de-Japanization'. If Japanization is for the sole purpose of explaining rendaku (in a circular way), then just assigning [+/–Rendaku] to each lexical item, regardless of the reference to the lexical strata, will work better. Then, we do not need to maintain the assumption in (i) (Rendaku is a basic phonological rule of NJ).

[12] e.g. *Migino uta issyu, hakase X...* 'As for the *waka* on the right, Specialist X...' (*Man'yooshuu* 16: 3836: left).

Japanization of non-NJ items is often invoked when the *o-/go-* selection to express politeness is discussed. When NJ nouns are expressed in polite form, the prefix *o-* is used, as in ***o**sake* 'sake', ***o**imo* 'potato', ***o**kane* 'money', etc. Polite SJ noun forms basically use *go-* prefixation instead, as in ***go**kenkoo* 'health', ***go**ryokoo* 'travel', ***go**syuppatu* 'departure', etc. However, some SJ nouns take *o-* to show politeness, such as ***o**tya* 'tea', ***o**sanpo* 'walk', ***o**kyuuryoo* 'salary', etc. They can be called Japanized in terms of non-NJ items falling into the NJ pattern, *o-* prefixation (though its definition will be circular), and in terms of one-way reclassification since NJ items never fall into the SJ pattern (*go-* prefixation). However, in rendaku cases, it is bi-directional and we have to account for why some NJ items 'departed' from the NJ pattern (rendaku) if we follow the Japanization assumption. The other issue here is that the Japanized items in politeness marking are not identical with those of rendaku. The three Japanized items in politeness marking do not undergo rendaku (e.g. *nihon**t**ya* 'Japanese tea', **nihon**d**ya*). It is hard to accept that one lexical item is Japanized in one rule and not in another with or without a clear definition of Japanization.

3.2 On [+/–Rendaku] Specifications

Lexical specification for the rendaku selection by the feature [+/–Rendaku] is preferable, considering the fact that the NJ–SJ distinction ([+/–Native] distinction) is often hard. It seems, for example, that Itô and Mester (1986) regard the SJ items, *toohu* 'tofu' (p.52), *huton* 'futon' (p.53), and *kenka* 'quarrel' (p.54, fn.5), as [+Yamato] (NJ) items.[13] Despite the fact that native speakers often cannot identify whether a word is NJ or SJ in some cases, they 'know' whether the item would or would not undergo rendaku.

Further, the only way to maintain the assumption of the [+/–Rendaku] specification would be to assume that the items which have split forms are assigned either [+Rendaku] or [–Rendaku] underlyingly, and include lexicalized compounds whose second items are the exceptions to this specification. However, this is not borne out. The results of the rendaku experiments below reveal that native speakers select rendaku/non-rendaku forms by analogy from existing compounds. That is, the rendaku selection is not lexically specified in each item, such as by [+/–Rendaku]. We cannot determine which form (rendaku/non-rendaku) is the 'basic specification' or the 'exception' for an individual item.

[13] It appears that Otsu (1980) classifies some SJ items into NJ vocabulary. He does not mention that his first rendaku examples include SJ items (*kasi* 'candy' (his (1), (1b) in this paper), *taiko* 'drum' (his (2), (1a) in this paper), and *tyawan* 'cup' (his (6))) and introduces a new set of SJ items to show that some SJ items undergo rendaku.

4. Rendaku Experiment

The main purpose of the experiments is to test whether native speakers follow the predictions that rule-based analyses pose when they pronounce novel compounds, and to find a basis for rendaku/non-rendaku selection.

4.1 Formats

I asked native Japanese speakers to decide on a pronunciation, either rendaku or non-rendaku, for novel compounds. All first items in compounds are real NJ items in current use.

The first experiments were held in the USA. I interviewed eight native speakers of Japanese and asked them to pronounce novel compounds (choices between rendaku and non-rendaku forms were not given). The subjects had spent three to seven years in the USA, and their ages ranged from 20 to 38. Four of them were male and the other four were female.

The second experiments were carried out at the International Christian University (ICU), in Tokyo, Japan. I asked subjects to fill out questionnaire sheets in which the novel compounds and choices between rendaku and non-rendaku forms were listed in hiragana with a meaning for each word and compound. The subjects were 14 students and 25 alumni (total 35), whose ages ranged from 18 to 47, but most (29 out of the 35) were in their twenties. Twenty of them were male and the remaining 15 were female.

When the two sets of results are given, e.g. (8 out of 8) (30 out of 35), the first is the results from interviews in the USA and the other is the results of the questionnaire in Japan. They can be distinguished according to the number of the total number of subjects (8 vs. 35). Some items were asked only in Japan. The birthplace and hometown of the subjects were not factors in determining rendaku tendencies.

4.2 Exceptional Rendaku/non-rendaku Forms 1 — Semantic Factor

The first two items test whether or not the analysis of the feature [+/–Rendaku] assignment to each item is relevant. The first item to consider is *kami* 'hair' (NJ) that has all rendaku forms in compounds except *kurokami* 'black hair', e.g. *maegami* 'forelock', *nihongami* 'Japanese hairstyle', *araigami* 'washed hair', etc. The second item is *ti* 'blood' (NJ) that has no rendaku form besides *hanadi* 'nosebleed', e.g. *ikiti* 'lifeblood', *namati* '(lit.) raw blood', *kaeriti* '(lit.) returned blood'.

If a rendaku selection is lexically specified by the feature [+/–Rendaku], *kami* 'hair' would be assigned [+Rendaku] and *ti* 'blood' [–Rendaku], with the lexicalized compounds of *kurokami* 'black hair' and *hanadi* 'nosebleed' as exceptions to the feature specifications. Hence, the prediction for a novel compound will be rendaku for *kami* 'hair' and non-rendaku for *ti* 'blood'.

The results reveal that those predictions are not borne out. For the novel compound, *siro* 'white' + *kami* 'hair' ('gray hair'), the majority chose the non-rendaku form *sirokami* (8 out of 8) (19 out of 23)[14]. For the novel compound *mimi* 'ear' + *ti* 'blood', the majority chose the rendaku form *mimidi* (7 out of 8) (30 out of 35). Let us summarize these in a chart:

(11) a. *kami* 'hair' = [+Rendaku] plus exceptional *kurokami* 'black hair'
prediction: rendaku for a novel compound
result: non-rendaku for *siro* 'white' + *kami* 'hair' → *sirokami*

b. *ti* 'blood' = [–Rendaku] plus exceptional *hanadi* 'nosebleed'
prediction: non-rendaku for a novel compound
result: rendaku for *mimi* 'ear' + *ti* 'blood' → *mimidi*

There would be no reasonable motivation to restate that *kami* 'hair' is actually [–Rendaku] and that a bunch of rendaku forms are lexicalized, or the opposite in the case of *ti* 'blood'. It is not only unreasonable but also incorrect because of other experimental results below. For the novel compound of *aka* 'red' + *kami* 'hair', the majority chose the rendaku form *akagami* 'red hair' (23 out of 35) as predicted. As for another novel compound *oo* 'big' + *ti* 'blood', half chose the non-rendaku form *ooti* '(lit.) big bleeding' (18 out of 35). The assumption of the feature assignment of [+/–Rendaku] to each item itself is thus questionable.

If the rendaku selection is not specified for each item, a question that naturally comes up is: "What makes native speakers select rendaku/non-rendaku forms?" The factor that made native speakers choose the unpredicted forms *sirokami* 'gray hair' and *mimidi* 'earbleed' seems to be the fact that they are parallel to other exceptional forms in meaning. It is reasonable to make a hypothesis as in (12) below.

(12) **Rendaku selection** (first version)
Native speakers refer to existing compounds and refer to a semantically parallel form when they determine the rendaku/non-rendaku form of a novel compound.

(13)		**existing form**	**new form**
	a.	*kurokami* 'black hair'	*sirokami* 'gray hair'
	b.	*hanadi* 'nosebleed'	*mimidi* 'earbleed'

Of course, 'existing' here means 'existing in the individual's lexicon'.

The statement in (12) indicates that if a person did not know the compound *kurokami* 'black hair' (and yet knows other compounds of *kami* 'hair'), he or she will select a novel compound with *kami* 'hair' in rendaku

[14] The total number of the subjects is 23, rather than 35, because one did not answer this question and the remaining 11 felt either given candidate of *sirakami* or *siragami*, where the first item *siro* 'white' undergoes a sound alternation, was preferred. Interestingly, at that time, 9 out of the remaining 11 chose the rendaku form (*siragami*), which is similar to the existing word for 'gray hair' *siraga*. It is also interesting in another sense; if the word *siro* 'white' is followed by *tama* 'ball', it is either *sirodama*, or *siratama* (see (3) above). The sound alternation in the first element is not correlated with the decision about rendaku/non-rendaku.

form. Similarly, if a person does not know the compound *hanadi* 'nosebleed' (and knows other compounds with *ti* 'blood'), he or she select a novel compound with *ti* 'hair' in non-rendaku form.

4.3 Exceptional Rendaku/non-rendaku Forms 2 — Phonetic Factors

It should be noted that the items *kuro* 'black' and *siro* 'white' are somewhat similar in sound as well, which suggests that not only semantics but phonetics may also be playing a role in selecting rendaku/non-rendaku forms.

The next examples are selected to test phonetic factors. There are existing compounds, which include *kusa* 'grass' (NJ) as the second item, *wakakusa* 'young grass' and *igusa* 'rush'. Hence, if phonetic similarity is a factor of rendaku reference, it is expected that phonetically similar novel compounds *aka* 'red' + *kusa* 'grass' and *ki* 'yellow' + *kusa* 'grass' will follow the existing pattern; *akakusa* for 'red grass' and *kigusa* for 'yellow grass'. The results can form to this expectation. Twenty-five out of 35 chose the expected non-rendaku form for 'red grass' (*akakusa*) and 25 out of 35 chose the expected rendaku forms for 'yellow grass' (*kigusa*). These results also support the hypothesis that rendaku is not specified for each word. The statement in (12) can be restated as in (14) below.

(14) **Rendaku selection** (second version)
Native speakers refer to existing compounds and refer to a semantically and/or phonetically parallel form when they determine the rendaku/non-rendaku form of a novel compound.

The expression 'phonetically parallel' does not only mean 'similar in sound'. The number of preceding morae may also be a factor. For example, in existing compounds, *hon* 'book' (SJ) undergoes rendaku only when the first item has three or more morae. e.g. *ehon* 'picture book', *seehon* 'book binding', *yoohon* 'Western book' vs. *mangabon* 'comic book', *bunkobon* 'pocket book', *tankoobon* '(kind of book)'.[15] The results of the novel compounding tests are: *karu* 'light' + *hon* 'book' → *karuhon* 'light book' (21 out of 35); *karugaru* 'light' + *hon* 'book' → *karugarubon* 'light book' (31 out of 35).[16]

4.4 Non-rendaku Forms and Rendaku Selectional Factors

The word *taka* 'hawk' (NJ) does not undergo rendaku in any compounds (*hagetaka* 'vulture', *yotaka* 'nighthawk', *kumataka* '(lit.) bear hawk'). Results from the novel compounding tests are: *oo* 'big' + *taka* 'hawk' → *ootaka* (8 out of 8) (33 out of 35); and *aka* 'red' + *taka* 'hawk' → *akataka* (8 out of 8) (33 out of 35). We do not need the de-Japanization hypothesis

---

[15] The sole exception is *syarebon* 'pun book' (Kindaiti et al. 1994: 524).

[16] The numbers given above indicate that the condition in (14) is not a decisive factor for rendaku, though it is very influential.

or the feature specification of [–Rendaku] on the item to account for this. In this case, there is no possible reference to other existing rendaku forms. Then the two items are compounded without undergoing rendaku.

The word *surume* 'dried squid' (NJ) does not occur in any compounds. Results from the novel compounding tests are: *oo* 'big' + *surume* 'dried squid' → *oosurume* (8 out of 8) (33 out of 35); and *aka* 'red' + *surume* 'dried squid' → *akasurume* (8 out of 8) (33 out of 35). This result, along with the *taka* 'hawk' case above, strongly suggests that native speakers do not create rendaku forms if there are no existing rendaku forms.

The statement in (14) does not work here because there are no existing possible references, though the items above follow a rigid pattern of non-rendaku. The rendaku condition must be like (15) below:

(15) **Rendaku condition** (final version)

If there is no possible reference to existing rendaku forms, the item does not undergo rendaku in a novel compound.

(Only when there are existing rendaku forms (in the individual lexicon), may the item undergo rendaku.)

The statement in (15) indicates that rendaku is not an automatic process of voicing (of NJ items) in compounds. In other words, the productivity of rendaku has been challenged. Some items (especially foreign items) do not undergo rendaku because they have no existing examples in rendaku form, or they have never been pronounced in rendaku form.[17] This is a fact of rendaku regardless of the lexical strata. It also indicates that rendaku selection is largely dependent on each individual because each individual refers to his or her own lexicon.

These generalizations support the view that native speakers simply memorize whether rendaku occurs for individual compounds and do not internalize the regularities in the behavior of many second items in compounds (Vance 1980b: 253), and that native speakers make the internal generalizations available to them (McCawley 1977: 55, 59f, Vance 1980b: 263). There is a consensus in *kokugogaku* (traditional Japanese linguistics) that rendaku used to be a very productive phonological rule in Japanese at one time in the past—but it subsequently ceased, leaving lexical residue (Hamada 1960, Okumura 1980, Endo 1989, etc.).[18] The condition in (15) supports that view stating that only when an individual refers to the lexical

[17] This view questions Lyman's Law as a synchronic factor as well. What (15) would say is that items which include a voiced obstruent never undergo rendaku because there are no rendaku forms of them in existing compounds.

[18] Endo (1989: 291) says that the system of rendaku had already ceased in the Kamakura Period (1192–1333). Hamada (1960: 7–11) says that rendaku is remnant of a phonological phenomenon in the pre-kana (kana = Japanese native syllabary) period (before 712), pointing out that the irregularity of rendaku is seen in the earliest Japanese literature in the eighth century.

remnant of rendaku, may he or she select rendaku forms for pronouncing new compounds.

5. Conclusion

I have shown that the validity of rule-based rendaku analyses is marginalized in two major ways. First, the information of lexical strata, or the distinction of [+/–Native], is not the factor determining rendaku. Second, rendaku is not lexically specified in each compounding item. I have shown that native speakers refer to existing compounds to select rendaku/non-rendaku forms for a novel compound. Although I could not delineate a particular environment in which rendaku occurs, I proposed a condition that states when rendaku is permitted (given as (15)). This axiom implies that rendaku is not a productive synchronic phonological rule. It contradicts the rule-based analyses of Otsu (1980) and Itô and Mester (1986), but supports the lexical analyses by Hamada (1960), Vance (1980b, 1987, 1996) etc.

References

Endo, Kunimoto. 1989. *Kokugo hyoogen to on'in genshoo.* (Expression in Japanese and phonological phenomena) Tokyo: Shinten-sha.

Hamada, Atsushi. 1960. Rendaku to renjoo. (Rendaku and *Renjoo* (sandhi)) *Kokugo-kokubun* 29:10. 1–16.

Hashimoto, Shinkichi. 1928. Hagyoo-shiin no hensen ni tsuite. (On changes of /h/) in Okakura sensee kanreki shukugakai (ed.) *Okakura sensee kinen ronbunshuu.* [reprinted in Hashimoto 1950. 29–45.]

————. 1944. Koma no inanaki. (Neigh of a horse) in Nihon bungaku-hoo kokkai (ed.) *Kokubungaku soowa.* [reprinted in Hashimoto 1950. 47–50.]

————. 1950. *Kokugo on'in no kenkyuu.* (Studies of phonology in National Language) Tokyo: Iwanami.

Ide, Itaru. 1982. Kodai no goi I. (Vocabulary in Nara Period (710–792) and before that) in Sakakura, Atsushi (ed.) *Kooza Kokugo-shi: Goi-shi.* (History of Japanese Vocabulary) 29–71. Tokyo: Taishukan.

Itô, Junko and Ralf-Armin Mester. 1986. The Phonology of Voicing in Japanese: Theoretical Consequences for Morphological Accessibility. *Linguistic Inquiry* 17. 49-73.

————. 1995. Japanese Phonology. in Goldsmith, John A. (ed.) *The Handbook of Phonological Theory.* 817–838. Oxford: Blackwell.

————. 1999. The Phonological Lexicon. in Natsuko Tsujimura (ed.) *The Handbook of Japanese Linguistics.* 62–100. Oxford: Blackwell.

Kokugo Gakkai. (ed.) 1980. *Kokugogaku daijiten.* (Encyclopedia of Japanese language study) Tokyo: Tokyo-Dô.

Martin, Samuel E. 1952. *Morphophonemics of Standard Colloquial Japanese.* Supplement to *Language, Language Dissertation No. 47.*

McCawley, James D. 1968. *The Phonological Component of a Grammar of Japanese.* The Hague: Mouton.

———. 1977. Acquisition models as models of acquisition. in Fasold, Ralph W. and Roger W. Shuy (eds.). *Studies in Language Variation.* 51–64. Washington: Georgetown University Press.

Kindaiti, Kyoosuke, Umetomo Saeki, Hatsutaroo Ooishi, and Masaaki Nomura. (eds.) 1994. *Shinsen Kokugo Jiten, 7th edition.* (New Japanese Dictionary) Tokyo: Shoogakukan.

Numoto, Katsuaki. 1986. *Nihon kanji-on no rekishi.* (History of Sino-Japanese sound) Tokyo: Tokyo-Dô.

Ohno, Kazutoshi. 1997. Rendaku -its complex status-. ms. University of Arizona.

Okumura, Mitsuo. 1952. Ji-on no rendaku ni tsuite. (On Rendaku of Sino-Japanese) *Kokugo-kokubun* 21:5. 9–22.

———. 1980. Rendaku. in Kokugo Gakkai (ed.). 925–926.

Otsu, Yukio. 1980. Some Aspects of Rendaku in Japanese and Related Problems. in Otsu and Farmer (eds.). 207–227.

Otsu, Yukio and Ann Farmer. (eds.) 1980. *Theoretical Issues in Japanese Linguistics.* MIT Working Papers in Linguistics; vol.2. Cambridge, MA: Massachusetts Institute of Technology.

Rice, Karen. 1997. Japanese NC Clusters and the Redundancy of Postnasal Voicing. *Linguistic Inquiry* 28. 541–551.

Sato, Kiyoshi. 1982. Wasei kango no rekishi. (History of Japanese-made Sino-Japanese) in Morioka, Kenji. et. al. *Kooza Nihongogaku 4*: *Goi-shi.* (History of Vocabulary) 70–91. Tokyo: Meiji-shoin.

Shinmura, Izuru. 1928. Ha-gyoo keishin-on enkaku koo. (Thoughts on the historical transition of /F/) in *Kokugo-kokubun no kenkyuu.* [reprinted in Shinmura 1971. 180–189.]

———. 1929. Kokugo ni okeru FH ryoo-on no katoki. (Transitional period of /F/–/h/ in the National Language) in *Miyake hakase koki shukuga kinen ronbun-shuu.* [reprinted in Shinmura 1971. 190–196.]

———. 1971. *Shinmura Izuru Zenshuu* 4. (Collections of Shinmura, Izuru) Tokyo: Chikuma shoboo.

Tamura, Suzuko. 1972. Gooseego ni mirareru onso kootai. (Phonemic changes found in compounds) *Kooza Nihongo Kyooiku* 8. 116–144. Tokyo: Waseda University Institute of Language.

Tsujimura, Natsuko. 1996. *An Introduction to Japanese Linguistics.* Oxford: Blackwell.

Ueda, Kazutoshi. 1898. Gogaku sooken. (New ideas in language) *Teikoku bungaku* 4: 1. Tokyo: University of Tokyo. [Reprinted in Ueda, Kazutoshi. 1903. *Kokugo no tame*: vol.2 (For National Language) as "P-on kou" (Thoughts on P sound)]

Umegaki, Minoru. 1980. Gairai-go. (Loan words) in Kokugo Gakkai (ed.). 135.

Vance, Timothy J. 1980a. Comments on Ôtsu. in Ôtsu and Farmer (eds.). 229–236.

———. 1980b. The psychological status of a constraint on Japanese consonant alternation. *Linguistics* 18. 245–267

———. 1987. *An Introduction to Japanese Phonology.* Albany: State University of New York Press.

———. 1996. Sequential Voicing in Sino-Japanese. *Journal of the Association of Teachers of Japanese* 30. 22-43.

Part III

Pragmatics, Discourse Analysis, and Sociolinguistics

A New Approach to the Analysis of the Sentence Final Particles *ne* and *yo*: An Interface Between Prosody and Pragmatics*

SANAE EDA
The Ohio State University

1. Introduction

This paper explores issues relevant to the understanding of the functions of Japanese sentence final particles (SFPs hereafter) , *ne* and *yo*, with focus on their interaction with sentence final intonation patterns. It argues that the "meaning" of *ne* and *yo* in each context can be derived as the result of the interaction between the lexical property of *ne* and *yo* on the one hand, and the sentence final intonation pattern on the other.[1]

---

*I would like to specially thank Mineharu Nakayama for helpful comments and suggestions. Address for correspondence: Sanae Eda (eda.1@osu.edu), Department of East Asian Languages and Literatures, Cunz Hall Rm. 208, 1841 Millikin Road, Columbus, OH 43210 USA

[1] Throughout the paper, the use of the plural form, SFPs, will refer only to the two particles, *ne* and *yo*, unless otherwise indicated. The scope of the present discussion is limited to the examination of the use of the SFPs at the sentence final position, not including the use of what Uyeno (1971: 48) terms the "interjective" use of SFPs. In addition, *ne* and *nee* are treated as variants of each other, following the assumption shared among the studies which have examined the SFP *ne*.

Researchers interested in Japanese SFPs have almost always pointed out the dialogue specificity of SFPs: that is, while they are used extremely frequently in spoken dialogues, their use in written text is limited to reported dialogues, or letters and children's literature emulating the spoken dialogues. Despite the recognition of the importance of the roles of SFPs as a marker in discourse to facilitate the communication, we are still waiting to see the proposal of a general and comprehensive theory which can account for all the aspects of the functions of SFPs.

This paper will advance our understanding of the functions of SFPs in the following three ways. First, recognizing the apparent inconsistencies which have existed among the previous theories of SFPs, it will provide an answer to the puzzlement of why *ne* and *yo* in some contexts behave as if they were the opposites of each other, and in some other contexts as interchangeable. Second, the proposed theory will provide an explanation for the fact that *ne* shows apparent variation in meaning under variation in intonation. Third, the proposed theory will readily explain the dialogue specific nature of SFPs and the obligatory uses of *ne* in certain context.

The examination of the intonation pattern with which the utterance is produced will play a crucial role in providing critiques on the existing body of literature on SFPs (in Section 2) and in suggesting a new way of analyzing SFPs (in Section 3).[2] The diacritics √!, √, /, !, and ^ will be placed in parentheses immediately following my own example sentences to indicate the appropriate intonation patterns to be used to make the utterance acceptable in the intended context. The inventory of the intonation patterns is based on Venditti et al. (1998), and will be discussed in Section 3.2 and 3.3. (Note the diacritics are of my own.) When the examples were taken from other works which did not specify the intonation, the diacritics are given in square brackets [ ] instead of parentheses ( ).

2. Previous Research on SFPs

In order to help us systematically analyze the nature of the "missing pieces" in the field, and to motivate the proposal of a more general and comprehensive theory which can fill the existing gaps, it will be meaningful to review literature relevant to the understanding of the functions of SFPs. Section 2 will, thus, present review the theories of SFPs which have been proposed to date.

[2] In discussing the sentence final intonation patterns, our investigation is limited to that of standard Japanese, spoken in Tokyo area.

2.1 Works Published Between 1975 and 1995

A chronological review of literature reveals that the works on the SFPs published between 1975 and 1995 can be divided into two general categories: 1) works which are based on the examination of the attribution of information and 2) those which focused on the communicative functions of SFPs. In this section, we will first examine these two major frameworks of analysis of SFPs, with a discussion on their shortcomings and inconsistencies.

Kamio (1978) is one of the most influential works which outlines the theory based on the notion, "speaker's territory of information," as a basis for analyzing "the relations between certain sentence forms and their uses in speech situations" (p. 213). Extending this line of analysis, the functions of the SFPs *ne* and *yo* have frequently been discussed in terms of the attribution of information (Kamio 1978, 1990, 1994, 1997; Oso 1986; Cheng 1987; Masuoka, 1991).[3, 4] The assumption on which their analyses are based is that the speaker's choice of the SFPs is determined on the basis of the speaker's evaluation of whose information (speaker or hearer) is being communicated in the utterance, and of the relative psychological distances between the speaker/hearer and the information. Noting that *yo* is typically used to convey the information which belongs to the speaker, and *ne* when the information belongs to the hearer, most works generated in this framework have proposed that the functions of *ne* and *yo* are the opposites of each other. Examples (1) and (2) illustrate these uses of *yo* and *ne.*

(1)	Satoo-san	wa	gakusee	desu	*yo.*	(√)
	Mr. Sato	TOP	student	is	SFP	
	"Mr. Sato is a student (I assure you)."					

(2)	Satoo-san	wa	gakusee	desu	*ne.*	(√)
	Mr. Sato	TOP	student	is	SFP	
	"Mr. Sato is a student, right?"					

Note, however, that *ne* can also be used in making a statement about the speaker's own experience or plan of action, as illustrated in examples (3) and (4), which is inconsistent with the functions proposed within the framework of analysis based on the attribution of information.

---

[3] This term was used by Katagiri (1997).

[4] Although Oso (1986) does not explicitly refer to the term "territory of information," her comment was apparently inspired by Kamio's influential work.

(3)	Watasi ga	gakusee no	koro	wa
	I NOM	student GEN	time when	TOP
	mainiti	tanosikatta	desu *ne*…	(^)
	every day	fun-PAST	is SFP	

"When I was a student, I had fun every day, you know..."

(4)	Kono hon,	asita	motte kimasu	*ne*	(√ , !)
	this book	tomorrow	bring	SFP	

"I'll bring this book tomorrow, okay?"

Theories which heavily relied on the contrast between the relative psychological distances between the speaker and the hearer cannot appropriately explain this apparent paradox of why *ne* can be used in both cases, when the information belongs to the hearer on the one hand, as was illustrated in example (2), and to the speaker on the other, as was illustrated in examples (3) and (4). In addition, regarding them as being the opposite for each other, they cannot well explain the instances in which *yo* and *ne* are used in the same utterance such as (5).[5]

(5)	Kono	sakana,	tabete	mo	daizyoobu	desu	*yo*	*ne*. (√)
	this	fish	eat	even	okay	is	SFP	SFP

"It's okay to eat this fish, don't you think?"

The shortcomings of analysis based on the information attribution such as these started to be pointed out in the early 1990's, the recognition of which lead some researchers to propose a different framework of analysis of SFPs based on the examination of their communicative functions (McGloin 1990; Izuhara 1993; Onoe 1997). Within the "new" framework of analysis, researchers tended to analyze the function of *ne* in terms of how its use increases the rapport between the speaker and the hearer, emphasizing that *ne* in such instances can be replaced by *yo*.

Although the second account can explain the uses of *ne* exemplified in (3) and (4), their weakness as a theory of SFPs lies in their partial reliance on the information attribution framework since it alone still cannot adequately explain the uses of *yo* and *ne* exemplified in (1) and (2). In other words, neither information attribution approach nor communicative function approach is complete and sufficient in explaining all the functions of the two SFPs, *ne* and *yo*.

---

[5] See Shirakawa (1992) for a fuller discussion on this issue.

The most serious deficit of the works mentioned so far is that they do not take into consideration the fact that *ne* shows apparent variation in meaning under variation in sentence final intonation, and that such alternation of intonation alone could negatively influence the acceptability judgment in discourse, other things being equal. For instance, let us examine the following examples taken from Kamio (1987):

(6) Ii tenki da *ne / nee.* [! , ^]
nice weather is SFP
'It's a beautiful day!"

(7) Anata wa kibun ga warui mitai desu *ne.* [!]
you TOP feeling-NOM bad look is SFP
'It looks like you are feeling sick, aren't you?'

If utterances (6) and (7) were produced with a full rising intonation instead of the intonations indicated in brackets, other things being equal, these utterances would "sound odd" in the same context. This variation of acceptability judgment clearly indicates that the examination of the relative psychological distance between speaker/hearer and the information being transmitted alone cannot adequately explain the functions of *ne.*

In this sense, it is difficult to expect any theory which fails to recognize the influence of sentence final intonation to be capable of providing us with a fuller understanding of the functions of *ne*. The following section, Section 2.2, will summarize some of the more recent theories, which attempted to look at the influence of intonation in analyzing the functions of SFPs, and their limitations.

2.2 Examination of SFPs and Their Interaction with Intonation

Starting in the late 1990's, researchers started to attempt to understand the functions of *ne* and *yo* in light of their interaction with discourse and intonation patterns (Katagiri 1997, 1998; Takubo and Kinsui 1996, 1998). Their approaches are uniquely different from the previous analyses of SFPs in that they propose that each intonation pattern carries certain meaning, *independently* of the grammatical and lexical elements, SFPs being one of such elements, and that the meanings of utterances can be derived as the result of the interaction between the grammatical and lexical elements on the one hand and intonation patterns on the other. The functions of *ne* and *yo* are defined in their analyses in a very simple way, and the examination of *ne* and *yo* focuses more on how their functions interact with the intonation patterns, and how the speaker's intentions, such as "question," "expressing agreement," "increasing rapport between the speaker and hearer," etc., are derived as the result of such interaction. This point characterizes their works as significantly different from others which also discussed the functions of SFPs in relation to the intonation patterns, such as Oso (1986), Jorden and Noda (1987), and Hubbard (1992).

One serious limitation of Takubo & Kinsui (1996, 1998) and Katagiri (1997, 1998) is, however, their reliance on too simplistic an analysis of intonation patters. In their frameworks of analysis, intonation patterns are divided simply into two categories; Katagiri examines the intonation patterns in terms of rising and falling, and Takubo & Kinsui categorizes them into "expectation for response" (hannô-yôkyû-kei) and "non-expectation for response (hi-hannô-yôkyû-kei). However, as we will discuss in detail in Section 3.2 and 3.3, an empirical study has revealed that the "rising intonation" alone can be further categorized into five distinct types (Venditti et al. 1998; Maeda et al. 1998), and that each type of rising intonation is associated with a certain set of semantic implications. In light of the availability of such data, this binary categorization is simply inadequate.

2.3 Need for a More Comprehensive Theory of SFPs

In this section, we have examined the inconsistencies and shortcomings that have hitherto existed among the theories of SFPs. A more comprehensive theory that accounts for all aspects of the SFPs *ne* and *yo* is urgently called for, and a candidate for such a theory needs to be able to provide explanations to the following behaviors of SFPs: 1) that *ne* and *yo* appear to have opposite meanings in some cases, and the same meaning in other, and 2) that *ne* shows apparent variation under differing intonation patterns. Section 3 will present a proposal for a general theory of SFPs by looking at the functions of SFPs in terms of their interaction with sentence final intonation patterns.

3. A Proposal of a New Analysis of SFPs

This section presents the two main elements of the proposed theory of SFPs. First, in section 3.1, the lexical properties of *ne* and *yo* are defined. Section 3.2 and 3.3 will describe the inventory of sentence final intonation patterns assumed in this theory. In Section 3.4 and 3.5, we will examine how the two elements interact with each other to convey the intentions of the speakers. Finally, Section 3.6 will discuss how the proposed theory overcomes the shortcomings of previous analysis of SFPs and how it can explain all the uses of *yo* and *ne* without any inconsistency.

3.1 Lexical Properties of *ne* and *yo*

The proposed framework assumes, first, that the "meaning" of each use of *ne* and *yo* can be derived as the result of the interaction between the lexical property of *ne* and *yo* on the one hand, and the sentence final intonation pattern on the other. The lexical properties of *ne* and *yo* are defined as follows:

> *Yo* is used to indicate to the hearer that the speaker has already accepted the propositional content of the utterance.
>
> *Ne* is a discourse marker which signals the speaker's expectation/request for an immediate response from the hearer, and also indicate that the speaker is leaving some room for the hearer to make comments on the propositional content of the utterance.

While the definition of *yo* is similar to that proposed by Takubo & Kinsui (1997), the definition of *ne* differs from their proposal. The added modification is intended to account for why the use of *ne* is obligatory in some contexts.

3.2 Inventory of Sentence Final Intonation Patterns

Another important assumption on which the proposed framework is based is that sentence final intonation patterns can convey paralinguistic information *independently* of the lexical and syntactic structures they interact with (cf. Pierrehumbert & Hirschberg, 1990; Katagiri 1996, 1997).

Studies attempting to seek the interface between pragmatics and prosody, motivated independently of the research on SFPs, have provided empirical data demonstrating how five sentence final intonation patterns were judged differently on eight semantic scales, indicating that different sentence final intonation patterns can cue different intentions of the speaker. In the experimental studies conducted by Venditti and her colleagues, the subjects were asked to listen to utterances (for example, *Naoya ni* "[this is] for Naoya," with a dative case marker *ni* at the utterance final position) produced with five intonation types: incredulity question rise (incredQ), information question rise (infoQ), prominence-lending rise (prom), insisting rise (insist), and rise-fall boundary movement (rise-fall). These five intonation types are schematically represented in Table 3-1 below (taken from Venditti and Maeda (1998, p.2); diacritics are my own). Subjects were then asked to rate each utterance in terms of how strongly they agreed or disagreed with eight statements, such as "the speaker is explaining something," and "the speaker is confirming something."

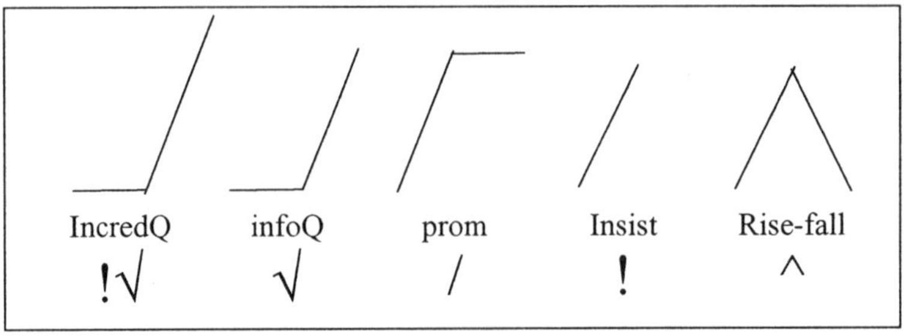

Table 3-1: Schematic Shapes of the Intonation Types

Their data is valuable in that the categorization of intonation patterns is based on the pitch modulation of the speaker's voice, which was observed in terms of its fundamental frequency (F0) contours. In addition, the semantic properties of each intonation pattern was assessed by a scientific method, and was not based on the subjective judgment of one or two individuals. The present framework follows Venditti and her colleagues, and analyzes the functions of *ne* and *yo* in terms of these five intonation patterns, rather than categorizing them simply into two, as was the case in Katagiri (1996, 1997) and Takubo & Kinsui (1996, 1998).

3.3 Characteristics of Two Sentence Final Intonation Patterns on Two Semantic Scales

For the purpose of illustration, let us examine more closely the characteristics of two intonation patterns, √ and **!**.

Taking a subset of the data presented by Venditti et al. (1998), Table 3-2 below summarizes the characteristics of sentence final intonation patterns, √ and **!**, rated on two semantic scales.

√	!
+ confirming	- confirming
- explaining	+ explaining

Table 3-2: Characteristics of Two Sentence Final Intonation Patterns on Two Semantic Scales

Note that these two intonation patterns cue the intentions of the speakers that are complementary to each other. For instance, the utterances produced with the so-called "information question contour" (√) were constantly perceived as indicating the speaker's intention of confirming something to the hearer, and the same utterances were rated negatively on the scale stating that the speaker was explaining something. The ratings of the "insisting" intonation (!) had a pattern exactly the opposite of that of √.

As for the physical manifestation of these two intonation patterns, the following two figures (Figures 3-1 and 3-2) show the F0 contours of utterances[6]: *hontoo ni nara no na no* (√) "Is it really [the one] from Nara?" and *hontoo ni nara no na no* (!) "It really is [the one] from Nara." While the pitch contour of √ is characterized by a full rise from the bottom to the top of the speaker's pitch range, ! contour is characterized by a rise to the mid point of the speaker's pitch range.

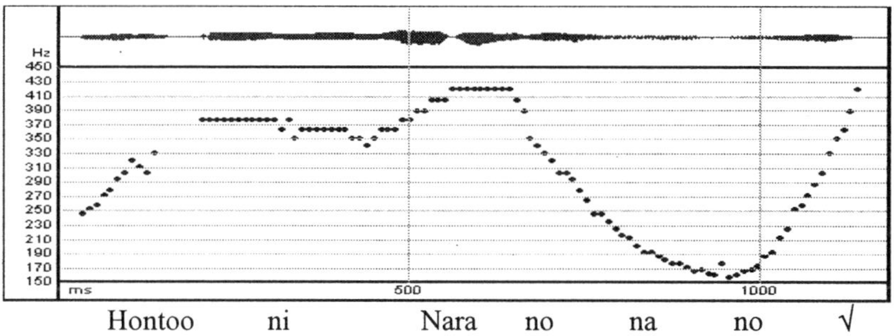

Figure 3-1: An Utterance with √ Intonation

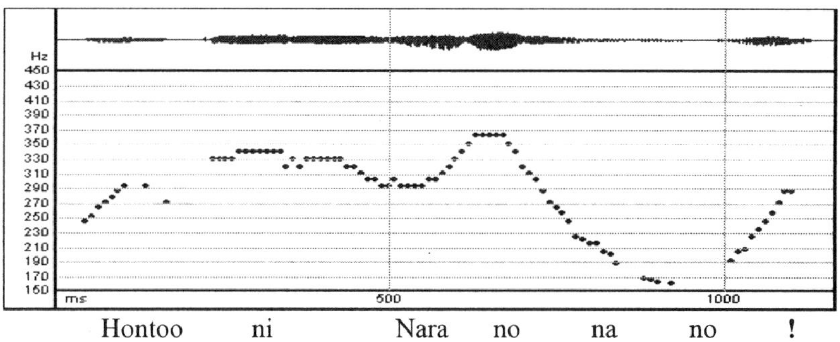

Figure 3-2: An Utterance with ! Intonation

A naïve native speaker of standard Japanese read the target sentences in an artificially manipulated context. The speaker was instructed to pay attention to what messages she needed to communicate, but no explicit instruction was given to manipulate the pitch modulation.

---

[6] I would like to thank Hiroko Niioka, a native speaker of Tokyo dialect, for her assistance in recording the utterances used in this paper.

3.4 Interaction Between Intonation and SFPs

Now, let us examine two utterances with SFP *ne* which differ minimally in the aspect of intonation: *hontoo ni Nara no na no ne* (√) "It is really [the one] from Nara, right?" and *hontoo ni Nara no na no ne* (**!**) "It is really [the one] from Nara, you see?"

A native speaker of Japanese would paraphrase the first utterance with full-rise intonation (√) as something like the following: the speaker thinks that the item under discussion is from Nara, but since she is not sure whether it is really the case, she wants the hearer to confirm her assumption. On the other hand, the latter utterance with **!** intonation will be interpreted as the following: the speaker and the hearer probably share the information, and the speaker is making a comment, assuming that the hearer would also be aware of this, that the item under discussion is from Nara. The F0 contours of these utterances are shown in Figures 3-3 and 3-4, respectively.

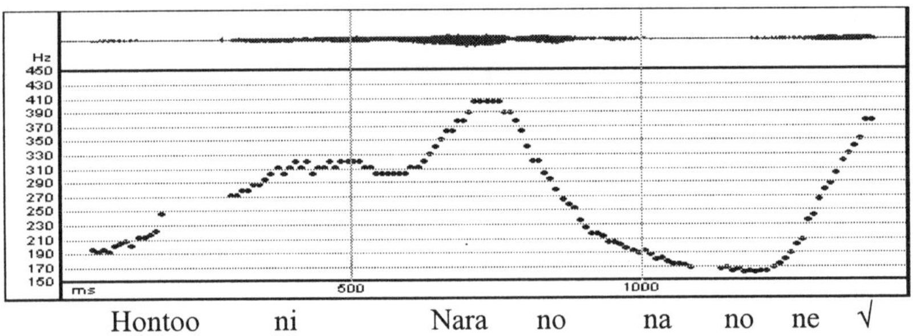

Figure 3-3: An Utterance with √ Intonation + *ne*

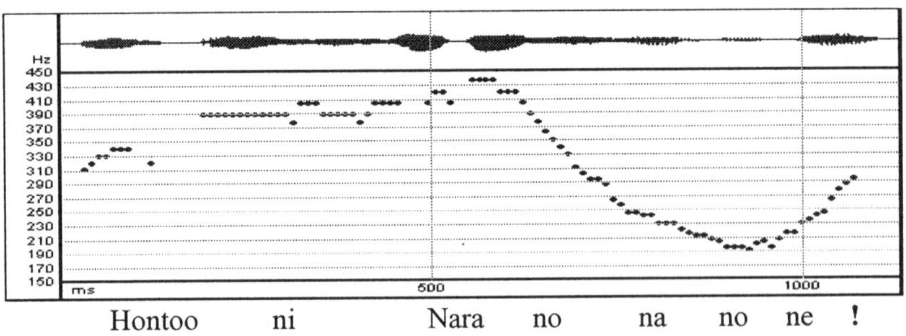

Figure 3-4: An Utterance with **!** Intonation + *ne*

A brief examination would reveal that the variation in meaning of *ne* in these utterances can be attributed to the sentence final intonation patterns associated with them.[7] Furthermore, observing the parallel between the two intonational minimal pairs, it is reasonable to predict that the speaker's intentions such as "confirming the assumptions" and "explaining, or making a statement," as summarized in Table 3-1 (in Section 3.2), are being communicated by the intonation patterns. This is strong evidence to show that functions such as "confirming" and "commenting," which have been analyzed in the past as an intrinsic part of the function of *ne* are actually obtained by the interaction between *ne* and the intonation patterns with which it appears.

3.5 Interaction Between Intonation and SFP *yo*

The SFP *yo* appears to differ from *ne* in one respect, namely, that *yo* is not readily influenced by the variation in intonation as *ne* is. Figure 3-5 below shows the F0 contour of an utterance, *hontoo ni Nara no na no yo* (√) "It is really [the one] from Nara, I am telling you."

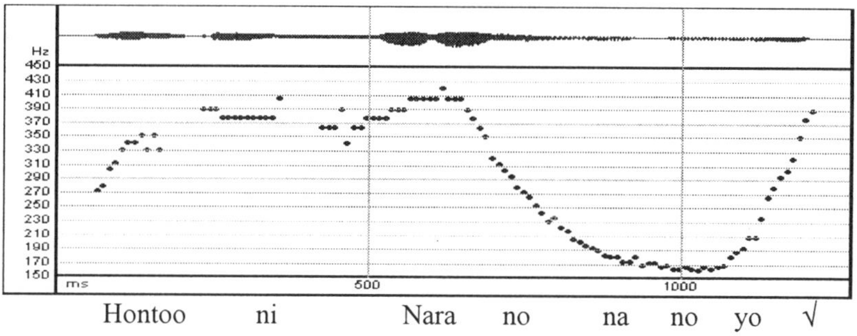

Figure 3-5: An Utterance with √ Intonation + *yo*

Comparing Figure 3-5 with Figures 3-3 and 3-4, we can see that while the SFP *yo* is produced with a full rising intonation, the utterance clearly conveys the sense that the speaker is "explaining" to the hearer the fact that the item under discussion is from Nara, and that the speaker is being emphatic about the information being communicated.

---

[7] The shapes of F0 contours shown in figures 3-3 and 3-4 differ also in their overall prosodic structures due to the additional intonation phrase boundary in the utterance shown in figure 3-3. This point, however, is beyond the scope of the current paper, and will be left as a topic for future investigation.

4. Discussion and Future Research

4.1 How does the Proposed Theory Overcome the Shortcomings of the Previous Analyses of SFPs?

As was discussed in Section 2.3, a candidate for a more comprehensive theory of the functions of *ne* and *yo*, or of any other SFPs, should be able to provide the explanation for the following "missing pieces": 1) that *ne* and *yo* appear to have opposite meanings in some case, and the same meaning in others and 2) that *ne* shows apparent variation under differing intonation patterns. The preceding discussion provides an answer to the second question. The first question requires more discussion.

Let us re-examine sentences (1), (2), and (3). Sentences (1) and (2) were in Section 2.1 as examples to illustrate the tendency within the information-attribution based theories to treat *yo* and *ne* as having the functions opposite of each other; example (1) shows the use of *yo* when the speaker considers the information being communicated to be closer to the speaker himself; in contrast, (2) shows the use of *ne* when the speaker is seeking confirmation of his assumption, the truth which the speaker assumes the hearer knows. These uses of *yo* and *ne* were explained in the information-attribution theories on the basis of the relative psychological distance between the speaker/hearer and the information. Sentences (3) and (4), however, exemplify the uses of *ne* which were "problematic" to the information-attribution theories, since the function of *ne* in these utterances could not be appropriately explained in terms of the attribution of information. This function of *ne* was explained by Izuhara and others in terms of increasing rapport between the speaker and the hearer.

A brief examination of the intonation patterns with which sentences (2), (3) and (4) are produced will clearly tell us that the variation in meaning of *ne* ("confirmation seeking" on the one hand, and "rapport" on the other) can be attributed to the variation in sentence final intonation patterns. More specifically, we can observe that *ne* can convey the sense of "confirmation seeking" when it appears with √ intonation, and it can convey the sense of "rapport" when it appears with **!** or ^ intonation. Furthermore, Table 3-1 (discussed in Section 3.3) shows that the speaker's intentions such as "confirming" and "explaining" which have been analyzed in the past as an intrinsic part of the function of *ne*, indeed are being communicated by the intonation patterns.

We have also examined in Section 3.5 that the variation in intonation patterns does not readily influence the meaning of the utterance that end with the SFP *yo* and this is the reason why *ne* and *yo* appear to have opposite meanings in some cases, and the same meaning in other. Thus, the proposed analysis explains all the functions of *ne* exemplified by (2), (3) and (4) without any inconsistency.

4.2 Suggestions for Future Research

It is important to acknowledge that some questions still remain unanswered: to what degree do the semantics of SFPs and of intonation patterns interact with each other? We have recognized that the semantics of two SFPs, *ne* and *yo*, are influenced to differing degrees by the variation in intonation. A more systematic examination of the interaction between the two elements, intonation and SFPs, will be necessary.

Another question that remains to be addressed is why sentence (4), in which the speaker communicates her plan of action, can be said with the √ intonation without sounding like a "confirmation question." For instance, compare sentence (4) with sentence (2), whose syntactic structure does not differ greatly from sentence (4); both sentences are simple declarative sentences with an SFP *ne*, and they are both said with the full-rising intonation to communicate very different intentions of the speaker. In order to answer this question, we will need to start looking at the SFPs and their functions in terms of the organization of discourse.

This framework certainly needs to be extended further to be able to provide a more general theory of SFPs, but it is hoped that this work is highly suggestive for a new direction in future research that goes beyond the limitations of current theories.

References

Cheng, Changhao. 1987. Shûzyoshi: Hanashite to kikite no ninshiki no gyappu o umeru tame no bunsetsu-zi. *Nihongogaku* 6:10. 93-109.

Hubbard, Maki. 1992. Question, Statement, and Roles of *ne*: Formulation of Utterances. *Journal of the Association of Teachers of Japanese* 26:2. 121-140.

Izuhara, Hideko. 1993. *Ne* to *yo* no kôsatsu: *Ne* to *yo* no komyunikêsyon kinô no kôsatu kara. *Nihongo kyôiku* 80. 103-114.

Jorden, Eleanor H. and Mari Noda. 1987. *Japanese: The Spoken Language*. Part 1. New Haven: Yale University Press.

Kamio, Akio. 1978. On the Notion Speaker's Territory of Information: A Functional Analysis of Csertain Sentence-Final Forms in Japanese, in G. Bedell, E. Kobayashi, and M. Muraki, eds., *Explorations in Linguistics: Papers in Honor of Kazuko Inoue*. 213-231. Tokyo: Kenkyusha.

—. 1990. *Joohoo no nawabari riron: Gengo no kinooteki bunseki.* Tokyo: Taishukan.

—. 1994. Theory of Territory of Information. *Journal of Pragmatics* 21. 67-100.

—. 1997. *Territory of information.* Philadelphia: J. Benjamins.

Katagiri, Yasuhiro. 1997. Syû-zyoshi to intonêsyon, in Spoken Language Working Group, eds., *Speech and Grammar.* 235-256. Tokyo: Kuroshio syuppan.

—. 1998. Dialogue Functions of Japanese Sentence-Final Particles. Paper presented at NSF Workshop on Syllable Structure and Gesture Timing: Sep. 19-20, 1998.

Masuoka, Takashi. 1991. *Modarithî no bunpô.* Tokyo: Kuroshio syuppan.

McGloin, Naomi Hanaoka. 1990. Sex Difference and Sentence-Final Particles. *Aspects of Japanese Women's Language.* 23-41. Tokyo: Kuroshio.

Onoe, Atsushi. 1997. Functions of *ne* and Its Uses by Learners. MA Thesis. Ohio State University.

Oso, Mieko. 1986. Goyoo bunseki 1 - "Kyoo wa ii tenki desu ne." "Hai, soo desu." *Nihongogaku* 5:9. 91-94.

Pierrehumbert, Janet and Julia Hirschberg. 1990. The Meaning of Intonational Contours in the Interpretation of Discourse, in P. R. Cohen, J. Morgan, and M. E. Pollack, eds., *Intentions in Communication.* 271-311. Cambridge, MA: The MIT Press.

Shirakawa, Hiroyuki. 1992. Shûzyoshi '*yo*' no kinô. (The function of the sentence-final particle *yo*.) *Nihongo-kyôiku* 77:7. 36-48.

Takubo, Yukinori and Satoshi Kinsui. 1996. Hukusû no sin-teki ryôiki ni yoru danwa kanri. *Ninchi Kagaku* 3:3. 59-74.

—. 1998. Danwa kanri riron ni motozuku *yo*, *ne*, *yo ne* no kenyû, in S. Dooka, Y. Niimi, K. Shirai, H. Tanaka, and R. Mizoguchi, eds., *Onsê ni yoru ningen to kikai no taiwa.* 257-271. Tokyo: Ohmsha.

Uyeno, Tazuko. 1971. *A Study of Japanese Modality: A Performative Analysis of Sentence Particles.* Doctoral dissertation, University of Michigan.

Venditti, Jennifer J., Kazuaki Maeda, and Jan P. H. van Santen. 1998. Modeling Japanese Boundary Pitch Movements for Speech Synthesis. Paper presented at the 3rd ESCA Synthesis Workshop.

From Place to Space to Discourse: A Contrastive Linguistic Analysis of Japanese *tokoru* and Korean *tey*

KAORU HORIE & YUKO SASSA
Tohoku University

1. Introduction[1]

Recently, within Functional-typological linguistics, the diachronic development of relational nouns (e.g. *front*) and locative adpositions in various languages has been extensively studied from the perspective of grammaticalization (Svorou 1993, Heine 1997). However, the lexical nouns encoding 'place', e.g. English *place*, have received relatively little attention within these typological studies on grammaticalization. It is partly because these nouns themselves do not positively participate in the grammaticalization process cross-linguistically (Soteria Svorou, personal communication).

In contrast, two 'place'-denoting nouns in Japanese and Korean, i.e. Japanese *tokoro* and Korean *tey*, are recruited to serve important grammatical functions in their respective languages. By presenting a contrastive linguistic analysis of the two 'place'-denoting nouns, this study will reveal striking differences in form-meaning correspondences between the two languages. The organization of this

---

[1] The authors thank Andrew Barke, Chun Chonghoon, Yongtaek Kim, JJ Nakayama, and Debra Occhi for insightful comments. The usual disclaimer applies.The current research project was partially supported by the Grant-in-Aid from the Ministry of Education, Science and Culture (No.10610522).

paper is as follows. Section 2 presents a morpho-syntactic and semantic characterization of "postadnominals", a special subclass of nouns to which *tokoro* and *tey* belong. Section 3 presents a contrastive linguistic analysis of Japanese *tokoro* and Korean *tey*. Section 4 argues that the differing patterns of semantic extension of *tokoro* and *tey* reflect the underlying difference between the two languages in terms of form-meaning correspondence. Section 5 presents the conclusion.

2. "Postadnominals" in Japanese and Korean

Japanese *tokoro* and Korean *tey* belong to a special subclass of nouns commonly found in both languages, traditionally referred to as *keisiki meisi* ('formal nouns') in Japanese and *uyconmyengsa* ('dependent nouns') in Korean (cf. Martin 1975, 1992). Typical examples of these nouns are Japanese *mono* ('thing') and its Korean counterpart *kes* ('thing, matter'). Unlike ordinary lexical nouns such as Japanese *yama* ('mountain') and its Korean counterpart *san*, these nouns encode highly abstract or general meaning and are normally preceded by modifiers such as demonstratives and/or predicate adnominal phrases, as illustrated below:[2]

(1) {ϕ?/*sono* *siroi*) *mono*-wa nan desu ka?
that white thing-TOP what COP:POL Q

(1') {ϕ?/*ku* *huyn*} *kes*-i mwues-i ey yo?
that white:ADN thing-NOM what-NOM COP SFP:POL

"What is (that white) thing?"

The Japanese and Korean nominals in question share sufficient morpho-syntactic and semantic similarities (i.e. being regularly modified by demonstratives/predicate adnominal forms, encoding general/abstract meaning) to merit comparison. For a lack of common terminology, I will use the term "postadnominals" (Martin 1992) to refer to the nominals in both languages.

Table 1 presents a selection of representative postadnominals in Japanese and Korean with their meanings given in parentheses:

Table 1. A selection of postadnominals in Japanese and Korean

Japanese	Korean
tokoro ('place')	*tey* ('place')
mono ('thing')	*kes* ('thing, matter')
koto ('matter, fact')	

Importantly, these postadnominals in Japanese and Korean have developed

[2] The following abbreviations are used. ACC(Accusative), ADN (Adnominal), CONJ (Conjunctive), COP (Copula) , DAT (Dative), DECL (Declarative mood), GEN (Genitive), GER (Gerund), LOC (Locative), NEG (Negative), NOM (Nominative), NOML (Nominalizer), POL (Addressee politeness), PRES (Present), QUOT (Quotative), SFP (Sentence Final Particle), TOP (Topic). ':' indicates that multiple grammatical functions are fused into one morpheme.

various grammatical uses, e.g. use as a sentential complementizer, as illustrated by examples (2) and (2'):

(2) Kankokugo-o oboeru *koto*-wa sonnani muzukasiku nai.
Korean alphabet-ACC memorize thing-TOP so difficult NEG

(2') Hankul-ul ikhi-nun *kes*-un kutaci elyep-
Korean alphabet-ACC memorize-ADN:PRES thing-TOP so difficult-
ci -anh-ta.
NOML-NEG-DECL
"Memorizing the Korean alphabet is not so hard". (Umeda 1991: 141)

Japanese and Korean postadnominals thus play a very important role in the lexico-grammatical structures of the two languages. However, it is important to note that the patterns of semantic extension and grammaticalization do not appear to be identical across the two languages. The next section closely examines the semantic and morpho-syntactic behaviors of two postadnominals encoding 'place', i.e. Japanese *tokoro* and Korean *tey*. The analysis of these 'place'-denoting nouns in Japanese and Korean will provide insight into the cross-linguistic similarities and differences between the two languages.

3. A Contrastive Linguistic Analysis of Japanese *Tokoro* and Korean *Tey*

This section presents a constrastive linguistic analysis of Japanese *tokoro* and Korean *tey* from the perspectives of semantic extension and grammaticalization, starting with the basic meaning then moving on to the meanings that are arrived at by semantic extension and grammaticalization.

3.1 Basic Meaning

Japanese *tokoro* and Korean *tey*, in their basic 'place' meaning, do not appear to be very different, as illustrated in (3) and (3') repeated below:

(3) Kootuu-no benrina *tokoro*-ni sunde iru.
traffic-GEN convenient place-LOC live:GER exist

(3') Kyothong-i phyenliha-n *tey*-ey salko iss-ta
traffic-NOM convenient-ADN place-LOC live:GER exist-DECL
"(I) live in a place where the transportation is convenient".

3.2 'Part of the Whole' Meaning

As pointed out by Teramura (1992: 314), Japanese *tokoro* can encode 'part of the whole', as shown below:

(4) Watasi-ga yomu *tokoro*-o moo itido yonde kudasai.
I-NOM read place-ACC again once read:GER please
"Please read the part (of the text) that I read".

(5) Kanozyo-no sinsetuna *tokoro*-ga ki-ni itta.
she-NOM kind place-NOM come to like:PAST
"I became fond of her kindness (lit. 'her kind *place*')".

Korean *tey* can encode the same 'part of the whole' meaning:

(4') Nay-ka ilk-un *tey*-lul tasi hanpen ilke-
I-NOM read-ADN:PRES place-ACC again once read:CONJ-
cwusipsio.
please:POL
"Please read the part (of the text) that I read".

(5') Kunye-uy chincelha-n *tey*-ka maum-ey tulessta.
she-GEN kind-ADN place-NOM come to like:PAST:DECL
"I became fond of her kindness (lit. 'her kind *place*')".

3.3 Extension into the Spatio-temporal Domain

It is cross-linguistically well-documented that spatial terms metaphorically extend into temporal domain, as aptly illustrated by the semantic development of spatial adpositions into temporal domain such as in the following English example (cf. Hopper and Traugott 1993):

(6) We're *behind* in paying our bills. (Hopper and Traugott 1993: 79)

Japanese *tokoro* and Korean *tey* also allow semantic extension from the purely spatial domain into the spatio-temporal domain. [3] However, the patterns of semantic extension are different between the two languages. Japanese *tokoro* can take on 'cotemporal' meaning when it co-occurs with immediately following case particles, such as accusative particle *o*, locative-allative *ni*, and locative-instrumental *de*, as shown below:

(7) Han'nin-ga kuruma-ni notte toosoosuru *tokoro-o*,
criminal-NOM car-LOC ride:GER flee place-ACC
gaadoman-ga mokugeki site i-ta.
security guard-NOM witness do:GER exist-PAST
"The security guard witnessed a criminal getting into a car and fleeing (lit. The security guard was watching *the place/scene of* the criminal)".

(8) Yuusyoku-o tabete iru *tokoro-ni*, denwa-ga kakatte kita.
dinner-ACC eat:GER exist place-LOC phone-NOM be placed came
"While we were having dinner, there was a call (lit. At the *place/point in time* where we were having dinner, there was a call)".

---

[3] The semantic extension of *tokoro* into spatio-temporal and textual domains has been discussed by previous researchers (e.g. Cu 1988, Matsumoto 1988, Teramura 1992, Ohara 1995, Ohori 1995, Yamanashi 1995, Horie1998, to appear). The analyses of *tokoro* presented in Sections 3.3 and 3.4 owe a great deal to the insightful works of HideoTeramura, particularly Teramura 1992.

(9) Kono mondai-o toita *tokoro-de*, kyoo-no zyugyoo-wa
this problem-ACC solve:PAST place-LOC today class-TOP
owari-ni si-yoo.
end-to do-PROPOSITIVE
"When you solve the problem (lit. At the *place/point in time* when you solve the problem), let's call it a day".

Tokoro in (7), which arguably functions as a sentential complementizer, has received the attention of numerous Japanese linguists because of its syntactic and semantic peculiarities (cf. Cu 1988). *Tokoro* in (8) and (9) functions as a situational/temporal conjunctive particle together with the immediately following locative particles *ni* an *de* respectively. In either of examples (7)-(9), the case particle is not omissible.

These patterns of semantic extension are not very productive with the Korean *tey*, as illustrated below:[4]

(7') Pemin-i cha-lul thako tocwuha-nun {*kes-ul/*tey-lul*}
criminal-NOM car-ACC ride:GER run-ADN:PRES thing-ACC/place-ACC
gatumayn-i mokkyekhay-ss-ta.
security guard-NOM witness-PAST-DECL
"The security guard witnessed a criminal getting into a car and fleeing".

As shown in (7'), Korean *tey*, which lacks the sentential complementizing function unlike its Japanese counterpart *tokoro*, must be replaced in this slot by yet another postadnominal *kes* ('thing') briefly mentioned in Section 2.

(8') Cenyek siksa-lul ha-nun {*cwung-(ey)* /*tey-(*ey)*} cenhwa-ka
evening meal-ACC do-ADN:PRES middle-LOC/place-LOC phone-NOM
wa-ss-e-yo.
come-PAST-CONJ-POL
"While we were having dinner, there was a call".

Example (8') shows that the combination of *tey* and the locative-allative particle *ey* is infelicitous. Instead, in the intended 'co-temporal' meaning, *tey* must be replaced by postadnominal *cwung* ('middle'), which can optionally be followed by the locative-allative particle *ey*. Interestingly, in (8"), *tey* is acceptable when it is not followed by *ey*. In that case, the combination of the present adnominal predicate ending *nun* and the immediately following *tey* is subject to the interpretation as a sentential connective *nuntey* (or its phonological variant *untey*), as shown below:

---

[4] One of the few attested comparable combinations in Korean is *tey-se* ('place-LOC') , which can encode "cotemporality", as in:
(a) Kol-ul neh-nun *tey-se* sihap-i kkuthnanta. (goal-ACC shoot-ADN place-LOC game-NOM ends:PRES:DECL) "When (one) shoots a goal (lit. *At the place/point in time* when (one) shoots a goal), the game ends". (Yongtaek Kim, personal communication).

(8") Cenyek siksa-lul ha-*nuntey* cenhwa-ka wa-ss-e-yo.
"While we were having dinner, there was a call".

Unlike (8'), where *tey* retains its nounhood, *tey* in the sentential connective *nuntey* in (8") loses its morpho-syntactic independence. The fact that *nun* and *tey* are not orthographically separated (in Romanization as well as in *Hankul*) attests to the boundedness of *tey* in *nuntey*. We will discuss *nuntey* in more detail in Section 3.4, but we would like to note that *nuntey* does not specifically encode 'co-temporality', unlike *cwung(ey)* in (8').

It must be noted that *tey* can co-occur with the locative-allative particle *ey* and encode the meaning 'on the occasion of, for the purpose of', as shown below:

(10) Meli aphu-n *tey*-(*ey*) i yak-i cohta.
head hurt-ADN place-LOC this medicine-NOM good:DECL
"When (lit. *On the occasion* when) you have a headache, this medicine is good".

(11) Yehayng ka-nun *tey*-(*ey*) philyoh-an kes-un
trip go-ADN:PRES place-LOC necessary-ADN thing-TOP
mwe-pni-kka?
what-COP:POL-Q
"What do we need when (lit. *on the occasion* when) we go on a trip?".

Tey in (10) was assigned a spatial interpretation ("Where your head hurts...") by some native speakers. In fact, the spatial interpretation of *tey* is more readily accessible when it is embedded in an interrogative sentence such as *Eti aphun-tey isse-yo?* ('where hurt:ADN-place exist:CONJ-SFP:POL'; "Does any *part* of your body hurt?")

Unlike Japanese *tokoro*, however, the locative-allative case particle *ey* in (10)-(11) is omissible. If *ey* is omitted, a reanalysis similar to (8") is possible. That is, *tey* and the immediately preceding present adnominal ending *nun* are interpreted as a single textual cohesion marker *nuntey*, as shown in (10a)-(11a):

(10a) Meli aphu-*ntey* i yak-i cohta.
"When you have a headache, this medicine is good".

(11a) Yehayng ka-*nuntey* philyoh-an kes-un mwe-pni-kka?
"What do we need when we go on a trip?"

In contrast, Japanese *tokoro* cannot be felicitously used in counterparts to Korean examples (10) and (11):

(10') Atama-ga itai {*toki/sai/*tokoro*}-(*ni*) kono kusuri-ga yoi
head-NOM hurt time/occasion/place-LOC this medicine-NOM good
"When you have a headache, this medicine is good".

(11') Ryokoo-ni iku {*toki/sai/*tokoro*}-(*ni*) nani-ga hituyoo
trip-LOC go time/occasion/place-LOC what-NOM necessity
desu ka?
COP:POL Q
"What do we need when (lit. on the occasion when) we go on a trip?"

Examples (10') and (11') suggest that *tokoro* is not acceptable regardless of whether it is used adverbially by itself or is immediately followed by the locative-allative particle *ni*. It must be replaced by overtly temporal postadnominals such as *toki* ('time') or *sai* ('occasion').

A comparison of Japanese examples (7)-(9) and Korean examples (10)-(11) reveals a noticeable difference between the two languages. Japanese *tokoro* obligatorily co-occurs with a case particles (e.g. *o*, *ni*, *de*) when it encodes spatio-temporal meaning. That is, *tokoro* and a case-marking particle are practically inseparable when spatio-temporal meaning is intended. In contrast, Korean *tey* is more regularly used without any accompanying case particle when it encodes spatio-temporal meaning. Furthermore, while the spatio-temporal meaning of *tokoro* ('location/point in time') is clearly traceable to the 'part of the whole' meaning discussed in Section 3.2, motivations for the semantic extension of *tey* into the spatio-temporal domain ('occasion') are less clearly identifiable except for the general tendency of semantic extension from spatial to temporal domains.

Finally, Japanese *tokoro* occurs in sentence-final position together with the copula *da* and can encode prospective, progressive, and 'hot news perfect' aspects (cf. Ohara 1995), depending on whether the immediately preceding verb form is imperfective *-ru*, periphrastic progressive *-te i-*, or perfective *-ta*:

(12) Tyoodo ima sensei-ni denwasu*ru* *tokoro* desi-ta.
just now professor-DAT call:PRES place COP:POL-PAST
"I *was just about to* call my Professor". (Prospective aspect)

(13) Ima syokuzi-o si*te* *iru* *tokoro* desu.
now meal-ACC do:GER exist place COP:POL (Progressive aspect)
"I'*m (in the middle of) having* a meal right now".

(14) Ima kaette ki*ta* *tokoro* desu.
now return:GER come:PAST place COP:POL (Hot news perfect)
"I *have just returned*".

These aspectual interpretations are manifested through the interaction of the inherent meaning of *tokoro* (specifically 'location/point in time') and the temporal meaning of each verb form immediately preceding it.

Korean *tey* does not yield sentence-final aspectual constructions unlike Japanese *tokoro*:

(12') Pangkum sensayngnim-kkey cenhwaha-l {*cham/*tey*}-
just now professor-DAT:HON phone-ADN:FUTURE verge/place-
i-ess-e-yo.
COP-PAST-CONJ-POL "I was just about to call my Professor".

(13') Cikum siksa ha-ko iss-nun {*cwung/*tey*}-i-
now meal do-GER exist-ADN:PRES middle/place-COP-
pnita.
POL:DECL
"I'm (in the middle of) having a meal right now".

In (12') and (13'), *tey* is replaced by postadnominals *cham* ('verge') and *cwung* ('middle'), which respectively are compatible with the particular aspectual interpretations.

3.4 Extension into Textual and Discourse Domains

As extensively discussed in grammaticalization literatures, a semantic change involves a shift from "meanings based in the described external or internal situation" to "meanings based in the textual situation", or a shift to meanings "increasingly situated in the speaker's subjective belief-state/attitude toward the situation" (Traugott and König 1991: 208-9). Judging from the synchronic usage, Japanese *tokoro* and Korean *tey* appear to have reached these later stages of semantic change, though in rather different ways.

Japanese *tokoro* encodes different types of textual meaning as sentential connectives by coalescing with the immediately following locative case particle *de* or nominative case particle *ga*. The degree of tightness of the coalescence differs between the two particles (cf. also Matsumoto 1988, Yamanashi 1995). The combination of *tokoro* and the locative case particle *de* encodes 'concession' and the particle is not omissible:

(15) Nando it-ta *tokoro-*(de)*, ano hito-wa kiite
how many times say-PAST place-LOC that person-TOP listen:GER
kurenai.
give me:NEG
"*No matter how* many times you say, he won't listen".

The combination of *tokoro* and the nominative case particle *ga* takes on a 'contrariness to expectation' meaning:

(16) Kare-o tazune-ta *tokoro-(ga)*, rusu dat-ta.
he-ACC visit-PAST place-NOM not in COP-PAST
"I visited him, *but contrary to my expectation*, he was out".

As shown in (16), the nominative case particle *ga* is omissible. When it is omitted, the contrast between the two events is slightly less pronounced than when it is present.

As can be predicted from its morpho-syntactic behavior discussed in Section

3.3, Korean *tey* does not show similar patterns of semantic extension. The concessive and contrastive meaning respectively expressed by *tokoro-de* and *tokoro-ga* in (15) and (16) are expressible by sentential connectives such as *tayssca* ('even though') and *teni* ('and then, contrary to one's expectation'):

(15') Myespen malhay-ss-*tayssca,* ku-salam-un
how many times say-PAST-even though that person-TOP
tule-cwu-ci-anh-nun-ta.
listen:CONJ-give me-NOML-NEG-PRES-DECL
"No matter how many times you say it, he won't listen".

(16') Ku-lul pangmwunhay-ss-*teni* pwucay cwung-i-ess-ta.
he-ACC visit-PAST-and then absence middle-COP-PAST-DECL
"I visited him, but contrary to my expectation, he was out".

Japanese *tokoro* coalesces with the immediately following nominative case particle *ga* or locative case particle *de* and yields conjunctions *tokoroga* ('however') and *tokorode* ('incidentally'):

(17) Ginkoo-ni itte mi-ta. *Tokoroga,* sudeni syattaa-ga
bank-TOP go:GER see-PAST however already shutter-NOM
simatte i-ta.
be closed:GER exist-PAST
"I went to the bank to see if it was open. *However*, the shutter of the bank was already closed".

(18) *Tokorode,* asu-wa donna go-yotei desu ka?
incidentally tomorrow-TOP what kind of HONORIFIC-plan COP:POL Q
"*By the way*, what kind of plans do you have for tomorrow?"

These conjunctions, as the orthography indicates, are each treated as one word. As extensively discussed by Matsumoto (1988), Japanese is abundant with these conjunctions which derived from the earlier more bound sentential connectives (e.g. *tokoro-ga*). These conjunctions have drawn much attention since they apparently go against the normal directionality of grammaticalization from more to less morpho-syntactic independence.

Korean has a sentential conjunction *kulentey* that covers both semantic domains of Japanese *tokoroga* and *tokorode*:

(17') Unhayng-ey kapo-ass-ta. *Kulentey,* imi syatha-ka
bank-to go see-PAST-DECL however already shutter-NOM
tathy-e-iss-ess-ta.
be closed-CONJ-
PAST-DECL
"I went to the bank to see if it was open. *However*, the shutter of the bank was already closed".

(18') *Kulentey*, nayil-un etten yeyceng-ipni-kka?
incidentally tomorrow-TOP what kind of plan-POL-Q
"*By the way*, what kind of plans do you have for tomorrow?"

Interestingly, *kulentey* includes *tey*. *Kulentey* obviously derives from the coalescent of the adjective *kuleha-ta* ('to be so') and the sentential connective *nuntey* by truncation (*kuleha* + *ntey* > *kulentey*) (Kim Yongtaek, personal communication).

Unlike Japanese *tokoro*, Korean *tey* does not show much variation in combinatory possibilities when it encodes textual cohesion. As briefly discussed in Section 3.3, *tey* invariably occurs with the immediately preceding *nun* and occurs in the form of *nuntey*. There are two possible sources of *tey* in *nuntey*, i.e. *tey* 'place' and *-ta* 'declarative sentence ending' (Bongshik Kang, personal communication). In this paper, we hypothesize that the adnominal ending *nun* and *tey* coalesces into a single sentential connective through the process of semantic extension from spatial to temporal domains.

The sentential connective *nuntey* is known for a variety of textual cohesive meanings. On the basis of numerous previous studies on *nuntey*, Yang (1999: 192) extracts two different types of textual meaning proposed in the literature, i.e. "contrastive relation" and "presenting background or establishing the situation". Examples (19) and (20) respectively illustrate the 'contrastive' and 'background' meaning of *nuntey*:

(19) Caknyen kyewul-un chwu-wess-*nuntey* olhay-nun
last year winter-TOP cold-PAST this year-TOP
ette-lnunci-yo?
how-MOOD-SFP:POL
"It was cold last winter; how is this winter going to be?"

(20) Cenpwu sa-lkka ha-*nuntey* com kkakka-
all buy-CONJ do-NUNTEY a bit give discount-
cwu-l swu iss-keyss-e-yo?
give me-ADN:FUTURE able-MOOD-CONJ-SFP:POL
"I'm going to buy them all. (So) could you give me a discount?"

Japanese *tokoro* is infelicitous in the counterparts to (19) and (20). Instead, sentential connectives such as *ga* ('but') or *kedo* ('but') need to be used:

(19') Sakunen-no huyu-wa samukat-ta {*ga/*tokoro*}, kotosi-wa doo
last year-GEN winter-TOP cold-PAST but/place this year-TOP how
desyoo ka?
MOOD:POL Q
"It was cold last winter; how is this winter going to be?"

(20') Zenbu ka-oo to omou {*kedo/*tokoro*}, tyotto
all buy-PROPOS QUOT think but/place a bit
makete kure masen ka?
give discount:GER give me POL:NEG Q
"I'm going to buy them all. (So) could you give me a discount?"

Clauses introduced by *nuntey* can occur by themselves without the accompanying matrix clauses (cf. Yang 1999) and can encode the speaker's subjective evaluation/opinion, as in (21), or convey indirectness, as in (22):

(21) I kulim cengmal coh-*nuntey*-yo.
this painting really good-NUNTEY-SFP:POL
"This picture is really good (and *I'm impressed*)".

(22) Ku chayk-un yeki eps-*nuntey*-yo.
that book-TOP here not exist-NUNTEY-SFP:POL
"We don't carry that book here (*I'm sorry to say*)".

4. Japanese *Tokoro* and Korean *Tey*: Whence the Differences?

Section 3 presented a contrastive linguistic analysis of the two nouns encoding 'place', i.e. Japanese *tokoro* and Korean *tey*, which play a very important role in the grammatical structures of the respective languages. The analysis presented in Section 3 reveals the rather different patterns of semantic extension of these nouns between the two languages, which are schematized in Figure 1:

Japanese *tokoro*
◎----------◎-----------◎-------------------◎---------------◎
tokoro *tokoro* *tokoro* *tokoro* *tokoro*, *tokoro-(ga)*
+particle +copula *tokoro-de*, *tokoroga*,
(*o*, *ni*, *de*) (*da*) *tokorode*
'place'-----'part'----'cotemporality/---'aspectual'----'textual'-------'subjective'
situation'

Korean *tey*
◎-----------◎-------------○ [--------------------------◎------------------◎]
tey-----------*tey*----------- *tey* [------------------------*nuntey*---------*nuntey*]
tey-(ey)

Figure 1. Hypothesized semantic extension link of *tokoro* and *tey*
(◎ 'meaning fully established'; ○ 'meaning not fully developed'; '[ ]' 'semantic link not established at this stage')

Although this study does not trace the diachronic development of Japanese *tokoro* and Korean *tey*, previous studies on semantic change and grammaticalization suggest how the original 'place' meaning is linked to the other "derived" meanings. In the case of Japanese *tokoro*, it is relatively easy to follow the link from the original 'place' meaning to the other more abstract/grammaticalized meanings via the 'part of the whole' meaning. In contrast, in the case of Korean *tey*, the link from the original 'place' meaning to the other more abstract/grammaticalized meanings is rather opaque. Furthermore, the semantic extension of *tey* from the original 'place' meaning is less productive than its Japanese counterpart *tokoro*, as shown by the tendency for *tey* to be preferentially replaced by semantically more specific postadnominals such as *cwung* ('middle'). Particularly problematic is the relationship between *tey* and *nuntey*, which are distanced by the absence of mediating semantic links.

Another noticeable difference between the two languages concerns the manner in which form-meaning correspondence is respected. When Korean *tey* takes on spatio-temporal meaning, it starts to lose its prototypical nominal marking, i.e. case-marking:

(11) Yehayng ka-nun *tey-(ey)* philyoh-an kes-un mwe-pni-kka?
"What do we need when (lit. on the occasion when) we go on a trip?"

When *tey* is used as a part of the sentential connective *nuntey*, it should not be followed by the locative particle *ey*:

(20) Cenpwu sa-lkka ha-*nuntey-(*ey)* com kkakka-cwu-l swu iss-keyss-e-yo?
"I'm going to buy them all. (So) could you give me a discount?"

In contrast, Japanese *tokoro* continues to retain its case-marking even when it takes on spatio-temporal meaning and textual meaning:

(9) Kono mondai-o toi-ta *tokoro-*(de)*, kyoo-no zyugyoo-wa owari-ni si-mas-yoo.
"When you solve the problem, let's call it a day (lit. 'At the *place/point in time* when you solve the problem, let's call it a day')".

(15) Nando it-ta *tokoro-*(de)*, ano hito-wa kiite kure-nai.
"*No matter how* many times you say, he won't listen".

(17) Ginkoo-ni itte mi-ta. *Tokoro-*(ga)*, sudeni syattaa-ga simatte i-ta.
"I went to the bank to see if it was open. *However*, the shutter of the bank was already closed".

These differences seem to point to a rather fundamental contrast between the two languages in terms of which form-meaning correspondence is handled. Korean tends to restrict one form to one meaning. Therefore, compared to Japanese *tokoro*, the range of semantic extension of Korean *tey* is restricted. When *tey* ceases to behave as a 'place'-referring noun and takes on adverbial meaning as in (20), it naturally starts to lose nominal properties such as case-marking. When a noun ceases to behave like a noun, it starts to behave differently syntactically as well. In contrast, Japanese is less restrictive in assigning one form to one meaning. One form (e.g. *tokoro*) can be assigned multiple meanings. The range of semantic extension is consequently wider in

Japanese than in Korean. Furthermore, even when *tokoro* starts to take on adverbial meaning (as in 9, 15), it can still continue to behave syntactically as a noun.

A similar contrast can be found in other different areas of the grammar of the two languages, e.g. functions of case-marking particles and word formation (cf. Horie 1998). For instance, Modern Japanese allows both nominative case-marked NPs and genitive case-marked NPs to encode subjecthood in adnominal embedded clauses, as in (23). The grammatical meaning of 'subjecthood' can thus be expressed by two forms in Japanese, although this phenomenon is restricted to adnominal embedded clauses:

(23) [Okane-{*ga/no*} aru] hito-wa raku da ga, nai
money-NOM/GEN exist person-TOP easy-but not exist
hito-wa kibisii.
person-TOP tough
"Those who have money can take it easy, but those who don't have a tough time".

In contrast, as extensively discussed by Horie and Kang (to appear), Modern Korean virtually restricts nominative case-marked NPs to encode subjecthood in matrix as well as adnominal embedded clauses, such as (23'). This is another reflection of the tendency to restrict one form to one meaning:

(23') [Ton-{*i/*uy*} iss-nun] salam-un phyenha-ciman
money-NOM/GEN exist-ADN:PRES person-TOP easy-but
eps-nun salam-un kosayng-i-ta.
not exist- ADN:PRES person-TOP hardship-COP-DECL
"Those who have money can take it easy, but those who don't have a tough time".

5. Conclusion

This study presents a contrastive linguistic analysis of the two 'place'-denoting nouns in Japanese and Korean, i.e. *tokoro* and *tey*, and finds that Japanese *tokoro* extends into various semantic domains (e.g. textual domain) without completely losing its nounhood (e.g. ability to be followed by case particle). The semantic extension pattern shown by *tokoro* accords with the tendency for one-to-many or many-to-one form-meaning correspondence to be tolerated in Japanese. Korean noun *tey*, in contrast, develops into a discourse cohesion marker by ceasing to behave like a noun, confirming the tendency of the Korean language to respect one-to-one form-meaning correspondence more strictly.

It is hoped that similar contrastive studies will be carried out in various domains of grammar and lexicon and will further explore the underlying differences between the two languages as well as the cognitive-cultural factors fostering cross-linguistic differences.

References

Cu, Le Van. 1988. *No ni yoru bun umekomi no koozoo to hyoogen no kinoo.* (Function of Structure and Expression of Sentential Embedding by *No*) Tokyo: Kurosio Publishers.

Heine, Bernd. 1997. *Cognitive Foundations of Grammar.* Oxford: Oxford University Press.

Hopper, Paul and Elizabeth C. Traugott. 1993. *Grammaticalization.* Cambridge: Cambridge University Press.

Horie, Kaoru. 1998. Functional Duality of Case-marking Particles in Japanese and its Implications for Grammaticalization: A Contrastive Study with Korean, in D. Silva, ed., *Japanese/Korean Linguistics* 8. Stanford: Center for the Study of Language and Information. 147-159.

Horie, Kaoru. To appear. Complementation in Japanese and Korean: A Contrastive and Cognitive Linguistic Approach, in K. Horie, ed., *Complementation: Cognitive and Functional Perspectives.* Amsterdam: John Benjamins.

Horie, Kaoru, and Bongshik Kang. To appear. Action/state Continuum and Nominative-Genitive Conversion in Japanese and Korean. *Modern Approaches to Transitivity.* Tokyo: Kuroshio Publishers.

Martin, Samuel E. 1975. *A Reference Grammar of Japanese.* New Haven: Yale University Press.

Martin, Samuel E. 1992. *A Reference Grammar of Korean.* Tokyo: Tuttle.

Matsumoto, Yo. 1988. From Bound Grammatical Markers to Free Discourse Markers: History of Some Japanese Connectives. *BLS* 14. 340-351

Ohara, Kyoko Hirose. 1995. What's in a Place? - Extended Uses of a Physical-world Noun in Japanese. *BLS* 21. 237-251.

Ohori, Toshio. 1995. Clause Integration as Grammaticalization: A Case from Japanese *Tokoro*-Complements. Paper presented at the Functional Approaches to Grammar Conference, U. of New Mexico, July 1995.

Svorou, Soteria. 1993. *The Grammar of Space.* Amsterdam: John Benjamins.

Teramura, Hideo. 1992. *Tokoro* no imi to kinoo. (Meaning and function of *tokoro*), in *Teramura Hideo ronbun syuu I - Nihongo bunpoo hen.* Tokyo: Kurosio Syuppan. 321-336.

Traugott, Elizabeth Closs, and Ekkehard König. 1991. The Semantics-Pragmatics of Grammaticalization Revisited, in E.C. Traugott, and B. Heine, eds., *Approaches to Grammaticalization.* vol 1. John Benjamins, Amsterdam.189-218.

Umeda, Hiroyuki. 1991. *Sutandaado hanguru kooza* 2. *Bunpoo to goi.* (Standard Korean series 2. Grammar and vocabulary) Tokyo: Taisyuukan.

Yamanashi, Masa-aki. 1995. *Ninti bunpooron.* Tokyo: Hituzi Syoboo.

Yong-Yae Park.1999. The Korean Connective *Nuntey* in Conversational Discourse. *Journal of Pragmatics* 31.191-218.

A Discourse Analysis of the Realization of Object NP Forms in Korean*

EON-SUK KO
University of Pennsylvania

1. Introduction

In Korean, the direct object is indicated by the object marker *-lul*. However, there are many cases where the object marker *-lul* is expected but does not occur. Moreover, the object itself undergoes ellipsis very often. Therefore, there are three possible ways of an object NP being realized in Korean[1]:

(1) Possible object NP forms
  a. NP-Acc
    cenhwase-lul nay cwun-tay
    phone bill-Acc pay give-DECL
    'Somebody is willing to pay the phone bill'

---

* I am indebted to Ellen Prince for her comments and encouragement. I also thank Jae-Woong Choe and Kimiko Nakanishi for helpful discussions, and Mark Liberman for allowing me to use the speech files of the Callfriend Korean database from the Linguistic Data Consortium. All remaining errors are mine.

1 A NP can be also realized with delimiters such as *-man, -nun, -to*, etc. However, I do not consider them as a separate category in this study since these forms occupy less than 10% of the frequency of object NP forms as will be shown in Table 1, and, more importantly, *-lul* will be argued to be one of such delimiters.

b. NP
tosilak ssalako kulayssnun-tey
lunch pack intend-DECL
'(I) was going to make lunch'

c. ϕ (zero-pronoun)
ne-to ϕ po-ass-ul-ci-to molu-keyss-ney
you-also it see-past-Acc-CONN don't know-DECL
'You could have also seen it'

The realization of objects and object marker of Korean provides evidence that the given/new distinction is not binary, as has been pointed out in Prince (1981, 1992). However, previous studies attempted to explain either the optional realization of the case marker on one hand (Lee & Thompson 1989, Lee 1995), or the distribution of zero-pronoun from the perspective of Centering Theory (Kameyama 1986), on the other. Thus, it has been overlooked that the possible NP forms of realization in discourse are at least three instead of being binary.

This paper examines the distribution of the object and object case marker in Korean by means of a quantitative analysis of naturally occurring data, and provides a unified analysis of what determines the optional or obligatory realization of objects and the object marker.

Contrary to previous researches which tried to identify the context in which the case marker drops, I assume that the bare NP is the basic form of the object realization, and that *-lul* is introduced as an operator for semantic reasons. Adopting the definition of 'focus' suggested by Vallduví & Vilkuna (1998), I argue that *-lul* is a 'kontrastive' focus marker which generates a set of alternatives that become available to semantic computation as some sort of quantificational domain. I will further argue that the distribution of the demonstratives and zero-pronouns can be explained using the cognitive hierarchy theory of Gundel et. al. (1993).

In the remainder of the paper, I will provide an analysis of the distributional pattern of NP forms in three different speech styles (section 2). I will then review previous analyses and address potential problems in analyzing the data in terms of information status theory (section 3). Adopting the notion of 'kontrast' from Vallduví & Vilkuna, and the 'cognitive hierarchy' from Gundel et. al. (1993), I will propose an analysis of the object NP forms in Korean (section 4).

2. Distribution of NP Forms in Different Speech Styles

In this study, three different styles of discourse that vary in terms of the degree of formality were investigated to explain the realization of object NP forms. They are as follows [2]:

2 Data (2a) were selected from the 100 telephone conversations collected by the Linguistic Data Consortium of the University of Pennsylvania as part of the Callfriend Korean project. A 30-minute conversation was transcribed and coded by the author and ten 30-minute conversations were audited to extract the bare NP and NP-Acc forms for further analysis. Tokens gath-

(2) Data
a. Informal telephone conversations between two people of the same honorific level, i.e. friends.
b. Informal narratives by four people freely expressing what they think about a certain topic in a newsgroup for housewives.
c. Four Formal TV news broadcast scripts.

To my knowledge, few previous studies looked at Korean newsgroup narratives as a subject of pragmatic studies, at least not to explain the realization of NP forms in Korean. However, with the growing number of population involved in internet-based communication in recent years, the way people address their opinions in newsgroups has become one of the established styles of communication. The data (2b) included in this study has interesting dual properties, i.e. although a written text, they use an informal speech style with the colloquial ending *-yo* instead of the formal *-ta*. It is thus expected that this speech style will show a pattern that stands between the informal (2a) and the formal (2c) data.

I found a total of 363 tokens where the object form is an issue as below:

Table 1. Distribution of object NP forms in three different speech styles

	Telephone conversation		Newsgroup		News broadcast	
object-lul (Acc. marked)	59	29%	44	64%	67	74%
object (Bare NP)	56	28%	10	14%	21	23%
zero-pronoun	68	33%	8	12%	3	3%
object-delimiter	20	10%	7	10%	0	0%
Total	203	100%	69	100%	91	100%

The results suggest that there is a close correlation between the elision (both of the case marker and of the object) and the style of the discourse: if the discourse is more formal, it is more likely to elide either the case marker or the object. Numerical details are as follows:

(3) The frequency of the occurrence of the Acc marker
News broadcast (74%) > Newsgroup (64%) > Telephone (27%)

It appears that the Acc marker *-lul* is deleted most frequently in telephone conversation. Following Lee & Thompson, I included the NP's incorporated with the light verb *ha*-'do' in counting the number of the bare NP's. [3]

ered from auditing were not included in the statistics of the Table 1. Data (2b) were captured from the newsgroup for housewives available from the internet server Chollian in Korea. Data (2c) were captured from the transcripts of the news broadcast available from the website of the Korean Broadcasting System (http://www.kbs.co.kr). The transcripts were audited to ensure the exact matching of the broadcast and the transcripts.

[3] The percentage of the nouns occurring with the Acc marker goes up as high as 93 % in the news broadcast if the incorporated nouns were excluded from the tokens, since news broadcast

An opposite tendency is found with the frequency of the zero-pronoun as illustrated in (4):

(4) The frequency of the elision of the object NP
Telephone (33%) > Newsgroup (12%) > News broadcast (3%)

As expected, the informal newsgroup narrative stands in the middle of the telephone conversation and the news broadcast in the frequency of both the occurrence of the Acc marker and the elision of the NP. This confirms the common observation that what determines the frequency of the realization and elision of these two factors is the degree of formality.

In the discourse of informal conversation, the distribution of the objects among the three possible types of NP realization is almost identical:

(5) Distribution of object NP forms in telephone conversation
overt case marked (29%), bare NP (28%), elided NP (33%)

Then, the question arises as to what determines the choice of the object NP forms among these three possibilities. This will be our subject of discussion in the remaining sections.

3. Previous Analyses and Problems

The distributional pattern of NP forms in the informal telephone conversation observed in the end of the previous section poses an interesting linguistic problem in that both the speaker and hearer should be able to reflect or infer what they may know or hypothesize about each other's belief-state from the linguistic form.

Traditionally a bare NP was considered as a form where the case marker is missing (Lee & Thompson 1989). Lee & Thompson provide an explanation for the non-occurrence of the Acc marker based on two styles of colloquial Korean, i.e. informal narratives and dialogues. In their analysis, the conditions that allow the elision of the Acc marker can be summarized as follows:

(6) Contexts for the non-occurrence of Acc marker (Lee & Thompson 1989)
a. Compounds: an incorporation of a direct object to a light verb *ha-* 'do'
...ilekhey nul <u>sayngkak</u> *ha*-ku iss-ta-ku
such always thought do-CONN exist-DECL-COMP
'I always think so'
b. Pragmatic particles: *-man* 'only', *-nun* 'topic', *-to* 'also', etc.
<u>pap</u>-un cal chac-a mek-na
rice-TOP well find-CONN eat-INDET
'whether (somebody) is eating well'

---

has the highest percentage of the verbs formed as a result of the nouns incorporated with the light verb *-ha* 'do'.

c. Grammatically and lexically determined bare nominals
ku ke kaps com pat-a tal-la-y
that thing price a little receive-CONN give-IMPER-IND

Lee & Thompson propose that the principle of 'sharedness between communicators' subsumes all the above contexts for bare nominals. That is, the greater the amount of 'sharedness', i.e. shared experience, shared context, and shared cultural background, the less necessary it is to specify grammatical relations.

Lee (1995) also makes a similar analysis of the optional realization of the case marker. He contends that an NP form with the Acc marker *-lul* signals that the event involved is rather *unexpected* and attention is paid to the NP. On the other hand, deletion of the case marker occurs when the event involving the NP referent is rather expected. In his view, formal and written text has a relatively low frequency of case deletion since not much is assumed familiar or expected.

As such, the notion of 'sharedness' has been an important notion in a given/new theory of information status (Clark & Haviland 1977, Prince 1981). In Prince (1992), it has been developed into a more refined theory of information status that considers the status of the hearer and speaker in a separate domain, which generates three possible dimensions of information status instead of the binary new/old. Prince suggests that, using the terminology of the familiarity scale[4] (Prince 1981), *brand-new* entities are discourse-new/hearer-new, *unused* entities are discourse-new/hearer-old, and *evoked* entities are discourse-old/hearer-old.

Applying this to Korean, we could then assume roughly the following sort of distributional pattern for NP forms in Korean:

(7) Application of Prince (1992)'s information status theory (to be modified)

	hearer-old	hearer-new
discourse-old	zero-pronoun	N/A
discourse-new	NP-ϕ	NP-lul

Such an explanation of the distribution of NP forms based on the information status theory seems to be supported by the acquisitional data. In a study of NP drop in children's speech, Cho (1995) found a tendency for subjects to be dropped most often, followed by object and dative drop. Since it is well known that subjects tend to represent old information and serve as a topic element, her result suggests that old information tends to drop more often than others do.

More support for such a direction of analysis can be found from the realization of NPs whose information status is *inferrable* as illustrated in (8a) (Prince 1992).

---

[4] Evoked > Unused > Inferrable > Containing inferrable > Brand new anchored > Brand new

(8) a. I got on a bus yesterday and the driver was drunk.
b. # I got on a bus yesterday and the student was drunk.
c. I got on a bus yesterday and a student was drunk.

Inferrables are like *hearer-old* entities in that they rely on certain assumptions about what the hearer knows, and they are like *discourse-old* entities in that they rely on there being already in the discourse-model some entity to trigger the inference. At the same time, inferrables are like *hearer-new* entities in that the hearer is not expected to already have in his/her head the entity in question.

The question then arises as to what linguistic form of NP's represent inferrables. In English, although it is not impossible to find cases where the inferrable entities are expressed as an indefinite NP, often they take the form of a definite NP form. That is, inferrables are expressed using the linguistic form which is typically used for *hearer-old* information.

In (8a), it is inferrable from the first part of the conjunction that the 'driver' was the one who drove the bus that I got on yesterday, and the inferrable NP took the form of a definite NP. If, however, a non-inferrable NP takes the form of a definite NP, the felicity of the whole sentence breaks down as illustrated in (8b) with the example of 'student'. Naturally, when a non-inferrable NP takes an indefinite NP form as in (8c), the construction is felicitous.

In Korean, where there is no definite article as in English, inferrables typically take a bare-NP form as the following examples illustrate:

(9) a. tolo-eyse wuncen ha-nun kes-to wihemhayse ...
driveway-on driving do-REL thing-also dangerous-CONN
'it is also dangerous to drive in the driveway'
b. # tolo-eyse cwum cwu-nun kes-to wihemhayse...
driveway-on dancing dance-REL thing-also dangerous-CONN
'it is also dangerous to dance in the driveway'
c. tolo-eyse cwum-ul cwu-nun kes-to wihemhayse...
driveway-on dancing-ACC dance-REL thing-also dangerous-CONN
'it is also dangerous to dance in the driveway'

In (9a), the act of 'driving' is inferrable since the most natural thing one can expect to do on a driveway is to drive. In (9b), however, the act of 'dancing' on the driveway is not something that a hearer can infer based on the speaker's beliefs about the hearer's beliefs and reasoning ability. Thus, when 'dancing' is accompanied with *-lul* as in (9c), 'inferrability' is removed and the construction is felicitous.

If we assume that the linguistic form an inferrable takes in different languages is sensitive to the information status associated with the NP form, the examples in (8) and (9) are consistent with the assumption that the bare NP in Korean is associated with hearer-old and discourse-new information as illustrated in (7).

However, it turns out that the information status model for Korean as illustrated in (7) is too simple and needs to be modified to be able to explain the following difficulties: First, the demonstratives are also discourse-old and hearer-old entities like zero-pronouns, but are nevertheless realized as a sentential element. Second, the NP-Acc form is actually often used for a discourse entity which was already evoked in the discourse segment, thus not a new entity any more. An extreme example of the second problem would be the demonstrative NP's followed by a case marker, i.e. *ku kes-ul 'that thing-Acc'*.

The first problem can be explained by adopting the cognitive hierarchy theory suggested by Gundel et. al. (1993), which provides a finer-grained hierarchy for Prince's notion of 'evoked' into 'in focus' and 'activated'. In section 4, I propose that objects can be dropped only when it is *in focus* and that demonstratives cannot be dropped since they occupy the next highest level of 'activated'.

The second problem is a more intricate and interesting one since it is paradoxical in that the stem, which is old information, can be followed by a suffix *-lul* which seems to represent new information. This paradox will be discussed in detail in the next section.

4. Proposal

4.1 *-lul* as a Delimiter: kontrastive focus

Here is a good place to carefully examine the notion of 'new' and 'old'. The notion of 'new' and 'old' used in literature can be divided into two separate components: the first one is about the 'newness' of a discourse entity—more specifically, how the information status of a discourse entity is encoded in terms of linguistic forms for a cooperative conversation between a speaker and a hearer. The second is how the information status of a certain syntactic constituent is conveyed through its location in a syntactic structure.

In the previous section, the example such as *ku kes-ul* 'that thing-Acc' has been pointed out as paradoxical from the perspective of the information status theory illustrated in (7) since the linguistic expression combines a new and old information at the same time. Interestingly, English also has exactly the same sort of paradox between new and old information as illustrated by the following example:

(10) It was *him* that I was thinking about.

The above *it-cleft* sentence is a typical example of the so-called focus-presupposition constructions [5] (Chomsky 1971), which structure the proposition that they convey into two parts: an open proposition as in (11a), and an instantiation of the variable in that open proposition as in (11b):

(11) a. I was thinking about *x*.
b. *x*=him

[5] Other examples of such constructions include Inversion (Birner 1994), Topicalization (Prince 1998), Gapping (Kuno 1976, Prince & Levin 1996), and so on.

The open proposition is generally taken to be 'old' information, already in the discourse-model or at least known or inferrable, while the focus is taken to be the 'new' information. The paradox here is that the focused entity in (10), i.e. him, is a pronoun which generally represents an 'old' discourse entity.

The interpretation of 'old' and 'new' in focus-presupposition construction thus needs to be defined as follows: The division of the sentence as 'new' and 'old' is to divide the sentence into the following two parts—an *open proposition* with a variable and the *instantiation* of the variable in the open proposition (Prince 1986). The open proposition is *old* in the sense of being 'shared knowledge' or 'salient', and the instantiation of the variable is *new* in the sense of not being a part of 'shared knowledge'. Thus in our example (10), what is *old* is the open proposition (11a), and what is *new* is the fact that 'him' is the instantiation of the variable *x*.

The notion of 'new'ness thus differentiated between discourse entities and constructions, let us consider the paradoxical example in Korean. I propose that the 'newness' of a NP associated with the Acc marker *-lul* is two-fold: it may come from the newness of the discourse entity, or from its operational property which performs an identificational function over a set of alternative members generated by *-lul*. In other words, I suggest that *-lul* is a focus marker in the sense of the alternative semantics of Rooth (1985) which is elaborated in Vallduví & Vilkuna (1998): a set of alternatives for the 'focused' constituent is generated as an additional denotation.

Before discussing the kontrastiveness of the NP-Acc form in Korean, let us briefly review the notion of 'focus' in Vallduví & and Vilkuna. They make a distinction between informational *rhematicity* and quantificational *kontrast*, which have been often used under the single term 'focus'. Informational *rhematicity* is defined as the new information of the sentence, the elements in the sentence that are contextually unbound, what pushes the communication forward (Firbas 1964), or what is asserted rather than presupposed. Languages differ in ways of realizing rheme/theme structurally utilizing syntactic, prosodic or morphological strategies.

Quantificational *kontrast*, on the other hand, is defined as an operator-like element whose exact semantic import varies from author to author: exhaustiveness (Szabolsci 1981), contrastiveness (Rooth 1992), and identificational operator (Horvath 1986). Thus, if an expression **a** is kontrastive, a membership set M={...,a,...} is generated and becomes available to semantic computation as a quantificational domain. The exact membership of M is determined both ontologically and contextually.

Importantly, kontrastiveness as defined by Vallduví and Vilkuna is orthogonal to informational rhematicity and thematicity. Therefore, a kontrast may be coextensive with a sentential rheme, in which case a given expression is doubly focal in the sense of being rhematic and kontrastive as illustrated in (12).

(12) John introduced $[\text{Bill}]_{R/K}$ to Sue.

In the above example, the effect of kontrast is merely 'identificational': as Rooth (1985) paraphrases it, if a proposition of the form 'John introduced *x* to Sue' is true, then 'John introduced Bill to Sue' is true. Informally it is defined as in (13):

(13) Identificational kontrast: if M={a,b,c} and P($x \in$ M), then P(a).

The orthogonality of kontrast and rheme is further shown by the fact that kontrast may be thematic as well. A well-defined type of such kontrast is the so-called 'contrastive topic' (Szabolcsi 1981, Gundel 1989), which is by definition thematic. Given their contrastive nature, they are often called 'focus' or 'new', but it has not been clear in what sense they are 'focal'. Vallduví & Vilkuna claim that since they are, by definition, thematic, they cannot be rhematic, but they can be indeed be kontrastive. It is illustrated by the following kind of data:

(14) $[\text{Beer}]_K$ I $[\text{LIKE}]_R$.

According to Vallduví & Vilkuna, thematic kontrast, just as any other kontrast, introduces a set M={...,a,...}. The interpretive effect obtained is that if property P holds of **a**, then other properties P' hold of the other members of M. This interpretive effect is described as follows (adapted from Ronat 1979):

(15) Thematic kontrast: if M={a,b,c} and P(a), then P'(($y \in$ M) $\neq$ a)

The notion of theme and rheme thus defined, let us turn our attention to how each language encodes such information. Different languages utilize different strategies for information packaging (Chafe 1976, Vallduví 1993). For example information structure exploits syntax in Catalan but prosody in English, whereas kontrast exploits syntax in Finnish and prosody in English.

I propose that, in Korean, kontrast exploits the *morphology* of an NP, i.e. the NP form is determined by kontrast rather than rheme. Specifically, I propose that *-lul* is used as an operator just like other delimiters such as *-man* 'only', and *-to* 'also' in Korean [6].

When a NP is kontrastive, it should be followed by an appropriate delimiter which serves as an operator of the related function. NP's followed by *-lul* is focal either in the sense of rhematic or thematic, or both. Importantly, rhematicity alone cannot determine the NP form since both bare NP's and *NP-lul* forms can be rhematic.

The following examples in (17) illustrate that NP's followed by *-lul* is kontrastive, which can be rhematic or not.

(17) a. A: Nana-hanthey $[\text{os}]_R$ ponay-ess-ni?
'Did you send *the clothes* to Nana?'
B: I'm sorry. I forgot to do it.
b. A: What is in the packet?
B: Nana-ka $[\text{os-ul}]_{R/K}$ ponay-ess-e.
'Nana sent *clothes*.'

---

[6] Chae (1999) comes up with similar analysis based on independently grounded syntactic arguments.

In (16a), *os* 'clothes' is a 'shared knowledge' between the two speakers, and it is not kontrastive but rhematic since it does not generate a membership set but pushes the communication forward. In (16b), however, *os-ul* 'clothes-Acc' is kontrastive since it identifies an element from a 'wh-set', analogous to the set of alternatives. It is also at the same time rhematic since it pushes the communication forward by instantiating an open parameter.

As mentioned, the operator-like interpretation associated with *-lul* is mainly identificational. Examples are illustrated in the following:

(18) a. Hankuk-eyse-nun cwulo yachay, kimchi conglyu-lul mek-unikka...
Korea-in-TOP mainly vegetable kimchi kind-ACC eat-CONN
'In Korea, they mainly eat *vegetable, kimchi kind of stuff*'
b. Hamburger 70 cen i-lanikka, 90 cen-ul ccik-ko iss-e
hamburger 70 cent be-CONN 90 cent-ACC type-CONN be-DECL
'I said hamburgers are 70 cents, but she's typing in *90 cents*'

In (18a), the comparable members of the generated set would be kinds of food such as beef, kimchi, noodle, and so on, among which a specific member is identified. Similarly, the set of alternatives generated in (18b) would include comparable amounts of price for a hamburger, among which a specific value is identified. Absence of the Acc in the above sentences would be infelicitous although grammatically well-formed.

Supportive evidence for viewing *-lul* as an operator comes from examples where adjuncts are followed by *-lul*. The following examples illustrate:

(19) a. Kyohoy ka-ass-ta o-ko?
church go-PAST-CONN come-Q
'Did (you) go to *church*?'
b. Kyohoy-lul ka-ass-ta o-a?
church-acc go-PAST-conn come- Q
'You mean if I went to *CHURCH*?'

In the above examples (19a-b), *kyohoy* 'church' is a complement of the verb *ka-* 'go', which would not take an accusative NP as its complement. Besides *ka-* 'go', there are several other verbs that can take complements of NP-Acc form (the so called *adverbial nominals*) such as *nol-* 'play', *kwulm-* 'starve', *ttena-* 'leave', etc. Under the traditional perspective that regards *-lul* as a simple case marker, it is not explained why intransitive verbs take accusative nominal complements, and that even optionally.

In the proposed analysis, these adverbial nominals are subject to the same explanation as the nominal complements for transitive verbs. That is, in (19a), which is taken from a naturally occurring conversation made on a Sunday, the speaker assumes that the hearer normally goes to church on Sundays. Therefore, it is not necessary for the discourse entity to generative a set of alternatives, which explains the lack of the delimiter *-lul*. In (19b), on the other hand, the speaker is implying that he has other places to go on

Sundays but not church. Thus, it is reasonable to assume that a set of alternative places is generated by the operator *-lul* in (19b).

Another point that I should address before closing this section is the ambiguity of focused constituents. In English, for example, the rhematicity of a NP signaled by H* may percolate up to a VP or an IP. Thus, in example such as (20), it may be ambiguous if the focus is narrow or broad.

(20) [[The PIPES]$_R$ are rusty.]$_R$

Likewise, in Korean, *-lul* may signal kontrast for a NP or a VP depending on the context. For example, look at the following hypothetic conversation in (21) taking place in a swimming pool.

(21) A: What's wrong with Nana?
B: [swuyeng hata [mul-ul mek-ess-tay]$_K$.]$_R$
swim do-CONN water-ACC drink-PAST-DECL
'She DRANK WATER(=almost drowned) while swimming'

In (21), although the Acc marker *-(l)ul* is morphologically associated with *mul* 'water', it is more reasonable to assume that the alternative set is generated for the whole VP, i.e. M={drowning, falling on the floor, injury from diving..}, rather than to assume a narrow focus on 'water' and generate an alternative set for it.

Compare with the following hypothetic conversation in a bar (22):

(22) Ne-nun bar-ey o-ase [mwul-ul]$_{K/R}$ masi-ni?
you-TOP bar-to come-CONN water-ACC drink-Q
'Are you drinking WATER in a bar?'

In this situation, it is reasonable to assume a narrow focus for 'water' and generate an alternative set such as M={milk, water, martini, beer...}, although it would be not impossible to assume a broad focus over the VP as well depending on contexts.

That *-lul* can operate over the whole VP is supported from the verbs that take cognate objects (cf. Choe 1999):

(23) Ne-nun ilen tey-kkaci o-ase cam-ul ca-ni?
you-TOP such place-even come sleep-ACC sleep-Q
'Can you SLEEP even when you came to such a place?'

For verbs taking cognate objects, there is no other option for the object than their cognates. Therefore, in such situation, it is more reasonable to assume that *-(l)ul* operates over the entire VP than that it has a narrow scope over the NP.

4.2 NP Forms and Cognitive Hierarchy

In this section, to explain the distribution of zero-pronouns and demonstrative NP, I propose to adopt the cognitive hierarchy of Gundel et. al. (1993).

Based on data from English, Gundel et. al. suggested the following mapping of cognitive hierarchy to NP forms:

(24) In focus (it) > activated (that, this, this N)> familiar (that N) > uniquely identifiable (the N) > referential (indefinite this N) > type identifiable (a N)

The above hierarchy appears to be similar to the familiarity scale of Prince (1981), but it differs in that it distinguishes the 'evoked' status of Prince into 'activated' and 'in focus'. A referent is defined as 'activated' when it is in current short-term memory, and as 'in focus' when it is not only in short-term memory but is also at the current center of attention.

In Korean, I propose that the zero-pronouns occupy a higher position in the hierarchy than the demonstratives, each corresponding to the 'in focus' and the 'activated' status, and that only the entities in the 'in focus' status are realized as a zero-pronoun. Bare NP's and NP's with a delimiter will come in the next position of the hierarchy, although I leave it open where exactly they map in the hierarchy of (24).

The following chunk of data, which is segmented for the sake of discussion, demonstrates how the proposed anlaysis would explain the realization of the NP forms in a naturally occurring conversation:

(25) a. A: e, Wuri **kaori-to** tuykye mek-ess-e
Mm, we kaori-also fry eat-PAST-DECL.
'Mm, we also had fried ***kaori fish***.'
B: **kaori**?
'***kaori***?'
b. A: Eng, keki ku semonakey sayngkin ceki mweya
uh, there that triangle-ADV shaped *like* what-Q
'Yeah, you know, that triangle-shaped ...'
B: ung, anuntey mikwuk-to **kulen-ke** mek-e?
Yes, know-but america-also such-thing eat-Q
'Yes, I know, but do they eat ***such things*** in America?'
c. A: eng, **kuke** wuri abbaka ceki pata ka kaciko ku naksilo capusin ke ketun
Uh, that my father *like* sea go and the reel-with catch thing-DECL
'Um, ***that thing***, my father went to the sea and fished with a reel'
d. B: eng, **kuke** capusy-ess-ta-ku?
what, that catch-PAST-DECL- Q
'What, ***that thing***, your father caught?'
e. A: kulayse appaka **ϕ** ssise kacikonun nayngcangkoe **ϕ** ellye noassessnuntey
so father ϕ wash then refridgerator ϕ freeze put-past-DECL
'So father washed ***it*** and then put ***it*** in the fridge to freeze, and'

cipey kase **ϕ** kacko wasstaka yopene **ϕ** hay mek-ess-e
home go ϕ bring-and come this occasion ϕ cook eat-past-DECL
'I went home and brought ***it***, and cooked and ate ***it*** recently'

In the above examples, all the underlined words refer to the same discourse entity, *kaori*, realized in various linguistic forms. (25a), the NP takes the form of a NP followed by a delimiter *-to* 'also', then a bare NP when it is no longer kontrastive. In (26b), it takes a form of longer demonstrative pronoun *kulen-ke* 'such thing' and then in (26c-d) a shorter form *kuke* 'that'. Finally in (25e), it is realized as a zero-pronoun as it occupies the highest position in the cognitive hierarchy of the speaker as the conversation moves on.

5. Summary and Further Issues

In this paper, I have reviewed the distributional pattern of NP forms in different speech styles and provided a unified explanation for three possible ways of realizing object NP forms in discourse utilizing the notion of kontrast (Vallduví & Vilkuna 1998) and cognitive hierarchy (Gundel et. al. 1993). The discussion made in this paper can be schematically summarized as follows:

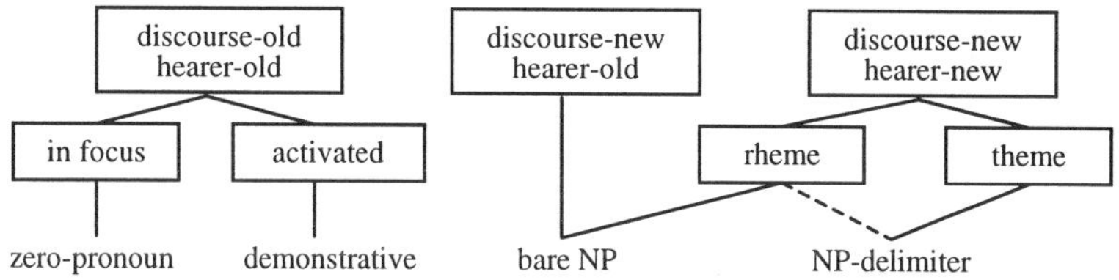

In principle, the proposed analysis should be extendable to the nominative case marker *-ka*. However, since subject position in Korean involves freer stacking of NP's and since cross-linguistically subject position and object position involve other different factors of information packaging, a further study is necessary before making a brute extension.

A radical extension of the proposal here would eliminate the morphological case in Korean. That is, a NP in Korean is only subject to structural case, and the case markers such as *-ka* and *-lul* are in fact an allomorphical realization of underlying information features, whose phonetic form is conditioned by the syntactic case of the stems to which they attach. Again, whether we can eliminate the property of a case marker completely from *-ka* and *-lul* is to be further investigated.

References

Birner, Betty. 1994. Information Status and Word Order: An Analysis of English Inversion. *Language* 70:2. 233-59.

Chae, Hee-Rahk. 1999. Adverbial Nominals and the *-ul/lul* Marker. A paper presented at the Harvard Symposium on Korean Linguistics.

Cho, Sook-Whan. 1995. Null Arguments and Mood Categories in Early Child Korean, in Y. Kim-Renaud, ed., *Theoretical Issues in Korean Linguistics*. 443-462. Stanford: CSLI.

Choe, Jae-Woong. 1999. The Focus and Scope of the Korean Delimiter *-man*. ms. Korea University.

Chomsky, Noam. 1971. Deep Structure, Surface Structure, and Semantic Interpretation, in D. Steinberg, and L. Jakobovits, eds., *Semantics: An*

Interdisciplinary Reader in Philosophy, Linguistics, and Psychology. 183-216. NY: Cambridge University Press.

Clark, Herbert and Susan Haviland. 1977. Comprehension and the Given-New Contrast, in R. Freedle, ed., *Discourse Production and Comprehension.* 1-40. Hillsdale, N.J: Erlbaum.

Firbas, Jan. 1964. On Defining the Theme in Functional Sentence Perspective. *Travaux Linguistiques de Prague* 1. 267-280.

Gundel, Jeanette. 1989. *The Role of Topic and Comment in Linguistic Theory.* New York: Garland.

Gundel, Jeanette, Nancy Hedberg, Ron Zacharski. 1993. Cognitive Status and the Form of Referring Expressions in Discourse. *Language* 69:2. 274-307.

Horvath, Julia. 1986. *FOCUS in the Theory of Grammar and the Syntax of Hungarian.* Dordrecht: Foris.

Kameyama, Megumi. 1986. *Zero Anaphora: the Case of Japanese.* Doctoral dissertation, Stanford University.

Kuno, Susumu. 1976. Gapping: A Functional Analysis. *Linguistic Inquiry* 7. 300-318.

Lee, Chungmin. 1995. Definite/specific and Case Marking in Korean, in Y. Kim-Renaud, ed., *Theoretical Issues in Korean Linguistics.* 325-342. Stanford: CSLI.

Lee, Hyo-Sang and Sandra Thompson. 1989. A Discourse Account of the Korean Accusative Marker. *Studies in Language* 13:1. 105-128.

Prince, Ellen. 1981. Toward a Taxonomy of Given-New Information, in P. Cole, ed., *Radical Pragmatics.* 223-255. New York: Academic Press.

Prince, Ellen. 1986. On the Syntactic Marking of Presupposed Open Propositions, in A. Farley, P. Farley, and K.-E. McCullough, eds., *Papers from the Parasession on Pragmatics and Grammatical Theory, 22nd Regional Meeting, Chicago Linguistic Society.* 208-222.

Prince, Ellen and Nancy Levin. 1986. Gapping and Causal Implicature. *Papers in Linguistics* 19. 351-364

Prince, Ellen. 1992. The ZPG Letter: Subjects, Definiteness, and Information-Status, in M. William, S. Thompson, A. Sandra, eds., *Discourse Description: Diverse Linguistic Analyses of a Fund-Raising Text.* 295-325. Amsterdam: John Benjamins.

Ronat, Mitsou. 1979. Pronoms Topiques et Pronoms Distinctifs. *Langue Française* 44. 106-28.

Rooth, Mats. 1985. *Association with Focus.* Doctoral dissertation, University of Massachusettes at Amherst.

Rooth, Mats. 1992. A Theory of Focus Interpretation. *Natural Language Semantics* 1. 75-116.

Szabolcsi, Anna. 1981. The Semantics of Topic-Focus Articulation, in T. Jannsen and M. Stokhof, eds., *Formal Methods in the Study of Language*, 191-205. Amsterdam: John Benjamins.

Vallduví, Enric. 1992. *The Informational Component.* New York: Garland.

Vallduví, Enric and Maria Vilkuna. 1998. On Rheme and Kontrast, in P. Culicover, and L. McNally, eds. *The Limists of Syntax.* 79-107. NY: Academic Press.

Code-switching in Japanese/English: A Study of Japanese-American WWII Veterans*

TOMOKO KOZASA
University of Hawaii

1. Introduction

The purpose of this paper is to analyze the strategic use of code-switching[1] by Japanese/English bilingual speakers. The data are collected from five Japanese Americans who served with allied forces during World War II (WWII). The data show, as much research implicates, that bilingual speakers use code-switching much the same way as monolingual speakers use style-shifting. Also, the choice of basic language in my data seems to reflect complex characteristics of Japanese Americans. This paper will investigate how basic language is chosen as a strategy to represent the speaker's identity or beliefs and will examine how bilingual speakers use code-switching as a conversational strategy. Whether used consciously or subconsciously, code-switching functions to reveal the speakers' emotions or beliefs.

* I am grateful to Jerry McMenamin, Yukiko Morimoto, Ritva Laury, and Shigeko Okamoto for an enormous amount of support and helpful comments on this work. I thank Ricky Jacobs for steadfast encouragement. I also thank two anonymous readers for comments on earlier drafts of this paper. All remaining errors are of course mine.

[1] The term 'code' is used not only referring to the language but also various kinds of speech variations; however, in this paper, I used the term 'code-switching' referring to bilingual speakers' language alternation within a conversation. Some scholars use different terms, such as 'code-mixing' or 'language-mixing' in the same sense of I use 'code-switching.'

2. Previous Work

Code-switching has been studied from various perspectives which indicates that code-switching is a dynamic activity and a central part of the communicative repertoire of bilinguals.

There are three major foci in the study of code-switching: grammatical constraints, functional or pragmatic effects, and the socio-psychological or sociolinguistic factors underlying code-switching. The analyses focusing on grammatical constraints deal mainly with syntactic structure (Myers-Scotton 1993a, Nishimura 1985, Poplack 1980). These studies explain only structural aspects of intra-sentential code-switching; that is, code-switching used within a sentence, and they do not describe the performance of code-switching as a whole.

Conversational functions of code-switching have been investigated by several researchers (Auer 1995, Blom & Gumperz 1972, Gumperz 1982, Nishimura 1995). Also, some studies have been done by examining extralinguistic factors such as setting, topic, interlocutor, and socio-psychological motivation (Bell 1984, Coupland & Giles 1988, Myers-Scotton 1993b, Le Page & Tabouret-Keller 1985). Finally, some researchers have attempted to find an interrelationship among these three factors (social/structural factors: Myers-Scotton 1993c, linguistic skill/ grammatical constraints: Poplack 1980). These interrelation studies, as well as a longitudinal research on bilingual children's linguistic behavior done by Zentella (1997), suggest that code-switching is a dynamic activity and that the performance of code-switching is involved several aspects.

Code-switching between Japanese/English has been studied intensively by investigating grammatical constraints (Azuma 1994, Nishimura 1985, Morimoto 1993, 1999). A pragmatic analysis has also been done by Nishimura (1995, 1997). She suggests that the speakers choose languages according to the interlocutor's ethnic identity. For example, *Nisei*[2] speak English with English speakers or other *Nisei*, but speak Japanese with Japanese speakers. However, my data do not fully support her conclusion. In section 4, I will discuss details of each informant's linguistic behavior and investigate what determines the behavior by examining the speakers' sociolinguistic background.

The main purpose of Nishimura (1995) is to provide a classification of the pragmatic functions of code-switching. She separates the instances of code-switching into three different types: 1) English nouns in Japanese, 2) Japanese nouns in English, and 3) English and Japanese mixed. She also suggests functions for each pattern: Habitual use and Filling lexical gaps for

[2] *Nisei* 'second generation' refers to people born in America but whose parents migrated from Japan.

English nouns in Japanese, Symbolic value for Japanese in English, and functions are categorized into six for English and Japanese mixed pattern, i.e., i) Reach-out Strategy, ii) Intensification, iii) Frame-marking, iv) Topic Introduction, v) Quotation, and vi) Function Undetermined. Nishimura concludes that the major functions of English nouns in Japanese are *habitual use* or *filling lexical gaps*. However, her conclusion is based on data collected from a single informant. Since each person's habits or lexical gaps vary, her claims are weakened by lack of evidence. Moreover, Nishimura argues that *Nisei* use Japanese phrases, such as *chotto* 'a little' or 'well, let's see' and *nanchuu no?* 'how do you say?,' as "ethnic identity symbols." She has observed that, "*Niseis* talk to each other this way [intersperse Japanese phrases and sentences sporadically] *constantly*" (1995: 165). If so, then *chotto* 'a little' and *nanchuu no* 'how do you say?' could be also habitually used by *Nisei*. I have noticed that my informants frequently used some English discourse markers similar to *chotto* 'a little' and *nanchuu no* 'how do you say?' such as *you know* or *anyway* while they were speaking Japanese. These English discourse markers cannot fit into Nishimura's classifications.

Morimoto (1993) also identifies conversational functions and sorts her data into 21 categories that are sometimes difficult to distinguish from one another. Gumperz (1982) points out that it is problematic to classify each instance of code-switching as having just one specific function. In other words, each instance of code-switching carries out multiple pragmatic functions.

3. Method of Data Collection

3.1 Informants

Five WWII veterans were interviewed for this study. One *Nisei* – Harry[3], and four *Kibei* – Bill, Frank, Kenji, and Mike. *Nisei* and *Kibei* are distinguished by their education background. *Kibei*, or *Kibei Nisei*, is a group of *Nisei* who were sent back to Japan to receive a Japanese education. When these people returned to the U.S., they were called *Kibei* in the Japanese-American society. Parents of *Nisei* often planned to return to Japan after their financial status improved and so decided to have their children educated in Japan to encourage their success in the Japanese society. It was common practice before WWII for *Nisei*, even those who did not go to Japan to get an education, to go to a Japanese language school in the U.S. Consequently, these *Nisei* became bilingual and bicultural. Because of this bilingual skill, almost 6,000 *Nisei*, mainly *Kibei*, have served in the U.S. Military Intelligence Service (MIS) (Falk 1995). These

[3] Persons' names are all pseudonyms.

Nisei's characteristics became quite complex, as they have gone through a severe identity crisis (Kitagawa 1967). Their linguistic behavior appears to be reflecting the complex characteristics.

3.2 Interviews

The analyses are based on narratives collected through oral interviews at each of the informants' houses. Labov (1972a, 1984) stresses that obtaining the high quality of recorded vernacular, in which the minimum attention is paid to speech, is the most important principle for speech variation studies. When a person tells stories of personal experience, or narratives, his/her speech becomes natural because the speaker's attention goes to the content rather than the manner of speech itself. The topics suggested by Labov (1972b) as modules to elicit good natural speech – death and the danger of death, marriage, and moral indignation – are included.

Each interview lasted about an hour to one and a half hours. I interviewed Bill and Mike three times each. The first interview was conducted mainly in English, the second time was in both English and Japanese. During these two interviews, I noticed that Bill used more English than Japanese and Mike more Japanese than English, so I tried to use more Japanese with Bill and more English with Mike during the third interview. During the interview with Bill, his wife (Michiko), who came from Japan after she finished high school, was sitting behind Bill quietly. The interval between the first and the second interviews was about two weeks, and almost six months between the second and the third interviews. To see their speech pattern in different settings, conversations among the four of us: Bill, Mike, Michiko, and I at Bill's place were also recorded.

About 45 minutes worth of narratives from Bill and Mike, 5 minutes worth of narratives from Frank and Harry, and about 10 minutes worth of conversations were transcribed for this paper.

4. Findings and Discussion

4.1 The choice of basic language as a discourse strategy

I observed through the interviews that each speaker's linguistic behavior was different from one another, some of them are contrary to the assumption I have built up while I immersed in Japanese-American society for more than ten years.

Nishimura (1985) describes her informants' choosing to speak Japanese to her despite her questions in English. She concluded that because they know she was a native Japanese speaker, they spoke Japanese to her. This conclusion agrees with my assumption and may explain the language choice of *Kibei* informant Mike. However, other informants' language choice varied from Mike's. Two *Kibei*, Frank and Kenji, used mainly English. Frank responded in English even to my greeting in Japanese. Kenji was mixing some Japanese in his English before and after the interview, but he did not use Japanese during the interview.

Bill also tried to use English more than Japanese. Even when he was speaking Japanese, once he switched to English, he tended to keep speaking English. His code-switching from Japanese to English in utterances which are longer than a sentence level were spontaneously done 90.6% of the time. Also, he used English more than Japanese to respond to my questions or backchannels (Table 1) almost three quarters of the time (73.4%). Bill chose English as his basic language, though he is a *Kibei*. As I mentioned above, Frank and Kenji, who are both *Kibei*, did not speak Japanese during the interviews. Their basic language was also English, not Japanese. These facts disagree with Nishimura's (1995) conclusion that the determiner of basic language is dependent on either interlocutors' ethnic identities or speaker's upbringing.

4.1.1 Reevaluating situational factors

Although situational factors such as setting, topic, and interlocutor's language may influence speakers' choice of basic language, these factors do not seem to be the key determiner of basic language in my data. The setting, an interview with a graduate student for her research, is an aspect to be considered for the speakers' language choice. Kenji, who is *Kibei*, hardly used Japanese during the interviews, although he used Japanese to me before and after the interview. So did *Nisei* informant Harry. Harry and I have known each other for more than three years and he often uses Japanese when he talks to me, yet when he told his war stories, he barely used Japanese. On the other hand, Mike, who is also *Kibei*, did not hesitate to use Japanese even during the interviews. The setting thus has some influences, but it does not seem to be a determiner of basic language by itself.

Topic, as well as setting, may have some influence on the speakers' choice of language. However, I have not found strong evidence to support topic as a determiner of basic language.

We cannot ignore the fact that the interlocutor's language influences the speaker's language choice. Since I found the linguistic behavior of Bill and Mike interesting, I tried to conduct interviews with them in different languages. The first interview was conducted mainly in English, and Bill hardly used Japanese. In contrast, Bill started using Japanese during the second interview, as I used both English and Japanese. Although Bill's basic language is English, his speech behavior changed depending on the interviewer's language. He responded in Japanese to my Japanese questions 22.8% of the time (Table 1).

Table 1 Code-switching in Response

Q – RES	Mike	%	Bill	%	Q – RES	Mike	%	Bill	%
JP – JP	3	6.1	18	22.8	EG – EG	9	18.4	20	25.3
EG – JP	8	16.3	1	1.3	JP – EG	0	0.0	18	22.8
Mix – JP	3	6.1	1	1.3	Mix – EG	1	2.0	7	8.7
EG – Mix	21	42.9	1	1.3	JP – Mix	4	8.2	13	26.5
Total	35	71.4	21	26.6	Total	14	28.6	58	73.4

Q = Questions or back-channels, JP = Japanese, EG = English

Mike, though his basic language is Japanese, responded 18.4% of the time in English to my English questions (Table 1). During the conversation among Bill, Mike, Bill's wife and I, Mike was using more English with Bill than with Bill's wife or me. The interlocutor's language does have some influence on the speakers' language choice. Mike's speech behavior could be explained with the *accommodation theory* (Giles 1973), as he spoke in Japanese with Japanese speakers, Michiko and me, and in English with English speakers. In contrast, Frank, another *Kibei*, did not use Japanese even in his conversation with me. Mike told me that he had tried to speak with Frank in Japanese, but Frank did not use Japanese at all with Mike either. This means that despite his knowledge of the Japanese language, Frank seems to always choose English as his basic language even when he speaks with other bilinguals.

In sum, situational factors seem to affect the speakers' language choice, yet they cannot be the strongest determiners. There must be something else which influences the speaker's language choice.

4.1.2 ACTS OF IDENTITY

The choice of basic language in my data seems to reflect the speakers' desire or belief of who they want to be or with whom they want to be identified. This idea refers to *acts of identity*. Le Page & Tabouret-Keller (1985) examine the relationship between code-switching and the speakers' identities and explain that speakers' linguistic behavior reveals the speakers' personal identities and how they perceive their roles in society. The choice of basic language could be a speakers' strategy to present themselves.

Mike and Bill's speech patterns are drastically different, even though they are both *Kibei* and have similar social backgrounds, I have therefore listed Mike and Bill's sociolinguistic background in order to compare how bilingual ability and attitude toward the language affect the language choice (Table 2)[4].

[4] Some of information was obtained through journals based on the interview done by National Japanese American Historical Society in 1996.

Table 2. Sociolinguistic background

	Mike	Bill
Matrix language	Japanese	English
Year of Birth, Place	1919, Sacramento Raised in Sanger	1919, Fresno Raised in Sanger
Occupation of Parents	Farm labor	Farm labor
Age: when he left for Japan	Nine years old	Six years old
Proficiency of Japanese at that time	Fair in conversation	Fair "had a language problem"
The number of years spent in Japan	One year	Nine years
Education in Japan	Grammar school	Grammar school, Middle school
Japanese School in the US	Every Sunday for eight or nine years	"wasn't too happy about it"
Education in the US	High-school : good	High-school : had a little difficulty
Proficiency of English when he came back	Fair	Limited; had to enroll in grammar school
Occupation	Farmer, Manufacture labor	Farmer
Main language at home	English	English but Japanese with his wife
Religion	Buddhist	Christian
Attitude toward the Japanese language	It is a wonderful language. He always wants to learn more.	It is not so important for his children to learn Japanese
Proficiency of language (self judgment)	Imperfect in both languages	Imperfect in both languages
Identity	Both Japanese and American	American
Favorite music	Enka (Japanese country music)	Nothing particular
Social groups	He is a member of a Buddhist temple in Fresno, he attends regularly at least once a month.	He regularly attends a church whose members are English speaking Nisei or Sansei.

Both Mike and Bill were born in 1919 and grew up in Central California. Their families were both farmers, and after the war they both worked as farmers. During WWII they were both sent to the Pacific by MIS. The surprising fact is that Bill seems to have had more environments to become a Japanese dominant speaker than Mike. Bill went to Japan when he was young enough to acquire the language, and spent nine years attending Japanese schools. He speaks Japanese with his wife. Mike, on the other hand, received a less formal Japanese education in Japan. He communicates with his family only in English. In fact, he was speaking fluent English with Bill, but prefers to speak Japanese with me.

Throughout the interview, I had the impression that Bill underwent a severe identity crisis. Toward the end of his staying in Japan, he sensed Japan was moving toward a militaristic society. He "started disliking" being in Japan. Though he had been identifying himself as an American, when he returned from Japan, he could not keep up in high school due to his lack of English language skills. Now he admires himself by saying, "*Washira eigo demo jozu ni natta* (I improved my English quit a lot)." In the Army he was force to do "dirty work," because "*Nihon-jin desu kara, kubetsu, sabetsu sarete irundesu* (because we are Japanese, [we are] segregated, discriminated)." Despite his belief that he is an American, he feels he was not treated as an equal to others. Now he associates with several English-speaking organizations such as JACL (Japanese American Citizens League), VFW (Veterans of Foreign Wars), and UJCC (United Japanese Christian Church). I have observed the VFW monthly meetings several times, and they are conducted only in English. I have visited UJCC a couple of times, and I have not observed anyone speaking Japanese among themselves, except for some *Nisei* greeting me in Japanese. Bill has been identifying himself as an American his whole life. Seemingly, he desires to be identified as a member of these English-speaking organizations. He thinks learning English in this country is more important than learning Japanese. He said, "you don't think there is no need for it (young Japanese-Americans don't think there is need for Japanese)," "I'd rather have a good command of English. English literature...," and "*Nihon-go wa iran na* (We don't need Japanese)." Consequently, he chooses English to speak with others, as if he presents himself as an ordinary American citizen or *Nisei.*

In contrast, Mike has a positive attitude toward Japan and the Japanese language. At the final session of the interviews, I asked him about his feelings toward the Japanese language. Mike is always looking for ways to improve his Japanese language skills, because "it [Japanese] is a wonderful language." He thinks the Japanese language is more eloquent for expressing complex feelings. He does not have any negative feelings about being Japanese or speaking Japanese with others, rather he is "proud to be Japanese." Furthermore, Mike is studying Buddhism by reading books written in Japanese. The Japanese language has a meaning to him; that is, teaching him religion. Mike identifies himself as an American as well, but he added he was not exactly the same as a white American. He is "proud to be Japanese." Mike's speaking Japanese with me reflects his feelings toward the Japanese language.

Among my informants, Frank is another *Kibei* who does not speak Japanese. He did not get a high-school education in Japan, but after he returned to the U.S., he went to a university and became an optometrist. During the war, he taught Japanese to American high-ranking soldiers, including university professors and Ph.D. students. During the occupation period, he was in Japan as a member of the U.S. intelligence department and associated with some Japanese political celebrities. His wife used to be an instructor at a university, and she does not speak Japanese in her daily life. Frank has been very active in JACL and VFW, and often makes speeches as a representative of these organizations. Frank has never thought about being Japanese or American, rather he wants to be a good human being. However, his continuous use of English gives me the impression that his emotional identity is that of an American. It is plausible to say that speakers' attitudes toward languages and consciousness of identity seem to be powerful determiners of code choice.

4.2 Code-switching as a strategy

4.2.1 Multiple functions of code-switching

Despite Nishimura (1955) and Morimoto (1993)'s attempts, it is impossible to determine a single function to each instance of code-switching. Each instance of code-switching seems to carry multiple functions.

We are able to observe the strategic use of code-switching in Mike's narrative. The following is a part of his story when he interrogated a captured Japanese soldier.

(1)[5] 1. Mike: Soshitara hitori no heitai wa kou
then one-CL GET soldier-TOP this way
'(What I saw was) one soldier

hanbun ***shoulder*** ga hahen de chigiretorun desu na
half -NOM shard by ripped DECL DISC
'lost a half of his shoulder by shards.'

Sorekara yoo miru to ***maggots***-ga orun desu yo.
then well look at -NOM exist-LEVEL DISC
'then I realized that there were maggots.'

Maggots yuutara Ninon-go de dou yuutara eenka shiran.
say Japanese in how to say good know not
'I don't know how to say maggots in Japanese'

5. ano uji yo. are ga zuibun orun desu yo.
well maggot DISC. that -NOM lots exist DECL DISC.
'well, *maggots*. There are lots of them.'

Hode "Itai ka?" yuute toutara,
Then painful -Q say asked

[5] The part of informants' utterances performed in English are indicated by using italicized bold face letters. The following abbreviations are used in examples: TOP = topic, NOM = nominative, GET = genitive, DAT = dative, PASS = passive, DISC = discourse marker, LEVEL = politeness, DECL = declarative, PAST = past tense, Q = interviewer's utterance or question marker, CL = classifier.

'Then " Does it hurt?," (I) asked, '

" ***No***, itai koto wa, koko wa itai kotowa..."
painful fact TOP here TOP painful fact TOP
"" No, it doesn't ..." '

Mou shindorun desu.
Already dead DECL
'It's already dead.'

Numb,

10. ***numb*** yuutara Nihon-go de dou yuutara eenka shiranga,
say Japanese in how to say good know not but,
'I don't know how to say *numb* in Japanese,'

wasuretaga, ***it's all numb***.
forgot but,
'I forgot, but, it's all numb.'

Words such as *maggots* (line 3) and *numb* (line 9) might be used because he could not think of a Japanese equivalent right away, as he admitted. Nonetheless, while he was repeating the word *maggots*, he re-called Japanese translation *uji* (line 5) for *maggots*. Therefore, the function of this code-switching can be identified as a filler or hesitation as well as filling lexical gaps. Also, before he used the word *numb*, he said " *Mou shindorun desu* (It's already dead)." Although it is not an exact translation of *numb*, what he tried to express is understood or even clearer to a native Japanese speaker than using exact translation *mahi* 'being numb.' This code-switching again demonstrates its multiple functions: filling lexical gaps and expressing exact nuances. The code-switching in the answer *"No"* in the line 7 is difficult to analyze. Since this is the response the Japanese soldier made and Mike's matrix language is Japanese in this story, Mike could have said it in Japanese. I could assume that the English word *no* might have become a part of Japanese-American's vocabulary, as Japanese people tend to avoid saying '*no*' in Japanese. I will leave the use of *no* an open question.

Strategic use of code-switching is also observed in Bill's narratives. The following example is a part of Bill's narratives about a Japanese lady whom he met in Japan.

(2) 1. Bill: ***But,*** hitori Osaka kara
one-CL from

ano ***ki***.. youchi-en no sensei-ga kite orarete
that .. kindergarten GET teacher-NOM come exist LEVEL
'But, there was a kindergarten teacher came from Osaka'

Ano ano.. ***Red Cross*** de hataraku noni na.

that that ..Red Cross at work for DISC
'that well, to work at Red Cross'

Sore ga washi uu.. asa.. yo..
it -NOM I ... morning
'that, I uh.. morning'

just about everyday, I used see her.

She says, " Hakujin ga kekkon shiyou yuun jyaga
white man-NOM marry do ask but
'" A white American proposed to me," '

do shimasho ka" yuute ne,
what to do -Q says DISC
what should I do?" she says

washi mo soke, " ***Don't get marry***," yuu te yuuta no yo.
I also then, say said GEN DISC
'I then said, " Don't get marry." '

Any, the people try to marry you,

is uneducated, kanya naimono ***you know,***
with no money

those kind of people, you know
so don't get involved with it, you know, yeah.

Bill switched back and forth between English and Japanese. Bill started to describe the lady in Japanese, then switched to English in line 6. It is understandable that the lady's quote was uttered in Japanese in line 7. However, Bill's own quote '*Don't get marry*' in line 9 is English. Since Bill was talking with a Japanese lady, this quotation must have been said in Japanese. Gumperz (1982) states that not all speakers use the language they actually used in the quoted or reported speech. The quotations in example (2) demonstrate Gumperz's claim. Auer (1995) suggests that code-switching in the quotation provides a contrast between the quote and the report speech. Bill might use a different language in the quote in line 9 to make a contrast, or to try avoiding saying an imperative sentence in Japanese, as it sounds too strong to the Japanese speaker.

It appears to me that Bill was trying to demonstrate the distinction between the Japanese lady and him, an American soldier, by using English, which was not her language. However, he said *kanya naimono* (a person with no money), in Japanese. We cannot determine any particular function for this code-switching. Bill's code-switching in (2) carries multiple functions.

4.2.2 Multiple functions in a "portmanteau sentence"

Nishimura (1985, 1995) has observed a sentence which is a hybrid structure from two sentences in different languages, which she calls a 'portmanteau sentence' as a below example.

(3) ***We bought two pounds*** gurai kattekita no (Nishimura 1995:167)
about buy-PAST DISC

This is possible because English has SVO word order while Japanese has SOV order, and because Japanese has postposition. A 'portmanteau sentence' is observed in the example in (2) line 7-8. Also, below examples (4) and (5) from Mike's narratives are portmanteau sentences.

(4) ***brought him back to Ninth Core-Headquarter*** no tokoro-e tsurete kite
-GET place-*to*-PostP bring come

(5) Washi-ga itta toki nya, ***1942*** no ***January 1st, I went there***.
I -AGT go-PAST when TOP GET

Morimoto (1993) has also observed this type of sentences in her data.

(6) ***We used to walk to*** kyuujo aruitari (Morimoto 1993:23)
stadium walk

(7) ***I would say [it was] about*** 15 gurai (Morimoto 1993:23)
about

Nishimura explains that the 'portmanteau sentence' occurs when the speaker attempts to reach out to two types of listeners at the same time. That is, the speaker uses the 'portmanteau sentence,' in order to accommodate both Japanese- and English-speaking listeners simultaneously. Nevertheless, in Morimoto and my case, the speakers did not use the 'portmanteau sentence' to accommodate two types of listeners since the speakers had only one interviewer. Portmanteau sentences also carry out multiple functions: a transitional point of code-switching and reiteration purpose, and are used strategically.

5. Conclusion

As we have seen, sociolinguistic background, especially affiliation and attitude, appear to be a strong influence for the speakers, and basic language seems to reflect their desire of who they want to be or with whom they want to be identified. It cannot be determined simply by ethnic identity of either the speaker or the interlocutor. We have examined setting, interlocutor's language, and speakers' sociolinguistic background. Every element seems to have some degree of influence, but the choice of basic language was strongly influenced by the speakers' subliminal ideas of identity. Some recent studies on style-shifting (Fought 1997, Schilling-Estes 1998) illustrate that the speakers' style-shifting reflects the speaker's perception of social norm: the speakers' awareness of how they are perceived in a society, how they want to be in the society. In this respect, we should treat code-switching and style-shifting as two points on a continuum. Code-switching is a central part of bilingual speakers' communicative repertoire and speakers use it to communicate their values.

Finally, my research is based on data from a group of Japanese-Americans who are WWII veterans and experienced a complex identity crisis. It is important to see if we can observe the same type of phenomena in other bilingual communities and environments.

References

Auer, Peter. 1995. The Pragmatics of Code-switching, in Lesley Milroy and Pieter Muysken eds., *One Speaker, Two Languages: Cross-Disciplinary Perspectives on Code-switching.* Cambridge: Cambridge University Press.

Azuma, Shoji. 1994. Word Order vs. Word Class: Portmanteau Sentences in Bilinguals, in Patricia M. Clancy, ed., *Japanese/Korean Linguistics* Vol. 2, 193-204.

Bell, Allan. 1984. Language Style and Audience Design. *Language in Society* 13. 145-204.

Blom, J. P. and Gumperz, John J. 1972. Social Meaning in Linguistic Structures, in John J. Gumperz and Dell Hymes eds., *Directions in Sociolinguistics.* New York: Holt, Renehart and Winston.

Coupland, Nikolas and Howard Giles. 1988. Introduction: The Communicative Contexts of Accommodation. *Language and Communication* 8. 175-182.

Falk, Stanley L. 1995. Personal Experiences Related at the 1993 MIS Capital Reunion, in Stanley L. Falk and Warren Tsuneishi eds., *MIS in the War Against Japan: The Nisei Veteran: An American Patriot.* Washington, D.C.: Japanese Americans Veterans Association.

Fought, Carmen R. 1997. *The English and Spanish of Young Adult Chicanos.* Doctoral dissertation, University of Pennsylvania.

Giles, Howard. 1973. Accent Mobility: A Model and Some Data. *Anthropological Linguistics* 15. 87-105

Gumperz, John J. 1982. *Discourse Strategies.* Cambridge: Cambridge University Press.

Kitagawa, Daisuke. 1967. *Issei and Nisei: The Internment Years.* New York: The Seabury Press.

Labov, William. 1972a. The Transformation of Experience in Narrative Syntax. *Language in the Inner City.* Philadelphia: University of Pennsylvania Press.

Labov, William. 1972b. The Design of a Sociolinguistic Research Project. Paper presented at the Sociolinguistics Workshop held by the Central Institute of Indian Languages in Mysore, India, May-June.

Labov, William. 1984. Field Methods of the Project on Linguistic Change and Variation, in J. Baugh and J. Sherzer eds., *Language in Use: Reading in Sociolinguistics.* New Jersey: Prentice-Hall Inc.

Le Page, R. B. and Andrée Tabouret-Keller 1985. *Acts of Identity: Creole-based Approaches to Language and Ethnicity.* Cambridge: Cambridge University Press.

Morimoto, Yukiko. 1993. Social Determinants and Syntax of Japanese-English Code Switching. ms., California State University, Fresno.

——. 1999. Making Words in Two Languages: A Prosodic Account of Japanese-English Language Mixing. *The International Journal of Bilingualism* 3.1. 23-44.

Myers-Scotton, Carol. 1993a. *Dueling Languages: Grammatical Structure in Code-switching.* Oxford: Clarendon Press.

——. 1993b. *Social Motivations for Codeswitching*: Evidence from Africa. Oxford: Oxford University Press.

——. 1993c. Common and Uncommon Ground: Social and Structural Factors in Codeswitching. *Language in Society* 22. 475-503.

Nishimura, Miwa. 1985. *Intrasentential Codeswitching in Japanese and English.* Doctoral dissertation, University of Pennsylvania.

——. 1995. A Functional Analysis of Japanese/English Code-switching. *Journal of Pragmatics* 23. 157-181.

——. 1997. *Japanese/English Code-switching: Syntax and Pragmatics.* New York: Lang.

Poplack, Shana. 1980. Sometimes I'll start a sentence in Spanish y termino en Español: Toward a Typology of Code-switching. *Linguistics* 18. 581-618.

Schilling-Estes, Natalie. 1998. Investigating 'Self-conscious' Speech: The Performance Register in Ocracoke English. *Language in Society* 27. 53-83.

Zentella, Ana C. 1997. *Growing Up Bilingual.* Oxford: Blackwell.

Part IV

Semantics

A Cognitive Approach to Connective Particles *-e* and *-ko*: Conceptual Unity and Conceptual Separation in Korean Motion Verbs

JEONG-HWA LEE
Sogang University

1. Introduction

The Korean connective particles *-e* and *-ko* connect two verbs to form a serial verb construction (SVC), as exemplified in (1a-b) and (2a-c):

(1)a.	*kutul-i*	*chimmolhan*	*pay-lul*	*kkul-e*	*olli-ess-ta*
	they-NOM	sunken	ship-ACC	pull-CONS[1]	raise-PST-DECL

'They pulled the sunken ship up.'

b.	*ku-ka*	*tongcen-ul*	*kwumeng-ey*	*mil-e*	*neh-ess-ta*
	he-NOM	coin-ACC	hole-LOC	push-CONS	put in-PST-DECL

'He pushed the coin in the hole.'

(2)a.	*ku-ka*	*mwun-ul*	*yel-ko*	*tat-ass-ta*
	he-NOM	door-ACC	open-ISOL	close-PST-DECL

'He opened the door and then closed it.'(sequential)

---

[1] I follow Rhee's distinction of the connective particle *-e* and *-ko*; *-e* is consolidating connective particle, glossed as CONS, and *-ko* isolating connective particle, glossed as ISOL (Rhee 1996:15).

b. *yescangswu-ka* *liekha-lul* *mil-ko* *tani-n-ta*
taffyseller-NOM wheeled cart-ACC push-ISOL go around-PRES-DECL
'The taffy seller goes around, pushing the two-wheeled cart.'
(co-extensive/continuous)

c. *kutul-i* *swul-ul* *masi-ko* *no-n-ta*
they-NOM alcohol-ACC drink-ISOL play-PRES-DECL
'They play, drinking (at the same time).'

This paper examines their distinct conceptual imports within the framework of Cognitive Grammar (Langacker 1987 and 1991). My claim is that *-e* refers to a conceptual unity of the sequence of two verbs, which represents a conceptually complex but unitary event. By contrast, *-ko* signifies a conceptual separation of an SVC, which involves two distinct events. This claim is based on the central theoretical claim of Cognitive Grammar that 'grammatical structure is inherently symbolic and that all valid grammatical constructs have some kind of conceptual import' (Langacker 1991:282).

Using Langacker's theoretical notions such as profile, base, trajector, and landmark, this paper also aims to provide two different schematic representations for both -e of conceptual unity and -ko of conceptual separation .

2. Semantic Manifestations for Conceptual Unity and Separation

The conceptual unity of *-e* and the conceptual separation of *-ko* are respectively supported and manifested by their semantic characteristics, e.g. iconicity in writing, intrinsic semantic relations of two verbs, unity of place and time vs. diffusion and positional SVC and locomotional SVC

2.1 Iconicity in Writing

The distance principle of iconicity (Dirven and Verspoor 1998; cf. Haiman 1985) accounts for the distinct conceptualizations of the two connective particles in an insightful way. The two verbs connected by the consolidating connective particle *-e*, which are conceptually fused together into a conceptual unity, are frequently put together without any space in writing between them. They form a verbal compound, as in (3a-c). By contrast, the two verbs connected by the isolating connective particle *-ko*, which are conceptually independent of each other establishing a conceptual separation, are linguistically put at some distance. In (4a-c), some space between the two verbs is recognized:

(3)a.	*ilk-ekata*	b. *mil-epelita*	c. *mil-ecwuta*
	read-CONS go(AUX)	push-CONS throw(AUX)	push-CONSgive(AUX)
	'read'(PROG)	push'(PERF)	'push'(BENEF)

(4)a.	*mek-ko masita*	b. *mil-ko tangkita*	c. *kkul-ko tanita*
	eat-ISOL drink	push-ISOL pull	pull-ISOL go around
	'eat and drink'	'push and pull'	'pull, going around'

Yang (1978: 338) confirms my claim that -*e* type holds "the higher degree of verbal compounding" than -*ko* type. It is also noticeable that the second verbs of the verb pairs connected by -*e* are frequently used for their figurative or idiomatic senses; *kata* 'go', *pelita* 'throw', and *cwuta* 'give' in (3a-c) function as progressive, perfective, and benefactive auxiliary verbs, respectively. By contrast, the two verbs connected by -*ko*, e.g. *mek-ko masita* 'eat and drink' in (4a), maintain their individual literal meanings, listing the two different events.

2.2 Intrinsic Semantic Relations of the Verbs

When two verbs are conceptually closely associated with each other, the connective particle -*e* should be used, as exemplified in (5a-b):

(5)a.	*ku-ka*	*uyca-lul*	*kkul-e*	*tangki-ess-ta*
	he- NOM	chair- ACC	pull-CONS	pull- PST-DECL
	'He pulled the chair.'			

b.	*ku-ka*	*mwuwu-lul*	*ppop-a*	*nay-ss-ta*
	he-NOM	radish-ACC	root up-CONS	take out-PST-DECL
	'He took out the radish.'			

In (5a), the motion verbs *kkulta* and *tangkita* are conceptually closely related within the semantic field of force-dynamic motion (expressing manner, cause and manipulation), and both are roughly translated as 'to pull' in English; the consolidating connective particle -*e* should be used because the verb *kkulta* is conceptually tightly connected with the verb *tangkita* by their intrinsic associations. The first verb in this SVC (i.e. *kkul-e tangkita*), *kkulta*, describes the slow and labored aspects of the event; and the second verb, *tangkita*, describes the quick and light aspects of the event. This SVC refers to a single event involving both a dragging aspect as well as tipping of the top of the chair and jerking it toward the trajector. The sequence *kkul-e tangkita*, which is conceptualized as a simultaneously occurring and "coextensive whole", represents a conceptually single event, contrary to ??*kkul-ko tangkita* (Sohn 1976:144)[2]. It is thus translated in a single English verb 'to pull'. This whole SVC means something like 'He drags and jerks the chair across the floor toward him'. The latter translation is not optimal because English requires a coordinate VP, which suggests two separate events. But the sense of the Korean sentence in (5a) really refers to a single event involving both a dragging aspect as well as tipping of the top of the chair and jerking it toward the trajector (Lee 1999). Another sequence of the two associated verbs, *ppopta* 'to root up' and *nayta* 'to take out' is also connected by *-e* in (5b).

By contrast, when two verbs conceptually opposed to each other, the connective particle *-ko* should be used to denote their conceptual separation.

(6)a. *ku-ka* *mwun-ul* *yel-ko* *tat-ass-ta*
he-NOM door-ACC open-ISOL close-PST-DECL
'He opened the door and then closed it.'

b. *ku-ka* *khal-ul* *ppay-ko* *neh-ess-ta*
he-NOM knife-ACC take out-ISOL put in-PST-DECL
'He took out the knife (from a container) and then put it in (the container).'

Since the two verbs in (6a), *yelta* 'to open' and *tatta* 'to close', have the opposite meanings, and *ppayta* 'to take out' and *nehta* 'to put in' in (6b) involve the opposite directions, it is not possible to integrate these contrasting events into a single conceptual unit. Thus, the connective particle *-ko* is used.

2. 3 Positional SVC and Locomotional SVC

I classify serial verb constructions with regard to the movement of the trajector into two types: **positional** and **locomotional** SVCs. A positional SVC contains the manner verb (e.g. *kkulta* or *tangkita*) connected with a path verb which does not involve the trajector's extended path. The positional SVC takes the consolidating connective particle *-e* rather than the isolating connective particle *-ko* because of its conceptual unity, i.e. the

---

[2] Sohn (1976:143) defines a compound verb in Korean as "a sequence of two or more verbs between which only the so-called infinitive suffix (*-e*, *-a*, or *-ø*) occurs without any pause intervening". His compound verb is identical with the SVC, connected by the consolidating connective particle *-e* in the present study. He points out that this compound verb functions as conceptualizing a group of actions as a coextensive whole.

positional motion (e.g. *ollita* 'to raise', *anta* 'to embrace', *mayta* 'to bind', *nehta* 'to put in', and *naylita* 'to lower') is simultaneous with, caused by, and inseparable from the pulling event in the same place.

Let us examine some examples of the positional SVC:

(7)a. *kutul-i* *chimmolhan* *pay-lul* *kkul-e* *olli-ess-ta*
they-NOM sunken ship-ACC pull-CONS raise-PST-DECL
'They pulled the sunken ship up.'

b. *kunye-ka* *chima-lul* *tangki-e* *nayli-ess-ta*
she-NOM skirt-ACC pull-CONS lower-PST-DECL
'She pulled her skirt down.'

In (7a-b), the trajector does not necessarily change its location, but may change its position in relation to the location of the landmark. Each sequence of a manner verb (*kkulta* or *tangkita*) and a positional path verb (*ollita* 'to raise' or *naylita* 'to lower') represents a conceptually single event in which the manner and path verbs are integrated by the consolidating connective particle *-e*. The components of the conceptually unitary event, e.g. *kkul-e ollita* 'to pull s.t. up', and *tangki-e naylita* 'to pull s.t. down', must occur at the same place at the same time, termed "unity of place" and "unity of time" (cf. Givón 1975; Langacker 1991). For example, in (7b), 'pulling her skirt' simultaneously occurs in the same place as 'lowering the skirt', and is unified into 'pulling her skirt down'. The positional path verb is literally glossed as a separate verb, as in *ollita* 'to raise' and *naylita* 'to lower'. However, because of the conceptual consolidation with the verb *kkulta* or *tangkita*, these path verbs should be more appropriately translated into English with the verbal particles *up* and *down* (Lee 1999).

Now, let us consider some examples of the positional SVC, connected by the isolating connective particle, *-ko*:

(8)a. **ku-tul-i* *chimmolhan* *pay-lul* *kkul-ko* *olli-ess-ta*
he-PL-NOM sunken ship-ACC pull-ISOL raise-PST-DECL
*'They pulled the sunken ship (up) and raised it.'

b. **kunye-ka* *chima-lul* *tangki-ko* *nayli-ess-ta*
she-NOM skirt-ACC pull-ISOL lower-PST-DECL
*'She pulled her skirt and lowered it.'

When the isolating connective particle *-ko* is selected, (8a-b) are not acceptable because these manner and path verbs cannot involve conceptually two separate motions. In this case, each of (8a-b) would be translated as a sequence of two distinct actions, e.g. 'pulled and raised' and 'pulled and lowered', which does not make sense for the situations above. For example, sentence (8a) is translated as 'They pulled the sunken ship (up) and raised it'. However, the pulling up of the sunken ship intrinsically involves raising.

A locomotional SVC is defined as consisting of the manner verb, e.g. *kkulta*, and a following locomotional (or translational) path verb, e.g. *kata* 'to go', *ota* 'to come', *tanita* 'to go around', *naota* 'to come out', and *nakata* 'to go out'. Unlike the positional path verb, e.g. *ollita* 'to raise' and *naylita* 'to lower', these locomotional path verbs describe the locomotion of the trajector. To be more specific, the grammatical subject fills two semantic roles in this SVC, i.e. AGENT for the manner verb *kkulta*, an agentive MOVER for the path verb, e.g. *kata* 'to go', *ota* 'to come' or *tanita* 'to go around'.

The locomotional SVC usually takes the isolating connective particle -*ko*, e.g. *kkul-ko kata* 'go, pulling', rather than the consolidating connective particle -*e* for the following reasons. With respect to the first verb, the pulling event itself does not explicitly make reference to the locomotion of the trajector, for example, the trajector's going, coming, or going around. For the event *kkulta*, the locomotion of the trajector (i.e. the extended path of the trajector) is interpretable from other collocational or contextual information, although it is an important semantic aspect of the event *kkulta*. The locomotion of the trajector is clearly designated by the locomotional path verb of a locomotional SVC. But the locomotional SVC does not establish a conceptually unitary event as much as the positional one, because it associates with conceptually two different events.

Now, consider some examples of the locomotional SVC connected by -*ko*:

(9)a. *mal-i* *swuley-lul* *kkul-ko* *ka-ss-ta*
horse-NOM cart-ACC pull-ISOL go-PST-DECL
'The horse went, pulling the cart.'

b. *kay-tul-i* *sselmay-lul* *kkul-ko* *wa-ss-ta*
dog-PL-NOM sled-ACC pull-ISOL come-PST-DECL
'The dogs came, pulling the sled.'

Sentences (9a-b) are completely acceptable with the isolating connective particle -*ko*. With the connective particle -*ko*, the pulling event designated by *kkul-ko* 'pulling' in (9a-b) is carried out along with the explicit locomotion of the trajector designated by a locomotional path verb, i.e. *ota* 'to come' and *kata* 'to go', and the landmark appears together with the trajector as a result of the SVC.

With the locomotional verbs *kata* 'to go' and *ttenata* 'to leave', (10a) and (10b) are strange or unacceptable because of the presence of -*e*:

(10)a. ??*kay-tul-i* *san-ulo* *sselmay-lul* *kkul-e* *ka-ss-ta*
dog-PL-NOM mountain-LOC sled-ACC pull-CONS go-PST-DECL
'The dogs went to the mountain, pulling the sled.'

b. **ku* *hwanca-ka* *hwilcheye-lul* *kkul-e* *ttena-ss-ta*
the patient-NOM wheelchair-ACC pull-CONS leave-PST-DECL
'The patient left, pulling the wheelchair.'

Note that the locomotional verbs, *kata* 'to go' and *ttenata* 'to leave' in (10a) and (10b), focus on the source of a movement in regard to the motion image schema of SOURCE-PATH-GOAL in that the trajector is conceived as departing from the speaker's position (cf. Lakoff 1987; Radden 1996). This source-focused semantics of the verbs *kata* 'to go' and *ttenata* 'to leave' does not coalesce with the goal-directed semantics of the verb *kkulta* (i.e. toward the source of force). This distinct semantics of the two verbs *kkulta* and *kata* (or *ttenata* 'to leave') makes it more difficult to connect the verb *kkulta* with the verb *kata* 'to go' (or *ttenata* 'to leave') by the consolidating connective particle -*e*. In nature, the events described by these verbs *kata* and *ttenata* involve the trajector's locomotion, which is conceptually independent of the event *kkulta*. When the consolidating connective particle -*e* in (10a) and (10b) is replaced by the isolating connective particle -*ko*, (10a) and (10b) become completely acceptable, presenting the two separate conceptual units.

Now, let us consider some examples of the locomotional SVC, connected by the consolidating connective particle -*e*, which is not common:

(11)a. ?*kay-tul-i* *san-eyse* *sselmay-ul* *kkul-e* *wa-ss-ta*
dog-PL-NOM mountain-LOC sled-ACC pull-CONS come-PST-DECL
'The dogs came, pulling the sled from the mountain.'

b. *ku-ka* *uyca-lul* *kkul-e* *wa-ss-ta*
he-NOM chair-ACC pull-CONS come-PST-DECL
'He came, pulling the chair.'

Although the verb *kkulta* is connected with the locomotional verb *ota* 'to come' by the connective particle -*e*, (11a) sounds better than (10a), because the goal directed semantics of the verb *kkulta* accords with that of the verb *ota*. But the SVC *kkul-ko ota* in (9b) is better than *kkul-e ota* in (11a) because this complex event in (11a) involves the trajector's obvious locomotional extended movement, as clearly specified by the locative noun phrase *san-eyse* 'from the mountain'.

By contrast, sentence (11b) is much better than (11a), although they have the same SVC *kkul-e ota*. Sentence (11b) has a different conceptualization from that of (11a) as follows. The verb *ota* 'to come' in (11b) is conceptualized as if it were similar to a positional path verb, e.g. *ollita* 'to raise' and *naylita* 'to lower'. Before the event *kkul-e ota* the landmark *uyca-lul* 'chair-ACC' is already located close to the trajector *ku-ka* 'he-NOM' (i.e. within the reach of the trajector's arm). Both trajector and landmark are visible to the speaker at the initial temporal point of this event, and can be also conceived as psychologically proximate to the speaker. The trajector *ku-ka* 'he-Nom' is thus conceived as involving a relatively very short locomotion over a very short time in a short distance. As a result of this event, the landmark is induced to move closer toward the source of force (trajector) and the speaker. Almost simultaneously, the trajector reaches the speaker's position with the landmark, and need not move very much in order to pull the chair toward the speaker. Therefore, the event designated by the SVC *kkul-e wa-ss-ta* in (11b) is possibly conceived as a complex conceptual whole.

3. Syntactic Evidences for Conceptual Unity and Separation

The conceptual unity and conceptual separation of the verb sequence are indicated by some syntactic manifestations, e.g. insertion of some linguistic element and scope of negation.

3.1 Insertion of some Linguistic Element

First, no other linguistic element can go between the two verbs connected by the connective particle -e because of it's consolidating power:

(12)a.	**ku-ka*	*namwu-wui-ey*	*iss-nun*	*ai-lul*	*kkul-e*
	he-NOM	tree-on-LOC	be-REL	child-ACC	pull-CONS

ttang-ulo *nayli-ess-ta*
ground-LOC lower-PST-DECL
'He pulled the child down to the ground who was on the tree.'

b. *ku-ka* *namwu-wui-ey* *iss-nun* *ai-lul* *ttang-ulo*
he-NOM tree-on-LOC be-REL child-ACC ground-LOC

kkul-e *nayli-ess-ta*
pull-CONS lower-PST-DECL
'He pulled the child down to the ground who was on the tree.'

(13)a. **ku-ka* *satali-ey* *oll-a* *ppali* *ka-ss-ta*
he-NOM ladder-LOC rise-CONS quickly go-PST-DECL
'He quickly climbed the ladder.'

b. *ku-ka* *satali-ey* *ppali* *oll-a* *ka-ss-ta*
he-NOM ladder-LOC quickly rise-CONS go-PST-DECL
'He quickly climbed the ladder.'

In (12a), the locative expression *ttang-ulo* 'to the ground' can not intervene between *kkul-e* and *nayli-ess-ta* because it cannot split the tightly integrated complex event *kkul-e nayli-ess-ta*. This also accounts for the unacceptability of (13a); the adverb *ppali* 'quickly' cannot go between the verb sequence *olla ka-ss-ta*. By contrast, other linguistic element can go between the two verbs connected by the isolating connective particle -*ko* because this SVC represents the conceptual separation of two distinct events, as exemplified in (14a-b):

(14)a. *mal-i* *swuley-lul* *kkul-ko* *yek-ulo* *ka-ss-ta*
horse-NOM cart-ACC pull-ISOL station-LOC go-PST-DECL
'The horse went to the station, pulling the cart.'

b. *ku-ka* *khal-ul* *ppay-ko* *tasi* *neh-ess-ta*
he-NOM knife-ACC take out-ISOL again put in-PST-DECL
'He took out the knife (from a container) and then again put it in (the container).'

3.2 Scope of Negation

The scope of negation supports the conceptual unity of the SVC connected by the connective particle -*e*.

(15)a. *ku-ka* *uyca-lul* *an-kkul-e* *tangki-ess-ta*
he-NOM chair-ACC not-pull-CONS pull-PST-DECL
'He did not pull the chair.'

b. *ku-ka* *namwu-wuy-uy* *ai-lul* *an-kkul-e* *nayli-ess-ta*
he-NOM tree-on-GEN child-ACC not-pull-CONS lower-PST-DECL
'He did not pull down the child on the tree.'

The scope of negation in (15a) is the whole sequence of *kkul-e tangkita*, not only *kkul-e* (cf. Sohn 1976). The scope of negation in (15b) is *kkul-e nayli-ess-ta*.

By contrast, the SVC connected by *-ko* has a different scope of negation which applies to only the first verb, and not to the whole sequence of the SVC, as exemplified in (16a-b). This argues for the conceptual separation of an SVC connected by *-ko*.

(16)a. *ku-ka* *swuley-lul* *an-kkul-ko* *ka-ss-ta*
he-NOM cart-ACC not-pull-ISOL go-PST-DECL
'He went, leaving the cart behind (without pulling the cart).'
lit. 'He did not pull the cart and went.'

b. *ku-ka* *hwilcheye-lul* *an-kkul-ko* *wa-ss-ta*
he-NOM wheelchair-ACC not-pull-ISOL come-PST-DECL
'He came, without pulling the wheelchair'
lit. 'He did not pull the wheelchair and came.'

The locomotional SVCs in (16a-b) are conceptually more loosely connected by *-ko* than the positional SVCs connected by *-e*.

4. Schematic Representations of *-e* and *-ko*

Now, let us examine how *-e* and *-ko* are schematically represented in the mind. Figure 1 and Figure 2 illustrate the schematic representations of *-e* and *-ko*:

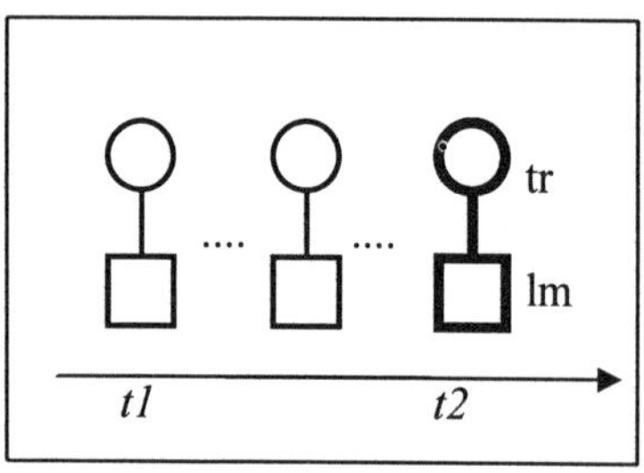

Figure 1. Representation of *-e*

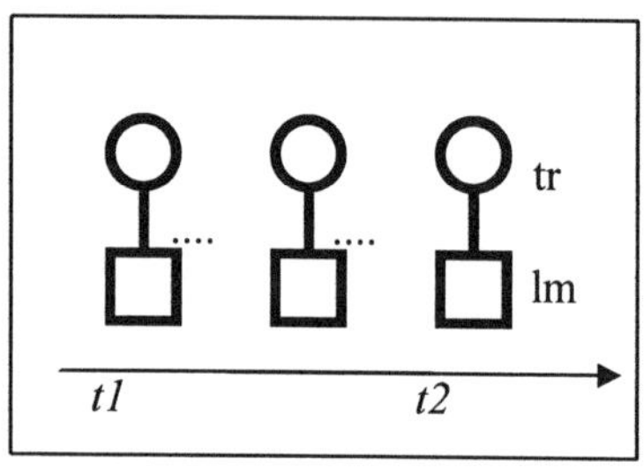

Figure 2. Representation of *-ko*

In Figure 1 and Figure 2, the three smallest circles and rectangles schematically represent the same trajector and landmark at the initial, intermediate, and final stages of an event, respectively. In Figure 1 and Figure 2, both the consolidating connective particle -*e* and the isolating connective particle atemporalize the temporally profiled process into non-finite participial relations. In other words, these connective particles convert a temporal process (e.g. *kkulta* 'pull') into an atemporal participle relation (e.g. *kkul-e* 'pulling' or *kkul-ko* 'pulling') by suppressing the temporal profiling. So, the temporal flow from t1 to t2 is not profiled in Figure 1 and Figure 2. The dots in Figure 1 and Figure 2 subsume all the intermediate stages of the event at different points in time.

For the schematic representation of -*e*, I adapt Lee's hypothesis (1996:85) that "the suffix -*e* functions as focusing on the final portion of a perfective process (translated into English)". In Figure 1, the connective particle -*e* only profiles the final state of an atemporal relation, with its initial and intermediate states or subevents unprofiled. I claim that with -*e*, profiling only the final state of the first event (e.g. *kkulta* 'to pull') in the SVC (e.g. *kkul-e naylita* 'to pull down') makes it easy to integrate this first event with the second event (e.g. *naylita* 'to lower'), establishing a conceptual unity. Only the profiled final portion of the component event (designated by *kkul-e* 'pulling') is selected as the initial facet of the composite event at the initial temporal point of t1, and is integrated with the second event (i.e. *naylita* 'lower').

Some linguistic manifestations support the claim that the particle -*e* focuses on the final portion of an event.

(17)a. *kongchayk-i*   *ccic-ki-e*   *iss-ø-ta*
notebook-NOM   tear-PASS-CONS   exist-PRES-DECL
'The notebook is in the state of being torn out.'

b. *say*   *han-mali-ka*   *cap-hi-e*   *iss-ø-ta*
bird   one-CLASS-NOM   catch-PASS-CONS   exist-PRES-DECL
'A bird is in the state of being caught.'

(18)a. *ku-ka*   *kongchayk-ul*   *ccic-e*   *noh-ass-ta*
he-NOM   notebook-ACC   tear-CONS   put-PST-DECL
'He put the notebook torn out.'

b. *ku-ka*   *say*   *han-mali-ul*   *cap-a*   *noh-ass-ta*
he-NOM   bird   one-CLASS-ACC   catch-CONS   put-PRES-DECL
'He put a bird caught.'

In (17a-b), the particle *-e* is conceptualized as profiling the resultant state of the first event. This small profiled portion of the first event is easily consolidated with the second event, constituting a conceptually single integral event (i.e., *ccic-ki-e iss-ø-ta* 'be in the state of being torn' and *cap-hi-e iss-ø-ta* 'be in the state of being caught'). Similarly, the particle *-e* combined with the verb *nohta* 'to put' in (18a-b) emphasizes the perfective and resultant meaning of a complex event (i.e. *ccic-e noh-ass-ta* 'put s.t. torn' and *cap-a noh-ass-ta* 'put s.t. caught')

Figure 2 represents the component structure of the isolating connective particle *-ko*. By contrast the particle *-ko* profiles the whole sequence of the initial, intermediate, and final states of the preceding event of an SVC. I claim that with *-ko*, profiling the whole sequence of a preceding event makes it difficult to integrate this preceding event with the following event as a whole. Therefore, the first event (connected by the particle *-ko*) is conceived as maintaining a separately conceptual unity, whether it is sequential, co-extensive, or simultaneous with the second event, as earlier exemplified in (2a-c), respectively.

A composite event (connected by *-ko*) can be related to tempòrality in three different ways, as illustrated in Figure 3:

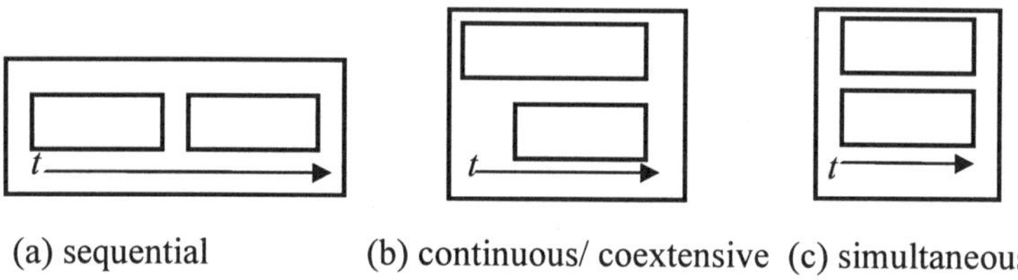

Figure 3. Temporality and Event Relation of *-ko*

In Figure 3, the shared property is that because of the profiling inheritance from the component structure *-ko*, the composite structure profiles the whole sequence of the component states of the first event. The preceding event of the composite event maintains its own conceptual unit, distinct from the second event. Thus, connected by *-ko*, the two verbs of an SVC describe conceptually two separate events.

This claim is supported by some linguistic evidences, as in (19a-b) and (20a-b):

(19)a. *ku-ka* *kongchayk-ul* <u>*ccic-ko*</u> <u>*iss-ø-ta*</u>
he-NOM notebook-ACC <u>tear-ISOL</u> <u>exist-PRES-DECL</u>
'He is tearing out the notebook.'

b. *ku-ka* *say* *han-mali-ul* *cap-ko* *iss-ø-ta*
he-NOM bird one-CLASS-ACC catch-ISOL exist-PRES-DECL
'He is catching a bird.'

(20)a. *ku-nun* *kohyang-ey* *ka-ko* *sip-ø-ta*
he-TOP hometown-LOC go-ISOL want-PRES-DECL
'He wants to go to his hometown.'

b. *ku-nun* *mwul-ul* *masi-ko* *sip-ø-ta*
he-TOP water-ACC drink-ISOL want-PRES-DECL
'He wants to drink water.'

The expression *V-ko issta* in (19a-b) focuses on the intermediate subevent with the final subevent unprofiled, highlighting the progressive or continuous character of the first event. The verb *sipta* 'to want' in (20a-b) signifies the hope and wish of a human being; the trajector wants to perform the first event designated by *kata* 'to go' or *masita* 'to drink'. In contrast to the perfectivity in (17a-b) and (18a-b), the first event designated by the imperfective mental verb *sipta* is not bounded in time, so the initial and final states are not clearly demarcated. An imperfective process does not describe any change through time. So, profiling the constant or expansible intermediate stage of the first event makes it more difficult to integrate this preceding event with the following event as a whole than profiling the final stage of an event.

5. Conclusion

This paper examined the conceptual imports of the two connective particles: with various semantic and syntactic evidences the connective particle *-e* refers to a conceptual unity of an SVC while *-ko* signifies a conceptual separation of an SVC.

Abbreviations

AUX	auxiliary verb	ACC	accusative
BENEF	benefactive auxiliary	CLASS	classifier
CONS	consolidating connective	DECL	declarative
GEN	genitive	IMP	imperfective
INSTR	instrumental	lm	landmark
ISOL	isolating connective	LOC	locative
NOM	nominative	PASS	passive
PERF	perfective	PL	plural
PRES	present tense	PROG	progressive

ORIENT	orientation locative marker	PST	past tense
PASS	passive marker	REL	relative
t	time	tr	trajector
TOP	topic marker	V	verb

References

Dirven, René. and Marjolijn Verspoor. 1998. *Cognitive Exploration of Language and Linguistics.* Amsterdam and Philadelphia: John Benjamins.

Givón, Talmy. 1975. Cause and Control: on the Semantics of Interpersonal Manipulation, in: J. P. Kimbal, ed., *Syntax and Semantics* 4. 59-89. New York: Academic Press.

Haiman, John, ed., 1985. *Iconicity in Syntax*. Amsterdam and Philadelphia: John Benjamins.

Lakoff, George. 1987. *Women, Fire, and Dangerous Things: What Categories Reveal about the Mind.* Chicago: University of Chicago Press.

Langacker, Ronald W. 1987. *Foundations of Cognitive Grammar vol. 1.* Stanford: Stanford University Press.

Langacker, Ronald W. 1991. *Concept, Image and Symbol: the Cognitive Basis of Grammar.* Berlin and New York: Mouton de Gruyter.

Lee, Jeong-Hwa. 1999. *A Cognitive Semantic Analysis of Manipulative Motion Verbs in Korean with Reference to English.* [Doctoral dissertation, Rice University]. Seoul: Hankuk Publisher.

Lee, Keedong. 1996. The [Verb-e kata] Construction in Korean. *Discourse and Cognition 3*: 83-99. (In Korean)

Radden, Guenter. 1996. Motion Metaphorized: the Case of *Coming* and *Going.* In E. H. Casad, ed., *Cognitive Linguistics in the Redwoods: The Expansion of a New Paradigm in Linguistics*, 423-458. Berlin: Mouton de Gruyter.

Rhee, Seongha. 1996. *Semantics of Verbs and Grammaticalization: the Development in Korean from a Cross-linguistic Perspective.* [Doctoral dissertation, University of Texas Austin]. Seoul: Hankwuk.

Sohn, Ho-min. 1976. Semantics of Compound Verbs in Korean. *Ene* 1:1. 142-150.

Yang, In-Seok. 1993. Pragmatics of Going-coming Compound Verbs in Korean. *Linguistic Explorations of Syntax, Semantics and Pragmatics*, 335-357. Seoul: Hanshin.

What does *ssik* in Korean Really Mean?

DAVID MCKERCHER & YOOKYUNG KIM
Stanford University

1. Introduction

In his dissertation, Jae-Woong Choe proposed that Korean *ssik* is an overt marker of distributivity (Choe, 1987). If we take distributivity to be a relation between two arguments, Choe's claim is that *ssik* marks a syntactic constituent as one of those arguments and forces a relation of distributivity. For example, the sentence in (1) has a distributive reading in which each child receives two gifts. Choe attributes the distributivity to the presence of *ssik* and proposed that *ssik* is the counterpart of English post-nominal *each*, also called shifted-*each*.

☆ We wish to thank Hanjung Lee, Eunjin Oh, and Myong-hi Chai for help with the Korean facts, and to Yukiko Morimoto and Masayo Iida for help with the Japanese examples. We are also grateful to David Beaver and Peter Sells for useful comments on our analysis and exposition of it. We are responsible for any errors in the facts or in the analysis of them.

(1) ai-tul-i senmul-ul twu-kay-ssik pat-ass-ta

child-PL-NOM gift-ACC two-CL-SSIK receive-PST-DECL[1]

'The children received two gifts each.'

Gil (1990) pointed out that Choe's analysis was incomplete because he overlooked an interpretation of the sentence in (1) where the children received gifts in pairs. Gil called this interpretation an example of "NP-internal distributivity."

We believe that Gil's NP-internal distributivity is the key to the meaning of *ssik* but we disagree with both Choe and Gil that *ssik* is a marker of distributivity. Our claim is that the function of *ssik* is to form multiple groups from the denotation of the noun it combines with and we argue that this function is independent of distributivity. Distributive readings are possible in sentences with NPs containing *ssik* for the same reasons that distributive readings are possible in their minimally different counterparts without *ssik*. While our paper is primarily concerned with Korean, we believe our analysis of *ssik* is relevant to its corresponding forms in other languages, particularly Japanese *zutu*.

In section 2, we discuss Gil's NP-internal distributivity and provide examples to clearly illustrate the grouping effect of *ssik*. We also include Japanese examples to show the similar behaviour of *ssik* and *zutu*. In section 3, we give the formal definition of the meaning of *ssik*, a definition that captures its multiple group forming function. In section 4, we consider a major prediction of the theory that *ssik* has this multiple group forming function: non-distributive readings should be possible for sentences containing *ssik*. In section 5, we provide additional facts—sentences containing *ssik*-marked NPs in an adverbial function—and point out how they fit with our analysis of *ssik*-marked NPs in argument position. We conclude in section 6 that the grouping function we propose for *ssik* is independent of distributivity and therefore *ssik* is not a marker of distributivity as claimed by Choe (1987) and endorsed by Gil (1990).

2. NP-Internal Distributivity

The Korean sentence in (2a) and its Japanese equivalent in (2b) are examples in which the most salient interpretation is one where there is distributivity of the object argument over the plural subject:

(2) a. John-kwa Mary-ka sakwa twu-kay-ssik-ul mek-ess-ta

John-and Mary-NOM apple two-CL-SSIK-ACC eat-PST-DECL

'John ate two apples and Mary ate two apples.'

---

[1] The following abbreviations appear in the glosses: PL for plural, NOM for nominative case, ACC for accusative case, DAT for dative case, GEN for genitive case, CL for noun classifier, PST for past tense, PRES for present tense, PROG for progressive aspect, PERF for perfective aspect, DECL for declarative mood, TOP for discourse topic, and COMP for complementizer.

b. John-to Mary-ga ringo huta-tu-zutu-o tabe-ta

John-and Mary-NOM apple two-CL-ZUTU-ACC eat-PERF

'John ate two apples and Mary ate two apples.'

In contrast, the Korean and Japanese sentences, in (3a) and (3b) respectively, illustrate distributivity of the subject argument over the event argument—two detectives per working event:

(3) a. hyengsa twu-myeng-ssik-i il-ul hay-ss-ta

detective two-CL-SSIK-NOM work-ACC do-PST-DECL

'Detectives worked in pairs.'

b. tantei huta-ri-zutu-ga sigoto-o si-ta

detective two-CL-ZUTU-NOM work-ACC do-PERF

'Detectives worked in pairs.'

Sentences of the kind in (4)—Korean in (4a) and Japanese in (4b)—have a range of interpretations.

(4) a. namca twu-myeng-i kapang sey-kay-ssik-ul wunpanha-ess-ta

man two-CL-NOM bag three-CL-SSIK-ACC carry-PST-DECL

'Two men carried three (SSIK) bags'

b. otoko huta-ri-ga sutukeisu san-ko-zutu-o hakon-da

man two-CL-NOM suitcase three-CL-ZUTU-ACC carry-PERF

'Two men carried three (ZUTU) bags'

Gil (1990) separated these interpretations into three types, given here in (5):

(5) a. **Interpretation A**: Two men carried three bags each (Direct object NP distributes over subject NP: three bags per man)

b. **Interpretation B**: Two men carried the bags three at a time (Direct object NP distributes over verb: three bags per carrying event, the men acting individually or collectively)

c. **Interpretation C**: Two men carried sets of three bags (The numeral for *three* distributes NP-internally over the head noun meaning *bag*; there can be one or many events, the men can act individually or collectively)

Gil illustrates Interpretation C in the following way: "Imagine, for example, the two men struggling together with a huge sack containing fifteen suitcases, tied together in five batches of three suitcases each" (Gil, 1990:387). In such a scenario, there is just one carrying event and the two men are working collectively as one group. The crucial feature of this interpretation is that the number of bags carried by the two men does not have an upper limit of six, but could be nine, twelve, fifteen, or some other multiple of three. Gil called this interpretation an example of NP-internal distributivity.

The sentences given below in (6) to (8) are the sorts of examples that illustrate Gil's NP-internal distributivity and which cannot be analyzed as distributivity over events or over another NP argument.[2] These examples also suggest that Korean *ssik* differs from English shifted-*each*, contra Choe (1987). Arguably, the sentences in (6) cannot be analyzed as three apples (or children) per dividing (or dispersing) event. Furthermore, the subject NP in (6a) is not semantically plural and so cannot serve as an argument in a distributive relation.

(6) a. John-i sakwa-lul sey-kay-ssik nanu-ess-ta
John-NOM apple-ACC three-CL-SSIK divide-PST-DECL
'John divided apples into groups of three.'

b. ai-tul-i sey-myeng-ssik hutheci-ess-ta
child-PL-NOM three-CL-SSIK disperse-PST-DECL
'Children dispersed in groups of three.'

The sentences in (7) are examples with stative verbs, with the consequence that there is no semantically plural event argument available for a distributive relation.

(7) a. kkoch-un sey-songi-ssik-i yeppu-ta
flower-TOP three-CL-SSIK-NOM pretty-DECL
'Flowers are pretty when they are in groups of three.'

b. sensayngnim-un haksayng sey-myeng-ssik-i
teacher-TOP student three-CL-SSIK-NOM
iss-ul ttay kipwun-i coh-ta
be-COMP when feeling-NOM good-DECL
'The teacher is happy when the students are in groups of three.'

Gil alluded to examples of the sort in (8), where there is enumeration of groups in stacked numeral constructions (cf. Gil 1990 and his "stacked numeral-plus-classifier phrases"). Note the use of *mwukkum*, the classifier used for counting group objects.

---

2 From here on we restrict the examples to Korean and the analysis to Korean *ssik*. However, we believe the claims we make about *ssik* and the meaning we ascribe to it extend to Japanese *zutu*.

(8) Na-nun chayk-ul sey-kwen-ssik ney-mwukkum sa-ss-ta
I-TOP book-ACC three-CL-SSIK four-CL buy-PST-DECL
'I bought four sets of three books.'

What the sentence in (8) shows is that once groups are formed, by use of the morpheme *ssik*, they can be counted. This is a prediction of an analysis of *ssik* as a group former. Choe's theory was that *ssik* is a morphological marker of distributivity in Korean and that it corresponds to English shifted-*each* (Choe, 1987:141). Yet the examples in (6) to (8) illustrate an important difference between Korean *ssik* and English shifted-*each*. In the next section, we take a step towards formalizing this difference by defining the function of *ssik* as a multiple group forming device.

3. *Ssik* as a Multiple Group Forming Device

The name "multiple group forming device" is intended to signify two key features of the morpheme *ssik*. The "group forming" part of the name means that, in set-theoretic terms, a set of elements is lifted to a set of sets of elements. In other words, groups are formed. Implicit in this idea of group formation is the requirement that the size of the groups be specified. As shown in subsection 3.2 below, the types of quantifiers that occur with *ssik* include the cardinal quantifiers such as *han* 'one', *twu* 'two', *myech* 'several', *manhi* 'many', and *kikkesshayya tases* 'at most five'. Quantifiers such as *taypwupwun* 'most', *motwu* 'all', and *twulta* 'both' cannot occur with *ssik* and we show below that this follows from the meaning we ascribe to *ssik*. A first approximation appears to be that the split is between weak and strong quantifiers, in the sense of Barwise and Cooper, 1981 (see also Keenan, 1987).

3.1 The Meaning of *ssik*

We formally define *ssik* as an operator which combines with a determiner denotation of type $\langle\langle e,t\rangle,\langle\langle e,t\rangle,t\rangle\rangle$ to form an expression of type $\langle\langle e,t\rangle,\langle\langle\langle e,t\rangle,t\rangle,t\rangle\rangle$. The notion of lifting the determiner denotation from the first type (a relation between sets) to the second (a relation between a set and a set of sets) is discussed extensively in van der Does (1993) and is also used in Verkuyl (1994, 1998). We follow van der Does and Verkuyl in making use of an operation which lifts the type of a determiner denotation and we assume that *ssik* is an overt marker of such an operation. In addition to the type-lifting, *ssik* provides the semantics of multiple grouping. It combines with the meaning of a quantifier phrase and returns a higher type denotation which means GROUPS OF n. The new expression can then combine with the denotation of a common noun (or noun phrase), resulting in a set of sets where each set is in the denotation of the noun and also satisfies the cardinality requirement imposed by the quantifier.

Our proposed definition of *ssik* as a multiple group forming device is given in (9a). For clarity, the two conditions are specified separately, in (9b) and (9c), and identified as to which part of the meaning they contribute[3].

(9) a. **ssik** $\Rightarrow \lambda D \lambda X \lambda \mathbf{R}$.Condition 1 & Condition 2

- D is of type $\langle\langle e, t\rangle, \langle\langle e, t\rangle, t\rangle\rangle$ (a quantifier relation), the denotation of the cardinal quantifier that combines with *ssik*
- X is of type $\langle e, t\rangle$ (a set of elements), the denotation of the noun
- **R** is of type $\langle\langle e, t\rangle, t\rangle$ (a set of sets), the type-lifted denotation of the verb phrase (cf. van der Does 1993 and Verkuyl 1998).

b. Condition 1: $|\mathbf{R} \cap \{Z : Z \cap X \neq \emptyset\}| \geq 2$ (multiple groups)

c. Condition 2: $\forall Z \in \mathbf{R}(Z \cap X \neq \emptyset \rightarrow D(X)(Z))$ (size of groups)

Condition 1 requires the number of sets in the denotation of the verb phrase containing members of the noun denotation to be greater than or equal to two. Condition 2 states that every subset of **R** (the denotation of the verb phrase) that contains members of X (the denotation of the noun) must satisfy the determiner denotation.

In order to see how the meanings combine to give the right result, consider the sentence in (10) with the constituent structure given in (11). We assume the case marking on the noun phrase is not relevant for the meanings we are deriving and hence we exclude case from the constituent structure and the derivation.

(10) namca sey-myeng-ssik-i anca-iss-ta
man three-CL-SSIK-NOM sit-be-DECL
'Men are sitting in groups of three.'

---

[3] Also for clarity we combine expressions of set theory and type theory. It should be clear that the entire meaning could be stated in pure typed lambda calculus, or Montague's Intensional Logic.

(11)

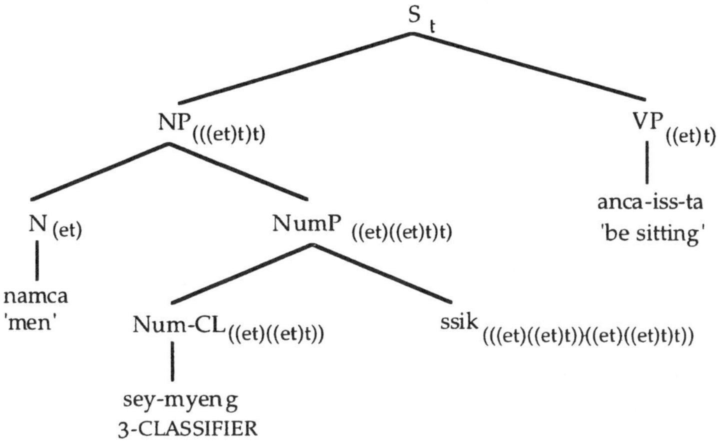

The denotation of a numeral is given in (12):

(12) Num-CL $\Rightarrow \lambda X \lambda Y.|X \cap Y| = n$

This has the type of a quantifier relation and holds of two sets if the cardinality of the intersection is equal to some number *n*. For example, the contribution of the Num-CL node to the meaning of the structure in (11), ignoring the classifier, would be as in (13): three members are in the intersection of *X* and *Y*.

(13) **sey-myeng** $\Rightarrow \lambda X \lambda Y.|X \cap Y| = 3$

We assume that in all cases the meaning of a mother node is obtained by function application of one daughter to the other. When the meaning of *ssik* which we proposed above in (9) combines with the meaning of *sey-myeng* in (13), as shown in (14a), we get the meaning in (14b) by lambda reduction:

(14) a. **sey-myeng ssik** $\Rightarrow$ ($\lambda D \lambda X \lambda \mathbf{R}.|\mathbf{R} \cap \{Z : Z \cap X \neq \emptyset\}| \geq 2$ $\& \forall Z \in \mathbf{R}(Z \cap X \neq \emptyset \rightarrow D(X)(Z))$) ($\lambda X \lambda Y.|X \cap Y| = 3$)

b. **sey-myeng ssik** $\Rightarrow \lambda X \lambda \mathbf{R}.|\mathbf{R} \cap \{Z : Z \cap X \neq \emptyset\}| \geq 2$ $\& \forall Z \in \mathbf{R}(Z \cap X \neq \emptyset \rightarrow |X \cap Z| = 3)$

The meaning in (14b) corresponds to the NumP node in the syntactic tree given in (11). This then combines with the meaning of the noun *namca* 'men' to give the denotation of the NP:

(15) a. **namca...ssik** $\Rightarrow [\lambda X \lambda \mathbf{R}.\ |\mathbf{R} \cap \{Z : Z \cap X \neq \emptyset\}| \geq 2$ $\& \forall Z \in \mathbf{R}(Z \cap X \neq \emptyset \rightarrow |X \cap Z| = 3)]$**[men]**

b. **namca...ssik** $\Rightarrow \lambda \mathbf{R}.\ |\mathbf{R} \cap \{Z : Z \cap \mathbf{men} \neq \emptyset\}| \geq 2$ $\& \forall Z \in \mathbf{R}(Z \cap \mathbf{men} \neq \emptyset \rightarrow |\mathbf{men} \cap Z| = 3)$

Given that the meaning of the verb phrase is simply **be_sitting**, then applying the function in (15b) to the verb phrase meaning gives (16):

(16) $S \Rightarrow |\,\mathbf{be\_sitting} \cap \{Z : Z \cap \mathbf{men} \neq \emptyset\}| \geq 2$ $\&\ \forall Z \in \mathbf{be\_sitting}(Z \cap \mathbf{men} \neq \emptyset \rightarrow |\mathbf{men} \cap Z\,| = 3)$

The formula for the sentence in (16) is true when two conditions are met. First, the number of sets containing men who are sitting must be greater than or equal to two. Second, every group which contains sitting men, contains exactly three sitting men. There may be women, children, cats, or squirrels also sitting with the men in various groups: the sentence is still true as long as the number of sitting men in each group containing men who are sitting is three.

3.2 Restrictions on the Quantifiers Occurring with *ssik*

At the start of section 3, we pointed out that there are restrictions on the type of quantifier that occurs with *ssik*. The sentences in (17) give the relevant data:

(17) a. ai-tul-i phwungsen-ul **han-**kay-ssik sa-ss-ta
child-PL-NOM balloon-ACC **one**-CL-SSIK buy-PST-DECL
'Children bought a balloon each.'

b. ai-tul-i phwungsen-ul **twu-**kay-ssik sa-ss-ta
child-PL-NOM balloon-ACC **two**-CL-SSIK buy-PST-DECL
'Children bought two balloons each.'

c. ai-tul-i phwungsen-ul **myech-**kay-ssik sa-ss-ta
child-PL-NOM balloon-ACC **several**-CL-SSIK buy-PST-DECL
'Children bought several balloons each.'

d. ai-tul-i phwungsen-ul **ceketo tases-**kay-ssik sa-ss-ta
child-PL-NOM balloon-ACC **at least five**-CL-SSIK bought
'Children bought at least/at most five balloons each.'

e. *ai-tul-i phwungsen-**tul**-ssik-ul sa-ss-ta
child-PL-NOM balloon-**PL**-SSIK-ACC buy-PST-DECL
*'Children bought balloons each.'

f. *ai-tul-i phwungsen-ul **taypwupwun-**ssik sa-ss-ta
child-PL-NOM balloon-ACC **most**-SSIK bought
*'Children bought most balloons each.'

g. *ai-tul-i phwungsen-ul **motwu**-ssik sa-ss-ta
child-PL-NOM balloon-ACC **all**-SSIK buy-PST-DECL
*'Children bought all balloons each.'

h. *ai-tul-i phwungsen-ul **twulta**-ssik sa-ss-ta
child-PL-NOM balloon-ACC **both**-SSIK buy-PST-DECL
*'Children bought both balloons each.'

These facts accord well with the meaning we have given to *ssik*. The example in (17e) is bad because the size of the group is not specified and the meaning of *ssik* requires a constituent which specifies the group size. If we disallow overlap of groups, then (17f-h) are bad because both conditions of the meaning of *ssik* cannot be satisfied simultaneously. For example, there is no situation where there are two or more groups where each group contains most of the balloons, assuming overlapping groups are not allowed.

3.3 NP-Internal Distributivity versus Multiple Grouping

At this point, it is important to return to Gil's NP-internal distributivity and ask how it differs from the multiple group-forming function described and formalized above in subsection 3.1. All that Gil offers in the way of a formal account of distributivity is what appears in (18):

(18) a. $[_X \ldots$ *ssik* $\ldots]$ distributes over $[_{Y[+pl]} \ldots]$

b. "In every occurrence of *ssik*, a constituent X containing *ssik* distributes over a semantically plural constituent Y disjoint from X" (Gil, 1990:387).

A precise formalization of (18a) is required in order to identify exactly how NP-internal distributivity differs from multiple grouping. However, even without the formalization of (18a), it is clear that multiple group formation is different. Gil has extended Choe's conceptualization of distributivity from the *inter*-phrasal level to the *intra*-phrasal level (Gil, 1990:387). On the other hand, our claim is that multiple grouping is not related to (interphrasal) distributivity. In other words the meaning of *ssik* is independent of whatever semantic mechanism gives rise to distributive readings. The most obvious prediction of this separation of grouping and distributivity is that non-distributive readings should be possible even in sentences containing *ssik*. In the next section, we argue that this is the case.

4. Distributivity with and without *ssik*

A major prediction of the theory that *ssik* functions as a grouping device and not as a marker of distributivity is that distributivity and grouping should be independent. A test of this prediction is to compare the number of readings of two sentences which differ from each other only in that *ssik* is present in one of the sentences. If *ssik* is not a marker of distributivity, then we expect the same number and types of readings for the two sentences. Furthermore, we expect there to be distributive readings in the absence of *ssik* and non-distributive (or collective) readings in the presence of *ssik*.

To test the prediction, we use Landman's system for counting readings (Landman, 1996) and we determine the possible readings of each member of the pair of minimally different sentences in (19).

(19)	a.	Namca	sey-myeng-i	kulim-ul	twu-chang	po-ass-ta
		man	three-CL-NOM	picture-ACC	two-CL	looked
		'Three men looked at two pictures.'				
	b.	Namca	sey-myeng-i	kulim-ul	twu-chang-**ssik**	po-ass-ta
		man	three-CL-NOM	picture-ACC	two-CL-**SSIK**	looked
		'Three men looked at pairs of pictures.'				

Tables 1 and 2 below present the eight logically distinct readings for the sentences in (19), based on Landman 1996. The notational conventions are as follows: 'C' indicates a collective (group) interpretation and 'D' indicates a distributive (sum) interpretation; 's' is for the subject NP and 'o' is for the object NP; the dash (–) between the subject and object NPs indicates that the scope mechanism described in Landman 1996 has not been invoked, whereas something of the form 'X(Y)' indicates that the scope mechanism has applied. 'X⊕Y' indicates the sum of X and Y and '↑(X⊕Y)' indicates the group individual consisting of X and Y. The arrow → indicates the relation LOOKED AT.

According to Korean speakers, the situation most easily evoked by the sentence in (19b) is given by reading #4, the Ds(Do) reading. Notice that since '1', '2', and '3' each represent two pictures, the total number of pictures looked at by men is a maximum of six. This is the same as the Ds(Co) reading in Table 1 for the sentence without *ssik*. The Cs–Do reading (#7) is a possible interpretation of the sentence, in a situation where the men as a group move from room to room in a gallery looking at a pair of pictures in each room. A minimally different scenario, in which the men look at pairs of pictures individually, is also a possible reading of the sentence. This is the Ds–Co reading in #6. If the groups of pairs of pictures are different, we have the more general reading Ds(Co) in #2.

1.	Cs–Co	$\uparrow(a\oplus b\oplus c) \rightarrow \uparrow(1\oplus 2)$	A group of three men looked at a group of two pictures.
2.	Ds(Co)	$a \rightarrow \uparrow(1\oplus 2)$ $b \rightarrow \uparrow(3\oplus 4)$ $c \rightarrow \uparrow(5\oplus 6)$	There are three men such that each man looked at a group of two pictures.
3.	Do(Cs)	$\uparrow(a\oplus b\oplus c) \rightarrow 1$ $\uparrow(d\oplus e\oplus f) \rightarrow 2$	There are two pictures such that each picture is looked at by a group of three men.
4.	Ds(Do)	$a \rightarrow 1$ $a \rightarrow 2$ $b \rightarrow 3$ $b \rightarrow 4$ $c \rightarrow 5$ $c \rightarrow 6$	There are three men such that for each man there are two pictures such that each man looked at each of those two pictures.
5.	Do(Ds)	$a \rightarrow 1$ $b \rightarrow 1$ $c \rightarrow 1$ $d \rightarrow 2$ $e \rightarrow 2$ $f \rightarrow 2$	There are two pictures such that for each of those pictures there are three men such that each of those men looked at that picture.
6.	Ds–Co	$a \rightarrow \uparrow(1\oplus 2)$ $b \rightarrow \uparrow(1\oplus 2)$ $c \rightarrow \uparrow(1\oplus 2)$	There are three men and there is a group of two pictures such that each of those men looked at that group of pictures.
7.	Cs–Do	$\uparrow(a\oplus b\oplus c) \rightarrow 1$ $\uparrow(a\oplus b\oplus c) \rightarrow 2$	There is a group of three men and there are two pictures such that that group of men looked at each of those pictures.
8.	Ds–Do	cumulative reading $a,b \rightarrow 1$ $a,c \rightarrow 2$ (among other situations)	There are three men who looked at a picture or pictures and two pictures which were looked at by a man or men.

Table 1: Logically distinct readings of the sentence
Three men looked at two pictures
(*Namca-ka sey-myeng-i kulim-ul twu-chang po-ass-ta*)

1.	Cs–Co	↑(a⊕b⊕c) → ↑(1⊕2⊕3⊕…)	A group of three men looked at groups of two pictures.
2.	Ds(Co)	a → ↑(1⊕2⊕3⊕…) b → ↑(4⊕5⊕6⊕…) c → ↑(7⊕8⊕9⊕…)	There are three men such that each man looked at groups of two pictures.
3.	Do(Cs)	↑(a⊕b⊕c) → 1 ↑(d⊕e⊕f) → 2 …	There are groups of pictures such that each group is looked at by a group of three men.
4.	Ds(Do)	a → 1 b → 2 c → 3	There are three men such that for each man there is a group of two pictures such that each man looked at that group.
5.	Do(Ds)	a → 1 b → 1 c → 1 d → 2 e → 2 f → 2 …	There are groups of two pictures such that for each of those groups there are three men such that each of those men looked at that group of pictures.
6.	Ds–Co	a → ↑(1⊕2⊕3⊕…) b → ↑(1⊕2⊕3⊕…) c → ↑(1⊕2⊕3⊕…)	There are three men and there are groups of two pictures such that each of those men looked at that group of pairs of pictures.
7.	Cs–Do	↑(a⊕b⊕c) → 1 ↑(a⊕b⊕c) → 2 …	There is a group of three men and there are groups of two pictures such that that group of men looked at each of those groups of two pictures.
8.	Ds–Do	cumulative reading	Not relevant since the number of pairs of pictures is not specified and cumulative quantification in the sense of Scha (1981) requires two numeral quantifiers.

Table 2: Predicted readings of the sentence
Three men looked at pairs of pictures
(*Namca-ka sey-myeng-i kulim-ul twu-chang-**ssik** po-ass-ta*)
Note that '1', '2', '3', etc. each represent a *pair* of pictures rather than a single picture as in Table 1.

The Do(Cs) and Do(Ds) readings (#3 and #5) are extremely difficult to imagine because they both require the object to take wider scope than the subject. Even for the English sentence *Three men looked two pictures*, the interpretation in which there are six men is difficult to elicit (for each of two pictures, there are three men who looked at it). The cumulative reading in #8 is not relevant here since the number of pairs of pictures is unspecified and cumulative quantification in the sense of Scha (1981) requires two numeral quantifiers.

Finally, consider the Cs–Co reading in Table 1. This is the double collective reading where a group of three men looked at a group of two pictures: there are three men and two pictures involved in the event. In the corresponding reading in Table 2, a group of three men looked at a group of pairs of pictures: there are three men and 2*n* pictures, where *n* is the number of pairs. Recall Gil's scenario of two men struggling together to move fifteen bags, tied together in sets of three. This involves one carrying event between a group of two men and a group of sets of three bags, fifteen in total. If we substitute looking at pairs of pictures for carrying trios of bags, we arrive at the Cs–Co reading in Table 2. Gil's NP-internal distributivity, then, amounts to the double collective reading.

Table 1 shows that distributive readings are possible without *ssik*, just as they are for English sentences without shifted-*each* such as *Three men lifted four tables*. We have seen the double collective reading of a sentence with an NP containing *ssik*. The conclusion is that *ssik* is not a marker of distributivity.

5. Adverbial Functions of *ssik*-Containing Phrases

In all the examples discussed so far, the NP containing *ssik* has been either the subject or object of the verb. But the distribution of *ssik*-containing phrases is somewhat broader. For example, they occur in NPs that function as adverbials, as shown in the examples in (20) to (22):

(20) John-i ku muncang-ul twu-pen-ssik ilk-ess-ta
John-NOM the sentence-ACC two-times-SSIK read-PST-DECL
'John read the sentence twice each time.'

(21) onto-ka i-to-ssik ollaka-n-ta
temperature-NOM two-degree-SSIK rise-PRES-DECL
'The temperature rises in increments of two degrees.'

(22) haksayng swu-ka sip-%-ssik chwu-n-ta
student number-NOM ten-%-SSIK reduce-PRES-DECL
'The number of students decreases by ten per cent each time.'

Up to this point, we have discussed examples which illustrate multiple grouping of the denotation of an argument of the verb. The examples in (20) to (22) illustrate multiple grouping of the degree adverbial which modifies the verb meaning. If *ssik* were absent in (21), the interpretation of the sentence is one where the temperature gradually increases and ends up two degrees higher than it was. With *ssik*, the interpretation is that the temperature increase is some multiple of two degrees and the increase is specified to be in increments of two degrees. That *ssik* induces both the multiplicity and the incremental nature informally supports our analysis of *ssik* as a multiple group forming device.

6. Conclusion

The 'projection' of distributivity is independent of the presence of *ssik*. Furthermore, distributivity is not necessary when *ssik* is present, giving rise to what Gil called NP-internal distributivity and what we call a multiple group forming function. We have provided a formal definition of *ssik* to capture this multiple group forming function.

References

Barwise, Jon and Robin Cooper. 1981. Generalized Quantifiers and Natural Language. *Linguistics and Philosophy* 4.159–219.

Choe, Jae-Woong. 1987. *Anti-Quantifiers and a Theory of Distributivity*. Doctoral dissertation, University of Massachusetts Amherst.

Gil, David. 1990. Markers of Distributivity in Japanese and Korean. In Hajime Hoji, ed., *Japanese/Korean Linguistics*. Center for the Study of Language and Information, Stanford, CA, pp. 385-393.

Keenan, Edward L. 1987. A Semantic Definition of "Indefinite NP". In Eric J. Reuland and Alice G. B. ter Meulen, eds., *The Representation of Indefiniteness*. MIT Press, Cambridge, MA, pp. 286-318.

Landman, Fred. 1996. Plurality. In Shalom Lappin, ed., *The Handbook of Contemporary Semantic Theory*. Blackwell, Oxford, UK, pp. 425-457.

Scha, Remko. 1981. Distributive, Collective and Cumulative Quantification. In J. A. G. Groenendijk, T. M. V. Janssen and M. B. J. Stokhof, eds., *Formal Methods in the Study of Language, Part 2*, Mathematical Centre, Amsterdam, pp. 483-512.

van der Does, Jaap. 1993. Sums and Quantifiers. *Linguistics and Philosophy* 16.509-550.

Verkuyl, Henk. 1994. Distributivity and Collectivity: A Couple at Odds. In Makoto Kanazawa and Christopher J. Piñón, eds., *Dynamics, Polarity, and Quantification*. CSLI Publications, Stanford, CA, pp. 49-80.

Verkuyl, Henk. 1998. Some Issues in the Analysis of Multiple Quantification with Plural NPs. In Fritz Hamm and Erhard Hinrichs, eds., *Plurality and Quantification*. Kluwer Academic Publishers, Dordrecht, The Netherlands, pp. 283-319.

Quantificational Elements and Polarity Licensing in Japanese*

SHRAVAN VASISHTH
The Ohio State University

1. Introduction

Negative polarity items (NPIs) are elements with a restricted distribution: they appear only in "affective" contexts (Klima 1964) like negation (e.g., *not*, *nobody*), questions, antecedents of conditionals (*if ... then*), and expressions like *less than four people,* among others. Some examples of NPIs are expressions like *budge an inch*, *lift a finger*, and *anything*. Examples in (1) show that these NPIs generally do not appear in affirmative sentences but do appear in the scope of negation (see (2)), and in other contexts (see (3)). (In all the examples below, the licensing environment is shown in **bold letters** and the NPIs in *italics*; bold letters do not indicate intonational prominence.)

1a. *Mary *budged an inch.*

b. *Mary *lifted a finger* to help.

2a. Mary did**n't** *budge an inch.*

b. Mary did**n't** *lift a finger* to help.

*I thank the faculty and students at Osaka University, in particular Takao Gunji, Shinako Imaizumi, Hiroshi Mito, Seiji Ueno, Michael Wescoat, and Akiko Yoshimura for their evaluation of the data, comments, and advice. I have also benefitted from discussions with David Dowty, Sanae Eda, Anna Feldman, Larry Horn, Michael Israel, Mineharu Nakayama, Asya Pereltsvaig, and Kiyoko Yoneyama. The usual disclaimer applies.

b. *This new book on semantics is *half bad.*

It turns out, however, that the presence of such a negative element is a sufficient but not a necessary condition for NPI licensing, and that English NPIs display a hierarchical behavior with respect to their licensing environments. As an illustration of this hierarchical behavior, consider the three NPIs *any*, *a bit*, and *half bad* and the constraints on their appearance in the presence of the licensors *few students*, *no-one*, and *not.*

14a. **Few students** are aware of *any* of these facts.

b. **No-one** is aware of *any* of these facts.

c. John has**n't** read *any* of these books.

15a. ***Few students** were *a bit* happy about these facts.

b. **No-one** was *a bit* happy about these facts.

c. John was**n't** *a bit* happy about these facts.

16a. ***Few amateur actors** were *half bad.*

b *Among the amateur actors, **no-one** was *half bad.*

c. This new book on semantics is**n't** *half bad.*

The above facts may be conveniently summarized in tabular form:

	any	a bit	half bad
few students	✓	*	*
no-one	✓	✓	*
not	✓	✓	✓

Table 1

Note that it is arguable whether *half bad* is in fact an NPI as claimed, *inter alia*, by McCawley (1988: 562-563), and it may turn out that English has very few or no NPIs that appear only with *not* or *n't* and do not appear with licensors like *no-one* (see (Israel 1998)). This view may well be correct and it may be that English NPIs have a distribution somewhat different from the one shown above (Yoshimura 1996). The point, however, is that NPIs in several languages (Dutch, German, and Hindi (Vasishth 1998), among others) display the kind of three-way distinction presented for English above. The specific claims for English are not crucial in this respect to the discussion that follows.

With this caveat in mind, what is required for the above data is an explanation of three facts: why is the NPI *any* permitted in the scope of all the three licensors *few students*, *no-one*, and *not*, as in (14); why is *a bit* allowed only in the scope of *no-one* and *not* but does not appear with *few students*, as in (15); and why does *half bad* appear only in the scope of *not* and not *few students* or *no-one*, as in (16). Zwarts, van der Wouden, and others, developing Ladusaw's ideas, have attempted to provide an answer to these

b. *Taroo wa **mosi** *bidoo-dani -demo/-mo* si-**tara** korosareru to sitte-ita.
Taro top if budge-an-inch-even do-then kill- pass that knew
'Taro knew that if he as much as budged an inch, he would be killed.'

c. Taroo wa moo-jiki sinu to i-warete mo *bidoo dani*-demo/-mo*
Taro top soon die that said-pass even budge-an-inch-even
si-**na**-katta.
do-not- past
'Taro didn't blink an eyelid on being told that he would die very soon.'

To summarize, if an overtly focused NPI appears in the scope of the NPI licensors *zyuunin tarazu* and *mosi ... ara*, it does so with *-demo*, and in the scope of negation it appears with *-mo*.

This apparently puzzling asymmetry among Japanese NPIs has a natural explanation in terms of the semantic properties of NPI licensors and NPIs in general. I discuss this in the following section.

3. A Hierarchy of Monotone Decreasing Expressions

The role of downward monotone or monotone decreasing expressions in NPI licensing has been well known since Ladusaw (1979). In this section, I begin by summarizing some facts about NPI licensing in English. These, along with related work on Dutch and German NPIs (see, e.g., (Zwarts 1996), and (van der Wouden 1994)), indicate that NPIs tend to present a hierarchical behavior in these languages. In the next three subsections, I discuss the notion of downward montonicity, its algebraic reformulation by Zwarts and van der Wouden, and its application to the NPI licensing issue in English. Then I show that the Japanese data presented above receive a natural account in terms of the Zwarts/van der Wouden view.

3.1 Some Facts about English NPIs

Some simple examples of NPIs from English are *any*, *a bit*, and *half bad*; see (van der Wouden 1994:141) and (McCawley 1988:562-563) for a detailed discussion of these and other NPIs. Comparing the pairs given in the (a) examples to those in the (b) examples in (11)-(13), it is clear that each of these NPIs must be licensed by the negative element *n't*. In (12b), although a literal reading is available in the positive context, the NPI reading is not; such NPIs are known as *minimizers* (see (Bolinger 1975)).

11a. John has**n't** talked about *any* of these problems.

b. *John has talked about *any* of these problems.

12a. John was**n't** *a bit* happy about these problems.

b. #John was *a bit* happy about these problems.

13a. This new book on semantics is**n't** *half bad*.

8a. *arukooru o *ittekitari to -demo/-mo* nonda no wa
alcohol acc one-drop even drank nl top
zyuunin tarazu datta.
ten-people less-than were

'Less than ten people drank even a drop of alcohol.'

b. **mosi** arukooru o *ittekitari to -demo/*mo* nond-**ara**
if alcohol acc one-drop-even drink-then
arutyuu ni-naru yo.
alcoholism become emph

'If you drink even a drop of alcohol, you'll slip into alcoholism.'

c. arutyuu ga naotte kara-to-iu-mono *ittekitari to*-demo/-mo*
alcoholism nom recover after-ever-since one drop even
nondei-**nai**.
drinking not

'He hasn't drunk a drop ever since he recovered from alcoholism.'

Even more restricted NPIs are bare NPIs *roku na*, 'satisfactory', and overtly focused NPIs like *bidoo dani mo s-*, 'to budge an inch'/'to blink an eyelid'. As shown below, *roku na*, appears only in the scope of negation and never with the other two licensors. All bare NPIs and most of the overtly focused NPIs fall under this class of NPI.

9a. *ano daigaku de *roku-na* ronbun o kaita-no-wa
that university at satisfactory thesis acc wrote-nl-top
zyuunin tarazu datta.
ten-people less-than were
'Less than ten people have produced a decent thesis at that university.'

b. ***mosi** *roku-na* NPI-no-ronbun ga a-tt**ara** yomi-tai mono da-ne.
if satisfactory NPI-poss-article nom be-then read-want nl cop
'If there is an article on NPIs that is worth reading, I'd like to read it.'

c. Taroo wa *roku-na* ronbun o kaita koto ga **nai**.
Taro top satisfactory paper acc wrote nl nom not
'Taro has never written a decent research paper in his life.'

An example of an overtly focused NPI having such a restricted occurrence is *bidoo dani mo s-*, 'to budge an inch':

10a. *siken ni otite *bidoo-dani-demo/-mo* sita no wa
test in fail budge-an-inch-even did nl top
zyuunin tarazu datta.
ten-people less-than were
'Less than ten (students) were upset upon failing the test.'

per, I consider three NPI licensing contexts, *zyuunin tarazu*, 'less than ten people', *mosi...-ara*, 'if...then', and *nai*, 'not'. These particular contexts are interesting because they reveal a clear pattern of NPI licensing based on their logico-semantic properties (discussed further on). In the next two subsections, we look at the behavior of these two kinds of NPI in the licensing contexts mentioned above.

2.2 *-mo/-demo* Alternation in Overtly Focused NPIs

NPIs like *hito-koto-demo/-mo moras-*, 'to say even a word', and *itiru-no-nozomi-demo/-mo*, 'even the slightest hope', are licensed in all the three contexts, but it is only in the scope of the licensor *nai*, 'not', that the affix -*mo* occurs; in the other contexts, the affix must be *-demo*. The following examples show this.

6a. gokuhi syorui ni kansite *hito-koto -demo/*-mo moras*ita no wa
confidential papers dat regarding one word-even leaked nl top
zyuunin tarazu datta.
ten-people less-than were
'Less than ten people revealed anything about the confidential papers.'

b. **mosi** syorui ni kansite *hito-koto-demo/*-mo morasi-***tara** kubi da-yo.
if papers dat regarding one word-even leak-then fired are
'If you say a word about the papers, you'll be fired.'

c. kono koto ni tuite wa *hito-koto*-demo/-mo morasa* **nai**-de-ne.
this fact dat about top one-word-even leak not
'Please don't say a word about this to anyone.'

7a. siken ni ukaru *itiru- no- nozomi-demo/*-mo* aru no wa
test in pass slightest-poss-hope-even have nl top
zyuunin tarazu da.
ten-people less-than are
'Less than ten people have the slightest chance to succeed in the test.'

b. Taroo ni **mosi** siken ni ukaru *itiru- no-nozomi-demo/*-mo* atta **nara** ...
Taro dat if test in pass slightest–poss-hope-even had then
'If Taro had the slightest chance of passing the test...'

c. siken ni ukaru koto ni tuite wa *itiru-no-nozomi-*demo/-mo* **nai**.
test in pass thing in regarding top slightest-poss-hope-even not
'There isn't even the slightest hope (of his) passing the test.'

However, not all NPIs pattern like the ones above. Consider the NPI *itteki tari-to-demo/-mo*, 'even a drop'. This appears in more restricted contexts; it is licensed only with *mosi ... -ara* and *nai*, but not with *zyuunin tarazu*. Again, only *-mo* occurs with the NPI when it is in the scope of *nai*, and only *-demo* occurs with the NPI in the scope of *mosi ... -ara*.

3a. I wonder **if** Mary will *budge an inch* to help.

b. **Nobody** *lifted a finger* to help.

Ever since Klima's work, many researchers have tried to provide a uniform characterization of NPIs and their licensing contexts, often taking radically differing approaches. Among them, Ladusaw (1979) has argued for a semantic constraint on NPIs, namely, the downward monotonicity property of licensing contexts (discussed below). In this paper we explore this semantic constraint in the context of Japanese NPIs. The paper is organized as follows: Section 2 introduces the different types of NPI in Japanese and presents the phenomenon of *-mo/-demo* alternation among NPIs; Section 3 presents the background for Zwarts' (1996) and van der Wouden's (1994) theory of NPI licensing, and shows that the Japanese data provide strong support for their view, modulo certain language specific differences; and Section 4 concludes the paper.

2. NPI Licensing in Japanese

2.1 Types of NPIs in Japanese

I will distinguish between OVERTLY FOCUSED NPIS, which always have a quantificational element *-mo* or *-demo* affixed to them (see (4) below) and BARE NPIS, which never have such an element (as shown in (5)).

4a. *dare mo* ko-**na**-katta.
anyone come-not-past
'No one came.'

b. Taroo wa *bidoo dani mo* si-**na**-katta.
Taro top budge-an-inch-even do-not-past
'Taro didn't budge an inch.'

5a. Taroo wa *roku-na* ronbun o kaita koto ga **nai**.
Taro top satisfactory paper acc wrote nl nom not
'Taro has never written a decent (research) paper in his life.'

b. Ken wa yasai *sika* tabe-**nai**.
Ken top vegetables apart from eat-not
'Ken doesn't eat anything apart from vegetables.'

Other examples of overtly focused NPI's are: *oyobi mo tuka-*, 'is no match for', *ki ni mo kake-*, 'pay no attention whatsoever to', *ittekitari-to mo*, 'even a drop', *hito-koto mo moras*, 'say a word', *itiru no nozomi mo*, 'even the slightest hope', *titto-mo*, 'the least bit'; and examples of bare NPIs are: *kessite*, 'at all', *metta-ni*, 'rarely', and *betu-ni*, '(not) particularly'. Due to limitations of space, we will consider only a subset of these here.

As mentioned earlier, NPIs are licensed only in certain kinds of negative contexts, like negation, antecedents of conditionals, and so on. In this pa-

questions. Before describing Zwarts' and van der Wouden's view of NPI licensing, it is necessary to review the phenomenon of monotonicity in natural language.

3.2 Monotonicity and Natural Language

Ever since Barwise and Cooper (1986), noun phrases (NPs) have been treated as generalized quantifiers, that is, as (higher order) set-theoretic entities consisting of collections of sets. Moreover, certain quantified NPs, such as *few N* and *at most n N*, happen to have the set-theoretic property of being closed under subsets: given a universe U, sets X and Y, and a (generalized) quantifier Q, if $X \in Q$ and $Y \subseteq X \subseteq U$, then $Y \in Q$. Such quantifiers are known as *downward entailing* or *monotone decreasing* (Barwise and Cooper 1986). Monotone decreasing quantifiers contrast with *upward entailing* or *monotone increasing* quantifiers such as *every N*, and *at least n N*, which have the property of being closed under *super*sets. Set-theoretically, upward entailment amounts to the following statement: if $X \in Q$ and $X \subseteq Y \subseteq U$, then $Y \in Q$.

As an example of downward entailing expressions, consider the sentence *few men ran*,which contains the downward entailing quantifier *few men*. Given the truth of this expression, we can conclude that the expression *few men ran slowly* must also be true. Here, the set of slow runners is in general a proper subset of the set of runners. The converse, however, is not true. That is, given that *few men ran slowly* is true, we cannot conclude that *few men ran* must also be true. In other words, we cannot reason from a set such as one characterizing the property of running slowly to one of its supersets, which in this case is the set characterizing the property of running. The discussion in this paper is limited to noun phrases as generalized quantifiers, which take the verb phrase denotation as argument. However, it is also possible to consider a determiner as a two-place relation which takes the noun and the verb phrase as arguments. In such a case, one can then speak of downward and upward monotonicity applying independently to both the first and second arguments of the determiner. For example, the generalized determiner *every* can be regarded as taking two arguments, a first argument, such as *woman*, with which it forms an NP *every woman*, and a second argument, such as the verb phrase *is running*, to form the sentence *every woman is running*. As the reader can verify, *every* happens to be downward monotone in its first argument, but upward monotone in its second argument: *every woman is running* entails *every tall woman is running* but not *every woman is running in the park*. In this paper, when talking about NPs as NPI licensors, in the case where I describe an NP as monotone decreasing, it should be clear that I am referring to the monotonicity property as applying to the second argument of the generalized determiner in question.

Zwarts (1996:175) and van der Wouden (1994:94-111) note that there is an alternative, boolean algebraic way of establishing whether an expression is downward monotone. I adapt their results in the following simplified schemas.

17a. SCHEMA 1 A functor f is monotone decreasing iff:
f(X *or* Y) $\rightarrow$ f(X) *and* f(Y).

b. SCHEMA 2 A functor f is anti-additive iff:
f(X *or* Y) $\leftrightarrow$f(X) *and* f(Y).

c. SCHEMA 3 A functor f is antimorphic iff:
(a) f(X *or* Y) $\leftrightarrow$ f(X) *and* f(Y)
(b) f(X *and* Y) $\leftrightarrow$ f(X) *or* f(Y).

Let us examine the English counterparts of the first two of these classes of functions. Looking first at monotone decreasing functors as defined in Schema 1, note first of all that Schema 1 corresponds to one half of the first of De Morgan's laws of negation, stated below. That is, monotone decreasing functors are weakly negative contexts, since they satisfy only part of De Morgan's first law.

18a. De Morgan's First Law: $\neg (A \vee B) \leftrightarrow \neg A \wedge \neg B$.
b. De Morgan's Second Law: $\neg (A \wedge B) \leftrightarrow \neg A \vee \neg B$.

In English, several NPs qualify as monotone decreasing on the basis of the test given in Schema 1; Zwarts (1996:176) lists twenty-one such NPs but we consider only two, *few N* and *at most n N*, by way of illustration. Applying Schema 1 to the expression *few men*, we find that it does indeed satisfy the schema.

19a. *Few men* drink or smoke $\rightarrow$ *few men* drink and *few men* smoke.

b. *At most two men* drink or smoke $\rightarrow$ *at most two men* drink and *at most two men* smoke.

Turning now to anti-additive functors as defined in Schema 2, notice that the definition corresponds to the first of De Morgan's laws in its entirety. In other words, these constitute a stronger negative context than monotone decreasing functors. Zwarts (1996:184) lists eleven NPs that qualify as anti-additive, but we consider only two for purposes of illustration: *no N* and *none of the N*.

20a. *No men* drink or smoke $\leftrightarrow$ *no men* drink and *no men* smoke.

b. *None of the men* drink or smoke $\leftrightarrow$ *none of the men* drink and *none of the men* smoke.

It is obvious from the above schemas that anti-additive expressions constitute a subset of monotone decreasing ones, since anti-additivity is simply a more restrictive condition than monotone decreasingness. The significance of this fact is that if an NPI is licensed in a monotone decreasing context, it must necessarily be licensed in an anti-additive one as well; however, the converse is not true, as we will presently see. Put another way, all anti-additive contexts, which satisfy the more restrictive biconditional in Schema 2, are also monotone decreasing ones, since they naturally satisfy the less restrictive implication of Schema 1; the converse is not true. A similar distinction holds between anti-additive expressions and antimorphic expressions (such as *not*): antimorphic expressions are a subset of anti-additive expressions. By transitivity, it follows that antimorphic expressions are a subset of monotone decreasing ones as well.

With these distinctions in mind, I now present a summary of van der Wouden's (1994) conclusions regarding negative polarity and its connection to downward monotonicity.

3.3 Strong, Medium, and Weak NPIs in English

To recall the case of English, shown in (14)-(16), *any* appears in all downward entailing contexts (i.e., monotone decreasing, anti-additive, and antimorphic), *a bit* only in anti-additive contexts (i.e., anti-additive and antimorphic), and *half bad* only in antimorphic contexts. Van der Wouden refers to NPIs like *any* as 'weak', those like *a bit* as 'medium', and those like *half bad* as 'strong'. The main idea is that weak NPIs appear in all weakly negative contexts (this encompasses the three kinds of negative contexts), medium NPIs appear in medium negative contexts (all anti-additive contexts, and therefore all antimorphic contexts), and strong NPIs appear only in strong negative contexts (antimorphic contexts). Van der Wouden thus defines three classes of NPI:

21a. Definition:
An NPI is Weak iff it is licensed in a monotone decreasing context.

b. Definition:
An NPI is Medium iff it is licensed in an anti-additive context.

c. Definition:
An NPI is Strong iff it is licensed in an antimorphic context.

The English facts indicate that the strong, medium, and weak distinction of NPIs is meaningful and sheds new light on the factors constraining the occurrence of NPIs in natural language. Moreover, van der Wouden claims similar results for Dutch, and Vasishth (1998) for Hindi. These results are summarized in Table 2 below.

	Weak NPIs	Medium NPIs	Strong NPIs
few students	✓	*	*
no-one	✓	✓	*
not	✓	✓	✓

Table 2

3.4 NPI Licensors in Japanese

Recall the three NPI licensors we have been considering in the case of Japanese: *zyuunin tarazu*, *mosi ... -ara*, and *nai*. As the following instantiations of Schemas 1-3 show, these are monotone decreasing, anti-additive,and antimorphic, respectively:

22. sake o nomu ka tabako o suu-ka sita no wa
sake acc drink or cigarette acc smoke did nl top
zyuunin tarazu datta →
ten people less-than were
sake o nonda no wa zyuunin tarazu datta si
alcohol acc drank nl top ten people less-than were and
tabako o sutta no mo zyuunin tarazu datta.
cigarette acc smoked nl also ten people less-than were
'Less than ten people smoked or drank → Less than ten people smoked and less than ten people danced.'

23. mosi o-sake o nomu ka tabako o suu no nara, okorimasu ↔
if hon-sake acc drink or cigarette acc smoke nl then be-angry
mosi o-sake o nomu no nara okorimasu
if hon-sake acc drink nl then be-angry
mata, mosi tabako o suu no nara okorimasu.
and if cigarette acc smoke nl then be-angry
'If you drink or smoke, I'll be angry ↔ if you drink I'll be angry and if you smoke I'll be angry.'

24a. Taroo ga sake o nomu ka tabako o suu-ka to-iu-koto wa nai ↔
Taro nom sake acc drink or cigarette acc smoke that top not
Taroo wa sake mo noma-nai, katu tabako mo suwa-nai.
Taro top sake also drinks-not and cigarette also smokes-not
'It is not the case that Taro drinks or smokes ↔
it is not the case that Taro drinks, and it is not the case that Taro smokes.'

b. Taroo ga sake mo nomi katu tabako mo suu to-iu-koto
Taro nom sake also drink and cigarette also smoke that
de-wa nai ↔
not
Taroo wa sake o noma-nai ka tabako o suwa-nai-ka
Taro top sake acc drinks-not or cigarette acc smokes-not
(no dochira) da.
either is
'It is not the case that Taro drinks and smokes ↔
it is not the case that Taro drinks, or it is not the case that Taro smokes.

Reconsidering the Japanese data in this new light, we find that these also separate into weak, medium, and strong NPIs, but overtly focused NPIs have their licensing environment morphologically marked: *-demo* marks non-antimorphic licensing contexts and *-mo* marks antimorphic ones. The majority of overtly focused NPIs are strong, as are all bare NPIs. The facts about overtly focused NPIs are summarized in the table below.

	Weak NPI-demo	Weak NPI-mo	Med. NPI-demo	Med. NPI-mo	Strong NPI-demo	Strong NPI-mo
Monotone dec.	✓	*	*	*	*	*
Anti-additive	✓	*	✓	*	*	*
Antimorphic	*	✓	*	✓	*	✓

Table 3

Thus, these data are consistent with the monotonicity thesis, and raise an interesting problem for purely syntactic accounts of NPI licensing in Japanese since these accounts typically rely only on configurational/structural relationships between licensors and NPIs. These data, however, point to a semantic constraint.

4. Concluding Remarks

In sum, this paper reveals a hitherto unnoticed asymmetry in Japanese NPI licensing and provides a semantic, cross-linguistically motivated account. This is not to say that structural (i.e., syntactic) effects are irrelevant in Japanese. Consider the case of double negatives. These were first noticed by Baker (1970). The issue is that NPIs can occur in the scope of two downward monotone expressions:

25a. **If** he *lifts a finger*, fire him.

b. **If** he does**n't** *lift a finger*, fire him.

Thus, an NPI is licensed if it is in the scope of at least one downward monotone expression (Ladusaw 1979), although in English it need not be the licensor closest to the NPI (see (Fry 1999)). In Japanese, the presence of *-mo* or *-demo* (which, as we have seen, are morphological markers of the licensing contexts), clearly tells us that the licensor is always the lowest c-commanding one. We illustrate this with a medium NPI below.

26a. *arukooru-o *ittekitari-to-demo/-mo* nonda-no-wa
alcohol-acc one-drop-even drank-nl-top
zyuunin tarazu datta.
ten-people less-than were
'Less than ten people had even a drop of alcohol.'

b. arukooru-o *ittekitari-to*-demo/mo* nondei-**nai**-no-wa
alcohol-acc one-drop-even drank-not-nl-top
zyuunin tarazu datta.
ten-people less-than were
'Less than ten people haven't drink even a drop of alcohol.'

(26a) is unacceptable since the medium NPI *ittekitari-to-demo/-mo* is in the scope of a monotone decreasing licensor; but in (26b), the lowest c-commanding licensor is the antimorphic *nai*, and we know that it is the licensor since the NPI has the affix *-mo* which is associated with antimorphic contexts when it occurs with NPIs.

Interestingly, Pereltsvaig (1998) has independently shown that Russian NPIs also have distinct morphological markers on NPIs for antimorphic and non-antimorphic licensing contexts (*ni-* and *-libo*, respectively). It turns out that Russian also shows the same pattern ((a) examples below are from (Pereltsvaig 1998:13), and (b) examples are via Pereltsvaig, p.c.): here, as in Japanese, the lowest c-commanding licensor is the one licensing the NPI:

27a. **Esli** vy *kogo-libo* vstretite, pozvonite mne.
if you who-libo-acc meet call me
'If you meet anyone, call me.'

b. **Esli** vy *ni-kogo* **ne** vstretite, pozvonite mne.
if you ni-who-acc not meet call me
'If you don't meet anyone, call me.'

28a. **Nemnogie studenty** chitali *kakoj-libo* zhurnal.
few students read-past which-libo journal-acc
'Few students read any journal.'

b. **Nemnogie studenty ne** chitali *ni-kakix* zhurnalov.
few students not read-past-imp ni-which-gen-pl journal-gen-pl
'Few students don't read any journal.'

In conclusion, although these data provide more evidence for the downward monotonicity thesis of Ladusaw and others (cf. (Pereltsvaig 1998)), more research is required to determine the precise interaction between syntax and semantics in the case of Japanese NPIs. Further research is also needed to identify other NPI licensors in the context of the claims made here. Moreover, the recent work of Israel (1998), among others, makes a compelling case against monotonicity as a basis for NPI licensing. Another interesting task that remains to be carried out is to re-examine the facts discussed above in the light of these other theories of NPI licensing.

References

Baker, Carl L. 1970. Double Negatives. *Linguistic Inquiry* 1.169-186.

Barwise, Jon and Robin Cooper. 1981. Generalized Quantifiers and Natural Language. *Linguistics and Philosophy* 4. 159-219.

Bolinger, Dwight 1972. *Degree Words*. The Hague: Mouton.

Fry, John. 1999. Proof Nets and Negative Polarity Licensing. Ms. Stanford: Stanford University.

Israel, Michael. 1998. *The Rhetoric of Grammar: Scalar Reasoning and Polarity Sensitivity*. Doctoral dissertation, University of California San Diego.

Klima, Edward S. 1964. Negation in English, in J. A. Fodor and J. J. Katz, eds., *The Structure of Language*, 246-323. Englewood Cliffs, NJ: Prentice Hall.

Ladusaw, William A. 1979. *Polarity Sensitivity as Inherent Scope Relations*. Doctoral dissertation, University of Texas at Austin.

McCawley, James D. 1988. *The Syntactic Phenomena of English*. Chicago: University of Chicago Press.

Pereltsvaig, Asya. 1998. Negative Polarity Items in Russian. Ms. Montreal: McGill University.

van der Wouden, Ton. 1994. *Negative Contexts*. London: Routledge.

Vasishth, Shravan. 1998. Monotonicity Constraints on Negative Polarity in Hindi, in M. Bradshaw, D. Odden, and D. Wyckoff, eds., *OSU Working Papers in Linguistics*, Volume 51, 147-166. Columbus: The Ohio State University.

Yoshimura, Akiko. 1996. *Buuru Tokusei to Hitei no Imironteki Kaisousei*. (Boolean Properties and the Semantic Hierarchy of Negative Contexts.) Ms. Osaka Gakuin University. (In Japanese.)

Zwarts, Franz. 1996. A Hierarchy of Negative Expressions, in H. Wansing, ed., *Negation: A Notion in Focus*. 169-194. Berlin: Walter de Gruyter.

Part V

Syntax and Acquisition

Resultatives and Language Variations: Result Phrases and VV Compounds*

NOBUKO HASEGAWA
Kanda University of International Studies

1. Introduction

In this paper, I will examine the characteristics of the resultative construction and some language variations seen in this construction. Typical examples of resultatives are given in (1), where a result phrase is italicized.

(1) a. Mary painted the wall (*red*).
b. Susan pounded the metal (*flat*).
c. Bill swept the dust *(*into the corner*).
d. The joggers ran the Nikes *(*threadbare*).

What is interesting in this construction is that with the presence of a result phrase the argument structure of a predicate seems to change and even intransitives can host an object as seen in (1d). (Cf. Jackendoff (1990), Carrier and Randall (1992), Levin

*Earlier versions of this paper were presented at the workshop on Complex Predicates and Argument Structure at University of Tsukuba in October 1998 and at the COE International Workshop at Kanda University of International Studies in November 1998, as well as at the Ninth Japanese/Korean Linguistics Conference at OSU in August 1999. I would like to thank the audiences for valuable comments. The research reported here has been supported in part by Grant-in-Aid for COE Research (08CE1001) from the Japanese Ministry of Education, Science and Culture granted to Kanda University of International Studies (Principal Investigator: Kazuko Inoue).

and Rappaport Hovav (1992), Goldberg (1995), to just mention a few.) Furthermore, as Kageyama (1993, 1996) and Washio (1997) observe, languages differ with respect to what types of predicates allow a result phrase and what construction type a language employs to express resultatives. English makes use of a result phrase such as AP and PP as in (1) and it forms resultatives rather freely irrespective of predicate types. Romance languages, however, neither transitives nor intransitives can involve a result phrase. That is, as shown in (2), resultatives in French are all not allowed. In Japanese, on the other hand, only the counterpart of (1a) can be expressed with a result phrase, as seen in (3a), but the counterparts of the other examples in (1), i.e., (3b-d), are not grammatical. Thus, only inherent accomplishment predicates or change-of-state predicates can make grammatical phrasal resultatives in Japanese. However, Japanese has another construction that expresses resultatives. Namely, V-V serialization, which involves a change-of-state or accomplishment verb for the second verb of a VV compound. This is shown in (4). Ungrammatical (3b) and (3d) become grammatical once the accomplishment verbs, *nobas-u* 'extend' in (4a) and *yose-ru* 'move.to' in (4b), attach to the verbs.

(2) a. *J'ai peint le mur rouge.
'I painted the wall red.'

b. *Jean a martelé le métal plat.
'John hammered the metal flat.'

c. *Il a marché les jambes raides.
'He walked his legs off (lit., stiff).' (Washio 1997)

(3) a. Hanako-ga kabe-o akaku nut-ta.
Hanako-NOM wall-ACC red paint-past
'Hanako painted the glass red.'

b. ?*Hanako-ga kinzoku-o taira-ni tatai-ta.
Hanako-NOM metal-ACC flat pound-past
'Hanako pounded the metal flat.'

c. ?*Taro-ga gomi-o heya-no-sumi-ni hait-ta
Taro-NOM dust-ACC room-GEN-corner-to sweep-past
'Taro swept the dust to the corner of the room.'

d. *Rannaa-ga kutuzoko-o usuku hasit-ta.
runner-NOM shoe soles-ACC thin run-past
'The runners ran the shoe soles thin.'

(4) a. Hanako-ga kinzoku-o taira-ni tataki-*nobasi*-ta.
Hanako-NOM metal-ACC flat pound-spead-past
'Hanako pounded the metal flat.'

b. Taro-ga gomi-o heya-no-sumi-ni haki-*yose*-ta.
Taro-NOM dust-ACC room-GEN-corner-to sweep-move.to-past
'Taro swept the dust to the corner of the room.'

In what follows, I will provide an analysis that accounts for these facts. The analysis I will propose is along the lines of Hale and Keyser (1993) and Chomsky (1995), incorporating some aspects of lexical conceptual structure into syntactic structure.

2. Resultatives and Verb Meanings

Before presenting a syntactic account of these facts, let us consider what type of eventuality the resultative construction expresses. To do so, I borrow the notation of Lexical Conceptual Structure (LCS). In (5), the four types of verbs in the sense of Vendler (1967) are represented in terms of LCS. Given these notations, the predicates with the result phrases in (1) may be expressed as in (6) (cf. Kageyama (1996), Rappaport Hovav and Levin (1996)).

(5) a. activity [x ACT (ON y)]
b. state [x BE state / at place]
c. achievement [BECOME [x BE state /at place]]
d. accomplishment
[x CAUSE [BECOME [y BE state / at place]]]
[[x ACT (ON y)] CAUSE [BECOME [y BE state / at place]]]

(6) a. [[x ACT ON<paint> y] CAUSE [BECOME [y BE red]]]
b. [x ACT ON<pound> y] → [[x ACT ON<pound> y] CAUSE [BECOME [y BE flat]]]
c. [x ACT ON<sweep> y] → [[x ACT <sweep>(ON y)] CAUSE [BECOME [z BE into the corner]]]
d. [x ACT<run>] → [[x ACT<run>] CAUSE [BECOME [y BE thin]]]

That is, though the original predicate types may vary, the resultative sentences in (1) have the LCS on the right of the arrows, expressing accomplishment eventualities. Some verbs, such as *paint* and the transitive use of *break* and *freeze*, are inherently of the accomplishment type, which is the case of (6a). Other predicates, such as *pound*, *sweep* and *run*, are originally activity predicates but they become accomplishment predicates with the presence of a result phrase. We would like to explore how this generalization expressed in terms of LCS can be captured in syntax. To do so, I would like to adopt Hale and Keyser's (1993) view that θ-roles and lexical relations are syntactically represented.

3. The Syntactic Representation of Resultatives

3.1 Lexical Relation and VP-Shell Structure

According to Hale and Keyser's view, an accomplishment eventuality and relevant

θ -roles are structurally represented as in (7):

(7)

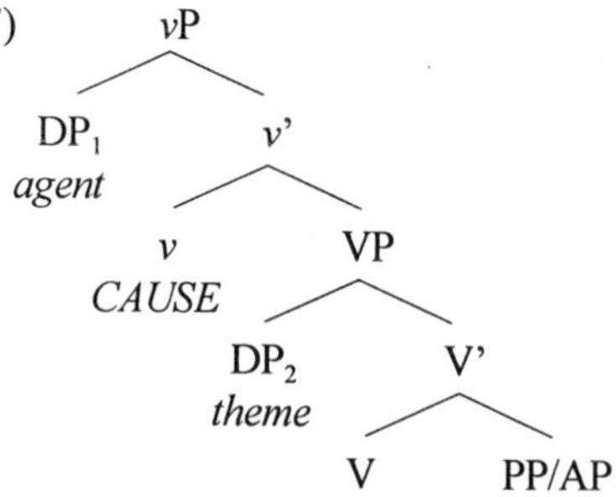

In this structure, *v* and VP are in a causal relation and *v* is a kind of a causative predicate that always implies a dynamic event expressed by the VP. The specifier (DP_1) of the causative *v* (with a VP complement) is identified as agent or causer and the specifier (DP_2) of the lower predicate V is taken to be a theme or patient argument, being involved in the event expressed by the VP. The complement of V, if it is a PP, indicates a location where the theme DP_2 is placed as a result of the event VP and if it is an AP, it indicates a state achieved as a result of the event. Thus, sentence (8a) with *put*, for example, is derived in the way shown in (8b) (see also Chomsky (1995)).

(8) a. Mary put the book on the shelf.

b.

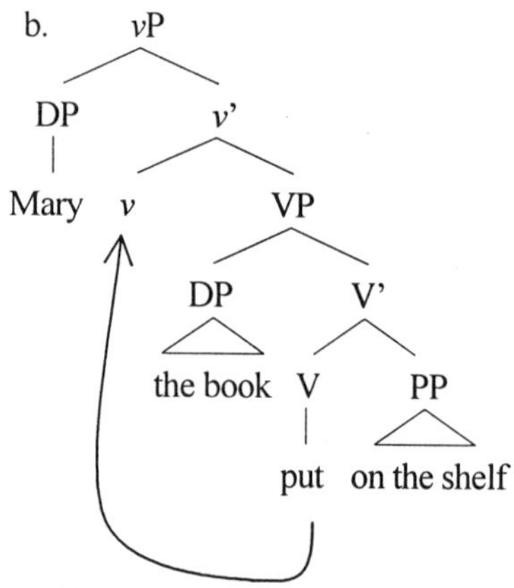

The verb *put*, which is under V, head-moves to *v* and the chain (or compound) of *v*-V is associated with the three arguments of *put*; namely, Agent *Mary*, Theme *the book* and resultant location *on the shelf*.

Here, I would like to extend this analysis further along the lines of Collins (1997) and assume that *v* is considered to be a functional category and it can be active or inactive: I use the notation [+Tr] for active *v*'s, which assign an external θ -role to

DP_1 and checks accusative Case of DP_2; [-Tr] is for inactive *v*'s, which neither assign an external role nor check accusative Case.[1]

In this system, the three types of predicates, transitives, unergatives, and unaccusatives, are assumed to have the structures in (9). Transitives and unergatives involve a *v* with the feature [+Tr] and unaccusatives have a *v* with [-Tr]. The lower verb V moves to *v* in both cases. With [+Tr] *v*, an agent external role is generated at the Spec of *v*. Here, I omit the structure above *v*P (i.e., TP) but I assume that the agent DP moves to Spec of TP and its nominative Case is checked by Tense before Spell Out. Furthermore, the object Case feature of the theme DP is checked covertly by *v*. When *v* is [-Tr], it does not assign an external role (i.e., there is no external agent argument) nor checks the object Case of the theme DP. The theme DP moves to Spec of TP overtly and its nominative Case is checked there:

(9) a. *activity predicates (transitives and unergatives)*
v [+Tr]: with external role, Obj Case checking

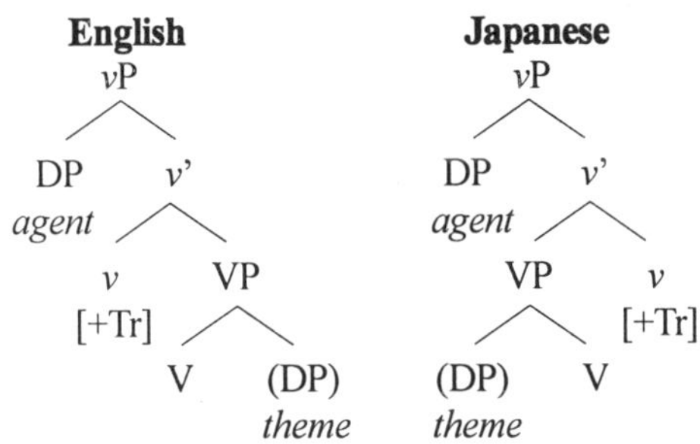

b. *unaccusative predicates*
v [-Tr]: no external role, no Obj Case checking

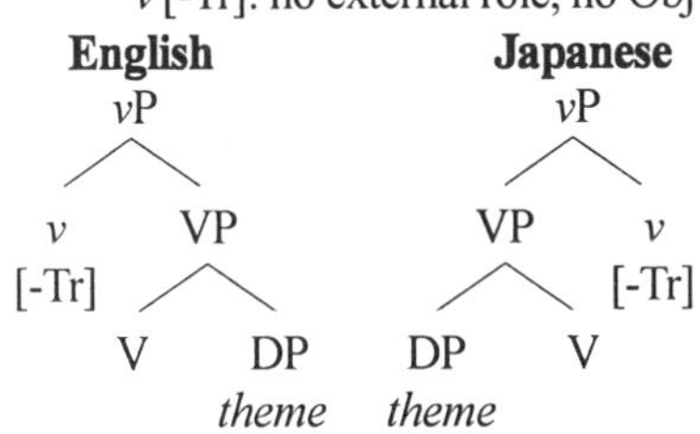

Within this system, the intransitive-transitive alterations of Japanese verbs exemplified in (10) are captured in terms of what morpheme resides at *v*. The pair in (11), for example, is syntactically represented as in (12), where the stem V *tao-* is accompanied by the *v* [+Tr] element, *-s-*, for the transitive (11a) and by the *v* [-Tr], -*re-*, for the intransitive (11b).

[1] Collins (1997) uses Tr and TrP instead of *v* and *v*P, respectively. Although I essentially follow Collins' system, I will continue to use *v* and *v*P in the following.

(10)

		v [-Tr]: Intransitive		*v* [+Tr]:Transitive		
a.	-e-	yak-e-ru	*ϕ*	yak-u		'burn'
		or-e-ru		or-u		'fold'
		war-e-ru		war-u		'break'
b.	-re-	tubu-re-ru	-s-	tubu-s-u		'crush'
		tao-re-ru		tao-s-u		'cut-down'
		kowa-re-ru		kowa-s-u		'destroy'
c.	-ar-	ag-ar-u	-e-	ag-e-ru		'rise/raise'
		sim-ar-u		sim-e-ru		'close'
		mag-ar-u		mag-e-ru		'bend'
d.	*ϕ*	ak-u	-e-	ak-e-ru		'open'
		tizim-u		tizim-e-ru		'shrink'
		tat-u		tat-e-ru		'stand'

(11) a. Hanako-ga hako-o taosi-ta. (tao-s-ita)
Hanako-NOM box-ACC push=down-past
'Hanko pushed down the box.'

b. Hako-ga taore-ta. (tao-re-ta)
Hanako-NOM fall-down-past
'The box fell down.

(12) a.

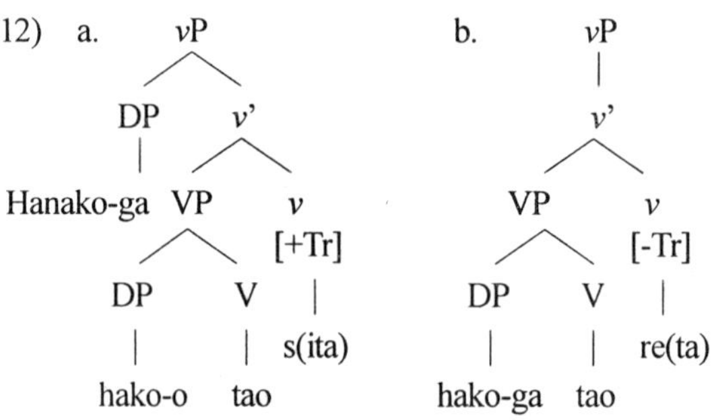

Given this system, the resultative construction can be structurally represented just like the *put* case in (8). That is, a result phrase takes place as a complement of the predicate V, designating an accomplishment event in collaboration with the V. However, there is one problem to be solved. That is, if the syntactic presence of a result phrase is the factor that determines whether a sentence conveys a resultative or accomplishment eventuality, there seems to be no way to distinguish true accomplishment verbs, such as *break* and *paint*, from activity verbs, such as *pound* and *sweep*, when there is no result phrase generated as a complement of VP. To put differently, the problem is how to distinguish the difference observed in (13): (13a) implies an accomplishment eventuality even without a result phrase, while without a result phrase (13b) only has an activity reading.

(13) a. Mary broke the glass.
b. Susan pounded the metal.

Another problem to be solved is how to account for language variations. Recall that in Japanese, phrasal resultatives are possible only with true change-of-state predicates like *nur-u* 'paint' but not with activity predicates like *tatak-u* 'pound'. This means that the occurrence of a result phrase in structure (8) is not free but must be licensed in a specific way. What needs to be done is to develop a system in which a result phrase is freely allowed in English but restricted only to true change-of-state verbs in Japanese.

3.2 Proposal

I would like to propose that the structure that gives rise to accomplishment eventuality is (14), rather than (8). That is, there is an independent result predicate projection (say, VrP with Vr as a head) between V and a result phrase (AP or PP) and this projection is responsible for connecting the result phrase and the verb V. I assume that the presence of VrP is universally available to accomplishment or change-of-state verbs but not to activity predicates. Let me elaborate this:

(14)

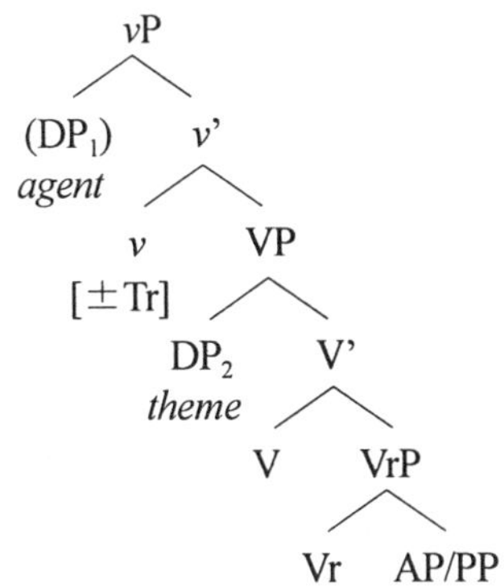

The basic function or meaning of Vr is to represent a resulting state, which is basically the same as what the semantic predicate BE does in the LCS representation such as (5). Vr has more than the function of BE in LCS, however. It connects the eventuality that V expresses and the state or location that AP/PP represents. Only when VP and AP/PP are connected by way of Vr, the resultative construction obtains. In order to connect these two, the mere presence of Vr is not enough but Vr must head-moves to the higher predicate V. Only when this Vr→V operation takes place, a result phrase is licensed.

The fact that true change-of-state verbs can take a result AP/PP freely both in English and in Japanese suggests that Vr→V raising always takes place for such predicates. This is captured if the derivation of inherent accomplishment verbs is what is shown in (15b).

(15) a. Mary painted the house red.

b.

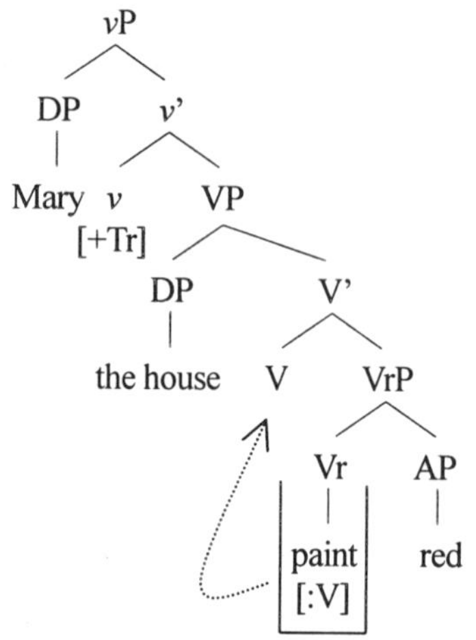

The category of true change-of-state or accomplishment verbs is Vr rather than V and they are generated under Vr and move to V. That is, these verbs universally undergo Vr-V movement. Assuming that movement is triggered by features, the feature responsible for the movement of Vr to V is a feature given to accomplishment verbs. I use the notation [:V] to indicate such a feature. Predicates with this feature are sort of bound morphemes and they must be raised to V. That is, the feature [:V], which needs to be checked off against the category V, forces the predicate with it to move to V. In other words, accomplishment or change-of-states verbs are verbs that have this feature.

Let us now consider the case of activity predicates. Recall that language variations are observed as to whether activity predicates allow a result phrase: English freely forms the resultative construction with activity predicates, while Japanese does not. As discussed in relation to (13), activity predicates do not imply a result state without a result phrase. This fact suggests that activity predicates are generated under V, not under Vr, and they do not have the feature [:V]. Thus, unless something mediates the activity V and a result phrase AP or PP, resultatives are not possible. In the case of Japanese, activity predicates cannot host a result phrase, which means that such a mediator is not available in Japanese. But in English, there must be a mediator. Let us assume that English has an independent but abstract predicate, say *Res*, which occurs under Vr and raises to V, where the activity predicate resides. The derivation of resultatives with an activity predicate is shown in (16b), taking (1d), repeated here as (16a), as an example.

(16) a. The joggers ran the Nikes threadbare.

b.

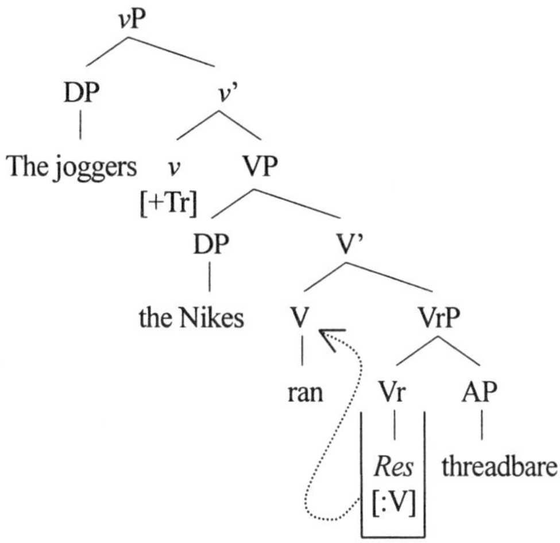

Thus, the difference between accomplishment verbs and activity verbs is not merely whether a result PP/AP takes place. What matters is at which predicate position a verb starts out. Activity verbs start out at V and accomplishment verbs at Vr. These two predicate types possess different feature specifications (with or without the feature [:V]) and only accomplishment verbs require head raising to V. To sum, the Vr→V operation is universally involved in change-of-state verbs, which explains why Japanese also exhibits resultatives with such predicates. Activity predicates, on the other hand, are generated under V and do not involve Vr. Hence, they do not license a result phrase. However, some languages such as English have an independent (abstract) predicate *Res*, which is Vr with [:V] and hosts a resultative phrase. Activity predicates can appear with a result phrase only when *Res* is available. Since Japanese lacks *Res*, Vr→V movement never takes place and phrasal resultatives are not observed with activity predicates.

Given this analysis, we can now account for the contrast in (13): accomplishment (13a) implies a result state without a result phrase, whereas (13b), which involves an activity verb, does not. As proposed above, accomplishment verbs always start out from Vr. Then even if no result phrase phonetically takes place, Vr is involved and the involvement of Vr means that it expresses an accomplishment eventuality regardless of whether a result phrase is present. This is the case of (13a). Activity verbs, on the other hand, do not start out at Vr but are generated under V. They can express an accomplishment eventuality only when the abstract predicate *Res* takes place under Vr and moves and adjoins to V. I assume that the abstract independent *Res* must be accompanied by (is subcategorized for) a phonetically realized result phrase. The absence of a result phrase in (13b) indicates that the abstract *Res* is not present, either. Hence, (13b) only expresses an activity eventuality.

3.3 An Account of VVCs in Japanese

The VrP analysis of resultatives presented above can be extended to resultative VV compounds (VVCs) in Japanese. As discussed, Japanese lacks the independent abstract predicate *Res*. However, I would like to claim that accomplishment or change-of-state verbs in Japanese can function similarly to *Res* of English. Note that typical VVCs such as the examples in (17) consist of an activity verb as the first element and a change-of-state verb as the second element (cf. Kageyama (1993, 1996), Li (1993), Matsumoto (1996), Nishiyama (1998)).

(17) *osi-hirak-u* 'push-open'
tataki-nobas-u 'pound-spread'
uti-koros-u 'shoot-kill'
arai-otos-u 'wash-remove'

Thus, it is reasonable to assume that VrP is involved for the second verb of VVCs. All we have to assume now for VVCs is that the second verb, the predicate that expresses a result state, starts out at Vr and the first verb, the one that stands for an activity or motion, is generated at V. What distinguishes VVCs and phrasal resultatives is whether V hosts an actual lexical item and whether Vr is abstract. In VVCs, V hosts a lexical item, which becomes the first verb of the VVC and Vr is not abstract but hosts a lexical item, which appears as the second verb in the compound. The initial structure and derivation for the sentence (4a), repeated here as (18a), are shown in (18b).

(18) a. Hanako-ga kinzoku-o taira-ni tataki-*nob*-*as*-ita.
Hanako-NOM metal-ACC flat pound-spead-transitive-past
'Hanako pounded the metal flat.'

b.

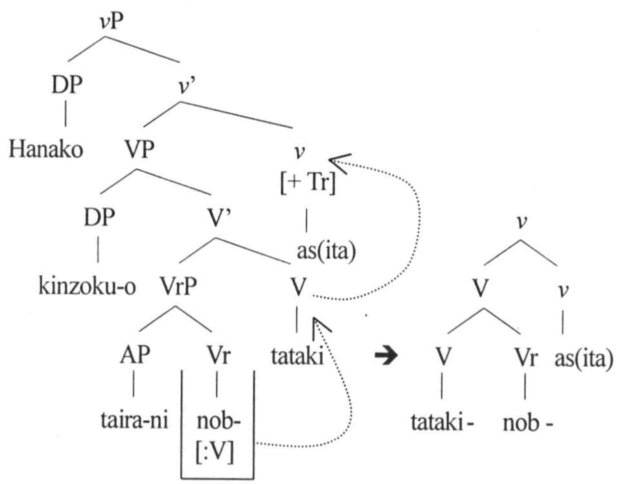

The derivation in (18b) resembles both the derivation of the accomplishment (15b) and that of the activity (16b). It is like (15b) in that the accomplishment (or change-of-state) verbs, *nob(as-ita)* 'spread' in (18b) and *paint* in (15b), are generated under Vr and they head-move to V (and to *v*). In (15b), however, V is empty, whereas in (18b) V is occupied by the activity verb *tataki* 'pound' and the VVC *tataki-nob-as-u* is formed when Vr adjoins to V (and then to *v*). The derivation of (18b) is similar to that of (16b) in that two separate predicates, namely an activity V and a resultative Vr, are involved. The difference is that in (18b), Vr is not an abstract predicate but an lexical change-of-state verb, whereas in the English example (16b), Vr is occupied by the abstract *Res*. Change-of-state verbs in Japanese can play the role of what the abstract *Res* of English plays.

As we saw, Japanese does not have the abstract *Res*; however, the examples in (19b) and (19c) with the verb *kom-u* 'go.in' suggest that Japanese does have an independent lexical Vr predicate, which is like *Res* but with a phonetic matrix. That is, *kom-u* is a lexical counterpart of *Res*:

(19) a. *Hanako-ga daigaku-ni kon-da.
Hanako-NOM university-to go.in-past

b. Hanako-ga baggu-ni hon-o osi-kon-da.
Hanako-NOM bag-DAT book-ACC push-go.in-past
'Hanako pushed the book into her bag.'
(b'.*Hanako-ga baggu-ni hon-o osi-ta.)

c. Taro-ga gakkoo-ni donari-kon-da.
Taro-NOM school-to yell-go.in-past
'Taro stormed into school (to complain).'
(c'.* Taro-ga gakkoo-ni donat-ta.)

The ungrammaticality of (19a) shows that *kom-u* cannot be used independently and it has to be always used as the second verb of a VVC. What *kom-u* does is host a goal phrase that is a kind of a result phrase (cf. Kageyama (1993, 1996)). This in fact is essentially what the independent *Res* does. Note that *os(u)* 'push' in (19b) and *donar(u)* 'yell' in (19c) are activity verbs and they alone cannot take a goal role, as the ungrammaticality of the parenthesized examples, (19b') and (19c'), indicate. The existence of predicates like *kom-u* seems to clearly indicate that the predicate *Res* under Vr is not a mere artifact but real: *kom-u* in Japanese is a lexical *Res* and English employs an abstract version of *kom-u*, namely, non-lexical *Res*.

3.4 Resultatives in Romance

This analysis of resultatives provides a way to describe Washio's (1997) generalization discussed in relation to (2), which is repeated here as (20). That is, in Romance languages, the occurrence of a result phrase is restricted and even accomplishment verbs do not allow a result phrase. Along with the French sentences in (20), Spanish examples in (21) are also ungrammatical.

(20) a. *J'ai peint le mur rouge.
'I painted the wall red.'

b. *Jean a martelé le métal plat.
'John hammered the metal flat.'

c. *Il a marché les jambes raides.
'He walked his legs off (lit., stiff).'

(21) a. *Juan pintó la pared blanca
'John painted the wall white.

b. *Juan martilleó el metal plano
'John hammered the metal flat.'

Note that the Japanese example (22) is grammatical, which corresponds to the (a) examples of (20) and (21):

(22) Taro-ga kabe-o akaku nut-ta.
Taro-NOM wall-ACC red paint-past.
'Taro painted the wall red.'

We have so far assumed that accomplishment verbs universally involve Vr and are to be generated at Vr and raised to V. If this is true, accomplishments in Romance must also involve Vr and be able to move to V. Then, the (a) examples in (20) and (21) must be allowed along with (22) in Japanese. The ungrammatical status of these examples suggests either of the following two: (i) Romance accomplishments are not true accomplishments but activity verbs or (ii) they behave just as in English and Japanese but the operation of Vr→V is not enough for a resultative to be licensed. It is hard to imagine that (i) holds, since the concept of "accomplishment" refers to a particular type of eventuality and it must be universally consistent. (ii), on the other hand, is quite probable, since there is a clear syntactic difference between Romance languages and English/Japanese; i.e., a result phrase in Romance must agree with the DP that it is predicated of. Though details must be worked out more carefully, I would like to assume here that whatever property Vr has as part of an accomplishment predicate is not good enough to mediate the agreement between a result phrase and a DP. Vr functions similarly to the semantic predicate BE of LCS but it is not identical with the lexical copulative *be* after all, which can mediate the agreement between a DP and a predicative adjective. This may appear rather stipulatory; however, there is evidence that suggests that agreement has to do with the ungrammaticality of (20) and (21). Compare the Spanish examples in (23) with (21a).[2]

(23) a. Juan pintó la pared de blanco / en blanco.
Juan painted the wall of white in white
'Juan painted the wall white.'

b. Juan rompió el vaso en pedazos.
Juan broke the glass in pieces
'Juan broke the glass into pieces.'

---

[2] These examples are due to Kimi Hoshino (personal communication). See also Hoshino (1996) for relevant discussion on resultatives in Japanese, English and Spanish.

(21a) and (23a) are identical except that ungrammatical (21a) has the agreeing adjective *blanca* 'white' while in (23a) the result phrase is in the form of PP *de blanco* or *en blanco* and there is no agreement between the PP and the DP *la pared*. Similarly in (23b), a result phrase is allowed with the accomplishment *rompió* 'break', if it is in the form of PP. Thus, even in Romance, accomplishment verbs can take a result phrase as long as no agreement is involved. The reason for the ungrammaticality of (20a) and (21a) is not due to the restriction on the occurrence of a result phrase but is due to the inability of Vr to mediate agreement between the result phrase and the DP that undergoes state changes. In this way, we can maintain the claim that change-of-state or accomplishment predicates universally involve Vr and a result phrase is licensed by the movement of Vr→V.

4. Summary

My proposal is summarized in the boxes below.

- The resultative construction has a structure that involves the resultative predicate Vr, which has the feature [:V].
- The predicate with the feature [:V] is raised to V. I.e., the feature [:V] is responsible for the movement Vr→V.
- Inherent accomplishment predicates are generated under Vr and have the feature [:V].
- Activity predicates are generated under V.
- English has the abstract predicate *Res* under Vr, which has the feature [:V] and is subcategorized for a result phrase (AP/PP).
- Japanese has a lexical *Res* (e.g., *kom-u* 'go.in') under Vr, which has the feature [:V] and is subcategorized for a location resultative phrase (PP).

Language Variations:

English

A result phrase freely takes placce irrespective of predicate types.

→ abstract Res exists.

Japanese:

A result phrase is allowed only with an inherent accomplishment.

→ no abstract *Res*

Romance:

A result phrase, if it is an AP, cannot take place even with an inherent accomplishment predicate. However, if it is a PP (or a phrase that does not need to agree with the DP that it is predicated of), it is allowed.

→ no abstract *Res*.

Vr (a predicate with [:V]) does not mediate agreement.

The VrP analysis with Vr-V movement thus successfully accounts not only for language variations observed in phrasal resultatives but also for the two types of resultative constructions in Japanese, VVCs and phrasal resultatives.[3]

References

Carrier, Jill, and Randall Janet H. 1992. The argument structure and syntactic structure of resultatives. *Linguistic Inquiry* 23.173-234.

Chomsky, Noam. 1995. *The minimalist program*. Cambridge, Mass.: MIT Press.

Collins, Chris. 1997. *Local economy*. Cambridge, Mass.: MIT Press.

Goldberg, Adele. 1995. *A construction grammar approach to argument structure*. Chicago: University of Chicago Press.

Hale, Kenneth, and Jay Keyser. 1993. On argument structure and the lexical expression of syntactic relations. In *The view from building 20: Essays in linguistics in honor of Sylvain Bromberger*, ed. Kenneth Hale and Jay Keyser, 53-109. Cambridge, Mass.: MIT Press.

Hasegawa, Nobuko. 1998. The Syntax of Resultatives. In *Report (2) Researching and verifying an advanced theory of human language*, 31-57. Knada University of International Studies.

Hoshino, Kimi. 1996. Kekka-koobun no gainen-koozoo (the conceptual structure of the resultaive construction). Master Thesis, Kanda University of International Studies, Chiba, Japan.

Jackendoff, Ray. 1990. *Semantic structures*. Cambridge, Mass.: MIT Press.

Kageyama, Taro. 1993. *Bunpoo to gokeisei (grammar and word formation)*. Tokyo: Hitsuji Shobo.

Kageyama, Taro. 1996. *Dooshi imiron: gengo to ninchi no setten (verb semantics: the interface between language and cognition)*. Tokyo: Kurosio Publishers.

Levin, Beth, and Malka Rappaport Hovav. 1995. *Unaccusativity: At the syntax-lexical semantic interface*. Cambridge, Mass.: MIT Press.

Li, Yafei. 1993. Structural head and aspectuality. *Language* 69. 490-504.

Matsumoto, Yo. 1996. *Complex predicates in Japanese*. Tokyo: Kurosio Publishers.

Nishiyama, Kunio. 1998. V-V compounds as serialization. *Journal of East Asian Linguistics* 7. 175-217.

Rappaport Hovav, Malka, and Beth Levin. 1996. Building verb meanings. Paper presented at a TACL meeting, Tokyo Metropolitan University.

Vendler, Zeno. 1967. *Linguistics in philosophy*. Ithaca, New York: Cornell University Press.

Washio, Ryuichi. 1997. Resultatives, compositionality, and language variation. *Journal of East Asian Linguistics* 6.1-49.

[3] For consequences of this analysis regarding the nature of the head movement operation proposed in this paper and the organization of grammar in terms of how so-called lexical and syntactic processes interact, see Hasegawa (1998).

More on Two Ways of Deriving Distributive Readings*

J.-R. HAYASHISHITA
University of Southern California

1. Introduction

Generative Grammar aims at discovering the formal properties that mediate between a string of sounds and the corresponding "meaning", and one of its working hypotheses is that the formal basis of "meaning" of a given sentence is represented in terms of the hierarchical relations among its constituents. The representation is called an LF (representation). Wide-scope distributive readings (hereafter DR's) are among the phenomena that have been extensively discussed in the investigation of the properties of LF. For expository purposes, let us use DR<α, β> to signify the DR for α over β. Consider (1).

(1) a. (At least) two students visited three professors (of USC).

b. $\exists X(X \subseteq \mathit{student} \wedge |X| = 2)\ \forall x(x \in X)\ [\exists Y(Y \subseteq \mathit{professor} \wedge |Y| = 3)\ \forall y(y \in Y)\ [\text{x visited y}]]$

* The main conclusion of this paper is the same as that of Hayashishita 1999. I would like to thank Hajime Hoji and Ayumi Ueyama, who helped shape the view presented here. Among many others who have helped me understand various issues in this paper are Joseph Aoun, Daisuke Bekki, Hagit Borer, Teruhiko Fukaya, Maria Gallardo, Shadi Ganjavi, Audrey Li, Susan Robinson, Barry Schein, Tim Stowell, Yukinori Takubo, and Yukiko Tsuboi.

c. $\exists Y(Y \subseteq professor \wedge |Y| = 3)\ \forall y(y \in Y)\ [\exists X(X \subseteq student \wedge |X| = 2)\ \forall x(x \in X)\ [x \text{ visited } y]]$

(1a) has DR<*two students, three professors*> as in (1b) and DR<*three professors, two students*> as in (1c). This fact is taken as evidence for the thesis that there are two LF representations corresponding to the form in (1a). In one LF, *two students* c-commands *three professors*, and in the other, *three professors* c-commands *two students*.

In this paper, I challenge the validity of this thesis, and argue that not all the DR's are derived solely on the basis of the hierarchical information at LF. I will argue in particular that there are two ways to interpret a given sentence (see (2)): (i) solely on the basis of its LF representation ($M_{(ethod)}$-I) and (ii) through Subject Predication, which forms a Subject Predicate representation (henceforth SP) partially based upon its LF representation (M-II).

(2) LF → $T_{(ruth)}C_{(condition)}$ (M-I)
LF → SP → TC (M-II)

M-I and M-II can both give rise to DR's; hence there are two kinds of DR's. However, only the DR's derived by M-I are a pure reflection of LF properties. The empirical materials I will put forth below in support of this claim come from Japanese.[1] In particular, it will be claimed that DR<NP_{cm}, NP_{nom}>[2] in the basic order (see (3a)) and that in the "scrambled"[3] order (see (3b)) can arise in different ways. The former must be derived by M-II while the latter can be derived by either M-I or M-II.

(3) a. DR<NP_{cm}, NP_{nom}> in [NP-NOM ... NP-CM ... VERB]

b. DR<NP_{cm}, NP_{nom}> in [NP-CM ... NP-NOM ... VERB]

2. The DR's in Japanese

Regarding the availability of DR's in Japanese, the standard generalization is that the basic order, [NP-NOM ... NP-CM ... VERB], yields DR<NP_{nom}, NP_{cm}> but not DR<NP_{cm}, NP_{nom}> while the "scrambled" order, [NP-CM ... NP-NOM ... VERB], yields both DR<NP_{nom}, NP_{cm}> and DR<NP_{cm}, NP_{nom}> (Kuroda 1969/70, Hoji 1985). However, Kitagawa (1990), Kuroda (1994) and Kuno et al (1999) challenge this generalization, pointing out that the basic order also yields DR<NP_{cm}, NP_{nom}>. Consider (4).

(4) (watasi-ga mitatokorodewa), [$_{NPnom}$ (sukunakutomo) ippon-no ya]-ga [$_{NPcm}$ itutu-no mato]-ni sasatta.

---

[1] In Hayashishita 1999, I present empirical materials from English in support of the general approach to scope interpretation adopted here.

[2] 'NOM' stands for nominative, and 'CM' accusative or dative. NP_{nom} signifies a subject NP, and NP_{cm} a non-subject NP.

[3] I use *the "scrambled" order* to refer to the surface order in (3b) without committing myself to any particular analysis.

'(what I observed was) [$_{\text{NPnom}}$ (at least) one arrow] pierced [$_{\text{NPcm}}$ five targets].'

If (4) is uttered in the situation where five targets are standing next to each other without overlapping, the most natural reading is DR<NP$_{cm}$, NP$_{nom}$>. That is, each of the five targets has at least one arrow that pierced it.

It will be shown however that there are two kinds of DR's: one kind is purely due to LF properties, but the other kind is not, and that DR<NP$_{cm}$, NP$_{nom}$> in the basic order is of the latter kind. Thus, if the Kuroda/Hoji's generalization is understood as capturing DR's of the former kind, the examples like (4) would not constitute counterexamples to it.

3. The Distinct Properties of DR<NP$_{cm}$, NP$_{nom}$> in the Basic Order

3.1 NP Types

The distribution of DR<NP$_{cm}$, NP$_{nom}$> in the basic order is limited; it is significantly more difficult to obtain if the NP$_{cm}$ is an NP of Type B in (5b); cf. Liu 1990 for the contrast of the same sort in English and Chinese.

(5) a. Type A
Toyota to Nissan 'Toyota and Nissan',
subete-no kaisya 'all companies', daremo 'everyone'
sannin-no otoko 'three men', dareka 'someone'

b. Type B
sanninizyoo-no otoko 'three or more men',
40%izyoo no gakusee '40% or more of the students',
kanarinokazu-no gakusee 'a good number of students'

In (6a), the NP$_{cm}$ is of Type A, while in (6b), it is of Type B.

(6) a. (watasi-ga mitatokorodewa), [$_{\text{NPnom}}$ (sukunakutomo) ippon-no ya]-ga [$_{\text{NPcm}}$ itutu-no mato]-ni sasatta. (= (4))
'(what I observed was), [$_{\text{NPnom}}$ (at least) one arrow] pierced [$_{\text{NPcm}}$ five targets].' ^{YES}DR<NP$_{cm}$, NP$_{nom}$>

b. (watasi-ga kiitatokorodewa), [$_{\text{NPnom}}$ (sukunakutomo) ippon-no ya]-ga [$_{\text{NPcm}}$ 15.5%izyoo-no mato]-ni sasatta (rasii yo).
'(from what I heard), [$_{\text{NPnom}}$ (at least) one arrow] pierced [$_{\text{NPcm}}$ 15.5% or more of the targets].' ^{NO}DR<NP$_{cm}$, NP$_{nom}$>

DR<NP$_{cm}$, NP$_{nom}$> is available in (6a), but not in (6b).

By contrast, DR<NP$_{cm}$, NP$_{nom}$> in the "scrambled" order is available irrespective of the NP types, as illustrated below.

(7) a. (watasi-ga mitatokorodewa), [$_{\text{NPcm}}$ itutu-no mato]-ni [$_{\text{NPnom}}$ (sukunakutomo) ippon-no ya]-ga sasatta. (Cf. (6a).)
'(Lit.) (what I observed was), [$_{\text{NPcm}}$ five targets], [$_{\text{NPnom}}$ (at least) one arrow] pierced.' ^{YES}DR<NP$_{cm}$, NP$_{nom}$>

b. (watasi-ga kiitatokorodewa), $[_{NPcm}$ 15.5%izyoo-no mato]-ni $[_{NPnom}$ (sukunakutomo) ippon-no ya]-ga sasatta (rasii yo). (Cf. (6b).)
'(Lit.) (from what I heard), $[_{NPcm}$ 15.5% or more of the targets], $[_{NPnom}$ (at least) one arrow] pierced.' $^{YES}\text{DR}<\text{NP}_{cm}, \text{NP}_{nom}>$

Note that the NP_{cm} is of Type B in (7b), yet the $\text{DR}<\text{NP}_{cm}, \text{NP}_{nom}>$ is available.

The preceding discussion can be summarized as in (8).

(8) Generalization

$\text{DR}<\text{NP}_{cm}, \text{NP}_{nom}>$ in the basic order is available only if the NP_{cm} is an NP of Type A in (5), while the one in the "scrambled" order is available irrespective of the NP types.

3.2 Freezing Effects

When $\text{DR}<\text{NP}_{cm}, \text{NP}_{nom}>$ obtains in the basic order, the interpretive possibilities of the NP_{nom} are limited. In particular, the NP_{nom} cannot be related to a dependent term by means of bound variable anaphora (Freezing Effects on Binding), or it cannot be distributed over another NP (Freezing Effects on Scope).

Freezing Effects on Binding are illustrated in (9).

(9) $[_{NPnom}$ kanarinokazu-no ginkoo]-ga $[_{NPcm}$ mittu-no zidoosya gaisya]-ni soko-no torihikisaki-o syookaisita.
'(Lit.) $[_{NPnom}$ a good number of banks] introduced to $[_{NPcm}$ three automobile companies] its customers.'
$^{NO}(\text{DR}<\text{NP}_{cm}, \text{NP}_{nom}> \& \text{BVA}<\text{NP}_{nom}, \text{soko}>)$[4]

In (9), $\text{BVA}<\text{NP}_{nom}, \textit{soko}>$ cannot co-occur with $\text{DR}<\text{NP}_{cm}, \text{NP}_{nom}>$. As indicated in (10), each of the relevant BVA and the relevant DR can obtain in the absence of the other.

(10) a. $[_{NPnom}$ kanarinokazu-no ginkoo]-ga $[_{NPcm}$ mittu-no zidoosya gaisya]-ni Toyota-no torihikisaki-o syookaisita.
'$[_{NPnom}$ a good number of banks] introduced to $[_{NPcm}$ three automobile companies] Toyota's customers.' $^{YES}\text{DR}<\text{NP}_{cm}, \text{NP}_{nom}>$

b. $[_{NPnom}$ kanarinokazu-no ginkoo]-ga Toyota-ni soko-no torihikisaki-o syookaisita.
'(Lit.) $[_{NPnom}$ a good number of banks] introduced to Toyota its customers.' $^{YES}\text{BVA}<\text{NP}_{nom}, \text{soko}>$

$\text{DR}<\text{NP}_{cm}, \text{NP}_{nom}>$ in the "scrambled" order, on the other hand, does not induce Freezing Effects on Binding. $\text{DR}<\text{NP}_{cm}, \text{NP}_{nom}>$ can co-occur with $\text{BVA}<\text{NP}_{nom}, \text{soko}>$, as illustrated in (11).

---

[4] $\text{BVA} <\alpha, \beta>$ signifies the bound variable anaphora between α and β.

(11) $[_{NPcm}$ mittu-no zidoosya gaisya]-ni $[_{NPnom}$ kanarinokazu-no ginkoo]-ga soko-no torihikisaki-o syookaisita. (Cf. (9).)
'(Lit.) to $[_{NPcm}$ three automobile companies], $[_{NPnom}$ a good number of banks] introduced its customers.'
$^{YES}(DR<NP_{cm}, NP_{nom}>$ & $BVA<NP_{nom}, soko>)$

(12) illustrates that $DR<NP_{cm}, NP_{nom}>$ in the basic order induces Freezing Effects on Scope.

(12) (kinoo-no paatii-de)$[_{NPnom}$ (sukunakutomo) sanninizyoo-no heddohantaa]-ga $[_{NPcm}$ hutari-no hito]-ni $[_{NP\alpha}$ yottu-no kaisya]-o syookaisiteita (n datte).
'(at yesterday's party) $[_{NPnom}$ (at least) three or more headhunters] were introducing to $[_{NPcm}$ two people] $[_{NP\alpha}$ four companies].'
$^{NO}(DR<NP_{cm}, NP_{nom}>$ & $DR<NP_{nom}, NP_{\alpha}>)$[5]

$DR<NP_{cm}, NP_{nom}>$ and $DR<NP_{nom}, NP_{\alpha}>$ cannot obtain simultaneously. When $DR<NP_{cm}, NP_{nom}>$ obtains, the only possible reading for (12) is (13).

(13) $\exists Y(Y \subseteq \mathit{person} \wedge |Y| = 2)\ \forall y(y \in Y)\ [\exists X(X \subseteq \mathit{headhunter} \wedge n \geq |X| \geq 3)\ \exists Z(Z \subseteq \mathit{company} \wedge |Z| = 4)\ [\forall x(x \in X)\ \exists z(z \in Z)$ [x was introducing to y z] $\wedge\ \forall z(z \in Z)\ \exists x(x \in X)$ [x was introducing to y z]]], where n is an integer close to 3.

It should be noted that $DR<NP_{nom}, NP_{\alpha}>$ is independently possible, as shown in (14).

(14) (kinoo-no paatii-de)$[_{NPnom}$ (sukunakutomo) sanninizyoo-no heddohantaa]-ga $[_{NPcm}$ Smith-san]-ni $[_{NP\alpha}$ yottu-no kaisya]-o syookaisiteita (n datte).
'(at yesterday's party) $[_{NPnom}$ (at least) three or more headhunters] were introducing to $[_{NPcm}$ Mr. Smith] $[_{NP\alpha}$ four companies].'
$^{YES}DR<NP_{nom}, NP_{\alpha}>$

$DR<NP_{cm}, NP_{nom}>$ in the "scrambled" order, on the other hand, does not induce Freezing Effects on Scope. $DR<NP_{cm}, NP_{nom}>$ and $DR<NP_{nom}, NP_{\alpha}>$ can obtain simultaneously, as illustrated in (15).

(15) (kinoo-no paatii-de) $[_{NPcm}$ hutari-no hito]-ni $[_{NPnom}$ (sukunakutomo) sanninizyoo-no heddohantaa]-ga $[_{NP\alpha}$ yottu-no kaisya]-o syookaisiteita (n datte).

---

[5] The reading that (12) lacks can be expressed as (i)

(i) $\exists Y(Y \subseteq \text{person} \wedge |Y| = 2)\ \forall y(y \in Y)\ [\exists X(X \subseteq \text{headhunter} \wedge n \geq |X| \geq 3)\ \forall x(x \in X)\ [\exists Z(Z \subseteq \text{company} \wedge |Z| = 4)\ \exists z(z \in Z)$ [x was introducing to y z]]], where n is an integer close to 3.

'(Lit.) (at yesterday's party) to [$_{NPcm}$ two people], [$_{NPnom}$ (at least) three or more headhunters] were introducing [$_{NP\alpha}$ four companies].'

^{YES}(DR<NP_{cm}, NP_{nom}> & DR<NP_{nom}, NP_{α}>)

The discussion in this subsection is recorded as (16). The discussion in Section 3 as a whole can be summarized as (17).

(16) Generalization

DR<NP_{cm}, NP_{nom}> in the basic order induces Freezing Effects, while the one in the "scrambled" order does not.

(17) a. DR<NP_{cm}, NP_{nom}> in the basic order

(i) It requires that the NP_{cm} be of Type A.
(ii) It induces Freezing Effects.

b. DR<NP_{cm}, NP_{nom}> in the "scrambled" order

(i) It is available irrespective of the NP types.
(ii) It does not induce Freezing Effects.

4. Hypotheses

4.1 Assumptions

Let us first spell out some basic assumptions. I assume that all of the NP's of Type A and Type B can be interpreted either as (18a) or as (18b).

(18) a. Generalized Quantifier (henceforth $NP^{I(ndividual)}$) (Barwise & Cooper 1981)

b. Group Existential (henceforth $NP^{G(roup)}$)

For the sake of concreteness, let us assume that there is some marking at LF to signal whether a given NP is interpreted either as NP^{I} or as NP^{G}.[6] Consider (19).

(19) sanninizyoo-no hito-ga kita. 'three or more men came.'

If *sanninizyoo-no hito* is marked as NP^{I} as in (20a), the TC is (20b). On the other hand, if it is marked as NP^{G} as in (20a'), the TC is (20b').[7]

(20) a. LF: [$_{NP}$ sanninizyoo-no hito]^{I}-ga kita.

b. TC: (20a) is true iff there is three or more x, x is a man, such that x came.

---

[6] There is no reason, other than an expository one, to assume the marking at LF. For example, one may assume that *sanninizyoo-no hito* is represented at LF either as (i) [$_{DP}$ sanninizyoo(-no) [$_{NP}$ hito]] or as (ii) [$_{DP}$ ec [$_{NP}$ sanninizyoo-no hito]]. When *sanninizyoo-no hito* is represented as (i), it undergoes QR, leaving a singular variable, and the NP^{I} interpretation is induced. On other hand, when it is represented as (ii), it is an indefinite, and bound by an existential closure; thus, the NP^{G} interpretation is derived.

[7] I leave open the issue of whether NP^{I} can be differentiated from NP^{G} by the introduction of event variables.

a'.LF: $[_{NP}$ sanninizyoo-no hito$]^G$-ga kita.

b'.TC: (20a') is true iff there is X, X is a set consisting of three or more men, such that X came.

The assumptions just made have the following consequences. When a given sentence is interpreted solely on the basis of its LF representation, (i) an NP α establishes bound variable anaphora with a dependant term β only if α is interpreted as NP^I, and (ii) the distributive reading for an NP α over an NP β obtains only if α is interpreted as NP^I.

4.2 Hypothesis (1) – The Scope Principle

We have seen in Section 3 that the distribution of DR<NP_{cm}, NP_{nom}> in the basic order is more limited than that in the "scrambled" order. I claim that there is a means which gives rise to DR<NP_{cm}, NP_{nom}> in the "scrambled" order but not in the basic order (M-I). Now the question is what M-I is. To answer the question, I maintain (21), following the standard assumption.

(21) A given sentence is always able to be interpreted solely on the basis of its LF representation.

I claim that when a given sentence is interpreted solely on the basis of its LF representation, the Scope Principle postulated in Reinhart 1976 and Huang 1982 holds. I restated their versions as in (22).

(22) The Scope Principle (M-I) (Cf. Reinhart 1976 and Huang 1982.)

An NP α takes scope over an NP β only if α and β are in A-positions, and α c-commands β at LF.[8]

Given (22), DR's are derived if an NP taking wide-scope is interpreted as NP^I.

Turning to DR<NP_{cm}, NP_{nom}> in the "scrambled" order, it is unanimously accepted that the "clause-internally scrambled" NP shows A-properties (Saito 1992, Yoshimura 1992, and Ueyama 1998). I assume, following Ueyama 1998 in particular, that the form in (23a) may be represented as (23b) at LF.[9]

(23) a. PF: NP-CM NP-NOM VERB

b. LF: NP-CM NP-NOM VERB (the NP's are in A-positions)

In (23b), the NP_{cm} c-commands the NP_{nom} in A-positions; thus, as long as the NP_{cm} can be interpreted as NP^I, DR's can be derived. Since all the NP's in Type A and Type B can be interpreted as NP^I, DR<NP_{cm}, NP_{nom}> in the

[8] I have provided a simplified version here without assuming QR. This assumption however does not affect the arguments in this paper.

[9] Saito (1992) and Yoshimura (1992) assume that an NP can show A-properties outside the theta domain of a verb when it is "fronted" by movement. Ueyama (1998), on the other hand, argues that the A-position outside the theta domain of a verb is "base-generated" independently of the existence of movement.

"scrambled" order obtains irrespective of the NP type. It also follows from (22) that $DR<NP_{cm}, NP_{nom}>$ in the basic order cannot be derived by M-I since the relevant c-command relation is absent.

4.3 Hypothesis (2) – Subject Predication

Let us address the question of how $DR<NP_{cm}, NP_{nom}>$ in the basic order is derived (M-II). First, I maintain (24).

(24) A given sentence may not be interpreted solely on the basis of its LF representation.

I claim that when certain conditions are met, a given sentence can be interpreted by means of Subject Predication in (25).

(25) The Subject Predication Hypothesis (M-II)

If a given sentence has the following LF representation, then at some cognitive level the "value" of α can be interpreted as the Subject of a Predicate *S*

$$\underset{(LF)}{[_S \ldots \alpha \ldots]} \Rightarrow \underbrace{[\text{the "value" of } \alpha]}_{\text{Subject}} \ \underbrace{\forall x\,(x \in X)}_{\text{Distributor}} \ \underbrace{\lambda y\,[_S \ldots y \ldots](x)}_{\text{Predicate}}$$

This hypothesis consists of two parts. First, from a given LF representation, a Predicate is formed by substituting a variable for an NP α whose "value" is to be the Subject. Second, some set γ is taken from the domain of the speaker's direct experience in the sense of Takubo and Kinsui 1997 to be the Subject of the Predicate, and γ must be able to be "associated with" α. It should be noted that an SP is not a syntactic representation but a cognitive representation of some sort.

I also propose (26) and (27) to account for Freezing Effects.

(26) The Predicate Formation Hypothesis

In constructing an SP from a given LF, all the NP's, other than the NP whose "value" is to be the Subject, are incorporated into a verb to form a Predicate of the Subject.

(27) A necessary condition for Predicate Formation

No NP's in a Predicate may be interpreted as NP^{I}.[10,11]

---

[10] The Predicate in this paper must be differentiated from the Predicate of a WA-topicalized phrase in Kuroda 1992: Ch.1, wherein Freezing Effects do not seem to be induced.

[11] I am suppressing the fact that when $DR<NP_2, NP_1>$ obtains in the configuration, [... NP_1 ... NP_2 ... [... NP_3 ... NP_4 ... VERB] ... VERB] (where each of the NP's c-commands the NP's to its right), Freezing Effects are not induced in the embedded clause; i.e., $DR<NP_3, NP_4>$ is possible. It seems that Freezing Effects are limited only to the NP's that are clause-mates of an NP whose "value" is to be a Subject.

To illustrate the claims, let us go through the derivation of DR<NP_{cm}, NP_{nom}> in (4).

(28) a. PF: [$_{NPnom}$ (sukunakutomo) ippon-no ya]-ga [$_{NPcm}$ itutu-no mato]-ni sasatta. (= (4))
'[$_{NPnom}$ (at least) one arrow] pierced [$_{NPcm}$ five targets].'

b. LF: [[$_{NPnom}$ (sukunakutomo) ippon-no ya]^{G}-ga [$_{NPcm}$ itutu-no mato]$^{I\ (or\ G)}$-ni sasatta]

c. SP: $\exists X(X = \Sigma \wedge X \subseteq target \wedge |X| = 5)\ \forall x(x \in X)\ \lambda y[$ (*at least*) *one arrow pierced* y](x), where Σ is one of the sets stored in the domain of the speaker's direct experience.

d. TC: (28c) is true iff there is a set X, X is one of the sets stored in the domain in the speaker's direct experience and is a set consisting of five targets, such that for all x, x is a member of X, such that x has the property that (at least) one arrow pierced x.

In order to interpret the sentence in (28a) by means of Subject Predication, it must be represented as in (28b) at LF where the NP_{nom} to be incorporated into a verb is represented as an NP^{G}. In constructing the SP in (28c), a set of 5 targets is chosen from the domain of the speaker's experience, and is taken to be a Subject, and the NP_{nom} is incorporated into a verb to form a Predicate. Each of the 5 targets is associated with the Predicate through a hidden distributor.[12] The TC in (28d) is calculated on the basis of (28c); thus, DR<NP_{cm}, NP_{nom}> obtains.

4.3.1 On Subject

I have put forth the hypothesis that DR<NP_{cm}, NP_{nom}> in the basic order must be derived by means of Subject Predication, and that a Subject is not a linguistic expression but an object (a specific group in the cases under discussion) in the domain of the speaker's direct experience and can be "associated with" the NP_{cm}. The intuition behind this hypothesis is that the function of the NP_{cm} is only to "check" whether a specific group taken from the domain is appropriate or not. For example, when the NP_{cm} is *gonin-no gakusee* 'five students', a group of six students or a group of five teachers cannot be taken from the domain as corresponding to this NP. Consider (29).

(29) Dialogue[13]

A: [$_{NP}$ gonnin-no kakkoii gakusee]-ga paatii-ni kita rasii yo.
'[$_{NP}$ five handsome students] came into the party, I heard'

B: sitteru. [$_{NPnom}$ (sukunakuomo) sanninizyoo-no onnanoko]-ga [$_{NPcm}$ soitura]-ni iiyotta n datte.

---

[12] I assume that the hidden distributor here is a concept outside the syntax.

[13] I thank Hajime Hoji for bringing this example to my attention (p.c. Oct. 1999).

'I know. [$_{NPnom}$ (at least) three or more girls] have approached [$_{NPcm}$ them], I heard.'

(30) $\exists Y(Y \subseteq \textit{handsome-student} \wedge |Y| = 5)\ \forall y(y \in Y)\ [\exists X(X \subseteq \textit{girl} \wedge n \geq |X| \geq 3)\ \forall x(x \in X)\ [x \text{ approached } y]]$, where n is an integer close to 3.

In (29B), the NP_{cm} is not a quantified expression, but the DR in (30) is available. I would like to claim that the DR in (30) is also due to Subject Predication.

Ueyama (1998) points out that the felicitous use of a *so*-series demonstrative requires a linguistic antecedent.[14] The point can be illustrated in (31), for example. The contrast as reported in (31) is pointed out in Kuroda 1979.

(31) Someone's Monologue (at 6:00 a.m. immediately after he woke up)
{#soitura/aitura}-no namae-wa nandattakke.
'what was their name?'

Given that the DR in (30) is available for (29B), we must conclude that a specific group of five handsome students taken from the domain of the speaker's direct experience is judged as appropriate to be a Subject by the "checking" of *soitura* 'them'. Thus, *soitura*, which cannot be referential by itself, can serve the "checking" function with the "help" of the utterance of (29A), which contains *gonnin-no kakkoii gakusee* 'five handsome students'.

We have seen in Section 3.1 that DR<NP_{cm}, NP_{nom}> in the basic order requires that the NP_{cm} be of Type A, but not of Type B. Given the Subject Predication Hypothesis, we can understand this generalization as follows: the NP's of Type A but not those of Type B can serve the "checking" function. This is a feasible conclusion. Consider the NP's of Type B in (5) once again, repeated here as (32).

(32) Type B
sanninizyoo-no otoko 'three or more men',
40%izyoo no gakusee '40% or more of the students',
kanarinokazu-no gakusee 'a good number of students'

The NP's in (32) either do not set an upper bound due to the lexical meaning of *izyoo* 'more' or do not specify the exact size (kanarinokazu 'a good number'); therefore, they "usually" do not denote a specific group. By definition, all the sets in the domain of the speaker's direct experience are specific groups; hence, the NP's of Type B fail to serve the "checking" function in a normal context. But if we supply some appropriate context so that the speaker can identify a specific group with an NP of Type B, they

---

[14] What Ueyama calls the "non-individual" use of *so* is being ignored in this discussion; see Ueyama 1998: Appendix D.

can also serve the "checking" function. For example, consider the following scenario. John and Ken are wondering whether they should rob some shops on 5th Avenue in New York. They agree that they will not execute the plan if more than five buildings on 5th Avenue are guarded. Ken goes to spy, and sees seven buildings guarded. He returns and says, *dameda, (sukunakutomo) hitori-no gaadoman-ga itutuizyoo-no biru-no mae-ni tatteita* 'well, (at least) one guard was standing in front of five or more buildings'.[15] In this situation, *itutuizyoo-no biru* denotes a specific group of seven buildings. As expected, DR<NP_{cm}, NP_{nom}> is possible in this situation.[16]

4.3.2 The Subject Predication Hypothesis and Categorical Judgment

Kuroda (1992: Ch.1) argues that two types of judgments (thetic and categorical judgments) correspond to two types of sentence forms in Japanese (the "WA-topicalized sentence" and the "non-WA-topicalized sentence"). Ueyama (1998: Ch.2 Section 2.4.3) claims that even in non-matrix clauses, where judgments are not relevant, some distinction must be made, corresponding to the thetic/categorical distinction. Let us rephrase her claim as follows: at some cognitive level, a thetic representation and a categorical representation are distinguished. I claim that Subject Predication in this paper forces a categorical representation. It is predicted therefore that DR<NP_{cm}, NP_{nom}> in the basic order becomes unavailable in the environments where a categorical representation is not allowed.

Ueyama (1998) claims, in our terms, that the embedded clause of the perceptual report construction in (33) expresses eventuality, and it must be realized as a thetic representation.

(33) John-ni [$_{S*}$ Mary-ga aruiteiru] tokoro-ga mieta.
'John saw [$_{S*}$ Mary walking].'

We then predict that DR<NP_{cm}, NP_{nom}> in the basic order is not possible within the embedded clause in the perceptual report construction. The prediction is indeed borne out. Consider (34).

---

[15] I thank Maria Gallardo (p.c. May 1999) for the context just given and relevant discussion.

[16] Ueyama (1998) points out in Appendix D.2.1 that NP's that are able to denote a specific group can be related to a singular-denoting dependent term without invoking weak crossover effects, as illustrated in (i); cf. (ii). She also demonstrates that the status of the examples like (i) becomes degraded in the environment where a thetic representation is forced (see Section 4.3.2). I suspect that the contrast between (i) and (ii) can be explained once we assume that Subject Predication is established in (i) but not in (ii).

(i) ?soko-no bengosi-ga subete-no zidoosya gaisya-o uttaeteiru (node, zidoosya gyookai-wa daikonran-ni otiitteiru). (= Ueyama's 1998 (80b))
'(Lit.) (since) its attorney has sued every automobile company, (the automobile industry has been thrown into a state of disorder).'

(ii) ?*soko-no bengosi-ga mittuizyoo-no zidoosya gaisya-o uttaeteiru (node, zidoosya gyookai-wa daikonran-ni otiitteiru).
'(Lit.) (since) its attorney has sued three or more automobile companies, (the automobile industry has been thrown into a state of disorder).'

(34) John to Bill sorezore-ni $[_{S*}[_{NPnom}$ (sukunakutomo) hutari-no gakusee]-ga $[_{NPcm}$ (USC-no gengogakubu-no) gonin-no kyoozyu]-ni hanasikaketeiru]-tokoro-ga mieta.
'John and Bill each saw $[_{S*}[_{NPnom}$ (at least) two student] speaking to $[_{NPcm}$ five professors (of USC Linguistics)]].'
$[_{S*}$ ^{NO}DR<NP_{cm}, NP_{nom}>]

One may wonder if DR <NP_{cm}, NP_{nom}> is ever allowed in the non-matrix context. As shown in (35), DR<NP_{cm}, NP_{nom}> is possible in the embedded clause.

(35) John to Bill sorezore-ga $[_{S}[_{NPnom}$ (sukunakutomo) hutari-no gakusee]-ga $[_{NPcm}$ (USC-no gengogakubu-no) gonin-no kyoozyu]-ni hanasikaketeita]-to hookokusitekita.
'John and Bill each reported that $[_{S}[_{NPnom}$ (at least) two student] was speaking to $[_{NPcm}$ five professors (of USC Linguistics)]]'
$[_{S}$ ^{YES}DR<NP_{cm}, NP_{nom}>]

Hence the unavailability of DR<NP_{cm}, NP_{nom}> in (34) cannot simply be attributed to the fact that the relevant sentence is embedded.

5. Two Alternative Analyses

I have argued, on the basis of the distribution of DR<NP_{cm}, NP_{nom}> in the basic order, that LF cannot be the sole basis for wide-scope construal (and for the interpretation of a sentence in general), proposing that certain instances of wide-scope construal (DR<NP_{cm}, NP_{nom}> in the basic order, for example) are due to Subject Predication, which is outside the syntax. In this section, I will provide further support for the proposal by reviewing two purely syntactic analyses of DR<NP_{cm}, NP_{nom}> in the basic order.

Suppose that the DR<NP_{cm}, NP_{nom}> in the basic order were derived by the covert A-movement of the NP_{cm}, as indicated in (36) below. The DR in the basic order in (36a) and that in the "scrambled" order in (37a) would then be based on the identical LF representation.

(36) a. PF: NP_{nom} ... NP_{cm} ... VERB

b. LF: NP_{cm} NP_{nom} ... t_{cm} ... VERB (the NP's are in A-positions)

(37) a. PF: NP_{cm} NP_{nom} ... t_{cm}... VERB

b. LF: NP_{cm} NP_{nom} ... t_{cm}... VERB (the NP's are in A-positions)

We would then predict that they manifest the same interpretive possibilities. However, as we have observed, the prediction is not borne out; Freezing Effects are induced in the former but not in the latter.

Recall that DR<NP_{cm}, NP_{nom}> in the basic order requires that the NP_{cm} be of Type A (Section 3.1). We also saw in Section 4.3.1 that even if the NP_{cm} is of Type B, the addition of an appropriate context makes DR<NP_{cm}, NP_{nom}> available. Thus, if we were to assume that the DR is derived by A-movement, we would have to state that the movement does not apply to the

NP's of Type B in general but it does when some appropriate context is conceivable. It seems rather difficult to determine the syntactic category the movement makes reference to. The same problem would arise for the covert A'-movement analysis.[17] Hence, the covert (A or A') movement analysis cannot be maintained.

It should also be pointed out that there are two additional sets of facts that can be accounted for by the Subject Predication Hypothesis but cannot be accommodated by the covert (A or A') movement analysis without further stipulations. Consider the configuration in (38).

(38) LF: NP_1 ... NP_2 ... NP_3 ... VERB, where all the NP's are in an A-position and each of the NP's c-commands the NP's to its right.

The Subject Predication Hypothesis makes the following predictions.

(39) a. When the NP_3 takes scope over the NP_2, it must also scope over NP_1.

b. Only one NP can take scope over its c-commanding NP; i.e., it is not possible that both the NP_2 and the NP_3 take scope over the NP_1.

The predictions are indeed borne out. Consider (40).

(40) a. $[_{\text{NP1}}$ (sukunakutomo) hutari-no gakusee]-ga $[_{\text{NP2}}$ (USC-no) sannin-no kyoozyu]-kara $[_{\text{NP3}}$ (Chomsky-ga kaita) nisatu-no hon]-o kariteita.
'$[_{\text{NP1}}$ (at least) two students] borrowed from $[_{\text{NP2}}$ three professors (of USC)] $[_{\text{NP3}}$ two books (which Chomsky wrote)].'

b. $^{\text{YES}}(\text{DR}<\text{NP}_3, \text{NP}_2> \& \text{ DR}<\text{NP}_3, \text{NP}_1>)$, but $^{\text{NO}}(\text{DR}<\text{NP}_1, \text{NP}_2> \&$ $\text{DR}<\text{NP}_3, \text{NP}_2>)$ (from (39a))

c. $^{\text{NO}}(\text{DR}<\text{NP}_2, \text{NP}_1> \& \text{ DR}<\text{NP}_3, \text{NP}_1>)$ (from (39b))

On the other hand, under the covert movement analysis, we must stipulate, for example, (i) that covert movement must go over at least one S (for (39a)), and (ii) that only one NP undergoes covert movement (for (39b)). Hence we have further arguments for the Subject Predicate analysis of $\text{DR}<\text{NP}_{cm}, \text{NP}_{nom}>$ in the basic order.

6. Concluding Remarks

In this paper I have argued that there are two ways of interpreting sentences: (i) solely on the basis of its LF representation (M-I), and (ii) through Subject Predication, which forms a Subject Predicate representation partially based upon its LF representation (M-II). M-I and M-II can both give rise to DR's; thus, two kinds of DR's. One of the significant implications of this paper is that if one wishes to probe into the nature of some LF properties on the basis of the availability of DR's, one must utilize the DR's derived by M-I, i.e., the DR's in the M-II free environments. I hope that the delinea-

[17] We also need to stipulate that covert movement is sensitive to the availability of a categorical representation (see Section 4.3.2).

tion of the M-II free environments accomplished by this work could serve as a useful tool for the investigation of the formal properties of natural languages.

References

Barwise, Jon, and Robin Cooper. 1981. Generalized Quantifiers and Natural Language. *Linguistics and Philosophy* 4.159-219.

Hayashishita, J.-R. 1999. Two Ways of Deriving Distributive Readings. To appear in *Proceedings of the 23rd Annual Penn Linguistics Colloquium*. University of Pennsylvania.

Hoji, Hajime. 1985. *Logical Form Constraints and Configurational Structures in Japanese.* Doctoral dissertation, University of Washington.

Huang, C.-T. James. 1982. *Logical Relations in Chinese and the Theory of Grammar*. Doctoral dissertation, MIT.

Kitagawa, Yoshihisa. 1990. Anti-Scrambling. Ms., University of Rochester. (A paper read at the Tilburg University Workshop on Scrambling, 10/19/90.)

Kuno, Susumu, Ken-ichi Takami, and Yuru Wu. 1999. Quantifier Scope in English, Chinese, and Japanese. *Language* 75:1.63-111.

Kuroda, S.-Y. 1969/70. Remarks on the Notion of subject with Reference to Words like Also, Even or Only. In *Annual Bulletin.* Research Institute of Logopedics and Phoniatrics, University of Tokyo, vol.3.111-129, and vol.4.127-152.

Kuroda, S.-Y. 1979. (Ko) So, A nituite (On (*ko*), *so* and *a*). In *Eigo to Nihongo to (English and Japanese)*. Kuroshio Syuppan: Tokyo. 41-59.

Kuroda, S.-Y. 1992. Judgment Forms and Sentence Forms. In *Japanese Syntax and Semantics*. Kluwer Academic Publishers: Dordrecht. 13-77.

Kuroda, S.-Y. 1994. Quantifier Scope in Japanese. Ms., University of California in San Diego.

Liu, F-H. 1990. *Scope Dependency in English and Chinese*. Doctoral dissertation, University of California, Los Angeles.

Reinhart, Tanya. 1976. *The Syntactic Domain of Anaphora*. Doctoral dissertation, MIT.

Saito, Mamoru. 1992. Long Distance Scrambling in Japanese. *Journal of East Asian Linguistics*, 1-1.69-118.

Takubo, Yukinori, and Satoshi Kinsui. 1997. Discourse Management in terms of Multiple Mental Spaces. *Journal of Pragmatics* 28.741-758.

Ueyama, Ayumi. 1998. *Two Types of Depend*ency. Doctoral dissertation, University of Southern California, distributed by GSIL publications, USC, Los Angeles.

Yoshimura, Noriko. 1992. *Scrambling and Anaphora in Japanese*. Doctoral dissertation, University of Southern California.

The Role of the Coordinators in Interpreting *ANY* in Korean*

YOUNGJUN JANG
Chungang University

1. Introduction

It is one of the basic facts about language that you need at least two items in order to use such coordinators as *and* and *or*. Based on this fact, I provide answers to the following pervasive and difficult questions: (i) Why does Korean *amwu-to* 'anyone' necessarily become a negative polarity item (NPI, hereafter)? And (ii) why should *amwu-na* 'anyone,' which is closely correlated to the NPI *amwu-to*, be invariably interpreted as free choice *any*? A couple of assumptions will be made for this purpose. First, the NPI *amwu-to* is best characterized if decomposed to be [*amwu* + *to*], of which [amwu] is an indefinite and [-to] is a conjunctive. Second, the morpheme *amwu* is placed on the bottom of a pragmatically defined scale which represents significance, degree, and/or amount, along the line of study conducted by Fauconnier (1975). Given that *-to* is a conjunctive coordinator and *-na* is a disjunctive coordinator, I show that the semantics of *amwu-to* (negative polarity) and *amwu-na* (free choice) are fully predicted from the compositional meaning of

*I have benefited from comments and questions from the participants at the 9th Japanese/Korean Linguistics Conference held at Ohio State University, July 31, 1999. In particular, I thank Daeho Chung, Sungshim Hong, Laurence Horn, Chungmin Lee, Yae-sheik Lee, and Shravan Vasishth for their help at various stages of my preparation of the paper. All errors, however, are my own. This work was supported by the Research Support Program of Chungang University.

their constituents, thereby offering a uniform analysis of them. In particular, I show that Lee and Horn's (1995) claim that *any* is an indefinite + *even* is too strong. Instead, I claim that *any* (and its Koran counterpart) is an indefinite plus conjunctive/ disjunctive coordinator and that the pragmatic scale is presupposed by the role of these coordinators.

2. Polarity Scale and Polarity Item Licensing in English

Analyzing superlatives, Fauconnier (1975) proposes a scalar theory of NPI licensing.[1] Section 2.1 discusses cases of positive polarity item licensing and section 2.2 deals with cases of negative polarity item licensing in English.

2.1 Positive Polarity Items

First, consider the following examples:

(1) a. John can solve the most difficult problem.
    b. John can solve an easy problem.

If someone can solve the most difficult problem, then he can naturally solve an easy one. This is the situation that we see in sentences given in (1). Negation of the sentences in (1) does not pose a special problem for our purpose.

(2) a. John cannot solve the most difficult problem.
    b. John cannot solve an easy problem.

The fact that John cannot solve the most difficult problem does not entail that he cannot solve an easy one. He may or may not. In other words, there is no semantic entailment relation between (2a) and (2b). However, something very interesting happens, if we put the focus element *even* into these sentences, as shown in (3).

(3) a. *John cannot solve *even* the most difficult problem.
    b. John cannot solve *even* an easy problem.

The question that we would like to raise is why (3a) is unacceptable, in sharp contrast to the acceptable (2a). To account for the unacceptability of (3a), we need to discuss the semantics of the focus element *even*. Before proceeding further, however, let me make sure that superlative expressions like *even the most difficult problem* are at the top of the polarity scale, which is given in (4)

[1] A scale approach to the polarity phenomena is found in various previous works including Israel (1996), Fillmore, Kay and O'Connor (1988), Kadmon and Landman (1993), Lee and Horn (1995), and references cited therein, among many others. Readers are referred to these works.

below.

(4) a pragmatic scale (for difficulty):
 the most difficult

 the least difficult (=easiest)

Notice that these expressions are acceptable only in affirmative sentences. Hence is the contrast between grammatical (2a) and ungrammatical (3a). What this means is that an element consisting of [*even* + an expression at the top of the scale] requires affirmation. This is a case of so-called positive polarity item (PPI, hereafter) licensing. Put another way, (3a) is unacceptable, because the PPI *even the most difficult problem* is not licensed: it should be used in an affirmative sentence, and not in a negative one.

It is important to note that *even* alone is not enough to license PPIs or NPIs, as shown in (5):

(5) a. I heard even the faintest noise.
 b. I didn't hear even the faintest noise.

In (5), the sentences are all acceptable, though the focus element *even* is used in the affirmative (5a) and in the negative (5b). So far, I have shown that the contrast between (2a) and (3a) is nicely captured in the scale theory.

2.2 Negative Polarity Items

Now consider the following pair of sentences, which involve the lowest point of the pragmatic scale (4).

(6) a. John cannot solve the easiest problem.
 b. John cannot solve a difficult problem.

If John cannot solve the easiest problem, then he may not in general be able to solve a difficult one. Therefore, it can be said that (6a) pragmatically entails (6b). Importantly, note that the examples in (6) are negative sentences. Let's see what happens, if we change the sentences into affirmative ones, which are given in (7):

(7) a. John can solve the easiest problem.
 b. John can solve a difficult problem.

In the very restricted context where the sentences are a statement about John or what happened, (7a,b) may be acceptable: (7a) may be paraphrased as, e.g., what John can do is solve only the easiest problem, and (7b), as what John can do is solve a difficult problem. In fact (7a) could be interpreted in two ways. One reading is the one mentioned just before. The other reading is something like "John can solve even the easiest problem." However, (7a) with the second reading sounds awkward. This kind of awkwardness becomes more conspicuous if we insert the focus marker *even* in this sentence. Consider the following:

(8) a. *John can solve *even* the easiest problem.
    b. John can solve *even* a difficult problem.

Why is it that the focus element *even* renders the acceptable (7a) unacceptable, as shown in (8a)? Why, on the other hand, is it that *even* does not render (7b) unacceptable, as shown in (8b)? It should be noted that expressions like *even the easiest problem* are on the bottom of the pragmatic scale (4), and further that these expressions can be allowed only in negative sentences. Compare the grammatical (7a) with ungrammatical (8a). A natural conclusion from these facts is that [*even* + an expression on the bottom of the scale] requires negation in order to be properly licensed. It now becomes obvious why (8a) is unacceptable: the phrase *even the easiest problem*, being an NPI, is not licensed by negation. The ungrammatical (8a) can be saved in a negative context, as shown in (9):

(9) John cannot solve *even* the easiest problem.

In sum, an expression on the bottom of the pragmatic scale, together with the focus element *even*, requires negation, thereby being an NPI. Given the pragmatic scale, the top of the scale is a potential positive polarity item, while the bottom of the scale is shown to be a potential NPI: potential because these expressions in English should be accompanied by the focus element *even*. A paradigm example in point is shown as the following, respectively.

(3a) *John can not solve *even* the most difficult problem.
(8a) *John can solve *even* the easiest problem.

Since *the most difficult problem*, in conjunction with *even*, constitutes a PPI, it can be licensed in an affirmative sentence. On the other hand, *the easiest problem*, in conjunction with *even*, is an NPI and therefore can be licensed only by negation. Combining the two, we obtain the following polarity scale:

(10) The Polarity Scale
the most (=positive polarity)
|
the least (=negative polarity)

The topmost endpoint of the scale represents a PPI and the lowest endpoint of the scale represents an NPI. The term 'most' and 'least' may flip-flop according to a given context.

3. Polarity Item Licensing in Korean

3.1 Positive Polarity Items

Superlatives in Korean behave the same way as their English counterparts do. For example, consider the following:

(11) a. John-un [kacang elyewun mwuncey]-to phwul swu iss-ta.[2]
John-Top most difficult problem-also solve can-Dec
'John can solve even the most difficult problem.'
b. John-un [shiwun mwuncey]-lul phwul swu iss-ta.
John-Top easy problem-Acc solve can-Dec
'John can solve an easy problem.'

If John can solve *kacang elyewun mwuncey* 'the most difficult problem,' then he may also be able to solve *shiwun mwuncey* 'an easy problem'. Note that the relation between (11a) and (11b) is exactly the same as one we have seen in the English example (1) earlier. Let me just put off the discussion about the roles of the particle *to* and accusative case marker *-lul*, both of which I believe are very crucial for our purpose.

With this in mind, consider what happens if we negate these sentences.

(12) a. *John-un [kacang elyewun mwuncey]-to phwul swu eps-ta.
John-Top most difficult problem-also solve can not-Dec
'John can not solve even the most difficult problem.'
b. John-un [shiwun mwuncey]-lul phwul swu eps-ta.
John-Top easy problem-Acc solve can not-Dec
'John can not solve an easy problem.'

[2]This paper adopts Yale romanization for transcribing Korean. The following abbreviations are used: Top=Topic, Acc=Accusative Case Marker, Dec=Declarative Sentence, Pst=Past Tense, Prp=Propositive, Cl=Classifier

The negated sentence (12a) is unacceptable, in contrast to the grammatical (12b). Then the same question arises: Why is negation not compatible with the superlative *kacang elyewun mwuncey-to* 'even the most difficult problem'? Notice that the particle *-to* is equivalent to English *also*. I will return to the discussion of the particle *-to* in more detail in Section 5.

Then the same explanation as the one provided for the English examples in (1) could be applied to the data in (12): That is, the superlative *kacang elyewun mwuncey* 'the most difficult problem' is placed on the top of the pragmatic scale and that it becomes a positive polarity item, which can only be licensed in an affirmative sentence. In the following subsection, we discuss the opposite endpoint of the pragmatic scale.

3.2 Negative Polarity Items

Now, let me discuss the cases at the opposite end of the pragmatic scale. Consider the following Korean data:

(13) a. John-un [kacang swiwun mwuncey]-to phul swu eps-ta.
John-Top most easy problem-also solve can not-Dec
'John cannot solve even the easiest problem.'
b. John-un [elyewun mwuncey]-lul phul swu eps-ta.
John-Top difficult problem-Acc solve can not-Dec
'John cannot solve a difficult problem.'

If John cannot solve *kacang swiwun mwuncey* 'the easiest problem', then he may probably not be able to solve a more difficult one. Compare these sentences with their affirmative counterparts in (14) below.

(14) a. *John-un [kacang swiwun mwuncey]-to phul swu iss-ta.
John-Top most easy problem-also solve can-Dec
'John can solve even the easiest problem.'
b. John-un [elyewun mwuncey]-lul phul swu iss-ta.
John-Top difficult problem-Acc solve can-Dec
'John can solve a difficult problem.'

Interestingly enough, the affirmative sentence (14a) is unacceptable, as was the English counterpart (8a). The reason is, once again, that the superlative *kacang swiwun mwuncey* 'the easiest problem' is placed on the bottom of the pragmatic scale and that [an expression on the bottom of the pragmatic scale + *-to*] constitutes an NPI. (14b), however, is not such case, because the expression *elyewun mwuncey* 'a difficult problem' is not placed on the bottom of the scale.

In sum, I have shown that some expressions including superlatives are placed at either extreme of the pragmatically defined scale and that an expression at the top of the scale constitutes a PPI, in conjunction with *-to*, while the one on the bottom constitutes an NPI, in conjunction with *-to*. In this regard, Korean is not different from English.

4. The Role of Coordinators *-to* 'also' and *-na* 'or'

4.1 The Meaning of the Conjunctive *-to* 'also'

In this section, I will get to the issue of why the particle *-to* renders an expression at either extreme of the pragmatic scale a polarity sensitive item. Recently Lee (1996) proposes a unified account of polarity phenomena, using the notions of concession via inclusion (which I refer to as a conjunctive coordinator) and a pragmatic scale. One big difference between Lee's and my analysis is in the treatment of the particle *-to*. While Lee treats *-to* as a concession marker[3], I take it to be a simple conjunctive coordinator, which entails by its nature existence of other potential member(s). Shi (1997) also offers an account on this issue, paying a special attention to the role of the particle *-to*. Consider the following examples:

(15) a. John-to Mary-to o-ass-ta.
John-also Mary-also come-Pst-Dec
'Not only John but also Mary came.'
b. John-to Mary-to oci ahn-ass-ta.
John-also Mary-also come not-Pst-Dec
'Neither John nor Mary came.'

According to Shi, the particle *-to* in (15a) renders *John* and *Mary* to be included in the set of people who came. Likewise, in (15b), *John* and *Mary* are included in the set of people who did not come, since the particle *-to* simply includes its complement in a set denoted by the predicate. Hence (15a,b) may be simplified as follows:

(16) a. come (John + Mary)
b. not come (John + Mary)

However, Shi does not explain why the composition [*amwu* + *to*] should invariably become an NPI in his analysis.

An essential meaning of the particle *-to* is inclusion, equivalent to English *also,* as Lee (1996) and Shi (1997) note.[4] In this regard, Lee and Horn's (1995) claim that *any* is an indefinite plus *even* is too strong. The meaning of the conjunctive coordinator –to in Korean is 'also' or 'too' but not 'even.' However, instead of adopting the term [+inclusion], I will refer to the

---

[3]Similarly Lee and Horn (1995) take *any* to be an indefinite plus *even.*

[4]Rullman (1996) discusses similar facts in Dutch, adopting the scalar theory.

particle *-to* as simply a conjunctive coordinator, because it is in sharp contrast to the disjunctive coordinator *-na* 'or' (see Jang and Kim (1997) and Lee (1996)). How then should we treat the combined forms *amwu-to* (NPI any) and *amwu-na* (free choice)? For ease of exposition, let me start with a simple case given by the pattern in (17):

(17) #John-to o-ass-ta.
John-also come-Pst-Dec
'John also came.'

The sentence (17) is unacceptable in a situation where there is no other person who came other than John. On the other hand, if there were at least one more person who came, then (17) would be acceptable. Therefore (17) entails that someone other than John, e.g. Bill, be a member of the set of people who came. In a nutshell, [x-to] entails that there should exist at least one more member denoted by the predicate, no matter whether it is explicitly mentioned or not. With this in mind, let us return to the example (8a), repeated below.

(18) a. *John-un [kacang swiwun mwuncey]-to phul swu iss-ta.
John-Top most easy problem-also solve can-Dec
'John can solve even the easiest problem.'
b. John-un [elyewun mwuncey]-lul phul swu iss-ta.
John-Top difficult problem-Acc solve can-Dec
'John can solve a difficult problem.'

Since the conjunctive coordinator *-to* conjoins an additional member to a set denoted by the predicate, there should exist at least one more member. Suppose that someone, e.g. John, can solve the easiest problem of a given set of problems. That does not entail that he may also be able to solve a more difficult one automatically. He may or may not. However, what is important is that there does remain a possibility that he cannot solve any other problem except the easiest one. In this case, the conjunctive coordinator *to* cannot be used. Hence the unacceptability of (18a).

To be more concrete, suppose that there are four problems with differing degrees of difficulty in such a way that A is the easiest problem and B, more difficult, C, even more, and finally D is the most difficult. To say that someone can "also" (i.e. *-to* in Korean) solve problem D entails that there should be at least one more problem, e.g. A, B, or C, that he can solve. However, being able to solve problem D does not always guarantee an ability to solve a more difficult one, namely A, B, or C. Therefore, the use of *–to* 'also is not appropriate in this situation.

Alternatively, suppose that John cannot solve the easiest problem, say D. In general if one cannot solve the easiest problem, then he may not be able to solve a more difficult one. In this situation, the use of the conjunctive coordinator *–to* implies that there must be at least one more problem that he can not solve, namely problem A, B, or C, in addition to the easiest one D. Therefore, (19), which is the negation of (18a), is fully acceptable in contrast to the unacceptable (18a).

(19) John-un [kacang swiwun mwuncey]-to phul swu eps-ta.
John-Top most easy problem-also solve can not-Dec
'John cannot solve even the easiest problem.'

Likewise, to say that someone can "also" solve problem A entails that there should exist at least one more problem that s/he can solve, e.g. B, C, or D. This is quite probable because one can usually solve an easier problem if s/he can solve a harder one. Put another way, problem A, combined with *also* (i.e. *-to* in Korean), becomes a PPI. Therefore, the following example is fully acceptable.

(20) John-un [kacang elyewun mwuncey]-to phwulswu iss-ta.
John-Top most difficult problem-also solve can-Dec
'John can solve even the most difficult problem.'

4.2 The Meaning of the Disjunctive *–na* 'or'

In contrast to the conjunctive coordinator *-to* 'also,' the disjunctive coordinator *-na* 'or' does not necessarily render its complement "included" into a set denoted by the relevant predicate. Consider, for example, the following:

(21) Mary-na John-i kal kes-i-ta.
Mary-or John-Nom will go thing-is-Dec
'Mary or John will go.'

In order for (21) to be acceptable, there should exist at least one member of the set of people who will go, e.g. *Mary* or *John*. Notice that the disjunctive coordinator *-na* can be used only if there should exist at least two members so that at least one of them (or both of them) could be the members denoted by the predicate. This is the very meaning of disjoint.

With this background in mind, consider the following examples:

(22) a. coffee-lul masi-ca.
coffee-Acc drink-Prp
'Let's drink coffee.'
b. coffee-na masi-ca.
coffee-or drink-Prp
'Let's drink coffee.'

By sentence (22a), the speaker literally proposes to drink coffee, insinuating nothing else. However, it is not the case that in (22b) the speaker simply proposes to drink coffee. Using the disjunctive *na* 'or,' the speaker implies that there would be other things to do or something else to drink. Remember the role of the disjunctive *na* 'or,' which signals existence of another choice to make. In addition, (22b) implies that drinking coffee is the most ready thing for the speaker to do. For example, the speaker could choose, e.g. to drink tea, eat a meal, or go to a concert. Among the things he could choose, drinking coffee is the easiest thing for the speaker to do. Only in this situation is (22b) acceptable. Take another example:

(23) a. phikonhani, cam-ul ca-ca.
being tired, sleeping-Acc sleep-Prp
'Since we are tired, let's sleep,'
b. phikonhani, cam-ina ca-ca.
being tired, sleeping-or sleep-Prp
'Since we are tired, let's sleep.'

In general, one of the most likely things to do, when one is tired, would be to take a nap, and not, e.g. reading a book, watch TV, or talk with friends. (23a) is a simple statement about the speaker's wish, implying nothing else. In other words, the speaker didn't mention whether there are other things s/he would do or like to do. In (23b), however, the speaker suggests that there are in fact many things for him/her to do, although it is not patently expressed. Among other various choices, the speaker chooses the easiest thing (or the most expected thing), i.e. sleeping. Hence the use of the disjunctive *-na* 'or,' in sharp contrast to the accusative case marker *-lul*, implies that there would be other choices that are not chosen. In short, [x-na] entails that there is at least one more potential member that could otherwise be chosen by the denotation of the predicate.[5] So far, I have shown that the disjunctive *-na* 'or' plays a special role in signaling the existence of potential members to choose from. In what follows, let us discuss the semantics of *amwu-na*, equivalent to the English free choice 'any.' In the previous sections, I suggested that *amwu* refers to something/someone least significant and hence is placed on the bottom of the pragmatic scale.

Then let's consider what happens if *amwu* 'any' and the disjunctive *-na* 'or' are combined, yielding *amwu-na* (free choice), as shown in (24):

[5]Note that the x in [x-na] is a variable, which can be filled with any indefinite to yield a universal quantifier. Thus *nwukwu-na*(literally who-or, meaning 'anyone') and *etten salami-na* (literally which person-or, meaning 'anyone') are all interpreted as a universal quantifier. See Jang and Kim (1997) for a detailed discussion.

(24) (Looking at a menu table)
A: mwuel mek-ci?
what eat-Q?
'What shall we eat?'
B: amwu ke-na mek-ca.
any thing-or eat-Prp
'Let's eat anything.'

What (24B) entails is that there is in fact at least one more choice, e.g. chicken soup, chowder soup, or mashed potato, or what not, which they could choose. The fact that he could choose the least (significant/likely) thing to eat, represented by *amwu*, suggests that he might otherwise choose a better thing to eat. Therefore, the speaker B could choose any of the items on the menu. Hence comes the name "free choice any."

5. The Semantics of *amwu* 'any'

The basic meaning of *amwu* 'any' is indefinite and seems to be used to denote something/someone not important or less important. Suppose there are people that I would like to see and that one specific person of the group is important to me. In this case, I do not refer to that particular person as *amwu*. Rather I would call him/her by name or by an appropriate title. There seems to be a general tendency that the more significant a thing/person is, the more specific is the expression used. Of course, there may be a situation in which we employ an indefinite/non-specific expression on purpose in order to show special emotions or for some other reasons. I will ignore such a special case. If the treatment of *amwu* 'any' as denoting something indefinite and less important is on the right track, then the pragmatic scale such as (10) is enough to explain the negative polarity nature of *amwu-to* (NPI any). In other words, *amwu* 'any' is placed on the bottom of the scale. Since *amwu* 'any' is placed on the bottom of the scale, it becomes an NPI , in conjunction with the particle *-to* 'also.' It is important to note that *amwu* 'any' is assumed to be the least significant: in the sense that if someone is likely to come (by default) that we don't even take into consideration the possibility of his not coming, then the person would not be considered to be significant. It would not be appropriate to say that *amwu* (=the most likely to come) "also" came, because there still remains a possibility that no one else came. Again, *-to* 'also' is possible only if there is at least one more member denoted by the predicate. Therefore (25) below, which is an affirmative sentence, is not acceptable.

(25) *amwu-to o-ass-ta.
any-also come-Pst-Dec
'(lit.) Anyone also came.'

On the other hand, it is quite appropriate to say that *amwu* (=the most likely to come) "also" did not come, because there may surely be at least one more person who didn't come, e.g. A, B, or C. Hence (25), which is the negation of the unacceptable (26), is fully acceptable.

(26) amwu-to ahn o-ass-ta.
any-also not come-Pst-Dec
'(lit.) Anyone also did not come.'

Alternatively, suppose that three students John, Mary, and Bill, are expected to be at school. However, suppose that no one was at school, when you got there. In this situation, you might say as follows:

(27) a. hakkyo-ey-nun John-to eps-ess-ta.
school-at-Top John-also be not-Pst-Dec
'John was not in the school.'
b. Mary-to eps-ess-ta.
Mary-also was not-Pst-Dec
'Mary was not there, either.'
c. Bill-to eps-ess-ta.
Bill-also was not-Pst-Dec
'Bill was not there, either.'

In addition, you can add something like the following:

(28) hakkyo-ey-nun kaymi hanmali-to eps-ess-ta.
school-at-Top ant one-also be not-Pst-Dec
'There was not even a single ant in the school.'

Of course, you might not have expected that you could find an ant in the school. You might simply have wanted to see John, Mary, or Bill, or all of them. The reason why (28) is often used by Koreans is as follows: Since ants are (thought to be) the most likely thing to be found almost anywhere (i.e. least significant), if you couldn't find an ant, then it is probably the case that you could not find the person you wanted to see. Therefore, *kaymi hanmali-to* is always used as an NPI in Korean. Compare (28) with (29) below:

(29) *hakkyo-ey-nun kaymi han mali-to iss-ess-ta.
school-at-Top ant one Cl-also be-Pst-Dec
'There was even an ant in the school.'

Sentence (29) would be acceptable, if interpreted in such a way that you are describing what situation the school is in. For example, if the school is abandoned so long without care that you could find even ants, then the sentence would be quite acceptable. This is another case of PPI in the sense that an ant is the most unlikely thing to be found in the school. It is important to note that the complement of the conjunctive *–to* and/or the disjunctive *–na* should be indefinite to be interpreted as negative polarity any or free choice any, respectively. For example, a definite complement of the conjunctive coordinator *–to* is not an NPI, as discussed in Chung (1993). Consider his example below:

(30) a. ku-nun macimak nam-un han salam-to an manna-ss-ta
he-Top last remain-Rel one person-also not meet-Pst-Dec
'He did not meet the person who remained last.'
b. ku-nun macimak nam-un han salam-to manna-ss-ta
he-Top last remain-Rel one person-also meet-Pst-Dec
'He met the person who remained last.'

Unlike the case in (28-29), the quantified expression *han salam-to* 'one person also' is modified by a relative clause and thus is a definite noun. (30a) is a negative sentence and (30b) is an affirmative one, but both of these allow the quantified expression *han salam-to*, suggesting that it is not a polarity sensitive item. Compare the sentences with the following:

(31) a. ku-nun han salam-to an manna-ss-ta
he-Top one person-also not meet-Pst-Dec
'He did not meet even one person.'
b. *ku-nun han salam-to manna-ss-ta
he-Top one person-also meet-Pst-Dec
'He met even one person.'

As shown in (31), indefinite expressions like *han salam-to* are NPIs in Korean. Then a question may arise with regard to the pragmatic scale: Why don't we have PPIs with quantifiers? Given the scale (10), NPIs are the lowest point of the scale, represented by the smallest natural number, namely one. However, since the biggest natural number cannot be represented on the scale, we have no quantified PPIs, as Choi (1998) notes. In short, the indefinite expression *amwu* is on the bottom of the pragmatic scale (for significance). Therefore, it becomes an NPI, only if accompanied by the conjunctive *-to* 'also.'

6. Conclusion

The main task of this paper was to answer the following two correlated questions: (i) Why should *amwu-to* (NPI any) in Koran be invariably an NPI? And (ii) Why should *amwu-na* (free choice any) always be interpreted as such? Based on Fauconnier's pragmatic scale, I showed that *amwu* means the least significant and thus is placed on the bottom of the scale. One of the main claims of this paper is that since coordinators like conjunctive *-to* and disjunctive *-na* presuppose existence of (an)other potential member(s) denoted by the predicate, the combined forms *amwu-to* and *amwu-na* give rise to a special meaning: That is, since *amwu-to* presupposes existence of at least two potential members and is placed on the bottom of the scale, it should be negated. An analogous example was shown using superlatives on the bottom of the scale, in conjunction with the conjunctive *to*. On the other hand, *amwu-na* entails a choice of the least significant option of the potentially multiple choices. Hence it is called a free choice any.

References

Choi, Kiyong. 1998. On a Negative Polarity Item *amwu* in Korean. *Studies in Generative Grammar* 8(2): 313-342.

Chung, Daeho. 1993. Negative Polarity Items in Korean: Formal and Distributional Types. Ms. University of Southern California.

Fauconnier, Gilles. 1975. Pragmatics Scales and Logical Structure. *Linguistic Inquiry* 6: 353-375.

Fillmore, C., P. Kay, and C. O'Connor. 1988. Regularity and Idiomaticity in Grammatical Constructions: The Case of *let alone*. *Language* 64: 501-538.

Israel, Machael. 1996. Polarity Sensitivity as Lexical Semantics. *Linguistics and Philosophy* 19: 619-666.

Jang, Youngjun. 1998. Don't You Need One More to Conjoin? *Journal of Korean Linguistics* 23: 3.535-561.

Jang, Youngjun and Il-Kon Kim. 1997. Disjunctive *-na* and Universal Quantifier Reading in Korean. *SICOL-97*: 478-485.

Kadmon, Nirit and Fred Landman. 1993. ANY. *Linguistics and Philosophy* 16: 353-422

Ladusaw, William. 1980. The Notion of Affectiveness and the Negative Polarity Licensing. *Journal of Language Research* 1: 1-15.

Lee, Chungmin. 1996. Negative Polarity Items in English and Korean. *Language Sciences* 18: 1-2.505-523.

Lee, Young-Suk and Laurence Horn. 1995. *Any* as Indefinite plus *Even*. Ms. Yale University, New Haven.

Rullman, Hotze. 1996. Two Types of Negative Polarity Items. *NELS* 26: 335-350.

Shi, Chung-Kon. 1997. The Licensing Condition of Negative Polarity Item in Korean. *Korean Journal of Linguistics* 22: 3.71-497.

Korean *WH* -phrases Void of Operator

AE-RYUNG KIM
Indiana University

1. Introduction

This paper intends to argue that a wh-phrase is not a WH-quantifier in Korean wh-questions. In section 1 I will describe the properties of WH-quantifier: [+OP] feature and [+Q] feature. In section 2, I will show that a Korea wh-phrase bears neither [+OP] feature nor [+Q] feature. Section 3 discusses what element carries the properties of WH-quantifier in Korean.

2. Properties of WH-quantifier

Since Chomsky (1976), it has been a general practice to treat a wh-question on a par with a quantified sentence with respect to semantic interpretation, i.e. it involves a quantifier. A wh-question (1a) is interpreted as (1b), which is parallel with the interpretation of a quantified sentence as in (2b).

(1) a. What did Mary buy t?
b. For which x, x a thing, Mary bought x?

(2) a. Mary bought everything.
b. For all x, x a thing, Mary bought x.

Chomsky (1976) treats the moved wh-phrase *what* as an operator and its trace as variable. Higginbotham & May (1981) formalize the interpretation (1b).

(3) WHx [thing (x)] [Mary bought x]

They treat the wh-phrase as a binary operator and call the "WH" WH-operator.

May (1985) establishes a mechanism to capture the syntactic parallelism between a wh-question like (1a) and a quantified sentence like (2a). He suggests LF representation, at which quantified phrases undergo Quantifier Raising (QR) – adjunction to IP or VP. Given the QR, the parallelism between a wh-question and a quantified sentence obtains in the level of LF and semantic interpretation (SI) as in (4).

(4) a. SS What did Mary buy t
LF $[_{CP}$ what$_i$ did $[_{IP}$Mary buy $t_i]]$
SI WHx [thing (x)] [Mary bought x]
b. SS Mary bought everything
LF $[_{IP}$ everything$_i$ $[_{IP}$ Mary bought $t_i]]$
SI ∀x [thing (x)] [Mary bought x]

At SS a wh-question and a quantified sentence are contrasted in involving movement and a trace. However at LF and semantic interpretation, their structures are identical. May (1985) points out that movement renders LF structures transparent to semantic interpretation: the operator *what*/*every* is located in the position to c-command its argument IP (nuclear scope) at LF.

Let's decompose the properties of ordinary quantifiers. "Quantifier" refers to existential (∃) and universal (∀) operators. They are distinguished from the other operators, for example negation (¬) in that the proposition quantifiers enclose should be an open proposition, i.e. the proposition must have a free variable bound by the quantifier. Natural language prohibits the formula $\forall[\varphi]$ or $\exists[\varphi]$ due to vacuous quantification. We may distinguish a quantifier from negation operator: both have a quantificational force ([+QF] feature) to assign to the proposition they enclose, but unlike negation operator, quantifier also has operator property ([+OP] feature) to bind a free variable. We saw that WH-operator in (1b) binds a variable and hence it has [+OP] feature. Since it renders a sentence interrogative, it has interrogative force [+Q] feature (following the long tradition). The terminologies "quantifier" and "operator" are alternatively used in general. However they are distinguished in this paper, and the WH-operator of H&M (1981) will be called WH-quantifier from now on. With the features [+OP] and [+QF], we may distinguish some operators.

(5)

	[QF]		[OP]
Existential quantifier	+	[+∃]	+
Universal quantifier	+	[+∀]	+
WH-quantifier	+	[+Q]	+
Negation operator	+	[+ ¬]	–
λ - operator	–		+

Though the WH-quantifier has both properties [+OP] and [+QF], it is commonly called quasi-quantifier. The reason may be that existential and universal quantifiers assign a truth condition to the proposition without changing the type, but WH-quantifier changes the type of proposition from $< t >$ to $<<s,t>, t>$. The denotation of WHx [$\varphi(x)$] is a set of propositions, while that of $\forall x/\exists x$ [φx] is a truth-conditional proposition.

3. Korean Wh-Phrases

I specified that the WH-quantifier bears [+Q] feature and [+OP] feature in the section 1. In this section I will show that Korean wh-phrases bear neither [+Q] feature nor [+OP] feature and hence they are not WH-quantifiers.

3.1 [+Q] Feature of Korean Wh-Phrases

Let me clarify the terms "wh-phrase" first. As is well known, there are some words that are used for both interrogative expressions and quantified expressions in Korean as well as Chinese, Japanese and other languages. I will refer to them as **wh-expressions** and wh-expressions with interrogative meaning will be called **wh-phrases**. Korean wh-expressions appear in two forms: without a particle (wh-∅) as in (6a) and with a quantificational particle (wh-∀/∃) as in (6b).

(6) a. **Nuku-∅**-ka wass-*ni*?
    Who-∅-nom came- Q
    'Who came?'
  b. **Nuku-inka/ina**-ka wass-*ni*?
    Who-∃/∀-nom came-Q
    'Did someone/everyone come?'

Since all Korean wh-phrases are in the form of wh-∅, we are mainly concerned of wh-∅ expressions.

A wh-∅ expression is triple-ambiguous as in (7).

(7) a. Nuku-∅-ka wass-*ni*?
    who-∅-nom came-Q
    '**Who** came?'
  b. Nuku-∅-ka wass-*ta*/ *ni*?.
    who-∅-nom came-dec /Q
    '**Someone** came.' / 'Did **someone** come?'
  c. Nuku-∅-ka wo-*tunci*, na-nun ku-lul hwanyongha-lketi-ta
    who-∅-nom come-no matter I-top he-acc welcome-will-dec
    '**No matter who** comes, I will welcome him.'

In (7a), the wh-∅ expression *nuku* is a wh-phrase, while in (7b) it is an existential quantifier and in (7c) it is a pseudo-universal quantifier. The main question in this section is whether *nuku* in (7) has the [+Q] feature inherently.

This question has received various analyses. A group considers wh-∅ expressions to have an inherent quantificational force. Among them, C-M Suh (1987) claims that all wh-∅ expressions are existential quantifiers in the lexicon and they are conversed to wh-phrases when they receive phonological prominence (high pitch accent). C-S Suh (1989) and D-H Chung (1996) prusue the opposite direction: from a wh-phrase to an existential quantifier. H-S Choe (1994) suggests that wh-∅ expressions are lexically ambiguous. Watanabe (1992) takes a similar line for Japanese wh-∅ expressions: a wh-phrase has a null quantificational element as a quantifier phrase has a particle *mo*'∀' or *ka* '∃'. The other group considers that wh-∅ expressions do not have an inherent quantificational force. Kuroda (1965) first suggests it and Nishigauchi (1990) elaborates it for Japanese wh-∅ expressions. Aoun & Li (1993), pointing out that Chinese wh-∅ expressions are ambiguous between wh-phrase and existential quantifier, claim that they are variables in that they do not have an inherent quantificational force.

I will argue that Korean wh-∅ expressions should be treated as variables along the line with the second group. We saw that a wh-∅ expression is interpreted as a wh-phrase in (7a) and an existential quantifier in (7b) in an interrogative sentence. However when two wh-expressions appear in the same clause, they must receive the same interpretation as in (8). I will call this phenomenon across-the-board effect. [1]

---

[1] S-W Kim (1989) judges (8c) as acceptable. In fact, it seems to me that both (8c) and (8d) can be forced from the sentence (8) in special occasions. H-K Wee (personal conversation) points out that (8c) reading is easier to get if *nuku* receives extra high pitch accent considering a wh-phrase receives high pitch accent. The reading (8d) obtains with extra high pitch accent on *mues*.

The wh-question (8c), repeated in (ia) is different from a regular wh-question (ib) or (ic).

(i) a. **Nuku-∅**-ka **mues-∅**-ul sass-*ni*?
'**Who** bought **something**?'
b. **Nuku-∅**-ka computer-lul sass-ni?
'Who bought a computer?'
c. **Nuku-∅**-ka **mues-inka**-ul sass-*ni*?
'**Who** bought **something**?'

"Nobody" can be an answer to a wh-question like (ib), and (ic), which has the same interpretation as (ia). However, "Nobody" cannot be an answer to (a).

The answer "Nobody" is not compatible with a wh-question when the whquestion is uttered in the context in which "somebody bought something/computer" is a shared information. It follows that (ia) is uttered in the context where "somebody bought something" has already been uttered. Then *mues* 'somebody' in (ia) is somehow old information rather than being novel. Due to the property, we could put aside (ia/8c) and the reading (8d) from our consideration.

(8) **Nuku-Ø**-ka **mues-Ø**-ul sass-*ni*?
person-Ø-nom thing-Ø-acc bought-Q
a. 'Did **someone** buy **something**?'
b. '**Who** bought **what**?'
c. *'**Who** bought **something**?'
d. *'**What** did **someone** buy?'

Though an interrogative sentence is compatible with both a wh-phrase and an existential quantifier as in (7a) and (7b), both cannot occur in the same clause as in (8c-d). If a wh-Ø expression were inherently a wh-phrase or an existential quantifier, the sentence (8) should be able to have four readings, and a wh-Ø expression should not be influenced by the quantificational force of the clause-mate wh-Ø expression.

In this respect, the following sentence (9) is contrasted to (8).

(9) **Nuku-Ø**-ka **mues-inka**-ul sass-*ni*?
person-Ø-nom thing-∃-acc bought-Q
a. 'Did **someone** buy **something**?'
b. '**Who** bought **something**?'

(9) involves a wh-Ø expression and a wh-∃ expression. Due to the particle –*inka* '∃', the quantificational force of *mues* is fixed as existential. The sentence is two-way ambiguous depending on how *nuku-Ø* is interpreted. When one of them has a fixed quantificational force '∃', the mixed reading (9b) is possible. If *mues-Ø* in (8) has inherent ∃-quantificational force like *mues-inka* '∃' in (9), (8c) should be acceptable. The contrast between (8c) and (9b) indicates that unlike *mues-inka*, *mues-Ø* does not have an inherent existential force.

A similar contrast with respect to across-the-board effect is manifested in a *tunci*-clause as in (10) and (11).

(10) **Nuku-Ø**-ka **mues-Ø**-ul senmulha-*tunci* Mary-nun kippeha-cian-ulketi-ta.
Person-Ø-nom thing-Ø-acc give-*no matter*, M-top be pleased-neg-will-dec
a. '**No matter who** gives **what,** Mary won't be pleased.'
b. *'**No matter who** gives **something** for her, Mary won't be pleased.'
c. *'**No matter what someone** gives, Mary won't be pleased.'

The comp –*tunci* must have a wh-Ø expression in the same clause as English *no matter* requires a wh-phrase. In (10b) and (10c), a wh-Ø expression has pseudo-universal interpretation, but they are out because the other wh-Ø expression is interpreted as an existential quantifier. However, (11) indicates that *tunci*-clause is not incompatible with an existential quantifier.

(11) **Nuku-inka**-ka **mues-Ø**-ul senmulha-*tunci* Mary-nun kippeha-cian-ulketi-ta.
person-Ø-nom thing-∃-acc give-*no matter*, M-top be pleased-neg-will-dec
'**No matter what someone** may give, Mary won't be pleased.'

The sentence (11) contains a wh-Ø and a wh-∃ *nuku-inka*. *Nuku-inka* has an inherent existential force, and *no matter*-clause is compatible with the existential quantifier. If a wh-∅ expression *nuku-∅* in (10) had an inherent existential force as *nuku-inka*, (10) should allow the mixed reading (10c) as (11) does.

We saw that a wh-∅ expression shows a clear contrast to a wh-∃ expression that has its own quantificational force. While the latter is not subject to across-the-board effect, the former is subject to. From the fact that a wh-∅ expression is subject to across-the-board effect, it follows that wh-∅ expression does not have its own quantificational force.

3.2 [+OP] Feature of Korean Wh-Phrases

Since Huang (1982), the standard analysis of in-situ wh-questions adopts movement of wh-phrases. Huang (1982) suggests that in-situ wh-phrases undergo QR-like movement at LF. The motivation for the movement is that "since we have assumed that quantificational sentences are subject to QR and since wh-questions are quantificational, there is little reason not to assume that wh-questions also have a similar quantifier variable representation at LF". The claim is based on the assumption that Chinese wh-phrases are WH-quantifier and movement of a wh-phrase establishes a quantifier-variable relation. Watanabe (1992) and Tsai (1994) consider wh-phrases as bearing both [+Q] feature and [+OP] feature, while in Nishigauchi (1990) wh-∅ expressions do not have a quantificational force but they bear [+OP] feature. Due to the [+OP] feature, he adopts movement of wh-∅ expressions.

Given that Korean wh-∅ expressions do not have an inherent quantificational force, there are two options we can take about the [+OP] feature of the Korean wh-phrase. One is it does not have [+OP] feature either. The other is that it still has [+OP] feature. It is hard to show that a wh-phrase does not have [+OP] feature directly. However, I will support it by showing that an analysis based on the assumption that the wh-phrase has [+OP] feature but [-Q] feature cannot be applied to Korean wh-∅ expression. Nishigauchi (1990) implicitly assumes that wh-phrase still has [+OP] feature, though it does not have a quantificational force. His analysis runs into an empirical problem with the quantificational force of Korean wh-∅ expressions.

Nishigauchi (1990) hypothesizes that all wh-∅ expressions move to Spec CP whose head has either [+Q] (ka) or [+(pseudo)∀] (*mo*). The quantificational force of a wh-∅ expression is determined by the comp(lementizer) that governs it. The movement is subject to locality condition, i.e. a wh-∅ expression moves to the closest Spec CP.

(12) a. Kimi-wa [**dare**-ga kite-*mo*] ika-nai *no*?
you-top who-nom come *no matter* go-no $Q_{y/n}$
'Are you not going, **no matter who** may come?'
* 'For which x, x a person, are you not going if you know whether x is coming?'
b. John-wa [[**dare**-ga kuru *ka*] sirteite-*mo*] ika-nai.
J-top who-nom come Q_{wh} know-even if go-not
'John will not go even if he knows **who** will come.'
* 'For all x, x a person, John will not go if he knows whether x is coming.'

Though there are two comp's to which a wh-∅ expression can move, it can move only to the closer comp. Hence *dare* in (12a) is quantified only by *mo* and *dare* in (12b) is quantified only by *ka*.

Let's apply Nishigauchi's analysis to the quantificational forces of Korean wh-∅ expressions. Since Korean wh-∅ expressions have three kinds of quantificational force, there should be three types of comp: comp's with [+Q], [+(pseudo)∀] and [+∃]. We have to assume all the wh-∅ expressions move to Spec CP, if they move, because they are indistinguishable. What comp has [+∃] feature? We saw that comp *–ni* is related to [+Q] and *-tunci* to [+(pseudo)∀]. A wh-∅ expression takes existential force unless it occurs with [+Q] comp or [+(pseudo)∀] comp. Hence all the comp's except the two have [+∃] feature. Given the assumptions, the ambiguity of following interrogative sentence seems to pose a problem to the adoption of Nishigauchi's analysis.

(13) Nuku-∅-ka wass-*ni*?
who-∅-nom came-Q
'**Who** came?' / 'Did **someone** come?'

A wh-∅ expression governed by the same comp can take two different quantificational forces. However, this ambiguity may be solved if we distinguish the interrogative comp *–ni* into two types: *-ni* with [+Q] and *–ni* with [+∃] – first adjustment. If *–ni* has [+Q], it becomes a wh-phrase; if *–ni* has [+∃] the wh-∅ expression becomes an existential quantifier.

Locality condition predicts the embedded wh-∅ expression should be existential in (14) because the closest comp has neither [+Q] nor [+(pseudo)∀].

(14) John-un [Mary-ka **mues-∅**-ul sassta-ko] saengkakha-*ni*?
J-top [M-nom thing-∅-acc bought-comp] think-Q
a. Does John think Mary bought **something**?
b. **What** does John think Mary bought?

Unlike the prediction, it can be quantified by the farther comp *–ni* with [+Q] in (14b). Some might justify (14b) by explaining that [+Q] must quantify a wh-∅ expression, and thus locality is overridden to save the derivation of (14) from crashing – second adjustment.

However, even the adjustment cannot work for the reading (15a).

(15) **Nuku**-∅-ka [Mary-ka **mues**-∅-ul sassta-ko] saengkakha-*ni*?
Person-∅-nom M-nom thing-∅-acc bought-comp thini-Q
a. '**Who** thinks Mary bought **what**?'
b. '**Who** thinks Mary bought **something**?'
c. 'Did **someone** think Mary bought **something**?'

If the matrix comp –*ni* has [+Q] feature, the matrix wh-∅ expression *nuku* is interpreted as a wh-phrase as in (15a) and (15b). The reading (15b) obtains if the embedded wh-∅ expression *mues* moves to the embedded Spec CP. The reading (15c) obtains if –*ni* has [+∃] force. The reading (15a) is derived by the embedded *mues* moving to matrix Spec CP. It violates locality condition, though –*ni* with [+Q] quantifies a wh-∅ expression. In spite of violation of locality condition, (15a) is perfectly acceptable. The adoption of Nishigauchi's analysis cannot account for (15a). The across-the-board effect as in (16) poses a similar problem.

(16) John-un [**nuku**-∅-ka **mues**-∅-ul sassta-ko] saengkakha-*ni*?
J-top [person-∅-nom thing-∅-acc bought-comp] think-Q
'**Who** does John think t bought **what**?'

A-R Kim (in preparation) develops a rigorous discussion for the quantificational forces of Korean wh-∅ expressions.

In addition to inexplicable quantificational forces of embedded wh-∅ expressions in (15a) and (16), Nishigauchi's assumption that a wh-phrase has [+OP] feature but [-Q] feature makes the semantic property of WH-quantifier parametric; in some language it has [+OP] and [+Q] and in others it has [+OP] but [-Q]. I have shown that Nishigauchi's analysis cannot cover some quantificational force of Korean wh-∅ expressions. Based on that I propose that Korean wh-∅ expressions have neither an inherent quantificational force nor [+OP] feature. Thus wh-phrase, a type of wh-∅ expressions, does not have either of the property. Under this proposal, a wh-phrase/wh-∅ expression is not an operator. It is not a referential expression, either. Aoun & Li (1993) treats wh-phrases as variables in that sense. I agree with them on the status of wh-phrases and I assume that Korean wh-phrases are variables.

4. Consequences

The semantic interpretation of Korean wh-questions is parallel with that of English wh-questions. That is, Korean wh-questions are interpreted as having a WH-quantifier. In the section 2, I proposed that wh-phrases do not have any property of WH-quantifier, and they are variable. Then what carries the property of WH-quantifier in Korean? In section 3.1 I will propose that wh-comp (complementizer of wh-questions) is the WH-quantifier. The proposal leads to separating interrogative comp into wh-comp and yes/no-comp (complementizer of yes/no-questions). In section 3.2 I will justify that the separation of interrogative comp is on the right tract.

4.1 WH-Quantifier in Korean Wh-Questions

Bresnan (1970) claims that there is a node c-commanding S at D-structure. She hypothesizes a phrase structure rule S' → COMP S. A comp is generated under the COMP node. Though in English the COMP is occupied by a null element, in Korean as well as Japanese and Chinese, it is occupied by a morphological element.

(17) a. Mary-ka **mues**-∅-ul sa-ss-*ta*.
M-nom thing-∅-acc buy-past-dec
'Mary bought something.'

b. Mary-ka **mues**-∅-ul sa-ss-*ni* ?
M-nom thing-∅-acc buy-past-Q
'What did Mary buy?'/'Did Mary buy something?'

Due to the different sentence-final morphemes *ta* vs. *ni*, (17a) and (17b) are distinguished as a declarative sentence and an interrogative sentence, respectively. Chomsky (1973) distinguishes COMP into two types: COMP → ±Q(WH). If COMP is [+Q] the sentence is interrogative and if it is [-Q] it is declarative. The sentences (17a-b) show that the distinction is morphologically realized in Korean.

Korean Kyungsang dialect and Chinese have two kinds of interrogative comp's as in (18) and (19), respectively.

(18) a. Mary-ka **mues**-∅-ul sa-ss-*na* ?
M-nom thing-∅-acc buy-past-$Q_{y/n}$
'Did Mary buy something?'

b. Mary-ka **mues**-∅-ul sa-ss-*no* ?
M-nom thing-∅-acc buy-past-Q_w
'What did Mary buy?'

(19) a. Zhangsan mai-le **shenme** *ma*?
Zhangsan buy-past thing $Q_{y/n}$
'Did Zhangsan buy something?'

b. Zhangsan mai-le **shenme** (*ne*)?
Zhangsan buy-past thing Q_{wh}
'What did Zhangsan buy?'

While (17b) is ambiguous between wh- and yes/no-questions, the ambiguity disappears in Kyungsang dialect as in (18). In this dialect, a sentence with *–na* is interpreted as a yes/no-question and a sentence with *–no* as a wh-question.The distinction between yes/no-comp and wh-comp seems to be systematic in this dialect. Past tensed (perfective) interrogative sentences are distinguished by *–na* vs. *–no* as in (18), and future tensed (imperfective) ones are distinguished by *–ka* vs. *–ko* as in (20).

(20) a. John-i (naeil) **mues-∅**-ul sa-lketi-*ka*?
  J-nom (tomorrow) thing-∅-acc buy-will-Q
  'Will John buy **something** (tomorrow)?'

b. John-i (naeil) **mues-∅**-ul sa-lketi-*ko*?
  J-nom (tomorrow) thing-∅-acc buy-will-Q
  '**What** will John buy (tomorrow)?

H-S Choe (1994) claims that *–(nun)ka* and *–(nun)ko* distinguish embedded yes/no- and wh-questions[2]. Interrogative comp's are distinguished by the vowel contrast [a] vs. [o] in Kyungsang dialect. I will assume that while Kyungsang dialect shows morphological difference between wh-comp and yes/no-comp, other dialects have lost it.

In Kyungsang dialect, a wh-question must end with a wh-comp *–no* or *–ko*. Since it is the wh-comp rather than wh-∅ expression that renders a sentence a wh-question, I hypothesize that wh-comp functions as the WH-quantifier. To accept the hypothesis we should verify whether wh-comp has the two properties of WH-quantifier, [+OP] and [+Q]. It is trivial to check wh-comp *–no* has [+Q] feature since all the interrogative comp's have [+Q] feature. Let's see wh-comp *-no* has [+OP] feature. If it has this feature, it must require a free variable it can bind. See the examples (21).

(21) a.*Ne-nun ku-lul mannass-*no*?
  you-top he-acc met-Q_{wh}
  'Did you meet him?'

b. Ne-nun **nuku-∅**-lul mannass-*no*?
  You-top person-∅-acc met-Q_{wh}
  '**Who** did you meet?'

c. Ne-nun ku-lul **eti-∅**-eyse mannass-*no*?
  you-top he-acc place-∅-in met-Q_{wh}
  '**Where** did you meet him?'

A sentence (21a) ends with wh-comp *–no*, but it does not have a variable, wh-expression, and it is ungrammatical. In (21b) a wh-∅ expression appears and it is grammatical. The sentence (21a) becomes grammatical when a wh-∅ expression is added as in (21c). (21) indicates that wh-comp *–no* must co-occur with a wh-∅ expression.

Given that wh-∅ expressions are variables and wh-comp must have a wh-∅ expression, we can claim that wh-comp has [+OP] feature. That verifies that wh-comp has both [+Q] feature and [+OP] feature and it is WH-quantifier. If

[2] In fact, some speakers of Kyungsang dialect use*–ka* for embedded wh-questions as well as for embedded yes/no-questions regardless of tense.

we are on the right track in assuming that wh-comp is WH-quantifier, (21a) can be ruled out with the same reason that rules out the following logical forms of quantified sentences.

(22) a. $*\forall$ [love (j,m)] b. $*\exists$ [love (j,m)]

In (22a) and (22b), the quantifiers do not bind a variable. Unlike predicate logic, they are not allowed in the natural language because the natural language prohibits vacuous quantification.

I have proposed that wh-phrases are variables and wh-comp is WH-quantifier in Korean wh-question. The proposal leads to assuming that quantificational-variable relation is based generated rather than to be established by wh-movement. Another assumption the proposal makes is that wh-comp is substantially different from yes/no-comp, which departs from the standard analysis of interrogative comp since Chomsky (1973). Next section shows that the distinction is on the right tract.

4.2 Wh-comp vs. Yes/no-comp

4.2.1 Theoretical Problem with Uniform Interrogative Comp

Chomsky (1973) adopts Bresnan's (1970) new category comp and defines comp with [+WH/Q] or [-WH/Q]. Comp with [+Q] represents interrogative clauses and comp with [-Q] represents declarative clauses. It has been a standard analysis to characterize interrogative comp with [+Q] uniformly. May (1985) assumes a well-formed constraint on wh-questions, Wh-Criterion to capture the close relation between a wh-phrase and [+Q] comp. Wh-Criterion requires that all [+Q] comp must dominate a wh-phrase and all wh-phrases must be dominated by a [+Q] comp. According to Wh-Criterion, wh-phrases are licensed as long as they are associated with an interrogative clause. In next section, however, we will see this licensing condition is too generous.

Chomsky's (1995) minimalism framework also treats interrogative comp uniformly. In this framework, an interrogative comp has a strong [+Q] feature in English (or even universally). The strong feature [+Q] of comp should be checked off before Spell-Out takes place. Wh-movement in wh-questions and Subject-Aux-Inversion in yes/no-questions are motivated to check off the strong [+Q] feature. In wh-questions, a wh-phrase enters into the checking domain by moving to Spec CP and checks off [+Q] of C^0. In yes/no-questions, I^0 enters into checking domain via adjunction to C^0. Since wh-questions and yes/no-questions have the same interrogative comp, [+Q] of C^0 can be disjunctively checked off: either by wh-movement or by $I^0 \rightarrow C^0$ raising. Let's see how the checking theory accounts for interrogative sentences.

(23) a. *John bought what?
b. Did John buy a book?
c. Who bought a book?

The sentence (23a) is ungrammatical because [+Q] feature of C^0 is not checked off. Neither a wh-movement nor $I^0 \rightarrow C^0$ raising takes place. In (23b) [+Q] feature is checked off via $I^0 \rightarrow C^0$ raising and in (23c) via wh-movement.

Chomsky (1995) notices that the disjunctive nature of checking mechanism allows gibberish questions like (24a).

(24) a. #Did John buy what?

b. What did John buy?

The question (24a) is not quite acceptable for a wh-question, though the strong [+Q] feature is checked off via the movement of *did* ($I^0 \rightarrow C^0$ raising). Chomsky (1995) defines sentences like (24a) as well formed but gibberish. In addition to generating gibberish questions, the disjunctive nature of checking mechanism rules out perfect wh-questions like (24b) due to violation of Last Resort Principle. Last Resort Principle demands movement to be driven only by the need to check off some feature. The wh-question (24b) involves both wh-movement and $I^0 \rightarrow C^0$ raising. The driving force of both movements is checking off [+Q] feature. Once [+Q] feature is checked off by either of the movement, the other movement should not occur because the driving force has disappeared. Hence, (24b) involving both movements violates Last Resort Principle. Feature checking within minimalism is based on the uniform interrogative comp, which leads to disjunctive nature of checking mechanism. Disjunctive checking mechanism results in generating gibberish sentences and incorrectly ruling out good sentences.

4.2.2 Empirical Support for Distinction of Interrogative Comp

We have seen that Korean Kyungsang dialect and Chinese reveal morphological distinction between wh-comp and yes/no-comp. We saw a theoretical problem with uniform interrogative comp in English. This section presents an empirical English example that challenges uniform treatment of interrogative comp.

English is a language in which only one wh-phrase can move to Spec CP at S-structure/before Spell-Out. If a clause has multiple wh-phrases, the others should stay in-situ like *whom* in (25).

(25) Who remembers who met *whom*?

In (25), embedded clause has two wh-phrases. Since Baker (1970) points out, it is generally agreed that the in-situ *whom* in (25) has ambiguous scope interpretations. It can take embedded scope and matrix scope. If *whom* takes embedded scope, an answer to (25) is like (26a). If *whom* takes matrix scope, (26b) could be an answer to it.

(26) a. Bill remembers who met whom.

b. Bill remembers who met Tom.

The scope ambiguity has been accounted for by two different analyses. One explains that the in-situ *whom* moves either to CP of embedded [+Q] comp or matrix [+Q] comp at LF (in most literature within GB framework). The other analysis relates the in-situ *whom* to [+Q] comp by an association like binding (Baker (1970), Chomsky (1995) and Bošković (1996)).

Both accounts for the scope ambiguity in (25) are based on the idea that in-situ wh-phrase is licensed by [+Q] comp. Keeping that in mind, let's consider the following sentence.

(27) Do you remember who met *whom*?

The sentence (27) is exactly same as (25) with respect to interrogative comp. Both matrix clause and embedded clause have [+Q] comp in (25) and (27). However, the in-situ *whom* in (27) can take only embedded scope. It means that the [+Q] comp of the matrix clause does not license the in-situ *whom* in (27). What causes the contrast between (25) and (27)? The matrix clause of (27) is yes/no-question, while that of (25) is wh-question. It follows that wh-comp licenses an in-situ wh-phrase, but yes/no-comp does not. In (25) and (27), wh-comp and yes/no-comp are apparently different with respect to licensing an in-situ wh-phrase.

We can find similar examples manifesting the contrast between a wh-comp and a yes/no-comp. These examples show it more straightforwardly.

(28) a. Who remembers that John met *whom*?

b. *Do you remember that John met *whom*?

(29) a. Who likes books that criticize *whom*?

b. *Do you like books that criticize *whom*?

Unlike (27), the embedded clauses in (28) and (29) are headed by [-Q] comp, hence the in-situ wh-phrase *whom* cannot be licensed by the embedded comp. Thus it must be licensed by the matrix comp for the sentences to be grammatical. The matrix clauses of (28a) and (29a) are wh-questions, and *whom* is licensed. On the other hand, (28b) and (29b) are yes/no-questions, and they are ungrammatical. It follows that *whom* is not licensed by [+Q] comp of yes/no-question. The contrast between (28-29a) and (28-29b) indicates that [+Q] feature of comp is not sufficient to license a wh-phrase. To account for the contrast between (28-29a) and (28-29b), wh-comp should be distinguished from yes/no-comp.

What property is responsible for the difference between wh-comp and yes/no-comp? Recall that wh-comp is WH-quantifier in Korean. WH-quantifier has [+OP] feature and [+Q] feature. Yes/no-comp makes a clause interrogative, but it does not require a wh-∅ expression, variable. Given the fact yes/no-comp may be characterized as [+Q/-OP]. The suggestion leads to adding [±OP] to the feature of comp, and modifying Chomsky's (1973) rule COMP →[±Q] into COMP → [±Q/±OP]. Then the new rule would categorize comp's into four types as in (30).

(30)

	[+OP]	[-OP]
[+Q]	Wh-comp	Yes/no-comp
[-Q]	Relative-comp	Declarative-comp

The comp of relative clause may belong to the category [-Q/+OP] in that the clause must have a trace, but it does not have interrogative property. Though this paper does not elaborate a rigorous discussion of the property of relative comp, it captures the similarity and dissimilarity between wh-questions and relative clauses. The suggestion may shed a hint for the contrast between wh-island and relative clause as observed in Chinese, Japanese, Korean, and Scandinavian languages.

5. References

Aoun, Joseph and Audrey Li. 1993. WH-Elements in-situ: SS or LF?. *Linguistic Inquiry* 24. 199-238.

Bošković, Željko. 1997. Sometimes in Spec CP, sometimes in-situ. Ms.

Bresnan, Joan. 1970. On Complementizers: towards a syntactic theory of complement types. *Foundations of Language* 6. 297-321.

Cann, Ronnie. 1993. *Formal Semantics: An Introduction*. Cambridge University Press.

Choe, Hyon-sook. 1994. Focus and Topic Movement in Korean. In K. Kiss ed. *Discourse Configureational Languages*

Chomsky, Noam. 1973. Conditions on Transformations. *A Festschrift for Morris Halle*. 232-286.

Chomsky, Noam. 1976. Conditions on Rules of Grammar. *Linguistic Analysis* 2: 4. 303-351.

Chomsky, Noam. 1995. *Minimalist Program*. MIT Press.

Chung, Daeho. 1996. *On the Representation and Licensing of Q and Q-Dependents*. Doctoral dissertation. USC.

Higginbotham, James and Robert May. 1981. Questions, quantifiers and crossing. *The Linguistic Review* 1. 41-80.

Huang, James. 1982. *Logical Relations in Chinese and the Theory of Grammar*. Doctoral dissertation. MIT.

May, Robert. 1985. *Logical Form: Its Structure and Derivation*. MIT Press.

Nishigauchi, Taitsuke. 1990. *Quantification in the Theory of Grammar*. Kluwer.

Suh, Chung-mok. 1987. *A Study on the Interrogative Sentences in Korean* (in Korean). Thap Press.

Suh, Chung-soo. 1989. *A Study of Korean Grammar* (in Korean). Hankwuk-mwunhwasa.

Tsai, Wei-Tien. 1994. *On Economizing the Theory of A-bar Dependencies*. Doctoral dissertation, MIT.

Watanabe, Akira. 1992. WH-in-situ, Subjacency and Chain Formation. *MIT Occasional Working Paper*.

Causativity and Two Types of Noncausative Psych-verbs in Korean

SANG-GEUN LEE
University of Wisconsin

1. Introduction

Psych-verbs have been of interest to syntacticians (Lakoff 1970, Akatsuka 1976, Belletti & Rizzi 1988, Pesetsky 1995 among others), since they exhibit exceptional properties such as the linking problem for Baker's (1988) UTAH, backward binding (Akatsuka 1976), and the Target/Subject Matter restriction effect (Pesetsky 1995). However, no previous analysis considers the fact that causativization sometimes increases the valence of a psych-verb in Korean, but sometimes does not, which raises an objection to the untested general assumption that all types of Korean noncausative psych-verbs are comprised in one group (c.f., Kim 1989, Kim 1990, Nam 1993).[1]

---

[1] Experiencer's emotional state can be expressed in two ways in Korean; bare-form psych-verbs and *-eha* form psych-verbs. The former, which is my concern in this paper, describes the internal emotional state of the experiencer, forming double nominative constructions (DNCs), and being traditionally analyzed as ordinary two-place predicate sentences (see Kim (1990) for the contrasts between them).

a. nay-ka holangi-ka mwusepta. (Korean bare form psych-verb)
   I-Nom tiger-Nom is afraid
   'I am afraid of tigers.'

b. nay-ka holangi-lul mwusep-eha-n-ta. (Korean *-eha* form psych-verbs)
   I-Nom tiger-Acc be afraid-do-Pres-Dec
   'I fear tigers.'

In this paper, I will provide an explanation for why some psych-verbs causativize differently from the others in Korean, and which part of the grammar is most responsible for the contrastive distribution of two types of noncausative psych-verbs. Specifically, instead of appealing to any special syntactic structures, as Pesetsky (1995) did, I propose that the contrast between the two types of noncausative psych-verbs in Korean concerning the T/SM restriction effect (i.e., *Causer-Exp-T/SM) be approached from the Lexicalist point of view, such as Levin & Rappaport's (1995) Lexical Semantic Representation.

2. Problems for Syntactic Approach to the T/SM Restriction

2.1 T/SM Restriction with Psych-verbs

Assuming that linking patterns between thematic roles (e.g., Agent, Patient) and grammatical functions (e.g., Subject, Object) are predictable from the lexical properties of predicates, one can postulate a principle to that effect like Baker's (1988) UTAH or something weaker.

(1) Uniformity of Theta Assignment Hypothesis (UTAH, Baker 1988: 46):
Identical thematic relationships between items are represented by identical structural relationships between those items at the level of D-structure.

However, pairs such as (2) challenge the Hypothesis, which has been known as Flip, originally reported by Lakoff (1970):

(2) a. *Bill* was angry at *the article in the Times.* <Exp <Theme>>
b. *The article in the Times* angered *Bill.* <Theme <Exp>>

In (2a), Experiencer is the subject, and Theme is the object, while Theme is the subject and Experiencer is the object in (2b), which suggests that for psych-verbs, linking is arbitrary. To avoid this problem and rescue the Hypothesis in (1), Pesetsky (1995) proposes that the thematic roles assumed in (2) should be redefined like (3).

(3) a. *Bill* was angry at *the article in the Times.* <Exp <Target/SM>>
b. *The article in the Times* angered *Bill.* <Causer <Exp>>

Given Pesetsky's (1995: 59) new thematic hierarchy, i.e., Causer > Experiencer > Target/Subject Matter, we can say that higher thematic roles in pairs like (3) are mapped onto the higher D-structure positions, rescuing UTAH. However, this solution also has its own potential problem, as Pesetsky himself admitted, which is called T/SM restriction effect.

(4) a. T/SM restriction effect (Pesetsky 1995: 60): If Causer-role is distinct from either Subject Matter or Target of Emotion, why can't Causer and Target/Subject Matter cooccur with the same predicate?

b. **The article in the Times* angered *Bill* at *the government.*
*<Causer <Exp <Target>>>

Pesetsky (1995) suggests that in English, Object-Experiencer predicates like *anger* and *sadden* are actually bimorphemic, a zero causative morpheme (CAUS) and a bound root morpheme (e.g., √anger, √sad), as represented in (5). A piece of evidence for this suggestion comes from Japanese data taken from Akatsuka (1976), where a causative morpheme is overtly realized as -*(s)ase*, as shown in (6):

(5) a.[[√anger]+CAUS]] --> anger
b. [[√sad]+CAUS] --> sadden

(6) sono sirase-ga Tanaka-o knasim-*ase*-ta.
that news-Nom Tanaka-Acc be sad-*CAUSE*-past
'That news saddened Tanaka.'

The point made by Pesetsky (1995) is that affixation of CAUS to its root morpheme takes place in syntax, specifically at S-structure. That is, the phonologically null morpheme, CAUS, in English Object-Experiencer (henceforce, causative) psych-verb sentences, starts its life as a preposition lower than main root morpheme in the cascade structure representation shown in (7). Movement of CAUS to its host morpheme requires adjunction to each preposition intervening between them, so that it observes the Head Movement Constraint (HMC) (c.f., Travis 1984). However, the movement of CAUS in (7) is blocked by an intervening nonaffixal preposition *at.* And thus the zero morpheme, CAUS, cannot raise to its bound root morpheme *√anger*, explaining the T/SM restriction effect.

(7) a. **The article in the Times* angered *Bill* at *the government.*
b.

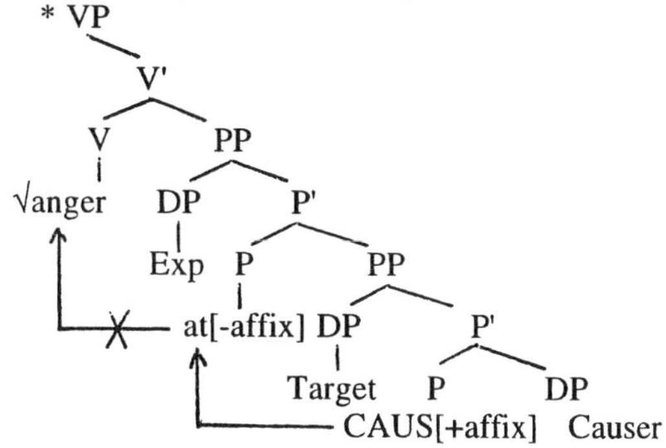

2.2 Problems Revisited

My concern in this paper is whether a better linguistic theory results from building complicated abstract representational structures such as the cascade structure (Pesetsky 1995) or adopting something simpler as phrase structure, and making use of other abstract informational structures, such as Lexical Semantic Representation (c.f., Levin & Rappaport 1995). Especially for an analysis of Korean psych-verbs, I will take the latter position from now on.

Aside from the potential difficulty in Pesetsky's (1995) analysis, (7b),[2] he does not seem to consider that in Korean (probably Japanese too)[3] there are actually two types of noncausative psych-verbs, one of which shows a totally different set of properties, especially with respect to the T/SM restriction. Note the contrast, especially in the grammaticality judgment between (8b) and (9b):

(8) a. *Sara*-ka *ku sosik*-i sulpessta. <Exp <T/SM>
Sara-Nom that news-Nom was sad
'Sara was sad about that news.'

b. *_ku sosik_-i *Sara*-eykey *casin-uy* *eleywun checi*-lu
that news-Nom Sara-Dat herself-Gen difficult situation-Acc

sulpu-keyhayssta. *<Causer <Exp <T/SM>>>
sad-made
'That news made Sara sad about her own difficult situation.'

c. *ku sosik*-i *Sara*-lul sulpu-keyhayssta. <Causer <Exp>>
that news-Nom Sara-Acc sad-made
'That news made Sara sad.'

(9) a. *Sara*-ka *pata*-ka kuliwessta. <Exp <T/SM>>
Sara-Nom ocean-Nom was (home)sick
'Sara was (home)sick for the ocean.'

b. *ku pata*-ka *Sara*-eykey *kohyang*-ul kulip-keyhayssta.
the ocean-Nom Sara-Dat hometown-Acc (home)sick-made
<Causer <Exp <T/SM>>>
'The ocean made Sara (home)sick for her hometown'

---

[2] In this D-structure representation, the Causer is still placed lower than the Target as well as the Experiencer. This kind of arrangement of thematic roles in (7b) violates Pesetsky's (1995) thematic hierarchy. To avoid this contradiction within his framework, he eventually needs to assume some extra mechanism, ending up with a more complicated phrase structure (see Pesetsky (1995: 208-209) for more details).

[3] Inoue (1972) reported that Japanese noncausative psych-verbs seemed not to be comprised in just one group. See the data in (10) and (11) taken from Inoue 1972) for the contrast between two types of Japanese noncausative psych-verbs.

c. **pata*-ka *Sara*-eykey/lul Ø kulip-keyhayssta. <Causer <Exp>>
ocean-Nom Sara-Dat (home)sick-made
*'The ocean made Sara (home)sick for.'

The data in (8) might lead us to conclude that the T/SM restriction is also observed even with Korean psych-verbs, however this conclusion does not seem to be extended to the other types of psych-verbs, as can be seen in (9b), which shows no T/SM restriction. Then, the real question to be answered is why a group of psych-verbs shows the T/SM restriction, while the other does not. The same observation has already been reported by Inoue (1972), but with Japanese data, (10) and (11):

(10) a. *taroo*-ga *sigoto*-o tanosindeiru.
Taro-Nom work-Acc is enjoying
'Taro is enjoying his work.'

---> b. *sigoto*-ga *taroo*-o tanosim-aseteiru
work-Nom Taro-Acc happy makes
'The work makes Taro happy.'

(11) a. *taroo*-ga *otooto-no kooun*-o netandeiru.
Taro-Nom brother-Gen good fortune-Acc be jealous of
'Taro is jealous of his brother's good fortune.'

---> b. **otooto-no kooun*-ga *taroo*-o netam-aseteiru.
brother's good fortune-Nom Taro-Acc jealous-making
*'His brother's good fortune is making Taro jealous.'

To sum up, noncausative psych-verbs in Korean (and probably Japanese too) are not comprised in just one class, to which no serious attention has been devoted until now. If this is the case, then the issue to be discussed is why a certain type of psych-verbs, (8b), especially in Korean, somehow seems to show the T/SM restriction effect, whereas the other type, (9b), does not?

3. Two Types of Noncausative Psych-verbs in Japanese/Korean

In this section, I propose that Japanese/Korean noncausative psych-verbs should be classified into two types, [+/- Transitive].

(12) Two types of noncausative psych-verbs in Korean
a. [+Transitive] type: kulipta (be (home)sick), pwulepta (be envious), heymosulepta (be disgusted)...
b. [-Transitive] type: sulputa (be sad), culkepta (be happy), koylopta (be sorry), cikyepta (be bored)...

(13) Two types of noncausative psych-verbs in Japanese (Inoue 1972)
a. Ordinary transitives: uram-u (be bitter), urayam-u (envy), netam-u (be jealous of), nozom-u (desire)...
b. Pseudo-transitives: tanosim-u (enjoy), kanasim-u (grieve), kurusim-u (suffer), nagek-u (regret)...

First, compare causativization with Korean ordinary (in)transitive predicates in (14) with causativization with two different types of noncausative psych-verbs in (8) and (9).

(14) a. *Sara*-ka *tali*-essta. -------> *Sora*-ka *Sara*-lul tali-keyhayssta.
Sara-Nom run-Past Sora-Nom Sara-Acc run-made
'Sara ran.' 'Sora made Sara run.'

b. *Sara*-ka *Seri*-lul ttayli-essta.
Sara-Nom Seri-Acc hit-Past
'Sara hit Seri.'
-------> *Sora*-ka *Sara*-eykey *Seri*-lul ttayli-keyhayssta.
Sora-Nom Sara-Dat Seri-Acc hit-made
'Sora made Sara hit Seri.'

Causative verbs in Korean necessarily involve one additional argument, Causer, in comparison with their corresponding noncausative verbs (c.f., Baker 1988), which is exemplified in (14). [+Transitive] psych-verbs undergoing causativization behave exactly like the ordinary transitive verbs, showing the same case alternation pattern and argument increase, as we have seen in (9). In contrast, the [-Transitive] type does not show any change in the valence (number of arguments) through causativization, as shown in (8), which convinces us that Korean [-Transitive] noncausative psych-verbs should not be analyzed as ordinary transitive verbs.

Consider the causativization of two types of Japanese psych-verbs, such as (10) and (11), and compare it with the pattern of causativization with ordinary transitive verbs, which is illustrated in (15).

(15) *taroo*-ga *tomodati*-o tazuneta.---> **tomodati*-ga *taroo*-o tazune-saseta.
Taro-Nom friend-Acc visited friend-Nom Taro-Acc visit-made
'Taro visited his friend.' 'Taro's friend made him visit.'

The pattern of causativization in (11) is in line with the regular causativization in (15), and thus the surface object in (11) can be said to be the true object. On the other hand, as pointed out by Inoue (1972), the second NP (NP2) in (10), which looks like a surface object, is not an ordinary object but a noun phrase denoting cause of emotion. This conclusion is further supported by the fact that the NP2's with [-Transitive] noncausative psych-verbs in Korean can be easily paraphrased with cause expressions like *-(u)lo* 'for' or *ttaymwuney* 'because of,' with no change of meaning (c.f., Nam 1993).[4] However, this is not true with [+Transitive] type, which is illustrated in (16):

(16) a. *Sara*-ka *ku sosik*-i/ulo/ttaymwuney sulpessta.
Sara-Nom that news-Nom/for/because of was sad
'Sara was sad because of that news.'

b. *Sara*-ka *kohyang*-i/*ulo/*ttaymwuney kuliwessta.
Sara-Nom hometown-Nom/for/because of was (home)sick
*'Sara was (home)sick because of her hometown.

The possibility of paraphrasing the NP2 (*ku sosik* 'that news') with a cause phrase in (16a) suggests that the NP2's with [-Transitive] type denote causes of such psychological states, which ordinary objects never involve.

4. Causativity of [-Transitive] Psych-verbs in Korean

According to lexicalist point of view (Chierchia 1989, Levin & Rappaport 1995 among others), the meaning of words itself reflects the deeper conceptual structures (e.g., Lexical Semantic Representation). In this section, I propose that NP2's with [-Transitive] noncausative psych-verbs at the level of surface structure are a reflection of the presence of cause event, which is one of the distinctive lexical properties of [-Transitive] type, and that the NP2's themselves be represented as Causer in the Lexical Semantic Representation (LSR).

Levin & Rappaport (1995) convincingly argue that only the core unaccusative verbs of change of state participating in the causative alternation (i.e., causative and inchoative alternation) are underlyingly causatives and thus dyadic in LSR, as shown in (17):

---

[4] Chungmin Lee (personal communication) pointed out to me that the possibility of paraphrasing the NP2's with a Korean causal phrase *-ttaymwuney* 'because of' should not guarantee the NP2's as being analyzed as adjuncts. I also agree with him on this opinion. Someone, such as Akatsuka (1976), might insist that the possibility can be provided as evidence guaranteeing the adjuncthood of the paraphrased elements (NP2's), which means that the sentences with [-Transitive] noncausative psych-verbs are simple (unergative) intransitives. However, if this is the case, then we will get into trouble with the obvious syntactico-semantic distinction between [-Transitive] psych-verbs and ordinary intransitive verbs. Rather, it might be more plausible to argue that the NP2's are obligatory adjuncts having causativity, which is in line with Grimshaw & Vikner's (1993) claim that obligatory adjuncts occur in passives with two parts of event structure, i.e., $[_{Event}$ [process] [state]], but never in actives.

a. *This house was built/designed/constructed.

b. This house was built/designed/constructed by a French architect.

In this paper, however, I stick to the claim that the NP2's with [-Transitive] noncausative psych-verbs, especially, unaccusative causative (I) psych-verbs are the Causer argument.

(17) a. Pat *broke₁* the window. (causative transitive verb)
b. The window *broke₂*. (unaccusative verb)
c. *break₁* : [x CAUSE [y BECOME BROKEN]]
d. *break₂* : ∃x [x CAUSE [y BECOME BROKEN]]

In line with Dowty's (1981) position for a lexical rule serving to predict how the form and meaning of a new added expression may be derived from that of an existing more basic expression, Levin & Rappaport (1995) further assume that existential quantification as a lexical binding (i.e., detransitivization) comes in with *break₂*, as represented in (17d), which makes it possible to derive an unaccusative (inchoative) verb in (17b).

I propose that in Korean, [-Transitive] noncausative psych-verbs participate in the same alternation and thus can be analyzed as unaccusatives with causativity in the lexical representation, whereas [+Transitive] noncausative psych-verbs are ordinary transitives without causativity, and being represented as such in LSR (c.f., Kim 1990).[5]

First, consider the contrast in grammaticality between (18a) and (18b):

(18) a. Sara-*ka/eykey* ku sosik-i sulpessta. (-Transitive)
Sara-Nom/Dat that news-Nom was sad
'Sara was sad about that news.'

b. Sara-*ka/*eykey* kohyang-i kuliwessta. (+Transitive)
Sara-Nom/Dat hometown-Nom was (home)sick
'Sara was (home)sick for her hometown.'

Referring to Croft (1993) and Dabrowska's (1994) claim that the "passiveness" of mental experiences is expressed with a dative experiencer, in (18a) the possibility of nominative-dative case alternation of [-Transitive] noncausative psych-verbs in Korean suggests that this type of psych-verbs has unaccusativity or passiveness in their lexical properties.[6] If this is the

---

[5] Kim (1990) convincingly argues that all types of (bare-form) noncausative psych-verbs in Korean as well as English are unaccusatives, based on the unaccusativity of those verbs. Then, her analysis cannot explain why some type of noncausative psych-verbs does somehow show the T/SM restriction, whereas the other type does not. After all, for the analysis of noncausative psych-verbs, I am not on any side, such as Akatsuka's (1976) intransitive analysis, Kim's (1990) unaccusative analysis, and transitive analysis (Lakoff 1970, Belletti & Rizzi 1988, Pesetsky 1995 among others).

[6] The contrast can also be well-represented by adopting Croft's (1993) two-way causal structure in (1) and (2) (see Lee (1998) for more details):
i. Object-motivated mental experience (expressed with [-Transitive] type)
a. nay-ka/eykey ku yenghwa-ka/ttaymwuney sulpessta.
I-Nom/Dat the movie-Nom/because of was sad
'I was sad about the movie.'
b. Causal structure: symmetric relation (bidirectionality)
Experiencer Stimulus
I <---------cause mental transition------ **the movie**
I -----------------FEEL (state)--------->**the movie**

case, then stepping further into the lexical properties of [-Transitive] noncausative psych-verbs in Korean, we can reach a systematic pattern (19a, b, c) of causative alternation, claiming with Chierchia (1989) and Levin & Rappaport (1995) that only the alternating unaccusative verbs are derived from underlyingly causative verbs.

(19) a. *ku sosik*-i *Sara*-lul sulpu-keyhayssta. (causative)
that news-Nom Sara-Acc sad-made
'That news made Sara sad.'

---> b. *Sara*-ka *ku sosik*-i sulpessta. (unaccusative causative (I))
Sara-Nom that news-Nom was sad
'Sara was sad about that news.'

---> c. *Sara*-ka sulpessta. (unaccusative causative (II))
Sara-Nom was sad
'Sara was sad.'

The data, especially in (19a, c), can be provided as evidence for the causativity with [-Transitive] noncausative psych-verbs in Korean, since the same pattern of causative alternation, which has been illustrated in (19a, b), is also observed in this case. Based on this observation, I propose that both subclasses, (19b, c), of [-Transitive] noncausative psych-verbs start from a single representation in LSR, as represented in (20):[7]

(20) *sulputa* 'be sad': (∃x) [x CAUSE [y BECOME *SAD*]]

What is crucial in my proposal for deriving two usages of unaccusatives, (19b, c), from a single lexical representation is then to assume that the existential quantifier in (20) optionally, not obligatorily, binds its variable, x, in Korean (see Dowty's (1981) lexical binding for details); if this binding takes place, the result will be detransitivized sentences such as (19c).

---

ii. Self-motivated mental experience (expressed with [+Transitive] type)
a. nay-ka/*eykey kohyang-i/*ttaymwuney kuliwessta.
I-Nom/ Dat hometown-Nom/because of be (home)sick
'I was (home)sick for my hometown.'
b. Causal structure: single asymmetric stative segment
Experiencer Target
I ---------FEEL (state)----- > **hometown**

[7] A member of the audience attending the 9th J/K Linguistics Conference reminded me to differentiate the lexical semantic representation of unaccusatives from that of passives. In my analysis, I assume with Grimshaw (1990) that the difference comes from where the (lexical) binding takes place; passivization involves binding a position (Agent) in the argument structure of the verb, thereby preventing the expression of that argument in the syntax. That argument, however, is still manifested in the form of *by* phrase, whereas the detransitivization of an unaccusative verb happens at the level of the Lexical Semantic Representation, and can never be present in the syntax. The contrast observed below can be attributed to this assumption.
a. The ship was sunk by Bill.
b. *The ship sank by Bill.

Otherwise, unaccusative causative sentences with NP2's like (19b) will be borne out. In other words, the NP2's with unaccusative causatives (I) in (19b) actually realize the Causer argument at the level of surface structure, which is originally introduced in the lexicon.

In contrast, [+Transitive] noncausative psych-verbs in Korean can be represented as ordinary transitives without causativity in the lexicon, as in (21):

(21) *pwulepta* 'be envious': [x BE *ENVIOUS* OF y]

A piece of evidence in favor of the analysis of Korean [-Transitive] noncausative psych-verbs as unaccusatives involves an issue of interpretation. According to Chierchia (1989) and Levin & Rappaport (1995), if unaccusative verbs such as *open, sink, break* are analyzed as containing a cause argument at some abstract level (e.g., LSR), it might be expected that some kind of special morpheme or modifier could be found that would reflect the presence of this Causer. Chierchia (1989) explicitly suggests that the Italian phrase *da se* 'by itself' (in the sense of 'without outside help') plays such a role. This is exemplified in (22), originally reported by Chierchia (1989) and cited by Levin & Rappaport (1995), and the English counterparts in (23) taken from Levin & Rappaport (1995):

(22) a. La porta si e aperta *da se*.
the door opened by itself
'The door opened by itself.'

b. La barca e affondata *da se*.
the boat sank by itself
'The boat sank by itself.'

(23) a. The plate broke by itself.
b. The door opened by itself.

Given their anaphoric nature, the Italian *da se* and English *by itself*, which modify a Causer, identify the Causer as Theme argument itself, *the door, the boat, the plate* here in (22) and (23). Ordinary intransitive verbs not participating systematically in the causative alternation (i.e., causative and inchoative) do not seem to have the same kind of interpretation when followed by this expression. For instance, the most natural interpretation of the sentence *Sara laughed by herself* is that Sara laughed unaccompanied (alone) rather than without outside help.

Extending Chierchia's (1989) original suggestion for the Italian *da se* to the effect that the Causer argument represented in the lexicon can be realized as an independent argument at the surface structure level, I propose that in Korean unaccusative causative sentences like (19b), the NP2's are real Causers, not just a reflection of the presence of the Causer in the LSR. This is because the NP2's are not brought to the surface structure level with any special morpheme or modifier identifying the NP2's (Causer) as Theme arguments themselves.

Overall, [-Transitive] noncausative psych-verbs in Korean are further classified into two subtypes, i.e., unaccusative causative (I) and (II), as illustrated in (19b, c), both of which start from the same lexical representation with causativity, whereas [+Transitive] noncausative psych-verbs are analyzed as ordinary transitives without causativity in the lexicon.

5. A lexical Approach to the T/SM Restriction

In section 2.2, I provided a pair of Korean psych-verb sentences, (10b and 11b), to show that Pesetsky's (1995) T/SM restriction effect is not uniformly observed in the Korean counterparts. This is because Korean [+Transitive] type does not show the effect at all from the very beginning, though Korean [-Transitive] type somehow does.

I propose that the contrastive behavior with respect to the T/SM restriction effect between [+Transitive] and [-Transitive] type psych-verbs in Korean results from different lexical representations, as shown in (20) and (21). I eventually claim that whether or not causativization in the syntax (c.f., Li 1990) increases the valence of a noncausative psych-verb in Korean should depend on the (non) existence of causativity in its lexical properties.

Suppose that a simple [-Transitive] noncausative psych-verb in Korean is represented as having causativity (or Causer) in the lexicon, and yet existential quantification over the Causer argument is not applied, as in the case of (24a).

(24) a. Unaccusative causative usage (I) of *sulputa* 'be sad'

LSR:	[x CAUSE	[y BECOME *SAD*]]
L-Binding:	|	|
Argument Structure:	<x>	<y>
D-S:	Causer	Exp

b. Unaccusative causative usage (II) of *sulputa* 'be sad'

LSR:	∃x [x CAUSE	[y BECOME *SAD*]]
L-Binding:	Ø	|
Argument Structure:	Ø	<y>
D-S:	Ø	Exp

Then, adding another Causer to the base sentence with causativity through causativization in the syntax is intolerable from a semantic point of view, resulting in vacuous causativization, which should be banned anyway. This situation might be roughly described in a more general way, I suggest, like (25) and (26):

(25) Vacuous syntactic operation hypothesis:
No vacuous syntactic operation, operation applied in the syntax but resulting in no change in the semantics, should be allowed.

(26) Vacuous causativization:
Syntactic causativization should not be applied to the base predicate having abstract causativity; if applied, vacuous causativization is brought about, which should be prohibited as per (26).

Given (25) and (26), we can now explain why sentences with [-Transitive] unaccusative causative (I) psych-verbs do somehow show the T/SM restriction effect. That is, the T/SM arguments (in Pesetsky's (1995) terms) in Korean [-Transitive] psych-verb sentences, such as (8a), can be redefined as Causer arguments from a lexicalist perspective, as shown in (27a). If one tries to causativize sentences like (27a), and adds another Causer argument to the same sentence, then the sentence will be ruled out in terms of (26), vacuous causativization. This is illustrated in (27b).

(27) a. *Sara*-ka *ku sosik*-i sulpessta. <<Exp> Causer>
Sara-Nom that news-Nom was sad
'Sara was sad about that news.'

b. **ku sosik*-i *Sara*-eykey *casin-uy eleywun checi*-lul
that news-Nom Sara-Dat herself-Gen difficult situation-Acc

sulpu-keyhayssta. *<Causer <<Exp> Causer>>
sad-made
'That news made Sara sad about her own difficult situation.'

c. *ku sosik*-i *Sara*-lul sulpu-keyhayssta. <Causer <Exp>>
that news-Nom Sara-Acc sad-made
'That news made Sara sad.'

The only way to avoid the vacuous causativization problem for [-Transitive] noncausative psych-verbs is to apply the operation, i.e., causativization, to the base sentences like (19c), which is derived from the lexical representation in (24b), with no Causer argument in their argument structure. In the derivation of (24b), there is only an Experiencer argument, which is associated with the subject at D-structure. If causativization is applied to (24b), the result will be like (27c). In contrast, one cannot expect the same intolerable situation to take place with Korean [+Transitive] psych-verbs, since they do not bear abstract causativity in their lexical representation, which I have already shown in (21). The whole derivation of Korean [+Transitive] noncausative psych-verbs will be like this:

(28) Ordinary transitive usage of *pwulepta* 'be envious of'

LSR:	[x BE *ENVIOUS* OF y]	
Argument Structure:	<x>	<y>
D-S:	Exp	T/SM

If a noncausative psych-verb is represented as having no abstract causativity in the lexicon, as in (28), causativization of the verb in the syntax does add an extra Causer argument, resulting in the change (or increase) of its valence as usual. This analysis eventually accounts for the reason [+Transitive] noncausative psych-verbs in Korean do not show the T/SM restriction effect, when they causativize in the syntax, as we have seen in (9b).

6. Conclusion

Concerning the T/SM restriction effect reported by Pesetsky (1995), according to which the [-Transitive] type somehow shows the same effect, while the [+Transitive] does not in Korean, I have explained this new T/SM restriction effect on Korean data from a lexical perspective, rather than syntactic perspective. I have done it without appealing to any complicated phrase structures or assuming any morphologically null pre(post)positions like the zero morpheme CAUS (Pesetsky 1995). Eventually, the analysis proposed here for the contrast between [+/-Transitive] noncausative psych-verbs in Korean supports the lexicalist idea that lexical representations and lexical rules can be viewed as a simple way to explain how the meaning of one existing basic expression is related to that of another.

References

Akatsuka McCawley, Noriko. 1976. Reflexivization: A Transformational Approach. *Syntax and Semantics* 5. 51-116.

Baker, Mark. 1988. *Incorporation: A Theory of Grammatical Function Changing*. Chicago: University of Chicago Press.

Belletti, Adriana. and Luigi Rizzi. 1988. Psych-verbs and Theta-theory. *Natural Language & Linguistic Theory* 6. 291-352.

Chierchia, Gennaro. 1989. A Semantics for Unaccusatives and Its Syntactic Consequences. Ms., Ithaca, NY: Cornell University.

Croft, William. 1993. Case Marking and the Semantics of Mental Verbs, in J. Pustejovsky, ed., *Semantics and the Lexicon*. 55-72. Dordrecht, Netherlands: Kluwer Academic Publishers.

Dabrowska, Ewa. 1994. Dative and Nominative Experiencers: Two Folk Theories of the Mind. *Linguistics* 32. 1029-1054.

Dowty, David. 1981. Quantification and the Lexicon: A Reply to Foder and Foder, in M. Moortgat, H. Hulst, and T. Hoekstra, eds., *The Scope of Lexical Rules*. Dordrecht: Foris Publications.

Grimshaw, Jane. 1991. *Argument Structure*. Cambridge, Mass.: MIT Press.

Grimshaw, Jane and Sten Vikner. 1993. Obligatory Adjuncts and the Structure of Events, in E. Reuland and W. Abraham, eds., *Knowledge and Language II*. 143-155. Dordrecht, Netherlands: Kluwer Academic Publishers.

Inoue, Kazuko. 1972. Agent and Source in Japanese. *Papers in Japanese Linguistics* 1:2. 195-217.

Kim, Sey-Jwung. 1989. Some Problems on Psych-adjective Sentences of Korean. *Language Research* 25:1. 151-165.

Kim, Young-Joo. 1990. *The syntax and Semantics of Korean Case: The Interaction Between Lexical and Syntactic Level of Representation.* Doctoral dissertation, Harvard University.

Lakoff, George. 1970. *Irregularity in Syntax*. NY: Holt, Rinehart & Winston.

Lee, Sang-Geun. 1998. On the Relevance of Mental Factors for Two-types of Noncausative Psych-verbs in Korean and their Reflection in Syntax and Semantics. Paper presented at the 1st International Conference on the Mental Lexicon. Edmonton, Canada.

Levin, Beth and Malka Rappaport. 1995. *Unaccusativity*. Cambridge, Mass.: MIT Press.

Li, Yafei. 1990, X^{0}-binding and Verb Incorporation. *Linguistic Inquiry* 21. 399-426.

Nam, Ji-Swun. 1993. For a Syntactic Classification of Adjectival Constructions in Korean 1: Psych-verb Constructions. *Language Research* 29:1 75-105.

Pesetsky, David. 1995. *Zero Syntax: Experiencers and Cascades.* Cambridge, Mass.: MIT Press.

Travis, Lisa. 1984. *Parameters and Effects of Word Order Variation.* Doctoral dissertation, MIT.

The Acquisition of Japanese Passives*

UTAKO MINAI
Tokyo Metropolitan University

1. The Maturation Hypothesis

There are a great number of studies on the acquisition of passive construction. Among them, a significant proposal was presented in Borer and Wexler (1987, 1992), which is called *The Maturation Hypothesis* (henceforth, referred to as MH). The observation of child passive in English leads them to the finding that children's performance shows less trouble on the adjectival passive as in (1a) than on the verbal passives as in (1b).

(1) a. The building was uninhabited.
    b. The building was destroyed.

The crucial distinction between (1a) and (1b) is that the derivation of (1b) involves the NP movement forming an A-chain, whereas that of (1a) entails

* I am deeply indebted to Hiroko Hagiwara, Heizo Nakajima, Ken-ichi Takami and Tetsuya Sano for their helpful suggestions and comments. I am also grateful to the members of Linguistic Circle of Tokyo Metropolitan University and of the Keio Psycholinguistic Workshop, and especially to the presenters and the attendants of 9th Japanese/Korean Linguistic Conference. Needless to say, all remaining errors and inadequacies are mine.

no such operation. Thus Borer and Wexler concluded that the children's problem lies in the formation of A-chain, and hypothesized that children at a certain age cannot form A-chain since their knowledge of A-chain has not yet matured. This explanation is consistent with the late emergence of full passive with *by*-phrase.

Given that the knowledge of A-chain is part of Universal Grammar (UG) which is assumed to be innate, and that MH presupposes the highly spontaneous development of the human linguistic program, it is necessary and fruitful to examine whether MH can account for the acquisition of other languages.

This paper is a preliminary report of the experimental study on the acquisition of Japanese passives. I will present a piece of supportive evidence for MH.

2. Previous Studies

2.1 Syntactic Analyses of Japanese Passives

Japanese passives have a variety of subcategories, and several categories have been widely assumed (Kuroda 1965, Howard and Niyekawa-Howard 1972, Inoue 1976, 1978, Hasegawa 1987 among others). I will adopt one of the recent analyses Kubo (1990) as my theoretical assumption.

Under Kubo's approach, the syntactic parallel can be seen between English and Japanese passive constructions. Let us consider (2).

(2) a. *accusative passive*

Kuma-san-ga$_i$ usagi-san-ni t_i tatak-are-ta.
bear-nom rabbit-*by* hit-pass-past
"The bear was hit by the rabbit."
$[_{IP}[_{NP}$ Kuma-san-ga$]_i[_{I'}[_{VP}[_{V'}[_{PP}$ usagi-san-ni $][_{V'}[_{NP}\ t_i]\ [_{V}[_{V}$ tatak-$][_{V}$ are$]]]]][_{I}$ ta$]]]$.

b. *possessive passive*

Kuma-san-ga$_i$ usagi-san-ni t_i boshi-o tor-are-ta.
bear-nom rabbit-*by* cap-acc take off-pass-past
"The bear had his cap taken off by the rabbit."
$[_{IP}[_{NP}$ Kuma-san-ga$]_i[_{I'}[_{VP}[_{V'}[_{PP}$ usagi-san-ni$][_{V'}[_{NP}[_{NP}t_i]$
$[_{N'}[_{N}$ boshi-o$]]][_{V}[_{V}$ tor-$][_{V}$are-$]]]]][_{I}$ ta$]]]$.

c. *gapless (indirect) intransitive passive*
Kuma-san-ga usagi-san-ni nak-are-ta.
bear-nom rabbit-*by* cry-pass-past
"The bear was affected by the rabbit's crying."
$[_{IP}[_{NP}$ Kuma-san-ga$][_{I'}[_{VP}[_{V'}[_{VP}[_{PP}$ usagi-san-ni$][_{V'}[_{V}$ nak-$]]]$
$[_{V}$ are$]]][_{I}$ ta$]]]$.

d. *gapless (indirect) transitive passive*
Kuma-san-ga usagi-san-ni denki-o kes-are-ta.
bear-nom rabbit-*by* light-acc turn off-pass-past
"The bear had the light turned off by the rabbit."
$[_{IP}[_{NP}$ Kuma-san-ga$][_{I'}[_{VP}[_{V'}[_{VP}[_{PP}$ usagi-san-ni$][_{V'}[_{NP}$ denki-o$]$
$[_{V}$ kes-$]]][_{V}$ are$]]][_{I}$ ta$]]]$.

Kubo's analysis is based on the involvement of A-chain in the derivation, as have been seen in English passives in (1). In the accusative passive (2a), the logical object is moved to the subject position, forming A-chain; in the possessive passive (2b), the possessor NP in the object NP raises into the subject position, which also forms A-chain. On the other hand, in the gapless intransitive passive (2c) and the gapless transitive passive (2d), there is no NP movement and A-chain formation in the derivation.

2.2 Studies on Child Passives in Japanese

There are some studies performed on the Japanese children's passives, which revealed the tendency supporting MH. Sugisaki (1997) and Minai (1997, 1998) tested the children's comprehension of the accusative passives as in (2a) and the gapless intransitive passives as in (2c), and showed the data that is consistent with the prediction under MH. However, those studies did not test all types of passives in Japanese, and, moreover, tested a limited number of children. It would be necessary to examine larger number of children, and to test wider range of Japanese passives as well, in order to examine the validity of MH.

On the other hand, Harada and Furuta (1998) is a significant study in the sense that they tested a larger number of children, and covered all of the four types of Japanese passives in (2). Their result, contrary to those of the previous ones and the prediction under MH, showed that children performed better on passives with A-chain (accusative and possessive passives) than on those without A-chain (gapless transitive and gapless intransitive passives).

They concluded that children seem to acquire the passives without A-chain earlier than those with A-chain.

However, from the standpoint of experimental arrangement, their study involves some problem. First, all of the passive subjects in their stimulus sentences are marked with topic marker *–wa*, not the unmarked nominative marker-*ga*, as shown in (3).

(3) a. Kuma-san-wa$_i$ usagi-san-ni t_i tatak-are-ta.
 b. Kuma-san-wa$_i$ usagi-san-ni t_i boshi-o tor-are-ta.
 c. Anpanman-wa usagi-san-ni Shokupanman-o homer-are-ta.
 d. Kuma-san-wa usagi-san-ni nak-are-ta.

Harada (1998, personal communication) explained that marking the subjects with *–wa* instead of *–ga* makes the passive sentences sound natural. However, subjects with *–wa* would make the subject NP pragmatically emphasized, and children's response, in turn, would be pragmatically biased.

Secondly, there is a problem in their control of the experimental situation. They performed a couple of experiments, but all of the four types of passives were not presented in each experimental session. For example, in one session, they tested only accusative, gapless transitive and gapless intransitive passives; however, the possessive passives were not presented in this session. In another session, on the other hand, accusative, possessive and gapless intransitive passives were served, but they tested no gapless transitive passives. Moreover, they used different tasks in each experiment. Thus, children's comprehension of each of the four types of passives was not elicited under a consistently controlled situation.

Given that Harada and Furuta's data seem to be elicited under an uncontrolled situation, it is necessary to reexamine Japanese passives again in a properly controlled circumstance. In the next section, I will survey my experimental study in which children's comprehension of a variety of Japanese passives was retested.

3. Experimental Study

3.1 Experimental Design

First, let us view the method and procedure of my experiment. Thirty-five Japanese children aged from 3 to 6 were tested in the experiment. Children were divided into 4 groups with respect to their age: 3-year-old group, 4-year-old group, 5-year-old group and 6-year-old group. There involved 8 children in 3-year-old, 4-year-old and 5-year-old groups each, and 11 children in 6-year-old group. They are pupils of three public nursery schools and two private kindergartens in Yamanashi prefecture in Japan. The experiment was performed in a quiet room in these nursery schools and kindergartens. Children were tested individually.

The task was two-choice picture selection. Children were presented a pair of pictures when each stimulus sentence was narrated. In one picture of each pair, the situation referred to by the sentences is depicted correctly, whereas in the other the subject (the NP with *–ga*) and the object (the NP with *–ni*) are reversed. Children were asked to choose the one picture in which the correct situation was described. The experimenter checked whether children correctly comprehended the meaning of each sentence. The entire session lasted from 15 to 20 minutes.

In order to control the experimental situation properly, I paid much attention especially to the following points. First, the experimenter checked whether children knew the animals appeared in the test sentences before we proceed the main session. Thus children were presented the pictures in which the animals referred to in the sentence were depicted at the first stage of the session. The experimenter asked children to tell the names of the animals, and checked whether they knew these animals. Second, in case children seemed to be tired or bored, we took a pause and waited till they got into a better condition.

The test materials used in the experiment are the following four types of the passive sentences: (i) accusative passives as in (2a): (ii) possessive passives as in (2b): (iii) gapless intransitive passives as in (2c): (iv) gapless transitive passives as in (2d). The nouns used in each sentence refer to animals that are popular among young children such as *kuma* 'bear' and *usagi* 'rabbit'. The verbs represent actions that are directly connected with children's everyday life such as *keru* 'kick' and *naku* 'cry'.

Six stimulus sentences of each type are used in the present study. In addition, the active counterparts of all of the accusative passives and possessive passives are served as control. Thus, children were presented 36 sentences in total, i.e., 24 passive sentences and 12 active control sentences.

In order to exclude pragmatic bias, all test sentences were presented to the children with the short contexts preceding the test sentences. The example is shown in (4). This is because it makes the passive sentence sound natural.

(4) *Kuma-san to usagi-san ga kenka o shimashita. Sono kuma-sanga usagi-san ni atakaremashita.*
"A bear and a rabbit were fighting. *The bear was hit by the rabbit.*"

Under MH, I hypothesized that passives with A-chain (accusative and possessive passives) are more problematic for children than those without A-chain (gapless intransitive and gapless transitive passives).

3.2 Results and Analysis

The results of the experiment are shown as follows. Table 1 and Figure 1illustrate the percentage of the correct response of all children.

Table 1: The percentage of correct responses

	Age 3	Age 4	Age 5	Age 6
active accusative	60.42	75.00	89.58	98.48
active possessive	68.75	72.72	64.58	93.94
accusative passive	54.17	60.42	60.42	69.70
possessive passive	37.50	45.83	56.25	59.09
gapless passive (Vi)	62.50	70.83	70.83	81.82
gapless passive (Vt)	62.50	72.92	79.17	68.18

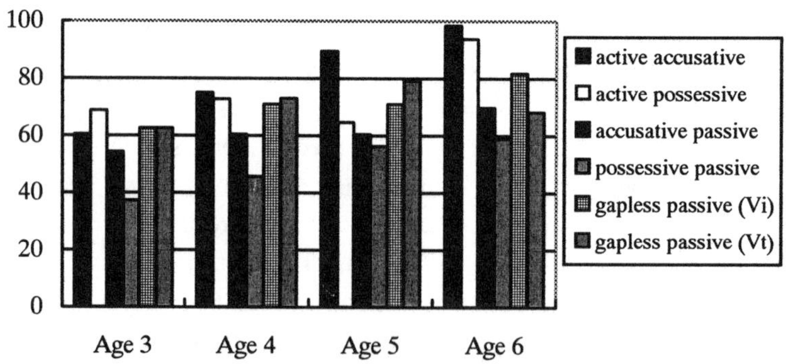

Figure 1: The percentage of correct responses

The data was analyzed according to the number of NPs involved in the sentences. Table 2 and Figure 2 show children's comprehension of the test sentences with two NPs, i.e., accusative and gapless intransitive passives. Their comprehension of the sentences with three NPs, namely, possessive and gapless transitive passives, is shown in Table 3 and Figure 3.

Table 2: Children's comprehension of sentences with two NPs: The percentage of correct response

	Age 3	Age 4	Age 5	Age 6
accusative passive	54.17	60.42	60.42	69.70
gapless passive (Vi)	62.50	70.83	70.83	81.82

Table 3: Children's comprehension of the sentences with three NPs: The percentage of correct responses

	Age 3	Age 4	Age 5	Age 6
possessive passive	37.50	45.83	56.25	59.09
gapless passive (Vt)	62.50	72.92	79.17	68.18

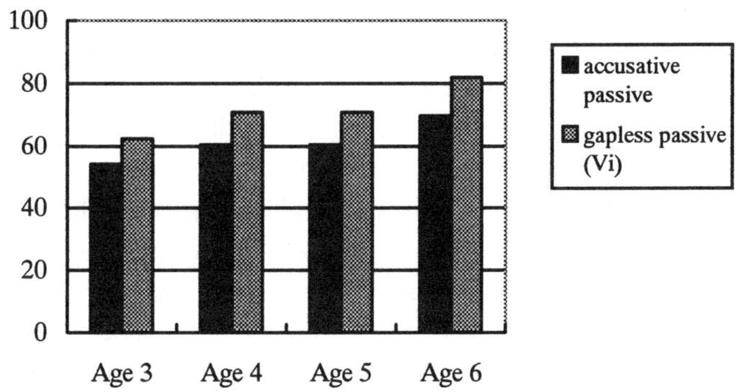

Figure 2: Children's comprehension of sentences with two NPs: The percentage of correct responses

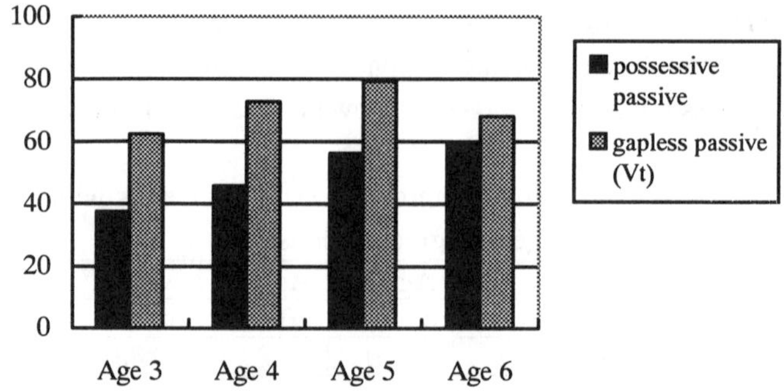

Figure 3: Children's comprehension of sentences with three NPs: The percentage of correct responses

In each group, children performed worse on passives with A-chain than on those without A-chain. Thus, my prediction was borne out, and the result was consistent with MH.

Moreover, I divided the children into the following three groups according to the rate of their correct responses: (A) those who performed better on passives without A-chain than on those with A-chain: (B) those who constantly showed good comprehension on all of the four types of passives: (C) those who performed better on passives with A-chain than on those without A-chain. Suppose that MH is on the right track. In theory, almost all of the children would fall into group (A), and the only children who have already acquired A-chain would be the members of the group (B). There would be no children who belong to the group (C). The whole scheme is pictured in (5).

(5) The grouping based on correct responses

	Age 3	Age 4	Age 5	Age 6	Total
(A)	6/8	6/8	7/8	6/11	25
(B)	1/8	1/8	0/8	4/11	6
(C)	1/8	1/8	1/8	1/8	4

In my experiment, 25 children (approximately 70 percent) fell into group (A), and 6 children into group (B). Only 4 children out of 35 turned out to be the members of the group (C). Roughly speaking, approximately 90 percent of the children fell into group (A) and (B). This suggests that almost all children showed the performance consistent with the prediction under MH.

In addition, another interesting fact on the acquisition of Japanese passives was revealed. Now, consider the four types of Japanese passives used in my experiment. They can be categorized into two types with respect to the number of argument NPs as well as the involvement of A-chain. The accusative passives and gapless intransitive passives have two argument NPs, while the possessive passive and gapless transitive passives have three argument NPs. Among the sentences with A-chain, comprehension on the accusative passive with two NPs was much better than that on the possessive passives with three NPs, especially in young children. This finding is shown in Table 4 and Figure 4. On the other hand, as illustrated Table 5 and Figure 5, among the two gapless passives, performance on gapless transitive passives with three NPs is roughly better than that on gapless intransitive passive with two NPs. This suggests that difference of the number of the NPs is not irrelevant.

Table 4: Children's comprehension of the passives with A-chain: The percentage of correct responses

	Age 3	Age 4	Age 5	Age 6
accusative passive	54.17	60.42	60.42	69.70
possessive passive	37.50	45.83	56.25	59.09

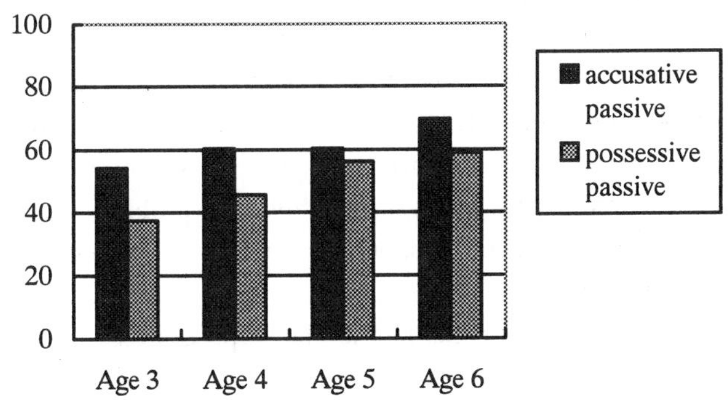

Figure 4: Children's comprehension of the passives with A-chain: The percentage of correct responses

Table 5:Children's comprehension of the passives without A-chain: The percentage of correct response

	Age 3	Age 4	Age 5	Age 6
Gapless passive (Vi)	62.50	70.83	70.83	81.82
Gapless passive (Vt)	62.50	72.92	79.17	68.18

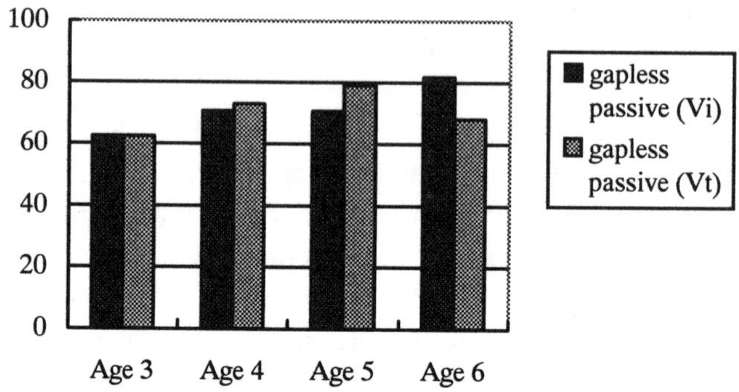

Figure 5: Children's comprehensiton of the passives without A-chain: The percentage of correct responses

Given this fact, there would be another problematic element for children as well as the involvement of A-chain. As described above, in the accusative passives, the logical object is moved to the subject position, whereas in the possessive passives, the possessor NP in the object NP is raised. Considering from the standpoint of the Case of the moved NP, we can reach the following conclusion. In the accusative passives, the Case of the moved NP switches from accusative to nominative. On the other hand, in the possessive passives the Case of the moved NP switches from genitive to nominative. Hence, it could be interpreted that the locus of the children's problem lies not only in the presence or absence of A-chain, but also in the type of Case-switch of the moved NP in Japanese.

One possible account for this fact is that in possessive passives, subject and object are not co-argument of the main verb. The passive subject, that is, the possessor of the object, is an argument in the object NP, but not the one of the main verb. Through the passivization it moves to the matrix subject position and becomes the sentence argument. This change would be a cause of the difficulty in the children's comprehension of these sentences.

4. Remaining Problem and Suggestions for Future Research

In the data reported in the present study, we found that there is the same tendency in passive comprehension of Japanese children as that of English acquiring children. That is, in both languages the passives with A-chain are more troublesome for the children at a certain age. This implies that in both English and Japanese a certain problem of children lies in passive constructions with A-chain.

Note that the present study revealed a significant finding, i.e., the fact that children showed much worse comprehension on the possessive passives than on the accusative passives. For this fact, such account is possible that the Case-switch of the moved NP would affect the children's comprehension. In the future research of the acquisition study of Japanese passives, this fact should be focused on, and the mechanism of the Case-switch should be examined and discussed.

Recent studies on children's A-chain knowledge would extend the possibility of the future acquisition study of Japanese passives as well. Babyonyshev et al (1994, 1998) reported the new supportive evidence for MH from the acquisition data on Russian unaccusatives. Japanese has the unaccusatives construction as well, which can be analyzed to involve A-chain in the derivation (Kageyama 1993, 1996). It would be fruitful to examine Japanese children's comprehension on the unaccusative construction.

On the other hand, the counterevidence was presented in some languages other than English (Demuth 1989, among others). Even in English, Fox et al. (1995) and Fox and Grodzinsky (1998) have shown that the presence or absence of A-chain did not affect children's comprehension of passives. They concluded that the children's problem lies in the involvement of *by* – phrase. Whether it is also the case in Japanese or not is an interesting issue for the future research.

References

Babyonyshev, Maria, Ronald Fein, Jennifer Ganger and Sergey Avrutin. 1994. Maturation of A-chains: Preliminary New Evidence from the Acquisition of Russian Unaccusatives. *MIT Working Papers in Linguistics* 23. 1-20.

Banyonyshev, Maria, Ronald Fein, Jennifer Ganger, David Pesetzky and KennethWexler. 1998. The Maturation of Grammatical Principles: Evidence from Russian Unaccusatives. Unpublished manuscript. MIT.

Borer, Hagit and Kenneth Wexler. 1987. The Maturation of Syntax, in T. Roeper and E. Williams, eds., *Parameter Setting*, 123-172. Dordrecht: D. Reidel.

__________. 1992. Bi-Unique Relations and The Maturation of Grammatical Principles. *Natural Language and Linguistic Theory* 10. 147-189.

Demuth, Katherine. 1989. Maturation and Acquisition of Sesotho Passive. *Language* 65. 56-81.

Fox, Danny, Yosef Grodzinsky and Stephen Crain. 1995. An Experimental Study of Children's Passives. *MIT Working Papers in Linguistics* 26. 249-264.

Fox, Danny and Yosef Grodzinsky. 1998. Children's Passive: A View from the *By*-Phrase. *Linguistic Inquiry* 29. 311-332.

Harada, Kazuko I. and Tomoko Furuta. 1998. On the Acquisition of Japanese Passives: Continuity vs. Maturation. *COE Annual Report*. 689-708. Kanda University of International Studies.

Hasegawa, Nobuko. 1988. Passives, Verb Raising, and the Affectedness Condition. *Proceedings of the West Coast Conference on Formal Linguistics* 7. 99-113.

Howard, Irwin and Agnes Niyekawa-Howard. 1976. Passivization, in M. Shibatani ed., *Syntax and Semantics 5: Japanese Generative Grammar*. 201-237. New York: Academic Press.

Inoue, Kazuko. 1976. *Henkeibumpo to Nihongo. [Transformational Grammar and Japanese.]* Tokyo: Taishukan.

__________. 1978. *Nihongo no Bumpo Kisoku. [The Grammatical Rules of Japanese.]* Tokyo: Taishukan.

Kageyama, Taro. 1993. *Bumpo to Gokeisei* [*Grammar and Word Formation*]. Tokyo: Hitsuji Shobou.

__________. 1996. *Doshi Imiron* [*Semantics on Verbs*]. Tokyo : Kuroshio Shuppan.

Kubo, Miori. 1990. Japanese Passives. Unpublished manuscript, MIT.

Kuroda, Shige-Yuki. 1965. *Generative Grammatical Studies in the Japanese Language*. Doctoral Dissertation, MIT.

Minai, Utako. 1997. *A Comparative Study on the Acquisition of English and Japanese Passives: A Case Study on Children's Knowledge of A-Chain*. B.A Thesis, Tokyo Metropolitan University.

__________. 1998. On Children's Knowledge of A-chain in Japanese --- A Preliminary Study. *Metropolitan Linguistics* 17. 52-74. Tokyo Metropolitan University.

Sugisaki, Koji. 1997. Japanese Passives in Acquisition. Unpublished manuscript, University of Connecticut.

Ni/ni yotte Variation in Japanese Direct Passives: A Syntactic, Pragmatic, and Historical Account

KIMI MIYAGI
The National Language Research Institute

1. Introduction

Japanese direct passives are formed by attaching the passive morpheme *rare* to a verb stem.[1] A demoted subject is optionally expressed in an adjunct phrase followed by either of the postpositions *ni* or *niyotte*. Examples follow.

(1) a. Yootienzi ga misiranu otoko ni/niyotte yuukais -are ta.
kindergartner Nom unknown man by kidnap Pass Pst
'A kindergartner was kidnapped by a stranger.'

b. Mise no kinko ga doroboo ni/niyotte nusum -are ta.
store Gen safe Nom thief by steal Pass Pst
'The safe in the store was stolen by the thief.'

Ni and *niyotte* are often interchangeable, as shown in sentences (1a) and (1b). In some sentences, however, one postposition is preferred or obligatorily chosen over the other, as illustrated in (2).

[1] Phonologically, *rare* becomes *are* when it is attached to a verb stem that ends in a consonant.

(2) a. Yuube otooto ga kuruma ni/*?niyotte hane -rare ta.
last night younger brother Nom car by hit Pass Pst
'Last night my younger brother was hit by a car.'

b. Hamlet wa 1600 nen ni Shakespeare niyotte/*?ni kak -are ta.
Top year in by write Pass Pst
'Hamlet was written by Shakespeare in 1600.'

The syntactic properties of Japanese passives, including indirect or adversative passives, have been extensively studied by Japanese linguists; however, the variation between *ni* and *niyotte* observed above has not been discussed in much detail in the literature. Recently, though, Hoshi (1991, 1994), following Kuroda (1965, 1979), has provided an account of the variation, attributing it to syntactic differences between *ni* and *niyotte* passives.

Providing an account of the variation between these passives is important because *ni* and *niyotte* are not always interchangeable; moreover, they do not convey exactly the same meaning, even when the alternation is possible. In this paper, I try to account for these phenomena in light of syntactic, semantic, pragmatic, and historical factors. In Section 2.1, I first examine Hoshi's syntactic distinction between *ni* and *niyotte* passives. In Section 2.2, I consider cases where *niyotte* is obligatorily used. Then, in Section 3, by employing the pragmatic notion of empathy, I explain the difference between these passives in terms of subjectivity vs. objectivity. Finally, I present some historical facts regarding the use of *niyotte* in passives and show how these facts are relevant to *ni* and *niyotte* variation.

2. Syntax of *Ni* and *Niyotte* Passives

2.1 Hoshi's (1994) Analysis

Hoshi notes some sentences in which *ni* and *niyotte* cannot alternate and argues that *ni* passives have syntactic structures that are different from those of *niyotte* passives. Consider the *ni* and *niyotte* passives in (3), which are quoted from Hoshi, 1994:150 (7b) and (7c) respectively.[2]

(3) Tyuui ga John ***ni**/ ni yotte haraw -are ta.
heed Nom by/by owing pay Pass Pst
*'Heed$_i$ was affected by John's paying it$_i$' (*ni* passive)
'Heed was paid by John.' (*niyotte* passive)

---

[2] The English translations of (3) are directly quoted from Hoshi.

The sentences in (3) include the verbal idiom, *tyuui o harau* 'pay attention'. Hoshi explains the difference in grammaticality exhibited by the *ni* and *niyotte* passives in (3) in the following way: a *ni* passive requires the subject to be an affectee that bears an Experiencer θ-role. The *ni* passive is ruled out due to a violation of this selectional restriction, because the subject *tyuui* cannot be an affectee.

According to Hoshi, the *ni* passive in (4), provided below, has the structure illustrated in (5a), whereas the *niyotte* passive counterpart has the structure in (5b).

(4) John ga Mary ni/niyotte nagur -are ta.
Nom by hit Pass Pst
'John was punched by Mary.'

(5) a. [VP$_1$ John$_i$ ga [V' [VP$_2$ PRO$_i$ [V' Mary ni [t$_i$ nagur t$_j$]]] areta$_j$]]

NP movement

θ-role assignment

b. [IP John$_i$ ga [VP (t$_i$) (Mary niyotte) t$_i$ nagur-are ta.]]

NP movement

By incorporating Larson's VP shell analysis, Hoshi accounts for the syntactic differences between (5a) and (5b) in the following way. In both passives, *rare* suppresses the external θ-role and absorbs the Case of the verb, *nagur.*[3] However, *rare* in (5a) optionally assigns an external θ-role; consequently, the VP shell (i.e., VP$_1$) is licensed, headed by *nagur-areta.* In the VP shell, the subject *John* is generated, and it is assigned an external θ-role by *rareta*[4]; moreover, it controls the PRO in VP$_2$. In (5a), the PRO moves to the Spec of VP$_2$ to satisfy Binding Conditions A and B. Contrastively, in (5b) the logical object of *naguru, John,* moves to the non-θ-subject position to receive Nominative Case. In this way, the subject *John* in (5a) is argued to be a base-generated θ-subject, while the subject *John* in (5b) is a derived non-θ-subject.

[3] Within the Minimalist Program (Chomsky 1995), passives are treated differently since all the movements take place for feature checking. Because Hoshi's account cannot be translated into the terms of the Minimalist Program, I discuss these phenomena within GB theory.

[4] Hoshi argues that *rare* excorporates from *nagur* to move to I at LF.

A major drawback of Hoshi's analysis is that it does not include the *ni* passives that have inanimate subjects such as (1b), despite the fact that they are grammatical. An additional example is provided in (6).

(6) Yakuintati no utiwabanasi ga hisyo ni nusumigikis-are ta.
officials Gen private talk Nom secretary by eavesdrop Pass Pst
'The officials' private chat was eavesdropped on by the secretary.'

Moreover, contrary to Hoshi's proposal, the θ- vs. non-θ-subject dichotomy does not seem to play a crucial role in sentence (7) below. Sentence (7), like (3), contains a verbal idiom, *hanasi no kosi o or(u)* 'spoil a story'.

(7) Mata hanasi no kosi ga Taroo ni/niyotte or -are ta.
again story Gen hip Nom by break Pass Pst
'Again a story (*lit.* a hip of the story) was spoiled by Taro.'

Just like the subjects in (3), the subject *hanasi no kosi* in (7) cannot be an affectee. The *ni* passive in (7) should therefore be ruled out in Hoshi's analysis. Contrary to his prediction, the *ni* and *niyotte* passives in (7) do not exhibit any grammatical contrast. Furthermore, regarding the PRO in the *ni* passive illustrated in (5a), Hoshi provides no syntactic evidence either for the existence of the PRO as a complement of the verb or for the NP movement of the PRO.[5]

The facts provided above demonstrate that Hoshi's assumption that *rare* in *ni* passives assigns an Experiencer θ-role to the base-generated subject is false. Consequently, the θ- vs. non-θ-subject distinction between *ni* and *niyotte* passives does not hold. There is, then, no reason to believe that *ni* and *niyotte* passives have different structures.[6] I assume that, regardless of whether a demoted subject is marked with *ni* or *niyotte*, direct passives in Japanese do not differ syntactically. In both passives, a subject is a logical object of the verb, which bears the θ-role the verb assigns. Both passives thus have a structure like that in (5b). Therefore, we can conclude that the *ni/niyotte* variation observed in direct passives is not due to different syntactic structures.

[5] Miyagi (1998) further discusses the problems of PRO and NP movement in Hoshi's analysis.

[6] Nakayama and Cipollone (1996) also reject the *ni/niyotte* dichotomy proposed by Hoshi, claiming that *niyotte* is not a variant of *ni*. They argue that *ni* is an equivalent of English passive *by* while *niyotte* is not, since it appears in both active and passive sentences with the meanings of "cause, reason, and source." Moreover, they include indirect passives in their discussion and show a distinction between passives with and without *ni*. See Nakayama and Cipollone (1996) for further discussion.

2.2 *Ni/niyotte* Variation and another Dative *Ni*-marked Clausemate

We must now look elsewhere for an account of the ungrammaticality of the *ni* passive in (3). Why is only the *niyotte* passive grammatical in (3)? The contrast seems to arise as a consequence of whether or not the verbs take a Dative *ni*-marked NP.[7]

Consider again the grammatical contrast between the *ni* and *niyotte* passives in (3), repeated as (8) below.

(8) Tyuui ga John niyotte/*ni haraw -are ta.
attention Nom by pay Pass Pst
'Attention was paid by John.'

Now compare (8) with sentence (7), which was previously provided to show that *ni* passives are possible even with non-θ-subjects. A noticeable difference between the verb *hara(u)* in (8) and *or(u)* in (7) is that *hara(u)* subcategorizes for a Goal NP, while the verb in (7) does not. A Goal NP is marked with Dative *ni* in Japanese. The *ni* passive in (8) is grammatical with an interpretation of the *ni*-marked *John* as a Goal argument, as in (9).

(9) Tyuui ga John ni haraw -are ta.
attention Nom Dat pay Pass Pst
'Attention was paid to John.'

This suggests that, even when the Goal NP is not present in the sentence, if the verb potentially takes a Goal NP, then *niyotte* is obligatorily chosen in the passive sentence, as illustrated in (10).

(10) Tyuui ga Mary niyotte/*ni (John ni) haraw -are ta.
attention Nom by Dat pay Pass Pst
'Attention was paid (to John) by Mary.'

The choice of *niyotte* is therefore forced in order to avoid possible confusion between the two *ni*-marked NPs, because the two *ni*'s are phonologically indistinguishable. If, on the other hand, the verb does not

---

[7] It should be noted that my discussion here concerns Dative *ni*-marked NPs only. I do not include postposition *ni*-marked NPs such as:

e.g. Mary ga John ni **paatii ni** manek -are ta.
Nom by party to invite Pass Pst
'Mary was invited by John to his party.'

In this sentence, the second *ni* in boldface is a postposition that could alternate with another postposition, *e* 'to'.

take a Goal NP, a demoted subject can be marked with either *ni* or *niyotte*. The verb *or(u)* 'snap, bend' in (7) exemplifies such cases.

All the passives with ditransitive verbs that take a Dative *ni*-marked Goal NP thus are subject to this restriction, as in (11).

(11) Sotugyoosyoosyo ga sensei niyotte/***ni** Mary **ni** tewatas -are ta.
diploma Nom teacher by Dat hand Pass Pst
'A diploma was handed to Mary by the teacher.'

When a sentence with a ditransitive verb such as *tewatas(u)* undergoes passivization, there are two possible NPs to become the subject—the direct object and the indirect object. If an Accusative *o*-marked direct object becomes the subject and a Dative-marked NP stays within the VP, a *ni* passive may result in a sentence containing two *ni*-marked NPs, as in (11). The two *ni*-marked NPs are both interpreted as Goal NPs, so that the interpretation crashes. Thus, in this case, *niyotte* is obligatorily used to mark a demoted subject. In contrast, when the Goal NP becomes the subject of a passivized sentence, either *ni* or *niyotte* can appear to mark the demoted subject.[8]

In fact, Dative *ni*-marked NPs which prohibit the occurrence of another *ni*-marked NP in the same clause are not limited to Goal NPs. Dative *ni*-marked Locative NPs also behave exactly in the same way as Dative-marked Goal NPs in this respect, as illustrated in (12).[9]

(12) Siroi penki ga John niyotte/***ni** yogoreta kabe **ni** nur -are ta.
white paint Nom by stained wall Dat paint Pass Pst
'White paint was painted on the stained wall by John.'

Therefore, it is the Dative *ni*-marked NP that prevents another clause mate NP—namely, a demoted subject—from being marked with *ni* in the passive, whatever thematic role the NP bears.

As exhibited above, when a passive sentence contains a Dative *ni*-marked argument, *niyotte* is obligatorily chosen to mark a demoted subject to disambiguate meaning. The obligatory use of *niyotte* in sentences (10),

---

[8] It should be noted that in a biclausal sentence, a *ni*-marked demoted subject of a matrix verb and a *ni*-marked argument of an embedded verb can co-occur in the same sentence.
e.g. John ga Mary ni Bill ni wabizyoo o kak -ase -rare ta.
Nom by Dat apology letter Acc write Caus Pass Pst
'John was made to write an apology letter to Bill by Mary.'
I do not discuss this any further in this paper.

[9] William O'Grady (p.c.) pointed out to me the possibility of the application of the same restriction to Dative *ni*-marked Locative NPs.

(11), and (12) must thus be motivated by sentence processing factors, rather than for syntactic reasons.

3. Semantic Explanation of *Ni/niyotte* Variation

3.1 Objectivity and *Niyotte* Passives

In Section 2, I argued that *ni* and *niyotte* variation does not arise syntactically. What then determines the preference for *ni* vs. *niyotte* in the sentences in (2)? It is now necessary to seek semantic and pragmatic explanations for the *ni/niyotte* variation. In this subsection, I consider the cases where *niyotte* is preferable. The *niyotte* passive in (2b) is repeated as (13) below.

(13) Hamlet wa 1600 nen ni Shakespeare niyotte/*?ni kak -are ta.
Top year in by write Pass Pst
'Hamlet was written by Shakespeare in 1600.'

Kuno (1983) accounts for the difference between passives with *ni* and those with *niyotte* by claiming that, while the latter represent a formal written style providing objective descriptions, the former do not. The passive sentences with *niyotte*, in fact, do sound formal and are often used to report information objectively. Thus, we find instances of *niyotte* passives in simple description of historical facts, as in (13), and in newspapers, news magazines, and textbooks, as in (14). I found (14) in the weekly news magazine, Syuukan Asahi; 6/12/1998.

(14) Meiji no soogoozassi o daihyoosi ta no wa
Gen all-round magazine Acc represent Pst one Top
Tokutomi Sohoo niyotte sookans-are ta "Kokumin no tomo".
by found Pass Pst citizen Gen friend
'What represented all-round magazines in the Meiji Era was *Kokumin no Tomo* that was founded by Sohoo Tokutomi.'

As shown here, objectivity is the reason that *niyotte* is preferable in sentences (13) and (14).

3.2 Subjectivity and *Ni* Passives

What about the case of (19a) where *ni* is preferable to *niyotte*? Consider again sentence (2a), repeated as (15).

(15) Yuube otooto ga kuruma ni/*?niyotte hane-rare ta.
Last night younger brother Nom car by hit Pass Pst
'Last night my younger brother was hit by a car.'

The reason why *ni* is chosen and sounds more appropriate than *niyotte* in sentence (15) is that the sentence involves subjectivity. What is described in (15) is a tragic and personal matter, so the event is expressed subjectively by the speaker. The speaker sympathizes with the subject and take his/her viewpoint to express the situation. In this way, the subject is entailed as an affectee by the speaker. The objective style with *niyotte* is thus not appropriate in these contexts.

The viewpoint under discussion here represents the speaker's attitude toward the participants in describing an event. Kuno (1987) argues that how the speaker views the situation is determined by the notion of *Empathy*. Kuno (1987:206 (2.1)) defines *Empathy* as follows.

(16) Empathy: Empathy is the speaker's identification, which may vary in degree, with a person/thing that participates in the event or state that he describes in a sentence.

According to Kuno, the degree of empathy can vary, ranging from 0 to 1. Identification to degree 1 means that the speaker totally identifies him/herself with the person he or she describes, whereas Identification to degree 0 is observed when the speaker describes the event objectively, with a total lack of identification with anybody described in the sentence. The notion of *Empathy* proposed by Kuno seems to be a very effective tool for characterizing the speaker's subjectivity in describing events in Japanese passives.

In sentence (15), the subject is a human, so it is naturally considered to be an affectee whose viewpoint the speaker is most likely to take. Interestingly, however, even when *ni* passives contain nonhuman or inanimate subjects, the sentences often convey affective meanings, as illustrated in (17).

(17) Atarasii kaapetto ga kodomotati ni yogos -are ta.
new carpet Nom children by spoil Pass Pst
'The new carpet was spoiled by the children.'

Although sentence (17) does not have overt affectees, these *ni* passives imply that there is an affectee or an experiencer of the event.

Kuno argues that in a passive sentence, a speaker empathizes more easily with the surface subject than with the demoted subject. This is true when a *ni* sentence includes an animate subject, as in (15). However, when the subject is inanimate, as in (17), the speaker might empathize with a syntactically absent but contextually understood experiencer (i.e., the owner of the carpet in (17)) and may express the situation from the experiencer's point of view.

The range of the speaker's identification with the experiencer varies from total objectivity to total subjectivity. The more objective the speaker is, the more *niyotte* is chosen; the more subjective he/she is, the more *ni* is used. The polarity between objectivity and subjectivity is realized in a sentence by the choice of *ni* or *niyotte* to indicate where the speaker places his/her viewpoint in describing the event.[10]

3.3 *Ni* and *Niyotte* Passives and Co-occurring Verbs

With respect to the environments in which a speaker's viewpoint is realized in *ni* passives, two factors seem to be involved. One is that, unlike *niyotte*, *ni* registers the speaker's empathy. The other is that some verbs are semantically empathy-loaded so that they naturally occur in *ni* passives. Verbs such as *nagur(u)* 'punch', *kenas(u)* 'criticize', and *yogos(u)* 'spoil' contain some elements of negative meaning and trigger the speaker's empathy; thus, they are empathy-loaded verbs. Verbs that have positive meanings such as *homer(u)* 'praise' and *kawaigar(u)* ' love' can also be considered to be empathy-loaded verbs.

Psych verbs such as *sitasimu* 'be familiar with' as in (18) below, are also often found in *ni* passives.[11]

(18) Andersen no doowa wa sekaizyuu no
Andersen Gen juvenile story Top whole world Gen
kodomotati ni sitasim -are te i ru.
children by enjoy Pass Ger Prog Pres
'Andersen's children's stories are enjoyed by children all over the world.'

Actually, the speaker of sentence (18) does not express his/her subjective view; yet, *ni* is preferred to *niyotte* in this sentence. This may be due to the fact that the psych verbs themselves express mental states—i.e., the emotions and subjective feelings of the participants in the events.

---

[10] Total objectivity may be realized in plain descriptions of historical facts. On the other hand, the situation where total subjectivity is expressed can be found in *ni* passives in which '*I*' is the subject and the speaker simultaneously.

[11] It should be noted that some psych verbs of a causative type such as *kanasimasu* 'make someone sad' do not form passives.

Contrastively, some verbs are neutral and do not seem to trigger a speaker's subjective viewpoint. Some Sino-Japanese + *suru* 'do' compounds[12] such as *kaketu-suru* in (19) exemplify such verbs.[13]

(19) Sono gian wa tasuu no giin niyotte kaketus -are ta.
that bill Top majority Gen Dietman by pass Pass Pst
'That bill was passed by the majority of the Diet.'

As shown in this subsection, *ni* passives are frequently found with empathy-loaded verbs, while *niyotte* passives often co-occur with semantically neutral verbs.

4. Historical Facts

The previous sections examined the synchronic phenomena of *ni* and *niyotte* direct passives. In this section, I investigate *ni/niyotte* variation in light of diachronic facts. The first question to be asked is whether such variation is found in historical texts. Historically, a *ni* that marks demoted subjects in direct passives is found even in Old Japanese as in (20a).[14] (20b) is from the early 11th century.

(20) a. Na ga haha ***ni*** kor -are a wa ik u.
your Gen mother by scold Pass I Top go Pres
(Manyoshu 14.3519)
'I'm leaving having been scolded by your mother....'

b. Arigataki mono. Syuuto ***ni*** home -raru ru muko.
rare thing father-in-law by praise Pass Pres son-in-law.[15]
(Makura no soshi 75)
'A rare thing. A son-in-law who is praised by his father-in-law.'

---

[12] Sino-Japanese nominals are of Chinese origin; the nominals by themselves function as nouns and become verbalized when incorporated into *suru*.

[13] In addition to sentence (19), the *niyotte* passive in (14), taken from a news magazine, also includes a sino-Japanese compound verb. It should also be noted that such compound verbs may appear in *ni* passives if they are empathy-loaded, such as *batoo-suru* 'lash'.

[14] According to Miller (1967), the Japanese language can be divided into the following periods. Old Japanese: before the 9th century
Late Old Japanese: the 9th to the end of the 12th century
Middle Japanese: the 13th to the end of the 17th century
Early Modern Japanese: the 17th to the middle of the 19th century
Modern Japanese: the middle of the 19th century to the present

[15] The morpheme *rare* changed its morphological and phonological form in the course of its historical development. In Old Japanese, passives were expressed with *y/ray(u)*; in Late Old Japanese *r/rar(u)* became prevalent. The contemporary form *rare* first appeared in Middle Japanese (13C) and became common in Early Modern Japanese.

Niyori and *niyorite,* which are the old forms of *niyotte*, are also found in Old Japanese; however, they are simply conjunctions, as illustrated in sentence (21) which is quoted from an 11th century text.

(21) .....yo o somuki te habe ru ga konogoro madou koto
world Acc avoid Ger be Pres but these days worried thing
habe ru **niyori**, ... (Genji Modogakari; Wakamurasaki)
be Pres Conj
'...(after her husband died, she) entered the priesthood, but because she has been sick these days.....'

Niyori(te), in fact, was never used as a marker for demoted subjects of passives until the middle of the 19th century. According to Kinsui (1991), the first use of *niyotte* or *niyori(te)* in passives is found in the translation from Dutch, *Waran bunten dokuhoo* 'Japanese Dutch Grammar Book', as in (22).

(22) Koko ni sikasinagara zyuuni no ippan no kisoku to
here in however twelve Gen general Gen rule that
sikooshite keiken ga kore nituite koosya naru
and experience Nom this about export be
gogakusya **niyorite** sadame -rare -te -ar u.
linguist by establish Pass Ger Stat Pres
'However, here are twelve rules that have been established by a linguistic expert who is experienced in this subject.'

The book was translated by Sooken Takenouchi in 1856 and *niyorite* in (22) is a direct translation of the preposition '*door*' that marks a demoted subject of passives in Dutch. We find many translations from Dutch into Japanese around this time. This is because Holland was the only western country that was allowed to continue trade with Japan when Japan stopped contact with the west, from 1639 to 1854. After Japan again opened its doors to western countries, a wide range of translations were done from Dutch, English, German, and French.

Kinsui points out that with the first use of *niyorite* as a demoted subject marker, *niyorite* or *niyotte* in passives is observed with high frequency in translations from western languages. From that time on, *niyotte* passives started to appear not only in translations, but in Japanese literature and in newspapers written by Japanese. [16]

---

[16] See Kinsui (1991) and Matsumura (1977) for further discussion regarding the changes observed in Japanese passives during the Meiji Era.

Thus, the use of *niyotte* in passives is a recent linguistic phenomenon in the history of Japanese. Until the middle of the 19th century, Japanese had only *ni* passives. As previously noted, *ni* passives in Japanese often express the experiencer's affectivity. Based upon these facts, some linguists such as Yamada (1908) and Mitsuya (1908) claimed that, originally, all Japanese passives were adversative, and that passives with inanimate subjects were brought into Japanese by translations of western texts in the 19th century.[17]

Contrary to this theory, however, is the fact that passives with inanimate subjects are found in old texts. The following examples are from Late Old Japanese.

(23) a. .....ookinaru ki no kaze ni hukitaos -are te.....
big tree Nom wind by blow down Pass Ger
'....the big tree was blown down by wind.." (Makura no soshi; 125)

b. Yomogi no kuruma ni osihisig -are tari keru ga......
mugwort Gen cart by push crush Pass Stat Pst Nom
'The mugwort which has been run over by a vehicle...'
(Makura no soshi; 223)

c. .....misu no soba ito arawani hikiage -rare
bamboo blind Gen edge very widely pull up Pass
taru o..... (Genji Monogatari; Wakana)
Stat Acc
'....the edge of the bamboo blind has been pulled up to show the inside openly....'

The passives in (23) have inanimate subjects; semantically, these sentences are quite neutral and no adversative meaning is expressed.

Regarding passives with inanimate subjects, Kosugi (1979) made an interesting observation. According to him, these types of passives written in *kana* letters that appeared in Late Old Japanese texts, particularly in the Heian Period (794-1192), almost always include the auxiliaries of 'state', 'existence', and 'continuance', *tari* or *ri* when the verbs express actions. In (23), (a) expresses a natural phenomenon, but (b) and (c) involve actions such as 'run over' and 'pull up'. Unlike (a), the passive morpheme in (b) and (c) is followed by *tari (taru)*; *tari* semantically plays a role to emphasize the resulting state, rather than an action that took place.[18] This suggests that the original Japanese passives with an action verb and an inanimate subject

---

[17] Kosugi (1979), Kinsui (1991), and Okutsu (1983) object to this theory.
[18] In later texts, *tari* or *ri* gradually disappear.

were plain descriptions of resulting state with no focus on the action itself nor on the agent who is responsible for the action.

The reason that *niyotte* was employed as an inanimate demoted subject marker in translations from western languages as in (22) is now understandable. The introduction of *niyotte* as a demoted subject marker provided Japanese with a tool to express events with a focus on the action, rather than the resulting state of the action, in passives.

5. Conclusion

In this paper, I examined the *ni/niyotte* variation observed in Japanese direct passives. I argued that *ni* and *niyotte* passives do not differ syntactically. Rather, the variation is a phenomenon that arises as a result of semantic and pragmatic interactions of *ni* and *niyotte* and co-occurring verbs.

Historically, *niyotte* was introduced into Japanese passives as a translation from Dutch about 150 years ago; before that, Japanese passives were not usually used to express an event objectively, with a focus on the action or the agent. In light of these historical facts, therefore, it can be said that the use of *niyotte* as a demoted subject marker is an innovation that arose to enrich the semantic and pragmatic dimensions of passives in Japanese.

References

Chomsky, Noam. 1986. *Knowledge of Language: Its Nature, Origin, and Use*. New York: Praeger.

Chomsky, Noam. 1995. *The Minimalist Program*. Cambridge: MIT Press.

Grimshaw, Jane. 1990. *Argument Structure*. Cambridge: MIT Press.

Hoshi, Hiroto. 1991. The Generalized Projection Principle and Its Implications for Passive Constructions. *Journal of Japanese Linguistics* 13: 53-89.

Hoshi, Hiroto. 1994. Theta-role Assignment, Passivization, and Excorporation. *Journal of East Asian Linguistics* 3: 147-178.

Hosokawa, Yukiko. 1986. Nihongo no zyudoobun niokeru doosashu no maakaa ni tsuite. *Kokugogaku* 144: 113-124.

Kinsui, Satoshi. 1991. Zyudoobun no rekishi nitsuite no ichikoosatsu. *Kokugogaku* 164:1-14.

Kokubungaku henshuubu ed., 1987. *Zyoshi to zyodooshi no techoo*. Tokyo: Gakutoosha.

Kosugi, Shoichi. 1979. Hizyoo no ukemi, in Ronbunshuu henshuu iinkai, ed., *Zyoshi, zyodooshi ronshuu*. Tokyo: Oohuusya.

Kuno, Susumu. 1983. *Shin nihon bunpoo kenkyuu*. Tokyo: Taisyuukan.

Kuno, Susumu. 1987. *Functional Syntax*. Chicago: The University of Chicago Press.

Kuroda, Sige-Yuki. 1965. *Generative Grammatical Studies in the Japanese Language*. Doctoral dissertation, MIT.

Kuroda, Sige-Yuki. 1979. On Japanese Passives, in G. Bedell, E. Kobayashi, and M. Muraki eds., *Explorations in Linguistics: Papers in Honor of Kazuko Inoue*. Tokyo: Kenkyusha.

Manyoshu. 1962. Tokyo: Iwanami Shoten.

Matsumura, Akira, ed., 1969. *Kotengo, gendaigo zyoshi, zyodooshi shoosetsu*. Tokyo: Gakutoosha.

Matsumura, Akira. 1977. *Kindai no nihongo: Edo kara gendai e*. Tokyo: Oikawa Tokuji.

Miller, Roy Andrew. 1967. *The Japanese Language*. Chicago: University of Chicago Press.

Mitsuya, Shigematsu. 1908. *Kootoo nihonbunpoo*. Tokyo: Meiji Syoin.

Miyagi, Kimi. 1996. *Passive, Affective, and Causative Constructions in Japanese*. Doctoral dissertation, Georgetown University.

Miyagi, Kimi. 1998. Syntax and Semantics of *Ni* and *Niyotte* Passives in Japanese. *Journal of Japanese Linguistics and Education* 5: 45-65.

Murasaki Shikibu. 1970-75. *Genji monogatari*. Tokyo: Shoogakkan.

Nakayama, Mineharu and Domenic Cipollone. 1996. *Japanese Ni vs. Niyotte Passive Dichotomy Revisited*. ms. The Ohio State University.

Okutsu, Keiichiro. 1983. Naze ukemi ka? *Kokugogaku* 132: 65-80.

Sei shoonagon. 1982. *Makura no sooshi*. Tokyo: Iwanami Shoten.

Sugimoto, Tsutomu. 1983. *Nihon honyakugoshi no kenkyuu*. Tokyo: Yasaka Shoboo.

Yamada, Takao. 1908. *Nihonbunpooron*. Tokyo: Hoobunkan.

Yoshida, Kanehiko. 1973. *Zyoodaigo zyodooshi no shiteki kenkyuu*. Tokyo: Meiji Shoin.

Some Evidence for a Zero Light Verb in Japanese [1]

YUTAKA SATO
International Christian University

1. Introduction

Martin (1975:178, 179) pointed out that there are nouns with 'individual valances' in Japanese that syntactically realize their arguments when directly followed by the 'dummy verb *suru* "do (it)"'; these nouns - named verbal nouns (VNs) by Martin - can '... be detached from *suru* by the object marker *o* or by certain particles of focus and restriction ...' Grimshaw and Mester (1988) formalized this phenomenon by stating that the dummy verb is a light verb with an empty argument structure, which inherits a VN's arguments to both θ-mark and Case-mark them like its own (even when the VN is detached from the light verb). The VN, highlighted in small capitals, in (1) and (2) is *setumei* 'explanation' and bears the argument structure (Agent, Goal, Theme). This VN can license (with the help of the light verb) arguments compatible with its argument structure, as shown in (1), but not an argument incompatible with it, for example, a Source, as shown in (2).

(1)	John	ga	Mary	ni	sore	ni-tuite	SETUMEI	(o)	sita.
	John	NOM	Mary	DAT	that	about	explanation	ACC	did

'John explained that to Mary.'

---

[1] I would like to express my thanks to the following people for their valuable comments on an earlier version of this paper: George Bedell, Mineharu Nakayama, Stephen Nolan, and Yoshie Yamashita.

(2) *John ga Mary kara sore ni-tuite SETUMEI (o) sita.
John NOM Mary ABL that about explanation ACC did
'*John explained that from Mary.'

The construction where a light verb verbally Case-marks the arguments inherited from a VN as in (1) - whether the VN is detached from the light verb or not - is called the Light Verb Construction (LVC) in this paper.

One of the most challenging problems with the VNs concerns the constructions in (3)-(5), where the VNs appear with verbally Case-marked arguments even without a light verb. The question is how a noun can license the verbal Case-marking of its arguments.

(3) John ga Ainugo o KENKYUU tyuu ni
John NOM Ainu ACC research middle in
'While John is/was doing research on Ainu, ...'

(4) John ga Amerika o HOOMON no ori ni
John NOM America ACC visit GEN occasion on
'When John visits/visited America, ...'

(5) John ga [PRO Nihongo o KENKYUU ni] iku.
John NOM Japanese ACC research to go
'John will go to do research on Japanese.'

The VNs in (3)-(5) appear to assign verbal Cases by themselves: they occur with an NP in the accusative, although no light verb appears in the same clause. Following Sells (1990), the examples in (3) and (4) are called the Temporal Affix Construction (TAC); the temporal affix in (3) and the temporal noun in (4) are underlined. The construction in (5) is called the Purpose Clause Construction (PCC), in which the purpose clause *Nihongo o kenkyuu* occurs as a complement of the postposition *ni*.

As extensively discussed by Sells (1990), the VNs are morphologically nouns, as can be seen from the fact that, unlike verbs, they do not inflect for tense (e.g. **KENKYUU-ta* 'research-PAST'), for example. Moreover, in the environments other than those given above (i.e. the LVC, TAC, and PCC), the VNs behave just like bona fide nouns, occurring only with genitively marked phrases. The sentence in (6) is such an example.

(6) Nihongo no/*o KENKYUU ga omosiroi.
Japanese GEN/ACC research NOM interesting
'To do research on Japanese is interesting.'

This sentence is ungrammatical if the VN's Theme *Nihongo* 'Japanese' is marked accusatively because the VN in (6) does not occur in any of the constructions exemplified in (3)-(5).

To capture the behavior of the VNs in (3)-(5), Iida (1987) claimed, not unreasonably, that nouns with argument structure assign verbal Cases when they are concatenated with a lexical item bearing a special aspectual feature, as shown in figure 1. The temporal affix in (3), the temporal noun in (4), and purposive *ni* in (5) are instances of such aspect licensers. This assumption is followed by Sells (1990), Manning (1993), and Dubinsky (1997). Furthermore, Sells (1990) and Dubinsky (1997) assumed that the VN in (1) is also aspectually licensed by the light verb and is responsible for assigning verbal Cases.

Figure 1.
Iida (1987:110), (43)

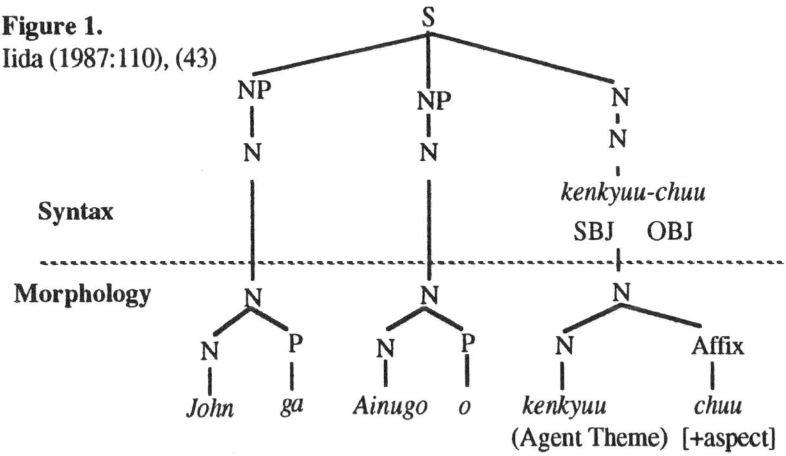

Similar proposals under which VNs verbally Case-mark their arguments on their own are made by Kageyama (1993) and Hasegawa (1991), but here I will focus on the position taken by Iida (1987) and others, where an aspectual feature renders VNs the ability to assign verbal Cases. I will call this approach the Aspect-Licensing Approach. The Aspect-Licensing Approach is quite radical in the sense that nouns with some aspectual feature can assign verbal Cases, just like verbs, despite the fact that, as stated by Iida, 'Current syntactic theories presuppose a categorial basis for case assignment.' What I will do in the rest of my paper is propose an alternative to the Aspect-Licensing Approach. My attempt, if successful, is to revert to the conservative Case assignment mechanism where nouns cannot assign verbal Cases. My approach is also in keeping with Grimshaw and Mester (1988), Hoshi (1997), and Uchida and Nakayama (1993), among others. I will present data from both adult and child Japanese to argue that a zero light verb is responsible for verbal Case-marking in the constructions where VNs appear to verbally Case-mark their arguments.

2. The Adult Data

The crucial adult data that argue for the presence of a zero light verb are given in (7) and (8), which are examples of a TAC that involves coordination with the disjunctive *naisi* 'or'. Note that these examples have structures that would be expected under the Aspect-Licensing Approach.

(7) Nihongo o [$_N$GAKUSYUU] naisi [$_N$KENKYUU] tyuu ni
Japanese ACC learning or research middle in
'While learning or doing research on Japanese, ...'

(8) ??[$_{NP}$Nihongo o KENKYUU __] naisi
Japanese ACC research or
[$_{NP}$Eigo o KENKYUU tyuu] ni
English ACC research middle in
'while doing research on Japanese or (doing research on) English, ...'

The example in (7), where only the VNs are coordinated, sounds much better than the example in (8), where both the disjuncts contain an accusatively marked NP as well as a VN. Although no examples like (7) and (8) were discussed in Iida (1987), I assume that the first temporal affix in (8) is gapped and that the gap can aspectually license the VN to assign accusative Case in the Aspect-Licensing Approach. Note that some kind of aspectual licenser (e.g. in the form of a gap) is needed after the first disjunct in order for the first VN to license the preceding accusative NP in Iida's framework.

One may argue that it is either the absence of a temporal affix after the first VN, or the coordination of the phrases headed by temporal affixes that is responsible for the marginality of (8). Neither of these, however, is the cause for its marginality, as shown in (9). The example in (9) has exactly the same structure as (8) but is perfectly grammatical; the only difference between the two examples is the disjunctive: it is *naisi* in (8), but it is replaced by another one *mata wa* 'or' in (9).

(9) [Nihongo o KENKYUU __] mata wa
Japanese ACC research or
[Eigo o KENKYUU tyuu] ni
English ACC research middle in
'while doing research on Japanese or (doing research on) English, ...'

It remains as a mystery under the Aspect-Licensing Approach why the disjuncts containing an accusative NP and a VN in (8) cannot be coordinated by *naisi*, while the VNs alone in (7) can.

Teramura (1992:350-355) pointed out that *naisi* only coordinates nominals, as shown in the contrast between (10) and (11). *Naisi* in the grammatical example in (10) coordinates two nominals, 'ball-point pen' and 'fountain pen,' or 'black ball-point pen' and 'black fountain pen.' On the other hand, if *naisi* coordinates two VPs in (11), 'buy a car' and 'sell a car,' the sentence turns marginal - while *mata wa* can coordinate them without any problem.

(10) [$_{NP}$ (Kuroi) boorupen] naisi [$_{NP}$ (kuroi) mannenhitu] de
black ballpoint or black fountain-pen INS
kaite kudasai.
write please
'Please write with a black ball-point pen or black fountain pen.'

(11) [$_{VP}$ kuruma o kau] ??naisi/mata wa [$_{VP}$ kuruma o uru]
car ACC buy or/or car ACC sell
toki
time
'When (you) buy a car or sell a car....'

The contrast between (10), on the one hand, and (11) with *naisi*, on the other, suggests that the contrast between (7) and (8) may have to do with a difference in syntactic category.

Suppose that the TAC in (3) has the structure in figure 2, where a zero light verb (Ø) occurs under V, combining with the VN to form a predicate complex. (There might be some functional categories above the VP, and the VN might have to incorporate into the light verb at some level; such details, however, will go beyond the scope of this paper and will not be discussed any further.)

Figure 2.

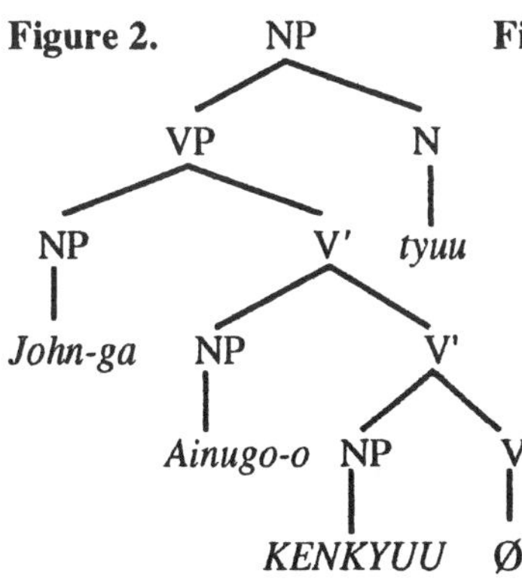

Figure 3.

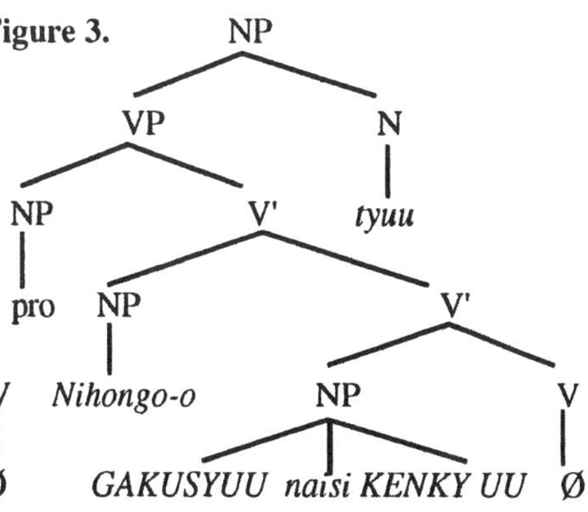

The structure is almost identical to the corresponding Light Verb Construction except for the phonological status of the light verb - that is, it is null in the TAC. The TACs in (7) and (8) under the Zero-Light Verb Approach would be those in (12) and (13), respectively.

(12) [$_{VP}$ Nihongo o [$_{NP}$ [$_{N}$ GAKUSYUU] naisi [$_{N}$ KENKYUU]] Ø]] tyuu ni

(13) ??[$_{VP}$ Nihongo o KENKYUU Ø] naisi [$_{VP}$ Eigo o KENKYUU Ø] tyuu ni

The two VNs in (12) (the structure of (12) is given in figure 3), *gakusyuu* and *kenkyuu*, are coordinated by *naisi*; coordinating them with *naisi* does not pose any problem because the VNs are nouns. The coordinated VNs combine with the zero light verb, and the zero light verb assigns accusative Case to the Theme argument of the two VNs, i.e. *Nihongo*. In (13) (the structure of (13) is given in figure 4), on the other hand, there needs to be a zero light verb in each disjunct to assign accusative Case - note that there is an accusatively marked NP in each of the disjuncts in (13). That is, both the disjuncts in (13) are verbals. But *naisi* can only marginally coordinate the verbals and, hence, (13) is degraded.

Figure 4.

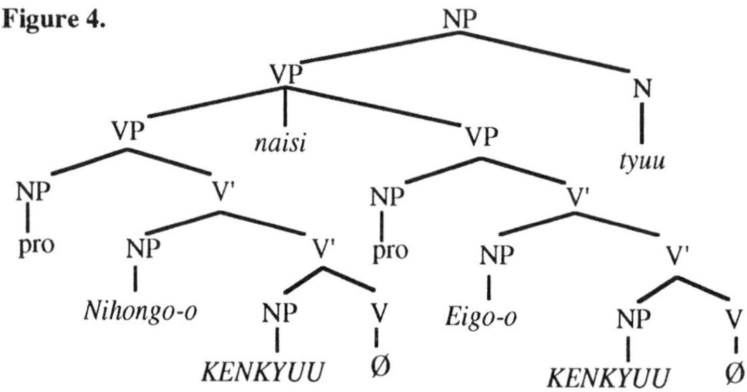

Gapping is assumed not to take place in the Zero-Light Verb Approach, although it was needed for (8) under the Aspect-License Approach in order for the VN to be aspectually licensed to accusatively mark the preceding accusative NP. This is because such gapping is unlikely to occur particularly in the case of compounds headed by a temporal affix, which triggers a special phonological process (i.e. regressive deaccentuation).

As has been shown above, the contrast between (7) and (8), or between (12) and (13), suggests that, despite the fact that VNs appear to verbally Case-mark their arguments by themselves in the TAC, there is in fact a zero light verb, which is responsible for verbal Case-marking.

Before turning to the child data in the next section, let us briefly observe another problem with the Aspect-Licensing Approach in adult Japanese, as shown in (14).

(14)	Hooan	syuugiin	o	TUUKA
	bill	House of Representatives	ACC	pass

'Bill passes the House of Representatives'

The example in (14) is a newspaper headline, where the VN alone (i.e., without aspectual licensing from an overt element) appears to verbally Case mark its argument. Manning (1993) noted in a footnote that 'aspect licensing is being provided by the discourse context.' But how it is formally done is not mentioned. Examples like (14) appear only in special styles in adult Japanese. But expressions like (14) abound in child language and in fact they appear initially and later develop into full-fledged LVCs. If that is the case, however, such data are a problem for the Aspect-Licensing Approach, because there is no (phonologically overt) element that aspectually licenses the VN in expressions like (14) and yet the VNs occur with verbally Case-marked arguments.

As has been just stated above, I assume in this paper that, if the Aspect-Licensing Approach is correct, it cannot allow a phonologically null aspectual licenser, particularly a phonologically null *suru*. This was similarly argued by Iida (1987). If one postulates a zero morpheme that aspectually licenses the VN in (14), however, such a zero morpheme is categorially a verb, as has been demonstrated by the contrast between (12) and (13). Moreover, such a verb is most likely a zero light verb because this zero morpheme alternates with the overt light verb in expressions like (15). That is, either the zero morpheme appears as in (14) or overt *suru* appears as in (15).

(15) Hooan ga syuugiin o TUUKA sita.
bill NOM House of Representatives ACC pass did
'The bill passed the House of Representatives.'

3. The Child Data

The child data I drew on were the utterances collected from one child Taachan, recorded by the National Language Research Institute (1982). Table 1 shows Taachan's production of VNs from 13 to 19 months of age. Examples of early production of VNs are given in (16), which are mostly onomatopoetic expressions and reduplicates. VNs, as stated above, are not uncommon even in the one-word stage.

Table 1 The number of tokens of Ns, VNs, and Vs in Taachan's speech (Yamashita, 1995, p. 86)

Age (months)	13	14	15	16	17	18	19	total
Ns (excl. VNs)	48	25	39	27	32	76	122	369
VNs	2	11	61	40	20	60	73	267
stative Vs	3	0	4	2	4	2	18	33
nonstative Vs	0	0	0	0	0	0	2	2

(16) **VNs appeared from 13 months to 19 months** (267 tokens/12 types): NENNE 'sleeping', DAKKO 'holding', NAINAI 'putting away', POI 'throwing away', SYANPUU 'shampooing', ZAA 'spilling', BAIBAI 'waving a hand and saying 'goodbye'', GAAGAA 'making noise of 'gaagaa (running a car)'', ONRI 'getting off', TATTI 'standing up', BOON 'throwing', BAA 'peekaboo' (Yamashita, 1995, p. 46)

These VNs in early speech appeared not only by themselves but also with an argument or adjunct, as in (17).

(17) Buubuu NAINAI.
car putting-away
'(I'm) putting away (the) car.'

Because utterances like (17) denote events, they seem to have a clausal structure rather than that of an NP. Put differently, if the arguments, adjuncts, and topics of a clause are called V-sisters[2] (borrowing Manning's (1993) terminology), the VNs in utterances like (17) appear to take V-sisters. If that is the case, however, it would pose a problem to the Aspect-Licensing Approach, because there are no overt lexical items in utterances like (17) that aspectually license the VN to take V-sisters. The Zero Light Verb Approach, however, can account for such data, claiming that a zero light verb occurs after the VN in (17). I will present three pieces of evidence in the following to show that the VNs in the early stages indeed take V-sisters and that the structure of utterances like (17) is that of a clause rather than an NP.

First, two-word utterances like (17), where a VN occurred with another element, appeared much earlier in Taachan's speech than those like (18), where a bona fide noun occurred with another element.

(18) Okaasan (no) syatu
mother GEN shirt
'Mother's shirt'

If the arguments and adjuncts of VNs in utterances like (17) were not V-sisters, but were N-sisters (i.e., a sister to a noun or a projection of a noun), however, they would have similar relationships to their heads as the specifiers or modifiers of bona fide NPs like (18), and both the patterns (e.g. (17) and (18)) should have emerged at about the same time in Taachan's speech. Compare the occurrences of the NP-N utterances with XP-VN utterances in table 2.

---

[2]V-sisters are sisters to V or sisters to a projection of V or I. Topics are assumed to occur in VPs as well as in IPs, following Brockett (1994).

Table 2 shows the frequencies of multiword utterances produced from 13 to 24 months. The NP-N utterances are those with nouns taking a specifier or nominal adjunct like (18), and the XP-VN utterances are those with VNs taking an argument, adjunct or topic like (17). No overt light verb appeared in the XP-VN utterances until 24 months of age. The first VN with an argument appeared at 13 months of age, and the first NP with a nominal modifier appeared at 22 months of age. The XP-VN utterances appeared nine months earlier than the NP-N utterances, but just as early as the XP-V utterances. The delay in emergence of NP-N utterances may have to do with obligatory genitive marking within NPs.

Table 2. Taachan's multiword utterances, 13-24 months (Sato, 1998)

Months	13	14	17	18	19	20	21	22	23	24	total
AP-N	0	0	0	0	0	24	119	95	25	11	274
NP-N	**0**	**0**	**0**	**0**	**0**	**0**	**0**	**10**	**9**	**16**	**35**
XP-VN	**1**	**1**	**0**	**1**	**2**	**3**	**16**	**6**	**14**	**16**	**60**
XP-V	2	0	0	0	1	1	51	7	5	31	98
XP-A	0	0	0	1	1	0	17	11	12	20	62
XP-*nai*	0	1	1	1	2	4	28	14	12	10	73
NP-NP	0	0	0	0	0	2	6	4	0	16	28
Adv NP	0	0	0	0	0	0	0	1	0	5	6
total	3	2	1	3	6	34	237	148	77	125	636

Secondly, some arguments and adjuncts of VNs in XP-VN utterances (without an overt light verb) appeared with overt morphological markers for V-sisters. The topic marker *wa* appeared on an argument and adjunct of a VN at 21 and 24 months of age, as shown in (19) and (20), and the postposition *de* appeared on an adjunct of another VN at 25 months, as shown in (21).

(19) Piipoo-piipoo wa NAINAI. (21 months)
ambulance TOP putting-away
'(I'm) putting away (the) ambulance.'

(20) Kyoo wa NAINAI. (24 months)
today TOP putting-away
'(I'm) putting (them) away for today.'

(21) Koko de KOTYO-KOTYO. (25 months)
here at tickling
'Tickle (me) here.'

The topics *piipoo-piipoo wa* 'ambulance' and *kyoo wa* 'today', and the locative *koko de* '(at) here' cannot appear within NPs but can appear only in clauses. In these examples, the VNs clearly cooccur with V-sisters without aspect-licensing.

Finally, the case-marking of the arguments or adjuncts of VNs (when not followed by an overt light verb) patterned in Taachan's early speech with the case-marking of bona fide V-sisters, rather than with bona fide N-sisters. Table 3 shows what case or discourse markers followed NPs when they occurred with a noun, verb, VN, or VN followed by *suru* in the multiword utterances from 24 to 26 months of age.

Table 3. Case marking in Taachan's utterances from 24 to 26 months[3]

	Months	24 mo.		25 mo.		26 mo.	
		freq.	%	freq.	%	freq.	%
NP-N	Bare	4	44.4	19	39.6	8	21.6
	Genitive	**5**	**55.5**	**29**	**60.4**	**29**	**78.3**
NP-V	**Bare**	**27**	**100**	**99**	**86.8**	**94**	**71.8**
	wa/mo	0	0	12	10.5	15	11.5
	Verbal cases	0	0	3	2.6	22	16.8
NP-VN	**Bare**	**7**	**87.5**	**10**	**90.9**	**10**	**90.9**
	wa/mo	1	12.5	0	0	0	0
	Verbal cases	0	0	1	9.1	0	0
	Genitive	0	0	0	0	1	9.1
NP-VN *suru*	Bare	2	66.7	9	60	6	100
	wa/mo	0	0	1	6.7	0	0
	Verbal cases	1	33.3	5	33.3	0	0

In the NP-N utterances, the NPs (i.e. bona fide N-sisters) were followed by a genitive marker 55.5% of the time at 24 months. In fact, morphological genitive case marking within NPs started at age 24 months. The proportion of genitive case marking was almost 80% at 26 months. In contrast, the verbs appeared with bare V-sisters (or bare NPs) most of the time: the bare NPs (i.e. NPs followed by no overt morphological case/discourse marker) appeared 100% of the time with verbs at 24 months; the proportion of bare NPs gradually decreased, but it was still 71.8% at 26 months. The VNs occurred with bare NPs at the constant rate of 90% of the time, and, hence, the case-marking patterns of the VNs were close to that of the verbs, but not of the bona fide nouns. The figures in table 3 suggest that Taachan clearly distinguished between the contexts for genitive case marking and verbal case

[3]Bare: NPs followed by no overt case/discourse marker; Genitive: NPs followed by a genitive marker; *wa/mo*: NPs followed by a discourse marker *wa* or *mo*; Verbal cases: NPs followed by a verbal case marker or a postposition.

The frequencies of the NP-N utterances for table 2 and 3 are different because five tokens of the compound noun *bataa-naihu* ('butter knife'), one token with a numeral quantifier, and one token with a demonstrative are excluded from the counts in table 3. Also only head-final utterances (without Right Dislocation) are counted for table 3.

marking. But, if that is the case, those VNs with V-sisters appeared without aspectual licensing from an overt lexical item.

To sum up, the arguments or adjuncts of VNs in NP-VN utterances without an overt light verb are easily analyzable as V-sisters. They almost always appeared as bare NPs, that is, just like bona fide V-sisters, while bona fide N-sisters were genitively marked more than 50% of the time. Some of them appeared with a topic marker or a postposition, which clearly shows that they were V-sisters, not N-sisters. Furthermore, those arguments or adjuncts of VNs emerged just as early as other bona fide V-sisters and much earlier than bona fide N-sisters. It follows that the arguments and adjuncts of VNs appeared as V-sisters without aspectual licensing in Taachan's early speech.

One may argue that the child Case-marking system is different from the adult's. That is, the child's first assumption is that VNs license verbal Case marking without aspectual licensing, and later s/he develops a mechanism that allows verbal Case marking only when aspectual licensing is available. If that is the case, one would expect overgeneralization of verbal case marking, as in (6). The example in (22) is the first and last example (recorded in the 26th months) of a VN with an argument occurring in an unambiguously genitive case marking environment.

(22) Ootobai no BUNBUN kikoeta no. (26 months)
motorbike GEN running heard SP
'I heard the running (sound) of a motorbike.'

In this example, the VN's argument is genitively marked. So no such overgeneralization was attested, although we only have one example up to 26 months of age. In addition, theoretically speaking, postulating a Case-assigning mechanism different from the adults' is less parsimonious and requires an explanation for how the child acquires the adult Case-assigning system only from positive evidence (Pinker 1984).

The zero light verb analysis postulates that children can guess in what environments a zero light verb occurs from positive evidence alone because a zero light verb appears in place of an overt one in the input. Because either an overt light verb or covert one assigns verbal Cases in the LVC, TAC, and PCC, Case-assignment is uniformly done by verbal elements, in both child and adult Japanese.[4]

Iida (1987:99) pointed out a problem with treating *kenkyuu* in the TAC in (3) as derived from *kenkyuu-si* by deleting *si*, pointing out that the verbal form *kenkyuu-si* cannot attach to the temporal affix *-tyuu*, as in (23).

[4]It is not clear, however, what licenses a zero light verb to occur. Considering the fact that the PCC is not possible and the acceptance of the TAC varies greatly in Korean, what motivates the occurence of a zero light verb may not be captured in formal syntax.

(23) *John ga Ainugo o KENKYUU si tyuu ni

(23)	*John	ga	Ainugo	o	KENKYUU	si	tyuu	ni
	John	NOM	Ainu	ACC	research	do	middle	in

'While John is/was doing research on Ainu, ...'

But such temporal affixes are limited to *-tyuu* 'during' and *-go* 'after'. Other temporal nouns like *tyokugo* 'right after' allow either a zero or overt light verb to appear in the preceding clause, as shown in (24).

(24) a.

[Sinsya	o	KOONYUU	Ø]	tyokugo	ni
new-car	ACC	purchase		right-after	at

'Right after purchasing a new car, ...'

b.

[Sinsya	o	KOONYUU	sita]	tyokugo	ni
new-car	ACC	purchase	did	right-after	at

'Right after (s/he) purchased a new car, ...'

Moreover, some verbs can indeed attach (with some difficulty) to *-tyuu* or *-go*, as shown in (25). *Kakinaosi-sase-rare* 'be forced to rewrite' in (25) is unambiguously a verb (or a syntactically derived complex verb) but it is never a noun.

(25)

?Sono	ronbun	o	KAKINAOSI-sase-rare	tyuu/go	ni
that	paper	ACC	rewriting-CAUSE-PASS	middle/after	

'When/after (s/he) is/was being forced to rewrite the paper, ...'

The ungrammaticality of examples like (23) can be accounted for by a prosodic condition proposed by Tsujimura (1992) and the phonological behavior of those temporal affixes, that is, they trigger regressive deaccentuation. Tsujimura (1992) demonstrated that the element that attaches to *-tyuu* or *-go* must be at least four morae long.[5] Assuming that the phonological process of deaccentuation can take place only within a word - which is not unreasonable because after all it unifies two accentuation patterns into that of one word - a phonologically overt element hosted by a deaccentuating affix must undergo incorporation into the affix at some level before the structure is assigned its accentuation.[6] Then, *si* alone incorporates into the temporal affix in (23), as shown in figure 5.

The whole verbal complex *kenkyuu si* cannot incorporate into the temporal affix because *kenkyuu si* can never exhibit the accentuation of one word, that is, the VN and the light verb, respectively, need to preserve their

---

[5]Tsujimura stated that such an element is a deverbal noun, but, as has been shown above, it is, in fact, a verb.

[6]I assume that a VN incorporates into a zero light verb and successively into a temporal affix at a level before the structure is assigned accentuation, when the temporal affix is either *-tyuu* or *-go*. This is because the VN needs to be deaccentuated by the temporal affix *-tyuu* or *-go*.

accentuation patterns, as pointed out by Poser (1992). The incorporation of the VN into the light verb, if it occurs at all, must take place at some level after the incorporation of the overt light verb into the temporal affix, as assumed by Kageyama (1993). If that is the case, *si*, the infinitive form of *suru*, being only one mora long, cannot meet the prosodic condition, resulting in ungrammaticality.

Figure 5.

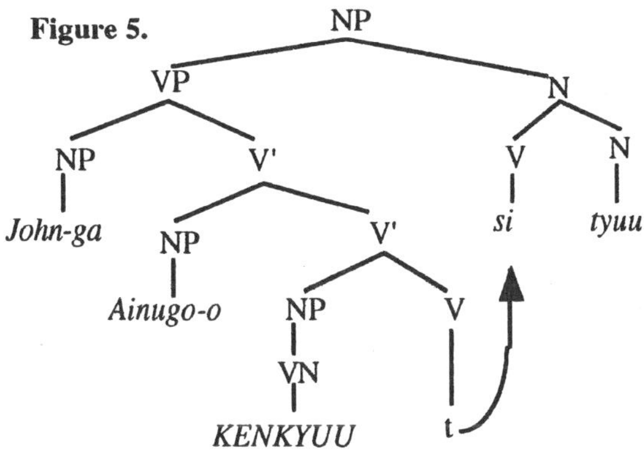

It follows from the above that a zero light verb always appears in the environments where an overt one does except for some phonologically exceptional cases (i.e. the cases of *-tyuu* and *-go*). Thus, children can rely on positive data to detect when the overt light verb is missing, whereby s/he can insure a position for a zero light verb in the syntactic structure of a sentence.

4. Conclusion

To sum up, I have shown using data from coordination that there seems to be a zero light verb in the TAC in adult Japanese. I have also shown from child data that VNs appear with V-sisters without aspectual licensing in early stages. Both facts, I believe, are better explained by postulating a zero light verb than an aspect-licensing lexical item.

References

Brockett, Chris. 1994. Mo: Quantificational evidence for non-quantificational analysis, in M. Koizumi and H. Ura, eds., *Formal Approaches to Japanese Linguistics 1* (pp. 45-59). MITWPL, Vol 24.

Dubinsky, Stanley. 1997. Syntactic underspecification and light-verb phenomena in Japanese. *Linguistics* 35:627-672.

Grimshaw, Jane and Armin Mester. 1988. Light verbs and θ-marking. *Linguistic Inquiry* 19:205-232.

Hasegawa, Nobuko. 1991. On head movement in Japanese: the case of verbal nouns. *Proceedings of Sophia linguistic society* 6:8-32.

Hoshi, Hiroto. 1997. Incorporation in Syntax and LF: The Case of Light Verb Constructions and Temporal Affix Constructions in Japanese, in H. Sohn and J. Haig, eds., *Japanese/Korean Linguistics*, vol. 6 (pp. 473-491). Stanford, CA: CSLI (Center for the Study of Language and Information).

Iida, Masayo. 1987. Case assignment by nominals in Japanese, in M. Iida, S. Wechsler, and D. Zec, eds., *Working papers in grammatical theory and discourse structure: Interactions of morphology, syntax, and discourse* (pp. 93-138). Stanford, CA: CSLI.

Kageyama, Taro. 1993. *Bunpoo to gokeisei [Grammar and word formation]*. Kasukabe: Hituzi Syobo.

Manning, Christopher. 1993. Analyzing the verbal noun: Internal and external constraints, in S. Choi, ed., *Japanese/Korean Linguistics*, vol. 3 (pp. 236-253). Stanford, CA: CSLI.

Martin, Samuel. 1975. *A Reference Grammar of Japanese*. New Haven: Yale University Press.

National Language Research Institute. 1982. *Yooji no kotoba shiryoo [The child's language data]*. Tokyo: Kokuritsu Kokugo Kenkyuujo.

Pinker, Steven. 1984. *Language learnability and language development*. Cambridge, MA: Harvard University Press.

Poser, William. 1992. Blocking of phrasal constructions by lexical items, in I. Sag and A. Szabolcsi, eds., *Lexical Matters* (pp. 111-130). Stanford, CA: CSLI.

Sato, Yutaka. 1998. A zero light verb in early child Japanese. *ICU Language Research Bulletin* 13:103-116.

Sells, Peter. 1990. More on light verbs and θ-marking. Manuscript, Stanford University.

Teramura, Hideo. 1992. *Teramura Hideo ronbun-shu* 1. Tokyo: Kurosio Syuppan.

Tsujimura, Natsuko. 1992. Licensing nominal clauses: The case of deverbal nominals in Japanese. *Natural Language and Linguistic Theory* 10:477-522.

Uchida, Yoshiko and Mineharu Nakayama. 1993. Japanese verbal noun constructions. *Linguistics* 31:623-666.

Yamashita, Yoshie. 1995. The Emergence of Syntactic Categories: Evidence from the Acquisition of Japanese. Doctoral dissertation, University of Hawaii.

Scrambling of Adjuncts and Last Resort*

KOJI SUGISAKI
University of Connecticut

1. Introduction

It has been assumed since Chomsky (1986) that movement operations are constrained by the principle of Last Resort, which states that movement is possible only when an element has some driving force to move. Given this assumption, scrambling in Japanese has been a serious problem, since it has been considered as a paradigm case of strictly optional movement (Harada 1977, Saito 1985). An example of scrambling in Japanese is given in (1); (1a) is a sentence with basic word order, and (1b) is an instance of long-distance scrambling[1], in which the object of the embedded clause appears in the sentence-initial position:

(1) a. John-ga [Mary-ga ano ringo-o tabeta to] itta.
John-NOM Mary-NOM that apple-ACC ate that said
'John said that Mary ate that apple.'

* I would like to thank Cedric Boeckx, Željko Bošković, Miwa Isobe, Howard Lasnik, Nobuhiro Miyoshi, Masao Ochi, and William Snyder for their valuable comments. I am also grateful to the audience at the 9th JK Linguistics Conference for stimulating questions. The usual disclaimers apply.

[1] Long-distance scrambling (i.e. scrambling that crosses clause boundary) is the main concern of this paper, and we do not discuss the cases of short-distance (i.e. clause-internal) scrambling.

b. Ano ringo-o John-ga [Mary-ga tabeta to] itta.
That apple-ACC John-NOM Mary-NOM ate that said

There are two recent approaches to this optionality of scrambling. One approach, discussed in Fukui (1993) and Saito and Fukui (1998), is to maintain the traditional view that scrambling is an optional movement, and to derive this optionality from the basic pattern of phrase structure in Japanese. The other approach, adopted in Bošković and Takahashi (1998, henceforth B&T), is to view the movement embodied in scrambling constructions as an instance of Last Resort. More specifically, they propose that scrambling is an LF lowering operation driven by the checking of theta-features.

B&T's analysis makes an interesting prediction with respect to the scrambling of adjuncts. As observed by Saito (1985), in the usual case adjuncts cannot undergo long-distance scrambling, and B&T attribute this to the lack of features that could motivate their LF movements. However, their analysis predicts that even adjuncts can be long-distance-scrambled if they have some driving force to "go back" to their own clauses. In this paper, I will argue that this prediction is borne out. Specifically, I will present some data from Japanese, which I believe are new, that show that long-distance scrambling of non-*wh* adjuncts, which is usually impossible, becomes possible when such adjuncts contain an item that has an independent driving force. I argue that these facts follow from and provide support for B&T's analysis of scrambling which claims that scrambling is a Last Resort operation.

This paper is organized as follows. In section 2, I summarize the approaches proposed by Fukui (1993) and Saito and Fukui (1998). Section 3 is a summary of B&T's analysis. In section 4, I discuss Tanaka's (1997) analysis of Japanese negative polarity item (NPI) *sika-nai*, which I crucially make use of in my data. In section 5, I present my data, which involve the interaction of adjuncts and the NPI *sika-nai*. Section 6 is the conclusion.

2. Scrambling as an Optional Movement: Fukui (1993) and Saito and Fukui (1998)

Fukui (1993) proposes the following "measure of cost" in order to explain the optionality of certain movement operations:

(2) *The parameter value preservation (PVP) measure* (Fukui 1993: 400)
A grammatical operation (Move α, in particular) that creates a structure that is inconsistent with the value of a given parameter in a language is costly in the language, whereas one that produces a structure consistent with the parameter value is costless.

It is assumed that if an application of Move α is evaluated as costless by the PVP measure, then it can in principle be an optional operation, but if an application of Move α is evaluated as costly by this measure, then this application must be "forced" (obligatory) and cannot be optional. Fukui discusses the interaction of the PVP measure with the head-complement parameter. Given this parameter, the PVP measure states that a movement that follows the direction of the complement creates a structure that is consistent with the value of the head-complement parameter in that language and hence in principle is optional. For example, in head-initial languages like English, rightward movements are predicted to be optional, whereas in head-final languages like Japanese, leftward movements are predicted to be free. Fukui claims that this prediction from the PVP measure correctly captures the distribution of optional movements in English and Japanese. English has the optional operations of Extraposition and Heavy NP Shift, which are rightward movements, and Japanese has scrambling, which is an optional leftward movement.

Saito and Fukui (1998) try to capture Fukui's (1993) basic intuition within the framework of the Minimalist Program (Chomsky 1995). They incorporate the head-complement parameter into the bare phrase structure theory (Chomsky 1994) as follows (Saito and Fukui 1998: 452):

(3) $K = \{\gamma, <\alpha, \beta>\}$, where $\gamma \in \{\alpha, \beta\}$.
   a. $\gamma = \alpha$: head-initial, left-headed
   b. $\gamma = \beta$: head-final, right-headed

(3) is a parameter attached to the operation *Merge*. Merge is a structure-building operation which combines two elements α and β and projects one of them as the "head". If the value (3a) is taken, when the elements α and β are combined by Merge, the right element α always projects as the head and this results in a head-initial language. If the value (3b) is chosen, the left element β always becomes the head and this results in a head-final language. In addition to (3), they adopt the following assumption from Chomsky (1995; Ch. 4):

(4) The operation Move is subject to Last Resort, whereas Merge is not (i.e. free).

Based on these two assumptions, Saito and Fukui claim that the application of Move that moves an element to the direction of the complement counts as "Merge" for the purpose of (4); only the application of Move that moves elements against the direction of the complement counts as "Move" with respect to (4). Thus, Heavy NP Shift in English and scrambling in Japanese, which follow the direction of the complement in each language, count as "Merge" and are exempted from the principle of

Last Resort.

The analyses proposed in Fukui (1993) and in Saito and Fukui (1998) are successful in capturing the distribution of optional movements in English and Japanese. However, if we restrict our attention to scrambling in Japanese, there is a property that remains to be explained. As Miyara (1982) and Saito (1985) observe, whereas arguments can undergo long-distance scrambling, adjuncts cannot:

(5) a. John-ga [Mary-ga isoide ano ringo-o tabeta to] itta.
John-NOM Mary-NOM quickly that apple-ACC ate that said
'John said that Mary quickly ate that apple.'
b. Ano ringo-o John-ga [Mary-ga isoide tabeta to] itta.
That apple-ACC John-NOM Mary-NOM quickly ate that said
c. Isoide John-ga [Mary-ga ano ringo-o tabeta to] itta.
Quickly John-NOM Mary-NOM that apple-ACC ate that said
'*John said that Mary quickly ate that apple.'
'John said quickly that Mary ate that apple.'

This contrast between arguments and adjuncts would require the following additional stipulation to Fukui's and Saito and Fukui's analyses, which argue that scrambling is an optional operation:

(6) Adjuncts cannot undergo long-distance scrambling.

3. Scrambling as an Instance of Last Resort: Bošković and Takahashi (1998)

In contrast to Fukui (1993) and Saito and Fukui (1998), Bošković and Takahashi (1998) argue that scrambling is an instance of Last Resort[2]. Specifically, they propose the following derivation with respect to long-distance scrambling (Bošković and Takahashi 1998; 350):

(7) Numeration → (a) → (c) (LF); → (b) (PF)
a. [$_{IP}$ Sono hon-o [$_{IP}$ John-ga [$_{CP}$[$_{IP}$ Mary-ga [$_{VP}$ [$_{V}$ katta]]]
that book-ACC John-NOM Mary-NOM bought
to] omotteiru]]
that thinks
b. sono hon-o John-ga Mary-ga katta to omotteiru
c. [$_{IP}$ John-ga [$_{CP}$ [$_{IP}$ Mary-ga [$_{VP}$ sono hon-o [$_{V}$ katta]]] to] omotteiru]
'John thinks that Mary bought the book.'

[2] Miyagawa (1997) also takes this position, and claims that A-scrambling is driven by "a Case agreement feature" and A'-scrambling is motivated by "something like focus." I will focus on B&T's approach in this paper.

In B&T's analysis, "scrambled" phrases are directly base-generated in their surface position and undergo LF lowering. This derivation is possible if we adopt the following assumptions. First, there is no condition that specifically bans lowering; certain lowering cases are ruled out by independent principles of grammar. For example, overt lowering is ruled out by considerations of linear ordering[3], and lowering of operators is excluded by the ban on vacuous quantification and the Proper Binding Condition. Second, as suggested by Lasnik and Saito (1992), movement does not leave a trace when no principle requires it. Third, movement into theta-positions is possible. In the pre-minimalist framework, such movement was ruled out by the Theta Criterion and the Projection Principle (Chomsky 1981), which require all theta-roles to be assigned at D-structure. Within the Minimalist system that dispenses with D-structure and S-structure, there is nothing intrinsically incompatible with movement into theta-positions. Fourth, theta-roles are formal features that have the ability to drive movements.

The first two assumptions make the LF lowering deriving (7c) possible. No principle requires this movement to leave a trace. Then, the Proper Binding Condition is inapplicable here, and hence the movement is legitimate. The latter two assumptions assign motivation to this LF movement. The LF movement deriving (7c) is an instance of movement into theta-position, driven by the need to check theta-features. In sum, B&T's analysis claims that long-distance scrambling is an LF lowering operation driven by the checking of theta-features.

B&T's approach to scrambling has various conceptual and empirical advantages. I note here one argument from each of these domains. One of the conceptual arguments for their approach is that their analysis makes scrambling fully consistent with the principle of Last Resort. Thus, they can eliminate an exception to this general principle. One of the empirical advantages is that their analysis provides a natural account for the impossibility of long-distance scrambling of adjuncts, exemplified in (5) and repeated here as (8):

(8) a. John-ga [Mary-ga isoide ano ringo-o tabeta to] itta.
John-NOM Mary-NOM quickly that apple-ACC ate that said
'John said that Mary quickly ate that apple.'
b. Isoide John-ga [Mary-ga ano ringo-o tabeta to] itta.
Quickly John-NOM Mary-NOM that apple-ACC ate that said
'*John said that Mary quickly ate that apple.'
'John said quickly that Mary ate that apple.'

---

[3] B&T suggest that if Kayne's (1994) theory of word ordering and Epstein's (in press) theory of c-command are adopted, an element that is attached to an embedded category will enter into no c-command relation with any higher elements, thus will cause an LCA violation.

In contrast to "scrambled" arguments, which have theta-features to drive their LF movements, adjuncts do not have any features (e.g. Case-features or theta-features) that could motivate their LF lowering. Thus, the principle of Last Resort prevents them from moving into the embedded clause.

B&T's account makes the following prediction with respect to the scrambling of adjuncts: adjuncts can be long-distance-scrambled only when they are assigned some driving force to lower into the embedded clause. B&T present one piece of evidence that confirms this prediction, which they attribute to Mamoru Saito (personal communication):

(9) ? Naze Mary-ga [John-ga sono setu-o sinziteiru ka] sitteiru.
Why Mary-NOM John-NOM that theory-ACC believes Q knows
'Mary knows why John believes in that theory.'
(Bošković and Takahashi 1998: 356)

In (9) the adjunct *wh*-phrase must be interpreted in the embedded clause, which is marked as interrogative. As specified, this sentence is only slightly marginal, even though this example involves long-distance scrambling of an adjunct. The grammaticality of this example is expected under B&T's analysis, since the adjunct *naze* has a formal feature (i.e. [+*wh*] feature) that is not checked in its base-generated, matrix IP-adjoined position and hence this feature can motivate the LF movement of *naze*.

In section 5, I present new evidence that provides further confirmation of B&T's prediction with respect to the scrambling of adjuncts. Before presenting my data, I will summarize in the next section Tanaka's (1997) analysis of Japanese NPI *sika-nai*, which plays a crucial role in my data.

4. Japanese NPI *sika-nai*

4.1 The distribution of *sika-nai*

-Sika is a negative polarity item (NPI) in Japanese which is licensed by the negative marker *nai* attached to a predicate. *–Sika*, taken together with *–nai*, means 'only'. Examples of the *sika-nai* construction are given in (10) and (11):

(10) a. John-sika ringo-o tabe-nai (koto)
John-NPI apple-ACC eat-NEG (fact)
'Only John eats apples.'
b. John-ga ringo-sika tabe-nai (koto)
John-NOM apple-NPI eat-NEG (fact)
'John eats only apples.'

(11) a. Hanako-ga [John-sika ringo-o tabe-nai to] omotta (koto)
Hanako-NOM John-NPI apple-ACC eat-NEG that thought (fact)
'Hanako thought that only John eats apples.'

b. Hanako-ga [John-ga ringo-sika tabe-nai to] omotta (koto)
Hanako-NOM John-NOM apple-NPI eat-NEG that thought (fact)
'Hanako thought that John eats only apples.'

In order to account for the distribution of *sika-nai*, various constraints have been proposed[4]. Tanaka (1997) has found that the distribution of *sika-nai* particles is constrained by various island constraints. First, *sika-nai* obeys the Complex NP Constraint:

(12) a. [[[Uma-ga biiru-o nomu]-koto]-sika omosiroku]-nai (koto)[5]
Horse-NOM beer-ACC drink fact NPI interesting NEG
'The only interesting thing is that the horse drinks beer.'
b. *[[[Uma-ga biiru-sika nomu]-koto]-ga omosiroku]-nai (koto)
Horse-NOM beer-NPI drink fact NOM interesting NEG
'Only beer is such that it is interesting that the horse drinks it.'
(Tanaka 1997: 149)

Second, *sika-nai* is constrained by *Wh*-island Condition:

(13) a. (?)Taroo-ga [Hanako-sika kuru]-to iwa-nai (koto)[6]
Taroo-NOM Hanako-NPI come COMP say NEG
'Taroo says that only Hanako will come.'
b. *Taroo-ga Hanako-sika kuru-ka(dooka) iwa-nai (koto)
Taroo-NOM Hanako-NPI come whether say NEG
'Taro says whether only Hanako will come.'
(Tanaka 1997: 150)

Third, *sika-nai* also obeys Adjunct Condition:

(14) * Taroo-ga [Hanako-sika LGB-o yomu]-mae-ni sono-hon-o
Taroo-NOM Hanako-NPI LGB-ACC read before the book-ACC
yoma-nai (koto)
read NEG
'Taroo reads LGB before only Hanako reads the book.'
(Tanaka 1997: 151)

In order to explain the fact that the distribution of *sika-nai* obeys various islands, Tanaka proposes the derivation shown in (16), essentially following

---

[4] For discussion of *sika-nai*, see Aoyagi and Ishii (1993), Kato (1979, 1994), Maki (1994), Muraki (1978), Oyakawa (1975), Takahashi (1990), Tanaka (1997), among others.
[5] Tanaka (1997) treats *–sika* as a focus marker. However, all other studies listed in note 4 treat this as a NPI. Following these studies, I gloss *–sika* as NPI.
[6] The example (13a) indicates that *sika-nai* is not clause bound. Tanaka (1997: 148) argues that *iwu* 'say' is a non-neg-raising verb and thus the example like (13a) would exclude the possibility of neg-raising.

Watanabe's (1992) analysis of *wh*-phrases in Japanese:

(15) Taroo-sika LGB-o yoma-nai (koto)
Taroo-NPI LGB-ACC read-NEG
'Only Taroo reads LGB.'

(16) a. Operator Movement (overt syntax)
Taroo-[sika t_i] LGB-o yoma-nai-Op_i
b. *sika*-phrase raising (LF)
t_i LGB-o yoma-nai-[Taroo-sika]$_i$

In overt syntax, an invisible operator moves from *sika*-phrase to the specifier of NegP to fulfill some sort of specifier-head agreement, and at LF, the entire *sika*-phrase moves to that position and replaces the operator. Hence, the distribution of *sika-nai* is constrained by islands for movements.

4.2. Adjuncts and *sika-nai*

In all the examples discussed above, *-sika* is attached to nominal elements. However, one interesting property of *–sika* particle that is not well discussed in the literature is that it can also attach to some (but not many) adjuncts. For example, manner adverbs like *yukkurito* (slowly) and *kyuuni* (suddenly), and frequency adverbs like *nikai* (twice) can host *–sika* particle:

(17) a. John-ga yukkurito booru-o nageta.
John-NOM slowly ball-ACC threw
'John threw a ball slowly.'
b. John-ga yukkurito-sika booru-o nage-nak-atta.
John-NOM slowly-NPI ball-ACC throw-NEG-PAST
'John threw the ball only slowly.'

(18) a. John-ga kyuuni nakidasita.
John-NOM suddenly started-to-cry
'John suddenly started crying.'
b. John-ga kyuuni-sika nakidasa-nak-atta.
John-NOM suddenly-NPI start-to-cry-NEG-PAST
'John started crying only suddenly.'

(19) a. John-ga nikai Mary-ni kisushita.
John-NOM twice Mary-DAT kissed
'John kissed Mary twice.'
b. John-ga nikai-sika Mary-ni kisushi-nak-atta.
John-NOM twice-NPI Mary-DAT kiss-NEG-PAST
'John kissed Mary only twice.'

This property of *–sika* particle, combined with Tanaka's hypothesis that *–sika* phrase moves to Neg at LF, makes an interesting prediction with respect to long-distance scrambling of adjuncts. This is the topic of the next section.

5. *Sika-nai* and the Scrambling of Adjuncts

We have seen in section 3 that B&T's analysis makes the following prediction with respect to the long-distance scrambling of adjuncts:

(20) Adjuncts can be long-distance-scrambled only when they are assigned some driving force to lower into the embedded clause at LF.

We have also seen Tanaka's analysis of *sika-nai*, which claims that *–sika* particle has the driving force to move the entire phrase to the specifier of NegP at LF. Furthermore, we have observed that there are several adjuncts that can host *–sika* particle. Given these, B&T's analysis predicts the following:

(21) Non-*wh* adjuncts, which are otherwise unable to undergo long-distance scrambling, can be long-distance-scrambled when they contain *–sika* particle.

The data that I have collected, which are given below, show that this prediction is borne out:

(22) a. Mary-ga [John-ga yukkurito booru-o nageta to] itta.
Mary-NOM John-NOM slowly ball-ACC threw that said
'Mary said that John slowly threw a ball.'
b. Yukkurito Mary-ga [John-ga booru-o nageta to] itta.
Slowly Mary-NOM John-NOM ball-ACC threw that said
'*Mary said that John slowly threw a ball.'
'Mary said slowly that John threw a ball.'
c. Yukkurito-sika Mary-ga [John-ga booru-o nage-nak-atta to] itta.
Slowly-NPI M-NOM J-NOM ball-ACC throw-NEG-PAST that said
'Mary said that John only slowly threw a ball.'

(23) a. Mary-ga [John-ga kyuuni nakidasita to] itta.
Mary-NOM John-NOM suddenly started-to-cry that said
'Mary said that John suddenly started crying.'
b. Kyuuni Mary-ga [John-ga nakidasita to] itta.
Suddenly Mary-NOM John-NOM started-to-cry that said
'*Mary said that John suddenly started crying.'
'Mary suddenly said that John started crying.'
c. Kyuuni-sika Mary-ga [John-ga nakidasa-nak-atta to] itta.
Suddenly-NPI Mary-NOM John-NOM start-to-cry-NEG-PAST that said
'Mary said that John only suddenly started crying.'

(24) a. Mary-ga [John-ga nikai Susan-ni kisushita to] itta.
Mary-NOM John-NOM twice Susan-DAT kissed that said
'Mary said [that John kissed Susan twice].'

b. Nikai Mary-ga [John-ga Susan-ni kisushita to] itta.
Twice Mary-NOM John-NOM Susan-DAT kissed that said
'Mary said twice that John kissed Susan.'
'*Mary said [that John kissed Susan twice].'

c. Nikai-sika Mary-ga [John-ga Susan-ni kisushi-nak-atta to] itta.
Twice-NPI Mary-NOM John-NOM Susan-DAT kiss-NEG-PAST that said
'Mary said [that John kissed Susan only twice].'

The contrast between (b) and (c) in (22) to (24) would be unexpected under Fukui's and Saito and Fukui's analyses, which would require the general ban on long-distance scrambling of adjuncts as in (6). On the other hand, this contrast is exactly what B&T's analysis predicts. Thus, the data presented above constitute another piece of evidence that supports B&T's Last Resort approach to scrambling.

6. Conclusion

In this paper, I have presented a new piece of evidence from Japanese that shows that there is no general ban on long-distance scrambling of adjuncts. My data have shown that even non-*wh* adjuncts can be long-distance-scrambled when they contain an item that has a driving force to lower into the embedded clause at LF. This generalization follows from and in turn provides support for Bošković and Takahashi's (1998) analysis of scrambling which claims that scrambling is a Last Resort operation.

References

Aoyagi, Hiroshi and Toru Ishii. 1993. On NPI Licensing in Japanese. Paper presented at *4th Japanese /Korean Linguistics Conference*.

Bošković, Željko and Daiko Takahashi. 1998. Scrambling and Last Resort. *Linguistic Inquiry* 29: 347-366.

Chomsky, Noam. 1981. *Lectures on Government and Binding*. Dordrecht: Foris.

Chomsky, Noam. 1986. *Knowledge of Language: Its Nature, Origin, and Use*. New York: Praeger.

Chomsky, Noam. 1994. Bare Phrase Structure. *MIT Occasional Papers in Linguistics* 5. Published in G. Webelhuth, ed., 1995, *Government and Binding Theory and the Minimalist Program*. Oxford: Blackwell.

Chomsky, Noam. 1995. *The Minimalist Program*. Cambridge, Mass.: MIT Press.

Epstein, Samuel D. In press. Un-principled Syntax and the Derivation of Syntactic Relations. In M.A. Browning ed., *Working Minimalism*. Cambridge, Mass.: MIT Press.

Fukui, Naoki. 1993. Parameters and Optionality. *Linguistic Inquiry* 24: 399-420.

Harada, Shin-ichi. 1977. Nihongo-ni 'henkei'-wa hituyoo-da.(Transformations are necessary in Japanese.) *Gengo* 6: 11-12.

Kato, Yasuhiko. 1979. Sika-nai Construction and a Theory of Binding. *Sophia Linguistica* 10: 92-104.

Kato, Yasuhiko. 1994. Negative Polarity and Movement. *MIT Working Papers in Linguistics* 24: 101-120.

Kayne, Richard. 1994. *The Antisymmetry of Syntax*. Cambridge, Mass.: MIT Press.

Lasnik, Howard. and Mamoru Saito. 1992. *Move α*. Cambridge, Mass.: MIT Press.

Maki, Hideki. 1994. Interaction of Negative Polarity Items and *Wh*-phrases: an Argument for the Linear Crossing Constraint. Ms., University of Connecticut, Storrs.

Miyagawa, Sigeru. 1997. Against Optional Scrambling. *Linguistic Inquiry* 28: 1-25.

Miyara, Sinsyo. 1982. Reordering in Japanese. *Linguistic Analysis* 9: 307-340.

Muraki, Masatake. 1978. The Sika nai Construction and the Predicate Restructuring. In J. Hinds and I. Howard eds., *Problems in Japanese Syntax and Semantics*. Tokyo: Kaitakusha.

Oyakawa, Takatsugu. 1975. On the Japanese Sika-nai Construction. *Gengo Kenkyu* 67: 1-20.

Saito, Mamoru. 1985. *Some Asymmetries in Japanese and their Theoretical Implications*. Doctoral dissertation, MIT.

Saito, Mamoru. and Naoki Fukui. 1998. Order in Phrase Structure and Movement. *Linguistic Inquiry* 29: 439-474.

Takahashi, Daiko. 1990. Negative Polarity, Phrase Structure, and the ECP. *English Linguistics* 7: 129-146.

Tanaka, Hidekazu. 1997. Invisible Movement in *Sika-nai* and the Linear Crossing Constraint. *Journal of East Asian Linguistics* 6: 143-188.

Watanabe, Akira. 1992. Subjacency and S-structure Movement of *Wh*-in-situ. *Journal of East Asian Linguistics* 1: 255-291.

Inalienable Possession Construction with 'do'

TAKAE TSUJIOKA
Georgetown University

1. Introduction

In Japanese, a verb that corresponds to English 'do', *su-*, can be used to mean 'wear' or 'put on' for objects such as jewelry and ties, as a substitute for verbs of clothing (Kageyama 1980). This is shown in (1).

(1) a. John ga aoi iyaringu o si-te i-ru
J. NOM blue earring ACC do-PART be-PRES
"John is wearing blue earrings."

b. John ga nekutai o si-te i-ru
J. NOM tie ACC do-PART be-PRES
"John is wearing a tie."

c. John ga yubiwa o si-te i-ru
J. NOM ring ACC do-PART be-PRES
"John is wearing a ring."

In (2), the same verb is used in expressions of inalienable possession:

(2) a. John ga aoi me o si-te i-ru
J. NOM blue eye ACC do-PART be-PRES
"John is blue-eyed."

b. John ga marui kao o si-te i-ru
J. NOM round face ACC do-PART be-PRES
"John is round-faced."

c. John ga nagai asi o si-te i-ru
J. NOM long leg ACC do-PART be-PRES
"John is long-legged."

For example, in (2a), *ao-i me* denotes an inalienable property of *John*.

The literature on Verbal Noun Constructions (Uchida & Nakayama 1993; Kageyama 1993), in which the argument structure of the verb *su-* is frequently discussed, treats *su-* in both cases as a similar instance of a thematically heavy verb. Interestingly, however, the counterpart of (1) is available in Korean, whereas that of (2) is ill-formed, as in (3) and (4).

(3) a. John-i phalan kwuykeli-lul ha-ko iss-ta
J.-NOM blue earring-ACC do-PART be-PRES
"John is wearing blue earrings."

b. John-i necktie-lul ha-ko iss-ta
J.-NOM tie-ACC do-PART be-PRES
"John is wearing a tie."

c. John-i panci-lul ha-ko iss-ta
J.-NOM ring-ACC do-PART be-PRES
"John is wearing a ring."

(4) a. *John-i phalan nwun-lul ha-ko iss-ta
J.-NOM blue eye-ACC do-PART be-DECL
intended reading: "John is blue-eyed."

b. *John-i tongkulan elkwul -ul ha-ko iss-ta
J.-NOM round face-ACC do-PART be-PRES
intended reading: "John is round-faced."

c. *John-i kin tali-lul ha-ko iss-ta
J.-NOM long leg-ACC do-PART be-PRES
intended reading: "John is long-legged."

The contrast between (2) and (4) is puzzling given striking typological similarities between Japanese and Korean, as instantiated in the parallelism between (1) and (3) itself.

In this paper, I will investigate whether it is correct to treat (2) on a par with (1), as well as why the sentences in (4) are unavailable in Korean.

2. Structural Discrepancies

Let us take a closer look at (1) and (2). For ease of exposition, I will refer to them as “Dressing Expression (DE)” and “Inalienable Possession Construction (IPC),” respectively. Given the surface identity of the two, one might posit that the IPC is somehow derivative of the DE - for instance, that ‘having blue eyes’ is ‘wearing blue eyes’, figuratively speaking. In other words, one might assume that the verb *su-* involved in the two cases is of a similar kind, the substitute for a garden-variety transitive verb denoting “wear”. As mentioned earlier, such grouping is often done, though in passing, in the literature on verbal noun constructions (Uchida & Nakayama 1993; Kageyama 1993).

There are two readily observable differences between the DE and the IPC, which have more to do with semantic/pragmatic factors than structural differences (Kageyama 1990, Tsunoda 1996). First, the modifier on the accusative-marked noun phrase is necessary for the sentences to be felicitous in the IPC, but not for the DE. (5) illustrates this point.

(5) a. John ga (aoi) iyaringu o si-te i-ru
J. NOM (blue) earring ACC do-PART be-PRES
“John is wearing (blue) earrings.”

b. John ga *(aoi) me o si-te i-ru
J. NOM (blue) eye ACC do-PART be-PRES
“John is *(blue)-eyed.”

The obligatoriness of modifiers, however, may have to do with a sort of pragmatic informativeness constraint like “Do not tell listeners what they already know”. Such a constraint was proposed by Ljung (1976) to account for similar restrictions on English bahuvrihi compounds such as *blue-eyed*. Presumably, every man has eyes, but not all men have earrings. Hence, without the modifier (5a) is still informative enough, but not (5b).

The second difference between the DE and the IPC has to do with the tense/aspectual forms of *su-*. The range of possible forms of *su-* is more restricted in the IPC than in the DE. While *su-* in the DE can appear in all the possible tense/aspectual forms in Japanese as shown in (6a) and (7a), *su-* in the IPC must accompany *-te iru* in the matrix context as shown in (6b). The *-ta* form is possible in the pre-nominal modification as shown in (7b):

(6) a. John ga aoi iyaringu o **su-ru/si-ta/si-te i-ru**

do-PRES/do-PAST/do-PART be-PRES

b. John ga aoi me o ***su-ru/*si-ta/si-te i-ru**

do-PRES/do-PAST/do-PART be-PRES

(7) a. [aoi iyaringu o **su-ru/si-ta/si-te i-ru**] syoozyo

do-PRES/do-PAST/do-PART be-PRES girl

"the girl who wears/wore/is wearing blue earrings"

b. [aoi me o ***su-ru/si-ta/si-te i-ru**] syoozyo

do-PRES/do-PAST/do-PART be-PRES girl

"the blue-eyed girl/the girl who is blue-eyed"

This contrast is largely due to the ambiguity of *si-te i-ru* in the DE. *Iyaringu o si-te iru* can be interpreted in two different ways: One is an eventive, progressive interpretation, which can be translated as 'putting on the earrings'. The other is a stative interpretation, 'wearing the earrings'. Those forms of *su-* available for the DE but not for the IPC all involve eventive readings. The narrower range of verbal forms available in the IPC may be attributed to the fact that there is no comparable event of 'putting on blue eyes'.

So far, the data in (5)-(7) can all be explained by pragmatic/semantic factors, and do not directly require structural accounts. However, a closer examination reveals that there are other differences between the DE and the IPC. As shown in (8b)-(10b), the accusative marked phrase in the IPC cannot be scrambled, topicalized, or relativized. In other words, the accusative phrase resists extraction. No such restriction holds for the DE.

(8) a. aoi iyaringu o John ga si-te i-ru (Scrambling)

blue earring ACC J. NOM do-PART be-PRES

"John is wearing blue earrings."

b. *aoi me o John ga si-te i-ru

blue eye ACC J. NOM do-PART be-PRES

(9) a. [aoi iyaringu wa] syoozyo ga t_i si-te i-ru (Topicalization)

blue earrings TOP girl NOM do-PART be-PRES

"As for the blue earrings, the girl is wearing them."

b. *[aoi me wa] syoozyo ga t_i si-te-i-ru

blue eye TOP girl NOM do-PART-be-PRES

(10) a. [OP$_i$ syoozyo ga t$_i$ si-te i-ru] aoi iyaringu$_i$ (Relativization)
girl NOM ACC do-PART be-PRES blue earrings
"the pretty earrings which the girl is wearing"

b. *[OP$_i$ syoozyo ga t$_i$ si-te i-ru] aoi me$_i$
girl NOM do-PART be-PRES blue eye

This contrast strongly suggests that there are some structural discrepancies between the DE and the IPC, despite their surface identity. Our task now is to present a structural account of the IPC which can accommodate the facts in (8)-(10).

3. Analysis

I propose that the observed syntactic differences are mainly due to two factors: First, the DE in (1) contains a thematic null verb, whereas no such verb is present in the IPC in (2). Second, the IPC involves relational nouns which act as predicative nominals, whereas the DE does not.

Adopting basic tenets of the Minimalist Program (Chomsky 1995), the structure for the DE (with stative reading) is assumed to be as in (11).

(11)

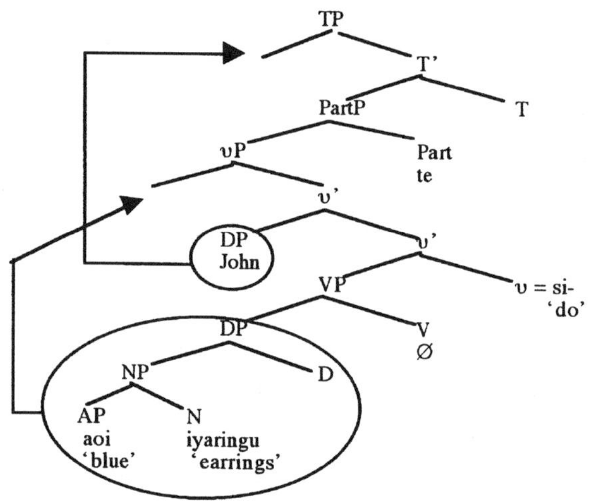

Following Chomsky (1995), I assume that the external argument is introduced by small υ, and raises to the Spec of TP to check Case and EPP features of T. The internal argument, on the other hand, is base-generated in the Spec of VP, and raises to the Spec of small υ to check Case features of small υ. In addition, there are some additional assumptions I make, which are rather immaterial to the present discussion. First, following Kinsui (1995), I regard *-te i-ru* in this case as a tensed version of the adjectival verb in Teramura's (1984) sense. Thus, *i-ru* here is a carrier of tense features. I postulate that *-te* projects a participial phrase, though its exact label is not crucial. Futhermore, I regard *-te* and the prenominal *-ta* with stative interpretation to be allomorphic variants (Tsujioka & Shibuya 1999). I also assume that there is a thematic, but phonologically null verb which corresponds to a verb of Dressing. On the other hand, *su-* (*si-* before *te*) is regarded as the spell-out of a functional category small *υ* when no phonologically overt verb raises to support it (Chomsky 1995; Kratzer 1996; Hale and Keyser 1993 among others).

Let us now turn to the proposed structure for (2a) shown in (12).

(12)

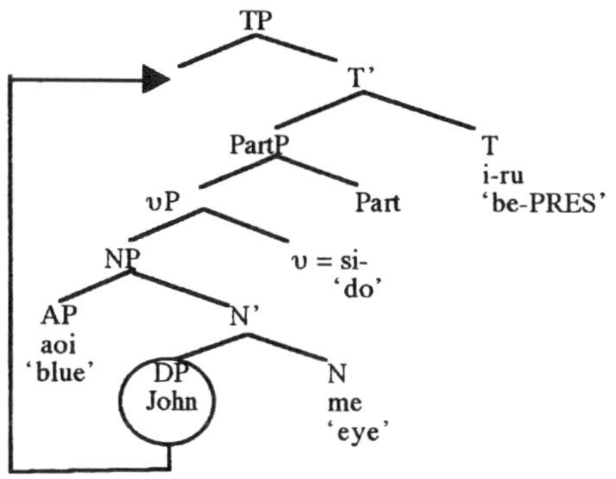

Following Tellier (1998), Vergnaud & Zubizaretta (1992), and Barker (1995) among many others, I assume that relational nouns such as body part nouns (e.g., *face, eye, leg*) take their own argument, conveniently labeled as "possessor". In (12), for example, *me* 'eye' is a relational noun, and theta-licenses the possessor *John.*

The first structural discrepancy between (11) and (12) is that there is a null V that corresponds to a default Dressing verb in (11), whereas no such verb is present in (12). This difference is evidenced in the fact that *su-* in (1a) can be substituted by a content verb, whereas *su-* in (2a) cannot.

(13) Substitution by a content verb (Tsujioka & Shibuya 1999)

a. John ga aoi iyaringu o mot/tuke/hame -te i-ru

J. NOM blue earring ACC have/wear/put on -PART be-PRES

"John has/is wearing/has put on pretty earrings"

b. *John ga aoi me o mot/tuke/hame -te i-ru

J. NOM blue eye ACC have/wear/put on PART be-PRES

Since there seems to be no semantic reason to postulate a null verb in the inalienable possession case, I propose that the relational noun phrase, being a predicative nominal, directly merges with small *υ*.

The second difference between (11) and (12) is as follows: the projection of a relational noun is categorically NP in (12), whereas the projection of a clothing nominal is a DP in (11). This claim is in accordance with a commonly-held view that predicative nominals project NPs, not DPs (Stowell 1989, Longobardi 1994). The fact that relational noun phrases are non-referential, and thus, incompatible with demonstratives or numerals, supports the predicative NP status of the relational noun projection.

(14) Compatibility with demonstratives or numerals

a. John ga sono/hutatu aoi iyaringu o si-te i-ru

J. NOM that/two blue earrings ACC do-PART be-PRES

"John is wearing that/two pairs of blue earrings."

b. *John ga sono/hutatu aoi me o si-te i-ru

J. NOM that/two blue eye ACC do-PART be-PRES

Finally, and most importantly, I claim that the nominative marked DP is base-generated as a sister to the relational noun *me* 'eye' in (12), whereas it is introduced as an external argument by the functional category small *υ* in (11). In (12), *John* moves to the Spec of T to check NOM Case features and EPP features of T. There are two pieces of evidence which together support this possessor raising analysis. Firstly, it is commonly argued that only thematically saturated noun phrases allow appositive modification (Vergaud & Zubizarretta 1992; J. H-S Yoon 1989; and J.-M. Yoon 1997). If such a view is right, the presence of appositive modification in the IPC shows that the thematic grid of the relational noun is satisfied within its projection. As I have already pointed out, the appositive modification in the IPC is not only possible but obligatory.

Secondly, if we assume that the possessor DP moves out of the relational noun projection in the overt syntax, that entails that the relational noun phrase contains a trace of the possessor DP as shown in (15).

(15) possessor$_i$ [$_{NP}$ t$_i$ RN]

Then, the non-extractability of the relational noun phrase observed in (8b-10b) can be naturally explained by (any re-interpretation of) the Proper Binding Condition (PBC) (Fiengo 1977; Lasnik & Saito 1992). As shown in (16), such movement creates an unbound trace (= bold-faced).

(16) *[$_{NP}$ **t$_i$** RN]$_j$ possessor$_i$ t$_j$

Under the possessor raising analysis, therefore, the ungrammaticality of (8b) is accounted for if one assumes that scrambling involves movement; scrambling of the relational noun DP renders the trace of the possessor unbound as shown in (16). In passing, I would like to point out that (8b) is predicted to be ungrammatical even under a theory of 'scrambling' that base-generates the ACC-phrase in its visible position (e.g., Boskovic & Takahashi 1998). This is because in order to realize the order of (8b), an illicit *overt* lowering of the possessor would be necessary.

Researchers have proposed possessor-raising analyses for various constructions across languages (Szalbolcsi 1983; Kitahara 1990; Ura 1996).

Here, inspired by Ura's (1996) minimalist interpretation of possessor-raising, I characterize the mechanism of possessor raising involved in (12) as follows: In the configuration shown in (17), the embedded category Y can become visible to attraction provided that there is no intervening features of the same kind left in X.

(17) [XP ... [YP ... Y ...] ... X][1]

4. Rejecting the Alternatives

In this section, I consider three alternatives to the proposed analysis and argue that each has difficulties in its application.

First, besides positing a trace of the possessor within the RN projection, there is another way in which the RN phrase can be thematically saturated: that is to assume that the RN theta-marks an internal empty pronominal, which is in turn bound by the possessor as schematized in (18).

(18) possessor$_i$ [$_{DP}$ pro/PRO$_i$ RN]

I refer to this kind of analyses as the *pro*-binding approach. The *pro*-binding account has often been proposed for the Possessive Dative Constructions in Romance (cf. Landau 1999).

The *pro*-binding analysis, however, does not make the right prediction about the non-extractability of the relational noun phrase. Under the *pro*-binding approach, one may postulate that the non-extractability of the relational noun phrase results from *pro* not being bound in the configuration in (19).

(19) [$_{DP}$ pro/PRO$_i$ RN]$_j$ possessor$_i$ t_j

However, we normally observe a reconstruction effect on local scrambling involving a subject binder as shown in (20).

(20) a. John$_i$ ga [pro$_i$ hahaoya] o tasuke-ta

J.-NOM mother ACC help-PAST

"John helped his mother."

b. [pro$_i$ hahaoya o]$_j$ John$_i$ ga t_j tasuke-ta

The binding relationship between *John* and *pro* is not affected by scrambling in (20b). Thus, if the same effect is applicable to (8b), scrambling is wrongly predicted to be possible in the configuration in (21).

(21) [DP [AP aoi] *pro*/PRO$_i$ me]] o [DP John$_i$] ga si-te i-ru (= *8b)

blue eye ACC J. NOM do-PART be-PRES

Next, let us consider another type of account often given for the so-called Korean External Inalienable Possessor Construction (EIPC), also

---

1 I assume that a predicative NP has Case-features. After Case-checking, it becomes invisible to further attraction (probably because its phi-features are uninterpretable and are, therefore, deleted). The embedded possessor DP phrase is then free to raise.

known as Multiple Accusative Construction shown in (22a). The Korean EIPC is relevant here since the non-extractability of the relational noun phrase is also attested in this construction as (22b) illustrates: the RN phrase *meli-lul* 'head-ACC' does not scramble over the possessor DP *Yenghi-lul*.

(22) a. Chelswu-ka Yenghi-lul meli-lul chi-ess-ta

C.-NOM Y.-ACC head-ACC hit-PST-DCL

"Chelswu hit Yenghi on the head."

b. *Chelswu-ka meli-lul Yenghi-lul chi-ess-ta

C.-NOM head-ACC Y.-ACC hit-PST-DCL

Unlike the IPC in Japanese, the Korean EIPC has attracted much attention in the literature. Most recently, Yoon (1997) proposes that the argument of the RN in this case is theta-licensed external to the RN projection. She argues that the thematically unsaturated RN phrase and the verb form a complex predicate as a result of Functional Composition (Di Sciullo & Williams 1987). According to Yoon, thematically unstaturated nouns project only up to NPs in Korean, and this categorical status of the projection is the key to explaining the non-extractability of the relational noun phrase. She claims that DPs, but not NPs, can undergo syntactic movement.

We do not extend Yoon's account of the Korean EIPC to the Japanese IPC for the following reasons. First, it is not clear to me how we can motivate that only DPs, and not NPs, are visible to syntactic movement, given that both are maximal projections. Second, Yoon's strongest argument for the claim that the RN phrase is thematically unstaturated in (22) comes from the fact that it rejects appositive modification as shown in (23).

(23) *?Chelswu-ka Yenghi-lul yeppen elkwel-ul chi-ess-ta

C.-NOM Y.-ACC pretty face-ACC hit-PST-DCL

Intendedreading: "Chelswu hit Yenghi's face, which is pretty."

However, as I mentioned earlier, the relevant construction in Japanese is compatible with appositive modification. This excludes the possibility of applying to the Japanese IPC those analyses which invokes complex predicate formation, since thematic unsaturatedness of the relational noun phrase is a hallmark of such analyses.

Finally, in Tsujioka & Shibuya (1999), we proposed that the observed non-extractability of the accusative nominal is due to the fact that *su-* in the IPC is a thematically 'light' verb and the nominal undergoes post-lexical incorporation into the light verb *su-*. However, this analysis encounters difficulty in the following respect. First, other reported instances of syntactic/post-syntactic incorporation primarily exclude case particles

(Shibatani & Kageyama 1988), while the accusative Case marker is present in the IPC. Second, if incorporation happens at LF, the effects must not be observed overtly, and thus, the non-extractability of the accusative marked nominal cannot be explained. Given these problems inherent the incorporation analysis, I abandon it in the present paper, and opt for the possessor-raising analysis.

5. Deriving the Japanese/Korean Differences

In Section 3, I proposed a possessor-raising analysis for the Japanese inalienable possession construction with 'do'. I now argue that such an account can deal with the contrast between Japanese and Korean, adopting Ura's (1996) proposal with respect to the parametric difference between accusative Case in Korean and Japanese.

Ura (1996) proposed that T, but not small *v*, may enter into multiple checking relations (i.e., allows multiple specifiers) in Japanese. In Korean, on the other hand, both T and *v* can enter multiple checking relations. This reflects the presence of the 'double-*o* constraint' in Japanese, but the absence of its counterpart in Korean. Thus, the configuration in (24a) is possible in both Japanese and Korean, whereas that in (24b) is only possible in Korean.

(24) a. both Japanese & Korean b. only possible in Korean

Now, adopting this proposal, we can postulate that Korean small *v*, being capable of multiple Case checking, induces a minimality effect, prohibiting the possessor DP from raising up to the Spec of T. This is schematized in (25b), in comparison to the Japanese case in (25a).

(25) a. Japanese b. Korean

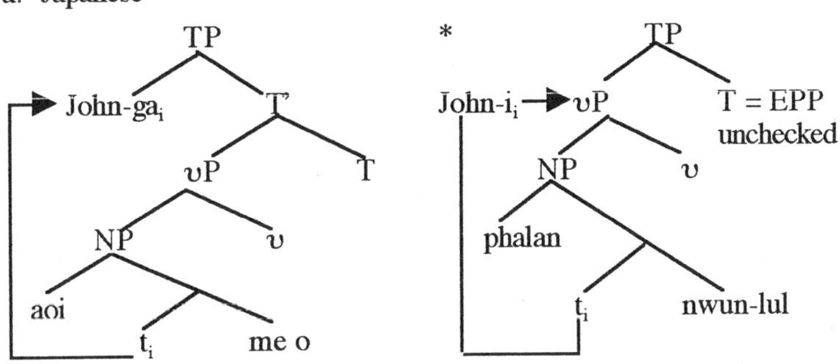

The possessor DP cannot raise to the Spec of TP because of the intervention by small *v*. When it does not raise, the EPP and Case features of T remain unchecked, rendering the derivation to crash. In other words, sentences such as (4) are never possible in Korean.

In this way, the possessor raising analysis can explain why (3) but not (4) is available in Korean: while (3) are canonical transitive sentences, (4) require possessor-raising which is not possible in the configuration in (25b). The reason why the Korean counterpart in (25b) is ungrammatical is tied to a well-known difference between the two languages, namely the availability of multiple accusative Case in Korean, but not in Japanese.

6. Discussion

Let us now turn to conceptual, as well as empirical implications of my proposal for the structure of the IPC in (12).

First, I mention two conceptual implications of my proposal. I have postulated that the ACC-phrase in (12) undergoes in-situ Case checking, in comparison to that in (11) which raises to the Spec of small *υ*. This proposal is in fact compatible with Chomsky's (1995) assumption that "Theta-theory is complementary to the theory of checking" (p. 312). An argument nominal, which is theta-licensed in its base-generated position, must undergo movement in order to be Case-licensed. On the other hand, I hypothesize that a predicative nominal, which does not by itself get theta-licensed, can be Case-licensed in its original position.

It should be noticed that in my analysis, small *υ* in (11) introduces an external argument, but not in (12). The case in (12) constitutes a clear exception to Burzio's generalization as the accusative Case and the external argument in this case do not co-occur. My speculation as to why the external argument is not introduced in (12) is as follows: I take small *υ* to be a predicate-forming function (cf. *Pred* in Bowers 1993). I also assume that small *υ* is sensitive to the event structure of the predicate and matches it with an appropriate external argument (e.g., eventive predicate <-> agent) via Event Identification (cf. Kratzer 1996). It is commonly assumed that unlike complex event nominals, relational nouns do not have event arguments. Then, it does not seem to be too far-fetched to posit that RNs, lacking an event argument, do not undergo Event Identification, and as a result, no external argument is introduced.

Second, there are two sorts of empirical implications: one is for existing studies of so-called "external inalienable possessor construction", and the other for so-called "bahuvrihi possessives".

The literature on various inalienable possession constructions makes a distinction between "External Inalienable Possessor Construction" (EIPC), as opposed to "Internal Inalienable Possessor Construction" (IIPC). The distinction has to do with whether the possessor DP is visible inside or outside the projection of RN as schematized in (26).

(26) a. IIPC: [Possessor ... RN] b. EIPC: Possessor...[RN]

(27) has examples of IIPC and EIPC. As I mentioned earlier, the Korean EIPC is a well-known example.

(27) a. Example of IIPC

[John no atama] (Japanese)

J. -GEN head

"John's head"

b. Example of EIPC

Chelswu-ka Yenghi-lul [meli-lul] chi-ess-ta (Korean)

C.-NOM Y.-ACC head-ACC hit-PST-DECL

"Chelswu hit Yenghi on the head."

There seems to be a consensus that something like (28) is correct for the structural analysis of the IIPC:

(28)

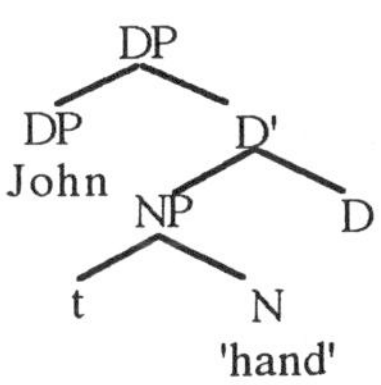

On the other hand, the structure of EIPC has been a matter of debate. Especially, how the external possessor is thematically licensed in the EIPC has provoked a great deal of discussion.

The Japanese inalienable possession construction with 'do' can be understood to be a type of EIPC, as it too has the configuration in (26b). However, as I argued in Section 3, it differs from the Korean EIPC as to the availability of appositive modification. In this paper, I did not attempt to provide an analysis for the Korean EIPC, nor a uniform analysis of EIPC. The facts of appositive modification suggest that EIPC may be a heterogeneous set of constructions which require different analyses.

Finally, I suggest that the base structure presented in (12) has a possible cross-linguistic counterpart in so-called bahuvrihi possessives. If the relational noun phrase incorporates into small υ, we get the bahuvrihi compounds seen in Germanic languages , as shown in (29).

(29) a. John is blue-eyed. (English)

b. John ist blauäugig (German)

If, on the other hand, only the relational noun head raises to small υ, we get the bahuvrihi expression in Yaqui in (30).

(30) vempo [teeve-m t] choon-ek (Jelinek 1998: 215)

they long-PL hair-[TR]-PERF

"They have long hair."

7. Conclusion

I have argued that the Inalienable Possession Construction with *su-* in (2) structurally differs from the Dressing Expression in (1). I have shown that the possessor raising analysis can handle both the Japanese-internal facts, as well as the Japanese/Korean contrast. In addition, I discussed the conceptual implications of the structure of the IPC in (12) for Case-checking of predicative nominals and the nature of small *υ*. Finally, I have suggested that the structure for the inalienable possession construction with *su-* potentially be extended to the bahuvrihi expressions in other languages.

References

Barker, Chris. 1995. *Possessive Descriptions.* Stanford: CSLI.

Bowers, John. 1993. The Syntax of Predication. *Linguistic Inquiry* 24. 591-656.

Bošković, Želko and Daiko Takahashi. 1998. Scrambling and Last Resort. *Linguistic Inquiry* 29. 347-366.

Burzio, Luigi. 1986. *Italian Syntax.* Dordrecht: Reidel.

Chomsky, Noam. 1981. *Lectures on Government and Binding.* Dordrecht: Foris.

Chomsky, Noam. 1995. *The Minimalist Program.* Cambridge, Mass.: MIT Press.

Di Sciullo, Anna Maria and Edwin Williams. 1987. *On the Definition of Word.* Cambridge, Mass.: MIT Press.

Fiengo, Robert. 1977. On Trace Theory. *Linguistic Inquiry* 8. 35-61.

Guéron, Jacqueline. 1995. On HAVE and BE, in J. Beckman, ed., Proceedings of *NELS* 25. 191-206. Amherst: GSLA.

Hale, Ken and Samuel Keyser. 1993. On Argument Structure and the Lexical Expression of Syntactic Relations, in K. Hale and S. Keyser, eds., *The View from Building 20.* 53-109. Cambridge, Mass.: MIT Press.

Jelinek, Eloise. 1998. Voice and Transitivity as Functional Projections in Yaqui, in M. Butt and W. Geuder, eds., *The projection of arguments*, 195-224. Stanford: CSLI.

Kageyama, Taro. 1980. *Nichiei Hikaku Goi no Koozoo.* Tokyo: Syoohakusha.

Kageyama, Taro. 1990. Nihongo to Eego no Goi no Taisyoo, in F. Tamamura, ed., *Nihongo no Goi to Imi: Kooza Nihongo to Nihongokyooiku 7.* 1-26. Tokyo: Meejisyoin.

Kageyama, Taro. 1993. Kanryoo Keiyooshi to Goigainenkoozoo. *Jinbun Ronkyuu* 43. 110-25.

Kinsui, Satoshi. 1994. Rentai Syuusyoku no *ta*-ni Tuite, in Y. Takubo, ed., *Nihongo no Meeshi Syuusyoku Hyoogen.* 29-65. Tokyo: Kuroshio.

Kitahara, Hisatsugu. 1993. Inalienable Possession Constructions in Korean: Scrambling, the Proper Binding Condition, and Case-Percolation, in P. M. Clancy, ed., *Japanese/Korean Linguistics 2.* 394-408. Stanford: CSLI.

Kratzer, Angelika. 1996. Severing the External Argument from Its Verb, in J. Rooryk and L. Zaring, eds., *Phrase Structure and the Lexicon.* 125-175. Dordrecht: Kluwer.

Landau, Ian. 1999. Possessor Raising and the Structure of VP. *Lingua* 107. 1-37.

Lasnik, Howard and Mamoru Saito. 1992. *Move Alpha*. Cambridge, Mass.: MIT Press.

Longobardi, Giuseppe. 1994. Reference and Proper Names: A Theory of N-Movement in Syntax and Logical Form. *Linguistic Inquiry* 25. 609-665.

Ritter, Elizabeth and Sara Thomas Rosen. 1997. The Function of 'have'. *Lingua* 101. 295-321.

Shibatani, Masayoshi and Taro Kageyama. 1988. Word Formation in Modular Theory of Grammar: Post-syntactic Compounds in Japanese. *Language* 64. 451-484.

Stowell, Tim. 1989. Subjects, Specifiers and X-bar Theory, in M. Baltin and A. Kroch, eds., *Alternative Conceptions of Phrase Structure*. 232-262. Chicago: Chicago University Press.

Szabolcsi, Anna. 1983/84. The Possessor that Ran Away from Home. *The Linguistic Review* 3. 89-102.

Tellier, Christine. 1990. Underived Nominals and the Projection Principle, in J. Carter, R.-M. Déchaine, B. Philip, and T. Sherer, eds., *Proceedings of NELS 20*. 472-485. Amherst: GSLA.

Tsujioka, Takae and Yoshiho Shibuya. 1999. Inalienable Object Construction in Japanese, in G. Booij, A. Ralli, and S. Scalise, eds., *Proceedings of the First Mediterranean Conference of Morphology*. 141-152. University of Patras.

Tsunoda, Tasaku. 1996. The Possession Cline in Japanese and Other Languages, in H. Chappell and W. McGregor, eds., *The Grammar of Inalienability*. 565-630. Berlin/New York: Mouton de Gruyter.

Uchida, Yoshiko and Mineharu Nakayama. 1993. Japanese Verbal Noun Constructions. *Linguistics* 31. 623-66.

Ura, Hiroyuki. 1996. Multiple Feature-checking: A Theory of Grammatical Function Splitting. Doctoral dissertation, MIT.

Vergnaud, Jean-Roger and Maria Louisa Zubizarreta. 1992. The Definite Determiner and the Inalienable Constructions in French and in English. *Linguistic Inquiry* 23. 595-652.

Yoon, Hye-Suk James. 1989. The Grammar of Inalienable Possession Construction in Korean, Mandarin and French, in S. Kuno, I.-H. Lee, J. Whitman, S.-Y. Bak, Y.-S. Kang, and Y-J. Kim, eds., *Harvard Studies in Korean Linguistics 3*. 357-368. Seoul: Hanshin.

Yoon, Jeong-Me. 1997. The Argument Structure of Relational Nouns and Inalienable Possessor Constructions in Korean. *Language Research* 33. 231-264.

Index

Other titles in the Japanese/Korean Linguistics Series Published by CSLI Publications

Previous volumes are available at your local bookstore. Additional information on these books as well as other CSLI Publications' titles can be found on our web site at http://cslipublications.stanford.edu. To receive our catalog, contact us at pubs@csli.stanford.edu

Japanese/Korean Linguistics, Volume 7

Edited by Noriko Akatsuka, Hajime Hoji, Shoichi Iwasaki, Sung-Ock Sohn and Susan Strauss

400 p. ISBN: 1-57586-117-8; ISBN: 1-57586-116-X (paper)

Asymmetry in the Interpretation of *-(n)un* in Korean (CHUNG-HYE HAN); Ventriloquism in Text and Talk: Functions of Self- and Other-Quotation in Japanese (SENKO K. MAYNARD)

Part I: Conversation: Turn-taking in Japanese Conversation: Grammar, Intonation and Pragmatics (HIROKO FURO) ; So? (On Japanese Connectives *sorede, dakara,* and *ja*) (MUTSUKO ENDO HUDSON); Co-Construction in Japanese Revisited: We *Do* "Finish Each Other's Sentences" (MAKOTO HAYASHI & JUNKO MORI); It Takes Two to Dance: The Interactional Determinants of NP Intonation Units with a Marked Rising Intonation (*hangimonkei*) in Japanese Conversation (TSUYOSHI ONO, ERI YOSHIDA, & MIEKO BANNO); *Hai* and *Ee*: An Interactional Analysis (NAOMI HANAOKA McGLOIN); Some Uses and Meanings of Utterance: Initial *iya* in Japanese Discourse (SCOTT SAFT)

Part II: Language and Culture: The Use and Non-Use of Honorifics in Sales Talk in Kyoto and Osaka: Are They Rude or Friendly? (SHIGEKO OKAMOTO); What the Language in Television Commercials Reveals About Cultural Preferences: A Glimpse into Japanese, American, and Korean Advertising Strategies (SUSAN STRAUSS & YONG-YAE PARK); Color Naming and Color Categorization in Korean (RODNEY E. TYSON)

Part III: Historical Linguistics: *Kakari* Particles and the Merger of the Predicative and Attributive Forms in the Japanese Verbal System (PETER HENDRIKS); The Correspondence Between the Form and

Meaning of Predicative Grammatical Categories in Classical Japanese (KATSUNOBU IZUTSU)

Part IV: Semantics and Pragmatics: An Analysis of Japanese *Ne* in Terms of the Theory of Territory of Information (AKIO KAMIO); The Complementizer *Toyuu* in Japanese (YOSHIKO MATSUMOTO); Where the Progressive and the Resultative Meet: A Typology of Imperfective Morphology in Japanese, Korean, Chinese and English (YASUHIRO SHIRAI); Pronoun Drop and Perspective in Japanese (SATOSHI UEHARA)

Part V: Syntax and Semantics: WH-Scope Identification via Quasi-Binding (DAEHO CHUNG); Attachment Ambiguity in Head Final Languages (YUKI HIROSE & SOON AE CHUN); Thetic Markers and Japanese/Korean Perception Verb Complements (HISAKO IKAWA); Syntactic Reflexes of Tripartite Structures of Generic Sentences (YOUNGCHUL JUN); Resultatives: English vs. Korean (SOOWON KIM & JOAN MALING); Branchingness and Phrasing in Japanese (KIYOMI KUSUMOTO); Is There a Genuine *Himself* Type Local Anaphor in Korean and Japanese? (GUNSOO LEE); On the Null Beneficiary in Benefactive Constructions in Japanese (NANAKO MACHIDA); The Japanese Dummy Verbs and the Organization of Grammar (KEIKO MIYAGAWA); Morphosyntactic Realization of Aspectual Structure (WILLIAM McCLURE); Predicate Cleft Constructions in Japanese and Korean: The Role of Dummy Verbs in TP/VP-Preposing (KUNIO NISHIYAMA & EUN CHO); Raising Asymmetry and Improper Movement (HIROMU SAKAI); Optimality and Economy of Expression in Japanese and Korean (PETER SELLS); The Laziest Pronouns (SATOSHI TOMIOKA); A Note on Scope Dependencies in Japanese Multiple *Wh*-questions (SHIN WATANABE); Semantics and Pragmatics of Contrastive Topic in Korean and English (HAE-KYUNG WEE)

Part VI: Phonetics and Phonology: Voicedness Alterations in the Tohoku Dialect of Japanese (SACHIKO OHNO); On the Irregular Behavior of *h* in Korean (SECHANG LEE); Correspondence in Korean Hypocoristic Truncation (SEUNG-HOON SHIN); Noun Faithfulness: Evidence from Accent in Japanese Dialects (JENNIFER L. SMITH); Focus Realization in Japanese English and Korean English Intonation (MOTOKO UEYAMA & SUN-AH JUN)

Part VII: Demonstrative Workshop: Formal Dependency, Organization of Grammar and Japanese Demonstratives (HAJIME HOJI)

Japanese/Korean Linguistics, Volume 6

Edited by Ho-min Sohn and John Haig

400 p. ISBN: 1-57586-089-9; ISBN: 1-57586-088-0 (paper)

Part V: Semantics: Verb Lexicalization Patterns in Korean—With Focus on Motion Conflation in Complex Verb Constructions (YOUNG-JOO KIM); On the Primacy of Progressive over Resultative State: The Case of Japanese *–teiru* (YASUHIRO SHIRAI); Groups as Event-oriented Entities (EUN-JOO KWAK); Topic and Focus in Korean: The Information Partition by Phrase Structure and Morphology (HYE-WON CHOI)

Part VI: Discourse: An Exploration of Sentence-final Uses of the Quotative Particle in Japanese Spoken Discourse (MAKOTO HAYASHI); An Expanded Concept of Speakerhood (DINA R. YOSHIMI); Japanese *keto*: Discourse Genre and Grammaticization (TOSHIHIDE NAKAYAMA & KUMIKO ICHIHASHI-NAKAYAMA); How 'Seeing' Approaches 'Knowing' in Korean, Japanese and English: An Analysis of *pota*, *miru*, and *see* (YONG YAE PARK & SUSAN STRAUSS); Discourse Motivations for Referential Choice in Korean Acquisition (PATRICIA M. CLANCY); On the Function of the Japanese Particle *wa*: New Light on Two Distinct Uses of the *te-wa* Construction (SETSUKO ARITA); A Cognitive Account of the Korean Morpheme *-se*: A Marker of Inclusiveness (SUSAN STRAUSS); The Discourse Function of the *-myen* Clause in Korean (CHANG-BONG LEE)

Japanese/Korean Linguistics, Volume 3

Edited by Soonja Choi

354 p. ISBN: 1-881526-22-4; ISBN: 1-881526-21-6 (paper)

Part I: Discourse and Acquisition: Other-Initiated Repair Sequences in Korean Conversation as Interactional Resources (KYU-HYUN KIM); Functions of the Filler *ano* in Japanese (HARUKO MINEGISHI COOK); The Structure of the Intonation Unit in Japanese (SHOICHI IWASAKI); Relative Clauses and Discourse Strategies (YOKO COLLIER-SANUKI); Some Observations in Humble Expressions in Japanese: Distribution of *o-* V(stem) *suru* and 'V (causative) *itadaku* (JUNKO MORI); Referential Structure in Japanese Children's Narratives: The Acquisition of *wa* and *ga* (KEI NAKAMURA); Grammatical Factors in the Acquisition of Complex Structures in Japanese (WENDY SNYDER)

Part II: Syntax and Semantics: Adjuncts and Event Argument in Restructuring (NATSUKO TSUJIMURA); On the Syntactic Properties of the Passive Morpheme in Japanese (HIROTO HOSHI); The Affected Construction in Korean and Japanese (TAEGOO CHUNG); Numeral Classifier Phrases Inside DP and the Specificity Effect (HISATSUGU KITAHARA); Floating Quantifiers, Scrambling and the ECP (MYUNG-

KWAN PARK & KEUN-WON SOHN); The Boundedness of Scrambling (SHUICHI YATABE); Case, Agreement, and *Ga/No* Conversion (SHIGERU MIYAGAWA); Analyzing the Verbal Noun: Internal and External Constraints (CHRISTOPHER MANNING); A Semantic Parameter: The Progressive in Japanese and English (WILLIAM McCLURE); Do *aru* and *iru* Exist as Verbs of Existence in Japanese? (SUSAN STRAUSS); Case-Marking in Korean Post-Verbal Negation (YOOKYUNG KIM); From Zero to Overt Nominalizer NO: A Syntactic Change in Japanese (KAORU HORIE)

Part III: Phonology: Rhythmic Lengthening and Shortening in Korean (HEE-BOK JUNG); Notes on Some Japanese-Korean Phonetic Correspondences (ALEXANDER VOVIN)

Japanese/Korean Linguistics, Volume 2

Edited by Patricia M. Clancy

510 p. ISBN: 1-881526-14-3; ISBN: 1-881526-13-5 (paper)

Part I: Discourse and Pragmatics: On the Clause-Linking to Construction in Japanese (SEIKO YAMAGUCHI FUJI); Functional Transfer in the History of Japanese Language (SHOICHI IWASAKI); Topicality in Korean Conversation: A Conversation Analytic Perspective (KYU-HYUN KIM); Linguistic Politeness and Cultural Style: Observations from Japanese (YOSHIKO MATSUMOTO); Idiomatic Conditionals in Japanese (SHIGEKO OKAMOTO); Cognition, Affect and Topicality of the Causal Particle *–Nikka* in Korean (SUNG-OCK S. SOHN); The Korean Modal Marker *Keyss* as a Marker of Affect: An Interactional Perspective (KYUNG-HEE SUH & KYU-HYUN KIM)

Part II: Phonology: The Phonological Word in Korean (EUNJOO HAN); Prosodic Approach on Korean Partial Reduplication (JONGHO JUN); Prosodic Word-Level Rules in Korean (ONGMI KANG); A Phonetically Based Analysis of [Voice] and [Fortis] in Korean (DAVID JAMES SILVA)

Part III: Psycholinguistics and Language Acquisition: Conditionality and Deontic Modality in Japanese and Korean: Evidence from the Emergence of Conditionals (NORIKO AKATSUKA & PATRICIA M. CLANCY); Word Order vs. Word Class: Portmanteau Sentences in Bilinguals (SHOJI AZUMA); Development of Locative Case Markers in Korean (SOONJA CHOI); The Organization of the Korean Syllable: Experimental Evidence (BRUCE L. DERWING, YEO BOM YOON & SOOK WHAN CHO); The Acquisition of the Japanese Subject Marker *Ga* and its Theoretical Implications (PATRICIA MAYES & TSUYOSHI

ONO); Processing of Japanese Relative Clause Constructions (HIROKO YAMASHITA, LAURIE STOWE & MINEHARU NAKAYAMA)

Part IV: Syntax and Semantics: Indefinite Wh Pronouns and the Morpheme *Mo* in Japanese(RURIKO KAWASHIMA); Scrambling and Scope in Japanese (MASANORI NAKAMURA); A Note on So-Called "Donkey Sentences" in Japanese: A Preliminary Study (SHIN WATANABE)

Part V: Syntax and Morphology: Inalienable-Type Multiple Accusative Constructions in Korean and Japanese (DONG-IN CHO); Case-Motivated Movement to Non-Argument Positions: Evidence from Japanese (STANLEY DUBINSKY); The Role of Pro in the *Ni* Passive in Japanese (HIROTO HOSHI); On Certain Differences in Comparative Deletion Between English and Japanese (YASUO ISHII); Inalienable Possession Constructions in Korean: Scrambling, the Proper Binding Condition, and Case-Percolation (HISATSUGU KITAHARA); Modal Phrase and Adjuncts (MASATOSHI KOIZUMI); Postverbal Adverbs and Verb Movement in Korean (JAE HONG LEE); The Syntax of Serialization in Korean (SOOKHEE LEE); Case Alternation and Word Order Variation in Nominal Clauses (YOUNG-SUK LEE); Uniform Pro Subject Analysis of Japanese Sentences (SHIGEO TONOIKE)